ETHNIC & RACIAL GROUPS

THE DYNAMICS OF DOMINANCE

Richard M. Burkey

University of Denver

Cummings Series in Contemporary Sociology
Consulting Editor: James F. Short, Jr.

Cummings Publishing Company
Menlo Park, California • Reading, Massachusetts
London • Amsterdam • Don Mills, Ontario • Sydney

ISBN 0-8465-0742-0
ABCDEFGHIJ-MA-7987

Cummings Publishing Company, Inc.
2727 Sand Hill Road
Menlo Park, California 94025

PREFACE

Ethnic and Racial Groups *is intended to be a primary text in undergraduate college and university courses, particularly for sociology courses focusing on the United States as the major emphasis. The book has two parts: Part 1, "Major Concepts and Processes," and Part 2, "Ethnic and Racial Dominance in the United States."*

Part 1 attempts to explain and describe the major concepts in this field, to illustrate them with examples from societies other than the United States, and to organize them into a conceptual framework. After extensive review of the meanings of the major concepts and after considerable thought and revision, the definitions of particular scholars are utilized while differing conceptions are examined in the notes at the end of the book. In some cases my definitions are a synthesis of several meanings, while in other cases I have enlarged or limited definitions, or invented new concepts. Two concepts that are popular in the field have been eliminated: prejudice and minority group. The many elements that have been ascribed to the overloaded idea of prejudice have been utilized as particular *concepts: racism, stereotyping, bias, social distance, personal distance, ethnocentrism, and others. Minority is used here only in the numerical sense of the term and attached to the idea of power with the concepts of dominant majority, dominant minority, subordinate majority, and subordinate minority; there are dominant or subordinate pluralities as well.*

One reason for writing this book was to present my efforts at understanding the major concepts. A second reason was to organize these concepts into some sort of framework rather than just examining them at random. The conceptual framework of Part 1 is based upon efforts to answer the following questions: (1) What are major dimensions of race and ethnic relations in all societies? (2) What is the meaning of racial and ethnic dominance? (3) What processes are involved in the origin of systems of racial and ethnic dominance? (4) What processes are involved in the maintenance or intensification of systems of racial and ethnic dominance? (5) What processes relate to the reduction or the termination of dominant-subordinate relationships based upon ethnicity or race?

Chapter 1 contains explanations and cross-societal examples of the basic units—races, ethnic groups, nationalities, and societies—and some interconnections between these units. In Chapter 2 five major dimensions of ethnic and race relations are explored: cultural differentiation, stratification, social distance, geographical segregation, and conflict and competition. Chapters 3 through 5 examine the processes involved in the origins, the maintenance, and the transformation of systems of racial and ethnic dominance, again utilizing examples taken from numerous societies, past and present. A third reason for writing this book was to put within a single cover not only an extensive case study of the United States but to provide material from other societies as well.

Part 2 attempts a somewhat different approach to race and ethnic group relations in the United States. Rather than organizing this section by chapters related to specific ethnic groups, or by using concepts as the focus of the chapter organization and then selecting illustrative examples at random from American history, the chapters in Part 2 are chronologically based on the origins, the maintenance, and the transformation of dominant-subordinate relations. Part 2, therefore, is a developmental case study of one society, the United States, using the conceptual framework of Part 1.

Part 2 begins with a chapter on the origins of the dominant group in the United States, the Anglo-Americans (or the "unhyphenated Americans"). The idea of an American ethnic group is controversial since many people believe that only "minorities" are ethnic, existing along with a nonethnic majority. In Chapter 7, the origins of the major subordinate groups are described, some of which became subordinate in the seventeenth or the eighteenth century and others as late as the end of the nineteenth. Chapters 8 and 9 focus on the manner in which dominant-subordinate relationships were maintained, and intensified in some cases, from the time a given group became subordinate to the end of World War II. World War II is a benchmark, and the remaining chapters (10 through 13) are concerned with post World War II changes: the social movements, protests, and revolts; the changes in government policies and an evaluation of their effectiveness; the evidence for the reduction of discrimination and other forms of inequality as well as the persistence of many elements from the past; and a presentation of the pluralist and the integrationist arguments for the direction of these changes.

As a final note, an alternative reading order of the chapters is possible and perhaps desirable for instructional purposes.

Introduction to the basic units and dimensions	*Chapter 1*
	Chapter 2
Origins of dominance and the case of the U.S.	*Chapter 3*
	Chapter 6
	Chapter 7
Maintenance of dominance and the case of the U.S.	*Chapter 4*
	Chapter 8
	Chapter 9
Transformation of dominance and the case of the U.S.	*Chapter 5*
	Chapter 10
	Chapter 11
	Chapter 12
	Chapter 13

I would like to offer my thanks and appreciation to professors William Key, Thomas Drabek, Rita Braito, and Judith McDowell for their encouragement and assistance in this endeavor. And above all, I want to thank my wife, Sally, for putting up with me during the research and the writing of this book. Being a sounding board and a critic are not elements included in a marriage contract.

Richard M. Burkey

CONTENTS

Contents

Part 1

MAJOR CONCEPTS
AND PROCESSES

INTRODUCTION

Part 1 of this book presents a conceptual framework for a conflict-dominance view of social relations, stressing order as well as disorder and competition as well as conflict. The following are the major ideas developed and illustrated in Part 1:

1. Virtually all complex societies, past and present, have been multiethnic, and many have racial divisons. Racial and ethnic membership can transcend a particular society.

2. In the great majority of complex societies, one ethnic group or race has been or is dominant, which means that the major positions within the state are occupied by members of that particular group; in addition, the culture of that group may set the standards for the others, and the majority of the wealth of the society may go to this one group.

3. Whether or not a dominant group exists, there are at least five major dimensions involved in the interaction between ethnic groups or between races: competition and conflict, some degree of cultural differences ranging from minor to extreme, some degree of social distance or sense of the appropriate forms of contact and interaction that should take place, some degree of residential concentration or dispersement of the groups (segregation), and some degree of inequality of power, privilege, prestige, and wealth between groups (stratification).

4. Dominant-subordinate relationships between ethnic groups or between races originate through conquest, immigration, enslavement, or annexation. Dominant-subordinate relationships are maintained or intensified by the use of discrimination; by legitimizing the system through the use of some ideology, particularly racism; by the unintended consequences of organizational policies; by the conformity of subordinate groups; and by the suppression of revolts. Dominant-subordinate relationships are reduced when subordinate groups acquire relative autonomy over their own affairs (pluralism) or when they are accepted into the institutional activities of the dominant group (integration). Dominant-subordinate relationships are terminated when a subordinate group gains political independence (secession); when a subordinate group ceases to exist because it has been absorbed into the dominant group (assimilation); when a subordinate group overthrows the government and becomes dominant (revolution); or when a subordinate group is exterminated or is expelled from the society.

5. Although each system of race or ethnic relations is unique and there is difficulty in predicting a system's development, three basic types of societies can be identified: empire societies, in which a dominant minority controls other groups as a result of conquest; national societies, in which a majority ethnic group is so dominant that the subordinate minorities are virtually "invisible"; and pluralistic societies, in which no dominant group exists, creating a tenuous equilibrium between relatively equal groups.

Part 1 elaborates on this brief overview, defining the key concepts and providing examples from several societies, past and present. This procedure should not be seen as an effort at comparative analysis. Examples can be misleading when events and processes are extracted from the context in which they have occurred and when a part is described without some idea of the reader's knowledge of the whole. Nevertheless, some cross-societal material will provide useful insights into the nature of race and ethnic relations. If nothing else, such material will allow us to escape briefly from our peculiar American trappings.

1

THE BASIC UNITS:
ETHNIC GROUP, RACE,
NATIONALITY, AND SOCIETY

ETHNICITY AND ETHNIC GROUP

Since prehistoric times, the concept of ethnic group has had a major effect upon the motives and actions of human beings. The term "ethnic group" has been given several meanings by social scientists and average citizens alike. It has been interpreted to mean a cultural group, an ancestral group, a racial group, a minority group, an immigrant group, any group that wears colorful clothing and dances at weddings, a group distinguished in certain ways from a supposedly nonethnic majority, or any combination of these meanings. The sociologists Shibutani and Kwan define an ethnic group as "those who conceive of themselves as being alike by virtue of their common ancestry, real or fictitious, and who are so regarded by others."[1]* They cite cultural and physical similarities as factors affecting this sense of ancestry, along with ethnic labeling imposed on individuals by members of the group and by outsiders. R. A. Schermerhorn also stresses ancestry in his definition of an ethnic group as "a collectivity within a larger society having real or putative common ancestry, memories of a shared historical past, and a cultural focus on one or more symbolic elements defined as the epitome of their peoplehood."[2] Schermerhorn's meaning limits an ethnic group to a segment of a society, while Shibutani and Kwan's definition permits an ethnic group to transcend a number of societies.

The idea of ancestral ties among a collection of people seems to be the essential element in defining an ethnic group. Although many social scientists use the concepts of ethnicity and ethnic group interchangeably, it might be useful to conceive of them separately yet utilize the idea of ancestry with both terms. Briefly put, ethnicity is an attitude or a set of *attitudes* (a

All numbered notes appear at the end of the book.

5

psychological concept), while ethnic group is *social* in nature (a sociological concept). This distinction needs further clarification.

Ethnicity: The Psychological Component

Human beings have defined individuals beyond their immediate families as being biologically related, and at the same time they have viewed other people as being strangers, aliens, or not of "my people." In many cases and under certain circumstances, this sense of ancestry, biology, or "blood" ties has taken precedent over all other factors that divide *Homo sapiens*, such as class, religion, gender, and ideology. As Shibutani and Kwan have written, "Men more easily believe that they are alike when they think they are descended from the same ancestors. Inherited attributes in themselves may not be important, for consciousness of kind may rest more upon a common culture. But what is presumed to be inherited is of decisive importance."[3] One can change occupations, move from one class to another, convert to a different religion, or take out citizenship in another society, but it is difficult for most to deny their ancestry, even if this option is open to them.

How does the meaning of ethnicity differ from the notion of "blood" ties within families and kinship systems? And in what ways are family and ethnic groups similar? According to Shils:

> Ethnicity is very much like the kinship tie–they are both primordial, being consti-
> tuted by the significance attributed to a presumed genetic connection and the
> primordial unit arising therefrom. Unlike kinship . . . ethnicity does not refer to a
> genetic link with a particular important person or persons. It is a link with a
> collectivity in which a vital, charismatic quality is diffused. It is thought to repre-
> sent the possession of some quality inherent in the ethnic aggregate and shared by
> all of its members.[4]

Ethnicity, therefore, is more diffuse, lacking specific genealogical ties, and ethnicity includes within this diffuse sense of ancestry a number of specific families and kinship systems.

What factors enable individuals to identify ancestrally with some other people and not others? Three significant aspects within the individual's environment contribute to ethnicity—language, culture, and physical appearance. Generally speaking, the greater the contrasts between two or more collectivities in one or a combination of these conditions, the greater the sense of and relevance of ethnicity.

1. *Language.* Similarities and differences in language are an important factor in ethnic group identification. One's own kind speaks one's own language and speaks it "correctly." Out-groups or "foreigners" speak other languages or, at the very least, give themselves away by a dialect or a lack of mastery of colloquial terms and linguistic nuances. When the contrasts are great, such as between English and Chinese, language differences are obvious clues to ethnic placement. When people share a language, contrasts are

minimal and subtleties of style and inflection and unique words or phrases will determine the relevance of ethnicity and ethnic group placement.

2. *Culture*. Culture may be defined as the shared symbolic meanings of specific social units or social collectivities. Particular social groupings, such as regions, organizations, religions, ethnic groups, classes, occupations, and whole societies, share a configuration of symbolic meanings, or ideas, and the material manifestations of some of these ideas (artifacts). A culture contains *norms*—ideas about expected forms of behavior either in the form of rules or as agreements; *values*—ideas about what is important, valuable, or desirable; *beliefs*—conceptions of what the world is and what it is not (what is, as opposed to what ought to be); *technology*—ideas often related to the use of tools involving "how to" or know-how (for example, how to build a bridge or an igloo; how to pass tests or climb the ladder in a bureaucracy). Culture generally becomes manifest as behavior (such as customs), but behavior is not synonymous with culture, since we often are forced into actions we do not value or we deviate from what is expected.

Many sociologists have defined ethnic groups simply as collectivities with distinctive cultures, ignoring or de-emphasizing the notion of ancestry. However, every group and every society has a culture. In addition, there are very few ethnic groups above the level of primitive tribes that do not have cultural variations based upon urban-rural differences, class differences, religious differences, or differences produced by residence within more than one society. Moreover, the culture of an ethnic group can change drastically even while the same ethnicity persists. Modern Greeks, Assyrians, and Egyptians have retained very little of their ancient cultures, yet there are still Greeks, Assyrians, and Egyptians. The identification with an ethnic group *name* is more important than the culture of a group; the name persists as a symbol even though the culture has changed.

Although culture does not distinguish ethnic groups from other types of groups, it is difficult to believe that ethnicity could long exist without at least a few highly symbolic elements of a cultural nature. Of particular importance in this regard have been distinctive food preferences, "folk" art and music, traditional occupational specializations, family names, and a "mythology" of the group's origins and history.

Ethnic groups in contact with each other may be culturally quite different, or there may be few differences to assist in creating or in maintaining ethnicity. When contrasts are minimal (as between Austrians and Germans, or between Anglo-Americans and Anglo-Canadians), the differences that do exist will be highly stressed.

3. *Physical Type*. In many cases of contact or interaction between members of different ethnic groups, physical, biological, or "racial" (that is, *selected* physical differences, such as skin color) contrasts exist. Differences in hair texture and color, nose shape, skin color, stature, or some other aspect of human physiology provide highly visible clues. When populations within large geographic areas such as in Asia or in Europe have had exten-

sive interaction for long periods of time, physical variations may be few or nonexistent. Under these circumstances clues to ancestral identification with others must be based upon cultural or linguistic differences.

In some cases of contact and interaction all three indicators of ethnic membership—language, culture, and biology—may exist. For example, Group A may speak a different tongue, have different skin color, and use quite different artifacts from those of Group B. However, in circumstances characterized by greater contact over a longer period of time, similarities tend to increase and differences to diminish. Miscegenation may blur color lines, cultural borrowing may create cultural overlap, and extensive communication may produce bilingualism in one group or another or the sharing of a common language. Other combinations of differences and similarities between languages, cultures, and observable physical differences (phenotypes) may exist. In Guatemala, for example, it is difficult to distinguish between working-class Indians and Ladinos (Spanish) on the basis of physical traits. Elements such as costume, diet, house architecture, and language are more significant. Differences in these traits of the Ladinos and Indians leave little doubt as to the group membership of individuals, even though phenotype has little relevance.[5]

Differences and similarities in terms of language, culture, and phenotype provide clues to one's ethnicity and to the ethnicity of others. However, even with these "objective conditions at work the boundaries of ethnic groups are often flexible. Some collections of human beings outside of one's immediate relatives seem to be closer than some others under certain circumstances, yet even those with seemingly distant ties become "kissing cousins" when contrasted with those "foreigners" that are around. Ethnicity is relative, relative to individuals and to a consensus among individuals depending upon circumstances. In Israel, a person may conceive of himself or herself as a Polish Jew, a European Jew (Ashkenazi), an Israeli, or simply a Jew. Spanish-speaking people in the American Southwest have divided themselves into Mexican-Americans and Spanish-Americans, but under Anglo dominance they are becoming Chicanos or Hispanos and many identify with *La Raza* (all peoples of Spanish language and culture throughout the world). Individuals in Egypt may define themselves in ethnic terms as members of a small tribe, as Egyptian, or as Arab.

Ethnicity may be conceived of as having levels, or concentric circles. Each level or circle has its own ethnic label, and the higher the level or the further out the circle, the more people are included. In the process of expanding the membership of one's group the differences are de-emphasized and the similarities are stressed. For example, Chiricahua, Gila, and Jicarilla are ethnic groups at a low level. When these groups are put into a contrast or conflict situation with, say, Kiowa, the members think of themselves as Apaches in a middle level of ethnicity. And Kiowa, Apache, Sioux and others may move to an even higher level (that is, a broader and more general level)—Indian—in contrast to whites.

Although one particular level or circle of ethnicity is generally the most relevant boundary of ethnicity, fluctuation can occur under special circumstances. Romans, Sicilians, Piedmontesc, and Neopolitans came to the United States in the late nineteenth century. The dominant Anglos made few distinctions between these groups; they were all Italians or, more pejoratively, wops. A higher level of ethnicity, the Italian-American, developed under these conditions. In their segregated communities within American cities, however, reversions to lower levels often occurred; for example, a Roman would not marry a Sicilian.

Likewise, Jews from Germany, who had come to the United States at an earlier period, considered themselves quite different from the newly arrived Jews from Poland and Russia. In fact, the term "kike" was first used by the German Jews to refer to these Polish and Russian immigrants.[6] However, when Gentile Americans used the term for both groupings and treated them the same, a higher level of ethnicity developed—Jewish-Americans.

A final example is ancient Greece, where a stable level of ethnicity existed for centuries based on city-state membership. Thus, citizens considered themselves Athenians, Spartans, Thebans, or Corinthians. With the Persian invasion (fifth century B.C.) and the threat to the existence of all of these groups from the "barbarians," a "higher" and more encompassing conception of ethnicity developed, uniting them under the name of Hellenes.[7] When the threat was over, Hellene became less relevant than the lower levels, and conflict between the groups near the end of the fifth century temporarily eliminated the relevance of being an Hellene.

Ethnicity, then, is *a set of attitudes related to a sense of ancestral identification with a segment of the world's population.* Like all attitudes, it varies among individuals. Some people are preoccupied with ethnicity, while others find it irrelevant or absurd. Some may consider a very limited number of people as members, while others may think in terms of all of humanity. Members of ethnic groups that are a majority of the society's population may not even consider themselves ethnic until a war breaks out and "tribal" loyalty becomes all important. Members of ethnic minorities, either dominant or subordinate, are generally more acutely aware of their own ethnicity and the ethnicity of others. But whatever the variation by individuals or the differences in the environment of individuals that enhance or diminish this sense of ancestry, ethnicity is attitudinal in nature.

Ethnic Group: The Social Component

An analogy can be used to explain the difference between ethnicity and ethnic group. Individual Catholics vary in their Catholicism. Some are devout, while others are only nominal Catholics. This Catholicism is a set of attitudes. But in addition there is the Catholic church, a social organization that has persisted and changed over a two-thousand-year period. The Catholic church as a social unit is more than simply the sum total of the attitudes of the individual members. Similarly, an ethnic group is more than the totality of the ethnicity of its members.

A group (any group) has characteristics or structural elements that cannot be explained in psychological terms, such as motive or attitude, and, in a sense, a group has its own reality (*sui generis*). There are at least three reasons for this relatively independent reality of groups. In the first place, individuals come and go, but the group goes on. Individuals are born into a group and they die within a relatively short period of time, thereby ending their membership; or individuals voluntarily join a group and later they leave. In either case, as long as there is not widespread loss of membership due to the sudden death of all of the members or a mass exodus within a short time, the group continues while the membership changes.

Second, the group has a more or less determining effect on the attitudes of the members. The group is not an effect of the sum total of attitudes; the attitudes, to some extent, are an effect of the group. Groups (some types of groups more than other types) often have rules, agreements, values, and beliefs that have existed for hundreds of years. The new members are socialized (or "educated") into the acceptance of these meanings, sometimes deep into their subconscious. Through this process of socialization new members, whether they are born into a group or are voluntary applicants, take on attitudes shared by current members (and attitudes once held by now dead members).

Third, in spite of this effect of the group structure upon attitude formation, there will be differences of opinion within any group. The toleration of divergent attitudes will vary according to the group. The more authoritarian groups will tolerate few exceptions to its norms or rules, and individuals with extremely dissenting views will have to keep those views to themselves or face the consequences. Attitudes are *predispositions* to behavior; they do not automatically result in behavior. In the more tolerant or democratic groups, greater toleration for diverse opinions will exist, but even within this type there will be limits. Whether authoritarian or democratic, the group reality is revealed. The behavior of members of a group is not simply the manifestation of all of the attitudes of the individuals, and a group can continue in spite of attitudinal disagreement among the members.

Ethnic groups constitute a particular type of group, yet they have these three essential qualities of all groups. An ethnic group is not an associational group or organization. It does not have a bureaucracy, a set of goals, a hierarchy of positions, or a specified division of labor, as in General Motors or the Catholic church (here the analogy between ethnic group and church breaks down). Because ethnic groups generally have a large number of members, all of the individuals cannot engage in face-to-face interaction with each other as they do in such groups as families, gangs, or fraternities —other forms of a group. Ethnic groups are a special and perhaps unique form of group; they are communities based upon ascription.

For the most part, individuals are born into an ethnic group, a group that may go back hundreds or even thousands of years. There is little the individual can do about this. The last part of Shibutani and Kwan's definition of an ethnic group states, "who are so regarded by others." The individual may reject his or her own group (denial of ethnicity in general or denial of ancestral affiliation with the membership group), but others are not going to permit this. That individual is a member whether he or she likes it or not. It may be possible to change membership (by becoming assimilated into another group), but only if all clues to one's original ethnic group are eliminated and all ties with friends and relatives are terminated. The first characteristic of an ethnic group is that members occupy an ascribed status rather than an achieved or chosen status.

A second characteristic of ethnic groups is their community nature. Individuals interact with other individuals within a territory as members of a community. All of the members of a given group do not have to live together within a single contiguous geographical space. Segments of the group often reside within different cities or towns not only in the same society but within communities found in a number of societies. Chinese, for example, are concentrated within numerous communities in the United States, Britain, Taiwan, South Africa, and Thailand, not to mention the People's Republic of China. But what is necessary for a *viable* ethnic group to continue is interaction with members of their own kind within a territory, even if this territory consists of neighborhood sections of numerous cities. Ethnic groups are not homogeneous units. Attitudes vary considerably, class differences are generally found, even religious variation exists. Nevertheless, to constitute a group, some interaction within the membership segments must occur, interaction related to the group's institutional activities: family life, friendship patterns, economic activities, religion, and perhaps even political behavior.

When a particular ethnic group is divided into numerous subcommunities, a lower level of ethnicity may predominate; but in the modern period forms of mass communication (ethnic newspapers, television with ethnic programs) may help to solidify ethnicity at a higher level as a community that transcends specific territories.

While ethnic groups are not organizations or associations, they do have such groups as divisions within them. The presence of organizations constitutes the third characteristic of ethnic groups. Ethnic organizations may be churches, lodges, clubs, businesses, political parties, banks, pressure groups or lobbies, or several other forms; however, this is not to say that these organizational types are always necessarily ethnic in nature—in the more integrated societies many of these will have a multiethnic membership. Nevertheless, ethnic groups have at least a few organizations based on a common ethnicity.

Ethnic groups that are a dominant majority, such as the Germans in West Germany, the French in France, and the Americans (or Anglo-Americans) in the United States, also have organizations. Dominant majorities may deliberately restrict membership in political parties, government, schools, and other organizations to their own members; the correct ethnic status becomes a necessary but not sufficient requirement for membership. If such discrimination is no longer legitimate, the more public organizations will be opened up and become multiethnic. But associations of a more intimate nature, such as private clubs, may remain restricted.

Based upon a modification of the definitions of Shibutani and Kwan and of R. A. Schermerhorn and the ideas that have been presented in this section, the following is a revised definition of *ethnic group*: *a community group based upon the ascribed status of a diffuse ancestry that is maintained by similarities of culture, language, and/or phenotype.* The definition stresses the following:

1. An ethnic group is a special type of group; it is a community of interacting members containing organizations and primary groups as subparts.
2. A diffuse sense of ancestry (ethnicity) constitutes the basis for membership.
3. The status of the members is one of ascription; individuals are labeled with an ethnic name by other members of the group and by members of other ethnic groups.
4. The ethnicity of the members and the labeling or classifying of individuals as ethnic group members are made possible by contrasts of culture, language, and/or phenotype between population segments.

As will be examined later, an ethnic group may be a minority, a plurality, or a majority of the population of a society. In some cases ethnic groups may transcend the boundaries of several societies, although this is rare. Ethnic groups may be dominant or be subordinate, or they may coexist with others as relative equals. A tribe is the same as an ethnic group, or it may be considered one form of ethnic group; a tribe generally has a belief that its members are descended from a single ancestor, but they perceive their biological ties with others beyond the clan level as relatively diffuse. And a nation is synonymous with ethnic group if stripped of its identification with a state or country.

Relationships between Ethnicity and Ethnic Group

Once the distinction between ethnicity and ethnic group has been made, a number of interesting relationships may be identified. The following are a few suggestions of possible interconnections between the two:

1. The more isolated an ethnic group, the less the salience or importance of ethnicity. In such circumstances the ethnic group is a viable

form of social organization with extreme importance for the determination of individual attitudes and actions, yet the members are not very "ethnic." When contact with other ethnic groups occurs and contrasts are noted, the salience of ethnicity will increase.

2. While ethnicity often transcends several societies, ethnic groups rarely do, given the restraints of societal boundaries upon community interaction networks. The level of ethnicity that most individuals identify with is the ethnic group; that is, the interaction network affecting the daily lives of the members. Higher levels of ethnicity (such as *La Raza*, Pan-Slavism, the notions of Arab, Indian, Pan-African, European), which some members may identify with, will not become ethnic groups unless community and organizational structures are created that will maintain and perpetuate this broader view of ethnicity.

3. Ethnic group intergration (integration *between* groups) often increases the salience of ethnicity for some members. When ethnic groups are "breaking down" (when cultural differences with other groups are being reduced, residential areas are becoming ethnically mixed, intermarriage is increasing), ethnicity, at least for some, becomes more significant. Individuals become worried about the possible demise of their group and thereby become "professional ethnics." "Get back to the old traditions and keep separated from the outsiders" becomes the battle cry.

4. The greater the conflict between ethnic groups, the greater the salience of ethnicity. Discrimination as one form of conflict, for example, is functional in maintaining and intensifying ethnicity.

Other relationships could be suggested. The distinction could prove to be useful.

RACE

Why are there physical variations between individuals, between ethnic groups, and between geographical areas? What are the differences and the similarities, if any, between the ideas of race and ethnic group? Do races have some real existence independent of what human beings think and classify, or are they "fictions in our brains"?

Biological Variations

Current evidence indicates that humans evolved in Africa from a primate species now extinct. At least one hundred thousand years ago, if not earlier, *Homo sapiens* came into existence. In the search for food, bands, clans, and tribes (ethnic groups) eventually became dispersed over much of the earth's surface. The greater the distance between any two ethnic groups, the greater the probability of differences in phenotype and genotype.

Phenotypes are readily *observable* physical traits, such as skin color, stature, and hair texture. The phenotype of an individual may, to a limited extent, be affected by environmental conditions, such as diet and climate, but for the most part the phenotype is a manifestation of that hereditary package of genes and chromosomes contained within the organism (the genotype). A specific gene can be manifested as a number of phenotypic traits, or a single observable trait can be the expression of a number of genes.

In four widely separated areas of the world, clusters of ethnic groups or tribes developed the greatest physical differences vis-à-vis each other. These areas were northern China, northern Europe, West Africa, and Australia. In between these areas, various gradations of the extremes existed, depending upon geographical and social barriers to sexual intercourse.

The biological variations were produced by the same evolutionary and hereditary mechanisms that created *Homo sapiens* and other species (closed breeding populations): (1) mutation—alterations in the composition of the genotype of individual organisms, primarily due to radiation; (2) isolation and inbreeding; (3) excessive population reproduction—reproduction of more members than can survive in an ecological system; (4) natural selection—the phenomenon of differential reproduction, a result of the fact that some genotypes in a population are better adapted to a given environment than others; (5) sexual selection—because certain phenotypic traits of males and females arouse sexual behavior, individuals with the more attractive traits are more likely to reproduce; and (6) genetic drift—fluctuations in the gene frequencies (genotype) due to chance or accident in small breeding populations.[8]

Among human beings, geographical barriers and social restrictions limited the sexual interactions between different populations. Mutations occurred, most of which were not perpetuated, but some of which made for greater adaption to the environment and became more stable over time. Since no human group has been isolated long enough to develop changes of the magnitude that would create a new species, only relatively minor variations have taken place within *one* species—*Homo sapiens*.

Certain "racial" traits resulting from the perpetuation of mutations seem to have survival value. Dark skin filters out excessive sunlight in tropical areas; light skin (skin with less melanin) in less sunny climes allows the limited ultraviolet rays of the sun to penetrate, thus providing an important source of vitamins C and D;[9] and the eye structure of the Oriental or Mongoloid may offer protection from the blizzards common in northern Asia. The hands of Eskimo have a higher temperature than those of Caucasians, a quite useful feature for their cold environment.

Regarding the other hereditary mechanisms, genetic drift was probably of minor importance in the differentiation of human populations, while conceptions of what is sexually attractive was (and is) of greater significance.[10]

Races: Real or Symbolic Constructs?

What has been described so far is the rather obvious fact that human beings differ physiologically, albeit in minor ways. But the idea of races is not quite the same thing as the evidence of physical variation. Although the term "race" has a number of meanings,* it has most commonly come to refer to categories of human beings classified together on the basis of a characteristic cluster of phenotypic and/or genotypic traits. Races, so conceived, are "boxes" in which the entire human population can be categorized.

The great majority of scientists in the eighteenth and nineteenth centuries (and a few today) believed that races were discrete categories or "real" units in nature that could be *discovered* and properly classified. These classifications, before Mendelian genetics developed, were based upon perceived correlations of *selected phenotypic* traits, primarily skin color, head shape (round or long), hair texture and color, nose shape, facial bone structure, and eye shape and color. (Earlobe connection, toe size, foot length, and other such variations that also exist among human beings were not taken into account.) With the development of the science of genetics, anthropologists and others have attempted to ascertain gene frequencies (the genotypic approach) and to use these patterns of genotype combinations in the continuing pursuit of ascertaining races. But, whether phenotypes or genotypes are utilized, scientists have not agreed in their classifications of the "racial" divisions of humankind. Classifiers have identified major races and minor races, major races and subraces, and major and miscellaneous races, with the number of such categories differing significantly. Table 1.1 (pages 16–17) shows but a few of such efforts at classification of the biological divisions within humankind.

Dobzhansky has explained the problem involved in racial classification:

Populations that inhabit different countries differ more often in relative frequencies of genetically simple traits rather than in having any single trait present in all individuals of one population and always absent in another population. Not only are the differences thus relative rather than absolute, but, to make things still more complex, the variations of different characters are often independent or at least not genetically correlated. Some populations may be clearly different in gene A but rather similar in gene B, while other populations may be different in B but less so in A. This makes the drawing of lines separating different races a rather arbitrary procedure and results in the notorious inability of anthropologists to agree on any race classification yet proposed. Race classifiers might have indeed preferred to find simple and tidy races, in which every person would show just the characteristics

---

*For example, the human race (that is, the human species) or the German race (that is, the German ethnic group or the German nationality).

Table 1.1
Three Classifications of Races

E. A. Hooten, 1946

A. White or Caucasoid Primary
   1. Mediterranean
   2. Ainu
   3. Keltic
   4. Nordic
   5. Alpine
   6. East Baltic
   7. Armenoid
   8. Dinaric
   9. Nordic-Alpine
  10. Nordic-Mediterranean
B. Composite, Predominantly White
   1. Australian
     a. Murrian
     b. Carpentarian
     c. Tasmanoid
   2. Indo-Dravidian
     a. Classic Indo-Dravidian
     b. Armenoid-Iranian Plateau
     c. Indo-Nordic
     d. Australoid or Veddoid
     e. Negritoid
   3. Polynesian

C. Negroid Primary
   1. African Negro
   2. Nilotic Negro
   3. Negriot (pygmy)
D. Composite, Predominantly Negroid
   1. Tasmanian
   2. Melanesian-Papuan
     a. Papuan
     b. Melanesian
   3. Bushman-Hottentot
     a. Bushman
     b. Hottentot
E. Mongoloid Primary
   1. Classic Mongoloid
   2. Arctic Mongoloid or Eskimoid
F. Composite, Predominantly Mongoloid
   1. Indonesian-Mongoloid
     a. Malay-Mongoloid
     b. Indonesian
   2. American Indian
     a. Brachycephals
     b. Dolichocephals

T. Dobzhansky, 1962

1. Northwest European
2. Northeast European
3. Alpine
4. Mediterranean
5. Hindu
6. Turkic
7. Tibetan
8. North Chinese
9. Classic Mongoloid
10. Eskimo
11. Southeast Asiatic
12. Ainu
13. Lapp
14. North American Indian
15. Central American Indian
16. South American Indian
17. Fuegian

18. East African
19. Sudanese
20. Forest Negro
21. Bantu
22. Bushman and Hottentot
23. African Pygmy
24. Dravidian
25. Negrito
26. Melanesian-Papuan
27. Murrayian
28. Carpenterian
29. Micronesian
30. Polynesian
31. Neo-Hawaiian
32. Ladino
33. North American colored
34. South African colored

Table 1.1 (cont.)

A. L. Kroeber, 1948

A. Caucasian or "White"
  1. Nordic
  2. Alpine
  3. Mediterranean
  4. Hindu
B. Mongoloid or "Yellow"
  1. Mongolian
  2. Malaysian
  3. American Indian

C. Negroid or "Black"
  1. Negro
  2. Melanesian
  3. Pygmy Black
  4. Bushman
D. Of Doubtful Classification
  1. Australoid
  2. Polynesian
  3. Ainu
  4. Veddoid (Indo-Australian)

SOURCES: A. L. Kroeber, *Anthropology* (New York: Harcourt, Brace & Co., 1948), pp. 155–56, 132. John Buettner-Janusch, *Origins of Man, Physical Anthropology* (New York: John Wiley & Sons, 1966), pp. 9–12, 367–74, 395–425.

that his race is supposed to possess. Nature has not been obliging enough to make the races conform to this prescription.[11]

One critic of the efforts to "discover" races has written: "The inventing and isolating of human 'races' is, although an amusing pastime, of no further service to physical anthropology; it can only hinder the progress of that science, whose primary aim is to explain the evolution of the species as a whole. 'Races as irreducible categories,' wrote Jean Pinot, 'exist only in the fictions in our brains.'"[12] On the other hand, another well-known physical anthropologist stated flat out: "Of course races exist! They exist today, and they probably existed in the Pleistocene as well. . . . subgroups of our species occur and are definable according to consistent, established genetic criteria. A race and a Mendelian population, from the point of view of geneticists, are the same thing."[13]

Whether or not races are real, the "idea" of race has had an extremely important effect on human interactions, particularly in the last five hundred years. Race has significance as long as human beings categorize and symbolize human groupings by selected physical traits and act upon these meanings. It is for this reason that race will be defined in this book as: *any collection of human beings defined as alike due to certain selected physical attributes and labeled as such*. Races are words, which is not to say that there is nothing "out there" to give rise to such symbols. Racial terms may be polite or offensive, used by scientists, administrators, or the ordinary person—white, black, colored, Caucasian, nigger, honky, gook, Oriental, and Nordic are examples of these terms. A society has as many races within it as there are names for them, not including equivalent terms like Negro and black. From this perspective such words bring races into existence.

SOCIETY AND NATIONALITY

Ethnic and race relations occur within and between societies. A society can best be conceived of as a *sovereign normative social unit*. All social units (communities, organizations, and other groupings) have a set of norms to which members are expected to conform. A society's norms, however, are sovereign—they take precedent over the norms of all subunits. Such norms may take the form of written law codes in complex societies or be the unwritten understandings of a primitive tribe. In either case political autonomy is the essential criterion for distinguishing a society from other social units.[14]

Although there are several ways in which societies may be classified, one useful typology is the division of all societies into three types: primitive (or folk), preindustrial (or agrarian), and industrial (or modern). A primitive society is nonliterate, is small in population, lacks formal government, and is based upon either food gathering and hunting or upon rudimentary agriculture. Today there are no more primitive societies (that is, primitive sovereign units) but numerous folk subsocieties do exist within the approximately 150 countries in the world. Preindustrial societies first appeared in the Near East around 4000–3500 B.C. and are generally characterized by writing; monumental technology; urbanization (about 5 to 15 percent of the population was urbanized before the nineteenth century); strata consisting of landowners, merchants, artisans, peasants, and slaves; and a state generally headed by a monarch. Several societies today remain basically preindustrial except for large cities uncharacteristic of the traditional type and the absence of slavery. Industrial society, which originated in Britain around 1800, is distinguished by a more flexible class system, mass communication, industrial technology, large-scale bureaucracies, and a high degree of urbanization, among other features.

As will be elaborated upon later, the overwhelming majority of complex societies (preindustrial and industrial) have been multiethnic, and in some cases multiracial as well. What has blurred or concealed this quality of complex societies has been the idea of "nationality" or "nation" that has developed in the last two or three hundred years. A nation has been conceived of as a people with common traditions and a sense of shared ancestry. The term "nationality" has often been used in the same manner. Since ethnic group, in the meaning that has been presented here, is synonymous with this meaning of nation, it is suggested that this meaning of nation be dropped. We will define *nationality* as *all of the citizens of a modern state*, regardless of their ethnic or racial status.

INTERRELATIONSHIPS

In summary, these are the four basic units that make up the subject matter of the field of race and ethnic relations: an *ethnic group* is a community group based upon the ascribed status of a diffuse ancestry that is maintained by similarities of culture, language, and/or phenotype; a *race* is a collection of human beings defined and labeled as alike due to certain selected physical attributes; a *society* is a sovereign or politically autonomous social system and, depending upon the presence or absence of certain sociocultural elements, may be classified as primitive, preindustrial, or industrial; and a *nationality* is all of the citizens of a modern state-society. There are a number of interconnections and relationships among these four social units, relationships that, in some cases, blur these analytical distinctions.

Ethnic Group and Race

The distinction between race and ethnic group is a useful one. Race is defined essentially by biological characteristics; ethnic group is defined in terms of behavior, culture, and language, in addition to an occasional reliance upon phenotype; ethnic groups constitute community interaction networks; races rarely do. In some cases the distinction between the two concepts is quite clear; in other circumstances there is a tendency for the two to merge. Four basic relationships between race and ethnic group may be identified.

In the first relationship, a race generally includes several ethnic groups. Races such as white, black, and yellow (or Caucasoid, Negroid, and Mongoloid) subsume diverse ethnic groups under a single rubric symbolizing phenotypic similarities. But even with this stress on physical differences there are cultural differences between races. When the cultures of European whites and their colonial offshoots, the whites of the Americas and Australia, are compared *as a whole* with the cultures that comprise the numerous ethnic groups of Africa and Asia, one can see that there *are* differences. At a very general level there are cultural differences between occidental, eastern, and African societies. Such differences *have been perceived* and reinforce the idea of race because of the correlation between cultural and phenotypic differences, if one is willing to ignore all of the cultural differences between ethnic groups within each of the races. Because of this and because phenotypic difference does, on occasion, indicate ethnic group status, the sharp distinction between ethnic group as cultural and race as physiological is more an analytical conception than a social reality.

The second relationship between ethnic group and race occurs when miscegenation (reproduction across racial lines) becomes frequent. As white

Europeans spread out from their native homelands to Africa, Australia, the Americas, and Asia, primarily as conquerors, they mated with the natives of these lands, producing children of mixed genotypes who became known as mestizos, half-breeds, or mulattoes. The same phenomenon occurred when members of numerous black ethnic groups were forcibly transported from Africa to the New World. Sexual relations between individuals from phenotypically different ethnic groups create a new race.

There are many examples of such racial categories coming into being as a result of sexual relations between members of different ethnic groups. In South Africa the union of Dutch and aboriginal inhabitants (the Hottentots and the Bushmen) produced a Dutch-speaking colored population, officially termed "colored." In India the product of Britishers and native inhabitants was the Anglo-Indian. Miscegenation between Europeans and imported black slaves in the New World created mulattoes, or coloreds. Sexual relations between Spaniards and Indians and Spaniards and blacks created the mestizo. And in the United States there are various mixtures of red, black, and white with such names as Clappers, Chicahominy, Nanticokes, Red Niggers, and Yellowhammers.[15]

It was stated previously that *in general* racial terms such as white or black included numerous ethnic groups as racial subdivisions. Mulatto and mestizo racial categories are exceptions. They are races, but there are no ethnic subdivisions within them; yet they are not ethnic groups, because they lack a sense of ethnicity. Most races are multiethnic color categories; a few are not. What is common to both of these forms of race is the importance that members of a society give to phenotype.

In the third major relationship between race and ethnic group, a race can become an ethnic group, although such a transformation is rare. Under circumstances of contrast and conflict, a collection of individuals classified together primarily on the basis of phenotype may develop a sense of ethnicity, which in turn may lead to a community, thereby creating an ethnic group. Such a process has occurred among the Anglo-Indians in India. According to Noel Gist:

> The many difficulties encountered by the Anglo-Indian minority, particularly discrimination by the British or even by other Indians, had the effect of arousing a sense of "community" among its members. This community consciousness, based on the ties of blood and culture, emerged in the eighteenth century and has continued to this day, fluctuating in intensity with the rise and fall of Anglo-Indian fortunes, the presence or absence of effective leadership in the group, and discriminatory acts against its members. Community solidarity was also enhanced by the wide cultural gap between the Anglo-Indians and the vast Indian majority, mainly Hindus and Muslims.[16]

The group that the Anglo-Indians identified with (their reference group) was the British, and the Anglo-Indians would have gladly been absorbed into this group if the British had let them; however, British social distance kept them marginal. The British looked down on these "breeds," and such arrogance was matched by "Anglo-Indian arrogance toward other Indians."[17] The marginal status created the climate for the emergence of a new ethnic group out of what was once a racial category.

The Métis (Red River Métis) of Canada are another race that became an ethnic group. The result of miscegenation between Europeans (English and French) and various American Indian ethnic groups in the seventeenth and eighteenth centuries, the Métis acquired a new cultural tradition including French and Indian elements and unique elements of their own creation. Today the Métis recognize few Indians or European kin and think of themselves as a separate people, neither white nor Indian.[18]

Both the Anglo-Indians and the Métis were once races with no internal ethnic divisions. It is this type of race that is most likely to acquire a sense of ethnicity and perhaps become a viable ethnic group. It is also possible for a multiethnic racial category to develop into an ethnic group. This transformation may be occurring within the race of Indian-Americans. Over two hundred ethnic groups in the United States were collectively labeled Indians by Europeans. Treated similarly by white settlers and government agencies in the nineteenth century, the Indian tribes failed, nevertheless, to acquire a sense of "Indianness" and were conquered, one by one. Today, however, there is evidence that a common sense of ancestral identity is developing, along with organizations to promote Indian interests, although Indian ethnicity and an Indian ethnic group are far from being realized at the present time.

The fourth and final relationship between race and ethnic group necessitates the invention of a new concept, a *racial-ethnic group*. In those societies in which a dominant ethnic group exists, a racial-ethnic group is defined as an ethnic group that is phenotypically divergent from the dominant group. Racial-ethnic groups in the United States include Black-Americans,* Japanese-Americans, and Chinese-Americans, among others, since they have all of the characteristic of ethnic groups yet are physically different from the dominant Anglos (or nonhyphenated Americans). Polish-Americans and Italian-Americans are not racial-ethnic groups because they are not physically different from the dominant group. Because of their greater visibility, racial-ethnic groups in the United States have been subjected to far greater forms of discrimination and to a greater intensity of discrimination than have the white immigrant groups from Europe and Canada.

---

*From this point on, "Black-Americans" will be capitalized. Black-American is not the equivalent of white American. Whites in the United States are a race; Black-Americans are an ethnic group, one group among many that make up the black race. In an earlier period in American history blacks lacked a common ethnicity, being made up of members from many African groups. In the last one hundred years ethnicity has developed along with community. Black-Americans are not just "colored WASPs."

Ethnic Group, Society, and Nationality

Throughout the development of human society, from simple food-gathering societies to complex industrial states, ethnicity has persisted. During 99 percent of the time humans have existed on this planet, ethnic group and society have been synonymous. In primitive or folk societies the tribe was the sovereign unit of social control. While ethnicity did not differentiate internal relationships, it was maintained and reinforced by intertribal contacts. When the state came into existence, with its written laws, tax collection apparatus, bureaucracies, military forces, and an ideology sufficient to override the loyalties of kith and kin (that is, the sacred monarchy), the control of a much larger and more diverse population was made possible.

With few exceptions, complex societies have been multiethnic. The ancient empire states were extremely heterogeneous. Even small city-states or medieval European kingdoms and duchies generally had minority groups which did not feel that they were ancestrally related to the majority of the population. Today, virtually all of the countries of the world are ethnically heterogeneous (Table 1.2). In some cases the members of one ethnic group constitute a majority of the total population, which includes one or more numerical minorities. In a few societies one group is a plurality of the population and the rest are minorities. And in other cases all of the ethnic groups are minorities in the numerical sense of the term.

Often all the citizens of a society are known by the name of one of the ethnic groups, a fact that may conceal the society's ethnic subdivisions. In France, for example, all of the citizens, collectively, are known as Frenchmen (nationality). The majority of the population is ethnically French, but several other ethnic groups reside within the territory of France. This situation is found in numerous other societies, such as West Germany, East Germany, Argentina, Poland, Mexico, and Sweden.

In the United States a similar condition exists. In polite company there are Mexican-Americans (or Chicanos), Black-Americans, Polish-Americans and many more. When all of the hyphenated groups are listed it is apparent that a large segment of the population is not included within these categories. What is that segment? Are they an ethnic group? Some rather inadequate terms have been used to label this segment—Anglos, Anglo-Saxons, old-stock Americans, native Americans, Yankees, whites, and WASPs (White Anglo-Saxon Protestants). But perhaps there is an American *ethnic group* as well as an American nationality. As will be examined in Part 2, an American ethnic group did emerge in the latter part of the eighteenth century. This group originated from an English core in the colonial period, began to perceive itself as different from the English, and absorbed many European immigrants as a result of its power and prestige. Following the idea of the hyphenated group, with the ethnic name being on the left side of the hyphen and the nationality name on the right side, perhaps we should recognize "American-Americans."

Table 1.2
Ethnic Makeup of Major Countries in the World

The Union of Soviet Socialist Republics: Great Russians (53% of the population in 1970); 119 other major ethnic groups, among them being—Ukrainians, Lithuanians, Letts, Poles, Estonians, Finns, Germans, Roumanians, Jews, Georgians, White Russians, Armenians, Iranians, Tartars, Kirghiz, Mongols, Latvians, Maldavians, Turmenians, Abkhasians, Uzbeks, Chuvash, Mari, Tadzhiks, Udmurts, Bashkirs, and Azerbaijanians, to name the major groupings.

The People's Republic of China: Chinese (with many linguistic, if not ethnic, subdivisions), Mongols, Tibetans, Mongol-Turks, Turkic-Tartars, Tungans, Lolo, Miao-Tye, Manchus, Koreans, Japanese (one-half million in Manchuria), etc.

Iran: Iranians (Persians), Kurds, Armenians, Turks, Turkomans, Jews, Syrians, Assyrians, Baluchis, etc.

Argentina: Argentines (Spanish culture), Irish, English, Italians, Spaniards (from Spain), Belgians, Germans, Swiss, etc., and a few Indian groups remaining from their Indian wars of the nineteenth century.

Laos: Thai (Lao, Lu, etc.), Meo, Khmu, Sek, Vietnamese, Yao, So, Lamet, Mon-Khmer, etc.

Nigeria: 250 groups, among them being Yoruba, Ibo, Kanuri, Tiv, Nupe, Ijaw, Hausa-Fulani.

Yugoslavia: Serbs, Croats, Slovenes, Macedonians, Montenegrins, Slovaks, Moslems, Albanians, Hungarians, Rumanians, Bulgarians, Ruthenians, etc.

France: French, Germans, Italians, Basque, Jews, Algerians, Bretons, Corsicans, and various groups from former French colonies in equatorial Africa.

The United States: Anglos, Irish, Mexicans (or Chicanos), Puerto Ricans, Germans, Cubans, Blacks, Swedes, Jews, Hungarians, Japanese, Chinese, Hawaiians, Eskimos, Italians, Poles, etc., and at least 200 Indian groups.

The United Kingdom: English, Welsh, Cornish, Irish, Scots, Indians (from India, Uganda), Pakistani, Americans, Italians, Jews, West Indians (blacks), etc.

Afghanistan: Afghans (or Durani), Pathans, Ghilzai, Tajiks, Hazaras, Kaffirs, Baluchi, Kohistani, Gujars, Parachas.

Ghana: Asante, Fanti, Efe, Gā, etc.

The Philippines: Filipinos, Chinese, Americans, Spanish, Japanese, several groups from Indonesia, and numerous primitive tribes.

Burma: Burmans, Shans, Chins, Indians, Kachins, Chinese, and Europeans of several kinds.

Brazil: Brazilians (Portuguese culture), Germans, Poles, Japanese, Negroes, Italians, and numerous Indian tribes in the Amazon region.

In other societies where the ethnic-nationality nomenclature is not different, perhaps the hyphenated ethnic group-nationality idea would produce clarification: German-Germans, German-Poles, Polish-Germans, and Polish-Poles, for example.

Some societies do not suffer from this confusion of nationality and ethnicity. In the United Kingdom all citizens are British. This name is different from those of the ethnic groups that constitute this society, such as the English, Scots, West Indians, Irish, Cornish, Welsh, and Indians. Yugoslavia, Czechoslovakia, and Nigeria are other countries in which the nationality name is different from any of their ethnic group members.

Membership within a society generally creates new ethnic groups. Members of an ethnic group in one society who emigrate to another become separated from their brethren. Societal boundaries discourage or prevent intersocietal communities, and in time a new ethnic group emerges. Irish immigrants to the United States became Irish-Americans. Mexican-Americans or Chicanos are not the same group as Mexicans in Mexico.

Ethnicity can certainly transcend several societies, even though intersocietal ethnic groups are rare. One can be Irish-American and Irish in general. Basque ethnicity transcends citizenship in Spain or in France, and Jewish ethnicity transcends numerous societies. However, functioning ethnic groups, as viable forms of social organization affecting the daily lives of their members, are generally unique subdivisions *within* a given society. This reality is often dramatically brought home to members who take a trip back to the country of their origins. Greek-Americans visiting Greece will have a higher-level ethnicity, but they will soon note the differences between Greek-Americans and Greek-Greeks. Sometimes even first-generation immigrants returning to their native land after a twenty-year absence will be shocked by what they find and what they failed to remember.

The final relationship between ethnic group, society, and nationality is more of a theoretical possibility than a recurrent reality. It is possible for all of the ethnic groups within a society to merge together as one group. Nationality and ethnic group become identical, as once happened with society and tribe. One possibility is the assimilation or absorption of all of the minority groups into the dominant group. The nationality name, which is the same as the dominant ethnic group's name, becomes the symbol of ethnic identification for all of the members of the society. Everybody in France becomes an ethnic Frenchman; Corsicans, Basques, and Algerians disappear. Another possiblity is that a nationality name that does not refer to any one ethnic group comes to be a new ethnic group; all of the groups disappear and everybody makes nationality the sense of ethnicity. For example, while at the present time there is no ethnic group in Yugoslavia called Yugoslavian, all of the groups could disappear and everybody would become ethnically Yugoslavian. No more Croatians, Serbs, or Macedonians would be found in the country, just one people—Yugoslavians. The merging of nationality and ethnic group is an ideal and constitutes the myth of the nation-state: one people under one government.

SUMMARY

Ethnicity is a set of attitudes related to a sense of ancestral identification with a certain segment of the world's population. The sense of ancestral or biological ties is diffuse in nature and is maintained and reinforced by intergroup contrasts of language, culture, and phenotype, which emphasize intragroup similarities.

An ethnic group is a community group based upon the ascribed status of a diffuse ancestry that is maintained by a shared culture, language, and/or phenotype. As a social unit, an ethnic group consists of a community network of interaction, along with organizations and primary groups as subdivisions. Group membership is due to ascription rather than choice.

Races are collections of human beings defined and labeled as alike because of physical attributes, such as skin color. A race may be either a multiethnic color category or, less frequently, a category of people created by miscegenation and lacking ethnic subdivisions or ethnicity. Biological variations with Homo sapiens *were created by the same general processes involved in all evolution—mutation, inbreeding, excessive population reproduction, natural selection, sexual selection, and genetic drift. The relative significance of each of these factors in producing physical variations within the one human species is not precisely known. Whether racial labels correspond to relatively clearly delineated categories of human beings as biological realities or are arbitrary symbolic constructions, the* idea *of race has been of extreme importance in affecting social relationships.*

A society is a sovereign normative unit. Whether this sovereignity rests in the customs and traditions of a nonliterate group or in the state of complex societies, political autonomy is the essential condition that distinguishes a society from other social units. Nationality, a term that has gained importance in the last few hundred years, refers to all of the citizens of a state-society, regardless of the ethnic or racial status of these members.

The following are but a few of the relationships between these basic units:

1. Ethnicity is generally related to an ethnic group within a particular society but may transcend the ethnic group and the society.

2. A multiethnic color category (one form of race) may develop into an ethnic group if a shared ethnicity develops and the individuals develop community networks based upon this ethnicity.

3. A race that is created by miscegenation and that lacks ethnic subdivisions (another form of race) may become an ethnic group if ethnicity develops along with forms of social organization.

4. When the nationality name is the same as the ethnic name of the dominant group there is a tendency to conceive of the society as homogeneous or as a nation-state.

5. Ethnic groups are generally subdivisions of societies; however, a few ethnic groups transcend two or more societies.

6. Nationality can be a higher level of ethnicity for many members of the various ethnic groups within a society. If lower levels of ethnicity disappear along with ethnic group divisions, nationality can become the basis for a new ethnic group: one people under one government.

2

THE BASIC DIMENSIONS
AND MODELS

INTRODUCTION

Needless to say, ethnic groups and races differ *from each other* in a number
of important ways, and *within* each group or race there are differences. At
the same time, members of these statuses carry on their institutional activities within and across the boundaries of ethnic group or race, meeting
and interacting with members of their own groups or with members of
out-groups. For example, groups often specialize in certain occupations as
opposed to others. Likewise, members of some groups exist predominantly
in one social stratum while others have a strata membership that approximates the overall societal distribution. Although most groups have rich
and poor members along with those of average income, others may be predominantly poor or predominantly rich. When any two groups are compared
they may show strikingly different customs, or, at the other extreme, there
may be little in the way of traditions to distinguish between them. Some
individuals may stress their ethnicity or race as paramount over everything
else, thereby affecting their political views and their choice of friends,
mates, and neighbors; yet in the same group other individuals might consider their race or ethnicity largely unimportant. Some individuals may
just try to get through each day as unobtrusively as possible, while others
may perceive out-groups as categorical enemies or at least as competitors in
the struggle for existence. Other examples of diversity within and between
groups could be given, but the point is that an ethnic group or a race is not a
homogeneous entity, and that there is considerable variation in the relationships between these categories of human beings.

How is it possible to come to grips with such complexity? Should we throw up our hands and argue that since every human action is unique (which it is) there is no way to make sense out of the uniquenesses?

First of all, it is possible to identify a number of very *general* characteristics or dimensions of race and ethnic relations, dimensions that, although highly variable, are nevertheless to be found whenever such groupings come together in the same society. Second, simplified types of relationships or "models" can be constructed that at least approximate the ongoing social life of real societies. Third, it is apparent that every identifiable, specific aspect of social life has a beginning at some point in history. And elements of society persist at least for a short period and often for many years. History also demonstrates that specific patterns or aspects of social life change and eventually disappear. Generally, while there may always be some form of government or religion, *specific* governments and religions have a beginning, they persist, they change, and then they cease to exist. The history of humankind is littered with discarded institutional practices. Nobody believes in or practices the religion of Osiris, Britain no longer has feudalism, and Athens is not a city-state. For our study of ethnic groups and race relations it will be useful to at least identify those general social processes that are involved in the beginnings (or origins) of relationships between groups within the same society, those processes that enable relationships to crystallize and to persist, and those processes that change and perhaps terminate a pattern that was once identifiable.

Eventually, more precise generalizations about ethnic and race relations can be devised, generalizations related to the dimensions, to the models, and to the idea of "stages" of development and change. Numerous predictions, based on probabilities and organized together in a logical manner, may someday reduce the apparent disorder in the field of race and ethnic relations. This last stage of scientific inquiry, however, is beyond the scope of this book.

The purpose of this chapter is to identify and to briefly explain five major dimensions, varying in degree and in form, that seem to exist whenever different ethnic groups and races coexist within the same system: stratification, spatial segregation, cultural differentiation, social and personal distance, and competition and conflict. In addition, three models or types of race and ethnic relations will be constructed: empire societies, national societies, and pluralistic societies.

STRATIFICATION

In every society, but particularly in complex societies (preindustrial and industrial), rewards have been unequally distributed among individuals, families, and social statuses (such as gender, occupation, age, organizational position, religion, ethnic group, and race). The generic term for the processes involved in such a distribution over periods of time and for the structure of such inequality at any given time is *social stratification*.

Rewards, generally, are what members of a society consider important or valuable, and, as such, are *scarce* commodities or conditions. Rewards are those factors which increase one's control over his or her destiny, increase alternative forms of behavior, reduce unpleasant obligations and tasks, enhance self-esteem, contribute to material comforts, and, in the broadest sense, make life more meaningful. At an abstract level the four major rewards are power, prestige, privilege, and wealth (PPPW). *Power* is the command of resources sufficient to secure compliance with, or to suppress resistance to, particular decisions or expectations.[1] *Prestige* is the extent of social honor or the estimation of social worth attributed to individuals, families, statuses, groups, and other forms of social units. *Privilege* can be defined as benefits, opportunities, and exemptions from obligations acquired by certain social units and individuals and denied to others.[2] And *wealth* consists of whatever is valuable, chattel or fixed, that can be possessed, controlled, accumulated, and exchanged (money and property).

The unequal distribution of a specific reward or a combination of rewards creates *strata*, or ranked divisions of reward distributions. The ranks may be delineated by sociologists or by the average citizen, and the boundaries between the divisions may or may not represent reality. The following are all strata: the rich and the poor; dominant and subordinate ethnic groups; the propertied class and the nonpropertied; the aristocracy and the commoners; the elite and the masses; the upper, middle, and lower classes (or social classes); those who earn less than three thousand dollars a year and those who earn three thousand to six thousand dollars a year; the governing class and the governed; "superior" and "inferior" races. Such divisions may be useful or not. They may be oversimplifications of complex reality, or they may be terms that accurately symbolize inequality. In any case, they are a symbolic way of defining reality as ranked categories of individuals or ranked social groupings rather than a gradation of inequality.

A specific form of strata is social class. Social classes are divisions of whole societies or communities within societies that represent divisions of a combination of rewards (in one meaning of this ambiguous term[3]). At least three social classes can be identified in almost all complex societies. The upper social class consists of individuals and families with the greatest amounts of power, privilege, prestige, and wealth. The lower social class includes those families and individuals who exist in relative poverty, who engage in the least desirable forms of labor, and who have the least power and privilege. The middle social class designates those individuals and families of moderate income who occupy organizational positions with limited power and who enjoy some privilege and prestige. In industrial societies the middle social class is primarily made up of individuals with relatively specialized and valued skills related to production or to the providing of services requiring greater training.

More than three social classes may be conceptualized, but for our purposes this crude model of inequality will be sufficient.

Ethnic and Racial Stratification

The acquisition of rewards varies from one ethnic group or race to another. This inequality may be manifested in several ways:

1. Ethnic groups and races are not proportionately distributed among the social classes. If an ethnic group constituted 5 percent of the population, and if ethnic group status made no difference, then we would expect 5 percent of the upper social class, 5 percent of the middle social class, and 5 percent of the lower social class to be occupied by members of this group. But proportional representation is rare, if not nonexistent, even in the most egalitarian of societies. In the more extreme systems of stratification, the proportion of members of one ethnic group or race in the upper and middle social classes will greatly exceed their proportion of the total population of the society. At the same time, one or more other groups will exceed their population ratio as members of the lowest social class.

2. Ethnic groups and races will differ in the percentage of their members who acquire specific rewards. When any single reward is divided into strata, each group will have a somewhat different percentage of members within these strata. With income, for example, 15 percent of group A may earn over $15,000 a year and 3 percent may earn $3,000 or less, while only 1 percent of group B may earn $15,000 or more and 20 percent may earn $3,000 or less. Years of education, an important factor in determining income because of its relationship to occupational placement, may be divided into strata and the ethnic composition of each strata examined. Thus, 25 percent of group A may have a college education, while only 0.5 percent of group B may hold a college degree. Power, if defined operationally as positions of policy making in organizations, can be similarly examined. Are all of the ethnic and racial groups of a particular community proportionately represented in the positions of power? The answer is generally no.

3. Ethnic groups and races generally differ in prestige. Although members of a society tend to rank their own groups the highest, there is often a general consensus on the rating of all of the groups. Some groups tend to be admired and emulated; others may be stigmatized as subhuman.

4. In some societies ethnic groups and races differ in privileges. Ethnic or racial status per se becomes relevant in such matters as voting, jury duty, owning property, or having a certain occupation, to name

but a few areas of social life in which some groups have privileges while others are denied them.

In a few societies ethnic groups and races have been relatively equal in terms of proportional representation within strata, although some degree of inequality exists. In these societies, which will later be described as *pluralistic*, privileges related to ethnic or racial status are illegal.

But the focus of this book is on the more extreme forms of ethnic and racial stratification, on societies in which there is a dominant group and one or more subordinate groups.

Dominance and Subordinance

Dominance and subordinance are terms derived from Latin. *Dominance* means the state of ruling, prevailing, controlling, or exercising influence over others. *Subordinance* refers to the condition of being below others in terms of rank, influence, and power. When two parties in a relationship differ in power, and, of lesser importance, in prestige, wealth, or privilege, over a period of time in numerous interactions, the relationship will be one of dominance and subordinance. Dominant-subordinate relationships are a frequent and enduring aspect of the social life of human beings as well as of many animal societies. Males have dominated females for thousands of years, the old have controlled the young, and old men have always run societies. The United States has dominated Latin America, teachers have dominated students, and officers have dominated enlisted men. Recently, Turks have dominated Greeks, English have dominated Irish, and white has dominated black and yellow.

In modern Israel the following relationship of inequality exists between the Ashkenazim (European Jews) and the Sephardim ("Oriental" Jews):

The general distribution of resources (such as income, education or occupation) between Ashkenazim and Orientals is roughly two to one. Disparity of power is much more considerable and discrete. Ashkenazim are in full control of the three power centers in the state—the state government, the Histadrut and the Jewish Agency—as well as the public and private sectors of the economy. In the intermediate power echelons, Ashkenazim are several times more overrepresented than Orientals. The ratio is five to one respectively. Only in the local power positions is there a roughly proportional representation (short of equality) of each group. The Ashkenazi group is also the dominant cultural group in a culturally diversified society. Aside from a few token examples like the humus *and* tabini *dishes and Yemenite traditional crafts, the Ashkenazi or western values and practices predominate. History texts used in Jewish schools hardly mention Oriental Jewry of the last 500 years. Literature is exclusively Ashkenazi. Musti follows suit. The prevailing social ideals are completely Ashkenazi—a small middle-class urban family, a kibbutz member, the sabra, the socialist society. The Oriental Jew cannot recognize himself in such images of Israel.*[4]

31

In this society the political, economic, *and* cultural dominance of one group over another is clearly established. But what if *all* of these three forms of dominance were not present? Is it possible for one group to be dominant in one area and not in another? What is the major criterion that will establish the existence of a dominant ethnic group or race in a given society?

The Criterion of Dominance: Control of the State.   The state has been the major locus of power and authority since its invention in the beginning of history. Members of the state have acted *as if* their policies and programs are in the interest of the total society and transcend the pluralism inherent in state societies. The state has regulated or eliminated other organizations. By instigating or tolerating the existence of various forms of discrimination, the state has intensified or maintained patterns of inequality. It has planned, organized, and controlled the economic sector. The state has conquered other states or primitive tribes, thereby bringing new ethnic groups and races into subordination. Although it has tolerated reform movements and radical movements as long as they did not go too far, the state has crushed them when they have been defined as dangerous. Even when the government of a state has fallen to a revolutionary movement, the state has not withered away but has become the necessary tool of the new elite. When the territory of a state becomes fragmented as a result of a successful secessionist movement, the secessionists must establish their own state to consolidate and to maintain their new position. And when the state is controlled by the economic elite (a ruling class), such control is deemed essential, for without it how could 1 percent of a population continue to exist in such splendor?

Because of the overwhelming importance of the state, the group that controls it has dominance. *A dominant ethnic group or race exists when the majority of the major positions of the state are occupied by the members of one ethnic group or race.* It makes no difference whether the dominant group is a majority, a plurality, or a minority of the total societal population. It also matters not if an ethnic group that is a minority of the population is proportionately represented in the state—for example, when a group constituting 5 percent of the total population occupies 5 percent of the state's major positions.

The Soviet Union provides an excellent example of state control, in this case by the Russians:

> From the beginning, but especially in recent years, Russians have held most of the leading positions in the security and "justice" ministries. In the general staff of the Soviet army, among generals and commanders of lower rank, Russians are overwhelmingly predominant. The foreign service has been completely dominated by Russians since the early 1930's. . . . A statistical approach to the question of Russian predominance tends to be misleading. It should be stressed that all important non-Russian members of the Communist party passed through the deep transform-

ing process of thorough Communist indoctrination and complete Russification. Acceptance of Russian culture is, indeed, an essential factor. . . . It is an established principle in the Soviet Union that only true converts to Russianism and Sovietism can occupy posts of importance in the Soviet government and the Communist party machinery, while all insincere and false converts are sooner or later accused of nationalist deviation or bourgeois nationalism and are removed or shot "to encourage the others."[5]

Russians dominate the central Communist Party and most of its regional subdivisions.[6] Although officially the U. S. S. R. is a federation of ethnic-based republics and according to Article 17 of the constitution each republic has the right "freely to secede" from the U. S. S. R., Article 14 transfers all major authority to the central government. The ethnic republics have minimal authority. "Permission to build a bridge in Bashkiria, to install water pipes in Tiflis, to run trolleybuses in Nalchik, to build a school in Tajikstan, or to construct an opera house in Ashkabad must be secured from Moscow before funds are released."[7] Ethnic autonomy in the republics amounts to no more than the right to employ the native tongue of the area as the official language of government and education.[8]

Control of the state by the members of one ethnic group, as seen in the Russian example, has a number of implications for other ethnic groups, as well as for the nonelite members of the dominant group. While an ethnically homogenous political elite is not always preoccupied with problems of an ethnic nature, their policies have an ethnic bias. At the very least this bias takes the form of a lack of sensitivity to the problems and interests of other ethnic group members, a lack of sensitivity that might be termed cultural arrogance. Members of the controlling elite formulate policies which, in their minds, have nothing to do with ethnicity, but are rather for the good of "society." They build dams in the sacred areas of an ethnic minority, instigate highway programs and urban renewal projects that devastate the community life of ethnic minority enclaves, enact criminal laws which reflect their views of what is criminal or noncriminal, and conduct national ceremonies and historical reenactments based upon their own ethnic view of history, which either neglects or insults the other ethnic groups.

Ethnicity is overtly relevant when members of the dominant group enact policies that they perceive to be beneficial to other groups with little or no consultation with members of these groups. When the minority "children" do not appreciate what has been done for them, the elite is likely to react with anger. Similarly, when members of subordinate ethnic groups protest or engage in violent acts because of such paternalism or because of discrimination, the elite may not perceive the ethnic basis of the reaction. Actions that an outside observer may perceive as an ethnic rebellion are often defined by the political elite as the results of *criminal* elements.

The ethnic bias of the political elite often becomes quite overt. Members of the elite may decide to forcibly acculturate a group, to forcibly segregate them, to institute increased programs of discrimination, to tolerate or encourage discrimination by nonelite members of their group, to forcibly expel a group, or, as the ultimate solution to a perceived threat to their interests (which, of course, is in the interest of society), exterminate the group. Even if subordinate ethnic groups are highly successful or highly integrated into a society, the possibility always exists that the state can turn against them—Germany turned against the Jews in the 1930s.

Since, by definition, subordinate ethnic groups or races do not have significant representation in the state, they are, in a real sense, at the mercy of those individuals who are in control of the government. State policies toward them can be favorable for periods of time and then drastically change; security for many subordinate groups must be tenuous. As will be examined in Part 2, the American government has vacillated in its policies toward the Indians—it has made them wards of government (1871), tried to turn them into individualistic Yankee farmers on family plots of ground (1884), put them on reservations to strengthen them politically and economically (1934), repossessed their reservations and moved the Indians into the cities (1954), and then moved them back to improved reservations (1970).

In the Philippines, from the time they established their dominance in 1571 until the Americans replaced them in 1898, the Spanish elite vacillated similarly toward the Chinese minority. The Chinese were initially welcomed and encouraged to immigrate in order to provide needed commercial enterprises and services. After ten years the drain of Spanish gold to China and the unanticipated success of the immigrants in commerce began to threaten Spanish dominance, and the Chinese in Manila were segregated. This was followed by the deportation of 12,000 Chinese in 1596. In 1603 23,000 Chinese were killed, and another 23,000 went to their deaths for revolting against having to pay a special tribute to the Spanish king for the privilege of living in the islands. In 1755 all non-Christian Chinese were expelled, and in 1823 new discriminatory taxes were levied against the Chinese, causing 800 more to leave the country and 1,083 to flee to the mountains. Later in the nineteenth century the Spanish government reverted to a policy of encouragement and the Chinese population increased from 8,000 in 1850 to 100,000 by 1885.[9] What the state giveth, the state can taketh away.

Who controls the state has significance also for nonelite members of the dominant group. Belonging to the same ethnic or racial group as members of the political elite does not guarantee rewards, although it helps. Our concern with ethnicity and race should not make us forget the relevance of other social factors, such as class and ideology. The Russian elite discriminated against and exploited Russian peasants as well as non-Russian groups. A common ethnicity does not eliminate class conflict, religious conflict, or struggles between church and state for rewards, and elite members of an ethnic group can often be harsher in their treatment of other members of their ethnic status than out-group members. Nevertheless, there are still a number of advantages or rewards for nonelite ethnic dominants. If the elite discriminate by ethnicity in their recruitment and enlistment of new elite, then a member of the dominant ethnic group has at least passed this minimal test of admission. Dominant nonelites also benefit from the relative absence of ethnic or racial discrimination against them. They may be coerced, exploited, or controlled on other grounds, such as religion, political views, or social class, but at least they are generally exempted from ethnic or racial discrimination.* Another advantage is that the lower-echelon positions within the major organizations will be more readily available to them—not only because of discrimination against other groups, but also because of their own cultural familiarity with the rules and skills necessary for such positions. Such an organizational position will in turn lead to other rewards, particularly a higher income. Nonelites also enjoy the advantage that their culture and language, in most cases, predominate in public life. The advantage of not having to learn a new language will be apparent to anyone who has struggled to master another tongue, a difficulty made worse by a "let them learn our language" attitude. If nothing else, even the poorest members of a dominant group can bask in the prestige of their group and the accomplishments of some of its members ("they are my people"). For a long time it was still better to be "poor white trash" than "poor black trash" in the American South. Because of the peculiar nature of symbols, a loser can bask in the accomplishments of winners because "we are the same people."

Factors That Intensify Dominance.   The minimal criterion for ethnic or racial dominance, as argued here, is the control and occupancy of at least the majority of the main positions of authority within the organizations of the state. Racial or ethnic group dominance is *intensified* if any or all of the following factors develop: (1) the dominant group occupies the major positions of authority in nonstate organizations; (2) the culture and language of that group set the standards for the whole society; (3) the majority of the society's total wealth goes to the members of this one ethnic group or race; and (4) privileges are obtained by this one group.

In complex societies there are always other important organizations besides the ones that constitute the state. Such organizations include churches, banks, corporations, universities, unions, guilds, businesses, public schools, and newspapers. Generally, when one ethnic group controls the state it also occupies the major positions within nonstate organizations.

*An interesting exception to this general advantage occurred in Argentina and Chile. The governments in these two states were composed primarily of native-born Creoles of Spanish descent, or "Argentines" and "Chileans." In the latter part of the nineteenth century and the early twentieth century they encouraged European immigrants to enter and improve their respective countries. Native-born Chileans and Argentines were discriminated against in several fields in favor of European foreigners, particularly in the areas of engineering and teaching. (Carl Solberg, Immigration and Nationalism: Argentina and Chile, 1890–1914 [Austin: University of Texas Press, 1970], pp. 74–76.)

There have been exceptions, however. In some societies economic enterprises may be dominated by members of ethnic minorities. In many societies outside of China the Chinese have predominated in commercial establishments. The ancient empires often allowed and even encouraged foreign or subordinate ethnic merchants and traders. In the nineteenth century Argentina encouraged emigration from Europe, and by 1914 29.9 percent of these foreigners owned 72 percent of the society's commercial firms and 65 percent of the industrial enterprises.[10] Indians in Uganda controlled the commercial firms both under the British and, later, under African rule. And in other states, such as Malaya, foreign investors have controlled the major economic enterprises. But these minorities and their significance in economic organizations are subjected to the policies of those who run the state. Minorities have been expelled, their property confiscated or their enterprises nationalized.

The significance of the state's being controlled by members of one race or ethnic group while the commercial sector is dominated by others can be seen in Uganda. Some 172,000 Asians in Uganda held British passports until the government ordered them to become naturalized citizens of Uganda or leave the country with only a minimum of possessions. Thousands have left, leaving their commercial enterprises to be taken over by Africans. President Idi Amin stated the matter quite succinctly: "Our top priority is to place the commercial sector in the hands of the indigenous African. All countries want their economies controlled by their own people and there is no reason why Uganda should be an exception."[11] Whether or not state organizations and nonstate organizations have been controlled by different ethnic groups, the state, with few exceptions, has exerted disproportionate power and influence over the other organizations.

In many societies where one ethnic group controls the state, its culture has been so overwhelmingly dominant in establishing "the spirit of the nation" that the dominant group has not even been defined as ethnic. It is the country or the "mainstream" of the country itself. The truly *ethnic* culture of the dominant group may be so closely identified with that of the society as a whole that it will not be exposed for what it is unless subordinate ethnic groups protest and generally assert their own cultures. As Enloe has written, "Only when minorities (or oppressed majorities) self-consciously assert the worth of their own cultures is the ethnicity of 'invisible' ethnic communities exposed. Ukrainian nationalism reveals the ethnic chauvinism of the Great Russians; Turkish nomads' resistance to the Red Army reveals the ethnicity of the Han Chinese; the black power salute challenges and exposes the ethnicity of Anglo-Saxon Americans."[12]

When linguistic dominance exists, the language of one ethnic group is the predominant or even the exclusive language of the governmental and legal processes and of the educational systems. Other languages may be tolerated in particular regions or areas inhabited by subordinate groups, but the language of the dominant group remains the language of the whole society.

The architecture of the politically dominant group has been another standardizing factor. Wherever the ancient Romans went, arenas, temples, and public buildings based upon the Greco-Roman synthesis found in Italy became conspicuously present, along with their famous roads. The Spanish conquerors of the New World ruthlessly destroyed much of the native Indian architecture and replaced it with the Baroque structures then prevalent in Spain. During the nineteenth century Victorian architecture became prominent in India and other parts of the British Empire.

There have been exceptions to the relationship between political and cultural dominance, but, again, these exceptions have existed as a result of the *policies* of the ethnic elite that controlled the organizations of the state. The Romans were never actively interested in romanizing their vast empire but allowed religious freedom and local customs to prevail. As long as the subordinate ethnic groups paid their taxes or tributes and obeyed a certain number of Roman laws applicable to everyone, cultural differentiation was permitted.[13] In some cases empires have been multilingual or bilingual, but this situation was *expedient*. The Persians, who were a small dominant minority in their empire, utilized both the Aramaic language and their own as the official languages.[14] Although the forced acculturation of other groups has been a recurrent policy, cultural dominance in all areas is not necessary for the continuing control of a society by a dominant ethnic group. In fact, the allowance of some degree of cultural differentiation in systems that contain highly diverse groups is quite effective in maintaining control and avoiding resistance.

The dominant ethnic group or race generally receives more than a majority of the total society's wealth. Such a distribution is not as rare as one would think. The upper class in preindustrial societies controlled 50 to 60 percent of the total wealth, and this group has generally been made up of the same ethnic or racial members that control the state. Even in industrial capitalistic societies such as the United States, 0.5 percent own one-third of the private sector wealth and the top 11 percent of this group own 60 percent of the society's wealth.[15]

The Republic of South Africa provides an example of wealth distribution on a racial basis. Europeans or whites make up around 20 percent of the population and are a dominant race by any criteria one can devise. Indians (from India) account for 3 percent of the population, 10 percent are coloreds, and blacks (Africans or Bantu speakers) make up 68 percent of the total. A rural white population of less than one-half million owns 87 percent of the land, while four million Africans are squeezed into the remaining 13 percent of the desirable land; the mean family income of whites is approximately thirteen to fourteen times that of Africans and five times that of coloreds or Indians; and in 1960 whites earned 67 percent of the national income, while Africans received 26.5 percent.[16]

Although the Republic of South Africa and the traditional empires may be extreme examples, the control of the majority of the wealth of a society by one group is not uncommon. If the upper class is relatively ethnically or racially homogeneous, a great step toward dominant control of the wealth has occurred. If an ethnic group or race makes up the *majority* of a society's population in addition to controlling the major organizational positions, the probability is quite high that that group will also control the wealth.

Thus, if the dominant ethnic group or race controls the *majority* of the positions of power and authority, if its culture predominates in the *majority* of the forms and situations of social interaction, and if the group owns or controls the *majority* of the wealth, then that group will be a "majority," even if it is a numerical minority of the population.

The last major condition that intensifies dominance is the acquisition of privileges. In many societies in which there is a dominant group, privileges related to ethnic or racial status per se constitute an important factor in stratification. Citizenship, owning property, voting, residing in particular areas, not being subjected to forced labor, paying low taxes or no taxes, and numerous other benefits may be acquired by the dominant group and denied to other groups. In some cases such privileges are institutionalized into the legal structure, but often they exist as informal benefits under a facade of democracy or equality. Intentional efforts to acquire and to maintain privileges involve the process of discrimination (which will be examined in some detail in Chapter 4). An esoteric example of a privilege extended to members of the race that controls the state is found in South Africa: while black miners in Kimberly are subjected to regular examinations of their rectums for stolen diamonds, whites are exempted from regular humiliation and subjected only to random searches.[17]

A Comparison of Ethnic Dominance and Racial Dominance

Which form of dominance, ethnic or racial, has the most severe consequences for the members of a subordinate group? This question is difficult to answer. Subordinate ethnic groups phenotypically quite similar to the dominant group have been subjected to coercion and violence. The Jews in Nazi Germany are an extreme example of this, the Irish under English domination a somewhat milder example. On the other hand, nonwhite ethnic groups in the United States and in the Republic of South Africa have experienced far greater oppression from the respective dominant groups than have white members. Yet in contrast to these two countries, subordinate races in Brazil suffer minimal discrimination. At this stage of comparative research it is safe to say only that race differences increase the probability of oppression of a subordinate race or a racial-ethnic group if conflict develops. Identifiability and a heightened sense of difference are key factors in race relations.

GEOGRAPHICAL SEGREGATION

The concentration or dispersion of ethnic groups and races in geographical space varies from society to society. The most extreme form of geographical segregation is found when ethnic groups or races live in particular regions separated by water barriers. Somewhat less extreme would be regional concentration in contiguous land areas. Ethnic regionalism is quite common in many societies whether a dominant group exists or not. In Yugoslavia the majority of each of the ethnic groups reside in their own regions—71 percent of Serbs in Serbia, 79 percent of Croats in Croatia, and 94 percent of Slovenes in Slovenia. Of the twenty-two cantons or regions in Switzerland, fifteen are predominantly German, one is overwhelmingly Italian, three are primarily French, and three are a German and French mixture. Ethnic regionalism is found in many other modern states: the Basques cluster in northern Spain and southern France; the Bretons remain in Brittany, France; the Scots, English, Welsh, and Cornish are concentrated in their respective areas of Great Britain; the French-Canadians live predominantly in Quebec Province; and the Lapps for the most part reside in the northern part of the Scandinavian states. Then there is the extreme regionalism of the U.S.S.R. In the past, at least, the United States has had a high degree of regional segregation of its minority populations: Mexicans in the Southwest, Blacks in the South, Irish in the East, Japanese and Chinese on the West Coast, Indians on reservations primarily in the West, and Scandinavians and Germans in the Midwest.

A condition of somewhat less geographical segregation exists when most of the groups are found within all of the regions, but some are more rural and others more urban, with some degree of segregation in the larger communities. The United States today approximates this degree of segregation. Geographical segregation is minimal when most or all of the specific groups are quite similar to the total national regional and urban-rural distribution, and when all or most of the groups are widely dispersed within cities rather than being concentrated within specific enclaves.

CULTURAL DIFFERENTIATION

Cultural differentiation is the extent to which ethnicity or race distinguishes and separates members of a society in terms of their beliefs, values, technologies, customs, norms, and artifacts. Language differences and similarities may be considered part of this dimension or, if the distinction proves to be useful, treated as a separate dimension.

Extreme cultural differentiation or cultural segmentation is generally correlated with geographical regionalism and the coexistence of quite different cultural systems, often from different traditions. Cultural diversity within the British Empire was enormous. Not only did Western, African, and Asian traditions coexist, but there was also diversity within each of these general cultural streams. In systems that are culturally differentiated to a high degree, different languages coexist and may even come from different language families.

Moderate or medium cultural differentiation exists when the cultures and languages of the various groups stem not from unrelated historical traditions, such as oriental and occidental, but from a similar historical background. This more moderate form of cultural segmentation is found within Belgium, Kenya, Czechoslovakia, and Switzerland, for example.

A low level of cultural differentiation or cultural integration exists when one language guides all forms of public interaction and there are few differences in culture traits related to ethnicity or race. A few highly symbolic linguistic nuances and customs serve to maintain ethnic identity in the absence of phenotypic variations.

Occupational specializations, when not affected by dominant group restrictions and coercion, are also indicators of cultural differentiation. In the ancient world Syrians and Greeks were predominant in the banking industry; Jews, Babylonians, Egyptians, and Greeks were the great merchants; Romans dominated engineering; and Egyptian doctors were the best in the world. In later periods to the present time many occupations have been ethnic specialties, hence, the prominence of Norwegian sailors and fishermen; Japanese gardeners, shipbuilders, and fishermen; Welsh coal miners; Basque sheepherders; Chinese merchants; English financiers; Swiss bankers; Jewish bankers in the Austrian Empire and Jewish comedians in the United States, to name but a few. And, of course, Irish priests are proverbial.

SOCIAL AND PERSONAL DISTANCE

Social distance refers to norms or "rules" that indicate "the expressed legitimacy and conventionality of specified modes of intergroup behavior."[18] Social distance involves questions of the *propriety* of particular forms of contact and interaction and the *frequency* of such contact. Social distance is manifested in all areas of social life: officers do not fraternize with enlisted personnel; social distance between employers and employees is reduced at Christmas office parties and then reestablished when the social occasion is over; work associations between members of different races are acceptable but personal friendships after hours are not; endogamy (marrying within the group) is universally emphasized; and people with higher status refer to people below them by their first names—a practice that is not reciprocal. Should there be contact, how much contact should there be, and what form of contact and relationships should take place? These are the issues of social distance, which varies according to the number of boundary lines that are established and the intensity in which the norms are sanctioned.

Personal distance is the "expressed intention to engage personally in specified modes of intergroup behavior."[19] Personal distance may correspond to social distance as *conforming* belief and behavior or be incongruent as *deviance*. In race and ethnic relations characterized by high social distance (that is, "caste" relations), it takes courageous deviants to violate social distance. Those individuals with low *personal* distance* who are willing to accept the consequences become the leaders in reducing *social* distance between groups. This is particularly true if such innovators are elite members of the community and if by their examples new precedents are established.

COMPETITION AND CONFLICT

The last major dimension of ethnic group and race relations involves the extent of and the changes in competition and conflict between members of the various groups within societies and across societal boundaries.

General Definitions

Within every social unit, of whatever size, and between social units of whatever type, some degree and form of competition exist. "Everywhere in nature, of which man is a part, there is a constant 'struggle for existence' . . . . All organisms strive to preserve life, to pursue their interests, to reproduce; this requires coming to terms with extant environmental conditions. Where there are insufficient resources to support all of the population, there is *competition*; the parties *independently* strive for values that are in short supply."[20] For some human beings competition is still for basics— roots, food, shelter, and a sexual partner. But for most human beings competition has been primarily over symbolic values—prestige, power, grades, wealth, job success, and the approval of significant others.

Competition is the striving for scarce objects or values in which attention is directed toward the obtaining of the objects or values rather than toward other human competitors of human obstacles to these goals. As such, it is a relatively impersonal social process in which individuals may not even be aware that they are engaging in competition with others. However, competitors may be known, and this variant of competition has often been termed *rivalry*.

But whether the competitors are known or unknown, some will fail and

---

Low personal distance means that race or ethnic status is a relatively unimportant factor in social relationships.

41

others will succeed. This is the lesson of competition, a process that in itself may be a value. But whether it is considered to be a desirable state of affairs or not, it is a frequent, if not ubiquitous, social process.

Conflict is a social relationship between two or more parties based on a perception of incompatible goals, which becomes manifest as behavior in efforts at coercion or injury or, when this is not possible, as accommodation. There are three major aspects of this meaning of conflict—the conflict relationship, conflict actions, and accommodation. A conflict relationship comes into existence when the parties in an interaction define their goals or interests in opposition to each other; goals or interests are incompatible, and the attainment of the goals of one party will have to be at the expense of the other. Incompatible goals may mean that *different* goals exist. The American Indian's goal of maintaining a hunting territory was incompatible with the goal of the white settler—to farm land. The goals of the Spanish in Mexico—to convert the natives and extract wealth—were incompatible with Aztec goals—to maintain their religion and their wealth. Incompatible goals may also mean that the parties share a *common* goal but that the goal is in short supply or unavailable to everyone. The achievement of the goal by one individual or group means that the other unit will fail; hence, a form of incompatibility results. There just isn't enough to go around, or greed prevails. Germany, France, and Great Britain had the same goal in Africa—to form colonies. Since they each wanted the whole of Africa, however, their goals were incompatible. (They eventually agreed to divide up the territory.)

Conflict *relationships* may be attitudinal, or they may take the form of written policies and ideologies. Such relationships become manifest in *behavioral* terms as conflict actions. Conflict action involves efforts to coerce, to injure, or to eliminate the opposition; the root of the word *conflict* means to fight. Such actions may be verbal, violent, or nonviolent. All of the following are forms of conflict actions designed to coerce or injure others: insults, strikes, boycotts, battles, petitions, assassinations, kidnappings, slander, lockouts, court suits, infliction of financial damage, destruction of property, discrimination, debates (in many cases).

When conflict actions fail to neutralize or to eliminate the opposition, when both parties realize that further acts will only be self-destructive, when compromises occur, or when one party decides to postpone goal attainment in order to regroup, another form of conflict behavior occurs—*accommodation*. A conflict relationship continues, but conflict actions diminish or end, at least temporarily. For one hundred years management and labor in the United States have been involved in a conflict relationship, a relationship that has vacillated or alternated between conflict actions and accommodation. From the time of Henry II to World War I, France and Britain were also engaged in such a pattern. In different areas of the country, and at different times, white-black relations in the United States have alternated between conflict actions and tenuous accommodation.

Conflict may be institutionalized or formalized within a society, as in the relationships between prosecuting and defending attorneys in court, between labor and management in the United States since 1935, between political parties, and between pro-football teams. In some situations conflict is not governed by rules, but the end is considered to justify the means, as in revolutions, rebellions, or war (war is essentially wide open, in spite of the Geneva Convention).

Conflict relationships and their behavioral manifestations may terminate when both parties face a common enemy or when compromises prove satisfactory; they always end when one party is totally exterminated or whipped into utter subjugation. But new conflict relationships may develop between the same parties at some later date.

Some form of conflict between *some* units is a ubiquitous social process in any human society, although its frequency has been overemphasized. Conflict is also a major source of social change—for better or worse, depending upon one's standards.

Forms of Competition and Conflict

When one thinks of group competition or conflict, as opposed to individual manifestations of these processes, one generally has in mind associational groups or organizations, such as armies, political parties, unions, and corporations. This type of group competition involves some degree of co-ordination between *all* of the individuals within a group under the leadership of the elite. However, ethnic groups, much less races, are not associations, although they may have such organizations within them. How, then, do these statuses compete and conflict? While competition in an associational group involves the *entire* group, competition and conflict between racial and ethnic statuses are for the most part *segmental*—that is, competition and conflict take place between individuals, associational groups, or social movements within the statuses.

In direct competition, race or ethnicity itself is the issue, as opposed to occupation, party, class, sex, or some other issue. In this conscious and direct competition a number of tactics have been utilized: buying from one's own people, forming organizations to promote the interests of one's own people, organizing schools to promote one's ethnic culture and to increase the sense of ethnicity of the young, getting the curriculum of the state schools to teach one's ethnic culture, working out forms of inheritance so that family members can maintain or increase the gains that have been won, seeking bills in government favorable to the "people's" cause, lobbying in Congress on ethnic grounds, increasing the population of one's group, seeking public office, and entering professions with the motivation to return and help one's people.

An excellent example of direct ethnic group competition with some elements of conflict occurred in the early twentieth century in the Austrian-

Hungarian Empire. For centuries the Germans were the dominant ethnic group, and other groups, such as the Czechs, the Slovaks, and the Magyars were subordinate by any number of criteria. Around the turn of the century the Czechs in Bosnia and Bohemia made their move. Czechs from all over the empire were encouraged by other Czechs to migrate to these provinces and to increase their birthrate. In lower Austria, between 1890 and 1900, the Czechs increased by 42 percent, while the total population increased by only 16 percent. One town—Budweis—had been solidly German for three centuries, but by 1915 the immigrations of Czechs and the lower birthrate of Germans produced a population of only 17,000 Germans, compared with 28,000 Czechs. In municipal elections the Czechs voted as a bloc and replaced many German officials. Czech banks were founded to lend money to Czech peasants to buy property, and once they acquired property the new owners encouraged friends and relatives to buy near them. Nationalistic Czech societies also bought up land to sell to Czechs, land that Germans unwittingly sold. Because many Czechs were able to speak both German and Czech, the central government appointed many of them to bureaucratic positions at the local level. By 1915 in Bohemia, only 5,305 of the 24,720 local state officials were Germans. Czechs boycotted German products to ensure that their money went only to the concerns and companies of their group; these concerns in turn gave large donations to nationalistic societies or to the newly founded schools. A large number of new, private schools were opened, and the Czech University at Prague was founded.[21] After the defeat of the Austrian-Hungarian Empire in World War I, the victors carved the empire into small states—one of which was Czechoslovakia, a state that owed its existence to the competitive successes of the Czechs in this region. Without conflict (World War I or a Czech secessionist movement), the Czechs as a dominant group (having their own state) would not have come into existence; however, competitive successes were in part responsible.

Ethnic group competition may also be *indirect* and not consciously motivated. In this form of ethnic competition, individuals, *as individuals*, not as representatives of their group, strive for scarce values. In this sense, there is no group competition, but *one's* ethnic status nevertheless makes a difference. An individual's success or failure is indirectly affected by his or her ethnic status, and the areas of competition one is likely to enter are affected by ethnic traditions, values, and skills that have become part of oneself.

Segmental ethnic and racial *conflict* is by definition direct, and takes numerous forms: battles between armies, riots, guerrilla warfare, discrimination, revolution, boycotts, strikes, the crushing of rebellions, enslavement, court litigation, and extermination, to name only the more important varieties.

Major Factors Affecting Success and Failure

What factors determine the successes and failures of different groups in the processes of competition and conflict? Understanding that competition and conflict involve interaction between specific groups and that these processes take place within ecological settings, a number of contributing factors can be suggested: specific cultural elements, the extent of group cohesiveness, organizational subdivisions, if any, and the relative sizes of the groups.

1. *Culture.* Since human beings are cultural animals, a specific cultural trait vis-à-vis others in a particular ecological and social context may be an important aspect of competitive success or failure. In industrial societies, for example, an "activistic" outlook is more conducive to competitive success than a "passivistic" outlook. Other things being equal, individuals and whole groups who subscribe to such values and beliefs as the work ethic, planning, the idea of progress, thrift, discipline, the belief that God helps those who help themselves, individualism, competition, and education are more likely to be successful in the struggle for rewards. Conversely, those who believe in fatalism ("whatever will be, will be," "if God Wills," "the Lord will provide"), work as a means only, familism (precedence of the family as a whole over the aspirations of any of its members), and having large families, and who devalue the efficient performance of mundane tasks, have an increased probability of failure in complex industrial societies. Such individuals are likely to be poor in industrial societies, unless they have inherited wealth or are subsidized by their parents or someone else.

Students of Japanese culture in America have noted the activistic orientation of the Japanese, who have been successful in the United States despite considerable discrimination. They took over areas of land in California and, utilizing Japanese farm technology, increased the yield in areas that other groups had defined as worthless. By 1940, second-generation Japanese-Americans exceeded the average education of the total population of the United States; now they are overrepresented in the professional and merchant occupations. Kitano has identified such activistic values as hard work, achievement, self-control, and thrift as elements of Japanese-American culture.[22]

In the nineteenth century the Argentines encouraged European immigration to their country. The competitive successes of the Europeans as opposed to the Argentines can, in part, be explained by cultural contrast. The Argentines held values typical of paternalistic and aristocratic societies; one writer in a work entitled *Eulogy to Laziness* emphasized that work and useful activity was "madness." "The aristocratic ideal in Argentina or Chile was to enjoy the leisure that the income from one's land made possible. The idea of dignity of labor, which the European cultural heritage of many immigrants emphasized, was weak."[23] The Europeans were industrious, working long hours, and believed that saving was a value. One Italian wrote that "in the struggle for a quick fortune . . . no fatigue is too great, no privation is too important."[24] "An Italian traveling in Argentina was shocked to discover our principles of economy, of saving, . . .the parsimony that for us is a point of honor, all those moral rules that oblige us to regulate our lives in provision for the future, are unknown in America."[25] As for the

Argentines, one writer exclaimed, "We don't know how to save. A census in 1887 found that of the 36,507 depositors in one of the nation's largest banks, only 7,565 were Argentines, while 16,132 were Italians and 5,831 were Spaniards."[26]

The specific beliefs of an ethnic group have sometimes contributed to conflict or competitive success or failure. An excellent example is the Moslem Arab idea that Allah's truth should be spread throughout the world, along with the belief that death in battle ensures heavenly salvation. When Moslems invaded India and opposed ethnic groups that believed in an endless round of reincarnation and passive adaption to a cyclical universe, there was no contest. The Aztecs believed that every encounter in which they were defeated was due to divine judgment and the fulfillment of an omen. They also believed that time came in cycles, that when one age came to an end all was destroyed and a new age began. In addition, they took prisoners to be sacrificed to the gods. The Spanish, on the contrary, took reverses as lessons from which to avoid defeat in the future, held to no such cyclic view of time, and adhered to the Western idea that war means killing the enemy in battle.[27] When these contrasts were added to the superiority of Spanish military technology, Spanish alliances with other Indian groups, and the belief that Cortes was the returned god Quetzalcoatl, a small number of Spanish soldiers were quite successful in conquering Mexico. Indeed, it *was* the end of an age for the Aztecs.

Differences in technology between ethnic groups in a given environment are another aspect of cultural variation that affects competition and conflict. Technology involves tool using and other skills whose effectiveness can be measured more readily than other cultural elements. In areas of human activity such as war, revolution, agriculture, and business, technological differences often play a decisive role. Military success in a conflict situation is often rooted in technology and the social organization of this technology. The use of armored warriors on horseback along with highly advanced siege devices made the Assyrians invincible for hundreds of years. The Persian archers were mainly responsible for the extension of Persian dominance and were eventually defeated by Alexander's Macedonians, who utilized large shields to protect themselves from arrows and placed twenty-foot-long spears across the shoulders of the men in front in a close-knit formation. English longbows defeated the flower of French knighthood, encased in armor, at the Battle of Crecy during the Hundred Years War. The German use of tanks to lead foot soldiers made possible the blitzkrieg through France and other European countries (a tactic ironically developed by Charles de Gaulle as a young colonel and accepted too late by the French General Staff). One could cite numerous other examples from the history of warfare in which superior technology coupled with superior military organization (discipline, communication, and planning) made the difference in war, one form of conflict actions.

Military technology, which is of prime significance in the establishment and maintenance of ethnic group dominance in numerous societies, is only one form of technology. In other areas technology also plays an important part in competition and conflict, and particular ethnic groups often develop technological specializations related to occupation. Jews have long been successful in commerce in many societies, and in the United States Jews play a disproportionate role in the clothing and the entertainment industries. Japanese-Americans have become skilled gardeners and truck farmers. The Japanese emerged from feudalism a little over a century ago and have become dominant in shipbuilding and electronics, to name only a couple of areas. The Greeks in the ancient world not only were master merchants who regularly cheated their Roman overlords but also had superior technological skills in the arts. The Parsis in India, often termed the Jews of India, are a small minority of highly successful professionals and merchants with a tradition of technological superiority in these areas. In numerous countries the Chinese, as minorities, have dominated the business sector because of their traditions of commerce and their know-how in this field. In Thailand:

> *Trade and industry in the kingdom are dominated by Chinese, and Chinese immigrants and their descendents do comprise the majority of the labour force in commercial occupations. Yet this is only part of the picture. The Chinese younger generation by reason of practical training, often in family enterprises, have the essential skills and know-how for business careers, far more than the average Thai, and it is natural that the former would be preferred by both Chinese and Western business concerns, even if no other considerations entered into their employment. Moreover, man for man, the Chinese are more diligent, more careful workers than the Thai. Even the Thai when they want a job done and done well—building a house, for example—will hire Chinese rather than Thai workers.*[28]

Cultural differences are relevant in explaining the general success of technologically advanced peoples in situations of conflict with primitives, as, for example, the English versus the aborigines in Australia or the Dutch versus the Hottentots in South Africa. Cultural differences also affect competitive success or failure when people from agrarian areas or from agrarian societies migrate to large, complex cities.

As primitive societies disappear and the world becomes increasingly standardized as a result of technological requirements and restraints, cultural variations diminish and thus become less significant in explaining inequality between groups in modern societies. In technologically advanced and complex societies, *structural* conditions such as the nature of the economy (the income distribution system, employment levels, access to occupations), the power distribution, and the existing discriminatory barriers become more significant as cultural variation diminishes.

In such circumstances it is important not to confuse the *effects* of structural inequalities upon groups with the idea of culture. People may behave in particular ways not because they have internalized some traditional culture but because their position allows them no choice. The heading of households by females among Black Americans (about one-fourth of black families) is not due to some valued social institution which is part of a culture (matriarchy). Black males experience structural situations of unemployment, poor jobs, and discrimination, which deny them the breadwinning role they value, a value shared by the females they are forced to desert. Female-headed families are a structural effect, not an institution.

2. *Group Cohesiveness.* The more cohesive an ethnic group, the greater the probability (other things being equal) that it will (as a whole) be successful in competition or in conflict with other ethnic groups. Group cohesiveness is the degree to which perceived group needs and interests take precedence over individual needs and interests. It is a function of the degree to which individuals *believe* that they can attain values at a lower cost by cooperation with other ethnic members. Cohesiveness is enhanced by the perception of common problems, particularly threats to a whole ethnic group's position or its existence, and by ethnocentrism (pride in one's group and in the achievements of its members, ranging from the belief that one's group is at least equal to other groups to the sense that one's group is superior to other groups). Cohesiveness diminishes when group members pursue mutually exclusive or individual ends; when class, ideological, or regional differences are perceived as paramount; or when individuals demean their own ethnic group and identify with or seek membership in another ethnic group.

3. *Organization.* Cohesiveness alone is not sufficient for success against out-groups. A spirit of unity can easily become ethnic self-hatred without effective organization. To organize means to establish coordination among divisions of labor and to mobilize resources in order to obtain common goals. The degree to which an ethnic group is organized can be determined by the number of associational groups within an ethnic group, the degree to which *each* of these is organized (coordinated, with resources mobilized, and with consensus on goals), and the extent to which the various associational groups work together to improve or maintain common ethnic interests. Ethnic associational groups take such forms as banks, schools, credit unions, labor unions, and civil rights organizations. For dominant ethnic groups, all of the organizations of the state are their organizations, a condition that obviously increases the probability of success.

Subordinate ethnic groups, faced with an entrenched dominant group, do not have an easy task in trying to improve their position within the society. Their organizations exist only with the tolerance of the state. In relatively democratic societies or in societies that accept some degree of pluralism, subordinate groups are allowed to form organizations for a wide variety of purposes, as long as such organizations do not threaten the state. Typical of many subordinate group organizations in democratic societies have been mutual aid or mutual benefit societies. As will be seen in Part 2, virtually all of the immigrant groups in the United States formed such organizations to lend money, to find employment, to provide insurance, and to help new arrivals adjust to their new surroundings.

When subordinate group organizations are perceived as a threat by the state, harassment and repression will take place. Organizations may be totally suppressed or forced to go underground in efforts to accomplish their goals, and their goals will often change in the face of such opposition.

4. *Population Size.* Knowledge, skills, and activistic values coupled with some degree of group cohesiveness and social organization are the major factors that affect the success or failure of ethnic groups in situations of conflict and competition. An additional factor is population size vis-à-vis other groups in the society. The population size has little significance except when combined with the above variables, since large, unorganized populations often can be as easily controlled as small groupings. But numbers do constitute a resource when group members have developed cohesiveness and organization and are equipped with technological skills.

Because of the possession of such attributes and their control of the state, dominant ethnic groups pose a severe obstacle to those groups in subordination. The latter may accept this position, seek to improve their relative stratification position without the possibility of becoming dominant, strive to replace the dominant group, or seek to become independent by seceding from the society. The irony of a subordinate group's seeking change is that in order to be successful it must often acquire those aspects of the dominant group in the society that have enabled the dominant group to maintain supremacy. This may mean drastic changes in culture and forms of social organization; if the subordinate groups retain traditional patterns, they may very well remain where they are.

Factors That Reduce Competition and Conflict

The factor of success or failure in situations of competition and conflict is a major explanation for human inequality and ethnic or racial inequality in particular. Equally important are those factors which reduce or eliminate the very possibility that such engagements will take place. To use the metaphor of a game, not only do teams win or lose, but the game may not be held at all, or one team may win by default.

Factors Reducing Competition. Competition between *all* members of *all* of the ethnic groups in *all* of the occupational specializations within a society does not exist. Cultural traditions, ethnic in-group sanctions and expectations, and discrimination combine to reduce ethnic group competition within specific occupations. Many ethnic groups value and compete for traditional occupations while ignoring other occupational areas. The Thai in Thailand, for example, value working for the government, while the Chinese in this society consider trade and industry far more desirable. Jewish-Americans value competitive engagement in the professions, in merchant activities, and in music. They meet other ethnic group competitors in these areas, of course, but they lose by default in other less-valued fields, such as athletics, agriculture, or ranching (a Jewish cowboy?). Irish-Americans, because of their own values and Anglo discrimination, have been successful as politicians, theater performers, police officers, and fire fighters, and they overwhelmingly dominate the Catholic priesthood (Mexican and Italian Catholics have lost to the Irish by default). On the other hand, Irish-American doctors, farmers, and bankers are negligible. Occupational restrictions in athletics have been reduced in recent years, and as a consequence Black-Americans predominate in such areas as basketball, football, track, and baseball. However, one rarely hears of successful black golfers, swimmers, tennis players, rodeo performers, or polo players, at least in the United States—a condition resulting, of course, from opportunity barriers, but also from values. And as an extreme example, Anglos and Jews competing in the field of physics do not have to worry about competition from Mexicans, Eskimos, Navahos, or Hawaiians.

It is difficult to isolate the effects of discrimination, differential social class placement, valued cultural traditions, and in-group expectations on occupational distributions among ethnic groups. But whatever the relative mixture of these factors for particular groups, occupational specialization by ethnicity or race reduces interethnic competition. And what is important for ethnic or racial inequality or stratification is the fact that some occupations bring more rewards than others. Failure to compete for the more rewarding positions, for whatever reasons, will mean a disproportionate membership in the lower social class. (It should be added that some marginal groups, such as the Lapps in Norway or the aborigines in Australia, really do not care about climbing the ladders of mainstream society; they just want to be left alone.)

Occupational specialization by ethnicity is not the only factor in reducing interethnic competition; there is also the individual aspect. For some individuals, competition per se is extremely important, even a compulsion. For others, competition is hell on earth, a continuing exposure of oneself to the terrible judgments of others. Withdrawal, retreatism, security, or escape may be preferable to the competitive rat race. Whether one values competition or not is often affected by one's success or failure in the competitive process. It is difficult to define competition as important and to enter the daily struggle when losing seems inevitable. An individual's decision to compete or not is related to his or her social class placement, and if certain ethnic groups are disproportionate within particular classes, ethnic relations are affected. Lower-strata members, particularly the older ones, generally have little desire to compete within the rules or at all. The lower class placement of individuals may be the result of an unfavorable definition of competition, or being born into the lower strata may offer so little chance of success that when someone asks, "Why don't you get out there and compete?" the response is apathy or a four-letter expletive. But if members of the lower class don't compete, or if they are so crippled they cannot, for whatever reasons, their inferior stratification position will be perpetuated. Upper-strata members thus win by default.

Factors Reducing Conflict. The major factor in reducing or preventing the establishment of a conflict relationship is *legitimacy*. Legitimacy is *the perceived rightness or justness of some social arrangement, practice, or policy* (legitimacy given to a role that exercises power becomes authority). When people feel the existing distribution of power, privilege, and wealth is right or just, they accept their situation, the legitimacy of it, and do not feel they are in conflict with their superiors. In the words of Lewis Coser, "Legitimacy is a crucial intervening variable without which it is impossible to predict whether feelings of hostility arising out of an unequal distribution of privileges and rights actually leads to conflict."[29]*

The sense of legitimacy is affected by doctrines of *legitimation*. Legitimation refers to all of those beliefs or ideologies that explain and hence justify some pattern of inequality. One of the oldest forms of legitimation related to gender inequality is sexism—all of those ideas that "explain" why men are superior to women. Legitimation may take the form of theological doctrines in which the existing system is justified in terms of God's will or as the result of reincarnation (Law of Karma in India). Inequality in American capitalistic society is explained by differences in individual ability and initiative: the system is open; you've no one to blame but yourself. And as will be seen in Chapter 4, the doctrine of racism has been useful in convincing subordinate groups and members of dominant groups that ethnic or racial dominance is legitimate.

An important factor related to legitimacy is the belief that democracy exists. According to Mayhew and Levinger, "if individuals believe that they have an influence on decision making, they are more likely to accept the decisions that are made. . . . If people believe that they rule, they can hardly revolt, for they could only revolt against themselves."[30]

When increasing numbers of subordinate status members perceive the illegitimacy of the existing social arrangements, then a conflict relationship is established. However, conflict *actions* may not be forthcoming if the power differential is perceived to be so great that actions will bring suppression or that the costs of engaging in conflict actions will far outweigh any possible gains.

In short, members of subordinate statuses will fail to perceive a conflict *relationship* if they believe the system to be legitimate. They will fail to engage in conflict *actions* if they feel they have little chance of success, as a rule (fanatics are exceptions).

Whatever the factors that reduce competition and conflict, systems of dominance and subordinance will continue in a structured and stabilized

---

*What Coser means by conflict is conflict actions.

form unless challenges are made and the challenges force some alteration. Dominant statuses or dominant groups rarely give up their superior positions for altruistic, moral, or egalitarian reasons.

INTERRELATIONSHIPS

Each of the dimensions of ethnic and race relations affects, and in turn is affected by, every other dimension. A few of these interconnections can be suggested, in the absence of sufficient empirical validation.

As was previously examined, the extent and form of cultural differentiation between ethnic groups or races is one of the major factors affecting success or failure in situations of competition and conflict. In turn, it is the thesis of this book that racial and ethnic inequality is predominantly the result of success or failure in innumerable situations of competition and conflict. Dominant and subordinate groups come into existence primarily as the result of conflict and competition; systems of dominant-subordinate relationships are maintained, even intensified, in interaction based upon the processes of competition and conflict; changes in the position of subordinate groups vis-à-vis each other or relative to the dominant group are essentially the result of these processes; and for the same reasons dominant groups can become subordinate.

What other possible explanation for ethnic and racial inequality can there be? Although individuals vary in intelligence, whole ethnic groups and races do not. Inequality is not due to biology. What about the capitalistic system? Is capitalism the cause of differential placement of ethnic groups and races among the social classes or the reason for the existence of dominant and subordinate groups? Some groups do better than others within these structural constraints, but replace it with socialism and ethnic inequality persists. Is ethnic or racial inequality the result of a ruling class conspiracy? Even if one grants the existence of a ruling class, this social class does not have to be made up primarily from one ethnic group, and ruling classes have been overthrown. Certain organizational practices and policies may place some groups at a disadvantage, but this is generally the effect of past discrimination (a form of conflict). The structural disadvantage will continue as long as the disadvantaged group or groups acquiesce. If the dominant group establishes the ground rules for competition and these are manifested in the structure of society, then subordinate groups must learn to play according to the rules or they must change the rules. In either case success or failure in competition and conflict will affect the outcome.

While cultural differentiation affects the competitive and conflict abilities of groups, it seems irrelevant to the existence or nonexistence of conflict itself. Groups quite different from each other as well as groups that are virtually indistinguishable can choose to engage either in cooperation or in the most violent forms of conflict. Primitive groups have been exterminated by extremely different and technologically advanced peoples; yet the virtually indistinguishable Jewish population of Nazi Germany met the same fate. Few differences separate the Basques from the rest of the Spaniards in Spain; nevertheless, they want independence (or some of them do). Violent conflict occurred between the aboriginal populations of North America and invading Europeans, while at the same time in the United States extreme black-white conflict occurred between races virtually undifferentiated on the basis of culture. The extent of cultural differentiation has little relationship to the development of conflict between groups.

A few other brief relationships between the dimensions of racial and ethnic relations may be noted. Conflict increases social distance, while, on the other hand, the reduction of conflict does not necessarily reduce social distance. The greater the regional concentration of ethnic groups within societies, the greater the probability of cultural segmentation and high social distance. Nevertheless, groups can be separate geographically and socially and yet be either relatively equal or grossly unequal. While high social distance is more probable between groups that are geographically separate and culturally distinct, there are exceptions: in the Old South in the United States, Black-Americans and whites with the same traditions lived in close proximity yet with a caste form of social distance unmatched anywhere, with the exception of India. Without geographical concentration, one form of conflict will not take place: secession, or the struggle to gain political independence within a territorial segment of an existing society; yet the existence of ethnic regionalism is a necessary but not a sufficient condition for secession. And the greater the inequality between groups, the greater the social distance; inferiors and superiors do not integrate no matter what the extent of brotherhood propaganda.

MODELS

In order to more fully understand the idea of racial or ethnic dominance and subordinance and the various dimensions involved in relationships between ethnic groups and races, complex reality can be reduced to three basic models or types of societies: empire societies, national societies, and pluralistic societies. The first two are characterized by the existence of a dominant ethnic group and are the main concern of this book.

Empire Societies

An empire society is a sovereign social system characterized by the existence of a *dominant* ethnic *minority* and several *subordinate* ethnic *minorities* residing in subsocieties that have been incorporated by conquest for the most part (a few subordinate minorities may be voluntary immigrants). The empire society is the result of the expansion of the military forces and the state of one ethnic group and the incorporation of previously sovereign social systems under the political control of the conquering group. In some cases the conquered society may have been itself an empire society (for example, the Aztec Empire).

Every empire society has a core and a periphery, a social-geographical distinction that will vary over the course of time in terms of the size of the respective territories and may disappear if large-scale internal migration takes place. Within the core resides the majority of the members of the dominant group, since this is the geographical base to which other territories and peoples have been added. Members of subordinate groups that have been relatively integrated with the dominant group will also be found within the core. The more recently conquered, the less integrated, and the more culturally discongruent peoples as a rule reside on the periphery. Territories on the periphery may be contiguous (connected with the core) or noncontiguous (separated by water or by other societies). The concentration of most of the members of any given group within a particular region is the general demographic pattern.

Within each region the members of the various ethnic groups practice diverse customs, speak different languages for the most part, and interact primarily within the confines of their own groups as they conduct their institutional activities.

What binds these subsocieties together is the existence of a common government with at least a few laws applicable to everybody, the conduction of foreign affairs by the central government, and the presence of at least a few members of the dominant group in all areas in the roles of administrators and "policemen." Since consensus on values, norms, and beliefs does not exist, force or the threat of force on the part of the state is the major factor in ensuring order. But the advantages of this order to subordinate groups is another factor that helps to maintain order. Some degree of economic interdependence may also operate as a bonding element (because of specialization the regional economies need each other).

For administrative purposes relatively ethnically homogeneous subsocieties may be treated as political divisions—provinces, satrapies, colonies, dependent kingdoms, territories, or some other such unit. However, for purposes of control and order it may be more expedient to put a number of ethnic groups and their territories within the same political subdivision or to split an ethnic group by establishing the boundary line through the middle of the group's communities.

Political divisions and subordinate groups are rarely treated alike by the central government, since controlling a complex empire requires constant attention and adaption to diverse peoples. The ever-present threat to empire societies is secession (the gaining of complete independence by one or more of the subordinate groups in a territorial segment of the society). A unit may be allowed some degree of home rule or local control over its immediate affairs, it may be ruled by a puppet leader of the same ethnicity as most of the people in the region, or it may be a colony—paternalistically administered and economically exploited. The cultures of the subordinate groups may be respected, or assimilation of the subordinate groups into the dominant group may be the policy. Both policies—toleration and assimilation—can exist simultaneously in different dominant-subordinate relationships.

Regardless of the government's relationship to the subunits and subordinate groups, they all are taxed or pay tribute, and they all are expected to acquiesce to the policies of the state.

There have been many major preindustrial empire societies.* Industrial empire societies, on the other hand, have been rare. The core, at least, of the British Empire became industrialized. In recent years the Germans, Italians, and Japanese have had short-lived empires, and Communist Russia (the U. S. S. R.) is a contemporary industrial empire state masquerading as a pluralistic society. With a few modifications of the empire model, the "Republic" of South Africa can be classified as an industrial empire society.

The British Empire at its peak, around 1900, was the epitome of the empire. In 1897, when Queen Victoria spoke of "her people," she

> *was referring to the nearly 400 million subjects living in all five continents, honoring a thousand religions, speaking a thousand languages–people of every race, culture, stage of development: occupying mud huts in the Australian outback, caves in the Kalahari Desert, exquisite manor houses in Nova Scotia; savages who did not know the use of money, Boers like Biblical patriarchs, Hindu princes of porcelain sensibility, ancillary kings, colonial magnates, Mediterranean noblemen, dung-smeared wizards, cannibals, Confucian scholars, Eskimos, Arabs–such a variety of peoples have never before, in the whole history of human affairs owed their allegiance to a single suzerain.*[31]

Within this single system, and a system it was in every respect, 387,400,000 individuals, divided into ethnic groups, races, classes, and religions, carried on their lives within 10,200,000 square miles of noncontiguous land areas under the supervision of a dominant minority, the British.

National Societies

In addition to empire societies, one other major type of society is characterized by the existence of a dominant ethnic group (and in some cases, a dominant race that includes the dominant ethnic group)—the national so-

---

Akkadian, Assyrian, Median, Acheamenid Persian, Macedonian (and its later independent divisions, all of which were characterized by a Greek-Macedonian minority rule: Antigonid, Seleucid, and Ptolemaic), Roman, Han Chinese, Sassanian Persian, Egyptian, Mongol, Arab, Seljuk Turkish, Ottoman Turkish, Parthian, Frankish (Carolingian), Great Russian (Czarist Russia), Ghana, Mali, Songhai, Asante, Toltec, Mayan, Portuguese, Spanish, Dutch, French, and British.

ciety. National societies, which developed primarily in the last two to three hundred years, have a dominant ethnic *majority* and one or more subordinate ethnic minorities. Not only do members of this dominant group control the state and the economy, but their language and culture set the standards for the entire society. Minorities are relatively invisible unless they are protesting in some form. Society and the dominant group seem to be synonymous. This extreme dominance in all aspects gives the impression of a true nation-state; however, in the words of Wagley and Harris:

> *Certainly there is no society in the world today where state and nation may be said to coincide, except as a convenient fiction for novelists and politicians. And yet, especially during the last few centuries, many conscious and unconscious efforts have been made to achieve the ideal of a national state. In the process, the cultural traditions, the language, and the physical type of one of the groups of a state society are proposed as the national language, the national culture, and the national physical type.*[32]

Cultural diversity, when compared to that in empire societies, is minimal, although a few of the subordinate minorities may be quite different from the dominant majority (for example, Eskimo in the United States, the Ainu in Japan, or the Lapps in Norway).

The language of the dominant group is the instrument of communication in all forms of public interaction. Members of subordinate minorities may still use their own language, but knowledge of the dominant language is essential for social participation outside of segregated minority enclaves.

Generally, the ethnic minorities are dispersed throughout all the regions of the society, although regional concentrations have existed in several national societies at certain times. The general trend, however, is toward a breakdown of regional concentration. Members of the ethnic *majority* are to be found in virtually all of the regions and the communities within the society.

Integration is the general policy of the government. By emphasizing a common nationality and the irrelevance of ethnicity or race, the government attempts to absorb the subordinate minorities into the dominant group mainstream. The educational system, the economic organizations, and the means of mass communication all contribute to this end. Dominant majorities are rarely tolerant of cultural diversity and "clannish" groups within their midst.

There are exceptions to the emphasis on integration in some national societies. (There are always exceptions to any model that extracts the predominant themes or patterns.) A group may be granted a pluralist status* because it is technologically backward, because nobody can quite figure out

---

*Recognition of the relative autonomy of a subordinate ethnic group by the government. See Chapter 5 for a more extensive treatment of this subject.

how to bring the group into the mainstream, or because the group is adamant about maintaining its integrity within its own communities. Generally, however, dominant group members view such an arrangement as expedient and temporary.

Another exception to the emphasis on integration and the eventual assimilation of the minorities is found with "pariah" groups or with groups defined as biologically inferior and hence contaminating. As long as such dominant group attitudes persist, the stigmatized subordinate group will be kept somewhat isolated socially and reduced to performing the most menial and unpleasant tasks of society. Stigmatized groups are not granted a pluralist status, since their culture and their identity are not worth recognizing.

Minorities generally hold to two levels of ethnicity simultaneously—their minority status and their nationality—and emphasize one or the other, depending upon the circumstances. The value of integrationism (intermingling with dominant group members in institutional activities) or of pluralism (maintaining ethnic integrity and autonomy) varies among subordinate group members.

Several contemporary national societies are the core of empire societies in which the periphery has been lost because of secession—France, Spain, Germany, Turkey, the United Kingdom, the Netherlands, and Portugal, to name a few. Other national societies are states that gained their independence from empires—Mexico, Peru and most of the other countries of Latin America, the United States, Canada, Australia, Greece, and Norway.

Additional subordinate groups have been added to the national societies through conquest, immigration, and annexation by purchase.

Pluralistic Societies

Pluralistic societies have no dominant ethnic group or race. No one group controls the majority of the positions of the state, nor does the culture of one group set the standards for the rest.

In this societal type the two quite different meanings of pluralism in the social sciences are applicable. In political science pluralism means a condition or state of balanced power between the major groups that constitute the society. When applied to *ethnic* relations (no state-society has ever had balanced power between races), the term means that all or most of the ethnic groups within a society exist in a tenuous accommodation or power balance. No one group is desirous and/or capable of establishing dominance over the rest. Formal or informal recognition of the multiethnic nature of the society is part of the political process and structure. Ethnic political parties are a common feature, as is ethnic representation in the legislature or executive bodies on an egalitarian or a proportional basis (proportional to population size). Governmental laws and policies are generally written in the languages of all of the major groups.

For sociologists in the field of ethnic relations, pluralism refers to a condition of the relative *autonomy* of at least most of the ethnic groups in the conduct of their institutional activities. Most of the population of each ethnic group is to be found within specific regions, a condition of spatial segregation conducive to institutional autonomy. Family and religious activities as well as other forms of social life take place within the confines of a given ethnic group. The cultures of the various groups differ from one another to some extent, but because of regional proximity all of the cultures generally stem from a common historical tradition. Fewer cultural differences exist than in empire societies but generally more than in the national type. Pluralism is not only a structural feature of pluralistic societies but a *value*, a desired state of affairs maintained and implemented by the state.

Although not extreme, some degree of ethnic inequality exists in the pluralistic society. Statistics on inequality by ethnic group are often incomplete or nonexistent, since governments in these societies do not officially recognize that inequality exists. Publicizing data on the income, education, and occupational distribution of different ethnic groups could upset the tenuous equilibrium.

Pluralistic societies, like some national societies, have come into existence through independence from empire societies—for example, Kenya, Nigeria, Yugoslavia, and Czechoslovakia. A voluntary federation of Germans, Italians, French, and Romanisch produced the most successful pluralistic society in the world—Switzerland. Belgium, with its delicate balance between Flemish (Dutch speaking) and Walloons (French speaking), is a creation due to the influence of France and Britain. It is quite possible that the demands of the Welsh, Cornish, and Scots for greater independence in Britain could very well transform this society into the pluralistic type.[33]

SUMMARY

There are at least five major dimensions of race and ethnic relations within any complex society: stratification, segregation, cultural differentiation, social distance, and competition and conflict.

One form of social stratification is racial or ethnic. In all multiethnic or multiracial societies these statuses have an affect on the placement of their members within the strata, ranging from extremely disproportionate distribution to one approaching equality. In addition to this form of ethnic and racial stratification, ethnic groups and races in many societies vary in the prestige of their cultures and body types, and in the extent of privileges they have acquired.

In many societies, quite possibly in a clear majority of them, one ethnic group or race dominates all of the others. A dominant group is the one whose members control and occupy the major positions within the organizations of the state. This political dominance is usually accompanied by cultural and economic forms of dominance. Dominant groups may be a minority of the total population, as in empire societies, or a majority, as in the national type of society.

The opportunities available to a subordinate group are affected to some degree by the group's relative placement within the strata and by the actions of dominant group members. Under extreme conditions of domination subordinate groups may be discriminated against, coerced into acquiring the dominant culture, forced into undesirable forms of labor, spatially restricted, or expelled from the society. Under less extreme conditions they may be allowed to compete, to maintain their cultures, and to move about freely, while having little if any involvement in the decision-making process that affects their existence.

In the geographical segregation dimension, ethnic groups and races may be highly concentrated within particular regions, or they may be dispersed throughout the society. Some groups may be predominantly urban while others are rural, or they may be quite similar in their urban-rural distribution. Within cities, groups may inhabit specific areas or sections, or they may be more generally distributed throughout the particular cities.

The cultural differentiation dimension ranges from extreme cultural segmentation to cultural integration. Groups may be quite culturally distinctive with entirely different traditions, or groups may share many cultural elements in common with little differentiation in shared meanings created by ethnic or racial divisions. Another possibility is that several groups may have few cultural elements to distinguish them while one or a very few other groups may be quite different from all of the rest.

Besides being more or less unequal, more or less spatially segregated, and more or less culturally differentiated, ethnic groups and races are more or less socially segregated or distant from each other. Social distance involves the acceptance of norms that define acceptable forms of interaction between members of different groups and the frequency of *such interaction. The greatest social distance exists in caste relations, while the least social distance generally exists between permissible marriage partners. Personal distance is individual, affected by the person's own images of ethnic or racial out-groups and the desirability or undesirability of certain forms of association with these out-groups. Personal distance may conform to the consensual social distance or be deviant.*

Some form of conflict and competition occurs between ethnic groups and races most of the time. Ethnic and racial group competition and conflict are segmental, involving individuals and subgroups for the most part. The major factors that contribute to conflict and competitive success or failure are social organization, cultural contrasts, the relative population sizes, and relative degree of group cohesiveness. The major reason, if not the sole reason, for the relative inequality of all of the groups within societies and for the existence or not of dominant and subordinate groups is success or failure in situations of competition and conflict.

Three basic models of ethnic and racial relationships can be constructed. In empire societies, a dominant minority incorporates a number of other subordinate minorities into a single political system, primarily by military conquest. Extreme cultural diversity, regional concentration, great social distance, and parallel institutions (except the state) are to be found. Such diversity and separation, which are potentially divisive, are countered by the laws imposed upon all units, by economic interdependence, and by the societal members' perception of the state's ability to maintain order while allowing a certain degree of ethnic autonomy. In contrast to empires, national societies have a dominant ethnic majority and are relatively integrated. Minority ethnic groups or races are often "invisible," thus giving rise to the myth of the nation-state. Pluralistic societies have no dominant ethnic group, and are characterized by balanced power between regionally concentrated and culturally divergent groups in a pattern that is generally structured and deemed socially valuable.

The remainder of Part 1 will focus on the empire and the national societies, concentrating on those processes involved in the origin of dominance (Chapter 3), those processes that maintain dominance (Chapter 4), and those processes related to the reduction or the termination of ethnic or racial dominance (Chapter 5).

3

THE ORIGINS
OF DOMINANCE

INTRODUCTION

All systems of social relationships have a beginning. In the case of *ethnic* dominance and subordinance the beginning can often be identified with relative precision—in some circumstances, such as the signing of an annexation treaty or the end of a decisive battle, the exact day can be determined. The emergence of a system of *racial* dominance is more likely to be gradual, to evolve over a long time period. In any case, the dominance of one group over one or more other groups has an origin, and the form of this origin significantly affects later patterns of social interaction.

Although there are similarities between the origin of ethnic dominance and the origin of racial dominance, important differences necessitate that each be examined separately.

ETHNIC DOMINANCE

A dominant-subordinate relationship between two ethnic groups usually originates when one group is incorporated in some manner into a new society in which the state is controlled by the members of another ethnic group. If the addition of the newly incorporated group changes the ethnic composition of the society from one ethnic group to two, the group that controls the state will become a dominant group. For example, the small city-state of Rome in the fifth century B.C. was probably uniethnic. After conquering the neighboring Sabines and incorporating them into the Roman system, the Romans became a dominant group. As the Romans expanded their empire, the incorporation of each new group constituted the origins of a particular dominant-subordinate relationship—for example, the Roman-Greek relationship, the Roman-Samnite relationship, the Roman-Gaul relationship.

There are four major ways, all involving some form of migration or movement through geographical space, by which ethnic groups become subordinate: through conquest, immigration, annexation, and enslavement.

Conquest

Although precise knowledge is lacking, it seems likely that the most common origin of dominant-subordinate relationships has been through the conquest of one ethnic group by the military forces of another. Conquest consists of two elements—invasion and occupation.

Generally, invasion is the migration of organized warriors, soldiers, or armed settlers into the territories of other ethnic groups, followed by some degree of violent conflict as the indigenous peoples attempt to resist this intrusion. The invading force may be multiethnic or it may be relatively homogeneous; it may even recruit indigenous ethnics to fight against their neighbors. The Spanish utilized a number of non-Aztec Indians in their conquest of Mexico, the Romans used members of other ethnic groups within their empire as auxiliaries, and the American cavalry units were often composed of a few Indian ethnics as scouts as well as black contingents in their wars against American Indian groups. In any case, the higher positions within the invading army are generally held by members of a dominant ethnic group, and the army is part of a state that is controlled by members of a dominant ethnic group. Invaders may also be composed of armed settlers who are not professional warriors, such as the Dutch farmers (Boers) who invaded the territories of various African ethnic groups in South Africa, or the American settlers in their wars against the Indians and the Mexicans.

Dominance has been established by the consequences of a single battle. As every schoolchild knows, the Normans defeated the Saxons at the Battle of Hastings in 1066, thereby reducing the Saxons to a subordinate status. A less well known occurrence was the Battle of Kinsale between the English and the Irish in 1603. From 1593 to 1603 the Irish had avoided a direct engagement with the English, relying instead on their guerrilla tactics in resisting English occupation. Finally, however, they decided to fight a formal engagement in the style of the times on a field near the town of Kinsale. "The Irish infantry tried to array themselves in the massive formations which had for so long brought victory to their Spanish allies in the great continental battles of the age, but they had never fought in that way before. They were slow and inexpert in their movements, and, to increase their difficulties, their horsemen deserted them." The English destroyed them piecemeal. "The battle of Kinsale had decided everything."[1] For the next three hundred years the Irish were subordinate to the English.

The success or failure of an invasion depends on the comparative resources of the groups in question and the organization of these resources. If the discrepancy is great, a single battle or a brief period of conflict will decide the issue. When power is more balanced, the invasion and occupation may take decades. In their efforts to subjugate the peoples of South Africa, the Dutch met fierce resistance from the Zulus. The Zulu people were disciplined warriors. Each Zulu soldier had to put in six months of military duty each year. Neglect of duty was punished by death. In battle their major tactic was to flank the enemy soldiers on both sides and then surround and annihilate them. The younger and less experienced but more enthusiastic members made the initial engagements; if they faltered, the veterans moved into combat. This formidable group resisted Dutch control of South Africa throughout the eighteenth and nineteenth centuries before they finally surrendered.[2]

Forms of migration other than the movement of troops may precede military conquest and are often a factor in precipitating the invasion. People from alien ethnic groups have been allowed to "occupy" particular areas within a society—various Europeans, for example, were given sections along the coast of West Africa to erect forts and warehouses related to the slave trade in the seventeenth, eighteenth, and nineteenth centuries; the English were granted trade privileges and the right to erect fortifications in Bengal, India, in the seventeenth century; thousands of Jewish immigrants were permitted to settle in particular areas of Palestine in the twentieth century; French missionary stations received permission for their establishment in Indochina in the nineteenth century; and the Mexican government encouraged American immigration into its northern territory, Texas. In time, all of these gratuitous acts by the indigenous elite led to military conflict and to the subordination of its people: African kingdoms were conquered by Europeans; the English expanded from their trading base to conquer most of India; the Jews gained their independence in the section they occupied and then conquered other sections of Arabic territory; the French conquered Indochina, justifying such actions as a means of protecting their missionaries; and the Americans in Texas gained their independence, Texas was annexed to the United States, and the annexation led to the conquest and dismemberment of Mexico. There seems to be a moral here.

Following military success, other forms of migration take place in the process of territorial occupation. At a minimum, military personnel and administrators are sent from the center of an expanding state-society to govern and tax the newly acquired areas and peoples. Other members of the occupying group also migrate to the new territory: entrepreneurs come to exploit the labor and resources of the land; farmers, miners, missionaries, clerks, and others may "follow the flag." Roman colonists in their newly acquired territories, British convicts sent to Australia, French businessmen and farmers finding opportunity in Algeria, and American miners entering the Dakotas are only a few examples of past migratory occupants.

Justifications for Conquest.   There have been numerous justifications offered for conquering other peoples, justifications that are noble, base, or just "good common sense," depending upon one's point of view. However, the initial result is the same: a territory is invaded and occupied.

Obviously, the extraction of wealth from the conquered areas or the acquisition of a new source of taxes and tribute has been either an explicit or an implicit motive for conquest. The ancient Assyrian king Tiglath-pileser I was quite explicit: "In my fierce valor I marched against the people of Qummuh, conquered their cities, carried off their booty, their goods and their property without reckoning. . . . The people of Adansh left their mountains and embraced my feet. I imposed taxes upon them."[3] Francis Bacon was somewhat cynical of religious justifications and stressed other motives in the conquest and subjugation of the New World: "It cannot be affirmed . . . that it was the propagation of the Christian faith that was the . . . [motive] . . . of the discovery, entry and plantation of the new world; but gold and silver, and temporal profit and glory."[4] Columbus managed to fuse the obtaining of gold and Christian duty in his letter to Ferdinand and Isabella: "Gold is most excellent. Gold is treasure, and he who possesses it does all he wishes to in the world, and succeeds in helping souls into paradise."[5]

However, several scholars have argued that modern European empires were based more on enhancing the power and prestige of the state rather than on economic exploitation. D. K. Fieldhouse, an English scholar concerned with European colonies, has written that "colonies were seldom deliberately acquired to produce wealth and they were retained irrespective of their 'profitability.' Empire in the modern period was the product of European power: its reward was power or the sense of power."[6] He argued that a formal empire was not necessary for successful economic exploitation, since this political structure never provided a degree of commercial monopoly sufficient to enable capitalists to sell at monopolistic prices at home or in the colonies; that European investors showed no marked preference for their own colonies and often received greater profits by operating in the colonies of others; and that colonial administrators, sensitive to public opinion at home, often restricted entrepreneurial activity.[7]

Fieldhouse's arguments apply to problems involved in the extraction of wealth, problems not possibly foreseen by empire makers motivated by economic gain. But certainly national prestige and power have often been a major motive for the expansion of the state from the earliest periods of human history. Much of the competition and conflict between European states in the last three hundred years is a result of this motive: *to increase the glory and prestige of the state.* In the New World, Africa, and Asia, numerous states competed to acquire colonies or possessions as symbols of national greatness, regardless of the cost. The competition over Africa by European states led to the Berlin West African Conference in 1884–1885 in order to develop ground rules for the staking of claims. The more powerful European states were successful in enhancing their national pride; in 1880 more than 90 percent of Africa was ruled by Africans, but twenty years later only Ethiopia and Liberia were ruled by Africans.[8]

Population pressure has also been used as a justification for conquest. A succinct summary of this argument was made by the German Wirth, in 1904, in his conception of lebensraum (living space), a concept later incorporated into the writings and speeches of Adolph Hitler. Wirth wrote:

> *A people needs land for its activities, land for its nourishment. No people needs it as much as the German people which is increasing so rapidly and whose old boundaries have become dangerously narrow. If we do not soon acquire new territories, we are moving towards a frightful catastrophe. It matters little whether it be in Brazil, in Siberia, in Anatolia or in South Africa, as long as we can once again move full of freedom and fresh energy, as long as we can once more offer our children wholesome light and air in plenty. Once more, as 2000 years ago when the Cimbri and the Teutons were hammering at the gates of Rome, sounds the cry, now full of anguish and unappeased desires, now arrogant and full of confidence—sounds more and more strongly cry "We must have lands, new lands!"*[9]

The defense and protection of the state, paradoxically, lead to conquest and the expansion of the state. In this justification for conquest, colonies have to be acquired in order to protect other colonies already acquired: the threats of peoples on the border of the state have to be eliminated; the expansion of other states in backward areas will make them more powerful and, hence, we must expand there first; we must protect our property and our citizens in these foreign states, etc. The Israelis conquered sections of Jordan, Egypt, and Syria to create more defensible borders. The English, after conquering India, felt it necessary to have colonies and bases in East Africa in order to protect India. The Americans conquered Cuba in order to protect American citizens and property and took the Philippines from Spain as a bonus. The Tudors of England conquered parts of Ireland to prevent domestic rivals and foreign enemies from using Ireland as a base of operations against them and to counteract the growing empire of Spain.[10] In 1864 the Russian foreign minister justified the conquests of what is now central Russia on the grounds of boundary security. As he pointed out, "subjugation of one tribe brought the civilizing power into contact with fresh tribes. To defend the new boundary it was necessary to crush the new raiders."[11] He quoted the military history of the British and the Americans to confirm his argument that such conquest is necessary when a civilized state comes into contact with barbarous peoples.[12]

This expansion through defense is often unplanned. The elite may not consciously set out to conquer the world but may somehow get involved in the affairs of other peoples and thus in war, the acquisition of territory, and the problems of order and new neighbors. "Rome did not really want to build an empire but eventually found itself saddled with a rudimentary one after the First Punic War; from then on, in the process of discharging new responsibilities thus acquired, all it could do was to go on conquering and subduing and civilizing for the protection of its new wards, and learn to enjoy it."[13] It has been said that Rome conquered the world in order to defend itself, and, although this is an exaggeration, there is a certain truth to it.

British involvement in India and subsequent developments in Africa also illustrate inadvertent involvement and the subsequent need for defense. In 1623 a private English company called the East India Company was given trade privileges in India, particularly in Bombay and Calcutta. This permission was given by the Mughal emperor, the king of a group of Moslem Turks who claimed a relationship to the Mongols of Genghis Khan and Timurlane and who had established dominance over India through conquest at an earlier period. In the late 1600s and early 1700s the Mughal Empire disintegrated after several Hindu princes revolted.

The English were tolerably ready to keep afloat in the troubles to come. Their settlements had been fortified, and a degree of friendship existed between them and the men who seized power in the provinces of the empire. The English had come as traders; then they became armed traders; soon they needed soldiers to defend their settlements; and, as the Mughal empire disintegrated, "spheres of influence" became necessary if the Company was to survive. Slowly, the rhythm of empire-building had imposed itself on the simplicities of trade.[14]

Racism* is another motive for conquest. Inferior peoples need protection, the argument goes, or exposure to the one true faith or the glories of a certain civilization, or they need to be subjugated because of their threat to others. In 1933, Franz von Papen, a member of the German government, justified the acquisition of colonies in Africa in paternalistic, racist terms:

Africa . . . includes among its inhabitants a number of tribes and races which are not yet ripe to govern or to manage themselves. Europe is, so to speak, the intellectual guardian of those peoples. To Europe has fallen the great task of bringing to them the blessings of civilization.[15]

He also added a few side benefits for the Germans: a source of food, a place to take care of surplus population, and wealth to meet foreign credit obligations.[16]

Chapter 4 will explain this concept in detail.

The American Senator Albert J. Beveridge justified American military actions at the turn of the century with a similar racist view:

[God] has made us the master organizers of the world to establish system where chaos reigns. He has given us the spirit of progress to overwhelm the forces of reaction throughout the earth. He has made us adept in government that we may administer government among savage and senile peoples. Were it not for such a force as this the world would relapse into barbarism and might. And of all our race He has marked the American people as His chosen nation to finally lead in the regeneration of the world. [17]

The Consequences of Conquest.   Later patterns of ethnic relations within a system of dominance are often related to the manner of its origins. The relationship between a dominant group and a subordinate group that began with conquest generally is quite different from one that originated with the voluntary immigration of a subordinate group. One important effect of conquest is the greater probability that subordinate groups will secede generations later. Since the conquered peoples are "charter members" of certain areas of a society, they are less likely to assimilate into the dominant group and are more likely to maintain a certain degree of cultural distinctiveness from the dominant group. When the circumstances are right, movements to gain their independence in their "occupied" territory are more probable than among those groups subordinated through immigration or slavery. This is particularly true of relatively large populations of relatively advanced peoples that have been temporarily occupied by a foreign group, as in the domination of Africans and Asians by Europeans.

Relative population size is an important factor in affecting later developments. If small tribes of primitives are conquered and their territories inundated by a large number of colonizing dominants, other consequences are more likely. The primitives may be decimated by disease and war, their lands may be appropriated, and they may be herded into human game reserves. Various forms of psychological and social disorganization may take place. Since they are generally incapable of being incorporated into complex economies, members of outside ethnic groups are often enslaved or encouraged to immigrate. Because of their small size and limited resources, their eventual independence from the dominant group is virtually out of the question; their alternative is to continue to exist on their impoverished reservations or to disappear into the dominant group mainstream. This pattern has been manifested in the Spanish conquest of Argentina, the Portuguese conquest of Brazil, the British conquests of Australia, Tasmania, and New Zealand, and the American and the Canadian conquests of their nonliterate populations. [18]

Failure and the Problem of Causation in Human Affairs.   Conquest is the result of successful invasions followed by occupation of acquired territory and its people. Invasions have been failures, however. History is filled with dramatic engagements in which armies have been defeated (thereby creating a quite different pattern of history to unfold than if they had been successful). The Greeks stopped the expanding Persians at the battles of Salamis (480 B.c.) and Plataea (479 B.c.). Moslem expansion into France and quite possibly the rest of Europe ended with the Battle of Tours (732 A.D.). German efforts to establish dominance over the British failed in the Battle of Britain (1941). The British themselves had been losers when, after successfully conquering India and Burma, they decided to add Afghanistan to the empire (1839). The invasion force met severe resistance, and by 1842 retreat was the only solution. Only one person survived to tell the tale of bitter cold, sniping, and ambushes. Afghanistan did not become subordinated to the British.[19]

Did history have to happen the way it did? Military historians have noted idiosyncratic events related to the outcomes of battles: the miscommunication of some message, the late arrival of a section of an army, a leader's cowardly retreat before the outcome is decided, and the consequent demoralization of the soldiers. In one sense of the term "causation," the outcome of a battle is said to be caused by a certain combination of factors that preceded the outcome. However, many causes of events in history are not generalizable; they are unique. Presumably, if a certain combination of factors seems to precede victory, for example, then social scientists would be able to predict the outcome of a particular battle in advance. The ability of social scientists to predict human behavior is limited to tenuous statements of probability, since unique events can always drastically alter their predictions. Predicting conflict success or failure is extremely difficult, whether the conflict action is an invasion or a revolt (revolt failures will be examined in Chapter 4). Until even some general factors affecting success or failure in conflict can be ascertained and used in prediction, we are left with a tautological explanation: the winners won because they were more powerful (that is, because they had more resources and more effective organization of these resources). How do we know they had more power? Because they won. Even when the generalizable causes can be ascertained there will be the unique factors.

Regarding the question "Did history have to happen the way it did?"— the answer is yes, unless we want to give up the whole idea of causation; however, the scientific study of human behavior and the course of human events will never be reduced to laws or precise mathematical equations.

Immigration

Immigration may be defined as the entering of a society by members of an ethnic group or race from another society in order to improve their position. Members of an ethnic group or race in one society emigrate to another with the hope of economic, political, or social betterment. Such families or individuals may be members of either a dominant or a subordinate group in their society of emigration, but, regardless, they become subordinate in a new dominant-subordinate relationship in the host society, if this society is characterized by the presence of a dominant group.

Emigration from one society (leaving) and immigration into another (entering) may or may not be based upon a prior commitment. Sometimes immigrants have signed labor contracts with firms in the host country prior to their embarkation. Such contracts generally specify the number of months or years of employment and whether or not permanent residence can occur when the contract expires, as governed by the laws of the host society. Immigration can also be an adventure. Individuals, families, or somewhat larger groupings may decide to emigrate with no guarantee that they will be allowed into the country or that they will find a source of economic livelihood. Promising letters from friends or relatives help in making this decision to leave one's native land, as does host country propaganda. The optimistic expectation of betterment becomes the motive for emigration, an expectation that may not be fulfilled.

Immigrants may see the new society as either a permanent or a temporary residence. Many young people who are unmarried or who leave their families may only be interested in acquiring enough wealth to be able to return to their native country after a number of years. They may change their minds, however, and decide to make the host society their permanent home, if they are legally permitted to do so. Others, generally whole families, have every intention to become citizens, to sink roots, and to be buried in their adopted homeland.

The decision to leave one's homeland and to take up temporary or permanent residence in another society, and not just any society, is dependent upon what the demographers term *push and pull factors*—factors that push individuals out of one country and pull them toward another specific society. Major push-pull factors have been economic. The emigrants may perceive their prospects of economic betterment within their native society to be nonexistent, or their economic condition may have taken a turn for the worse. Class or ethnic discrimination may be a barrier to the more remunerative forms of employment. Widespread unemployment, depression, inflation, or crop failures are also push factors. In some cases, such as the potato famine in Ireland in the 1830s, sheer survival may be the impelling motive for emigration. In the last 100 to 150 years, industrialization and population increases have been the underlying causes of economic instability. Mechanization of agricultural techniques has displaced farmers in rural areas who must seek employment in the urban centers of their own society or leave altogether. Advances in medical technology that have reduced infant death and prolonged life expectancy have created population surpluses that cannot be absorbed in a society's existing economic system.

Despite industrialization and rapid economic growth, societies in northern and western Europe in the late eighteenth and nineteenth centuries could not find employment for their increasing populations. As a result, the

United States, Australia, Algeria, New Zealand, and Latin America became the new homes of millions of displaced Europeans. Between 1846 and 1932 alone, an estimated 51,660,000 Europeans left Europe.[20]

Between 1945 and 1955 eight million Europeans, primarily from Austria, Germany, Greece, the Netherlands, and Italy, became residents of other societies. The host countries for these immigrants in rank order of number of immigrants received were: the United States, Canada, Australia, Israel, Argentina, the United Kingdom, Brazil, France, and Belgium.[21] Although economic betterment was the major motive, many emigrated for political reasons as well.

Since the 1960s there has been a major movement *within* Europe—from the poorer and underdeveloped countries of the south to the more industrialized countries of the north. At the end of 1966 5 million Europeans resided in countries other than their "own," with the largest segment being Italians (2 million). France was the leading recipient of such immigration, with a foreign population of 2.2 million.[22] Although the majority of these immigrants are contract laborers and will return to the native countries after their work permits expire, many will be or have become permanent subordinate minorities.

Economic pull factors include opportunities for advancement, cheap land, job vacancies, the demand for certain specialties, higher real salaries (in terms of higher purchasing ability), reduced rates for passage, or contractual guarantees. Underpopulated areas experiencing industrialization, as Argentina, Canada, the United States, and Australia did in the nineteenth and early twentieth centuries, need large supplies of cheap labor and families to settle in vast underpopulated and unpopulated areas. The United States needed not only cheap labor for the industries of the East but colonists to settle in the West to overcome Indian resistance to settlement and to make the area productive.

Agents of governments or of private companies have actively recruited in other societies in order to acquire labor or colonists. In the eighteenth century Catherine the Great sent out agents who successfully encouraged thousands of Germans to colonize sparsely settled lands on the Volga through the use of subsidies and tax exemptions.[23] Private companies and state governments in the United States in the nineteenth century and the first decade of the twentieth century sent numerous agents to Europe to seek immigrants. French industrial companies in search of manpower sent agents into Poland in the 1920s and 1930s. Largely because of their success, the Polish population of France increased from 45,000 in 1921 to 508,000 by 1931. Polish miners were particularly useful, since "they proved more docile than native labor and did not demand salaries commensurate with the strenuousness and health hazards of the occupation."[24] Since World War II the French government has actively sought permanent residents to fill the demographic void left by low birthrates and the effects of the war.[25]

In some societies in which dominance has been established through conquest, the subordinate populations are plentiful enough as a source of labor;

however, they may lack the necessary skills for what the economic elite requires, or they may be unreliable workers. Under such circumstances other ethnic groups are recruited from other societies. South Africa, for example, brought in people from India, the Malay Archipelago, China, and Madagascar. Similarly, French planters in Indochina and Polynesia, American planters in Hawaii, and British industrialists and planters in Burma and Malaya encouraged immigration of Indians, Chinese, Japanese, and Portuguese to fill economic niches.[26] Many of these immigrant groups become "middlemen" minorities in the system of ethnic or racial stratification—in between the dominant group and the conquered populations.

Although economic push-pull factors have been predominant in creating emigration and immigration, other circumstances and conditions have also been important. Persecution by the government of a society or the anticipated consequences of a change in government have been factors in pushing people out of their birth places. Russian governmental efforts to suppress the culture and identity of Poles and Jews in the nineteenth century sent thousands of members of these groups to the United States. Similarly, the Moslem Turkish harassment of Lebanese Christians drove large numbers to the United States, Argentina, and Chile (85,000 Lebanese entered the United States between 1900 and 1915).[27] Turkish oppression also caused 320,000 Christian Armenians to flee to other countries in the Middle East or to Europe.[28] Political factors may impel dominant group members to emigrate as well. Over 50,000 Spaniards left Spain for North Africa during the Spanish Civil War, and another 14,000 became permanent residents of France. Mussolini's dictatorship sent 70,000 Italians to North Africa, and over 60,000 Czechs fled to the western zones of Austria and Germany following the Communist takeover of the Czechoslovakian government in 1948.[29]

Political pull factors essentially amount to the emigrants' perception that a government in another society allows greater political freedom and does not engage in or support discrimination and suppression of their group.

With very few exceptions, newly arrived immigrants seek out members of their own group who have arrived previously. Thus, immigrant enclaves form and grow, either in urban neighborhoods or in towns and rural areas. Although discrimination may be a factor, this spatial segregation occurs even in the absence of discrimination. The immigrant ethnic enclave performs the important functions of reducing cultural shock and of acclimating the recent arrivals to their new surroundings. Pasquale d'Angelo, an Italian immigrant to the United States, explained his view of the little Italies:

We fellow townsmen in this strange land clung desperately to one another. To be separated from our relatives and friends and to work alone was something that frightened us, old and young. So we were ready to undergo a good deal of hardship before we would even consider breaking up the gang.

As soon as they step outside of the Italian colony they are almost as helpless as babies, owing to their lack of knowledge of the language, customs, and laws of this country. That is one of the fundamental reasons why these people, in the open air, working in the fields—prefer the gray life of the slums; anything rather than to be separated from the rest of their countrymen. It is the instinct that makes all living creatures band together in time of storm.[30]

The immigrant colony becomes the base of operations from which entries into the larger society eventually may be made.

The largest immigration movements have generally involved the dispossessed or the unskilled. Hence, immigrants often have entered the lower strata, a position which may be temporary. If relatively successful, they may acquire sufficient wealth and return to their native land, perhaps in a higher stratum in the society of their origins. If they remain, they or their descendents may acquire the language of the dominant group and sufficient skills to improve their socioeconomic position. Upward mobility should not be conceived of solely in individual or family terms, however. What is often of extreme importance is the collective energies of the group, in the form of organizations to promote their own interests and to remove dominant group barriers to advancement. But upward mobility is accompanied by diminished internalization of the minority culture; in fact, its loss may be a prerequisite to mobility. Advancement also requires leaving the comforting but restricting confines of the ghetto. In time, unless new members from the old country replenish these segregated areas, they disappear one by one. However, ethnocentrism, sufficient population maintenance, and economic opportunity within such segregated enclaves may prevent their absorption or disappearance for centuries. The Volga Germans remained intact in their own communities from the middle of the eighteenth century to the end of World War II, when they were forcibly dispersed by the Soviet government. Similarly, the Swiss-German Amish in Pennsylvania and other states have maintained their communities in relative isolation from the mainstream.

Becoming subordinate through immigration may be preferable to remaining in one's native land. On the other hand, the new society may be oppressive and restrictive to the immigrant. Dominant group practices and behaviors, particularly the policies and actions of elites, will determine whether or not immigration was worth it.

Annexation

The term *annexation*, in its broadest sense, means the incorporation of all or a segment of one society into another. If the incorporating society has a dominant group, then the ethnic groups within the incorporated, or annexed, society become subordinate at the point that sovereignty is transferred.

The most frequent manner in which annexation occurs is through conquest or defeat in war. Annexation will be used here, however, to mean the acquisition of territories by all means other than victory in battle. Annexation, in this limited meaning of the term, is the least frequent condition under which groups from different societies come together in a dominant-subordinate relationship.

The major means of annexation, other than by conquest, have been by purchase, by plebiscite, by petition, and by the establishment of a protectorate. These forms are generally peaceful (that is, they lack violent coercion); nevertheless, conflict and power differentials are often involved in some manner.

Purchasing territory from another society is quite rare. The United States has been the major country to acquire new land this way—Florida from Spain, the Louisiana Purchase from France, and Alaska from Russia. Another example is the German purchase of the Caroline and Mariana Islands from Spain in the late nineteenth century.

Annexation by plebiscite consists of allowing the people of a disputed area to decide themselves whether they want to remain within their present society or join another. In this manner, the nothern section of the German province of Schleswig voted in 1919 to join Denmark by a vote of three to one.[31] Needless to say, this League of Nations–sponsored election would not have occurred if Germany had not been defeated in World War I.

When territory is acquired by petition, the government of one society asks the government of another to incorporate it. The United States acquired Texas and Hawaii through this procedure. In 133 B.C., in a very unusual petition, the king of Pergamum (a kingdom in what is now Turkey) asked Rome to incorporate his society upon his death. Rome willingly obliged.

A more common form of annexation is the establishment of a protectorate over a powerless society by a more powerful one. Such an arrangement may be welcomed by the annexed society or may be imposed upon it in such a manner that resistance is futile. Under the authority of the League of Nations, Britain acquired areas of Africa taken away from Germany after World War I, as well as Palestine, a territory previously dominated by the defeated Turks. New Zealand became a part of the British Empire in 1840 when a majority of the Maori chiefs of the island signed a treaty with the British government giving up their independence in return for British protection.[32] Other islands in the South Pacific were annexed as protectorates in the nineteenth century—Tahiti, New Caledonia, and the Society Islands by the French; Eastern Samoa by the Americans; and the Marshall Islands by Germany. Generally, protectorates are allowed relative internal independence as long as order is maintained, but their relations with other countries are the concern of the central government. In time, however, political or economic dominance over domestic affairs by the central government is generally intensified.

Enslavement

Slavery is a legal status in which a person is the possession of another person, or chattel property. A slave can be "bought, sold, traded, leased, mortgaged, bequested, presented as a gift, pledged for a debt, included in a dowry, or seized in bankruptcy."[33] Slave status was imposed upon individuals captured in a war or kidnapped in slavery raids, it was used as a punishment for crime, and it was hereditary. Slavery probably existed informally before becoming a legal status, but as an institution and as a form of stratification it goes back to the earliest civilizations and has existed in some degree* in virtually all preindustrial societies. Although as a rule slaves performed the most menial tasks, they were also artisans, teachers, clerks, and even officials in government; it was their position as chattel property rather than the type of labor they performed that defined the slaves' status. Slavery was a condition of servitude "which no man, woman, or child, regardless of status† or wealth, could be sure to escape in case of war or some other unpredictable and uncontrollable emergency."[34]

If anybody could become a slave in the earlier preindustrial societies, of what significance is slavery in the origins of ethnic dominance-subordinance? Although slave status was sometimes imposed by members of an ethnic group upon their own kind, the more frequent practice was to enslave foreigners, as war captives or captives acquired through raiding expeditions in foreign lands. In the oldest civilized society, the Sumerian (Iraq), "the very words for slave meant 'male (or female) of a foreign country.'"[35] In ancient China, according to Davis, slaves were a criminal class, sharply differentiated from the "good" population:

> *To kidnap or wrongfully sell a "good" person was a serious crime, and the victim was not considered to have been an authentic slave. But since foreigners were thought to be something less than human, the Chinese had no compunction about enslaving Koreans, Turks, Persians, and Indonesians.*[36]

In the tenth and eleventh centuries A.D. the Germans linguistically distinguished "the *servi* of their own nationality from the captives who arrived from the east, and who were apparently given a far lower status. The foreigners were called *sclavi*."[37] Later, the Slavs, an ethnic group with numerous lower levels of ethnicity, were enslaved to such a degree that their name became the common term for this status—slave.

Because the major sources of new slaves were wars between societies and raiding excursions into foreign lands, the slave population of a given preindustrial society would consist primarily of foreigners; very few members of a dominant ethnic group would be slaves in their own society. In this way, members of an ethnic group in another society would become subordinate within a new system of dominant-subordinate relationships.

However, slavery was not conducive to the perpetuation of ethnicity. The slave status was not subdivided into viable ethnic communities, and being

---

In terms of numbers of slaves, and in terms of proportion of slave to free in the total population of a given society.

†*Meaning prestige rather than position.*

born into slavery did not permit one's effective socialization into the ethnic culture of one's ancestors. Slaves went with their masters, and although friendship patterns between slaves often would be based on a common ethnicity, friends could be separated at any time. Legal position overrode ethnicity, dividing human beings with the same culture and language into slave and free.

Until the last four hundred years or so, the slave category per se did not have a racial basis. It was always multiethnic, of course, and in certain societies phenotypic differences between some of the ethnic groups were present: nevertheless, *anybody* could be enslaved. As Europeans flocked to the New World, however, slavery became reserved, with few exceptions, for peoples with black skin. By the 1700s in North and South America, the term "black slave" was redundant.

In the next section the origins of *racial* dominance and subordinance will be examined, with particular emphasis on enslavement based upon race.

RACIAL DOMINANCE

Racial dominance is always the outgrowth of ethnic dominance. Ethnic dominance is established in some manner, generally by conquest, in a society where phenotypic differences exist between a few or several of the ethnic groups. In time (or immediately) racial classifications may develop whereby phenotype takes precedence over cultural and linguistic characteristics in the allocation of rewards. This development of racial stratification out of ethnic dominance occurs in one or more of the following processes:

1. The dominant ethnic group grants privileges to phenotypically congruent subordinate ethnic groups but continues to discriminate against or exploit those phenotypically discongruent ethnic groups. Under such circumstances those subordinate groups that are physically similar to the dominant ethnic group become somewhat integrated under the bond of a common color vis-à-vis those other phenotypically diverse subordinate groups. Racial labels are attached to the severely disadvantaged populations, which are then perceived in their common physiognomy rather than in their ethnic diversity.

An example from the United States will clarify this process. Anglo-Americans became the dominant ethnic group by secession from the British Empire. Continuing the pattern set by their British ancestors, they conquered a large number of Indian ethnic groups and imported members of diverse black ethnic groups from Africa as slaves. In the nineteenth century immigrants from numerous ethnic groups in Europe added to the polyglot population of the expanding society. In addition, a small number of Mexicans became incorporated into the society as a result of the conquest of Mexico and the annexation of about one-half of Mexico's territory. Black skin and slavery became synonymous, and the differences between the black ethnics were eliminated by the oppressive socialization practices of the slavery system. The Indian groups were defined as "Indians," or red men, on the basis of their color and their cultural similarities, in contrast to the Americans. The ethnics from Europe, who were physically and culturally similar to the dominant Americans, never experienced the hostility and discrimination suffered by Asian immigrants (Chinese and Japanese), black slaves, Indians, and culturally and sometimes physically discongruent Mexicans. Hence, color categories were formed—black, white, yellow, brown, and red. Mexicans occupied an ambiguous racial status—sometimes white, sometimes "Indian," and sometimes "brown." White was the dominant racial status; nonwhite, or various types of nonwhite, became subordinate. Color became the significant factor in the allocation of rewards, however. Ethnic dominance was not eliminated—Anglos continued to dominate and to discriminate against the Irish, the Jews, the Italians, etc.—but such discrimination was mild in comparison to discrimination against nonwhites.

Similarly, in South Africa today the dominant Afrikaners and the subordinate English are *white*, a color bond that is intensified by similar European traditions but weakened by linguistic differences and by conflicting interests. The conquered ethnic inhabitants are *black*, a label also related to their similar cultures in contrast to the cultures of the whites. Race is all important today, but the system began with ethnic dominance.

A variant of this first process occurs when the dominant ethnic group is physically different from all of the subordinate ethnic groups, which are physically similar to each other. Such was the case with the Spanish conquest of a number of Indian groups, such as the Aztec, Mayan, Toltec, Mixtec, and Zapotec tribes. All of the conquered groups were classified together as Indians and as a subordinate racial "caste."

2. The offspring of the sexual unions between dominant ethnic group members and members of phenotypically discongruent subordinate groups are defined as a special category (mixed, or "breeds"), even though such people may be socialized into the culture of the dominant ethnic group. These "breeds," or "mestizos," generally occupy an intermediate stratification position in the society. Race is the reason for their relative inequality, since they are generally linguistically and culturally similar to the dominant group.

3. The third process producing a racial system out of ethnic dominance is relevant only to blacks brought to the New World as slaves. Members from ethnically diverse groups from Africa were forcibly brought to areas in the New World that were dominated by particular European ethnic groups or their descendents. The black skin of the slaves and the white skin of their superiors was an obvious and extreme situation of contrast.

Once racial categories have crystallized and become more important than ethnicity, the incorporation of members of other ethnic groups into the society will have a racial basis. New groups becoming part of a society through immigration, conquest, annexation, or enslavement will be fitted into the racial stratification system that has been established.

SUMMARY

There are four major ways in which ethnic groups from different societies become members of the same society in a system of dominant-subordinate relationships:

1. Conquest.   *The military forces of one society invade and occupy another society. The ethnic groups within the conquered society then become subordinate to the invaders. Conquest has been justified as a means of acquiring economic resources, of enhancing the power and prestige of the state, of relieving population pressure and the necessity of defending and protecting the state, and of improving the conditions of "inferior" peoples.*

2. Voluntary immigration.   *Members of ethnic groups from other societies voluntarily emigrate to a new society in the hopes of improving their condition. If they enter a society that has a dominant ethnic group, the immigrants become subordinate. Emigration-immigration is affected by push-pull factors: unfavorable political, economic, or social conditions push members of a group to leave their society; perceived advantages of the host society pull them to that society.*

3. Annexation.   *When the government of one society annexes other societies or segments thereof, by purchase, plebiscite, petition, or by establishing a protectorate, the ethnic groups residing within the annexed territory become subordinate (unless, of course, the members in the incorporated territory are members of the dominant group in the society that has acquired the territory).*

77

4. Enslavement. *Members of ethnic groups in other societies who are taken into captivity by force become subordinate within the society of their masters. Slave status has traditionally predominated over ethnic status, preventing the formation of viable subordinate ethnic group communities. Nevertheless, ethnicity has been an important factor in slavery, since people rarely enslave members of their own ethnic groups.*

Racial dominance, or racial inequality in general, is initially the outgrowth of ethnic dominance. Subordinate groups that are phenotypically similar to the dominant group may be given greater privileges and receive much milder treatment than subordinate groups that are phenotypically divergent from the dominant ethnic group. Phenotype thus becomes the most important factor in determining the allocation of rewards, and a system of racial inequality emerges. Once this system of racial inequality has been established, new members of the society, incorporated by whatever means (conquest, immigration, enslavement, or annexation), become part of the racial system. In addition, miscegenation between members of the dominant ethnic group and members of phenotypically divergent subordinate groups may create new racial units within the system. While ethnic stratification can exist without racial stratification, systems in which race is paramount always coexist with ethnic stratification.

4

THE MAINTENANCE
OF DOMINANCE

INTRODUCTION

Once a dominant ethnic or racial group has come into existence, or a *particular* dominant-subordinate relationship has been established, dominance may continue for centuries. To maintain dominance is, by definition, to keep control of the state, to occupy the key positions in other organizations, to continue to acquire a majority of the society's wealth, and to ensure that the dominant group's culture continues to set the standards for others. At the very least the state must remain in the hands of members of one group. To intensify dominance is to increase the relative inequality of one or more subordinate groups vis-à vis the dominant group and to increase the controls and restrictions placed upon one or more subordinate groups.

Whether the maintenance of dominance is defined as desirable or as a social problem, what processes, conditions, and practices function to maintain or to intensify a system of racial or ethnic dominance? The following factors, particularly in combination, seem to be the most important: discrimination, racism, structural disadvantage, the conformity of subordinate groups, and the suppression of revolts.

DISCRIMINATION

Although broader meanings exist,[1] discrimination will be defined here as *intentional efforts to restrict or to require actions of selected ethnic groups or races within a society.*

Selective Restrictions or Requirements

Discrimination is selective in that some groups have restrictions or requirements placed upon them while one or more others are exempted, a condition made possible by a power relationship. The most common form of discrimination consists of efforts to *restrict* the activities and alternatives of a subordinate group—in voting, public accommodations, organizational membership, occupational position, residency, educational attainment, and numerous other areas of social life.

Less frequent but no less discriminatory are requirements that particular groups engage in certain activities or perform obligations not required by members of other ethnic or racial statuses. Selective requirements have taken such forms as paying higher taxes or tribute, engaging in forced labor, obeying curfew laws, wearing or carrying some stigmatic symbol, having to move to certain reserved land areas, or showing deference to members of the dominant group in public interaction.

These forms of discrimination occur as a result of *intra*-actions of a dominant group. Such intra-actions might include passing discriminatory laws, voting to exclude members of another group or status from an organization, or placing restrictive advertisements for jobs in newspapers (no Ethians* need apply).

*Inter*group confrontations occur between dominant and subordinate group members and may involve overt or covert actions. *Overt* discriminatory confrontation can take the form of arrest, harassment, or even murder by authorized members of state—the police or the military. In Natal, a province of South Africa, any gathering of more than ten blacks for reasons other than religion is broken up by the police in accordance with a 1928 law.[2] Africans are required to carry identification with them at all times, and each day an average of 1,750 Africans are jailed or fined for violation of this requirement (ten days or fifteen dollars).[3] The police in the American South prior to World War II enforced "racial etiquette." One example of this was the informal norm that black drivers must give the right-of-way to white drivers. Although there was no such rule in the legal code, blacks who violated it were arrested for "careless driving." More severe actions taken by the state would include mass arrests and imprisonment and the use of the military to remove a whole group to some other area of the society or to expel the group members. Nonofficials in the society may also engage in violent forms of overt discriminatory confrontation, such as lynchings, attacks on the communities of the disadvantaged group, murder, and beatings.

Nonviolent overt confrontation is more common. A personnel director may simply say to an unwanted applicant, "We do not hire Ethians." Hotel or restaurant personnel may simply ignore an unwelcome customer or flatly tell the customer to keep out. A tavern keeper in Connecticut had an effective method of punishing Negroes who had the audacity to come and ask for a beer: "put a head on their beer, serve them in a different glass to show you don't want them around, break the glass when they're finished."[4]

*The term Ethian is a name we can use as a substitute for the name of any particular ethnic group or race.

In overt discriminatory confrontation, whether violent or nonviolent, there is no effort to hide or disguise one's discriminatory intentions. *Covert* techniques, on the other hand, are subtle, devious, and disguised, although the intent is the same. Racial minorities in the United States have experienced much covert as well as overt discrimination. A person is not hired because of "lack of qualifications"; a hotel registration card is lost; an applicant is informed, "We're all out of voter cards—come back later," "The hotel is all filled up," "I'm afraid you do not qualify for the loan," or "I'm sorry, but the house has just been sold."

Whether discriminatory actions occur *between members of a dominant group* in the form of creating strategies, policies, laws, or tactics, or whether they occur *between members of the different statuses as a confrontation*, the idea of restricting or requiring is involved. Even violent confrontation is the result of efforts to initiate some discriminatory decision, to punish somebody for violation of the norms, or to provide a lesson to the entire group: keep your place.

Not every member of a dominant group can discriminate, nor is it necessary. A power relationship is necessary for discrimination to take place, and power of great magnitude resides primarily in the executive positions of large-scale organizations. Discrimination by the elite has greater consequences than discrimination by the nonelite. Members of the elite have the major responsibility for the existence and the continuance of discrimination, either in the role of policy makers or in the condoning of discriminatory actions on the part of subordinates. It is certainly true that the elite is influenced by the rank and file or by the masses, particularly in democratic societies. Nonelite members of the dominant group can influence and even coerce the top members of the state and other organizations to carry out discriminatory programs. Nevertheless, the opposite is generally the case. Whatever the extent of pressure from below, the members of the elite, in the final analysis, are the major sources and implementors of discrimination.

Discrimination Is Intentional

Discrimination is a form of conflict and therefore is intentional. It is to be distinguished from other social conditions and policies that may perpetuate inequality but that are unintentional. Intentional efforts to restrict or to require actions of subordinate groups stem from two basic perceptions of reality: the perception of advantage and the perception of threat.

The Perception of Advantage.   Discrimination often has been perceived to have certain economic, political, and/or psychic advantages. Economic advantages or rewards are the most readily apparent, and they take two general forms—the reduction or elimination of competition and the maximization of profit or income. The economic elite has utilized ethnic or racial subordinates—groups that either have been conquered or have been encouraged to immigrate into the society—as sources of cheap labor. The cheaper the labor, the greater the profits. Such groups also help the economic elite to discipline and control its own ethnic working class by increasing the labor supply and thus driving down wages or by acting as strike breakers (scabs) against unionized members of the dominant ethnic working class.

Dominant group members of the working class can obtain economic advantages if subordinate group members are utilized to do the most menial and unrewarding tasks at the lowest pay scales. In this way the dominant group members form an aristocracy of labor.[5] One author has estimated that white workers in the United States gain about $15 billion per year from discrimination against nonwhite workers.[6]

In South Africa, Afrikaner workers and English-speaking labor groups found it highly advantageous to unite as whites against all African groups. The increasing use of nonwhite miners by mine owners produced a number of labor strikes in the 1920s under the slogan of Workers of the World Unite to Defend a White South Africa. Over 60 percent of whites before 1930 were poor or close to it. Through their efforts to influence the government, laws have been passed that protect white labor from competition with nonwhites; today there are very few whites in the lower stratum.[7]

In a study of the American South, Norval Glenn concluded that

> *the evidence is convincing though not conclusive that many whites in Southern urbanized areas benefit occupationally and economically from the presence and subordination of a large disadvantaged black population. The primary beneficiaries apparently are middle-class Southern housewives and white workers in proprietary, managerial, sales, and upper-level manual occupations. A majority of these beneficiaries apparently have intermediate rather than high income.*[8]

Another form of economic reward for certain members of dominant groups is reduced competition in commerce. Business competition is always risky, and discrimination helps to cut down the risks. At one time or another in Thailand the Chinese could not (1) be retail agents of tobacco, wine, sugar, or canned goods produced by government factories; (2) be butchers; (3) sell cloth to Buddhist monks; (4) sell pork at retail; (5) own coffee shops; (6) own ships trading within Thai waters; (7) fish in Thai waters; (8) drive vehicles for hire; or (9) collect bird nests (used in bird's-nest soup, a Chinese gourmet delicacy).[9] When ethnic discrimination is coupled with other devices, such as fair trade laws, monopolistic practices, and high tariffs, the old adage seems valid—competition is what is left after businessmen get through with it.

Economic advantages in these areas and in numerous other areas are often merely *perceived* advantages. The real or objective consequences of such discrimination may be dysfunctional for the economy of a society as a whole and have negative effects on dominant individuals. In market economies the low wages created by discrimination diminish the levels of consumer purchasing ability and hence potential demand. Lower levels of production, employment, and profits are often the result. Reliance upon menial labor at low wages also discourages technological innovation—innovation that can increase production and the standard of living for everyone.

Few individuals, however, realize the collective consequences of their individual decisions, and even when one does know what the consequences will be, immediate self-interest may be more important. In the United States

the white man who hears an estimate that discrimination against Negroes reduces the gross national product by several billions annually is not likely to be greatly concerned, especially if he knows that discrimination enhances his relative standing in the economic hierarchy. Discrimination keeps the total economic pie smaller, since it prevents the most efficient utilization of human resources, and it may even keep the whites' share of the economic pie absolutely smaller. However, it keeps the whites' share relatively larger, and from their point of view this may be more important.[10]

Racial and ethnic dominance also has political and social advantages. Subordinate ethnic groups often are convenient scapegoats for the various social and political ills of a society. Politicians can stir up latent prejudices against such groups to get elected, and divided political parties can be unified against the common "enemy." The limitation of the electorate to the dominant group helps to ensure that their privileges and lifestyles will not be threatened by groups considered alien.

The French taught the natives in their African colonies to assist in government but restricted their education to the necessary skills and paid them less than French employees. Prior to the 1890s the French elite had subscribed to the principle of the complete assimilation of conquered peoples. If the conquered aliens were educated and transformed into Frenchmen, the argument went, then the French Empire would become an integrated whole and would avoid the disintegrative tendencies inherent in pluralistic societies. However, the realities of colonial rule turned this policy of total assimilation into lip service and then into limbo (total assimilation was resurrected after World War II). The task of administering and controlling huge sections of Africa required extensive personnel, and the importation of Frenchmen would have greatly exceeded the colonial budgets. "The cheapest solution clearly was to train African personnel to undertake all but the top administrative tasks and to hire them on a much reduced salary scale."[11] A complete European education would be dangerous and, indeed, useless for groups that were to remain subordinate. The policy was economically advantageous in that it saved money. Political advantage was gained because the top positions were reserved for Frenchmen, yet government tasks could be carried out.

Finally, there are psychological advantages to racial and ethnic discrimination. The lower classes within the dominant group can take some consolation from the fact that there are people below them. Likewise, the acquiescence of a subordinate and powerless female to the sexual demands of a dominant male certainly enhances the male's self-esteem, particularly if he has been rebuffed by females in his own group. The deference shown to colonial administrators by the "natives" in the various European empires is another example of the psychological benefits of dominance. In South African restaurants African waiters have greeted the white person with the question "What does master desire?" In the United States, "Southern Negroes traditionally have showed deference to all whites, regardless of age, occupation, education or economic standing, so that no white person was without an ever-ready source of ego-enhancement."[12] John Dollard, a well-educated Northerner, reported in his study of a Southern town in the United States that it was impossible not to respond with self-satisfaction and exhilaration to the deference of the Southern Negro.[13]

The Perception of Threat. Discrimination against subordinate groups may develop or be intensified when such groups appear to be a threat not only to dominant group advantages but to the very existence of the dominant group. Dominant groups may perceive subordinate groups as threatening because of their competitive ability, their potential for revolt, a belief that they have been engaged in subversive activity, or fear of being contaminated by association.

One tactic of discriminatory control is to forcibly segregate the dangerous group, a tactic that may involve widespread movement of the population. In the Republic of South Africa intertribal or interethnic rivalries among blacks have diminished and a broader African ethnic community is emerging. As whites have perceived this threat to their supremacy they have moved Black ethnic groups such as the Zulu, the Sotho and the Xhosa in large numbers to separate reservations, or Bantustans. Blacks are prohibited from residing in major cities, and high-rise hostels have been built on the outskirts of a few cities to house the workers used in the cities by day. Several all-black towns and cities have also been created, the largest being Soweto, a city of one million people just outside of Johannesburg.[14] Divide and dominate.

During and shortly after World War II, on the grounds of collaboration with the Germans, eight ethnic groups in the USSR were forcibly removed from their ancestral territories and relocated in the vast reaches of Siberia. An estimated two-fifths of the populations involved, primarily old people and children, died in these transfers, with casualties amounting to almost a half million.[15]

The United States has also segregated subordinate groups. During the eighteenth and nineteenth centuries, Indians were moved from one area to another and prohibited from leaving their "reserved" areas; blacks have been segregated into sections of cities and at certain times have been prohibited from entering certain states; and over one hundred thousand Japanese-Americans were forcibly removed from the West Coast during World War II and placed in "relocation centers" in a number of interior western states.

When the population of subordinate groups increases, dominant groups may begin to feel threatened by fears of competition, "mongrelization," or increases in social problems, such as crime. Immigration control then becomes a necessity. The American elite encouraged immigration of Europeans and Asians in the nineteenth century and then closed off immigration to Southern Europeans, Eastern Europeans, and Asians in the early part of the twentieth century. Australia and Great Britain have, in recent years, restricted the immigration of "colored" peoples into their states. The French government, troubled with urban problems, has instituted a policy that employers must provide adequate housing to immigrant workers and pay them French wages; the policy is intended to cut down on immigration from North Africa when employers find that they no longer can hire Arabs or Berbers at low wages with no obligation for their housing. In 1950 Thailand passed a law limiting the number of aliens to only 200 per year in order to restrict the immigration of the Chinese, a highly competitive group.

Expulsion of most or all of the population of some ethnic groups from a state because they are perceived as a threat (or both because they are perceived as a threat and because the dominant group sees advantages to be gained from their expulsion) has been an infrequent but always a tragic form of discrimination. One of the most extreme incidents was the expulsion of the Jews from Spain in 1492. Approximately 100,000 Jews that had not "converted" to Christianity were forced out of the country. Their money was confiscated, their synagogues were transformed into churches, and their cemeteries were turned into pasture.[16] In recent years several countries have reduced the populations of subordinate groups that are perceived as dangerous. In the USSR, 14 million Germans were expelled at the close of World War II, and thousands of Turks were forced to leave other communist states.[17] Asians have been expelled from Kenya and Uganda, ostensibly for refusing to give up their British passports for African ones. Their control of the middle-level occupations, their competitive skills, high birthrate, and high degree of social distance (known as "clannishness") have led to the expulsion of all of those Asians that refused to turn over their British passports. The restrictions on Commonwealth immigration into Britain (1968) have complicated their fate even further, causing many to become stateless persons.[18] If all of the members of an ethnic group are expelled, a particular dominant-subordinate relationship is terminated, of course. But when this is not the case, dominance over the remainder of the group has been maintained, even intensified, although the society as a whole may have lost a valuable resource.

Conformity.   But not everybody within a dominant group perceives discrimination as advantageous or views subordinate group members as threats. There is a third cause of discrimination, also intentional—conformity. Because they fear the consequences of nondiscrimination, or perceive the legitimacy of such discrimination, many members of a dominant group who can discriminate will generally do so. Conformity to discrimination is more likely when such restrictions or requirements have become institutionalized.

Institutionalized Discrimination

Most efforts at discrimination are sporadic, temporary, and unsystematic. The government may institute some discriminatory program and then rescind it later. A group may be persecuted for a period of time and then ignored. *Individuals* may refuse to sell their homes to out-group members. Or the elite in some organizations may discriminate against a given group while other organizations may not.

However, discrimination has been institutionalized in numerous societies, such as the traditional empires, the Republic of South Africa, and the United States. According to one definition, "to institutionalize is to establish, standardize, and give social sanction to some particular pattern of social values, relationships, and behavior. Institutionalization is the process by which certain parts of the culture pattern are established, standardized, and given social sanctions which make them mandatory for those persons and groups concerned."[19] When institutionalization occurs, discrimination takes the form of *norms*. In stable systems of ethnic dominance two norms exist which are the converse of each other for any effort at restrictions or requirements of behavior—the discriminatory norm and the privilege norm. For example, the voting restrictions placed upon blacks in the United States (discrimination) become simultaneously a privilege of whites (an opportunity or exemption from an obligation that is denied to others). Thus, the privilege norm is "only whites shall vote," and, conversely, the discriminatory norm is "blacks shall not vote." Group A does not have to pay tribute, Group B does; Group A has the privilege of serving on a jury, Group B does not; Group A is entitled to due process in the courts, Group B is not, etc. In this sense, one group's privilege is another's discrimination.

Privileges and their discriminatory counterparts may be formal or informal norms. *Formal* norms are institutionalized into the legal systems of societies, communities, and organizations. Such norms may take the form of laws that have been enacted by legislative bodies or by heads of state, or have been formulated by the courts. They may also occur as rules in the constitutions or manuals of organizations and associations. *Informal* norms, on the other hand, are the unwritten understandings, customs, and expectations, of a highly stable and consensual nature, that are found among members of particular social groupings. Informal norms are often more binding and more effectively sanctioned by the members of a group than are formal norms, although they may lack the legitimacy afforded to formal norms.

Examples of formal norms (privilege and discriminatory counterpart) may be found within many state societies at one time or another. In the United States most of the cities and states in the South passed numerous discriminatory ordinances between 1890 and 1915. Jews in Poland in the 1920s were forbidden by law to acquire land, to become citizens, and to engage in certain enterprises. At an earlier period in Italy the formal edicts of Pope Paul IV (1555–1559) restricted Jews to a walled ghetto, prohibited them from owning real estate, and forced all who had such property to sell within six months. In 1775 Pope Pius VI renewed older edicts and added a few special restrictions for the Jews of Rome: they were not allowed to ride in carriages, erect tombstones, or sing dirges at funerals.[20] In Ireland the Penal Code of 1692, imposed by the English, denied the following to Irish Catholics: voting, entering the Irish Parliament, entering the learned professions, obtaining commissions in the army or navy, opening or teaching in a school, selling or manufacturing arms of any type, producing or selling books or newspapers, having more than one priest per parish, having more than two apprentices, leaving an estate to a child, or owning a horse worth more than five pounds.[21] In South Africa today there are more than three hundred formalized norms discriminating against blacks, including prohibitions against joining unions, striking, conducting a school that is not registered, or watching a carnival organized by students of a white university.[22]

In the Spanish colonies of the New World there were a number of formalized privileges (rights) for Spaniards and Creoles (persons of native birth but of Spanish descent) that were legally denied to Indians, free mulattoes, and Negroes. Indians could not carry weapons or ride horseback.[23] Free mulattoes and Negroes could not appear on the streets after dark, carry arms, have Indians as servants, hold public office, or be admitted to craft guilds; mulatto and Negro women could not wear luxurious clothes, silk, gold, or pearls.[24] The Indians of Peru were forced to labor for the state or for private parties eighteen weeks every seven years (in principle, but in practice they often remained away from their homes for years); other Indians were forced to labor in mines, in factories and estates, and on public works (an estimated 8,085,000 perished in the mines alone during the colonial periods).[25] The Indians were also formally required to pay tribute of a set amount; however, by custom, tribute was exacted from them more than once a year, and they *had* to buy goods from the local provincial administrators (or *corregidores*). Articles were arbitrarily selected by the official to be bought by particular Indians, including sick mules, damaged goods, or European items quite irrelevant to Indian life (razors, hair powder, mirrors, ribbons, silk stockings, etc.). If they could not or would not pay, their lands were seized or the men were forced into labor.[26] The priests also did their share of discriminating. Indians had to pay higher fees for baptism, burial, and marriage; the priests invented new festivals in honor of saints that would necessitate new collections of money;[27] and the Mexican Church Council of 1555 denied Holy Orders to Indians as well as to mestizos and blacks.[28]

Informal privileges and discriminatory norms are generally more common than formal ones, particularly in democratic societies where formalized and blatant discrimination would go against egalitarian ideologies. These informal norms vary somewhat as to consensus among dominant group individuals, according to the time period, region, or social status, but are nevertheless binding rules for those groups that do subscribe to them. Informal norms may exist in lieu of formal norms or be in violation of the formalized norms. Prior to the civil rights laws of the 1960s in the United States, it was informally understood that particular occupations were reserved for whites (prestigious and remunerative occupations were a privilege) while menial tasks were "Negro jobs." Laws against occupational discrimination have considerably reduced such practices, but they do still exist on an informal basis.

Prohibiting blacks from serving on juries in the United States was against the law following the Civil War, however, informal discrimination was quite effective in keeping them off juries. In 1910 Gilbert Thomas Stephenson sent out letters to jury commissioners inquiring about Negroes on jury duty. One reply from a county in Florida stated that "Negroes do not sit on the jury in the county, and have not since the days of 'Carpet-Bag Rule.' I do not think a county in the State permits a Negro juryman."[29] Another commissioner from Alabama wrote:

> [*Once*] *a Negro was drawn as a grand juror (by mistake) who appeared and insisted upon the court's impaneling him with other jurors, which was done in accordance with law, the court having no legal right to discharge or excuse him. My recollection is he served two days, when he was taken out at night and severely beaten, and then was discharged on his own petition by the court. This will convey to your mind that Negro jurors are not very wholesomely regarded and tolerated in this county. The fact is, Negroes have never been or never will be allowed to sit on juries in this county.*[30]

Informal discriminatory norms and privileges are often involved in the elite recruitment of other elites. The elites recruit new elites on the basis of congruence—congruence of the attributes and qualifications of the potential member with those of the recruiters. The informal rule is that such membership is a privilege given only to those who have the "right" qualifications, and the "right" ethnicity or race is often a *minimal* test for admission.

When discrimination is institutionalized and normative, conformity is expected—conformity by members of *both* subordinate and dominant statuses. Violators of the norms are deviants. For the dominant status member who deviates, negative sanctions can take the form of epithets ("Ethian lover"), fines, scorn, legal proceedings, ostracism, or even imprisonment. In South Africa, for example, the education of blacks is illegal except under government auspices, and whites who spend a few hours a week in their own homes teaching African servants to read are guilty of a criminal offense.[31]

When employers state that they are not prejudiced but that they must discriminate or lose business, they are often quite sincere as well as realistic. Subordinate status members who object to the restrictions or requirements may suffer similar sanctions, along with the possibility of bodily assault and death.

When subordinate group members consistently conform to what is required of them, particular forms of discrimination *rarely lead to confrontation*. The example of jury duty discrimination in the United States illustrates this point—the jury commissioner couldn't recall when there had been any Negro seeking to serve on the jury, with the one exception. Similarly, Matthews and Prothro in their study of voting registration by southern blacks wrote, "Far lower rates of Negro registration are found in counties with little if any racial violence. Here Negro subordination may be so total that violence is not required to keep the Negro 'in his place' and outside of the polling booths."[32]

When discrimination has been institutionalized for an extensive period, subordinate group "deviance" will be so unexpected that members of the dominant status may be quite uncertain what to do. Kohn and Williams did a study of forty-three situations, focusing primarily on restaurants and taverns. They state that "in white neighborhoods infrequently visited by Negroes, for example, we found many restaurant and tavern managers who had never faced a situation where it was necessary [to decide] whether or not to serve Negro patrons."[33] The study involved sending a Negro couple (members of the research team) into these bars and recording the reaction of the whites. Following are the notes of one white observer in one of the situations:

Proprietor (amazed): "Well, how do you like that!"
Bartender (turning): "What?"
Proprietor and Blonde (simultaneously): "Those two jigs that just walked through here." "Two colored people just went in."
Bartender (in surprise): "Where'd they go?"
Blonde: "Into the dance hall."
Enter Jane, a second waitress, from kitchen.
Jane: "I'm not going in there. What can we do? This never happened before." (To proprietor) "What'll we do? (anguished) Do I have to serve them?"
Proprietor: (peering through service peephole from bar to dance floor): "Let 'em sit."
Bartender: "Yes, stay away from them. I didn't see them. Where'd they go?"

Blonde: "They're at the table for six. What are we going to do?"
Jane: "I'm not going in there. This is awful."

. . . .

Proprietor: "Just let them sit." For the next several minutes, the proprietor inquired anxiously from time to time, "What are they doing now? Did they go?" Each time he looked more amazed. Said to me, "Never in my time here did we have any of them at the bar."
[They continued to ignore them. Finally the proprietor told the bartender to get rid of them, and the Negro couple complied with the request. One white customer felt that they had rights and should have been served. The bartender threateningly told the man: "Pick up your change and drift. You want to drink with them? Go on down to the C.D. bar. Lots of them there" The white man left. The customers, proprietor, and bartender all felt that the whole incident was planned.][34]

The Consequences of Discrimination

The effects of discrimination upon subordinate groups vary depending upon the *number* of restrictions or requirements imposed, the *type* of discrimination (such as economic, political, residential), the *duration* of such discrimination, and the *effectiveness* of these dominant group actions. In this context, effectiveness refers to the extent to which a discriminatory effort accomplishes what is intended and the extent of resistance to such actions. Voting restrictions, for example, would be maximally effective if the targets do not vote or protest. Likewise, if the targets are required to engage in a compulsory labor program for a period of time and they do so, again without protest, maximum effectiveness is achieved.

However, the effectiveness of discrimination rarely approaches such perfection. Not only do subordinate groups often protest or react violently to such efforts, but, more commonly, in extreme systems of dominance, they practice subterfuge. In the Philippines, for example, the dominant Filipinos have placed a number of economic restrictions on the alien Chinese since World War II. Many Chinese have avoided such discrimination, however, by the use of bribes to acquire citizenship.[35] Similarly, Japanese aliens in California around the turn of the century were denied the right to own property by a discriminatory law. Their solution was to put property in the names of their children who had become American citizens. The black author Richard Wright has described his subterfuge in acquiring library books in the pre–World War II American South. Since blacks were not allowed to check out books, he would write a note to the librarian that said "Please let this nigger boy have the following books." Then he would sign out the books, using a fictitious name, supposedly a white man's.[36]

When relatively effective, discrimination can limit social mobility, prevent political actions, or create a low level of education and literacy. Discrimination can also create segregation in residency, prevent a group from increasing its size, and keep subordinate groups out of particular organizations and occupations. In addition, being the target of discrimination per se can have psychic consequences such as low self-esteem, neuroses, and psychoses for those ill-equipped to handle such stresses.

The consequences of discrimination can be direct or indirect. Consequences are direct when they correspond to the actual intended consequences. Indirect consequences are those effects of direct discrimination in one area of social life upon another. For example, if discrimination in an industrial society only took the form of restrictions on education, the following areas would be indirectly affected: job placement, income, property ownership, and residency.

Direct and indirect consequences should not be confused with their cause, discrimination. Discrimination is the *effort* at restricting or requiring actions of a selected group, not whatever results that may or may not occur. The existence of various forms of inequality does not prove the existence of present discrimination. Inequality may be the result of past discrimination, of the unintended consequence of organizational policies,* or of differences in competitive abilities. Similarly, segregation is not necessarily the result of discrimination; segregation has often been voluntary.

RACISM

Actions taken by members of dominant groups and the very existence of a dominant-subordinate system of relationships need to be justified, to be legitimated, or to be made "right." One major belief that has served this purpose is the doctrine of racism. Racism has been utilized to justify all forms of discrimination and numerous governmental policies directed against or "for" subordinate groups. The greater consensus on this legitimating belief within a society, the greater the probability that dominance will be maintained. This is particularly true if large numbers of subordinate group members, as well as members of the dominant group, accept the validity of this belief. In this sense racism is functional in the perpetuation of a system of dominant and subordinate relationships.

The Meaning of Racism

The concept of racism has been defined and utilized in a number of ways. What is common to most of these meanings is the idea of the existence of superior and inferior groups and the belief that this presumed difference justifies certain actions on the part of the superior group. Theorists differ as to whether this superiority-inferiority doctrine is based on biological heredity or upon both biology and environment; whether racism is only a doctrine or if the term encompasses actions too, and whether racism is limited

*Unintended consequences of organizational policies and practices will be labeled "structural disadvantage" and explained in a later section of this chapter.

to races or includes both racial and ethnic statuses. In addition, the term has been used as an inclusive concept to cover virtually all forms of race and ethnic relations—"prejudice," discrimination, inequality, and the unintended disadvantageous consequences of the operation and policies of organizations upon a racial group.[37]

Racism will be defined here as *the belief or doctrine that one people must control or act upon another people because of the superior and inferior attributes of the respective groups*. The following points will make this meaning clear:

1. *Racism is a belief system*. At the individual level racism takes the form of attitudes. At the sociocultural level racism is expressed in speeches, scholarly studies, newspaper articles, or verbal statements between individuals. Racism is a doctrine, an ideology, or an "ism" that is more or less developed and systematized. Whether or not such beliefs become manifest as discrimination or violent conflict is dependent upon the power of the groups in question and the consensus on the validity and the respectabililty of the doctrine. The National Socialist German Workers' Party (Nazis) subscribed to a racist ideology for many years before it was in a position of power to implement its beliefs.

2. *Racism applies to ethnic groups as well as to races*. As explained in Chapter 1, the distinction between race and ethnicity is useful but is often blurred. In addition, the most severe practices of dominance were directed against European Jews by the German Nazis and justified on superior-inferior grounds, even though the two groups were phenotypically indistinguishable. If racism is limited only to color categories or to racially identifiable ethnic groups, then we need another term for the doctrine of the superiority and inferiority of ethnic groups. "Ethnicism" is far too awkward and unnecessary.

3. *Racism involves both biological and environmental determinism*. Human beings past and present have disagreed about the causes of the differences between ethnic groups and races. Are behavior, character, and mental ability due to biological inheritance, to the forces of environment, or to some combination or interaction? Are behavior, ability, and character fixed and unalterable, somewhat modifiable within biologically fixed limits, or quite plastic and adaptable? Is one or more of these elements—behavior, character, and mental ability—more mutable than the others? There has been a wide variation of interpretation on these issues.

Particular ethnic groups and whole races have been viewed as separate species that are different because it is their *nature* to be different, like lions, foxes, and chickens. Such a nature is believed to be fixed by divine creation or by evolution. Thus, inferior groups are immutable and subhuman.

An example of this kind of thinking is the ancient Greek view of barbarians. Said Euripides, "It accords with the fitness of things that barbarians are slaves by nature." According to Professor Simon Davis, "in the eyes of the Greeks the barbarians were not only foreigners, but inferior beings: between man and beast."[38] Barbarians were biologically inferior, yet the overwhelming majority of these peoples were not physically different from Greeks.

With the increased contact between phenotypically diverse ethnic groups in the last four to five hundred years, the idea came about that observable physical traits and mental characteristics were intrinsically interconnected. In 1913 Dr. James Bardin of the University of Virginia proclaimed: "Mental characteristics are as distinctly and as organically a part of a race as its physical characteristics and for the same reason: both depend ultimately upon anatomical structure."[39] Hence, education and an improved environment are a waste of time for such groups.

On the other hand, a nineteenth-century American sociologist, Franklin H. Giddings, was more optimistic in his environmental view: "The Negro is plastic. He yields easily to environing influences. Deprived of the support of the strongest races, he still relapses into savagery, but kept in contact with the whites, he readily takes the external impress of civilization, and there is reason to hope that he will yet acquire a measure of its spirit."[40]

This view holds that human nature is extremely flexible, capable of a great deal of modification. However, say others, environmental exposure over a long period of time can fix human groups into some pattern of behavior. The eighteenth-century Scottish historian William Robertson believed that the American Indians were fixed into a life of indolence and a retarded mental state because of the lack of environmental challenges. Because "the desires of simple nature are few, and where a favorable climate yields almost spontaneously what suffices to gratify them, they scarcely stir the soul, or excite any violent emotion." They "waste their life in listless indolence."[41] Similarly, an Australian archbishop told his audience in 1904: "The Papuan race [of New Guinea] is unquestionably of an inferior nature. It has lived too long a prey to *original* sin."[42] An interesting ancient view of the power of the environment upon character and mental ability was given by a Roman consul to his troops before an engagement with the Gauls of Greece:

> *Our forefathers had to deal with genuine Gauls, born in their own lands; but they are now degenerate, a mongrel race, and, in reality, what they are now named, Gallograecians; just as in the case of vegetables and cattle, the seeds are not so efficacious in preserving their original constitution, as the property of the soil and climate under which they are reared, are in changing it. . . . Everything is produced in higher perfection in its own native soil; whatever is planted in a foreign land, by a gradual change in its nature, degenerates into that by which it is nurtured.*[43]

And carrying the power of environment to an extreme, people have believed that environmental forces can even alter physical traits. According to

Reverend Samuel Stanhope Smith in 1787, the features of house and field slaves differed because of their different social positions.[44] Professor Robert Bennett Bean published an article in the *American Anthropologist* in which he argued that the Jewish nose developed as a result of "continued excessive sexual indulgence" and that once developed it was perpetuated through sexual selection.[45]

It should be apparent that diverse reasons have been given for the supposedly inferior or superior natures of human groups. It is not necessary to restrict the idea of racism to biological determinism or to the even narrower view that phenotype and mental ability are interconnected. As will be seen in the following section, what is more important is how the "inferior" group is defined—as dependent or as a threat.

4. *Racism involves the idea of action to be taken*. In addition to the belief in superior and inferior groups, racism includes the idea that inferior peoples must be controlled (restricted, made harmless, cared for), exploited, or eliminated (expelled, exterminated). These actions taken against inferior groups are believed to be necessary for the good of the superior group's society or to be beneficial to the inferior peoples, an inescapable duty or an inevitable consequence of such differences.

If sufficient power exists, racism may be the motivation for such actions *or* a rationalization of actions already taken. Racism may be a genuine factor in bringing into existence conflict and discrimination, or it may be a cover-up for other motives, such as profit, political advantage, or social advancement.

Whatever the relationship between cause and effect, the doctrine of racism includes two essential elements: beliefs about inferior and superior groups *and* beliefs that some pattern of action should be taken if possible. It is one thing to make jokes about or even express extreme hatred of an out-group; it is quite another thing to conceive or plan actions that should be taken against the group.

The following statement contains the essence of the doctrine of racism: The Ethians_____(*fill in name of group*) are_____(a threat, dependent upon us, in need of our guidance) because of their_____(biological inferiority, environmental or cultural inferiority); *therefore*, we must _____ (civilize, restrict, exterminate, expel, control, resocialize, use, help, uplift) them because it is _____ (our duty, God's will, necessary for the good of society, necessary for our survival, for their own good, inevitable).

Images of "Inferior" Peoples

There are several recurring conceptions about peoples defined as inferior, and they all involve stereotypes. Stereotypes are standardized pictures or images in our minds consisting of certain qualities we attribute to social categories.* Inferior or superior attributes of ethnic groups or races can involve intellectual qualities (brilliant, backward, dull), moral qualities (frugal, industrious, stingy), aesthetic qualities (musical, passionate, stodgy), political qualities (radical, authoritarian, freedom loving), or physical qualities (beautiful, ugly, thick skulled, athletic, bleached out).[46] Large and heterogeneous categories of human beings are reduced to a selected number of attributes, attributes that may be applicable to some extent to a segment of the group but that hardly constitute a realistic description of the whole group.

It is easy to stereotype because we all rely upon symbols and language as intervening factors between raw reality and ourselves. In the words of Shibutani and Kwan:

> All men live in a symbolic environment, a substitute world in which objects and events fall into an orderly scheme. Life is much too complicated for any individual to respond to each item he encounters in terms of its distinctive characteristics. Each object is unique, but there is rarely time enough to examine it with care before handling it. Hence objects and events must be classified, and men act as if all of the items in each category have the same characteristics.[47]

Stereotypes of "inferior" peoples can be classified into two general types, depending upon whether the out-group is defined as threatening or as dependent: conflict racism and paternalistic racism.

Conflict Racism. Conflict racism develops when the inferior out-group is defined as a threat. At the very least the out-group is believed to be a frustrating burden, a pariah in the bosom of society that does not pay its way, contributes little, and therefore is a cancerous threat to the system. In the more extreme definition of a threat, the group is perceived as downright dangerous. It is a peril to everything held sacred, a threat to life and property and to the continued existence of one's society. It may be useful to distinguish between a number of subtypes of this general type:

1. *The Treacherous Savages* (or The Wild Beasts, or The Dangerous Barbarians). These people are considered vicious, dangerous, and treacherous. They lack any civilized or human sentiments, either because of their culture or because of their subhuman qualities. Male and female alike are animalistic in their sexual drives and have no inhibitions. No civilized woman is safe from the sexual appetites of the "bucks," and the females breed like rabbits. In their natural habitats their basic animal instincts serve them well, making them a dangerous enemy. They never can be truly tamed or civilized,

*Stereotypes are not limited to images of ethnic groups or races. We all have negative or positive images of such categories as southern sheriffs, librarians, professors, men or women, hippies, New Englanders, etc.

and given any opportunity they will kill, rape, and rob their protectors. Therefore, a good savage is a dead savage.

The Roman historian Titus Livius (Livy) provides several examples of the barbarian or savage stereotype in the ancient world. An Athenian pleaded with a Roman general for assistance against the "savage" but phenotypically similar Aetolians, saying, "They have nothing Grecian but the language, as they have nothing human but the shape. They live under customs and rites more brutally savage than any barbarians, nay, than wild beasts themselves."[48] A Roman official attempted to convince the Campanians that they should remain loyal to Rome and not join Hannibal's army of Carthaginians and other mercenaries, for Hannibal used "a body of soldiers who are not even natives of Africa, destitute of all laws, and of the condition and almost the language of men. Savage and ferocious from nature and habit, their general has rendered them still more so . . . by teaching them to live on human flesh."[49]

When the English settled Australia and Tasmania the aborigines were at first "charming primitives." As the English settled more and more land, however, these indigenous tribes became nuisances. When violent conflict erupted, those settlers most directly affected began to define the aborigines as wild beasts. In 1858 a historian and English settler on the island of Tasmania wrote that the earliest colonists on the island of Tasmania

> *describe, with exultation, their new acquaintance, when writing to their friends; how peaceful, light-hearted, and obliging. They are charmed by their simplicity; they sleep among them without fear: but these notes soon change; and passing from censure to hatred, they speak of them as improvident, importunate, and intrusive; as rapacious and mischievous; then as treacherous and blood-thirsty–finally as devils and beasts of prey. Their appearance is offensive, their proximity obstructive: their presence renders everything insecure. Thus the muskets of the soldier, and of the bandit, are equally useful; they clear the land of a detested incubus.*[50]

The American Indian was perceived in a similar way during the White-Indian Wars; this will be examined in detail in Part 2.

2. *The Sinister Foes.* "Sinister foes" have many of the attributes of the "treacherous savage"; however, they are not uncivilized barbarians or primitives, nor are they beasts in the state of nature, although animalistic aspects are sometimes cited. Sinister foes are the product of advanced civilizations and, hence, are more dangerous adversaries. Although dangerous, they are inferior. They are cunning, deceitful, immoral, arrogant, mercenary, clannish, and treacherous. But they are also organized, a factor which intensifies their threat to society. Such an image may be ascribed to dominant or to subordinate groups within a society, or to alien peoples in other societies. Sinister foes have to be defeated and crushed in battle, or, if they are internal foes, their sinister conspiracies must be ended by the state—through restrictions, imprisonment, or extermination.

The Jews, in various times and places, have been perceived as the epitome of the sinister foe. The following is a condensation of pages 417–50 in *Mein Kampf*, utilizing the exact words of Adolph Hitler, who was certainly the epitome of all racists:

> *The Jew is not creative, only a thief of other's culture. He is a parasite in the body of other peoples, using their language and culture but always remaining Jewish. He is the moral enemy of all light and the despiser of all true culture. The Jew is usurious, a blood-sucker, a flatterer, a master of lies and deceit. He wants to take over the world by ruining the racial foundations of the peoples to be enslaved, by systematically demoralizing women and girls, by working methodically for revolution, by applying all knowledge which he takes in the schools of others in the service of his race, and by destroying the bases of any national self-dependence and defense. Jews have no thought of a Jewish state in Palestine, only a central organization that is withdrawn from the seizure of others to be used as a refuge for convicted rascals and a high school for future rogues. Ultimately, the Jew pulls down into the gutter everything which is truly great, overthrowing all conceptions of beauty, sublimity, nobility, and quality, and pulls all people down into the confines of his own swinish nature.*[51]

3. *The Indolent Hedonists*.   The indolent hedonists (or, more colloquially, the shiftless bums), as the label implies, are lazy and concerned only with the pleasures of the moment (they do not "defer gratification"). They also beat their wives, carry knives, and are dirty, disease ridden, ignorant, sexually promiscuous, and superstitious. They haven't done a decent day's work in years and can lie, cheat, and steal with ease. They have all of the morals of an alley cat and none of its virtues. They are pariahs and parasites living off welfare and other handouts, and are burdens to the taxpayers. The males manifest their preoccupation with their masculinity by fighting, drinking, and copulating; the females are filthy bitches in heat. They neither plan for the future or remember the lessons of the past—life is for the moment.

Given the corrupting nature of such peoples, they must be restricted from entering society and/or expelled. Social controls must be severe enough to keep this menace in check, and their assimilation is out of the question.

The qualities of the indolent hedonists are often ascribed to recent immigrant populations, who may very well be uneducated, illiterate, and unskilled. Many Ashkenazic Jews in Israel have been concerned about the influx of Arabs and Sephardic Jews from Morocco. In 1949 a journalist had this to say:

> *A serious and threatening question is posed by the immigration from North Africa. This is the immigration of a race the like of which we have not yet known in this country. Still more serious is their inability to absorb anything intellectual. . . . Here is a people whose primitiveness reaches the highest peak. Their educational level borders on absolute ignorance. . . . They are completely ruled by*

primitive and wild passions. . . . In the living quarters of the Africans in the camps you will find dirt, card-games for money, drunkenness and fornication. Many of them suffer from serious eye, skin, and venereal diseases; not to mention immorality and stealing. Nothing is safe in the face of this asocial element, and no lock can keep them out from anywhere.

But above all these there is a basic fact, no less serious, namely, the lack of all the prerequisites for adjustment to the life of the country, and first of all—chronic laziness and hatred of work. . . .[52]

David Ben-Gurion is quoted as saying in the mid-sixties: "Those from Morocco had no education. Their customs are those of Arabs. They love their wives, but beat them. . . .Maybe in the third generation something will appear from the Oriental Jew that is a little different. But I don't see it yet. The Moroccan Jew took a lot from the Moroccan Arabs. The culture of Morocco I would not like to have here."[53]

The epitome of this type of racism in the United States was the Anglo view of the Mexican-American before World War II, a view that proliferated in the newspapers, in magazine articles, and in scholarly journals. The following is from an article in the *Atlantic Monthly* in 1899:

No one can tell what a Greaser thinks; no one can say what masked batteries of passion live back of his well-mastered eyes. To trust a Greaser is to take a long jump into utter darkness. . . . If he had no fleas to bite him, he would be likely to die of ennui. . . . If you sleep beneath his roof, keep one eye on his handy knife. That is the Spanish of his nature and his creed, and illustrates the uncertainties of life in a neighborhood where forgiveness of sin is a marketable commodity.[54]

Paternalistic Racism

In this form of racism the out-group is defined as *dependent*; its members need to be protected and controlled for their own good, as well as for the good of society. They are retarded in their innate capacities, or they have lacked the proper environmental stimuli and contact with superior peoples to enable their advancement. Such an evaluation calls forth a fatherly or "we know what is best for you" response. These people must be protected from losing their innocence, cared for, and administered to by the superior peoples; usually they perform useful but simple tasks. There are a number of variations of paternalistic racism:

1. *The Charming Primitives.* Often when technologically advanced groups first come into contact with peoples of limited technology, there is a period in which the "primitives" are seen as interesting, amusing, charming, exotic, or even noble in some respects. Such peoples are defined as backward for the most part, but a certain amount of genuine admiration for their less complex lives may be expressed by the superior people. Of course few, if any, of the superior individuals throw off their clothes and join the group. The primitives merely provide a temporary source of amusement and respite from civilized tasks.

Primitive peoples are believed to be naturally more sensuous, rhythmic, and sexual than civilized peoples. They seem to copulate at a moment's notice, with unconstrained fervor; they seem to be forever dancing and singing, and they practice interesting, even exotic, customs and rites. Although much of their behavior stems from their traditional culture, a culture seemingly without any rules or constraints, they are naturally more "expressive," although lacking in the forms of sophisticated intelligence found in the "civilized" or "superior" races.

2. *The Retarded Adults or the Simple Children.* Under extreme systems of dominance a people may be viewed as childlike or retarded in intellectual growth. Such retardation may be considered either inherent in the biology of the group or the result of an inadequate invironment. Biological retardation has more severe consequences because of its fixed nature. In 1910 Professor Howard Odum, a sociologist at the University of Virginia, described the biological retardation of Negroes and the policies of education that must be based upon this fact of life.*

> As a rule, after Negro children become older than ten or twelve years, their development is physical rather than mental; whatever of mental ability in the child gave promise of worth to be recognized in later years is crowded out by the coarser physical growth.
>
> Text books are needed which are especially adapted to the Negro mind, texts based on the most accurate and sympathetic knowledge of the characteristics of the Negro. . . .[55]

Any effort at education with any hope for success, according to Odum, "must be obtained before the pupil goes beyond fourteen years of age; here the physical brain in the Negro reaches its maturity, and nearly all that can be done for a generation must be done by methods suited to the children."[56]

Inferior peoples that are retarded as a result of mental factors can, with considerable help, manage to become civilized. A Portuguese economist in 1950 succinctly stated this form of cultural racism and its implications for the blacks of Angola:

> This raw native has to be looked at as an adult with a child's mentality—and as such he must be considered. He needs to be tutored as if he were a minor, taught to feed and clothe himself properly and to withstand the dangers that face him on all sides, shown how to get the most of his own land by the best methods, guided in the choice of work suited to his abilities—in short, educated, physically, morally, and professionally.
>
> What he consequently requires is protection and teaching, until he grows up and, as a civilized man, can take his place beside us.[57]

*Professor Odum drastically altered these racist beliefs at a later period but was representative of many intellectuals of his time in pre–World War I America.

Retarded adults who are "childlike" are expected to act like children, to be respectful to "adults" (that is, superior people), and not to be naughty, or they shall have to be punished. They can be a trial to their "parents," but they can also be loved. Of course they must perform their "chores."

3. *The Domesticated Animals.* Retarded adults are at least human beings, but under certain conditions peoples may be defined as animals—beasts of burden, capable of domestication and of performing useful tasks. In Brazil such sayings exist as: "The Negro doesn't sit down, he squats"; "the Negro doesn't marry, he gets together"; and "the Negro is an ass and a brute."[58] Studies of the stereotypes held by the French regarding Algerians involve the "beast of burden" idea along with more human attributes,[59] and slaves, regardless of ethnicity or race, have generally been described in such terms.

4. *The Pathological Victims.* In this conception of inferior peoples, inferiority is the result of *past* victimization that has created a number of pathological traits which continue to exist in the present. These victims drink excessively, engage in violent crime, drop out of school, and lack motivation and job skills. They are highly promiscuous and thus produce large numbers of illegitimate children. The families are disorganized, with absent fathers and domineering mothers who lack control over the numerous children. They score low on intelligence tests, are deficient in language skills, and are particularly prone to mental illness. Although such conditions have been ascribed to groups on the ground of biological inferiority, in this view these pathological conditions are due to the historical racist practices of the dominant group. Terms like "cultural deprivation," "social pathology," and "social deficiencies" are utilized as euphemisms for inferiority, and the pathological conditions take on legitimacy in the form of statistics.

At first glance such a view does not seem to be racist. Contemporary social scientists in the United States have statistically documented such conditions as found among blacks, Chicanos, and Indians. It is also a fact that white dominance over nonwhites in the United States has been severe. Further, all of the available evidence in the sciences supports the theory that the behavior and attributes of *groups* are due to environmental influences, not biological imperatives.

Elements of racism emerge in such a view, however, if the differences defined as "pathological" (that is, inferior) are the result of an ethnocentric evaluation, or if the structural causes that continue to create these conditions are ignored while the victim is blamed for these same conditions. With regard to the latter, Stephen and Joan Baratz have written:

> Liberals have eagerly seized upon the social pathology model as a replacement for the genetic inferiority model. But both the genetic model and the social pathology model postulate that something is wrong with the black American. For the traditional racists, that something is transmitted by the genetic code; for the ethnocentric social pathologists, that something is transmitted by the family.[60]

In a similar vein, Kenneth Clark has raised the issue of whether the social deprivation view has not had consequences similar to the effects of biological racism in the field of education:

> *To what extent are the contemporary social deprivation theories merely substituting notions of environmental immutability and fatalism for earlier notions of biologically determined educational unmodifiability? To what extent do these theories obscure more basic reasons for the educational retardation of lower-status children? To what extent do they offer acceptable and desired alibis for the educational default: the fact that these children, by and large, do not learn because they are not being taught effectively and they are not being taught because those who are charged with the responsiblity of teaching them do not believe that they can learn, do not expect that they can learn, and do not act toward them in ways in which help them to learn.*[61]

The pathological victim view of a people becomes a form of paternalistic racism when programs are developed to "help" these unfortunates, programs administered by members of the dominant group with little or no consultation with or participation by members so defined as victims. "Helping" a people, regardless of the sincerity of the motives involved, can be as debilitating to a group as old-fashioned exploitation. The paternalism is intensified when structural causes of the group's condition are ignored and the cause is attributed to the group itself—its inadequate culture or its family patterns. Dominant group social workers and governmental administrators become missionaries to the primitives to eliminate their cultural deprivation, to modify their behavior, and to create a "nonpathological" family life. In short, the view is that (1) these people are pathological, (2) it is our ancestors' fault, and (3) therefore, it is our duty to treat them and make them into useful citizens.

These are the major forms of racism that have been expressed in numerous societies, past and present. Racism has been a motive for and rationalization of ethnic and racial dominance. In its legitimating function racism has been a major factor in the maintenance and the intensification of dominance.

STRUCTURAL DISADVANTAGE

An intended consequence of discrimination is the maintenance or intensification of stratification between a dominant and a subordinate group. Ethnic and racial inequality also can be perpetuated by circumstances we shall refer to as structural disadvantage. Structural disadvantage is *a condition created by organizational policies and practices that have the unintended consequences of restricting the alternatives of members of one status more than those of members of another.* Such policies and practices are generally institutionalized, but rather than being intentionally restrictive, as discrimination is, they are believed to be fair, just, instrumental, and technologically sound. They are often quite traditional and accepted without reflection about their possible consequences for certain groups as opposed to others. In the United States and in other industrial societies such disadvantaged groups have included racial and ethnic minorities, women, the handicapped, and the left-handed.

Examples of structural disadvantage created by organizations are numerous. Colleges require entrance examinations. Because of the effects of past discrimination or contemporary discrimination in lower educational levels, some minorities are more likely to fail the exam than dominant group members. In addition, the test itself may contain items biased in favor of the ethnic group or class of the test makers. Many public school systems use a track system. Students are labeled according to their ability as measured by tests and then placed in a particular track—such as modified, terminal, college bound, and advanced placement. Again, lower-class students and minorities are more likely to find themselves in the modified or terminal tracks. In the recruitment procedures for organizational positions a common practice is to consult other established members regarding potential candidates. This "old-boy network" functions to limit the pool of potential candidates. Delegates to political conventions are often appointed or elected on the basis of their standing in the community or the amount of money contributed to the party. Poorer people, including a disproportionate number of minorities, are excluded. A recession occurs and a number of workers in a company are laid off on the principle of seniority—the last to be hired are the first to be fired. Because of past discrimination, because of the effects of discrimination in some other area, or because of previous lack of interest for whatever reasons, members of minorities (and women) are likely to be recent employees and hence a greater proportion of their members will be dismissed.[62]

Structural disadvantage is primarily the result of social class placement. The unequal distribution of ethnic groups or races within the stratification system will create greater disadvantages for members of some groups than for others. Even in the absence of discrimination, structural disadvantage will occur because of the social class biases of most organizational practices and policies. Discrimination can be eliminated, but ethnic or racial structural disadvantage of some sort will always exist unless (1) all groups have the same percentage of members in each social class as they do in the society as a whole, (2) all subordinate groups have been assimilated into the dominant group, and, of course, (3) there are no social classes. Ethnic group or racial class distribution is the result of present direct or indirect discrimination, the effects of past discrimination, or the existence of primitive or preindustrial cultures in an industrial society. Because of the social class basis of structural disadvantage, some members of the dominant group will also suffer disadvantages or restrictions, and if such a group is a dominant *majority*, it is quite likely that, *numerically*, more of this group will be so affected.

Many may object to the term "structural disadvantage" because practices that are intentionally discriminatory and those which are unintentionally discriminatory have similar consequences. When it seems unimportant to distinguish the two, the word "discrimination" may be used to cover both. Or the more nebulous but dramatic term "institutional racism" may be used to include all forms of institutionalized practices that are disadvantageous, intentional or not, and in which racism as an ideology is or is not involved.[63] Important analytical distinctions are lost, however, when such diversity is subsumed under such all-encompassing terms.

Two final points. First, although many practices are unintentionally biased or unnecessary (such as IQ tests and "old-boy" recruitment), valid technological or instrumental requirements and practices do exist. In any industrial society, regardless of whether ethnic dominance exists or not, certain skills are required, and individuals have to measure up if they are to occupy these positions. Even in the total absence of discrimination some groups will be more disadvantaged than others in the competition for positions within an industrial structure.

Second, as will be examined in the next chapter, changes in structure and hence in relative disadvantage occur, as with numerous other issues, in the arena of conflict. If disadvantaged statuses (women, minorities, the aged) accept their condition, they will remain subordinate. If they don't and are successful in conflict actions, changes will occur. However, resistance to change is also a fact of life. If minorities want to replace the seniority system with a lottery when recession occurs, then conflict success or failure will decide whether the recently hired will gain advantages or whether the more senior personnel will maintain theirs.

CONFORMITY OF SUBORDINATE GROUPS

Subordinate groups must adapt in some manner to their circumstances. These circumstances include the expectations of dominant group members, particularly the elite, and a relatively powerless stratification position. In some relationships subordinate groups are expected to accept a variety of forms of discrimination, to discard their culture, or to adopt an extreme form of subservient behavior in the presence of dominant group members. In other relationships subordinate groups may be given relative freedom to live in their traditional manner as long as they pay their taxes or tribute and accept the authority of the state.

Adaption in a very general sense has two basic forms—conformity and resistance. Within any given subordinate group both forms of adaption will be found at any particular time, with variations in the percentage of individuals engaging in one or the other and in the specific form of conformity or resistance.

As long as subordinate groups conform—as long as they do not protest, revolt, or challenge the system but behave in ways expected of them—dominance will be maintained. And violent resistance, as will be seen in the next section, is generally suppressed, often leading to an intensification of dominance.

At least five major factors, singly or in some combination, are responsible for conforming behavior among subordinate groups: subordinate group perception of benefits, the process of cooptation, the development of a fatalistic belief system within subordinate groups, adherence to a traditional culture within segregated communities, and the fear of coercion.

Subordinate Group Perception of Benefits

In spite of the negative connotations of the terms "dominance" and "subordinance," being a member of a subordinate group in many societies has not always been a disaster or even an unbearable experience. Members of subordinate groups have perceived benefits and advantages in a system of dominance and subordinance, particularly if their previous experience has been worse or if other groups are in a worse position.

Even empire societies were not always tyrannical systems. In many of these societies ethnic groups found the only degree of order, stability, and protection they had ever experienced. Many groups were allowed to live according to their traditional culture undisturbed. Their standard of living and the opportunity to make money were often improved. The governments of some of the empire societies created new jobs, raised educational standards, granted citizenship rights, and reduced disease.

In the more open national societies there have been similar reasons for subordinate group conformity or even active cooperation. Numerous immigrant groups have found a greater probability of economic advancement and freedom from political persecution as subordinate members within alien societies than in their countries of origin, where they were "dominant." The United States, for example, for members of many immigrant groups, has indeed been a land of much greater opportunity than their original homelands.

The Process of Cooptation

Dominant elites have often found it advantageous to exempt certain members of subordinate groups from discrimination and to grant them the privileges of the dominant group (even elite privileges). These selected individuals acquire certain benefits denied to other members of their groups, and, by draining off minority individuals of leadership capability to act as a buffer against the frustrations and hostilities of other members of their groups, the dominant group minimizes sources of potential disorder. This process of discrimination exemption in return for cooperation may be termed *cooptation*.

In empire societies the cooptation of leaders of conquered peoples is quite frequent.

Many conquerors have found that it is easier to rule their subjects indirectly by controlling the traditional sources of power in the subordinate group. Parts of India and Malaya, for example, were ruled by the British through native princes, and after World War II there were still over 300 sultans and regents in the Dutch East Indies. In such colonies the social organization of subordinate groups is left largely undisturbed. Since the people are permitted to pursue the values of their own culture, they can achieve satisfactory careers. They are therefore less likely to rebel. . . . Such officials enjoy many benefits denied others of their ethnic group. In some communities they are accepted in the elite circles of the dominant group. Furthermore, they retain high status among their own people. Since they can enjoy some measure of self-respect, they are less likely to become leaders of a revolt.[64]

Lord Lytton, viceroy of British India (1876–1880), stated the necessity of such cooptation: "Politically speaking, the Indian peasantry is an inert mass. If it ever moves at all, it will move in obedience, not to its British benefactors, but to its native chiefs and princes, however tyrannical they may be. . . . To secure completely, and efficiently utilise, the Indian aristocracy is, I am convinced, the most important problem now before us."[65] Another member of the ruling British elite in India, John Strachey, made quite clear the distinction between cooptation and native rule:

Let us give to the Natives the largest possible share in the administration. . . . But let there be no hypocrisy about our intention to keep in the hands of our people those executive posts—and there are not many of them—on which, and on our political and military power, our actual hold of the country depends. Our Governors of provinces, the chief officers of our army, our magistrates of districts and their principal executive subordinates ought to be Englishmen under all circumstances that we can now foresee.[66]

Such a candid view of dominance is refreshing.

The kinds of privileges that coopted individuals in the traditional empires could gain in return for their cooperative efforts can be illustrated from the Spanish Empire in the New World. Hereditary Indian chiefs were addressed as don, exempted from tribute, clothed well, allowed to acquire Spanish titles of nobility, given the right to servants, allowed to bear arms, and given the privilege of riding a horse. For such privileges, many of these Indian chiefs assisted Spanish officials or *corregidores* in the exploitation of the Indians.[67]

Coopted individuals may be members of the ruling elite of a once independent society (chiefs, nobles, aristocrats) who are allowed to continue as puppet rulers, or they may be members of subordinate groups who have risen from the ranks. The aspirations of such relatively mobile individuals can be put to good use by members of the dominant elite. Granted dominant

105

privileges (or at least some privileges) the can become quite loyal to the regime. Every conquered people has its collaborators.

In national societies minority leaders can be appointed to governmental positions in return for their cooperation in "getting out the vote" for the majority group politician. They may even head government bureaus that are directly or indirectly related to their own group or to other minorities as well. Large businesses may find that a few minority members in visible positions will give the companies a favorable image when egalitarian policies are in vogue.

It is in this manner that some subordinate group members will find themselves superior (in terms of rewards) not only to other members of their own groups but also to many dominant group members. In return for these advantages they are expected to denounce the relevance of ethnic status or to maintain an image of in-group loyalty while implementing the decisions of the dominant group elite.

It should be emphasized that cooptation only exists when discrimination against a group is still practiced and some members of this group are exempted from the discrimination, among other rewards. When discrimination has not occurred or has been eliminated, the successes of some subordinate group members and their close association with the dominant group elite should *not* be defined as cooptation. Upward mobility is not necessarily Uncle Tomism.

The Development of Fatalism

In certain systems of ethnic and racial dominance, members of subordinate groups may conform because they believe nothing can be done about their position, that it is fate or the will of God. Religions which stress that nothing can be done about present circumstances and that one must wait until the next incarnation or a heavenly paradise can aid in this form of conformity. The idea that someday a messiah will deliver one from opression also functions to maintain conformity, since messiahs are notoriously long in coming. Fatalism, as a belief system, is a product of grinding and stable oppression, but once developed it becomes a major factor in producing conformity to the oppression.

Segregation and Conformity

Under certain circumstances a high degree of voluntary segregation on the part of subordinate groups is a factor contributing to their conformity to the system. If the dominant group approves of subordinate group segregation, then this ethnic closure is not only what the subordinate group members believe to be desirable but is also what is expected of them by the dominant group. In this circumstance conformity exists because of the congruence of subordinate group behavior with dominant group expectations. There is, however, a second circumstance involving the conformity of subordinate groups to their traditional cultures that is extremely significant in the maintenance of dominant-subordinate relationships. As explained previously, particular cultural factors are significant in affecting a group's competitive and conflict ability. Conformity to a traditional culture will contribute to continuing subordination if this culture was an important cause of the group's original subordination. Put crudely, if a group retains its culture, it will remain inferior. It will not develop new skills and new forms of social organization to effectively threaten the favored position of dominant group members.

There are a number of reasons why certain subordinate groups will attempt to isolate themselves from dominant groups. One important reason is to maintain their culture and to prevent its contamination from the outside. Ancestral ways of life are sacred ways of life. At the social level subordinate groups can avoid competing with dominant group members in a game they believe to be rigged against them. And by avoiding the dominant group the subordinate group can minimize potential sources of dangerous conflict. Psychologically, this ethnic closure helps powerless individuals to adjust to their inferior position in society. A sense of autonomy can be gained which would not be present in the larger society, personality-damaging rebuffs can be avoided, and some sense of achievement in occupational pursuits can be obtained within the limited opportunities available. For these segregated individuals "the social support they find in their individualized acceptance of each other counters the categorical rejection they experience with the dominant group.[68]

Conforming to a traditional culture within a limited and restricted social environment can have its benefits for subordinate group members, but there are costs as well. As Judith Kramer has emphasized:

Its [the subordinate group's] enclosure is sheltering, of course, but it may also be limiting. Minority members may not explore the changing reality of the larger society as a result. Unaware of new opportunities, they may fail to qualify themselves for further participation in dominant institutions. The stress placed on categorical status by the minority community itself can be stifling. In counteracting categorical status, the community gives as much priority as the larger society does, thereby reducing the social options available within the minority context.[69]

Whether or not the costs of conforming to a traditional culture within a segregated subsociety outweigh the benefits of such enclosure, dominance is maintained.

There is one circumstance in which extreme voluntary segregation does not relate to conformity and hence to the perpetuation of a group's position. Segregated communities may serve as "preparedness centers," where competitive abilities may be increased, strategies for reform or for radical change may be formalized, and social movements may be organized with greater protection from the surveillance of the state. Segregation, as such, does not necessarily create conforming behavior, but when such closure emphasizes tradition, stability, and fatalism, rather than competition, conflict, and change, it does function in the interests of the dominant group.

Fear of Coercion

Some subordinate groups have existed in an atmosphere of intimidation and in an ever-present fear of coercion by dominant group members and the state. Under these conditions subordinate group members conform to the expectations of the dominant group because of fear of the consequences if they do not. Sometimes even the slightest insult to a dominant group member has produced organized attacks upon whole minority communities. A government policy of tolerance may become one of coercion, seemingly without provocation.

Avoiding such provocations through conformity and segregation may forestall dominant group coercive actions, but even these forms of behavior may not suffice. Powerless groups have become scapegoats for circumstances beyond their control, such as plagues or depressions. Nevertheless, they may continue to hope that conformity to dominant group expectations and avoidance of contact with dominant group members will allow peaceful coexistence.

Black-American communities in the United States before World War II existed under a continuing threat of coercion. Swimming on a beach reserved for whites or failure to show the proper deferential behavior could bring about violence aginst anybody who happened to have black skin. Likewise, Armenians in the Ottoman Empire were never certain of what effects their conduct would have upon their Turkish overlords. But the Jews in Christendom were the classic case of a subordinate group living with the constant fear of out-group violence. Pogroms (out-group attacks upon Jewish communities) have been numerous in Europe over a two-thousand-year period. Even during the interludes of peace the threat of violence always remained. In the Middle Ages, according to Durant:

> . . . *a generation after each tragedy the Jews were again numerous, and some were prosperous. Nevertheless their traditions carried down the bitter memory of those tragic interludes. The days of peace were made anxious by the ever-present danger of pogroms; and every Jew had to learn by heart the prayer to be recited in the moment of martyrdom.*[70]

Completely powerless people have little choice but to conform. Times change, however, improvements in the stratification system are made, and increasing numbers of subordinate group members may come to perceive that discrimination and their share of the reward distribution are unjust. Opposition or resistance to the system may be defined as necessary and, more important, as possible. However, the decision to conform or to resist is a difficult choice. As Schermerhorn has written: "Neither is a sure thing. Opposition could bring additional gains, but it could also inflict a withholding of benefits. Subservience may bring peace yet could equally well encourage an additional turn of the screw." [71]

SUPPRESSION OF REVOLT

Periodically, within any system of dominant-subordinate relations, at least some members of subordinate groups will protest, demand change, riot, or commit other acts of rebellion. No matter how effective the discrimination or the government efforts to control population size and settlement or to regulate culture, no such system is completely immune from threats to order and to the continuance of dominance. In fact, these very efforts, along with inequality, are the basic sources of such discontent. Threats to public order range from spontaneous and sporadic acts by a few foolhardy individuals to highly organized movements with a realistic possibility of accomplishing changes, from protest and rebellion of members of only one group to a concerted coalition of many groups, and from nonviolent resistance to violent actions.

Armed uprisings pose the most serious threat to the continuance or maintenance of dominance. They must be suppressed. Such suppression may only be temporary, to be followed by later efforts at insurrection. Or suppression may be so total that the subordinate group will never again attempt such actions. The government may learn something from the violence and make a few concessions that to some extent satisfy the rebels, or it may institute new and more effective methods of social control.

Because of their instability, their cultural diversity, and the presence of "charter member" groups that have become subordinate as a result of conquest, empire societies have been particularly prone to rebellion. The following are a few examples of famous revolts that were suppressed. Because they were failures the system of dominance was maintained. Only in hindsight can we say that defeat was inevitable. There have been revolts in other societies and other times that have been successful as forms of conflict actions, successes that have transformed ethnic relations.

In 66 A.D. Jews revolted against their Roman masters. After a long siege of Jerusalem the Romans managed to break into the city. It has been estimated that over 116,000 Jews were killed in battle and by starvation and disease. The temple was destroyed, the property of those who had revolted was sold, and a tribute to pagan gods was placed upon the rebels. This suppression was not sufficient to produce conformity. In 131 A.D. the emperor Hadrian announced his intent to build a shrine to Jupiter on the site of the destroyed temple and issued orders that would ban circumcision and public instruction in the Jewish law. A final uprising took place. The Romans destroyed 985 towns, and an estimated 580,000 Jewish men, women, and children died in the process. With the end of the revolt a ban on Jewish observance of the Sabbath and other holidays became the law, along with the bans on circumcision and education.[72] The screws were tightened, and the Jews would not revolt again.

In 1780 the Indians revolted in the Spanish Empire provinces of Peru and Ecuador. After several Indian military successes and Indian massacres of whole towns, the Indian leader was captured and beheaded. His brother took over command, and during the next two years at least eighty thousand people on both sides were killed. One city that was controlled by the Spanish, La Paz, suffered two sieges, lasting 190 days and 75 days, respectively. Eventually (1783), the Spanish armies defeated the Indians and executed their leaders.[73] Exploitation of the Indians continued.

The Russian Empire under the czars had its share of revolts. A major uprising was that of the Poles in 1863. Prior to this year Czar Alexander II had granted the Poles some measure of autonomy, a decision that raised the expectations of the Poles, who then demanded an independent Poland. Guerrilla war broke out, guided by leaders operating safely from Paris. Aid from France and England was expected, but it was not forthcoming. By 1864 the uprising was over; thirty thousand Poles had been killed in battle and some fifteen hundred rebel leaders were executed.[74]

The British Empire experienced several major revolts that were suppressed. One of the most famous rebellions was the sepoy mutiny in India between 1857 and 1859. Sepoys were Indian (Hindu, Muslim, and Sikh) soldiers in the employment of the British. The uprising stemmed from rumors that the British officers were determined to forcibly convert the sepoys to Christianity and that the grease used to lubricate the barrels of the new Enfield rifles was made from cows (an offense to Hindus) or pigs (an offense to Muslims). In addition, it had been prophesied that British rule would end exactly one hundred years after it began (1757). The rebel soldiers captured two major cities, and the successes encouraged nonmilitary Indians to join the rebellion. The revolt was suppressed in 1859 and followed by mass execution of the rebels. The army made two changes to reduce the possibility of later uprisings by native soldiers: the proportion of natives to the British was not to exceed two to one, and artillery would henceforth be under the exclusive control of British troops.[75]

Another historic revolt against British rule occurred in the Sudan (a territory south of Egypt) between 1881 and 1898. A religious sect, the dervishes, led a rebellious social movement against the British under their leader, the Mahdi (The Guided One of the Prophet). After the city of Khartoum fell to the sect, British troops finally arrived and met the dervishes at the Battle of Omdurman on September 2, 1898. A fanatic frontal assault of spear-carrying rebels was met by British machine guns, rifles, and artillery. The results of this battle destroyed this effort at independence: eleven thousand dervishes killed, sixteen thousand wounded, and four thousand prisoners taken; the British had forty-eight casualties.[76]

Other notable but ill-fated uprisings against ethnic dominance in empire societies have been: the revolts in the Philippines against the Spanish in 1585 and 1587;[77] the rebellion of the Armenians in Russia and Turkey in the 1890s, led by the Armenian Revolutionary Federation;[78] the uprising of the Bondelzwarts (or Hottentots) against the Germans in German East Africa in 1903, which resulted in the total extermination of the natives;[79] the rebellion of the Magi in this same territory in 1905, producing the death of 120,000 rebels;[80] and the uprisings of the Hungarians against the Austrians in 1849.[81]

National and pluralistic societies are not immune to such revolts. Between 1961 and 1975 the Kurds of Iraq engaged in a revolt to win independence and failed. Basques in Spain are currently in rebellion. The Ibo in Nigeria failed in their efforts to establish a new country, Biafra. And the United States in recent years has seen the suppression of black revolts in major cities (1964–1968), the ill-fated effort of the Chicanos in New Mexico to regain the lands they consider theirs (1966–1967), and the violence at Wounded Knee (1973) when the American Indian movement demanded the return of South Dakota to the Indians. In the nineteenth century the United States witnessed slave revolts, rebellions by Indian groups, and guerrilla actions of Mexicans in the Southwest.

All of these actions were failures from the point of view of the subordinate groups. Dominance was maintained by the successes of the dominant groups.

These five factors (discrimination, racism, structural disadvantage, subordinate group conformity, and suppression of revolt), particularly in combination, seem to be the most important in maintaining a system of ethnic and racial dominance. A word of caution, however: nothing is certain, nor do these general processes and conditions *necessarily* function to maintain dominance. Out-group discrimination may lead to in-group cohesiveness and to demands for change. Cooptation may inadvertently train members of subordinate groups to become leaders of their own groups. Segregated communities can be training centers for later programs involving competition and conflict with the dominant group. Structural disadvantage does not have to be accepted by subordinate groups and may lead to demands for changes in organizational policies. Racist doctrines may be openly challenged by subordinate group members and become the highly symbolic focus for conflict. And the brutal suppression of a revolt can be the major cause of a later revolt that is successful. Systems of dominance do change and even terminate.

SUMMARY

Once dominance has been established it can continue for extensive periods of time. Ethnic and racial dominance is maintained and often intensified by five major factors: discrimination, racism, structural disadvantage, subordinate group conformity, and the suppression of revolts.

Discrimination may be defined as intentional efforts to restrict or to require particular social actions or activities of some groups as opposed to others. Such efforts take two forms: (1) between members of one group in the planning and implementation of these restrictions or requirements, and (2) confrontations between members of different statuses. Discrimination is generally practiced by members of a dominant group against members of subordinate groups, since it takes power to discriminate. Because of their special positions in society, members of the elite are the major implementors of discrimination. Discrimination may be overt or covert, formal or informal, regular or sporadic. Discrimination is based upon perceptions of advantage (particularly the reduction of competition), perceptions of threat, or the necessity to conform to the expectations of other dominant group members. The consequences of discrimination may be direct or indirect. Direct consequences are those effects intended by the discriminatory efforts, and indirect consequences are the unintentional effects of the direct consequences upon other areas of social life. The less the resistance to discrimination, the greater the possibility that such efforts will accomplish what is intended and the greater the effects upon other forms of ethnic and racial stratification.

Racism is the major motive or rationalization for discrimination and dominance in general. Racism is the belief that one people must control or act upon another people because of the superior and inferior attributes of the groups in question. Inferiority and superiority may be perceived as a result of biology, environment, or some combination of the two. The reasons offered as explanations of superiority and inferiority are not as important as how an "inferior" group is defined—either as a threat or as dependent. Groups defined as threatening evoke a conflict racist ideology. Groups defined as dependent stimulate a paternalistic set of stereotypes. Groups identified as dependent have been redefined as threatening when changes in social relationships have occurred. Racism functions to legitimate dominant systems, and the greater the consensus on such beliefs by members of dominant and subordinate groups, the greater the probability that the system will continue.

A third factor is structural disadvantage, which is a label for those organizational practices that have the unintended consequences of restricting the alternatives of members of one status more than members of another. Even in the absence of discrimination, dominant group advantages can be perpetuated by the institutionalization and traditional acceptance of certain organizational practices. Although such practices are not intentionally designed to promote ethnic or racial inequality or to restrict the life chances of certain statuses, they nevertheless do so.

Dominance is also maintained by the conformity of subordinate group members to the expectations of the dominant group, to the governmental policies and laws of a society that are concerned with perpetuating dominant-subordinate relationships, and to a traditional culture. Besides the perception that such arrangements are legitimate, subordinate group conformity has been engendered by cooptation, by perceived benefits from such behavior, by the development of a fatalistic belief system, by extreme voluntary segregation which perpetuates a traditional culture, and by the fear of dominant group coercion of subordinate group deviance.

In spite of discrimination, structural disadvantage, racist legitimation, and the conforming behavior of most subordinate group members, periodic protests and revolts do occur. Governments may react with programs to reduce the sources of discontent without basically changing the system, or military force may be used to quell resistance. Revolts have to be suppressed if dominance is to be maintained. In human history there have been far more unsuccessful rebellions than victories, and, with the tremendous centralization of power in the modern states, ethnic or racial insurrections in the future seem unlikely to result in anything but suppression.

5

THE
REDUCTION
AND TERMINATION OF DOMINANCE

INTRODUCTION

No system of human relationships is permanent, and ethnic or racial dominant systems are no exception. Such systems are transformed when dominance is reduced or when subordinate-dominant relationships are completely terminated.

Patterns of dominance and subordinance are *reduced* when a subordinate group gains greater autonomy over its affairs (pluralism) and when discrimination against the group is decreased or eliminated and improvements in stratification placement are made (integration). Particular dominant-subordinate relationships are *terminated* when a subordinate group gains political independence (secession), when a subordinate group overthrows the dominant one and reverses the relationship (revolution), when a subordinate group loses its ethnic or racial identity and thereby ceases to exist (assimilation), when a subordinate group is eliminated due to disease and homicide (extermination), when a subordinate group is forced to leave the society (expulsion), when victorious countries after a war break up a defeated country into smaller states (dismemberment), or when an alien group enters a society and subordinates all of the groups, including the formerly dominant one (conquest).

Before these processes and conditions are described, however, the one aspect of race and ethnic relations that cuts across most of these forms of transformation must be discussed separately: the interaction between social movements and governments, which defines or creates social problems.

SOCIAL MOVEMENTS, SOCIAL PROBLEMS, AND GOVERNMENT POLICIES

Social movements, based upon such factors as social class, sex, and political ideology, as well as on race and ethnicity, have arisen in numerous societies, both past and present. Members of these movements have demanded changes, and governments have reacted to those demands, particularly when there has been a threat to "law and order." Through this interaction of government and social movements, social problems are defined or created and efforts are made to solve them. In this conflict relationship one party may be a social problem or a source of problems for the other. Although significant social change does not always occur, conflict relationships have been major factors in altering social systems.

Social Movements

A social movement is an organized collective venture that transcends a local community and involves systematic efforts to bring about desired social change.[1] Examples of social movements are numerous: the Fenian movement in Ireland, the fascist movement in Italy, the French Revolution, women's liberation, the ecology movement, the communist movement, passive resistance in India, the agrarian reform movement in ancient Rome, the pan-Slavic movement, and the civil rights movement, to name only a few. All of these examples of collective behavior transcend a particular community and are regional, societal, or even international in scope. They involve one or more social organizations with specific programs, as well as sympathetic followers who are not members of the organizations. Depending upon what changes are desired, social movements may be classified as reactionary (when they seek to restore some conception of the past), reform (when they wish to modify the present system to produce a greater congruence between established values and structural opportunities), and radical (when the goal is drastic alteration or elimination of the system in order to establish new values).*

Prior to the formation of a social movement, increasing numbers of people perceive that something is wrong and that something needs to be changed, but precise articulation is often absent. This feeling of discontent is generally prompted by social and cultural changes. New ideas from other cultures may filter into a society, producing an awareness that what is doesn't have to be. Technological changes may be disrupting established social relationships or the environmental conditions of human existence. Individuals may perceive that their positions are threatened by such

*This is only one classification of social movements.

technological changes or by other conditions, such as economic instability, war, governmental insensitivity, or out-group unrest.

Social movements begin to form not only when established positions are threatened but also when *improvements* in conditions have occurred. Expectations of even greater improvements develop, and a return to previous modes of existence becomes out of the question. But expectations often rise faster than the actual changes, producing a discrepancy between what is and what ought to be. If setbacks occur, even greater stress develops as the result of the discrepancy between what are now defined as legitimate aspirations and the failure of the existing institutional structure to meet these expectations.

Social movements may also stem from a weakening of a society's power structure. Subordinate categories may then perceive a greater probability of goal attainment in light of such instability.[2]

Social movements emerge under one or more of these conditions when ideologies are articulated and organizations are formed. Ideologies contain beliefs about the nature of reality and the legitimacy of such reality, and a program of action that will create the desired changes.

The success or failure of social movements occurs in the interaction between members of the movement along with their distant supporters and members of the institutionalized elite along with their adherents. The outcome of this confrontation will institutionalize new "truths" and practices into the social order or replace the old elite with a new leadership that generally becomes as interested in maintaining order and the system as its predecessors; or the movement's efforts to bring about change will fail, leaving its members dead, cowed, or apathetic. In any case, the social movement terminates.

Social Problems

The major functions of a social movement are to define social problems (the function of the ideology) and then to solve them (the function of the organization guided by the ideology).* A social problem may be defined as *a perceived social condition that has been negatively evaluated and that requires collective action for its intended solution*. At least a few people believe that a condition exists (although others may not agree), judge it as undesirable (although others may evaluate it as progress or as normalcy), and believe that the problem can be reduced or eliminated by collective action of some sort (although others may believe that nothing can be done). These three elements are all necessary for a social problem to come into being.[3] Social problems are therefore relative to the definers, and a solution is dependent upon success in conflict.

Social movements are not the only problem definers. Government, established organizations, and unattached intellectuals are also important. However, anybody can define social problems.

Reducing or eliminating the undesirable condition requires a collective effort in ascertaining targets believed to be responsible for the condition and overcoming the resistance of the targets. At the same time the collective effort must seek to gain supporters for its point of view. Overcoming resistance and gaining support involve the general tactics of persuasion, bargaining, and coercion. People must be persuaded to change their behavior, either by appeals to reason or by propaganda. Bargaining, which consists of compensation for the changing of behavior (in short, a deal), may also be utilized. If all fails, coercion, consisting of threats or the actual use of force, can be applied to change or even to eliminate resistance.

Social movements are one form of collective action and are to be found among dominant as well as subordinate groups. The social movement seeks to undermine the legitimacy of an existing social condition or pattern of relationships and to replace this "problem" with a more desirable state of affairs, to turn what is into what ought to be.

Government Reaction

The development of a social movement forces the government of a society to react to this potential threat to law and order. One reaction is to define the social movement as a social problem. If the movement is perceived as dangerous to societal stability and the position of the governmental elite, suppressive efforts will be initiated. Another reaction, however, is to accept the legitimacy of the movement's definition of social problems, at least verbally. When this is the case a government may ostensibly become involved with the movement but make only minimal efforts to solve the problem or problems. For example, the government might pass laws without sanctioning power, set up a committee to study the problem, or establish a new bureaucratic agency without sufficient resources to be effective. By this tactic the government resists change yet pays lip service to the goals and values of the social movement. Or a government can become actively involved, utilizing all of the powers of the state to eliminate the condition defined as a social problem.

Governments make decisions and more or less effectively implement decisions related to subordinate ethnic or racial social movements. But in addition to *reacting* to social movements, governments often *initiate* policies regarding social problems in the area of race and ethnic relations. History demonstrates that virtually *any* condition involving races or ethnic groups can be a social problem to government: high cultural differentiation between the dominant group and a subordinate group, or the opposite, low cultural differentiation; an integrated condition or a segregated condition; the existence of dominant group privileges or the lack of dominant group privileges; racial or ethnic inequality or racial and ethnic equality. Efforts by subordinate groups to gain independence or to acquire dominance by revolution are always social problems to governments. What is consistent

117

among all of these conditions is that a threat to the stability of the system is a social problem. Government policies and programs designed to solve the problem are always intended to be "functional," that is, to maintain the system. Depending upon the circumstances, governments may attempt to integrate ethnic groups or races, segregate them, give them some degree of autonomy, expel them, or even exterminate them.

Governments are not omnipotent, however. In spite of the resources government can bring to bear upon what it perceives to be the social problems, government can be ineffective and inefficient. Policies can be confused, discord among the elites can create a stalemate, personnel are often incompetent, and budgets may be inadequate for the task. Conditions and circumstances of an ethnic or racial nature may have low priority among government programs. And government efforts can produce unintended results: efforts to suppress a group may increase the possibility of revolt, a program of integration may intensify segregation, and a policy to reduce the relative inequality of a group can make the subordinate group more competitive and a threat to dominance. Government inefficiency is more common than exceptional, and humankind has benefited accordingly.

Social movements, government, and the creation of social problems are all involved in the transformation of systems of ethnic and racial dominance. And along with these more or less organized attempts to create social change, the day-to-day decisions and actions of individuals and groups have their collective consequences. Once-stable patterns of dominant and subordinate relationships are transformed, but not always in the intended direction.

INTEGRATION AND ASSIMILATION

Integration as a social *condition* may be defined as the general irrelevance of racial or ethnic status in most areas of social life in distinguishing and separating members of two or more groups or all of the ethnic and racial groups within the total society.[4] Integration as a social *process* is the reduction of differences between members of two or more groups and the increasing irrelevance of race or ethnicity to these members in affecting interaction in their institutional activities.

In ethnically or racially heterogeneous societies, integration occurs between a few particular groups before becoming widespread. The integration process first takes place between those groups with certain areas of similarity—a common religion, a common race, a common language—or between groups with similar historical traditions. In the United States, for example, integration between Swedes, Danes, and Norwegians occurred before the integration of these Scandinavians with Anglo-Americans.[5] American Indian ethnic groups are integrating within this racial category far more than they are integrating with whites.

Integration between particular groups generally begins at the secondary level of relationships (at work, in the public arena). Subjectively, the ethnic or racial status of coworkers and fellow members of political or other organizations becomes increasingly unimportant to more and more members of the group. Objectively, statistics reflect greater ethnic or racial diversity in organizational and occupational membership.

Integration at the primary (personal) level of human relationships then follows. Subjectively, particular ethnic or racial out-groups become acceptable as member's of one's neighborhood, as guests in one's home, as personal friends, or as marriage partners. A point is reached when these out-group statuses no longer seem to be out-group—they are irrelevant. Objectively, neighborhoods and communities are more mixed (yet not perceived to be mixed), and intermarriage rates increase (and the idea of "inter" declines as a relevant symbol).

In time the integration process creates integrated conditions between collections of groups and, as these collections of groups coalesce, the entire society *may* eventually be characterized as ethnically or racially integrated.

It should be emphasized that integration is not irreversible. Before the rise of the Nazi party, Gentile and Jewish Germans in Germany were highly integrated, but Nazi policies drove the groups apart. Large influxes of immigrants into several of the groups within a society can also arrest or reverse integration.

Integration may be perceived not only as a social condition and a process but also as a value, a social problem, or a government policy, regardless of the actual structural circumstances between groups. Integration as a value is a desirable condition. The value may correspond to the actual state of affairs or be a desired goal to be obtained in the future. For those who wish to maintain their ethnic integrity and autonomy, integration will not be a desirable condition but a social problem to be rectified or avoided. And in many national societies integration may be the official view of reality or a goal to be attained. When integration is the official view of reality, the government ignores whatever ethnic or racial diversity that exists, does not compile statistics with racial or ethnic breakdowns, and prevents organizations in the private sector from making these distinctions. This official view may correspond to actual conditions of integration, or it may be pure mythology—if we ignore the heterogeneity in the society, maybe it will disappear.

Important aspects of integration as a general process are acculturation, social distance, and personal distance.

Acculturation

Acculturation is *the increase in cultural similarities between two or more groups created by the adoption of elements from each other.* Acculturation occurs for the most part because members of one group voluntarily adopt those cultural elements of another group which they perceive as prestigious or useful. But acculturation may also occur as a result of coercion. These "borrowed" traits may become additions to a group's culture, but more often they replace traditional forms (for example, one religion may replace another). Such "influencing may be reciprocal or overwhelmingly one-way."[6]

Behaviorally, *one-sided* acculturation occurs as individuals in each succeeding generation find little relevance in the "old ways," fail to learn the language of their parents, and transmit to their own children fewer and fewer of the beliefs, values, and practices of their ancestors. Instead, more and more of the traits and complexes of another ethnic group are transmitted. If a group is not racially distinctive, it can totally disappear when no traditional elements are left. However, as long as some elements persist that are symbolic to a group's identity, and the *name* of the group continues to be used as a label for this identity, total assimilation can be avoided. A. L. Kroeber gives an example of a highly acculturated ethnic group that still retains its identity—the Jews of Cochin India (who are internally differentiated by racial castes—white, black, and brown):

> *The Cochin Jews are at once well fitted into southern-Indian civilization and separate from it where they want to be, which chiefly is in religion and group identity. They live in a ghetto street, but from choice. They all learn to read Hebrew, the Blacks as sedulously as the Whites, for prayers and services, but all talk Malayalam along with the rest of Cochin. Rice is their staple food, as it is in all southern India; but they will never mix curries of meat with those of milk, in conformity with the orthodox Jewish injunction. They chew betel, paint their nails, play rummy, but have preserved their Hebrew ritual and festivals scrupulously. There is much acculturation, but also a wholly successful maintenance of the integrity of a minority group and of a subculture around an intact nucleus of religion.*[7]

Because of the increased similarity in behavior patterns, acculturation reduces the significance of ethnic statuses in social interaction—hence the lack of "clues" used in identification. However, racial-ethnic groups and races within a society are phenotypically distinguishable. Two or more races may be culturally similar, yet race is still relevant as a motive for discrimination or for segregation (voluntary or coerced).

The Reduction of Social and Personal Distance

As explained in Chapter 3, social distance refers to norms that indicate "the expressed legitimacy and conventionality of specified modes of intergroup behavior."[8] Personal distance, on the other hand, is the "expressed intention to engage personally in specified modes of intergroup behavior."[9] Integration in particular areas, such as education or occupation, or integration in general is accomplished when social distance has been eliminated—when there are no rules or norms related to ethnic or racial status other than the norm that making distinctions on the basis of race or ethnicity is inappropriate. When social distance between groups has been reduced and eventually eliminated, those individuals who maintain high personal distance become the deviants. They continue to make improper and invidious distinctions based upon irrelevant statuses and may be labeled bigots, Neanderthals, or mentally ill by others.

To say that a society or that any two given groups have become racially or ethnically integrated is not to say that other factors, such as religion, class, occupation, gender, and age are unimportant. These factors may or may not continue to divide members of a society; racial and ethnic integration means simply that racial and ethnic statuses cease to be of little importance.

Ethnic Group Assimilation

Integration proceeds piecemeal—between some groups as opposed to others, from secondary to primary relations, from political and economic processes to friendship and family patterns. During this process, the ethnic groups still exist; however, dominance is *reduced*. When integration has proceeded in all areas to a maximum degree, assimilation may occur, although an outbreak of conflict or a fresh immigration of less acculturated members may renew differentiation. Assimilation *terminates* a dominant-subordinate group relationship.

Assimilation may be viewed from a group or from an individual perspective. Assimilation at the group level is an end state characterized by the elimination of an ethnic group name—either one group has disappeared into another (absorption), or two or more groups have come together as a new group with a new name (fusion). Assimilation at the individual level is the change of ethnic identity. An individual no longer identifies with the group of his or her ancestors but with a new group and is accepted into this new group.

Absorption-assimilation consists of the disappearance of one ethnic group into another. Such an end state has its beginnings with the "passing" of a few individuals who have managed to eliminate all clues to their former membership group and have acquired the necessary traits of the reference group. This "passing" may involve changing one's name, having plastic surgery, learning a new language, or moving away from friends and relatives. If one successfully passes, individual assimilation has occurred, but the former membership group continues. With increasing integration, however, the term "passing" is no longer appropriate, since either one-sided or reciprocal acculturation has eliminated distinguishing cultural aspects. As more and more of its members change their identity or take on a dual identity, the size of the group being assimilated gradually diminishes.

Eventually nobody identifies with this group's name; assimilation is then total. But long before this final stage is reached the group will have ceased to be viable, either as an interest group or as a community.

A. L. Kroeber has described the total assimilation of a Jewish colony in China, a process that took several hundred years:

> *In 1163 a colony of Jews from Persia settled at K'aifeng in Honan. Five hundred years later they were still there, as attested by a stone inscription, and had just rebuilt their synagogue under imperial sanction. Two centuries more, however, and they were preserving only a consciousness of being Jews and some scrolls of their Law. The last rabbi had died about 1830 and the synagogue was pulled down by 1850. The colony no longer knew Hebrew, could not therefore read their scrolls, were uncircumcised, had lost their pedigrees, and were indistinguishable in names, dress, and often in features from Chinese. They had become poor, and this may have contributed to the relative rapidity of their final assimilation.* [10]

In the United States, a number of European ethnic minorities have virtually disappeared into the American ethnic group, with the exception of a few enclaves (this phenomenon will be examined in more detail in Part 2). English-Canadians, Danes, Scots, and Germans have ceased to be viable ethnic groups in contemporary America, and thousands of *individuals* in the last one hundred years have changed from these and other identities to that of Americans, except, perhaps, for the sake of nostalgia on particular occasions.

Because acculturation is generally in the direction of the more prestigious culture and because this group is often, but not necessarily, the dominant political group, the absorption of subordinate groups into dominant groups has been the most prevalent form of assimilation. The direction has sometimes been reversed, however, thus eliminating a dominant group. Two examples have been the Manchu and the Fulani. The Manchu established dominance over the Chinese in 1644, and over the next three hundred years they adopted the Chinese bureaucratic system of rule, Chinese customs, and Chinese names. Only their clan system prevented their complete disappearance, but for all practical purposes Manchu dominance was over. [11] The Fulani established dominance over the Hausa in West Africa by 1802; however, their empire was highly decentralized and within these segmented areas Fulani intermarried and acculturated, soon losing their distinguishing physical as well as cultural traits. [12]

The second type of assimilation, fusion, is characterized by the merging of two or more groups into one under a new name. Collections of individuals whose ancestors may have fought each other become fused together as one people. The process consists of increasing acculturation between the groups in question, the reduction of personal and social distance, the invention of unifying myths of origins, and the gradual acceptance of a new name as the symbol of the group. Great Britain offers an example of the termination of dominance through fusion. Normans from France had established dominance over Anglos, Saxons, Jutes, and Danes in the year 1066. In time these groups fused together as Englishmen. Norman dominance and the subordination of the other groups was terminated. As Englishmen, however, they established new dominant-subordinate relationships with hundreds of other groups.

Can There Be Racial Assimilation?

If the word "race" refers to a collection of people that are labeled with a designating term because of perceived physical traits and is either a multiethnic color category or an in-between color division with no internal ethnic subgroups, then is it possible for racial assimilation to occur? *Individuals* have changed racial status by "passing," but is there such a phenomena as racial *group* assimilation? Can one race disappear into another (absorption-assimilation)? Can several races fuse together under a new racial symbol, resulting in the loss of the older terms (fusion-assimilation)? Miscegenation, or the diffusion of genes, a process that makes racial categorization increasingly difficult, has certainly occurred, but do races, *as symbolic constructs*, disappear?

One problem in studying racial change is that the *idea* of race has only been important in the last five hundred years. Although this may seem like a long time, few changes have occurred in multiracial societies to provide scholars with data from which generalizations may be made. However, in at least one society—Mexico—racial changes have occurred that may shed some light on whether or not the concept of assimilation is applicable to race. The following outline of racial changes in Mexico is summarized from *Race and Racism*, by Pierre van den Berghe:

1. Five racial castas *developed in Mexico, shortly after the Spanish Conquest: European Spaniards who "were presumably pure whites"; American Spaniards or creoles who were "regarded as whites . . . but most[ly] were descended from mestizos who had been recognized by their Spanish fathers"; mestizos, who "were the illegitimate products of unions between Spaniards and Indians and between Indians and Negroes, as well as of the second and third generation mixtures between mestizos and the other nonwhite groups"; Indians; and Negroes and mulattoes.*

2. Spanish culture spread rapidly throughout the population, producing cultural homogenization.

3. The mestizo population has grown tremendously while the Indian population has diminished. " 'Pure' Indians declined from 98.7 percent of the total in 1570 . . . to 29.2 percent in 1921 (the year of the last racial census), and to an estimated 20.0 percent in 1950. The mestizos increased correspondingly to something like four-fifths of the modern Mexican population."

4. The racial terminology became complex, "passing" occurred in great numbers, and miscegenation was widespread from the beginning. "Concern for physical appearance gave rise to an elaborate nomenclature based on skin color, hair texture, and facial features. Afro-mestizos were sometimes distinguished from Indian-white mixtures by the term zambaigo. *Finer distinctions of shades of pigmentation and types of crossing between Indians and whites gave rise to such terms as* mestizo blanco, castizo, mestizo prieto, mestizo pardo, *and* mestindio.

"Although this complex terminology was obviously the result of concern for racial appearance, the very minuteness of the distinctions militated in fact against the formation of rigid lines and facilitated 'passing' and racial 'upgrading.' Thus Afro-mestizos tried to pass for Indians or Indian-white mestizos, for Indian 'blood' was regarded as superior to Negro 'blood,' and by the early nineteenth century the very distinction between Afro- and Indo-mestizo had lost its meaning. Similarly, the mulato blanco *and the* castizo *could often pass for creoles and sometimes did so by fraudulently changing the baptismal records which, as rule, recorded the* casta. *By the late eighteenth century passing had become common enough to blur the difference between creoles and mestizos and to make the* casta *system fairly nominal."*

5. Race has little relevance in modern Mexico, although color is reflected still in the class division. "Racial characteristics have so little social relevance in modern Mexico and the complex interplay of race and culture through the dual process of miscegenation and hispanization have so homogenized the Mexican population that race and ethnic relations in that country have received scant attention from social scientists. . . . European-looking Mexicans are disproportionately represented in the upper and middle classes; however, dark mestizos and Indians are found in significant numbers at all class levels. Although there probably is some slight residual tendency toward racial homogamy, physical appearance is not an appreciable factor in social mobility or, more generally, in social behavior. . . . Mexico has indeed become a nation of bronze."[13]

Can what occurred in Mexico be described as racial assimilation? Comparing this case with what has been characteristic of ethnic assimilation, we can find certain similarities. A number of racial terms are no longer utilized, a fact which signifies that those races have disappeared in Mexico. The descendants of people once classified into several racial categories have been absorbed into the increasingly larger category of mestizo, and mestizo has become synonymous, to a great extent, with Mexican. And like ethnic assimilation on a grand scale that produces ethnic irrelevance in internal affairs, race, which was once extremely significant in Mexico, has become irrelevant, for the most part, in differentiating the contacts and activities of the Mexican population. A final point of similarity is the reduction of clues that permit categorization. In ethnic group assimilation the clues take a variety of forms, including language, dialect, costuming, and customs. In the Mexican case of races, these cultural giveaways were also reduced and eliminated by a ruthless hispanization, and the physical differences were blurred and reduced by extensive miscegenation.

It seems that the concept of assimilation may indeed be applied to race as well as ethnicity; however, there is one important difference. In Mexico the racial terms increased from five or six to twenty or more before they all disappeared. According to the nominalistic approach to the idea of race that has been utilized throughout this book, this means that the number of races increased before they decreased. Such a development has never occurred, to this author's knowledge, in ethnic group relations. If the Mexican case indicates the way in which racial assimilation will occur in other societies, black-white-red-yellow assimilation in the United States may be preceded by its own expanding nomenclature (for example, yellowish brown, brownish black, reddish white, light brown, medium black, whitish yellow).

Integrationist Social Movements

An integrationist social movement is *a movement whose members seek to obtain equality through the elimination of discrimination and structural disadvantage and to become integrated into the institutional activities of the dominant group*. The members may disagree as to whether or not assimilation is to be the ultimate goal; the immediate concern is equality and integration at the secondary level. Members of such movements define themselves as reformist and may often receive support or active involvement from liberals in the dominant group who perceive the legitimacy of such reform. Integrationist movements often use institutionalized procedures, such as court cases, lobbying, and political campaigning, as well as noninstitutionalized means to achieve their goals. Discretion must be used in choosing noninstitutionalized means, since an unwise choice may antagonize members of the dominant group and thus jeopardize integration.

Integrationist movements are to be found in both empire and national societies, although movements within the latter are more common and more likely to be successful because of the congruence of the government's and the movement's goals. The nineteenth-century integrationist movement in British India was a failure. In 1876, the Indian Association was founded. Its demands were moderate: installation of lavatories in the third-class coaches, elimination of discrimination against Indians in the civil service, a union between Muslims, Hindus, Christians, and Parsis for the country's welfare, and the prevention of the removal of import duties on cotton cloth from England. The British community was opposed to any attempt at integrating the higher levels of the civil service. Faced with such resistance, a new organization was founded—the Indian National Congress. Supported by some English liberals, the congress attempted to represent a middle class of Indians in their efforts to eliminate discrimination in several occupations, including the civil service. These gradualist demands met with little success, and by 1905 "the divorce of the moderate leaders from the trend of the times had become almost absolute. Their reasonable demands impressed neither the government nor other nationalist bodies. In the emotional excitement of Hindu revivalism, secret societies, and growing economic frustration, their ideas appeared spiritless and futile."[14]

An excellent example of an integrationist movement in a national society is found in Israel today.[15] The major organization of the movement is the

Black Panthers, a group ranging from two hundred to ten thousand, according to differing estimates, and composed of young, lower-class Sephardic Jews, primarily from Morocco. Formed around January of 1971, the group's general goal is full integration with Ashkenazic Jews (the dominant group). Specifically, the Sephardic Jews charge discrimination in numerous areas and demand open enrollment in the schools, longer instruction time in schools with better teachers, a more widespread system of scholarships, more courses in Sephardic history and literature, easier mortgage payments, higher welfare payments, reclassification of their draft status, redefinition of their family status to that of recent immigrants, and job training programs in order that they may enter the professions and the skilled industrial occupations. Their tactics involve vociferous public demonstrations and threats of more violent action.

A second major group protesting discrimination is the National Young Couples Association, an essentially Sephardic group that dissociates itself from the Panthers. Oriental Jewish politicians not affiliated with either organization have demanded greater representation in all power positions of the society.

The government and the great majority of the Ashkenazim have generally reacted negatively. In the first demonstration of the Panthers in February of 1971, the leaders were arrested and the group was defined as criminal, subversive, and radical. Ashkenazim in general and the state in particular have denied both the existence of such discrimination and the ethnic basis of such complaints. According to Smooha, "Ashkenazim condemn these ethnic overtones as nonsensical, irrelevant, pathological and irresponsible. Ashkenazic spokesmen are willing to consider only those demands which are defined in the traditional class terms. The new ethnic rhetoric is very threatening because it has wider emotional appeal and might be used more effectively in mobilizing the Oriental masses."[16] The government has made a limited response in the area of housing, but "what actions are taken seem to be done more for their publicity value than for their substantive effect."[17] Problems of national security are offered as the major reason why adequate funds are not provided to make significant changes. It remains to be seen whether this Sephardic integrationist movement will have significant effect upon a society preoccupied with national defense in an Arab world.

In the United States the major integrationist movement has been the civil rights movement, which began in the 1950s and which will be examined in greater detail in Part 2. The civil rights movement has been composed of numerous organizations, some dating before World War II, representing Black-Americans and Mexican-Americans: the National Association for the Advancement of Colored Peoples (NAACP), the Urban League, the Southern Christian Leadership Conference (SCLC), the Congress of Racial Equality (CORE)*, the American G.I. Forum, the League of United Latin American

Since the middle 1960s CORE has been a pluralist organization.

Citizens (LULAC), the Mexican American Political Association (MAPA), and several others.

The social problems for integrationist movements are their relative inequality, the failure of the larger society to incorporate and integrate their group, and practices of discrimination which restrict their membership and prevent their obtaining the full benefits of the larger society. The solution of problems for integrationist movements involves efforts to break down specific opportunity barriers and to make ethnic or racial distinctions irrelevant through the use of reform tactics.

The Government, Integration, and Assimilation

For various reasons, governments of empire and national societies have been guided by a policy of the integration or even the total assimilation of all subordinate groups into the dominant one. In past empire societies assimilation, or at least integration of some of the groups, reduced the necessity for military control. In the nineteenth and twentieth centuries homogeneity has been perceived as helpful in accomplishing national goals and in eliminating racial and ethnic conflict. For example, a 1971 pamphlet of the Australian Immigration Department referred to the goal of "a socially homogeneous and cohesive population" unmarred by "self-perpetuating enclaves and undigested minorities."[18] In the Soviet Union the current emphasis on ethnic pluralism is but a temporary expedient. The Russians are to be the "elder brother" or the vanguard of the working class as they work toward "a higher stage of development when national groups are to disappear as distinct cultural and linguistic entities and be fused 'into a single common socialist culture with a single common language.' "[19] It is not difficult to conceive just what this culture and language are to be.

In "underdeveloped" national or pluralistic societies that are undergoing modernization or industrialization,[20] multiethnicity can be a barrier to such "progress." Resources have to be mobilized and decisions centralized in the national interest. Some ethnic groups may want to become involved and obtain the fruits of modernization; others may want to retain their traditional ways. Some may be useful; others may be dangerous. Decisions have to be made regarding which groups are vital to the program of modernization, which group or groups, if any, can be ignored, and which groups will pose security problems for the state. The participation of all of the groups may not be necessary. Cynthia Enloe has written:

Modern development requires mobilization but not necessarily the mobilization of every group in society. Groups that government must mobilize are those possessing the skills and resources essential for whatever social and economic change is deemed crucial (for example, groups with the greatest technical expertise, capital for investment, communication control, and administrative experience) and those

intimately associated with the nation's identity. Groups whose energies and coop-
eration are least needed to ensure development at a given time are those most likely
to be given a formal autonomous region or ignored. Groups possessing attributes
that make their integration imperative either will be lured into assimilation or
coerced into submission.[21]

In the industrial societies the segregation of some groups from the rest of society may be desirable. Such groups may wish to maintain their traditional ways and do not value incorporation into the industrial economy. But even if the policy makers do not include particular groups in the economic system, such groups will be affected somewhat by industrialization. The American Eskimo increasingly use snowmobiles and rifles instead of dog sleds and harpoons, and their once isolated territories are being encroached upon by industrial populations and white settlements. In Scandinavia hydroelectric projects and airstrips have cut into the reindeer areas of the Lapps (who call themselves the Samit). As a result, only eight thousand of the thirty-four thousand Lapps still follow the herds, while the rest are miners and lumberjacks. Faced with such industrial intrusion, one Lapp exclaimed, "We are not Norwegians, Swedes or Finns. We are different—and we intend to stay that way."[22] All one can say about this optimism is "good luck."

In the 1920s the government of the Soviet Union decided that no group would be left out of the drive for modernization and homogeneity. In a series of five-year plans, goals were set for the elimination of illiteracy, the collectivization of agriculture, the elimination of private enterprise, the secularization of Soviet life, and the industrialization of the entire society. Nothing was to stand in the way of the gigantic collective effort, including ethnic groups. In Central Asia, thousands of Kazah people starved to death while awaiting a decision as to whether nomads should first be collectivized and then settled into agricultural communities or whether they should be settled before being collectivized. Others were swept into the new industries of the Ural and Siberia.[23] Any "non-Russian was guilty of nationalism if in any way he stressed the differences that separate his nation from the Russian nation; of cosmopolitanism if he stressed any cultural links that bind his nation to any nation whose country is outside the Soviet Union."[24]

The Soviet government, of course, did not rely solely upon coercion. Bargains were made with various groups, and propaganda was incessant.

Propaganda has been effective in other societies trying to assimilate subordinate groups into the dominant one. One form of propaganda is an appeal to cultural nationalism. In this approach cultural elements, historical events, and personages primarily related to the dominant group's history and culture are glorified as representative of the *entire* society. This "superpatriotism" and glorification of the fatherland or motherland ignores for the most part the cultural and historical traditions of the minorities. Such efforts to reduce cultural differentiation by suffusing the entire state-society with the culture and history of the dominant group is a common feature of many modern national societies.

Argentina affords a representative example of cultural nationalism. In the nineteenth century, the elite of Argentina had actively encouraged large-scale immigration from Europe in order to populate this sparsely settled country and to provide a source of labor. Around 1910, this dominant group elite found itself in a dilemma—the immigrants and their descendants were challenging the elite's social and political predominance, but immigration was essential for the economy and the prosperity of the elite. The solution was cultural nationalism, symbolized by the gaucho—a figure that had been devalued but now became important—in order "to convince the public that the cultural values of the Argentine elite represented the true national character."[25] The primary agent of cultural nationalism was the public school system. "The central idea of Argentine nationalistic education was that the elementary and secondary curricula should emphasize Argentine history and geography, national civic problems, and the Spanish language. Instruction in these subjects should not merely furnish factual information, but should stress patriotic traditions and legends that would stimulate the child's love for his country." All of the devices familiar to students in American public schools were utilized in Argentina also—an oath of allegiance, a patriotic song ("Viva la patria") sung at the close of classes—as well as the Day of National Heroes honoring fallen Argentine patriots.[26]

Such arrogant cultural indoctrination—arrogant because the dominant group's heroes, myths, beliefs, and glorified historical events are defined as synonymous with those of the entire multiethnic society—may be, and has been, quite effective in reducing all forms of ethnic differentiation. This certainly was the case in Argentina: "By the 1930s first-generation immigrant children were fervently identifying with creole culture. The sons of Italians, Spaniards, and Russians enthusiastically studied gauchesque literature, shouted patriotic slogans, and even adopted some old Argentine customs. . . ."[27]

Cultural nationalism has been quite effective in the United States. Faced with a similar immigrant problem, "Americanism," symbolized by Uncle Sam, has been propagated by the public school system. Anglo heroes, Anglo values, and the Anglo view of history have indoctrinated millions of minority children, resulting in their assimilation into the dominant American mainstream. (In recent years, however, an increasing awareness of their own ethnic identity has increased the alienation of numerous ethnic groups in the face of such Anglo nationalism.)

Discrimination, a major process in the maintenance of dominance, can also be utilized to produce integration and assimilation. Following World War I, Italy acquired a section of Austria (South Tyrol).

Under Italy's Fascist government (1923–1943) attempts were made to Italianize South Tyrol, first, by transferring large numbers of Italians to the area and, second, by interfering with the customs and economy of the German-speaking inhabitants. In governmental positions and in public services Germans were replaced by Italians. The use of German in the schools was forbidden, street names and public signs were changed to Italian, and Germans were forbidden to engage in various cultural activities, such as the wearing of traditional costumes or membership in German social clubs. With the gradual industrialization of South Tyrol, Germans were generally excluded from employment in the new industries and power projects. . . . [28]

Discrimination against Jews in the Soviet Union has been a government program to absorb this divergent group, a practice that goes back to the czars. And in the nineteenth century the United States forbade Indians to practice their religion or to use their language on various reservations.

When subordinate group members desire integration, or even assimilation, and this is the policy of the state, coercion is not necessary, except, perhaps, to overcome the resistance of some *dominant* group members who do not want to integrate with "undesirables" or who object to what they perceive as government favoritism to other groups. When subordinate groups do not want to be incorporated into the larger society and do not want to disappear as an entity, governmental integration programs may become more coercive. Force can only be a preliminary measure, however. In the final analysis, true integration must be voluntary.

Integration reduces the extent of the dominant-subordinate relationship as discrimination and racism are diminished and eliminated. Assimilation of subordinate groups terminates these particular patterns of dominance. And, in a few cases, a dominant group itself can cease to exist if it assimilates into a subordinate group.

PLURALISM

In its most general sense, pluralism as a social *condition* is a structural arrangement whereby two or more ethnic groups have relative autonomy in the conduct of their institutional activities. In empire and national types of societies the dominant group always has this autonomy, but at least one subordinate group in a given society should be relatively autonomous if any degree of pluralism can be said to exist. If *all* of the groups within a society have a high degree of autonomy in their institutional activities and no one group controls the state, then a pluralistic society exists. This is not the case in the national and empire-type societies, however. At any given time within these two types of societies a quite varied structural arrangement can exist. Some subordinate groups may have a highly dependent, controlled or colonial status in which most or all of their institutional activities are affected by the whims of dominant group administrators and officials.

Other subordinate groups in the society may be highly integrated with the dominant group or may be in the process of becoming so. And one or more other subordinate groups may have acquired the conditions of autonomy that may be termed a *pluralistic status*, which *is the acquisition of some degree of autonomy that is formally or informally recognized by the state*.

A pluralistic status involves relative autonomy, and three major forms of autonomy can be distinguished: cultural and linguistic, political, and economic. Cultural and linguistic pluralism means that the government formally or informally acknowledges a subordinate group's right to linguistic and cultural autonomy in the conduct of its institutional activities. The government grants to a group support and protection of freedom of religion, freedom to practice traditional customs, the right to use one's own language in education, and the right to transmit to children the values, beliefs, and norms of the group. Political pluralism can consist of any or all of the following: local government or home rule by the subordinate group except where foreign affairs is concerned, subordinate group control of law enforcement in the group's own community or subsociety, and formalized proportional representation of the subordinate group in the central government. Economic pluralism, which is rare, could consist of the control of a regional ethnic economy without regulation by the central government, or a favored status in terms of employment to improve the group's stratification position (use of quotas, affirmative action programs, or more extreme, preferential treatment or "reverse discrimination").

"Transformation" by pluralism implies a change from a previous exploited, dependent, or colonial status to one of greater autonomy. When a pluralist status has been genuinely obtained, subordinance to a dominant group is reduced; the group now has far greater freedom and control over its own destiny. Yet it remains subordinate to some extent, since it does not control the state and its autonomy is not absolute. The state will still require taxes to be paid, the young men of the group will have to serve the state in time of war, treasonable or subversive activities will not be tolerated by the state, and further "separatist" efforts (secession) will be dealt with by all of the power of the state. But dominant group members are subjected to the same restrictions on their freedom. What is particularly relevant to a subordinate group with a pluralist status is the ever-present threat of a change in government policy.

Pluralism should not be confused with the mere existence of cultural differences, nor with the presence of more than one ethnic group in the society. There is always some degree of cultural differentiation between ethnic groups within a society, and virtually all complex societies are multiethnic. Extreme cultural differences existed between the British and the subordinate groups in its African and Asian colonies, which by no means had a pluralistic status. On the other hand, it is quite possible for a subordinate group with minimal cultural differentiation from the dominant group to have a pluralist status—as with the Scots and the English, for example.

The key word in the idea of pluralism is *autonomy*. No matter what the differences in culture or the number of groups in the society, the question to ask is, does the group (or do the groups) have relative independence over its destiny, or is it subjected to the decisions and actions of alien ethnic or racial out-groups? This is the test for the existence of pluralism.

Pluralism, like integration, is not only a structural condition in society, it also is a value. In its broadest meaning, pluralism is the value of acquiring or maintaining a pluralistic society: there should be no dominant group; all groups should be equal members of a federated society. More narrowly, pluralism is the value of acquiring or maintaining the autonomy of one's own group. As a value, pluralism constitutes the ideology (an "ism") of pluralist social movements.

Pluralist Social Movements

A pluralist social movement is *the movement of a group toward structural autonomy by eliminating dominant group discrimination and by acquiring governmental recognition and support of the group's right to control its own institutional activities.* The movement may focus on one group, several groups, or all of the groups in society in its desire to obtain this right. To members of a pluralist movement, dependency, integration, and exploitation are all undesirable social conditions.

In one form of the pluralist movement the primary focus is cultural and linguistic. A subordinate ethnic group wants to arrest acculturation, to develop or reactivate a distinctive culture, and to gain autonomy in the practice and implementation of this culture. In Ireland, for example, the Gaelic League was founded in 1893 to revive and restore Irish as the spoken language, to sponsor the development of Irish literature, and to convince other Irish people to avoid imitating the English and to prevent any anglicization efforts on the part of the English.[29] Today in Wales, members of the Welsh Language Society have disrupted court proceedings, demanding that they be held in the Welsh language; repainted English signs in Welsh; protested the rule that Welsh cannot be spoken to prisoners; and climbed a British Broadcasting Company television antenna to dramatize the need for a Welsh language channel.[30]

In another form of the pluralist movement the primary focus is political and economic. This type of pluralist movement may center around the demand for home rule or political control of an ethnically homogeneous region, control that falls short of sovereignty. An excellent example of a movement to obtain home rule has been occurring in Scotland since 1850. In 1707, the Act of Union eliminated Scotland and England as sovereign states and created the kingdom of Great Britain with the capitol and the central government in London, England. Since that time, some forms of pluralism have developed between the Scots and the dominant English. Scotland has its own educational system, court system, banking system, and the Scottish Trades Union Congress. But the Scots have demanded even greater autonomy. The modern pluralist movement began in 1850 when a minister in Edinburgh, James Begg, issued a pamphlet describing his views of social problems:

> We are sinking in our national position every year, and simply living on the credit of the past . . . . A people that might match the world for energy, and who have heretofore stood in the first rank of nations, sinking under a combination of increasing evils—the efforts of ministers paralyzed—our universities locked up, dwarfed, and comparatively inefficient—crime increasing—drunkenness and Sabbath-breaking making progress—Christianity languishing—pauperism threatening to swallow up the whole property of the country—hundreds of our best people flying from our shores under the pressure of want, or at the command of tyranny—the great national resources of our whole country locked up in the iron embrace of feudal despotism—little intelligence amongst the people to understand this, far less to battle with it—the very passes of our mountains interdicted—the fishing of our rivers monopolized—our public grounds and gardens shut up—the Parliament of England despising us, our natural guardians joining in the oppression.[31]

In 1853, the Scottish Rights Society was founded, followed by the Scottish Home Rule Association in 1886 and the Scottish National Party in 1934. All efforts to introduce home rule in Parliament have failed. Since 1946, the demand has changed from home rule or political pluralism to secession or political independence.

In the United States, the largest segment of the Black Power movement is pluralist.* Groups such as CORE (Congress of Racial Equality) and the Black Muslims have demanded equality and local control and are opposed to integration. Several American Indian groups are demanding a quasi-autonomous status for all reservations, with Indians completely in charge of all affairs directly related to the Indian people.

The social problems defined by pluralist movements are the threat of the loss of ethnic identity (through assimilation), the subordinate group's relative inequality in the society, and the group's lack of control over the decision-making processes. Solutions involve efforts to maintain or increase the subordinate group's cultural, spatial, and institutional integrity and to improve its stratification position. The movement must convince members of the subordinate group that these are desirable goals. Out-group targets are primarily the government and the economic elite. Pluralist movements employ means that may be defined as reform or as radical by the establishment, but most members of pluralist movements perceive themselves as reformist.

The Government and Pluralism

Governments generally grant a pluralist status to one or more subordinate groups because of expediency, not because of the value of such an arrange-

*The term "Black Power" includes pluralist, secessionist, and revolutionary divisions.

ment. If certain troublesome groups are granted concessions, resistance will be reduced and the overall system of dominance can be maintained more effectively.

In the Austrian Empire a drastic form of political pluralism developed between the Austrians (Germans) and the Hungarians (Magyars). For several hundred years the Hapsburg Empire in central Europe was dominated by the Austrian Germans: ". . . all the social elements of distinction and the ruling classes were Germans—the nobility of the Alpine regions, all-powerful at court, the upper clergy and bureaucracy, the middle classes and the liberal professions, as well as the better part of the proletariat. Every facet of the social prism reflected a German image. The other races seemed absent, the Polish and Czech aristocracy never appeared in Parliament, or, if they did, it was without their national flag . . . ."[32] But gradually the other ethnic groups, particularly the Magyars, the Czechs and Poles, increased in size and in importance. With the defeat of the Hapsburg army at the hands of the Prussians in 1866, considerable territory inhabited by primarily German-speaking people was lost, and the Germans became a very precarious dominant minority. German power was threatened; the solution was to divide the empire, granting equal status to the Hungarians, so that both sections shared a common monarchy. "The policy of *divide et impera*, by way of dividing the empire into two parts in order to save the rule in one half by surrendering it in the other to an undesirable yet much needed ally, became the necessity of the day."[33] This extreme political segmentation produced by conflict created the hyphenated Austrian-Hungarian Empire in 1867.

By the nineteenth century the Ottoman Turkish Empire had become quite weak as a result of wars with Russia, Great Britain, France, and other powers. Between 1821 and 1829 the Greeks had engaged in a war for independence (secession) from the empire and had been successful because of their own efforts and because of assistance from these powers. In order to prevent further defections, the Turks granted relative political autonomy to two subordinate groups—the Serbs in 1830 and the Bulgarians in 1878.

A government may grant pluralism out of weakness; in other cases, however, it may use pluralism to isolate a group. In Rumania, where Rumanians constitute 86 percent of the population, a decision was made in 1952 to isolate the Hungarian minority (9.4 percent of the population) in order to institute an economic development program more effectively. Transylvania, the region where most Hungarians resided, was given a quasi-autonomous political status. In 1956, an uprising in Hungary forced the Rumanian government to rethink this decision; its own Hungarian minority could be a problem. What followed is illustrative of the manner in which the government can reverse or change its relationship with subordinate groups in a relatively short time. The political status of Transylvania was eliminated and the area was divided into three counties. Rumanian was introduced as the sole language of education, law, and public services in the area, and Rumanians were encouraged to settle in Transylvania (where they now constitute 65 percent of the population in the area).[34] Pluralism was out; assimilation has now become the guiding policy of this national society. A pluralist status is an arrangement that, once acquired, must be jealously maintained against possible erosion of such privileges by the government or against a sudden and drastic alteration of government policy.

In systems of racial or ethnic dominance a government may grant pluralism as a temporary arrangement until the goal of integration or assimilation is met. Pluralism may be used as a facade to conceal ethnic dominance and the elimination of ethnic diversity. Such is the case in the USSR; the Soviet Union is an empire masquerading as a pluralistic society.

SECESSION

The reduction of dominance by pluralism is relatively rare compared to termination by independence. Under conditions of pluralism, the subordinate group elects to remain within the state-society; secession means separation and total political independence.

Secessionist movements are efforts to acquire political independence (or sovereignty) in a territorial segment of the existing state-society. Such movements often are outgrowths of unsuccessful efforts at integration or at pluralism. For the most part, the ethnic members of the movement are charter residents of conquest. An interesting and rare exception to this general pattern was the Texan secession from Mexico in 1835. As will be examined in more detail in Part 2, Americans *immigrated* into a northern province of the Spanish Empire (and later, Mexico), rapidly outnumbered the Mexican population in the area, revolted, and gained independence after the Battle of San Jacinto. But far more common than any other form of ethnic or racial movement is the independence effort of a charter member group.

The British Empire has been plagued by successful and unsuccessful efforts at secession. The colonies in North America were lost in 1783, after the success of the French-supported American independence movement. Britain lost India in 1947, after twenty years of efforts to prevent this secession. The Hindu leader of the secessionist movement was Mahatma Gandhi, whose basic tactic was *satyagraha*: "To draw suffering on oneself and thus shame one's opponent into a change of heart, to die—but not to kill—for the truth."[35] Muslims also desired independence and feared that the withdrawal of Britain would make them subordinate to the Hindu Indians. The desire for their new country, Pakistan, was stated by their leader, Muhammad Ali Jinnah: "Mussalmans are a nation according to any definition of a nation, and they must have their own homelands, their territory, and their state."[36] Taking advantage of Britain's problems in World War II, the Indians began widespread civil disobedience in 1942, along with riots and sabotage. In spite of efforts at suppression—60,000 were arrested and 940 killed—resistance was too severe to be controlled by a people engaged in a European and Asian war. In 1947 two states were created, India and Pakistan.[37]

Secessionist movements have plagued other European colonial powers since World War II. Algeria became independent from France in 1962, after thirty-five to forty years of nationalistic efforts. Between 1925 and 1962 a number of organizations such as the Etoile Nord Africaine (ENA, North African Star), the Parti du Peuple Algérien (PPA, Party of the Algerian People), and the Front de Libération Nationale (FLN, National Liberation Front) carried out protests, propaganda, assassinations, and eventually guerrilla warfare.[38]

The French had lost Indochina a little earlier, in 1954. After Japan surrendered in 1945, the French attempted to reassert control over this colony, which dates back to the nineteenth century. Ho Chi Minh and his guerrilla army had resisted Japanese dominance, and by the end of the war his movement had widespread support, with an ideology based primarily on national independence rather than on communism. Determined to hold on to the southern part of Viet Nam (around Saigon), where they had the greatest investments, the French installed Bao Dai as a puppet emperor and, with American military equipment and financial aid, fought back against the Vietminh. In 1951 Senator John Kennedy wrote: "In Indochina we have allied ourselves to the desperate effort of a French regime to hang on to the remnants of empire. There is no broad, general support of the native Vietnam Government (i.e., of Bao Dai) among the people of that area."[39] By February of 1954, the French agreed to negotiate a settlement, and a conference in Geneva was arranged for April. Before this conference took place, however, other events intervened. French paratroops landed in the middle of enemy territory at Dien Bien Phu and by April were surrounded and defeated. France lost Indochina, and the Americans took it upon themselves to prevent the southern portion from falling to the Vietminh and the National Liberation Front—an effort doomed to failure, as later events demonstrated.[40]

The last of the European powers in Africa, Portugal, was engaged in violent conflict in Angola and Mozambique from 1961 to 1974. In Mozambique, the black secessionist movement was headed by Front for the Liberation of Mozambique (Frelimo). The black guerrilla armies attacked convoys, blew up trains, used the friendly countries of Tanzania and Zambia as bases, and generally did what all guerrilla armies do—kill and terrorize. The Portuguese government, determined to retain colonies in order to stand up to the influence of Spain, pitted sixty thousand trained commando troops against the seven thousand members of Frelimo. One tactic of the government was to herd native populations into protected resettlement villages (called *aldeamentos*) to deprive the guerrillas of cover, supply, and shelter. By 1972, over a million people were relocated into nine hundred such fortified and controlled villages. But eventually the drain on the impoverished

Portuguese economy was too much, and Mozambique and Angola were granted independence in 1974 and 1975, respectively.[41]

Another example of the many secessionist movements that have been successful in recent years involves a former subordinate group that had become dominant through secession—the Pakistanis. In 1947 they gained independence from Britain and the state of Pakistan was created—a state made up of two noncontiguous territories separated by a thousand miles of India. In West Pakistan the dominant Pakistanis made up the majority of the section, while in East Pakistan the Bengalis made up most of the population but were controlled by the government in West Pakistan. A Bengali movement for home rule took the form of the Awami League, which in 1970 won an overwhelming majority at the polls. Following the election, the league began to implement its program in which the central government in West Pakistan would only be concerned with defense and foreign affairs. On March 25, 1971, a West Pakistani army invaded East Pakistan, arrested the leader of the league, and reportedly killed around 200,000 Bengalis. Deaths soared after the initial invasion; estimates ranged from 1 to 1½ million. India was inundated with 10 million Bengali refugees, a problem which prompted India to support the Bengali movement for independence. In late 1971 the new country of Bangladesh was created out of East Pakistan.[42] In 1973, it was reported that two other ethnic groups in Pakistan (formerly West Pakistan) were being encouraged by Afghanistan to secede—the Pathans and the Baluchi.[43]

These examples of independence movements reinforce the argument that virtually all complex societies have been and are multiethnic; that all complex societies, regardless of type—empire, pluralistic, or national—have a *continuing* problem of maintaining cohesiveness and order in the face of this multiethnicity; and that ethnic stratification is a unique form of inequality, not to be dismissed or subsumed under the idea of class. Regarding the latter point, Stanley Lieberson has written:

> *The most fundamental difference between ethnic and other forms of stratification lies in the fact that the former is nearly always the basis for the internal disintegration of the existing boundaries of a nation-state. On both theoretical and empirical grounds, only ethnic groups are likely to generate a movement toward creating a separate nation-state. Ethnic groups are the only strata that have the inherent potential to carve their own autonomous and permanent society from the existing nation without, in effect, re-creating its earlier form of stratification all over again. Political separatism offers a solution to disadvantaged groups in an ethnic stratification system that is not possible for groups disadvantaged on the basis of age, sex, or economic stratification.*[44]

Social problems for secessionist movements are numerous: discrimination, exploitation, potential loss of ethnic identity, dominance by out-group members, and the unresponsiveness of government. The solution is radical—complete independence through coercion of government officials and the supporters of the establishment. A necessary condition, but not a sufficient condition, for the success of such a movement is territorial segregation. Most of the members of a group must reside together in a geographical space that can become the basis for the new society. When this condition has been met, the movement must acquire enough resources and cohesiveness to resist successfully all efforts of the state to prevent the movement from attaining its goals.

If secessionist movements succeed, their leaders become heads of state, statues are erected to them, and legends take form. If they lose, the leaders are executed or imprisoned as criminals and are soon forgotten. Such is the outcome of success or failure in this form of conflict resolution.

REVOLUTION

A revolutionary movement is a collective effort to overthrow the government of a state, to establish one's own members in positions of power in this society, and then to plan to carry out some program of social change. Revolutionary movements, unlike secessionist movements, seek not to establish a new state-society out of a territorial segment, but to take control of the entire existing society. While secessionist movements can only be based upon ethnicity or race, revolutionary endeavors have been based upon class as well as race and ethnicity, and, in some cases, on a combination of these.* As for the idea of social change, all that is necessary is that there be a *program* for changes. Significant changes may or may not occur when a new group is in power, since there is a tendency for new members of the establishment to act in ways quite similar to those of the old elite. Revolutionary programs are often ignored as the new elite becomes more preoccupied with maintaining themselves in power and crushing dissent.

While ethnic or racial secessionist movements are quite common, ethnic- or racial-based revolutions are rare, and successful revolutions are even rarer. To this author's knowledge, only three ethnic-based revolutions were successful in the preindustrial empires, one of which had a racial aspect. In 555 B.C., under their leader, Cyrus, the subordinate Persians revolted and overthrew the Median Empire, transforming the entire state-society into the Persian Empire.[45] More than a thousand years later, in 750 A.D., Persians subordinate to the Arabs took over the empire society by killing off all of the members of the existing Arab ruling family (the Ommiads or Umayyads)

---

*Major revolutionary movements based upon class were the French Revolution in the late eighteenth century and the revolution in Russia in the early twentieth century. The American "revolution" was not a revolution but a successful effort at secession. If it had been a revolution as defined above, Americans would have marched into London, taken over the government, and replaced the English as the dominant ethnic group in the empire.

and established themselves in power as the Abbasid dynasty. In Will Durant's words, "after a century of humiliation, Persia conquered her conquerors."[46] Around 1500 B.C. in ancient Egypt, after several hundred years of contact, Egyptian armies conquered Negro-inhabited territory to the south. These black people, called *Nehsiu* by the Egyptians, were subordinated and forced to work the gold mines of the area. Approximately eight hundred years later an army of *Nehsiu*, or Ethiopians, took advantage of a weakened Egypt and established dominance over much of what was left of the Egyptian Empire. Egyptianized blacks took over the highest positions and ruled for sixty years.* [47]

There has been one successful ethnic revolution in modern times, and this was a peaceful reversal—the acquisition of power in South Africa by the Afrikaners (people of Dutch descent). With their victory in the Boer War, 1899–1902, the English established dominance over all the Dutch and Black areas. The British believed that they "would imperialize, anglicize, absorb and liberalize the Afrikaner majority, and out-populate them, a feat of which the British had proved capable in the preceding century. The reverse process began."[48]

From the first, the Union was controlled by Afrikaner politicians; the British political tradition atrophied. . . . The price of appeasing Afrikaner resentment, and of splitting Afrikaner leadership, was that henceforth the British were never ruled by one of themselves, or even had much representation in the cabinet. In 1949, Dr. Jansen, the minister of native affairs could tell a Nationalist party Congress [Afrikaner] with deadly truth: "It is now almost forty years since Union, and the English-speaking section of this country has not produced one leader of consequence in the political sphere . . . . Never so far have the majority of them been inspired by a true and pure South African spirit, and yet it has suited them to make use of Afrikaans-speaking leaders to carry out their imperialistic colour policy." If that had been their game, it was in 1949 certainly played out.[49]

The English allowed the Afrikaans language to have equal position with English, and Afrikaans thus became the effective medium of politics and administration. While the British (and Jewish-British) specialized in business, the Afrikaners increasingly moved into governmental posts. As the Afrikaners diligently increased their political power, the English made

Another glimpse of ancient racism comes from this relationship between the brown Egyptians and the blacks. An Egyptian king wrote, "He is really unmanly who is pushed back at his [own] frontier, since the Nehsi hears [only] to fall down at a word. It is the [mere] answering him that makes him retreat. . . . They are not really people [worthy] of respect; they are poor and broken of spirit." (John A. Wilson, The Culture of Ancient Egypt [Chicago: University of Chicago Press, Phoenix Books, 1951], p. 137). Evidence exists of blacks being killed and buried as sacrifices in the tomb of a high Egyptian official. The Egyptologist, John A. Wilson, writes that "the Egyptians had carried into the Middle kingdom an emphasis on social justice and the rights of the common man, but they still thought the Egyptians were the only proper humans and that foreigners were akin to animals. They did not carry their concern for individual rights with them into their colonies" (Ibid., p. 140).

class distinctions among themselves, creating a poor English class and a wealthy class that never severed its ties with England. In a classic example of "the grasshoppers and the ants," the Afrikaners worked while the English "turned South Africa into a playground for themselves."[50]

Since establishing themselves in power, the Afrikaners have crushed all black efforts to be equally revolutionary. In the 1950s and early 1960s, a number of organizations and movements demanding integration or some form of political pluralism were suppressed by the government of the Union of South Africa (the Republic of South Africa after 1961). The major organizations demanding change were the African National Congress (ANC) and the Pan-Africanist Congress (PAC). "The suppression of the ANC and the PAC and the mass arrests of demonstrators and political activists in the early 1960s convinced many Africans that the only successful way to deal with government repression was to resort to violent means. Driven underground, both the ANC and the PAC authorized the creation of subordinate organizations whose purposes would range from sabotage to armed revolt.[51] Two of these subordinate organizations—the Spear of the Nation and Poqo—along with an unaffiliated organization, the African Resistance Movement (RAM), engaged in terrorist activities and the sabotage of public utilities. All of these efforts have been suppressed by the government, primarily through police infiltration and paying for information. Over thirteen hundred persons were sent to prison in 1965.[52] In 1976 and 1977 there were major student riots in Soweto and other cities. Whether the white government can be overthrown, if some form of territorial separation controlled by Africans will occur, or if the solution is integration remains to be seen.

A little more common but still far from frequent is a revolutionary movement based on class *and* ethnicity or race. According to Cynthia Enloe, the greatest potential for this mixed form of revolution occurs in a country

in which ethnic boundaries are coterminous with socio-economic class lines, one ethnic group clearly dominates and exploits a numerically large but powerless have-not sector, and the oppressed group is integrated into the country's economic system and has symbolic significance for national identity. Only under these conditions will an ethnic group stand a good chance of spearheading a revolution.[53]

She points out that this mixed form was present in the revolution in Mexico in 1910, in which the mestizos and Indians made up the bulk of the peasantry; in the revolution in Cuba under Castro in 1958, in which dispossessed Negroes provided great support and involvement; and in the revolution in Bolivia in 1952, in which "peasant" and "Indian" were interchangeable terms. Enloe adds, "Though the legacy and plight of the Indian crystallized revolutionary fervor in Mexico and Bolivia, in neither country were Indians the principal actors or commanders in the revolution. Perhaps for this reason, the Indians' immediate circumstances were not radically altered when the revolution ended."[54]

CONQUEST AND DISMEMBERMENT

When alien groups from another society invade and occupy a society controlled by a dominant group, the dominant group becomes subordinate. Not only is conquest a major cause of the *origin* of subordinate groups, it also *terminates* the dominance of a group in a society that has been incorporated into a new system. As for the subordinate groups in the society that has been conquered, they merely change masters.

Dominant-subordinate relationships may also be terminated by dismemberment, which is the reduction of the territory of a defeated state by the victors following a war. The victorious state may annex some of this territory or it may create new sovereign systems. In the territorial changes following World War I, Czechs, Serbs, Croatians, Slovaks, South Slavs (Yugoslavs), and Slovenes were freed from the dominance of the Austrians and granted sovereignty. Most Poles became dominant once again in their new state. The subordinance of the Danes in Schleswig to the Germans was terminated when Schleswig was given to Denmark. Germans became subordinate in Czechoslovakia, Poland, and France (Alsace-Lorraine). And German dominance over numerous African peoples was terminated. The results of World War II terminated the short-lived dominance of the Germans over many of the peoples of Western Europe, the dominance of the Italians over the peoples of Libya and Ethiopia, and Japanese dominance over much of Asia. These brief empires were dismembered by the victorious powers.

The fifth major form of ethnic social movements—irredentism—is often a factor in dismemberment. An irredentist movement may be defined as "any movement which aims to unite politically with its co-national mother state a region under foreign rule."[55] R. A. Schermerhorn has explained irredentism:

> *Ordinarily this [irredentism] refers to a situation where ethnics residing in a nation-state which they do not rule, share the language, customs, and sense of nationality with fellow ethnics who rule a neighboring state. The latter, on the well-known nationalist assumption that a nation should be ethnically homogeneous, regards its "fellow nationals" as unfortunate subjects of a "foreign" power to be redeemed and united with their colleagues by political or military means. While they are subjugated they are unredeemed (irredents) but this is an inherently unstable position which history is bound to correct. It is therefore a duty to promote national aspirations and loyalty among the unredeemed, stirring them to rebel against their rulers so that they can unite with fellow nationals in a fully redeemed nation.*[56]

141

Europe has been the major center for irredentist movements, which occur within the society in which the group is a minority as well as in the "mother state." For example, "unredeemed" Italians in Trieste, Tyrol, and Trentino, all part of Austria, wanted to become incorporated into Italy, and the Italian-Italians shared this wish. Other examples have been the Danes in Schleswig, Germany; the Serbs in Bosnia (the Austrian Empire); the French in Alsace-Lorraine (lost to Germany after the Franco-Prussian War of 1870); the Greeks in Crete (part of Turkey); and the Germans in the Sudetenland (Czechoslovakia). War between "nation-states" provides the means of redemption. However, even though war brings some children back into the fold, new groups become subordinate minorities, which now have to be redeemed. So the quest for the unobtainable—the truly homogeneous nation-state—goes on.

EXPULSION AND EXTERMINATION

A particular dominant-subordinate relationship can be terminated by the total expulsion of a subordinate ethnic group from the society. The classic example of this was the expulsion of the Jews from Spain in 1492 (see page 85).

An even more extreme method of terminating a dominant-subordinate relationship is to exterminate the subordinate ethnic group. Shibutani and Kwan have described one such incident on the island of Tasmania, part of the British Empire in Australia:

> *The British colonists in Tasmania viewed the natives as a degenerate "race." Some of them hunted the aborigines as sport or to provide meat for their dogs; they chained up the women, raped, and then killed them. When the natives retaliated, a full-scale war began. Finally, to stop the slaughter, the governor offered a bounty of £5 for every adult and £2 for every child captured alive. The colonists formed a cordon of 5,000 armed men, stretching from one end of the island to the other, to capture every native, but only two were caught. Later on, a man who had won the confidence of the Tasmanians persuaded them to give themselves up. The 203 survivors were segregated, and the last of them died in 1876.*[57]

Ethnocide has been occurring in Brazil in recent years, according to Lucien Bodard. With the complicity of the Brazilian SPI (Service for the Protection of the Indians), entire tribes have been exterminated by machine gunning from the air, gifts of poisoned food, and gifts of clothing deliberately infected with deadly bacteria. Bodard lists twenty Indian ethnic groups that "have been exterminated, annihilated, and have vanished." Several others have been reduced to the point of extinction.[58] Extermination is the ultimate solution for a society with "minority problems."

SUMMARY

Dominance is reduced by integration or by pluralism. Dominant-subordinate relationships are terminated by assimilation, secession, revolution, dismemberment, expulsion, extermination, or conquest. Many of these processes of transformation involve interaction between the government of a society and subordinate group social movements.

A social movement is an organized collective venture that transcends a local community and that involves systematic efforts to bring about desired social change. Social movements develop in situations of discontent and social change. They crystallize when ideologies and organizations are created that define the social problems and the solutions to these problems.

A social problem is a perceived social condition that has been negatively evaluated and that requires collective action for its intended solution. Once the undesirable social condition is perceived, the problem becomes one of a discrepancy between what is and what ought to be. The causes of this condition are formulated and a solution is presented. From the point of view of the problem definers, solving a social problem means utilizing collective action to change or to eliminate particular behavior patterns. Resistance to the solution must be overcome and the behavioral causes of the problem must be changed. This is accomplished through persuasion (propaganda or rational argument), bargaining, coercion, or some combination of the three. People in a society disagree about what is, what ought to be, and how to get from what is to what ought to be. What is a social problem for some may be progress or a condition of normalcy for others. And the efforts at solving a social problem can create new social problems for at least some members of the society (whether they are members of a dominant group or a subordinate group), or can have consequences other than those intended. Any pattern of race or ethnic relations may be considered a social problem—integration, segregation, equality, inequality, assimilation, pluralism, secession, extermination, discrimination, or conflict in general.

Governments as well as social movements are problem definers.

Governments may define the social movement as the problem and seek to suppress it, or they may accept, at least overtly, the legitimacy of the demands for change. If they accept the legitimacy of the social movement's goals, governments may avoid action, give half-hearted attention to the problems (deliberately or because of inefficiency), or use all of the machinery of the state to assist the movement. Whatever the decision, except nonintervention, if government action is to be effective, its goals must be clear and agreed upon, resources have to be mobilized efficiently, the effects of the government's efforts must be ascertained, and any laws passed to eliminate the problem must be enforced with sufficient sanctioning power. Persuasion, bargaining, and coercion are utilized by governments as well as by social movements, and governments can be as ineffective as social movements in directing or in impeding social change.

One way in which dominance is reduced is through integration. Integration, as opposed to segmentation or pluralism, is characterized by the increasing irrelevance of race or ethnic status in distinguishing and separating members of a society. Integration, which is not irreversible, generally takes place first between certain groups that have something in common and then between members of the total society. It also proceeds from secondary relations to primary relations. Integration involves the reduction of cultural and behavioral differences through the process of acculturation, the reduction of inequality, and the reduction of social and personal distance. Integration may occur on an unplanned basis or develop as a result of efforts by integrationist social movements or by the government. An integrationist social movement is one whose members seek to obtain equality through the elimination of discrimination and structural disadvantage and to become integrated into the institutional activities of the dominant group. Governments may foster integration to achieve a homogeneous society, to reduce conflict, or to diminish resistance to government programs, particularly modernization.

A second way in which dominance is reduced is through pluralism, particularly political pluralism. Pluralism is a relationship between a dominant group and one or more subordinate groups that is characterized by the relative political and cultural autonomy of subordinate groups. Through pluralist social movements or by governmental action, subordinate groups acquire the ability to control their own internal affairs. A subordinate group's acquisition of home rule, the right to use its own language in its area, and the right to engage in or control its own institutional activities, such as education, are all aspects of pluralism that can develop in a society still characterized by the presence of a dominant group.

Secession, particularly within empire societies, is a major and relatively frequent process that terminates particular dominant-subordinate relationships. Secessionist movements, which can be based only upon race or ethnicity, since territorial concentration is a prerequisite, are efforts to acquire political sovereignty in a territorial segment of a state-society. With very few exceptions, the members of such movements are charter members of the area that have been incorporated into another society through conquest. Secession has been widespread throughout Asia and Africa since World War II.

A rare form of terminating particular dominant-subordinate relationships has been revolution. A revolutionary movement is a group's effort to overthrow the government of a state, establish its own members in positions of power, and then to carry out some program of social change. Such a movement has generally had a class basis, a few have been related primarily to ethnicity or race, and in some cases in recent years both class and ethnicity have been involved.

A third way in which dominance is terminated is by the conquest of a society headed by a dominant group. An alien group establishes dominance and the former dominant group becomes subordinate.

Dominant-subordinate relationships can be terminated by territorial changes imposed upon the vanquished by the winning states in a war. The victorious state may dismember the defeated society and either grant sovereignty to the territorial segments or incorporate them into the society of the victorious state. Groups within these territorial segments change their status. Dominance may continue within the territorially reduced society, but over fewer subordinate groups.

Finally, dominance may be terminated by the expulsion or extermination of subordinate groups.

Part 1 has examined the basic units—ethnic groups, races, nationalities, and societies—and the basic dimensions—stratification, segregation, cultural differentiation, social distance, and competition-

conflict—involved in the relationships between races and ethnic groups. The basic processes involved in the origin, the maintenance, and the transformation of those systems characterized by the existence of a dominant group have also been described.

Part 2, Ethnic and Racial Dominance in the United States, is a case study of one society, utilizing the processes and the conceptual framework that has been developed in Part 1.

ETHNIC AND RACIAL DOMINANCE IN THE UNITED STATES

INTRODUCTION

Part 2 is a case study of the United States from the beginning to the present time utilizing the conceptual framework and definitions developed in Part 1. The essential ideas of Part 2 can be summarized as follows:

1. There is an American ethnic group *which has constituted a majority of the* American nationality. *This ethnic group originated in the eighteenth century, and throughout most of the nineteenth century it was made up of people of British descent, along with individuals from other Northern European ethnic groups who had de-emphasized the country of their own or their ancestors' origins. Other groups were "hyphenated" Americans in polite company or groups given derogatory names in less civil surroundings.*

In the twentieth century, the meaning of what constituted an ethnic "American" expanded to include members of Southern and Eastern European groups; however, a racial emphasis restricted the American ethnic group to whites who had mastered the English language.

2. Americans, or Anglos, became dominant in the United States with the successful secession from the British Empire. Black slavery in the southern section of the United States was intensified, and Americans expanded to the west subjugating Indian ethnic groups through conquest. In 1848, Mexico was partitioned following a military invasion; a small population of Mexicans then became a subordinate group in the United States. Following the Napoleonic Wars, and until 1930, millions of individuals from numerous ethnic groups in Europe, Asia, Canada, and Mexico entered the U. S. as voluntary immigrants. And American domination was extended over the island territories of Hawaii, Puerto Rico, the Philippines, and Cuba as the result of conflict.

3. All of the subordinate groups resided within segregated communities, partly from coercion and partly from personal choice. Except for most members of Northern European Protestant ethnic groups, the subordinate groups experienced varying degrees of discrimination from the dominant Anglos. Relatively elaborate doctrines of racism were developed to justify such domination, particularly over those ethnic groups that were phenotypically identifiable.

4. In the twentieth century before World War II, dominance over the white ethnics was reduced, but dominance over the racially designated ethnics intensified. Black-Americans in particular experienced the establishment of a highly structured and racist system of apartheid (separate and unequal).

5. Due to the effects of World War II, both at home and abroad, there developed a new stage in the pattern of race and ethnic relations in the United States. The social movements involving, for the most part, Blacks, Indians, and Chicanos forced changes in government policies. The elimination of discrimination and the integration of the "minorities" (some minorities) became the expressed goals of the federal government.

6. Today, although the value of pluralism is in vogue, the major trend seems to be one of transforming a once-stable system of Anglo dominance by integration. The integration process, however, remains retarded in the case of four subordinate groups: Black-Americans, Mexican-Americans, Indian-Americans, and Puerto Ricans living in the continental United States.

7. In studying this 300-year-old system of race and ethnic relations, it is misleading to conceive of American history as one of white v. black or white v. nonwhite. Anglos dominated all groups. Few members of the non-Anglo white ethnic groups have been in positions of power that would enable them to discriminate against nonwhites. Although the racially identifiable ethnic groups ("racial-ethnic" groups) have experienced the greatest oppression at the hands of the dominant Anglos, a preoccupation with broad racial categories has concealed the essentially ethnic nature of the dominant-subordinate relationships.

6

THE ORIGINS
OF AMERICAN
DOMINANCE AND ETHNICITY

INTRODUCTION

There is an American *ethnic* group, in the past known as the "real" Americans but today more politely referred to as the Anglo-Americans or WASP (White Anglo-Saxon Protestants). American ethnicity should not be confused with American nationality. All groups in the United States are of American nationality, but this "we are all Americans" belief masks the conflict relationships between the dominant ethnic Americans and all of the other groups that ever received a hyphen. Perhaps we all *should* be considered one people, but this has not been the case. The situation is analogous with calling administrators and teachers "educators," or clerks and executives "management." A common label is an effective device, whether intended or not, in preventing the establishment of a conflict relationship and in maintaining the superiority of the dominant segment in a relationship.

Chapter 2 presented models of empire and national societies. How does one classify the United States? In the *nineteenth* century, the United States was an empire society. Americans established dominance over hundreds of ethnic groups within contiguous and noncontiguous territories by military conquest. It is true that numerous ethnic groups entered this country as voluntary immigrants, but many traditional empire states have had their immigrants. Nineteenth-century America did diverge from the empire model by virtue of the fact that Americans (that is, ethnic Americans) have always been a dominant *majority* rather than a dominant minority. But the Russians are a majority of the population in their empire society; a few exceptions from models of complex reality are inevitable. Some empire societies have assimilated subordinate groups, while others have granted subordinate groups some measure of independence, and within many empire states different practices have existed for different groups. Thus, the strong emphasis on assimilating white Europeans into the American group should not be taken as a major divergence from the empire model. The essential characteristic of the empire type of society is the prevalence of conquest.

Internally, the United States in the twentieth century has developed into a national society. This development does not mean that subordinate groups have been eliminated; it does mean that the United States, in the second half of the twentieth century, has become more integrated. Discrimination has been reduced, regional segregation by ethnicity is no longer significant, cultural differences between groups are minimal, and there is a more proportional distribution of the groups within the class system. One reason why post–World War II America is more integrated is that it has quit conquering other peoples, another reason for classifying it as a national society.

The concern of this chapter is, first, how Americans became independent from the British Empire and dominant within the new society, and, second, what factors were involved in the ethnogenesis of the American group. In short, the concern is with the origins of the dominant American group.

THE ETHNIC MIX OF THE BRITISH COLONIES

By granting royal charters to favored personages, Great Britain developed a number of English colonies on what is now the eastern seaboard of the United States, an area claimed by Britain on the basis of the explorations of John Cabot (1497–1498). After the initial failure to establish a permanent colony on Roanoke Island in Virginia in 1587, successful colonies were initiated in Jamestown, Virginia, in 1607; in Massachusetts in 1619; and later in Pennsylvania, Maryland, and the Carolinas. Immigrants from the established colonies formed new ones in Connecticut, Rhode Island, and part of Maine and New Hampshire. In the meantime, the Dutch founded colonies in New Amsterdam (New York), beginning in 1614, and the French settled, primarily as fur traders, along the St. Lawrence, the Great Lakes, the Mississippi, and in the Mississippi Delta.

In 1644, New Amsterdam, a wedge between the English colonies of the north and south, fell to the English armies and navy. In 1664, with the addition of New York, thirteen independent colonies answerable to the British throne existed, a colonial empire surrounded by the French to the north and west and by the Spanish in Florida to the south.

By this time the colonies were already multiethnic, although the English were a majority. In the years to follow, prior to the secession, other European groups immigrated to this British foothold, increasing the ethnic mix. While Europe suffered from unemployment, the colonies had labor shortages. Utilizing a variety of strategies, such as giving fifty acres of free land to every person who brought somebody over, exempting immigrants from taxes for a period of time, offering bounties to defray the costs of passage, and providing free tools and land, the colonies attracted thousands of Europeans.[1] Between 1717 and 1776 approximately 250,000 Scotch-Irish left Ulster and settled in New England and Pennsylvania. Germans from the Rhineland also settled in Pennsylvania in such large numbers (they later became known as the Pennsylvania "Dutch") that by the time of the Revolution about one-third of all Pennsylvanians were Germans and another one-third were Scotch-Irish.[2] French Huguenots—many after a generation of living in England, Germany, or Holland—scattered themselves throughout the colonies. Earlier a smattering of Sephardic Jews, primarily merchants, had emigrated to New Amsterdam from Portugal and Spain, Brazil, Holland, and England. Later other Sephardic Jews entered the British colonies and were joined by Ashkenazic Jews from Poland, Amsterdam, and London. There were only 2,000 to 3,000 Jews in America by the end of the eighteenth century, only 30 Jewish families in New York in 1773, and not a single rabbi by the time of the independence.[3] Swedes became established in the New World in 1638 when some 500 of them founded New Sweden in Delaware. After being taken over by the Dutch in 1655, they became part of the English colonies when New Amsterdam fell to the British. In 1790 about 1 percent of the new country's population and 9 percent of the state of Delaware was Swedish.[4] It has been estimated that by 1776 the colonies contained around 2 million people of European descent. The estimated proportions of this population by major ethnic groups were: English, 60 percent; Irish and Scotch-Irish, 17 to 18 percent; Germans, 11 to 12 percent; Dutch, 7 to 8 percent; and Scotch, French, Swedes, and others, 2 to 5 percent.[5] Ninety-nine percent of all of these groups were Protestant.[6]

The English were the dominant group. They were ethnically identified with those English in the Old World, and many of the rich sent their children to school in England. It was their language, institutions, and government that dominated the colonial societies. As dominant ethnic groups have a tendency to do, they made things difficult for other groups, in spite of the need for labor and defense of the frontier. According to Maldwyn Jones, "at one time or another, immigrants of practically every non-English stock incurred the open hostility of the earlier comers."[7] The French Huguenots, were Protestant, but they were also French, and the English and French had a tradition of hostility in Europe, which carried over into their relationship in the New World. Doubting the loyalty of the French Huguenots, the English compelled them to move farther away from the frontier in New York. Several Huguenots were imprisoned in Pennsylvania for security reasons, and a settlement in Rhode Island was attacked and dispersed by a mob in 1691.[8] German-speaking areas were considered divisive, even dangerous, to many English. Benjamin Franklin feared germanization in Pennsylvania: "Why should the Palatine Boors be suffered to swarm into our settlements and, by herding together, establish their Language and Manners, to the

Exclusion of ours? Why should Pennsylvania, founded by the *English*, become a Colony of *Aliens*, who will shortly be so numerous as to Germanize us instead of our Anglifying them. . .?"[9] Opposition to the Scotch-Irish was relatively severe in New England and acted to divert many of them elsewhere. A mob in 1729 attempted to prevent ships from Londonderry and Belfast from landing in Boston, and five years later another mob pulled down an Irish church in Worchester.[10]

Such incidents of inter-European ethnic relations were, of course, minor in comparison to these transplanted Europeans' treatment of Indians and blacks. Further, hostility and discrimination between the colonial whites diminished as a number of factors brought them together into a new ethnic group—the Americans. The first of these factors was the war for independence.

THE AMERICAN SECESSION AND ESTABLISHMENT OF DOMINANCE

Prior to 1763 the British colonies were part of a relatively lax mercantile system established by the English Board of Trade, a system which, although somewhat restrictive of colonial enterprise, did offer advantages. This mercantile system, based on the relationship between a colony and the mother country, was summarized by the following statement of a member of the English Board of Trade in 1726:

> *Every act of a dependent provincial government ought therefore to terminate in the advantage of the mother state unto whom it owes its being and protection in all its valuable privileges. Hence it follows that all advantageous projects or commercial gains in any colony which are truly prejudicial to and inconsistent with the interests of the mother state must be understood to be illegal and the practice of them unwarrantable, because they contradict the end for which the colony had a beginning and are incompatible with the terms on which the people claim privilege and protection.*[11]

Two of the important restrictions placed upon the English colonies were designed to protect the woolen and iron industries in Britain from colonial competition. According to the Woolen Act of 1699, no woolen goods could be exported from the colonies or between the colonies. The production of pig iron and raw iron in the colonies was encouraged by the government in London, but the act of 1750 denied to colonials the right to erect new slitting and rolling mills, plating forges, and steel furnaces.[12] Another set of restrictions protected the hat-making industry of Britain. In 1732 restrictions specified that no hat could be put on board a ship or cart for export to England; that no one could make hats unless he served as an apprentice for seven years; and that no master could have more than two apprentices.[13]

In a number of acts of trade and navigation, American merchants and shippers were likewise restricted (in principle, anyway). Certain raw materials from the colonies—including tobacco, sugar, ginger, ship masts, lumber, copper ore, beaver furs, molasses, hemp, iron, and raw silk—could be shipped only to England and in English ships. The northern colonies could never supply England with the volume of raw materials that the southern colonies did and fell increasingly into debt as imports of finished goods from Britain exceeded exports of raw materials. Thus, northern colonials came to depend upon trade with the French, Dutch, and Spanish settlements in the Caribbean—a trade that became the cornerstone of the northern economy and that involved the exchange of colonial lumber, fish, and work animals in exchange for slaves, sugar, molasses (for rum distilleries of New England), cotton, ginger, and specie (cash).[14]

If such acts, and others, had been rigidly enforced by the English government, the social movement that resulted in colonial independence would have occurred much sooner. But policy enforcement was lax, and violations, particularly in the trade with the non-British colonies in the West Indies, were the rule rather than the exception. In addition, such mercantile policies were not entirely negative, even when enforced. Colonies became prosperous as a result of preferential tariff rates, which gave them a virtual monopoly in the British market in such areas as naval supplies, indigo, whale oil, lumber, iron, and tobacco. Colonists could also buy certain English commodities at a cheaper price than could English citizens in Britain.[15] As to political rights, "North American Britishers . . . enjoyed more liberties and rights than did Britishers in Great Britain."[16] Morison summarizes the relative position of the American colonies vis-à-vis other colonies and countries of the time:

King and Parliament had undisputed control of foreign affairs, war and peace, and overseas trade. Parliament canalized colonial trade into channels that it deemed profitable to all. In almost every other respect, Americans had acquired home rule. Their assemblies had secured the exclusive right to tax their constituents, to appoint officials such as colonial treasurers and fix their salaries; to commission military officers and raise troops or not as they chose; to control their own schools, churches, and land systems. They had acquired far-more autonomy than Ireland then enjoyed, and infinitely more than the colonies of France, Spain, or any other country ever had before the next century. And they confidently expected to acquire more control over their destinies as they increased in population and wealth.[17]

The seeds of the American "Revolution" began with the French and Indian War (1754–1763). Prior to this war (called the Seven Years' War in Europe), England and France had engaged in a number of conflicts in Europe and in North America—King William's War (in Europe: War of the League of Augsburg), 1689–1697; Queen Anne's War (in Europe: War of the Spanish Sucession), 1701–1763; and King George's War (in Europe: War of the Austrian Succession), 1744–1748—none of which decisively settled whether the French or English would be dominant in North America. Unlike the previous conflicts, the last war between the French and English in the New World began in America, not Europe. American expansion into what was then considered the West was stopped by the French and their Indian allies, as the French laid claim to the entire area north of the Ohio River. Attempting to wrest a newly built French fort at the site of what is now Pittsburgh (Ft. Duquesne), English colonials and British regulars under General Braddock were severely defeated by French-Canadian militia, which consisted of a few French officers and a large number of Indians. The defeat brought over to the French side most of the Indians of the Northwest, who increased their raids on the colonial settlements. In spite of numerous military setbacks, the situation began to change in favor of the British as the new prime minister, William Pitt, concentrated British efforts in the New World, leaving their Prussian allies to contain the French in Europe. Largely as a result of a naval blockade that prevented the arrival of French reinforcements and the extreme population difference (80,000 widely scattered Frenchmen versus 1,300,000 concentrated Englishmen), the French were defeated outside of Quebec City (1759), virtually terminating the war in the New World. Nevertheless, the war continued in Europe, the West Indies, and the Far East until 1763. In 1763 the Treaty of Paris eliminated the dominance of the French in the New World. With the exception of a few islands, most of the territory became part of the British Empire, and France ceded Louisiana to the Spanish as compensation for their aid and their loss of East and West Florida to Britain.[18]

The significance of this French defeat for the British colonies has been excellently stated by Gipson:

> *This victory not only freed colonials for the first time in the history of the English-speaking people in the New World from dread of the French, their Indian allies, and the Spaniards, but, what is of equal significance, opened up to them the prospect, if given freedom of action, of a vast growth of power and wealth with an amazing westward expansion. Indeed, it is abundantly clear that a continued subordination of the colonies to the government of Great Britain was no longer considered an asset in the eyes of many Americans by 1774, as it had been judged by them to be in 1754, but rather an onerous liability.*[19]

In a similar vein, Gareth Stedman Jones has written, "The white settlers accepted the British mercantile system until they were strong enough to do without it. The purpose of American independence, as John Adams put it in 1774, was the formation of 'an independent empire.'"[20]

But the British government was not about to give the colonies free reign over their destinies. The government began more rigorously to enforce the older decrees and to add new restrictions. In 1761 the navy was ordered to stamp out smuggling in the West Indies trade, and colonial courts were required to issue writs of assistance (open search warrants) to aid in apprehending these "smugglers." The policy of "salutary neglect" was ended.[21] Southern colonial plantation owners needed land speculation in the West to account for their debts to English merchants when tobacco profits, in particular, had declined. (Individual Americans were indebted to English merchants at the outbreak of the Revolution by an estimated £5 million, of which at least five-sixths were debts of southern planters).[22] Land speculation in the West and in Canada was closed to Americans by the Proclamation Acts of 1763 and 1774, based on the arguments that an invasion of the West would cause new wars with the Indians and that the colonists should remain concentrated and consume British products rather than opening up trade outlets down the Mississippi. In 1762 the British government garrisoned ten thousand soldiers in the colonies, ostensibly as protection against Indians on the frontier, but most were stationed far from the frontier. In 1775, to pay for such "protection," the British imposed an internal tax on most paper products, including newspapers, diplomas, and playing cards. This Stamp Act was the first such tax, other than external customs duties, and raised widespread opposition; it was repealed in the following year (1776). A number of duties were levied on certain English manufactures, such as paint, glass, and paper. Although these duties were not out of keeping with the colonial system, they were also strongly opposed and eventually repealed (Townshend Acts, 1767–1770).

As the expectations of Americans rose (as a result of the defeat of the French) and their traditional freedoms were violated, protests increased. One such important incident occurred in Boston. In 1773, the East India Tea Company was granted the sole right to sell 17 million pounds of tea in America, thus driving out of business Americans who carried, imported, or sold into retail channels British tea, or who smuggled foreign tea into the country. The granting of this monopoly was a precedent, one that could not be ignored. After a group of Americans "disguised" as Indians destroyed much of the tea owned by this company, the British blockaded Boston until the city paid for the destroyed tea.

The social movement spread. At first it was disorganized and sporadic and focused on the elimination of such restrictions. But by 1776 secession seemed to many Americans to be the only alternative.

Since both support of and opposition to secession cut across class lines, the American "Revolution" was not a revolution in the class sense (as the later French Revolution was), although many members of the lower classes and those on the frontier perceived a separation from Britain as an opportunity to eliminate disfranchisement, entail and primogeniture, and landlord oppression. Nor was the Revolution an ethnic revolution, if such a term means that a subordinate ethnic group overthrows the government and puts members of its own group into government positions; no American troops ever occupied London. It was also not an ethnic secession movement, as typified by such modern colonial movements as the gaining of independence from France by the Algerians or the secession of Nigeria and Kenya from the British Empire. The Americans were not a subordinate ethnic group; the only truly subordinate groups in the colonies were the blacks and the Indians. If an analogy has to be made, the Revolution was more akin to the recent secession of Rhodesia from British control; but even here there are important differences. The Revolution was a civil war in the sense that one segment of the state society (the empire) was engaged in war with another; within the colonies civil war also existed as Loyalist and Patriot partisans engaged in considerable conflict.[23] It was a unique occurrence: members of a dominant ethnic group, augmented by assimilated members of other European groups, successfully gained independence from a powerful state and in the process added to the development of a new sense of ethnicity.

When the war itself is examined, even from hindsight, it is difficult to see why the secessionist movement was successful. All of the factors that have been stressed previously as significant for success in conflict seem to be absent—centralized social organization, strong commitment, superior technology, and financing. Americans outnumbered the English troops, and the war was fought on familiar territory; these were the only American advantages. Desertion was commonplace, and many commanders never knew how many men they could field for a given battle. Militias refused to fight too far from their home areas. Boorstin says that "men went home just as they were beginning to understand their duties, and it was often necessary to recruit a new army in the face of the enemy."[24] The troops had little discipline (compared with the typical European armies of the day), and disputes about rank were continuous. Money and equipment were in short supply, a condition made worse by the penurious Continental Congress. Very few ships existed, and virtually all of them were eventually sunk or captured. Finally, Loyalist fought Patriot, particularly in the Carolinas.

Virtually all of the major battles—such as Ticonderoga, Monmouth, and Camden—resulted in American defeat. The American victory at Trenton (December 1776) was against Hessian allies of the English, and the victory at King's Mountain in South Carolina (October 1780) was against Loyalist troops. The only major victories against British regulars were at Princeton (January 1777), Saratoga (October 1777), and Yorktown (October 1781), and at Yorktown the French navy and a French army played a major role in the surrender of the British forces.

Why, then, did the British government give up the effort to retain its colonies in North America? Boorstin suggests the following answer:

Today the most persuasive answer is not that the Americans won but that the British lost—or perhaps that they simply gave up, having seen the long-run hopelessness of their cause. The American terrain (together with the colonial dispersion, which meant that there was no jugular vein to be cut by British force) led the British to realize that to subdue America was beyond their means. Within the first four years of the Revolution, every one of the most populous towns—Boston, New York, Philadelphia, and Charleston—had fallen to the British and had been occupied by their regular troops, but always without decisive effect. The American center was everywhere and nowhere—in each man himself. In addition, the French brought crucial aid to the American militia and irregulars, and the spectre of a permanent American alliance with France haunted the British Empire.[25]

In the treaties signed in Paris (1783) between Britain and its various enemies—the colonists, Spain, France, and the Netherlands—Britain ceded Florida to Spain, France obtained Senegal in Africa, and the erstwhile colonies acquired all of the territory bounded by the Mississippi River, Canada, and Florida.

THE DEVELOPMENT OF AMERICAN ETHNICITY

The ethnogenesis of Americans began prior to the war for independence and was intensified by the secessionist effort. Swedish language pockets existed along the Delaware and Dutch language areas were found in the rural Hudson Valley until the nineteenth century, but many individual members of these groups had assimilated into the emerging American group by the time of the Revolution. Since they were widely dispersed and since few new immigrants had come from France after the initial immigration, the French Huguenots had virtually disappeared as a viable ethnic group by 1776. French surnames existed in some places, but many had changed their names. Maldwyn Jones points out that "Paul Revere, for instance was descended from a Huguenot family named Rivoire; James Bowdoin, one of the revolutionary leaders in Massachusetts, was the son of an immigrant named Pierre Baudoin; and John Greenleaf Whittier's mother came from a family of Huguenots who had changed their name from Feuillevert to Greenleaf."[26]

The conflict with Britain intensified this fusion process. In the words of Russel Blaine Nye:

The Revolutionary conflict brought the final phase of colonial unification. In 1776, the term "British American," formerly used by the colonists in their communications with Britain to describe themselves, disappeared with the Declaration of Independence, and along with it the term "United Colonies." "Our great title is Americans," wrote Paine. Noah Webster, twenty years later, reminded his countrymen that "we ought not to consider ourselves as inhabitants of a particular state only, but as Americans."[27]

As to the distinctions between the colonists, the emerging view was stated by Patrick Henry in 1774: "The distinctions between Virginians . . . and

New Englanders are no more. All America is thrown into one mass. I am not a Virginian, but an American."[28]

Not all colonists, however, identified with the term "American." Those individuals loyal to Britain (Loyalists or Tories) continued to perceive themselves as English, or, more generically, as British. But with the success of the Revolution this element of the population was virtually eliminated; ". . . even before the start of major hostilities Loyalists were boycotted, insulted, tarred and feathered, forced off their estates and out of their homes, and suffered the ruin of business or occupation."[29] When major cities eventually fell to American troops and the British were forced to evacuate, thousands of Tories emigrated to Canada, Nova Scotia, London, East Florida, and the British West Indies.[30] Howard Mumford Jones estimates that over seventy-five thousand Loyalists were lost to the country, and the great majority of these were of the upper stratum—doctors, lawyers, merchants, surgeons, printers, apothecaries, military men.[31] At the end of the war, ". . . the several states passed legislation forbidding Tories to practice their professions, teach school, engage in business, collect rent, and so on; and most states banished them and confiscated their real estate and property. . . ."[32] American ethnicity was intensified in this conflict with the Loyalists as well as with the British state.

The ethnogenesis of Americans also developed as a defensive and positive reaction to British prejudice toward colonists during the war and after, in American and in Europe.

Franklin remarked bitterly in 1775 that an American "was understood to be a sort of Yahoo," and noted "the base reflections on American courage, religion, understanding, etc. in which we were treated with utmost contempt." Few Americans were willing to forgive or forget the British general's arrogant sneer that with "a few British regulars" he could "geld all the American males, some by force and the rest with a little coaxing." The British tradition of condescension and rudeness to colonials, well illustrated by Dr. Samuel Johnson's remark that he could "love all mankind, except an American," continued after the war in the remarks of dozens of travelers, reviewers, and commentators, ranging from the ill-tempered poet Tom Moore (who in 1814 found America, "one dull chaos, one unfertile strife") to Sidney Smith's famous gibe of 1818 that "prairies, steamboats, and gristmills" should be the "natural objects for centuries to come" of American culture. James Fenimore Cooper, while traveling on the Continent a few years later, found twenty-three instances in which Englishmen had written insulting remarks after American names on hotel registers.[33]

Few Americans today realize the extent of American antipathy toward the British, and the English in particular, throughout most of the nineteenth century.

In 1783, after independence and prior to unification under the Constitution in 1787, John Jay wrote in the Federalist Papers: "Providence [had] been pleased to give this one connected country to one united people—a people descended from the same ancestors, speaking the same language, professing the same religion, attached to the same principles of government, very similar in their manners and customs. . . ."[34] The statement was intended to help in the achievement of a centralized and sovereign nation-state but was somewhat premature. It is apparent, of course, that this "one united people" did not include the large population of African slaves and those pockets of subordinated Indians.

The eventual acceptance of the Constitution and the formation of the American Republic further enhanced the sense of an American identity. Without this unification it would have been quite probable that, under the loosely organized Articles of Confederation, the members of the states would have reverted to lower levels of ethnicity and considered themselves first and foremost Virginians, New Yorkers, Georgians, etc.

Another factor in American ethnogenesis was the sharp drop in immigration from Europe during the wars between France and England (1793–1814), immigration that could have reinforced the ethnicity of Germans, Dutch, and other Europeans. The British believed that few ships were truly neutral, and stop-and-search practices were common. Because of the hazards of ocean travel, an average of only three thousand immigrants arrived in a given year. This hiatus in immigration enabled a consolidation of those groups already highly integrated by the events of independence. In Maldwyn Jones's words, "the limited scale of immigration during the first generation of national independence enabled those immigrants who had still been imperfectly assimilated at the time of the Revolution to take a long stride toward Americanization. Deprived of their customary accessions from abroad, non-English groups steadily lost in distinctiveness and cohesion. An especially significant sign was the snapping of those linguistic ties which more than anything else had bound together immigrants of common origin and had kept them apart from other Americans."[35]

In summary, the major factors that created a new ethnic group—the Americans—were the conflict with Britain, not only in the war for independence but also in the War of 1812; the elimination of the Tory population; the unification of the states under the Constitution; and the hiatus in immigration from the end of the Revolution to around 1820. Additional factors were the contrast between free whites and slave blacks, "heathens" from a strange land; the Protestant religion of the overwhelming number of Americans and their anti-popeism attitudes; and the conflict with the native inhabitants of the New World, collectively termed Indians, redmen, or just savages.

AMERICAN CULTURE AND CHARACTER

Prior to the mass immigration of the nineteenth and twentieth centuries and the extension of American sovereignty into the Pacific Ocean, the events of America's early history had produced a new ethnic group. This new group was essentially English with a name change. The culture, with a few modifications as a result of the colonial experience, was English. From the English tradition came common law, representative government, the belief in the sanctity of property and contract, the university system, trade unions, small-town government, private schools ("public" in England), and much of what constitutes the Puritan ethic.[36] The English language overwhelmingly dominated; before 1800 little borrowing from other languages had occurred and a few uniquely American phrases had been coined. According to Boorstin:

> *The resistance of the American language during the colonial period to borrowing and the invention of words shows the strength of the forces toward a uniform English speech. Wholesale assimilation of foreign words might have produced a semi-English patois, a pidgin English or a papiamento, like those in the Caribbean or in parts of South East Asia. But this never happened.*[37]

The "only strikingly new character which the English language had acquired in America was its uniformity."[38] The numerous dialect variations found within England diminished in the colonies. A writer in 1770 emphasized this uniformity:

> *The colonists are composed of adventurers, not only from every district of Great Britain and Ireland, but from almost every other European government. . . . Is it not, therefore, reasonable to suppose that the English language must be greatly corrupted by such a strange intermixture of various nations? The reverse is, however, true. The language of the immediate descendants of such a promiscuous ancestry is perfectly uniform and unadulterated; nor has it borrowed any provincial, or national accent, from its British or foreign parentage.*[39]

Later, when Americans were exposed to numerous other ethnic groups, a number of foreign words were incorporated into a changing American language. In addition, new words were coined that more clearly separated the American language from its English base. American, like Australian, has become different from the parent language in several respects, and this more distinctive tongue with the regional dialects that have developed is one more factor in the creation of an American ethnicity.*

Another major source of American culture and language, besides the

---

Daniel Boorstin has compiled a list of new American words and phrases and foreign language borrowings. Originating at different times and different places, most of the following were Americanisms by 1850: to cave in, to flare up, to flunk out, to fork over, to hold on, to stave off, to take on, to tote, to yank, to corner (a market), to boost, to peter out, to face the music, to engineer, to itemize, to fly off the handle, to knuckle under, to get the drop on, to strike it rich, to dress fit to kill, to handle without gloves, to stay on the fence, to get the hang of it, skedaddle, hunky-dory, rambunctious, slam-bang, kerflop (kerthump, kersplash, kerchunk), humbug, loafer, caucus, lynch, help (servants), squatter, rock (stone), OK, jigger, barroom, saloon, slim (as in slim chance), plumb crazy, horse sense, true-blue, know-how, knock-down and drag-out, in cahoots, a land-office business, set 'em up, it's not my funeral, chip on his shoulder, pull the wool over her eyes, barking up the wrong tree, and pan out well.

British base and the borrowings from other ethnic groups that became incorporated into the society of the United States, was the eighteenth- and nineteenth-century preoccupation with the Roman and Greek classical tradition. A large number of American public buildings have been built in the style of Greek or Roman temples. Classical place names have been given to many towns and villages—for example, Ithaca, Rome, Troy, Syracuse, Utica, Alexandria, Augusta, and Athens. A few states—such as Pennsylvania, Virginia, and Georgia—are Latin derivatives. The government of the United States is a republic (*respublica*), headed by a president (*praesidens*); the legislature is a congress (*congressus*) and the upper body is a senate (*senatus*); the government meets in a capitol, a term that originally designated a temple on a hill; Federalist and Republican are Latin derivatives, while Democratic comes from the Greek; the great seal of the United States depicts an eagle (although the Roman eagle was not the American bald eagle), and includes several Latin phrases: *E pluribus unum, Annuit coeptis,* and *Novus ordo seclorum*. American coins have been stamped with depictions of eagles (symbol of ancient Rome), the Roman fasces (double axe and reeds, which together were symbolic of Roman power), goddesses, and presidents in classical Roman profile. Statues of American political leaders in the nineteenth century were often in imitation of Romans, complete with toga, sandals, and laurel wreath. George Washington has been depicted wearing a Roman cloak and carrying the fasces (1789), as a Roman general seated in a chair with sword underfoot and reading from stone law tablets (1815), and seated with toga, a sheathed sword, and his finger pointing to heaven (1841).[40] This Roman influence was not accidental. Many writers and interpreters of the American scene, past and present, have compared the Americans to the Romans as great assimilators, engineers and builders, astute politicians, empire builders, pragmatists, and stoics.

What does constitute American character? Are Americans the modern Romans? Is it possible to ascertain a number of values, beliefs, and personality traits that are predominantly subscribed to or internalized by ethnic Americans? If it is understood that no single individual must necessarily adhere to the total number of such elements, that some individuals may not subscribe to any of these traits, and that individuals do not necessarily practice what they preach, it is still possible to come up with a number of traits or elements that are typically American. In fact, there is a relatively wide consensus on what constitutes the American character, not only

---

Notable borrowings (without acknowledgment as to copyrights) have been: from the French—bayou, cache, chute, rendezvous, crevasse, prairie, rapids, butte, depot, picayune, sashay, shanty; from the Spanish—bronco, canyon, calaboose, cinch, corral, adobe, alfalfa, bonanza, fiesta, frijole, lariat, lasso, loco, mesa, mustang, padre, patio, plaza, pronto, rodeo, savvy (from sabe), sierra, sombrero, stampede, vamoose, vigilante; from the German—kindergarten, nix, ouch, loaf, bum, bub, dumb, fresh (impertinent), shyster, lager, bock, stein, sauerbraten, sauerkraut; and from the Indians hundreds of place names, such as Illinois, Omaha, Miami, Biloxi, and Mississippi (The Americans: The National Experience [New York: Vintage Books, 1965], pp. 281–92).

among American writers but also among foreign visitors to the United States.

The historian John D. Hicks has summarized the views of a number of foreigners who traveled in the United States in the early nineteenth century. To these visitors, Americans seemed provincial because they knew little and cared even less about the world outside of the United States. They were inclined to be boastful about their country, and patriotism was a national obsession. To these visitors, the American was technically quite ingenious, a jack-of-all-trades who seemingly could master any problem. "The American practice of moving houses, for example, struck foreigners with peculiar force. Houses in Europe usually stayed where they were built; in America one might meet them coming down the street."[41] American manners were somewhat crude by European standards, and even in this early period of the country foreign visitors were fascinated and sometimes appalled by the Americans' "quick lunch" and their habit of bolting their food. Americans seemed to be restless, continuously on the move, forever in a hurry, and resentful of delays. The were identified as highly optimistic about the future, not impressed by efforts at aristocratic demeanor, and far more likely than Europeans to treat all women, regardless of class, with respect and courtesy. Individual freedom, individual effort, and pride in what had been accomplished were also major traits, in the observations of the travelers.[42]

In the opinion of Max Lerner, writing in the 1950s, Americans* are mobile, restless, this-worldly as opposed to other-worldly, more secular than sacred, and optimistic. Americans believe in progress, have a sharp sense of time and how to use time (don't waste it, save it), respect material success and technical skills, believe in whatever can be touched, grasped, and measured, and have a "taste for comfort and a belief that the means, if not the goal, of life are found in a higher living standard."[43]

In 1949 Ralph Barton Perry[44] delineated what he perceived to be the major elements of American character. Individualism seemed to be the most pronounced trait; in Perry's view, however, this individualism is more of a "collective individualism." That is, the individual is not isolated or solitary but part of cooperative collective efforts; yet within the collectivity the individual is distinct, not just part of the herd. According to Perry, Americans

*Both Lerner and Perry seem compelled to include all Americans (nationality) in their unit of analysis of character traits, even though such traits do not seem to be applicable, particularly in the nineteenth century, to Mexican-Americans, Indian-Americans, Italian-Americans, Irish-Americans, or Black-Americans, for example. Today, of course, many members of these minorities, particularly in the middle class, do share many of these elements. However, this present circumstance is probably indicative of their acculturation and integration into the dominant American mainstream. In the nineteenth century, cultural differentiation between the minorities and the majority was far greater than today. If one is to speak of the acculturation or the assimilation of minorities into American society, one must have a standard of comparison—that is, some culture that minorities are moving toward and an idea of which elements are being "borrowed" from the dominant group while being lost in the minority cultures. The position here is that these ethnic American (as opposed to national American) traits plus the utilization of the American language are the bench marks in the measurement of the extent of acculturation.

judge and expect to be judged by the standard of success, with a major emphasis on material success. Americans value bigness—big mountains, big buildings, big populations, big volumes of production. They also value competition and industry, and even losers expect and are expected to win somewhere, someday. Americans "feel themselves to be on the march; toward precisely what is not always clear, but anyway toward something bigger and better."[45] Perry quotes an engineer working on the Grand Coulee Dam who is reported to have said, "If a hard mountain gets in the way, move it. If it's just a soft mountain, freeze the darn thing, forget it, and keep on going."[46] Perry identifies another trait that has been observed by many (and made part of an extensive analysis of character by the social psychologist Kurt Lewin)—Americans have open personalities; they expose to total strangers or to people of short acquaintance aspects of themselves that Europeans conceive to be intimacies:

The American is often found distasteful because he is disposed instantly, or on short acquaintance, to disclose not only his name, but his business and his biography. He gives himself away—prematurely, it is felt. He does not wait to assure himself that his confidences are desired; nor does he insist on reciprocity. But that which underlies this trait, intrusive as it may sometimes be, is the fact that the American has nothing to conceal, and assumes that this is equally the case with others. There is a basic trust and a desire to establish a friendly atmosphere. This expresses not only a repugnance to silence and aloofness, but a desire to put the other man at his ease. The American impulse is to introduce oneself to everybody and everybody to everybody else, and so include everybody in the group of social intercourse.[47]

Perry also perceives that Americans have a tendency toward uniformity. This has been accentuated by mass communication in today's world, but it seems to be "an old and persistent American trait."[48] In 1837 James Fenimore Cooper stated that "the American ever seems ready to resign his own opinion to that which is *made to seem* to be the opinion of the public."[49]

In 1941 Lee Coleman conducted a survey of the literature from the earliest period in American history to 1940 and found a core of agreement about American values, although numerous other values were also found. His core consisted of disregard for the law and an emphasis on action, associational activity, democracy, equality as a fact and as a right, practicality, uniformity and conformity, prosperity, puritanism, religion, freedom of the individual, and local government.[50]

In his examination of American society the sociologist Robin Williams emphasized the following traits: stress on activity and work, external conformity, value placed on achievement and success, a tendency to see the world in moral terms, efficiency, humanitarianism, value placed on material comfort, belief in progress, avowal of equality, belief in racism and group superiority, patriotism, dignity, value placed on bigness (big means better), work as an end in itself, generosity, identification with the underdog, practicality (impractical is an American curse-word) and active control of the environment.[51]

Although there is some disagreement among these writers and authors, or a difference in emphasis, it does seem possible to identify some major traits of the American character that were present in the past and continue to exist today, although, perhaps, in a somewhat diluted form as a result of affluence. At the risk of stereotyping, we may say that the American character tends to be:

1. activistic; ready to coerce nature; ready to get to the heart of the matter
2. practical or pragmatic
3. competitive
4. individualistic, yet, paradoxically, valuing external conformity
5. Calvinistic and democratic, adhering to values of progress, hard work, material success, bigness, democracy, accomplishment, freedom, and equality
6. optimistic
7. religious (but believing that God helps those who help themselves and that the specifics of religion are up to the individual)
8. open and gregarious
9. patriotic, ethnocentric, and racist
10. preoccupied with time
11. prone toward the technological

Two jokes illustrating American character in contrast to that of other ethnics may not be totally irrelevant. Four individuals of different ethnic backgrounds (English, American, German, and French) were cast upon a deserted island. The Frenchman went looking for grapes, the German drew up a list of rules, the American started to build a shelter, and the Englishman stood around waiting to be introduced. Four individuals of the same ethnic statuses were instructed to write a book on elephants. The Frenchman wrote *Sex Habits of the Elephant*, the German wrote a five-volume study entitled *The African Elephant and Its Habitat*, the Englishman titled his work *Hunting Elephants in the British Empire*, and the American's volume was called *How to Build Bigger and Better Elephants*.

THE AMERICAN EMPIRE

With independence from Britain and unification under the Constitution, the United States began to expand to the west, to the north, and to the south as thousands of Americans, aided by members of other ethnic groups, spread out of the territorial boundaries of the United States established in the Paris Treaty of 1783. At the forefront of the migration to the west were settlers, miners, and other adventurers, who in some cases followed and in other cases preceded the American army. In the path of this expansion stood numerous Indian ethnic groups, some nomadic and some sedentary agriculturalists, all obstacles to be removed.

Expansion into Canada, where thousands of displaced Loyalists had fled after the Revolution, was stopped by the military action of Canadian settlers and the British army in the War of 1812. Florida was purchased from Spain in 1819 after American infiltration and military action under Andrew Jackson made Spanish control quite tenuous. Napoleon, having recently acquired a huge section of land west of the Mississippi from Spain, turned around and sold it to the United States government. In neither case were the Indian groups consulted as to ownership rights. The Mexican government encouraged Americans to settle in its northern province of Texas, and the American settlers returned this favor by seceding. Ostensibly disputing with Mexico over the border of the newly annexed state of Texas, but covertly desiring California, American troops invaded Mexico between 1846 and 1848, captured Mexico City, and took away approximately one-half of its territory, again, a territorial claim made without consulting the resident Indians, who disputed it.

In the process of expansion into the lands acquired from France by purchase and from Mexico by conquest, various Indian ethnic groups were defeated or coerced into signing treaties guaranteeing them special reserves of land. Virtually all of the treaties were eventually violated by the Americans and European immigrant group members, as Indian "reserved" land became valuable.

Throughout the expansion, Black-Americans were used to do many of the most difficult labor tasks, and Chinese and Irish were used as railroad builders. Over 30 million immigrants from virtually every society in Europe entered the lower stratum, primarily, but rapidly became more proportionally distributed throughout the class system as they took advantage of this expanding land of opportunity.

With the purchase of Oregon territory from the British, the "internal expansion" of the United States was completed. This internal expansion is rarely treated in the history textbooks as imperialism. One reason for such an oversight has to be racism. The aboriginal inhabitants, widely dispersed as they were, have not been considered conquered ethnic groups. Imperialism, to many scholars, has meant the conquest and occupation of civilized and densely populated state-societies, a meaning which ignores the conquests of folk peoples by the more traditionally defined empire societies. The Mexican conquest has also been overlooked as imperialism. Because a payment was made to the Mexican government for the acquired territory (a payment under duress), that territory has been treated as an annexation by purchase.

Another factor, perhaps, in ignoring the empire quality of this internal expansion is the very idea of "internal." For many Americans, America has seemed to have a territorial "essence," to be a territory just waiting to be filled up. In the nineteenth century the idea of "sea to sea" was not uncommon, even before the war with Mexico, and for some the territorial "essence" included Mexico and Canada. In the twentieth century the outline of the continental United States is familiar to all Americans. This outline seems to have been predestined; hence, an "internal" expansion to occupy its essential size and shape seems to have been not only justified but necessary.

Territorial expansion and the subordination of new peoples continued into areas not contiguous with the American territorial essence. In 1867 William Seward, the secretary of state, purchased Alaska, a territory he regarded as the northern flank in his aim to dominate the Pacific. Another aboriginal people, the Eskimo, became a subordinate group with this purchase. American sugar planters staged a revolution in Hawaii in 1893, deposed Queen Liliuokalani, and asked to be admitted into the Union (the admission took place in 1898). In the Spanish-American War of 1898 other island territories were added—Cuba, the Philippines, and Puerto Rico. The Pacific and the Carribean had become American lakes and validated Alexis de Tocqueville's prophetic words of an earlier period: "When I contemplate the ardor with which the Anglo-Americans prosecute commerce, the advantages which aid them, and the success of their undertakings, I cannot help believing that they will one day become the foremost maritime power of the globe. They are born to rule the seas, as the Romans were to conquer the globe."[52]

In 1935 the editors of *Fortune* wrote:

It is generally supposed that the American military ideal is peace. But unfortunately for this highschool classic, the U.S. Army, since 1776, has filched more square miles of the earth by sheer military conquest than any other army in the world, except only that of Great Britain. And as between Great Britain and the U.S. it has been a close race, Britain having conquered something over 3,500,000 square miles since that date, and the U.S. (if one includes wresting the Louisiana Purchase from the Indians) something over 3,100,000. The English-speaking people have done themselves proud in this regard.[53]

As for the political structure of the expanding empire, the Americans invented a novel formula for growth—after a territory has achieved a certain population size, admit it as a state equal to the others.

The venerable theory according to which colonies were founded for the benefit of the mother country, the doctrine according to which they were to remain subordinated, was thrown aside; a new form of expansionism was substituted, one which provided for organic growth, for the birth of new living cells to be grafted onto the main body politic, of which they became part and parcel. . . . with the temporary excep-

tion of the Philippines, American expansion shed the "colonial" coloration typical of European-style expansion; territorial acquisitions and possessions were not mere garments worn for the benefit of the mother country but became part of the flesh and blood of the United States.[54]

This view of organic growth must be tempered, however, with the realization that each territory was treated as a colony by the central government and the eastern economic establishment until it was admitted as a state. And there are some Westerners who still believe that the western United States is an economic colony of the East.

SUMMARY

As early as 1783, when the war for independence had ended, and certainly by 1820, a new ethnic group had come into existence—the Americans. This ethnic group was a fusion of a number of white Protestant European ethnic groups: the English, Scots, Welsh, Scotch-Irish, Irish, Germans, Dutch, French, and Swedes. Thirteen colonies of the British Empire in the New World formed the environment in which this ethnogenesis took place. The English element predominated in language, government and law, religion, and numerous customs and traditions.

Probably the most important factor in the formation of the American ethnic group was the conflict with Britain. After the British and colonial armies defeated the French, the colonies were no longer hemmed in on the eastern seaboard. However, the British mercantile system, which had previously given the colonists advantages, now became a system of liabilities hindering American expansion. As the government in London began to enforce old decrees and to place new restrictions on American economic and political activity, the conflict between the colonies and Britain intensified. By 1776, secession seemed to be the only answer for a majority of the "British" colonists. With the aid of the French, independence was accomplished by 1783. The conflict with England intensified the colonists' sense of being different from the mother country, aiding the formation of an American ethnicity, and the military success created a new country under the control of a dominant group.

A number of other factors contributed to the fusion of the white Protestant Europeans. A great majority of the colonists who still defined themselves as English or British were forced, through discrimination, to leave the new country. A constitution was written, unifying a loose federation of virtually sovereign states into one political system. Immigration from Europe dropped significantly between 1790 and 1820, allowing for the ethnic mix to gel. War with Britain from 1812 to 1814 further emphasized the differences between "American" and British. The American language became more distinctive, moving away from English accents and acquiring new words and phrases. A preoccupation with ancient Greece and Rome added other cultural elements to an American culture and widened the cultural gap between England and the United States. The contrasting factors of the "redmen" on the frontier, the subordinate Indians within the settled territory, and the presence of slaves from pagan Africa also contributed to the development of a distinctively American culture. Although black pockets of European ethnicity still remained, by 1820 the great majority of citizens of the new country were subscribing to a new ethnicity—American; only the racial groups were excluded from membership.

As a result of these factors and the problems of coping with an expanding frontier, ethnic Americans developed a number of distinctive character traits, including activism, pragmatism, individualism, optimism, ethnocentrism, and adherence to such values as technology, bigness, equality, material success, and hard work. And in their relationships with the subordinate groups in their midst, the Americans became one of the most racist ethnic groups in human history.

The Americans, after 1783, expanded through conquest and annexation to the Pacific Ocean, were stopped in their invasion of Canada, but by 1900 had added several island territories to the American Empire. To settle the newly acquired and sparsely inhabited territories, and to supply cheap labor for a burgeoning industrial capitalism, the United States encouraged immigration from Europe, Canada, and Asia. These immigrants became citizens of the United States and acquired an

American nationality, *but they retained a foreign* ethnicity. *In time, many of their descendants, particularly those from northern Europe but also those from southern Europe, acquired an American ethnicity as well as an American nationality.*

There were never any "Anglos" or "Saxons" in this country as identifiable ethnic groups, much less any "WASPs." There was, *however, an American ethnic group that was distinct from all the hyphenated groups. Failure to understand the concept of American ethnicity as distinct from American nationality has led to the myth of the nonethnic majority and the ethnic minorities. The "we are all Americans" belief masks the dominance of the ethnic Americans over all of the other groups that ever received a hyphen.*

7

THE ORIGINS OF SUBORDINATE GROUPS
IN THE UNITED STATES

INTRODUCTION

Groups from other societies have become incorporated into American society in a dominant-subordinate relationship by all of the possible processes—conquest, immigration, enslavement, and annexation. Conflict is of course intrinsically related to conquest and enslavement, but it was also found in the reasons for the emigration of some of the European groups, in the reception of some of the immigrants when they arrived, and in the events surrounding American annexation of certain territories. Nineteenth-century America had all of the characteristics of an empire society.

THE INDIANS

Ethnic Divisions and Indian Culture

Prior to European contact with the New World, an estimated 850,000 to 1 million Indians occupied the area now called the United States (and between 15 and 20 million occupied all of North and South America). The term "Indian," as everybody knows, was applied to the diverse groups of the New World by a lost Italian who thought he had reached India. As such, it was a racial term classifying together thousands of ethnic groups, some food gatherers and hunters, some advanced horticultural peoples, and other members of preindustrial state-societies. In the "United States" alone, an estimated 200 to 250 ethnic groups existed (estimates vary because of different levels of ethnicity; for example, Apaches may be counted as one group or as six), and there were at least 200 mutually unintelligible languages among the Indians north of Mexico.[1] Table 7-1 lists the major ethnic groups in what is now the United States according to their geographical area around the time of their first contacts with whites.

Despite the sociocultural differences among these various ethnic groups, most of them shared a number of general characteristics that contrasted with European characteristics. A rather common conception was that humans were part of nature, which was an integrated totality including gods, spirits, animals, vegetation, and human beings, alive and dead. In this view humans did not stand in a "mind-object" relationship to nature or in opposition to nature, as in the European world view. Competition existed between groups, but there was a strong emphasis on sharing and cooperation within the groups. Wars between groups lacked most of the elements of European wars—standing armies, protracted sieges, efforts at conquest, large numbers of casualties. Indian wars were more in the form of raids to acquire booty, to protect tribal hunting grounds, or to rectify some dishonor.[2] Private property was de-emphasized or nonexistent, and land was generally the common property of the tribe. Although chiefs and medicine men existed as leaders, such men could not speak for the entire tribe without consultation with and the agreement of members. Indian groups were far more democratic, in this respect, than Europeans could understand.[3] These were the common characteristics at an abstract level. The more specific differences, however, were far more important to the various groups, and these, coupled with traditional animosities, prevented the concept of Indian as ethnic from developing even after all groups were subordinated by conquest or by the threat of starvation.

The Indian Wars

At the risk of overgeneralizing and ignoring important variations, we can cite a number of general characteristics of the violent conflict between whites and Indians in America:

1. White ethnic group members acquired unity *as whites* in the conflict with Indians, a unity not even approximated by the Indian tribes. Josephy comments on this point:

> *In the Western Hemisphere, Indians, to the whites, were all the same, and the newcomers disagreed among themselves only over the extent to which the native populations differed from, or seemed to be inferior to, Europeans. On their part, the Indians, with rare exceptions, had no such unifying influence nor any conception of being involved in a total conflict of one race against another. Their own centuries-old differences, rivalries, feuds, and jealousies were readily discernible to the white men, who facilitated their own conquests by pitting one native group against another. . . . Many Indians, for various motives, even welcomed white newcomers and brought eventual ruin on themselves by the use they made of the whites. In repeated instances native leaders who were unable to foresee the ultimate*

173

Table 7.1

Major Indian Ethnic Groups in the United States

The following is a distribution of the major Indian ethnic groups in what is now the United States at about the time they made contact with whites. In cases where an Indian name is generic (denoting a higher level of ethnicity), subdivisions are given in parentheses. Many of these groups overlapped the geographical areas cited.

New England
Pennacook, Nipmuc, Penobscot, Passamaquoddy, Massachuset, Shinnecok, Wampanoag, Nauset, Niantic, Narraganset, Pequot, Mohican, Mohegan, Wappinger, Abnaki

New York, Pennsylvania, Ohio
Erie, Susquehannock, Huron, Tionotatis, Wyandotte, Iroquois (Mohawk, Onondaga, Cayuga, Oneida, Seneca), Manhatte

Delaware, Virginia
Delaware, Nanticoke, Pamunkey, Chicahominy, Mattapony, Saponis, Nottaway, Conoys, Pamlico, Powhattan, Shawnee, Monacans, Catawbas, Tutelo, Tuscarora, Susquehanna

Michigan, Indiana, Illinois, Iowa
Sauk, Fox, Potawatomi, Ottawa, Illinois, Moneton, Kickapoo, Iowa, Ojibwa (or Chippewa), Winnebago, Kaskaskia, Peoria, Miami, Weas, Piankashaw

Minnesota, Wisconsin
Santee (or Eastern) Sioux (Mdewakanton, Sisseton, Wahpekute, Wahpeton), Menominee

Carolinas, Georgia
Lumbee, Cherokee, Tuscarora, Hitchitis, Yuchis, Yamasee, Muskogis (called Creek by English), Pamlico

Florida
Seminole, Apalachee, Nimucua, Miccosukee

Louisiana, Alabama, Mississippi
Tunica, Chitimacha, Natchez, Alabama, Mobile, Choctaw, Chickasaw, Houma, Biloxi

Arkansas, Texas
Arkansas, Quapaw, Caddo, Kichais, Waco, Comanche (Yamparika, Kotsoleka, Nakoni, Kwahadi, Penateka), Tawaconi, Tonkawas

Kansas, Nebraska, Colorado, Missouri, Wyoming
Osage, Missouri, Kansas, Otos, Omaha, Ponca, Pawnee, Arapaho, Cheyenne, Kiowa, Ute, Oglala Sioux

Dakotas, Montana
Crow, Shoshoni, Teton Sioux (Oglala, Brule, Hunkpapa, Miniconjou, Sans Arc, Two Kettle, Blackfoot), Prairie Sioux (Yankton, Yanktonai), Mandan, Hidastas

California
Hupas, Yurok, Yaqui, Pomo, Chumash, Yokut, Miwok, Panamint, Tolowa, Mattole, Wiyot, Karok, Shasta, Yanas, Salinan, Achomawis, Atsugewis, Patwin, Maidus, Miwok, Wintun, Costanoan, Tubatulabal, Cahuilla, Serrano, Gabrielino, Fernandeno, Juaneno, Nicoleno, Luiseno

Washington, Oregon, Idaho
Chinookan, Salish, Nez Perce, Suquamish, Spokane, Klamath, Modoc, Klikitat, Yakima, Palouse, Walla Walla, Umatilla, Kusa, Tlingit, Tillamook, Killamucks, Clatsops

Table 7.1 (continued)

Nevada, Utah
Paviotso, Paiute, Ute, Gosiute, Chemehuevis, Monos, Kawiisus, Panamint, Washos
New Mexico, Arizona
Hopi, Zuni, Mohave, Navaho, Yuma, Pimas, Yavapais, Papago, Apache (Mescalero, Chiricahua, Gila, Pinal, Aravaipa, Jicarilla), Havasupais, Cocopas, Chemehuevis, Halchidhomas, Maricopas, Pueblo (Picuris, Taos, Nambe, Jemez, Acoma, Laguna, Chochiti, Zia)

> *consequences appealed for white help against rival chiefs and bands; others be-*
> *came slave catchers, tribute collectors, fur traders, petty administrators, overseers*
> *over other Indians, and mercenary fighters in the employ of whites, and in the traffic*
> *of European arms and manufactured goods they destroyed other Indian groups*
> *with relish.*[4]

Similarly, Robert Utley, in his books on the American army and the Indian wars, has written: "They viewed themselves not as Indians, but as Sioux or Nez Perce or Apache. They fought one another more often and more violently than they fought the whites. Alliances sometimes brought them together against an enemy, red or white, but not for long. Never did the perception of a fatal threat to the race overcome the traditional rivalry and particularism of tribes to inspire Indian resistance rather than simply tribal resistance."[5]

2. The pattern of conflict took the following general form: infiltration by white civilians into Indian territory, conflict between civilians and Indians and between the army and the Indians, conflict resolution in the form of a treaty guaranteeing the territorial integrity of the Indian groups in some reserve, violation of the treaty by civilian infiltration and then the United States government as the reserved lands became valuable, conflict, resettlement of Indians in different areas with treaty guarantees or concentration of Indians in the same area. This pattern followed the path of white settlement in the following order: expansion within the original thirteen colonies, expansion to the Mississippi River, the traveling *through* the Midwest (the Great American Desert) to settlement in Texas and the Pacific coastal areas, settlement of the Great Plains or the Midwest, settlement in the arid lands of Arizona and New Mexico.

Josephy elaborates on this general pattern:

> *Every means and method was utilized in the long effort to dispossess the Indian. In*
> *some areas, land was brought or traded fairly; elsewhere intrigue, deception, legal*
> *chicanery, or outright confiscation were the rule. If the Indians resisted, militias*
> *with superior arms or organized troop units of the governments involved usually*
> *came to the assistance of the settlers. Treaties of peace invariably wrung from the*
> *defeated Indians the land the settlers had wanted. The pattern had variations, and*

175

on occasion the Indians won temporarily or were able to compromise or restrain white aggression long enough to bargain for retention of part of their homelands as preserves.[6]

The treaties were based upon the assumption that a chief could speak for his entire group and that the entire group would therefore be bound by the stipulations of the treaty. Chiefs were coerced or bribed to give up tribal territories and in some cases to lead their people hundreds of miles to some alien and unwanted section, a reserve to be theirs "as long as the grass shall grow and the waters shall run." Given the nature of Indian social organization, many younger braves often refused to accept such terms and would continue to fight, a protraction of the conflict that would end up with the same results. "Up to 1868, nearly four hundred treaties had been signed by the United States government with various Indian groups, and scarcely a one had remained unbroken."[7]

Land and mineral resources led Americans and members of European ethnic groups into tribal territories, thus necessitating the breaking of the treaties, often on the grounds that Indian war parties were the initial abrogaters of the treaty. This assumption always neglected the fact that white intrusions prompted the Indian war parties.

3. Conflict between whites and Indians primarily took the form of guerrilla tactics by Indians against white settlements, isolated homesteads, and frontier outposts and the army's use of scattered forts along the expanding frontier to offer refuge to civilians and to serve as a base of offensive operations into Indian territory.

With few exceptions, most Indian war parties were small, ranging from five to thirty men under the loose leadership of any warrior with sufficient prestige to organize such a party.[8] Given the size of most of the bands and tribes and their war parties, casualties had serious consequences; hence, large-scale confrontations were only possible through tribal alliances, and even then most would be avoided. The Indians also avoided close combat unless victory was assured or their families were endangered. Hit-and-run tactics were well suited to the Indians' style. Because they knew the terrain far better than their enemies did, they were able to carry out effective ambushes and throw off their pursuers. By ranging far and wide with smaller parties, Indians could raise havoc and create panic far beyond what their numbers might otherwise accomplish. For the troopers, the Indians' reluctance to engage in armed confrontation made necessary long and arduous efforts at pursuit, with only occasional skirmishes. One army officer observed that "in a campaign against Indians, the front is all around, and the rear is nowhere." Another officer described the typical experience of war on the plains: "We travelled through the country, broke down our men, killed our horses, and returned as ignorant of the whereabouts of Mr. Sanico [a Comanche chief] as when we started." An Indian war was a "chapter of accidents."[9]

From the colonial period throughout the Indian wars in the Far West and the Plains, the army made use of forts, quite similar to those which the Romans used in Germania.* Civilians on the fringes of settlement demanded these reassuring structures, and in many areas of hostile Indian concentration their use as a defensive measure was a necessity. When warfare moved to the Plains and the Southwest, most military strategists favored the use of roving units of cavalry to ascertain the enemy's whereabouts and to attack his settlements. Certainly the emergence from the fort of a large body of mounted troops and its movement through Indian lands to show the flag were highly ineffective. Every Indian within miles would know of its coming, and settlements were easily and rapidly moved to avoid detection. Nevertheless, settlers demanded the forts, and Washington complied.[10]

By 1850, most tribes had treaty arrangements with the government, and the forts were utilized as encampments of "policemen" rather than of military conquerors. At midcentury the task of soldiers in the forts consisted primarily of rounding up "hostiles" (individuals and bands acting on their own) and ascertaining "criminal" liabilities.[11] However, from the late 1850s until the end of the Indian wars, the forts were utilized as bases of operation in "total war." As a result of pressure from western settlers and the army's own frustrations at being a policeman, a new policy based upon earlier precedents was developed. "If a tribe or band could not keep its members from raiding white people . . . then the whole group should be held responsible and punished accordingly."[12] Such a policy produced, by definition, a much larger "enemy" that could be conquered rather than just policed. After the Civil War, the army launched winter campaigns from the forts; in winter the Indian was most vulnerable. Following the successful tactics of Philip Sheridan and William T. Sherman in total war against the South, the army made no distinction between combatant and noncombatant. Food, clothing, and shelter were destroyed, animals were seized, and lands were devastated, leaving the Indians the option of surrendering or starving. Although the killing of women and children was never a policy of the army, such incidents did occur in the total-war campaigns. Total-war tactics were effective and demoralizing and eventually brought the Indian wars to an end in the 1880s. The ecological effect of these wars was devastating. The buffalo of the Plains, which was essential for Indian survival, was almost totally and deliberately eliminated. An estimated 13 million bison existed on the plains in 1867; by 1883 there were only two hundred left. With their source of shelter and food gone, Indians had no recourse but to accept the handout of rations on their reservations.

4. Those white civilians closest to the conflict were generally in favor of Indian extermination or, at the very least, group punishment for the hostile

---

*Forty-four forts and military posts alone were built in Apache territory; some were only used one or two years before they were closed down.

actions of any individuals or bands; whites much farther removed were more sympathetic to the Indian plight and in opposition to white injustices. The soldiers were caught in the middle of these differing expectations of their role; moreover, the soldiers had great respect for the Indian warrior from a military point of view.

"A good Indian is a dead Indian" was a widely held norm by most frontier civilians and by some army personnel in any period of the lengthy Indian wars. The killing of Indian children on the grounds that "nits breed lice" was also common. The major atrocities against Indian encampments and individuals were committed by civilians or by civilian militias. A miner in Arizona wrote:

> No treaty or flag of truce is too sacred to be disregarded, no weapon too cruel or cowardly to be used or recommended by Americans. If it is said that the Indians are treacherous and cruel, scalping and torturing their prisoners, it may be answered that there is no treachery and no cruelty left unemployed by the whites. Poisoning with strychnine, the wilful dissemination of small pox; and the possession of bridles braided with the hair of scalped victims and decorated with teeth knocked from the jaws of living women—these are heroic facts among many of our frontiersmen. [13]

Frontier newspapers reflected public opinion about Indians. After the Sand Creek Massacre in Colorado, the *Rocky Mountain News* (December 17, 1864) acclaimed the "heroes" (a hundred Indian scalps had been displayed in a local theater).[14] In 1876 the *Arizona Citizen* editorialized that "the kind of war needed for the Chiricahua Apaches is steady, unrelenting, hopeless, and undiscriminating war, slaying men, women, and children . . . until every valley . . . shall send to high heaven the grateful incense of festering and rotting Chiricahuas."[15]

People who held such views were, of course, "prejudiced" (what a weak and insipid term in such contexts). But such conceptions were hardly "irrational" or due to "inadequate socialization." Indians made few distinctions among whites in their raiding parties and committed untold atrocities themselves, as the accounts of pioneers make quite clear. To say that they were justified in their actions because of the invasion of their homelands and because of the actions of whites against them is a rational statement to make in hindsight or from the comforts of the settled East. But for those actually engaged in violent conflict, extreme categorical antipathy was understandable in both camps and even necessary for survival as conflict escalated. Such extreme racism was normative on the frontier, and those who held nonracist views (the "Indian-lovers") were often subjected to extreme sanctions (for example, the miner who gave his views on white atrocities in Arizona was beaten and driven out of Arizona).

Those far removed from the conflict were often appalled by the actions of the Westerners as reported in the eastern papers. Numerous groups demanded justice and fair play. Between the Westerners and the Easterners the army was placed in the impossible situation of "damned if we do and damned if we don't." Many officers and men, though hardly believers in the brotherhood of man, saw the Indian as "degraded and inferior but still a human being upon whom a great wrong was being afflicted." The soldiers, "wrestling with their own consciences, buffeted by extremes of opinion, had to fight an enemy with whom they sympathized in wars provoked by their own countrymen."[16]

In summary, the following general characteristics of white-Indian conflict existed over a 250-year period: white unity against red disunity; treaty making and treaty violation; guerrilla tactics against forts and military expeditions from the forts; and clashes of opinion between those whites engaged in the conflict and those removed from it, with the army caught in the middle.

Major Battles

Although most of the encounters between white and red were skirmishes between soldiers and bands of Indians or between raiding parties of Indians and white settlers, there were several major battles and key events involving wholesale transportation of Indians. For the sake of brevity, these battles and major events will be itemized and briefly described, beginning with the first major encounter following American independence from the British Empire.

1. *The Battle of Fallen Timbers, 1794.* After independence, the British refused to give up several forts in the Great Lakes area. The Indians in the region supported the British, since British forts offered protection from the land-hungry Americans. General Anthony Wayne and an army of two thousand advanced into the area and met an approximately equal number of Indians from various groups— Shawnee, Ottawa, Chippewa, Miami, Sauk, Fox, and Potawotami—along with seventy Canadian regulars. In forty minutes the battle, fought on a field of fallen timbers, eliminated Indian resistance in the "Northwest."[17]

2. *Removal of the Great Lakes Indians.* With authorization by President Thomas Jefferson and implementation by government officials headed by William Henry Harrison, governor of the Indiana territory, over 48 million acres of Indian lands were taken by white settlers by 1809, and numerous Indian groups were forced across the Mississippi River.[18]

3. *Battle of Tippecanoe, 1811.* In Illinois, Tecumseh, chief of the Shawnee and head of an alliance of several other tribes, attempted to resist such land grabbing as a violation of the treaty signed after

the Battle of Fallen Timbers in 1795. William Henry Harrison and eleven hundred soldiers defeated the alliance at Tecumseh's village near Tippecanoe Creek.[19]

4. *Removal of the Southern Indians and the Seminole War, 1817–1842.* Gold was discovered on Cherokee lands in Georgia, and the state legislature passed a law depriving the Indian of the right to be a witness or a party in a legal suit with whites. Legally helpless, the Indians saw their lands appropriated for a price of $5,600,000. Military troops forced the highly acculturated Cherokee across the Mississippi in the dead of winter, a forced march that killed one-fourth of the fifteen thousand Cherokee. In the next few years other southern Indians were removed to the West—the Choctaw (1830), Chicasaw (1832), and Creek (1835). The Seminole of Florida resisted, instigating the Seminole War (1833–1842), and retreated to the swamps, where they remain today.[20]

5. *The Black Hawk War and the Bad Axe Massacre, 1831–1832.* At the same time that most of the southern Indians were being displaced, Sauk and Fox tribes were forced out of Illinois and across the Mississippi into Iowa. After a bitter winter, Chief Black Hawk and a large group of Indians, including 600 women and children, came back to the native lands. In a war that lasted two months, Black Hawk attempted to go back to Iowa under a flag of truce. The Indians were massacred in the river, leaving only 150 of the original 1000 alive.[21]

6. *California, 1849–1859.* With the acquisition of California from Mexico in 1848 and the discovery of gold in 1849, thousands of whites inundated California. Viewing the Indians "as vermin who had to be eliminated from the California scene," whites raped Indian women and forced them into prostitution, murdered Indian children, and enslaved the males. Between the years 1849 and 1859 an estimated seventy thousand Indians were killed or died of disease.[22]

7. *Oregon and Washington, 1850–1877.* The Puget Sound tribes fought back against railroad incursions into their lands and attempts to confine them to reservations. By 1858, most of their chiefs had been slain in battle or hanged, the tribes herded onto smaller reservations, and their lands opened up for settlement. In 1872, the Modocs were defeated and exiled to California. In 1877, the Nez Perce refused to be moved to a smaller reservation, rebelled, and under military attack attempted to reach sanctuary in Canada. After defeating several armies they were eventually caught near the border and defeated in a five-day battle.[23]

8. *The Plains, the Rockies, and the Cheyenne-Arapaho War, 1860–1865.* By the 1860s white settlers were turning to areas previously consid-

ered undesirable—the Great American Desert (or the Plains) and the Rocky Mountains. Instead of just passing through on the way to the coast, they began to settle in increasing numbers. By 1876 over two hundred pitched battles had taken place in this territory.[24] Then a major war occurred in Colorado, after the discovery of gold in the Pike's Peak area brought one hundred thousand miners into Cheyenne and Arapaho territory. The Indians resisted this invasion, devastating the countryside and isolating Denver, the territorial center. By 1864, the Indians had suffered severe losses and asked for a truce. They were sent to a new reserve at Sand Creek, Colorado. In November of 1864, the Colorado militia attacked 500 sleeping Indians and massacred 450. At a later governmental inquiry, a trader testified that "they were scalped, their brains knocked out; the men used knives, ripped open women, clubbed little children, knocked them in the head with their guns, beat their brains out, mutilated their bodies in every sense of the word."[25]

9. *The Navaho Campaign, 1864.* While the Arapaho and Cheyenne were raiding in Colorado, the Navaho were pillaging in Arizona. Colonel Kit Carson, in a winter campaign, eventually trapped a large contingent in a canyon. Upon surrender, the Navaho were forced to march on foot three hundred miles to a new reservation in New Mexico. Four years later the Navaho were permitted to return to Arizona, where they accommodated themselves by becoming peaceful ranchers and shepherds.[26]

10. *The Little Big Horn, 1876.* The discovery of gold in the Black Hills brought thousands of whites into the Dakotas and Montana in violation of a Sioux treaty of 1868. In December of 1875 the Bureau of Indian affairs responded to the threat of war by ordering the Sioux groupings and the Cheyenne to confine themselves to specific reservations. A deadline for compliance was set for January 31, 1876. When the deadline had passed and Indian groups still roamed the area, Generals George Crook and Alfred Terry were ordered to seek out the major concentration under Chief Crazy Horse. In June of 1876 General Crook's division was defeated by Crazy Horse on the Rosebud River in Montana. After this battle several groups moved to the valley of the Greasy Grass (the Little Bighorn area), where their encampment was discovered. Major Marcus Reno attacked the south end of the camp, while Colonel George Armstrong Custer and 265 men attacked from the other side. Reno's contingent met severe opposition and his men retreated in a rout. The Indians then turned back and surrounded Custer and his men. Custer's entire division was killed. After another year of skirmishes and the army's use of total-war tactics, Chief Crazy Horse and 900 starving Oglala surrendered in April 1877.[27]

11. *The Apache War, 1863–1886.* In the early 1860s the discovery of mineral reserves in Arizona brought in thousands of prospectors and adventurers. When a peaceful band was attacked in violation of a treaty signed in 1863, "every Apache band in central, western, and southern Arizona took to the warpath."[28] Mining and settlement ceased as the Indian groups raided and pillaged, forcing most of the whites into the fortified towns of Tucson and Prescott. However, in 1872 General Crook initiated a new campaign against the Apache, using troops highly trained in Indian warfare and supplementing each company with 30 to 40 Apache scouts. Thus equipped, mobile contingents struck out in different directions with orders to kill any hostiles and drive them into mountain areas to be bottled up. The tactics were effective, although it took eleven years to completely subdue all of the bands, many of which used Mexico as a base of operations. The last great chief of the Apache, Geronimo, surrendered in 1884. In 1886 Geronimo and 382 peaceful Apaches from his reservation were shipped by train to a steamy concentration camp in Florida.[29]

12. *Epilogue: Massacre at Wounded Knee, 1890.* The wars were over. However, in 1890 a nativistic religious movement had spread to the Dakotas from Nevada—the ghost dance movement. The ghost dancers believed that Christ had returned as an Indian, that all of the grass and buffalo would be restored to them, and that white man's bullets would not harm them if they wore certain shirts. By dancing they would be taken into the air, suspended while the whites disappeared, and then set down among the ghosts of their ancestors on the new earth. In an effort to stop the movement, the whites forced a group of Indians to go to a military camp at Wounded Knee Creek in South Dakota and eventually took the Indians to a military prison in Omaha, Nebraska. The refusal of one Indian to surrender his rifle on the morning following their arrival at Wounded Knee led to an outbreak of shooting by the soldiers. When the firing was over, one-half of the Indians were dead or seriously wounded; one estimate placed the final total of dead at three hundred. Thus ended the massacre at Wounded Knee, December 29, 1890, and with it violent conflict between whites and Indians in the nineteenth century.[30]

ORIGINS OF SLAVERY

Many white Europeans and Americans have had a misconception that, prior to European conquest, Africans south of the Sahara were divided into numerous primitive and wandering tribes. This misconception includes the stereotype of peoples, often with bones in their noses, dancing to native drums, hunting game, engaging in magical rituals, living in grass huts, painting their bodies with dyes, clay, or dung, and on occasion engaging in cannibalism. Such primitive food-gathering and hunting bands *have* existed in Africa from the earliest periods of human evolution and may still be found; ritual cannibalism, however, was rare. Stereotypes are segmental; that is, the characteristics of a segment of a population are generalized to the entire population. In fact, two other types of societies have existed simultaneously with these primitive types. Like Asia, Europe, and the Americas, Africa has had neolithic or horticultural societies and preindustrial or agrarian types.

In West Africa, where the great majority of the New World slaves originated, all three types of societies existed at the time of the first European contacts in the fifteenth and sixteenth centuries A.D. The major preindustrial state-societies in existence at the beginning of the Portuguese and Spanish slave trade were: Wolof, Aguafo, Fetu, Asebu, Fante, Congo, Agona, Ife, Ga, Benin, Oyo, Mali, Songhai (Songhay), Dahomey, Ndongo (Angola), Mbundu, and Asante (Ashanti). Some of these states, such as Mali, were already on the decline (Mali was fragmented and by 1540 was reduced to a small principality by the Tuareg, Mossi, and Songhai peoples), while others, such as Songha and Asante, were on the rise as empires (Songha was overthrown and ended by the Moroccans around 1600, and Asante fell to the English in the latter part of the nineteenth century).

Like the overwhelming majority of preindustrial societies, these African kingdoms practiced slavery. Since blacks captured and enslaved other blacks, race was not the issue in Africa. Ethnic groups fought one another as they did in Europe, and slaves generally were not members of the dominant ethnic group. In addition, slavery within Negroid-African states (as opposed to Arab-African states) had more in common with European serfdom than with the chattel property systems in the Americas. In Ashanti an Englishman found "a slave might marry; own property; himself own a slave; swear an oath; be a competent witness; and ultimately become heir to his master . . . . Such briefly were the rights of an Ashanti slave. They seemed in many cases practically the ordinary privileges of an Ashanti free man . . . . An Ashanti slave, in nine cases out of ten, possibly became an adopted member of the family, and in time his descendants so merged and intermarried with the owner's kinsmen that only a few would know their origin. . . ."[31]

In 1441 two Portuguese explorers led a raid upon a section of West Africa and brought back twelve captives. One of these captives described his native land to Prince Henry the Navigator, whereupon Prince Henry received support from the Pope for further raids and possible conquests. The Pope welcomed this new opportunity for a crusade and granted "to all of those who shall be engaged in the said war, complete forgiveness of all their sins."[32] By 1460 the number of black slaves imported into Portugal had increased to around five hundred annually; by the second decade of the sixteenth century the number of slaves taken to Portugal had risen to such an extent that perhaps the majority of the population south of Lisbon were blacks. Thus, the European-African slave trade introduced a new and devastating era to West Africa.

The Great Circuit

In 1501 the first slaves, including both blacks and whites, were sent from Spain to Hispaniola (Haiti and the Dominican Republic). In 1510 the Spanish king issued orders for the transportation of two hundred slaves from Spain to the West Indies, in 1515 the first shipment of slave-grown sugar was sent from the Indies to Spain, and in 1518 the first cargo of African slaves came directly from Africa to the West Indies.[33] The Great Circuit had begun.

The Great Circuit

> consisted of the export of cheap manufactured goods from Europe to Africa; the purchase or seizure of slaves on the Guinea Coast and their transportation across the Atlantic; the exchange of these slaves for minerals and foodstuffs in the West Indies and Americas; and, lastly, the sale of these raw materials and foods in Europe. By this triangular system three separate profits were taken, all high and all in Europe: the first profit was that of selling consumer goods to the slavers; the second derived from selling slaves to the planters and mine-owners of the Americas; while the third (and biggest) was realized on the sale of American and West Indian cargoes in Europe.[34]

The development of sugar and tobacco planting and later cotton, and the tremendous increase in demand for these and other products in Europe, intensified the slave trade from Africa. One historian estimates that the number of slaves who landed in the New World increased from 125,000 between 1501 and 1600 to 1,280,000 between 1601 and 1700, and to 6,265,000 between 1701 and 1810.[35]

Other European nations rapidly entered the system and challenged Portuguese and Spanish dominance. The English shipped their first slave load from Africa to the New World in 1562. In 1593 the Dutch launched attacks against the Portuguese in Africa and captured Portuguese forts in Ghana. Other peoples, such as the Swedes, the Turks, the Arabs of Oman, the Danes, the French, and the Brandenburgers ("Germans"), contested for profits in this exploitation of human beings.[36]

It should be understood that Europeans did not invade West Africa, capture natives, and ship them off to the New World. The African kings and the elite of the various West African states were involved in the Great Circuit from the outset. These states were too powerful to be conquered by Europeans and would not be conquered until after the slave trade was virtually terminated by the English navy in the early nineteenth century. Europeans built forts on the coast of Africa only with the permission of the African kings, and even the types of material used in building the forts was sometimes specified by these kings and chieftains. The land upon which the forts were built was rented, and Europeans had to pay duties on all imports or give presents before they were allowed to trade.[37]

Europeans seldom ventured into the interior or too far from their assorted coastal castles and forts. Because of the African controls on the construction of forts, the shortage of skilled labor, and the scarcity of stone, few of these forts could have withstood any prolonged attack by Europeans or by Africans. Most of them were in appalling disrepair; the timber was rotted by the climate or eaten by ants and the dampness made the brick walls bulge and crack. The main purpose of the castles and forts was to make a brave show, to keep the slaves in storage secure, and to deter African forces tempted by the stocks of trade goods the forts contained. The guns on the bastions were often low on gunpowder, and many were useless due to rust and rotten carriages. A major castle housed a governor or chief factor (agent or broker), a number of merchants, coppersmiths, surgeons, chaplains, shipwrights, officers and troops, and slave help, along with the slaves awaiting transportation. In the British Royal African Company the period of residence was approximately three years, with the possibility of living no longer than five years because of the diet, disease, and the climate. With little for the Europeans to do but guard the slaves and barter with African chiefs in purchasing new slaves, excessive drinking and lethargy was typical.[38] This is hardly a picture of European colonialism or imperialism. European empires in Africa came much later.

As Africans became addicted to European goods such as gunpowder, liquor, tobacco, guns, and cloth, their ability to resist European slave demands diminished. "African chiefs found that the sale of their fellow-men was indispensable to any contact or commerce with Europe. Unless they were willing—and not only willing, but active in delivery—the ships went elsewhere. . . . Trapped in this unforeseen and fatal circumstance, pushed by their desire for European goods (and firearms often became essential to chiefly survival), or blackmailed by the fear that what one or two might refuse their rivals would consent to give, the rulers of coastal Africa surrendered to the slave trade. They struggled against its worst excesses from time to time; but the trade was always too strong for them in the end."[39]

The great majority of slaves were of a different ethnic group from that of their captors, but as the Great Circuit intensified some Africans even sold their own ethnic members into slavery. A report to an English committee in 1789 stated that "the Kings of Africa . . . incited by the merchandise shown them, which consists principally of strong liquors, give orders to their military to attack their own villages in the night . . . ."[40] Sometimes domestic slaves were resold to the Europeans, or criminals might be sold as punishment. But the great majority were war captives of alien ethnic group members captured on numerous raids along the coast or the interior.

The individuals thus captured and sold into slavery by the African elite were, therefore, members of behaviorally diverse ethnic groups (groups as different as various Europeans were from each other). It is not certain from which ethnic groups slaves in the New World came, but the following were probably involved: Mandingo, Nupe (or Tapas), Yoruba (or Nagos), Susu, Bambaru, Tuculor, Fulani, Kissi, Senufu, and Ibo. Certainly countless other tribes had members that became part of the populations in the Americas. In addition, these slaves came from various classes and from different types of societies. They were nobles, peasants, village farmers, warriors, merchants, and primitive food gatherers and hunters. In any case, the shock of the passage, the dehumanizing effect of the auction block, the separation of families, the treatment in the mines and fields, and the socialization of children into the slave systems all worked to break down such differences.

Captured slaves would be take to the forts and castles in wooden neck stocks or in chains and then imprisoned in these forts to await the second stage of their journey, or the middle passage. A voyage across the Atlantic in the sixteenth, seventeenth, eighteenth, and nineteenth centuries was a dangerous and arduous undertaking under the best of circumstances. For the slave the passage was unbelievably dehumanizing and often disastrous for health or life. The following is a description of a typical middle passage:

> *Every slave, whatever his size might be, had only five feet six inches in length, and sixteen inches in breadth, to lie in. The floor was covered with bodies stowed or packed according to this allowance. But between the floor and the deck or ceiling were platforms, or broad shelves, in the midway, which were covered with bodies also. The height from the floor to the ceiling, within which space the bodies on the floor and those on the platforms lay, seldom exceeded five feet two inches, and in some cases it did not exceed four feet.*
>
> *The men were chained, two and two together, by their hands and feet, and were chained also by means of ring-bolts, which were fastened to the deck. They were confined in this manner at least all the time they remained upon the coast, which was from six weeks to six months, as it might happen. Their allowance consisted of one pint of water a day to each person, and they were fed twice a day with yams and horse-beans. Instruments were kept on board to force them to eat, when sulky.*
>
> *After meals, they jumped up in their irons for exercise. This was so necessary for their health that they were whipped if they refused to do it, and often danced thus under the lash. They were usually fifteen or sixteen hours below deck out of twenty-four. In rainy weather they could not be brought up for two or three days together. If the ship was full, their situation was then inexpressibly distressing. They drew their breath with anxious and laborious efforts. Thus crammed together, some died of suffocation, and the filth and noisomeness occasioned putrid and fatal disorders; so that the officers who inspected them in a morning, had occasionally to pick dead slaves out of their rows, and to unchain their carcasses from the bodies of their fellow-sufferers, to whom they were fastened.*[41]

Following this middle passage came the last stage of the slave's journey—the auction and the transportation to the owner's residence or plantation. At the slave auctions (generally in sea ports) those slaves not already accounted for in advance and slaves already in the New World who were being resold were subjected to humiliating inspections of their teeth, muscles, and limbs, and were sold to the highest bidder. Typical newspaper ads in the United States indicate the subhuman or animal status of the African slave: "Negroes for sale—a negro woman, 24 years of age, and her two children, one eight and the other three years old. Said Negroes will be sold separately or together, as desired. The woman is a good seamstress. She will be sold for cash or exchanged for groceries." An ad for fifty slaves in 1796 stated: "They are not Negroes selected out of a larger gang for the purpose of a slave, but are prime, their present Owner with great trouble and expense, selected them out of many for several years past. They were purchased for stock and breeding Negroes, and to any Planter who particularly wanted them for that purpose, they are a very choice and desirable gang."[42]

Upon arrival at the plantation or at places that specialized in "resocializing" slaves, the blacks went through a "seasoning" process to break their spirit and to produce the docile and hard-working animal that the white dominants desired.

Many blacks, depending upon their personalities or past statuses, resisted such animalistic treatment at one or more stages of this process. Documentation of fifty-five mutinies aboard slave ships exists, along with references to at least two hundred more.[43] Other blacks sank into lethargy or chose death as an alternative. Death by starvation was one such choice, but even here the extreme dominance-subordinance of the system prevented some slaves from dying: metal forceps were used to pry open their mouths while food was stuffed in.

As a result of this treatment and the conditions of passage, the death rate of slaves was extremely high. In 1789 the English Privy Council estimated the mortality rate for the middle passage at 12.5 percent, the deaths in harbors before the slaves were sold at 4.5 percent, and deaths during the seasoning process at 33 percent. "If these figures are correct . . . then only one slave was added to the New World labor force for every two purchased on the Guinea Coast."[44]

The total number of black slaves taken from Africa to the New World is unknown. Estimates range from 11 million to 50 million (Philip D. Curtin reckoned a total of 11,300,000; W. E. B. Du Bois, Robert R. Kucyhski, Roland Oliver, J. D. Fage, and Robert Rotberg estimated approximately 15 million; other writers have accepted 15 million as the minimal amount with the probable total as 50 million; others have believed it was even higher than this.)[45]

The Beginnings of Slavery in America

In 1619 a Dutch frigate unloaded twenty Negroes at the English colony in Jamestown, Virginia, an event noted by John Rolfe: "About the last of August came in a dutch man of warre that sold us twenty Negars."[46] The evidence seems to indicate that the first Negroes in American colonies were not slaves, in the sense of being chattel property, but were indentured servants; chattel slavery did not develop until later in the seventeenth century, as a result of informal practices and piecemeal court cases. Were these first Negro indentured servants treated the same as white servants? This is not known; however, Jordan suggests that from the first Negroes were clearly distinguished from whites. "A distinct name is not attached to a group unless it is regarded as distinct. It seems logical to suppose that this perception of the Negro as being distinct from the Englishman must have operated to debase his status rather than to raise it, for in the absence of countervailing factors present, the need for labor in the colonies usually told in the direction of non-freedom."[47]

As the cost of labor and the demand for labor increased, and as the Great Circuit expanded south of the colonies, some Negroes were not freed from their indentured servitude but made servants for life. In 1640, in Virginia, two white servants and one black servant ran away and were subsequently captured. The two whites were given four additional years of service, but the black, a man named John Punch, was ordered by the court to serve his master for the duration of his natural life.[48] Other court records in 1635 and in the late 1640s indicate that some Negroes were freed from bondage while others were held for longer terms than whites.[49] In 1639 Maryland passed a law stating that "all persons being Christians (Slaves excepted)" over eighteen years of age who were imported without indentures would serve four years.[50] Even at this early period being a Christian did not guarantee eventual freedom, and in 1667 a Virginia statute made this quite clear— "conferring of baptisme doth not alter the condition of the person as to his bondage or freedome."[51] A few years earlier, in 1664, Maryland passed a law stating that "all Negroes and other slaves shall serve Durante Vita."[52] In the first decade of the eighteenth century, most of the colonies had passed laws making Negro slaves, and the children of female slaves,* slaves for the duration of their lives.

After independence from Britain, the egalitarian ideas of the Revolution helped abolish slavery in the North by 1817.[53] Slavery was also on the defensive in the South and seemed about to terminate; however, a new type of cotton (Sea Island cotton) and a new invention for separating the seeds from the fibers of this cotton intensified slavery and the opposition of the southern elite to its abolition. The economic historian Faulkner explains this development:

> *Losses incurred by the planters in the War of Independence, the exhaustion of the soil in the coast states, and the influx of white settlers from the North into these regions all tended to make the system less profitable. These influences, augmented*

Slavery had to go through the female line, since many of the fathers of children born to slave women were whites, hence producing a free mulatto class. In addition, given the conditions of slavery, the father, black or white, could not always be ascertained.

by the Revolutionary theories unfavorable to slavery, led many Southerners to question its economic and moral basis, but it was still firmly entrenched in 1781 in the rice and indigo fields of the Carolinas and Georgia, although its hold on the tobacco plantations had been weakened. The factors which contributed beyond all others to revive an apparently dying institution were the introduction of Sea Island cotton and the invention of the cotton gin (1793) simultaneously with the coming of the Industrial Revolution. The first gave the planters of the coast regions an opportunity to recoup their waning fortunes, the latter made it possible to raise profitably the inland short-fibered variety; and both led to the rapid extension of cotton culture into the uplands and westward. [54]

Slavery was particularly suited to the raising of cotton, and new land was continually needed to ensure profits. King cotton, the increasing value of slaves as workers and as an investment per se, and the demands for new lands all combined to intensify slavery for blacks, to eliminate the possibility of emancipation short of violence, and to spread the "peculiar institution" to the West.

The number of slaves increased rapidly in the United States as a result, and by 1850 the slave population had reached 3,204,313, with 2.5 million engaged in agriculture (primarily cotton growing). [55]

Early Forms of Racism

Embryonic forms of racism existed in England *prior* to the slave trade and in the very beginning of English contact with Africa. The belief that black skin was due to God's curse on Ham, the son of Noah, was prevalent. The English association of blackness with evil and dirt, the heathen religions of Africa and the strangeness of African customs and behavior *in combination* added up to savagery in the eyes of many British. [56] Many of the English colonists quite possibly held to these vague and unsystematic conceptions of black inferiority. Some early laws speak of mulattoes as "an abominable mixture." [57] Negro "lustfulness" was an image in English and some European writings. In 1526 a Spanish Moor disclosed that "the Negroes . . . lead a beastly kind of life, being utterly destitute of the use of reason, of dexteritie of wit, and of all arts. Yea, they so behave themselves, as if they had continually lived in a Forrest among wild beasts. They have great swarms of Harlots among them; whereupon a man may easily conjecture their manner of living." [58] Jean Bodin (1566) "concluded that heat and lust went hand in hand and that 'in Ethiopia . . . the race of men is very keen and lustful.' " [59] Jordan concludes that the "depiction of the Negro as a lustful creature was not radically new, therefore, when Englishmen first met Negroes face to face." [60]

As slavery developed, these incipient beliefs and attitudes solidified into a justification for slavery and were reinforced by black behavior resulting from the slave condition. Until the 1830s, however, these racist beliefs were based upon environmental determinism. Black inferiority and even skin color were considered products of environmental forces. According to Frederickson, "the belief that black mental, moral, and psychological characteristics were the result of environment was not effectively challenged in the period [the eighteenth century] and persisted as a respectable ethnological doctrine until the 1830s and 1840s."[61] The *biological* doctrines and their more severe consequences will be examined in the next chapter.

Although very few African blacks were enslaved and brought to the United States after 1810, as a result of constitutional restrictions and British efforts to end the slave trade, the natural increase of the American slaves and the spread of slavery to the territories posed numerous problems for American society. And these problems could not be resolved without violent conflict—the Civil War.

NEW SPAIN AND CONQUEST OF MEXICO

The northern part of the Spanish Empire in what is now the United States consisted at one time of all of the territory west of the Mississippi River to the Pacific Ocean and north to Canada, and the areas of Louisiana and Florida. This territory was sparsely settled by Spanish and, after 1821, by Mexicans in the territory that remained under Mexican control. Communication with the government in Mexico City was difficult because of the enormous distance and the rudimentary forms of transportation. And, of course, such territorial claims were disputed by the Indian inhabitants.

As late as 1850, after all of this territory had been taken by the Americans, there were only about seventy-five hundred Mexicans in California, sixty thousand in New Mexico, five thousand in Texas, and one thousand in Arizona.[62] These remote regions were settled by members of all the castes, the ratio varying in particular areas. In California, well over half of the Spanish-speaking settlers were mestizos and Indians; of the forty-six founders of Los Angeles in 1781, only two were Spanish, and they had Indian wives.[63] In New Mexico the "majority of the original settlers from Mexico in 1598 were males who, over the years, mixed with the Pueblo Indians of the region, as well as with Mexican Indians who settled in the area."[64]* This sparse settlement of a vast area would be their undoing in their competition and conflict with the land-hungry and expansionist Americans.

This racial mixture is mentioned because of distinctions made within the Spanish-speaking population of the Southwest and by Anglos in this area. In spite of the fact that miscegenation between Spanish and Indians in Mexico began in the earliest period of contact, the idea has persisted that there are segments of the Spanish-speaking population that are pure or primarily Spanish and other segments that are basically Indian in terms of race. Those segments that prefer to emphasize their Spanish biological and cultural heritage have used such terms as Spanish-American and Hispano. The term Spanish-American was very popular in New Mexico between 1910 and 1930 when the charter member Spanish speaking wanted to keep themselves separate from the recent immigrants from Mexico. But neither the charter member group nor the immigrants

American Expansion into New Spain

Americans had begun to emigrate into various areas of New Spain after independence. By 1790, several thousand Americans had farms in the Spanish territory between Natchez and New Orleans and made up a majority in this area. The bishop of Louisiana complained in 1800 that "the Americans had scattered themselves over the country almost as far as Texas and corrupted the Indians and creoles by the example of their own restless and ambitious temper.[65] The good bishop also believed that Americans had their eyes on the whole of Mexico. Within a few years more Americans had entered the state of Coahuila (of which Texas was a part), bringing their slaves and arrogantly demanding local government with English common law. Independence from Britain had given the Americans territory to the east bank of the Mississippi. But the west bank and the outlet at New Orleans were controlled by the Spanish, and numerous conflicts occurred between Spaniard and American in the river traffic. Even as far west as California a few hundred Americans were to be found. Along with other ethnic adventurers (Scots, Germans, French, and English) the Americans married daughters of the Spanish upper class, acquired citizenship and land, and adopted the Spanish fashions of the day. When the war came, however, they quickly discarded their Spanish veneer and became instrumental in overthrowing the government of California.[66]

In 1800, in a secret treaty, Spain ceded to France a huge section of its northern empire—from the Mississippi to the Rocky Mountains north to Canada (49° parallel) and south to Texas (near the Red River). Failing to overturn a newly established Negro republic in Haiti and realizing that in a war with Britain the new territory was indefensible, Napoleon sold this "Louisiana Territory" to the Americans. With this annexation by purchase, the Spaniards and French that remained in the area became subordinate.

Florida, now cut off from the western Spanish territory, was placed in a precarious position—it was protected by military forts and supplies from the Spanish Caribbean, but its Spanish inhabitants were far outnumbered by immigrant Americans (not counting the Indians). In this period, what is now Florida was divided into West and East Florida, with the Perdido River as the approximate boundary. The governor of West Florida had invited

---

from Mexico are racially pure; both groups are Indian-Spanish mixtures (Jack D. Forbes, "Mexican-Americans," in Mexican-Americans in the United States, *ed. John H. Burma [Cambridge Mass.: Schenkman Publishing Co., 1970] p. 7). Today many Spanish-speaking people have reacted against the term "Spanish" with its downgrading of the Indian heritage. To these people, "Mexican" is not a pejorative term but one that captures the mixed heritage with a proper stress on the Indian element. According to Forbes, the Spanish conquerors almost always referred to the Aztecs as Mexicans; it is an old and noble term. Other terms that give proper acknowledgment to the Indian element are Mexicano and Chicano. Many Anglos and many Spanish-speaking people have believed that Indian blood is contaminating; such a belief is racist.*

American settlers into his area, the first of similar mistakes made by Spanish and Mexican government officials. Jefferson wrote in regard to this misguided decision, "I wish a hundred thousand of our inhabitants would accept the invitation. It will be the means of delivering to us peaceably what may otherwise cost us a war."[67] Claiming that West Florida was part of the Louisiana Purchase (a claim disputed by the Spanish government), Americans revolted in 1810, with the assistance of the American government, and in 1812 West Florida was incorporated into the United States.[68]

East Florida presented more of a problem, but its fate was the same. In 1812 a Georgian by the name of George Mathews instigated a revolt, took over Amelia Island, and lay siege to St. Augustine, assisted by American troops. The United States government lent tacit approval of the undertaking by its silence; but public knowledge of the event, coupled with political repercussions, led President Monroe to break the silence. The area was to be restored to Spanish authority; however, American troops would remain to protect the rebels from reprisals.[69] In time, however, Tennesseans and Georgians who had been waiting for support from Washington had their opportunity. In 1817 a band of Seminoles conducted a raid in the United States and then returned to their base in East Florida. General Andrew Jackson invaded the territory on the pretense of pursuing Indians, captured the fortified cities of St. Augustine and Pensacola, ejected the Spanish governor, and garrisoned the cities with American troops. In February of 1819, convinced that Florida was lost, Spain ceded all of the land east of the Mississippi River (it had never recognized the loss of West Florida) in return for $5 million.

The Texas Secession

Texas was next. The first conflict action in Texas was a victory for the Spanish. During the War of 1812 a group of Americans and revolutionary Mexicans invaded Texas from Louisiana without authorization from the American government and against the orders of the governor of Louisiana. This "army" of 850 men met disaster against Spanish troops at the Medina River in August of 1813. Only 93 escaped; the rest were killed or captured.[70]

In 1821 Mexico became independent from Spain. The new creole government, which evidently had not learned from its Spanish predecessors, issued sixteen major land grants to American citizens to encourage the settlement of Texas. One of these was the grant given to Moses Austin and his son Stephen: 177 acres for each of three hundred families, 13,000 acres of prairie pasture, and 65,000 acres for the Austin family's private domain.[71] Freebooters like Sam Houston, the Bowie brothers, and Davy Crockett followed. Outnumbering the Mexicans in Texas and resenting the controls from Mexico, they made an abortive attempt at secession in 1826, when Texas was renamed the Republic of Fredonia. A few years later the government of Mexico made slavery illegal, closed off immigration of Americans into Texas (this was difficult to enforce), imposed new custom duties, and replaced the federal system (which had given the Texans some autonomy) with a centralist regime. In 1835 the Texans declared their independence, established a provisional government, and expelled the Mexican garrison at San Antonio.

The president of Mexico, Santa Anna, personally led an expedition of 3,000 men against the fortified mission at San Antonio, garrisoned by 180 Texans under the command of William Barret Travis. The Alamo had twenty-one cannons, and its defenders were armed with rifles having a range of two hundred yards. The Mexicans had eight to ten cannons, and the soldiers were equipped with smoothbore muskets having a range of around seventy yards. On March 5, 1836, the Alamo fell to the Mexican army after refusing to surrender for a logical reason: Santa Anna had proclaimed that "the foreigners who are making war on the Mexican nation in violation of every rule of law, are entitled to no consideration whatever, and in consequence no quarter is to be given them . . . ."[72] One Texan escaped alive (a man by the name of Louis Rose), and seven Texans, including Davy Crockett, surrendered; all seven were executed.[73]*

A short time later the Mexicans captured another Texan garrison, at Goliad. Marching eastward, the Mexican army pursued a Texan army under Sam Houston across the Colorado River and then the Brazos River. Near a ferry crossing on the San Jacinto River, the armies finally clashed. After a preliminary skirmish, the Mexican army of 1,400 men entrenched themselves about three-fourths of a mile from the camp of the Texans. The following morning, April 21, 1836, Houston gave orders to destroy a bridge vital to the Mexicans for continuing reinforcements and vital to the Americans if retreat became necessary. With retreat no longer possible, 700 Texans on horse and on foot attacked the Mexican fortifications in a wild charge. In the short melee that followed the Texans were overwhelmingly victorious. Houston reported 630 Mexicans killed, 208 wounded, and 730 prisoners taken as against a Texan loss of 2 dead and 23 wounded.[74] The relative losses were probably exaggerated, and the historian Fehrenbach disagreed with the prisoner count: "Few prisoners were taken. Instead those who surrendered were clubbed and stabbed, some on their knees. The slaughter . . . became methodical: the Texas riflemen knelt and poured a steady fire into the packed, jostling ranks . . . ."[75] The president of Mexico was captured eight miles away while crawling through the grass dressed as a common soldier.

As the result of this one battle, Texas became an independent country on May 5, 1836, and the following year, on March 3, 1837, President Andrew Jackson signed the congressional resolution that recognized this new state-society. This was one of the few times in history when an immigrant group was successful in a secession. With their new president, Sam Houston, Texas remained a sovereign state for nine years. When Texas was annexed to the United States in 1845, the development of a potential new ethnic

Nine Mexican Texans also died defending the Alamo.

group, Texans, was arrested and its American ethnicity reasserted (but even today Texans have a quasi sense of peoplehood).

Two other conflicts between Americans and Mexicans before the major war are noteworthy. In the 1820s and 1830s groups of Texas "adventurers" invaded New Mexico and Arizona and contended for the rich pasture lands in some of these areas. Hundreds of Mexican families were forced off their land and into Mexico, lynchings took place, and Texas cowboys shot up several villages.[76] The second incident occurred after the commander of the Pacific fleet saw a highly undiplomatic note from the president of Mexico to President Tyler. Assuming that war with Mexico was inevitable, the commander sailed to Monterey and forced the city to surrender. The city was returned to the Mexicans when the embarrassed commander found out that no such war had been declared; he was four years too soon.[77]

The Mexican War, 1846–1848

James K. Polk was elected president on an expansionist and manifest-destiny platform. Perceiving a British and a French threat to American interests in the Pacific, Polk offered to purchase California and New Mexico and to fix the southern boundary of Texas at the Rio Grande. In addition, Polk offered to cancel Mexican debts to the United States, pay $5 million for New Mexico, and pay whatever was necessary for California. The proposition was rejected.

On January 13, 1846, American troops under Zachary Taylor invaded Mexico by crossing the Nueces River, which had been the southern border of Texas for a century. When a Mexican detachment crossed the Rio Grande and engaged in a skirmish with the American troops, Polk used the incident to prompt Congress into declaring war on Mexico in May 1846.[78] With an American fifth column in California initiating the conflict actions and an American naval force "recapturing" Monterey, all of California fell by the end of 1846.

As California was being conquered, General Zachary Taylor crossed the Rio Grande and captured Monterrey (in Nuevo León) in September 1846, waited for reinforcements, and then defeated Santa Anna at nearby Buena Vista in February of the following year. Fearing that Taylor might become a presidential candidate, Polk selected the aged general Winfield Scott to lead the major attack into Mexico City. Taylor would sit in northern Mexico while another army would capture the capitol and end the war.

A few weeks after Buena Vista, General Scott and an army of approximately 10,000 men laid seige to Vera Cruz after arriving by sea. On March 26, 1847, the city fell, and Scott began his movement to capture the Mexican capitol, following much the same route and the same strategy that Hernando Cortez did: he left supplies and severed communication, producing no possibility of retreat or reinforcements. After a series of troop movements on both sides—the Mexicans attempting to fortify all roads to Mexico City and the Americans seeking to find the path of least resistance—

segments of the armies met in the Battle of Contreras. According to Scott, the victory opened up the road to the capitol with only a loss of 60 Americans killed or wounded as opposed to 700 Mexicans killed and 813 prisoners taken. Finding a fortified village in the path of invasion, the American army chose to attack rather than to flank it, taking it with severe casualties (1,056) but leaving Mexico City exposed a few miles away.

At this point the campaign stalled. Scott was expecting President Santa Anna to surrender the capitol, based upon an earlier agreement whereby Santa Anna would display a show of force in attempting to stop the advance and then would give up the city for a secret payment of $1 million. The wily president had really wanted more time. A British delegation arranged a truce between the two armies on August 24.

When the news arrived that Santa Anna was not preparing to evacuate but was fortifying the city, the Americans renewed their attack on September 8. Two routes were possible to take the city, one through flooded fields and the other by attacking Chapultepec (a plateau, surrounded by a wall on the top, with a palace in the center). The army decided on a frontal attack on Chapultepec. Advancing through a grove of trees below the hill while another division was bombarding the top and then using scaling ladders, the Americans eventually managed to break into the walled area and capture the fortress. The demoralized army of Santa Anna withdrew from the capitol to the town of Guadalupe Hidalgo. The war was over (September 14, 1847), Santa Anna was deposed by his own people, and his successor signed the Treaty of Guadalupe Hidalgo on February 2, 1848.[79] Approximately one-half of Mexico (918 million square miles) was ceded to the United States in return for a payment of $15 million. This was a small payment considering that the war was ostensibly fought because of a border dispute and that the United States acquired the future states of Arizona, New Mexico, Utah, Nevada, California, and part of Colorado. At the moment of the treaty's ratification by the American government on March 10, 1848, the approximately seventy-five thousand Mexican residents of this appropriated area became citizens of the United States and a subordinated minority. In what was left of Mexico these people would be known as "our brothers who were sold," and "as late as 1943 maps were still used in Mexican schools which designated the old Spanish borderlands as 'territory temporarily in the hands of the United States.' "[80]

One segment of the Mexican population had become subordinated as a result of conquest. In the twentieth century, several million more Mexicans would become subordinate as a result of voluntary immigration.

THE IMMIGRANTS

With the acquisition of territory from the Indians and from Mexico, and with the development of industrialization following the Civil War, there was a compelling need for an increased population. The demand for menial labor far exceeded the scarce supply, which was mainly in the black population. Extensive agricultural land existed for the taking in highly underdeveloped and underpopulated states and territories. Natural increase of the native population was insufficient for developing this land; immigration from other societies seemed to be the answer.

From 1820 to 1930, some 32 million Europeans, close to 3 million Canadians, 1 million Asians, and at least 750,000 legal immigrants from Mexico entered the United States. When immigrants from other areas of the world are included, 37.7 million people entered the United States by 1930, and the overwhelming majority became citizens. After a sharp drop in immigration due to the Great Depression and World War II (down to 1.5 million, 1931–1950), another 7.3 million immigrants came to the United States between 1950 and 1974.[81] Fifty percent of the total immigration between 1820 and 1974 occurred during a forty-year period—from 1881 to 1920. Table 7.2 lists twenty-five countries of origin ranked according to total immigration to the United States between 1820 and 1974, with a total to 1930 and the peak decade of each.

Table 7.2

Immigration, 1820–1974: Rank Order of 25 Countries and Peak Decades

Country	Peak Decade	Total to 1930	Total to June 1974
1. Germany	1881–1890 (1,452,970)	5,907,893	6,948,299
2. Italy	1901–1910 (2,045,877)	4,651,195	5,259,026
3. Great Britain	1881–1890 (807,357)	4,212,710	4,839,562
a. England	1881–1890 (644,680)	2,619,435	3,125,910
b. Scotland	1921–1930 (159,781)	726,887	816,003
c. Wales	1901–1910 (17,464)	72,647	94,575
d. not specified		793,741	803,074
4. Ireland	1851–1860 (914,119)	4,578,941	4,719,358
5. Canada	1921–1930 (924,515)	2,897,201	4,037,114
6. Russia (USSR)	1901–1910 (1,597,306)	3,341,991	3,349,313
7. Austria-Hungary[a]	1901–1910 (2,145,266)	3,172,461 to 1911	—

Table 7.2 (continued)

Country	Peak Decade	Total to 1930	Total to June 1974
8. Mexico	1921–1930 (459,287) and 1961–1970 (453,937)	755,936	1,849,399
9. West Indies[b]	1901–1910 (107,548)	431,423	1,341,052
10. Sweden	1881–1890 (391,776)	1,116,239	1,269,462
11. Norway	1881–1890 (176,586)	763,986	854,965
12. France	1901–1910 (73,379)	582,375	740,626
13. Greece	1911–1920 (184,201)	421,489	619,550
14. Austria (after 1910)	1911–1920 (453,649)	486,517	609,121
15. Hungary (after 1910)	1911–1920 (442,693)	473,375	529,609
16. Poland	1921–1930 (227,734)	397,729	499,176
17. China	1871–1880 (123,201)	377,245	478,602
18. Portugal	1911–1920 (89,732)	252,715	399,845
19. Japan	1901–1910 (129,797)	275,643	386,582
20. Turkey	1901–1910 (157,369)	360,171	381,253
21. Denmark	1881–1890 (88,132)	332,466	362,491
22. Netherlands	1881–1890 (53,701)	246,619	355,527
23. Switzerland	1881–1890 (81,988)	290,168	345,795
24. Spain	1911–1920 (28,958)	166,865	243,761
25. Belgium	1901–1910 (41,635)	153,388	200,138

SOURCE: *1974 Annual Report, Immigration and Naturalization Service* (Washington, D.C.: Government Printing Office), Table 13, pp. 56–58.
[a]Statistics after 1910 kept separately for Austria and Hungary; see numbers 14 and 15
[b]Not a country.

The overwhelming majority of these immigrants became part of the lower stratum of American society and, simultaneously, became members of subordinate ethnic groups. Encouraged by the economic and political elite of the dominant American group, they settled in patterns of voluntary segregation, for the most part, in the cities and the rural areas of America. Their labor would be a significant factor in urbanization and industrialization and in creating the powerful American state of the twentieth century. Each group would encounter some degree of discrimination and prejudice from the native Americans, particularly from those Anglos that competed directly with them. Many of the second generations of the immigrant groups would, in turn, give a similar reception to those who came later.

The major pull factors that encouraged this massive immigration from most of the countries of Europe, from the neighbors to the south and the north, and from Asia were numerous. Above all, there was economic opportunity. Even though immigrants' wages were low compared to those of the dominant Anglos, they were often much higher than what the immigrants had received in their societies of origin. In some cases, immigrants had to lower their customary standard of living, but this situation was temporary for many.

Economic opportunity in the United States was widely publicized in Europe by agents of businesses and state governments. Railroad companies needed immigrants to buy railroad land grants, to construct the tracks, and to work the trains. Immediately following the Civil War railroad agents toured northern Europe to encourage emigration to the United States. As for merchants, "nearly everyone who had something to sell or something to produce hoped to make money out of immigrants. Merchants looked to immigration for a growing supply of customers, and organized in various localities to attract it."[82] Factories needed labor and were quite successful in their efforts to acquire immigrant workers from Europe—between 1870 and 1920 roughly one out of three workers in the manufacturing and mechanical industries was an immigrant.[83] State governments, particularly of those states with low population density, also got into the act. Twenty-five out of the thirty-eight states in the 1860s and 1870s had official programs to encourage immigration into their states.[84]

Encouraging letters from relatives in America, publicity by steamship lines, low passage rates, and the lifting of emigration restrictions in several European countries also contributed as pull factors. And, according to Jones, a form of irrational collective frenzy occurred in some European areas as the inhabitants "were simply carried along by a force they did not understand."[85]

When European emigration declined in the 1920s because of improvements in the economies of Europe and immigration restrictions passed by the American government, there was a greater demand for Mexican labor. The demand for cheap Mexican labor was greatest in the Southwest but intense in other parts of the country as well. The vegetable and fruit industry of the Southwest, which began in 1900, was made possible only by Mexican labor.[86] During the 1920s Mexican labor spread out from the Southwest to the plantations of Mississippi, to the sugar beet areas of Colorado, to the steel mills of Ohio and Pennsylvania, and to the automotive industry in Detroit.[87] So great was the demand for this menial labor that labor smugglers would enter Mexico and bring out thousands of illegal workers that would be "sold" to employers for fifty cents to a dollar. Work teams were locked up at night under armed guards to prevent them from being stolen and sold to other employers.[88] In order to prevent the loss of the vital labor force to other parts of the country, Texas passed the Emigrant Agent Law in 1929. The law made it a criminal offense to recruit Mexican workers in Texas and send them to some other state. Such was the competition within the American business community for this source of profit.

The major push factors were also economic. They varied according to time and place but usually involved population increases and pressure on the food supply, the reduction of the yield and size of family agricultural land, and the decline in demand for artisan skills. The population of Europe doubled between 1750 and 1850 as a result of medical technology. Italy's population increased by four million during the thirty-year period from 1890 to 1920. Asia was also experiencing a rapid growth. As the population increased, opportunity diminished and the old ways became adequate. Small family plots in China, Japan, and particular areas in Europe could no longer sustain their members. In Ireland, for example, because of the system of subletting, the average farm size was ten acres or less.[89] In Germany, the farms could not support all of the sons, forcing many to go to the growing cities as a proletariat or to emigrate. Enclosure (the erection of fences) was occurring in much of Europe, transferring arable land into pasture land. Large-scale agricultural developments reduced the number of family farms, and industrialization in Germany and England made the skills of the artisan class obsolete. In addition, since the farming class was faced with hard times, it no longer had agricultural surpluses to exchange for the services and products of the artisans. In Germany, for example, "between 1840 and 1847 one sixth of all the weavers of Württemberg went bankrupt. Carpenters, saddlers, masons, and blacksmiths found little to do, and their incomes declined."[90] Natural disasters in some areas, such as the potato famine in Ireland and the floods in China, added to the economic problems of particular groups.

Political factors, although of less importance, also provided motives for emigration. The failures of the revolutions of 1848 in Germany, Austria-Hungary, and Italy and the collapse of several Irish nationalism movements at various times sent many "radicals" to the United States for asylum. China was also racked by political and social unrest at the time of a large-scale Chinese diaspora in the nineteenth century. In Mexico, the revolution

Table 7.3

Estimated Rank Order of 20 Ethnic Groups by Size of Immigration, 1820 to 1930, and Major Areas of Concentration

Ethnic Group	Est. Total to 1930	Peak Decade	Major Areas of Original Concentration
1. Germans	5,900,000	1881–1890	Midwest; Great Lakes; New York State; Pennsylvania
2. Italians	4,600,000	1901–1910	Northeast; California; Louisiana
3. Irish	4,500,000	1851–1860	Northeast; Illinois; California
4. Poles	3,000,000	1911–1920	Midwest; New York State, Chicago; New York City; Buffalo; Detroit
5. Canadians	2,800,000	1920–1929	Widely dispersed
6. Jews	2,500,000	1901–1910	New York; Midwest (German Jews)
7. English	2,500,000	1881–1890	Widely dispersed; New England and Great Lakes area in particular
8. Swedes	1,200,000	1881–1890	Midwest; Minnesota in particular
9. Scots and Scots-Irish	1,000,000	1921–1930	Widely dispersed; industrial centers
10. Norwegians	770,000	1881–1890	Midwest; Puget Sound; San Francisco
11. Mexicans	760,000	1921–1930	Texas and California; Southwest
12. Yugoslavians (Serbs, Croats, Slovenes)	750,000	1901–1910	Pennsylvania; Ohio; Illinois; Michigan; New York

of 1910 eliminated the system of peonage, thereby freeing thousands of peasants from traditional restrictions on their employment.

While extensive numbers of Scandinavians and Germans settled in the rural Midwest and the majority of the Mexican immigrants settled in the small towns and rural areas of the Southwest, the heaviest concentration of foreign-born was in the large urban centers. In 1860, for example, approximately 50 percent of the populations of Chicago, Milwaukee, New York, San Francisco, and Detroit were immigrants. At this same time, 60 percent of St. Louis were foreign-born, while one-third of the residents of Baltimore, Boston, and New Orleans were foreigners.[91] This pattern of urban settlement continued into the twentieth century, even among immigrants who were farmers in their countries of origin.

Table 7.3 (continued)

Estimated Rank Order of 20 Ethnic Groups by Size of Immigration, 1820 to 1930, and Major Areas of Concentration

Ethnic Group	Est. Total to 1930	Peak Decade	Major Areas of Original Concentration
13. French	580,000	1901–1910	Widely dispersed; Louisiana
14. Hungarians (Magyars)	500,000	1901–1910	New York; New Jersey; Pennsylvania; Illinois; Michigan
15. Greeks	400,000	1911–1920	New York
16. Chinese	375,000	1871–1880	West Coast; San Francisco
17. Danes	330,000	1881–1890	Midwest; twentieth-century immigrants widely dispersed in industrial centers
18. Japanese	275,000	1901–1910	West Coast; particularly California
19. Finns	275,000	1901–1910	Minnesota; Michigan
20. Portuguese	250,000	1911–1920	New England; New York

SOURCES: *1974 Annual Report, Immigration and Naturalization Service* (Washington, D.C.: Government Printing Office), Table 13, pp. 56–58. The identification of major areas of original concentration was derived primarily from Charles H. Anderson, *White Protestant Americans* (Englewood Cliffs, N.J.: Prentice-Hall, 1970).

NOTE: Estimating the immigration totals of some of these groups poses few problems since they came from a country in which they made up the overwhelming majority of the population (for example, Italians from Italy, or Danes from Denmark). Other groups, such as Jews and Poles, came from Russia, Prussia, and Poland, and are listed in immigration statistics from the country of origin, not the ethnic group. Jews are a special problem, since there were German-Jews, Polish-Jews, Russian-Jews, and many others. At least half as many Mexicans could be added to the total if we counted illegal immigrants.

Except for the Mexicans in the Southwest, the South received only a small fraction of the immigration total. The large concentration of blacks in the South, whether under the slavery system or the apartheid* system, discouraged immigrant settlement. Passage from Europe was far easier to northern ports, and the North and the West offered greater opportunity—cheap land, large-scale employment opportunities, as well as lack of black competition. In addition, most white Southerners in the nineteenth century had racist reasons for not wanting immigrants. In 1850 one southern editor warned that immigrants "are a curse instead of a blessing; they are generally a worthless, unprincipled class—enemies to our peculiar institutions."[92] Another southern newspaper editorialized that "the immigrants, do not, like our ancestors, fly from religious and political persecution, they come

*A system of extreme segregation coupled with extreme subordination. See Chapter 8.

merely as animals in search of a rich and fresher pasture . . . . They will settle in large masses, and, for ages to come, will practice and inculcate a pure (or rather impure) materialism."[93] According to Boorstin, "many Southern spokesmen traced national political ills (and the declining influence of the South) to the European immigrant influx, among other unwelcome changes."[94] The only southern state to attract a significant number of immigrants was Louisiana. Italians in particular settled in this unique state, giving Louisiana more Italians than any other state west of the Mississippi except California.[95]

In the early twentieth century, many Southerners changed their minds about immigrant settlement in Dixie. Cotton mills, railroads, and other industries were expanding, a.id an increased labor supply was necessary. Racism was not gone, however, as some Southerners hoped that the immigrants would not only solve their labor problem but accelerate the exodus of blacks from the South.[96] Agents from the South were sent to Europe, conventions were held, and extensive literature was distributed; however, the campaign met with "pathetically little success," as most immigrants continued to stay away.[97]

Table 7.3 summarizes the estimated immigration of twenty ethnic groups in order of their total immigration from 1820 to 1930 and lists their major areas of original concentration. Table 7.4 illustrates the concentration in thirty-year periods of several selected ethnic groups. Both the spatial concentration and the time period concentration are important factors in creating viable ethnic communities.

One final point needs to be explained regarding the entrance of immigrants into the United States: the idea of the "old" and the "new" immigration from Europe. At the beginning of the twentieth century, it was widely believed that the year 1880 (or the decade from 1880 to 1890) was a watershed in immigration from Europe. Supposedly, before 1880 immigrants to the United States came from northern Europe (the "old" immigration), but after this date the source of immigration was southern and eastern Europe (the "new" immigration). This idea was accompanied by the belief that the "new" immigration had a higher percentage of males and was less permanent, more illiterate, and more unskilled than the "old." These ideas primarily stemmed from the work of a government body known as the Dillingham Commission and functioned to intensify the idea that the United States was being inundated by diverse and unassimilable foreigners.

It is true that more immigrants came from southern and eastern Europe · after 1880 than from northern Europe (59 percent of the total immigration between 1880 and 1929 came from eastern and southern Europe, while only 41 percent of the total in this period came from northern Europe). It is also true that few immigrants came from southern and eastern Europe before 1880 (only 2 percent of the total immigration from southern and eastern

Europe came before 1880; 98 percent came after this date). However, the idea that the 1880s saw the demise of northern European immigration is not true. As has already been noted, 41 percent of the total immigration between 1880 and 1929 came from northern Europe, a figure that hardly indicates a sharp drop-off. But, more important, more people came from northern Europe after 1880 than before (47.8 percent of all northern European immigrants came before 1880 and 52.2 percent came after).[98]

The statistical evidence about illiteracy, sex ratio, and unskilled labor was misleading because of the artificial geographic division and the collapsing of the categories of ethnic groups within these two divisions. Maldwyn Allen Jones explains this statistical fallacy:

It was undeniable that Italian and Slavic immigrants, for instance, were predominantly male, unskilled, illiterate, and transient. But there were larger percentages of males among German, Scandinavian, and English immigrants than there were among Jewish, Bohemian, and Portuguese; Bohemians, Moravians, and Finns had lower percentages of illiteracy than had the Irish and Germans; Englishmen, Germans, and Scandinavians showed a greater tendency to return to Europe than did Armenians, Dalmatians, Jews, and Portuguese; Jews had a higher percentage of skilled laborers than any group except the Scots, and the Irish had a smaller percentage than the Italians.[99]

Table 7.4

Immigration in Thirty-Year Periods as Percent of Total to 1930 and as Percent of Total to 1974: Selected Ethnic Groups

Ethnic Group	Thirty-Year Period	% of Total, 1820–1930	% of Total, 1820–1974
1. Germans	1861–1890	50%	42.5%
2. Italians	1891–1920	82%	72%
3. Irish	1841–1870	46.5%	45%
4. Greeks	1901–1930	95%	65%
5. Swedes	1881–1910	78%	68%
6. Mexicans	1901–1930	96%	39%
Mexicans	1951–1974	—	55%
7. English	1861–1890	50%	42%
8. Canadians	1901–1930	64%	46%
9. Japanese	1901–1930	90%	64%
10. Chinese	1861–1890	66%	52%

SOURCE: Compiled from the *1974 Annual Report, Immigration and Naturalization Service* (Washington, D.C.: Government Printing Office, Table 13, pp. 56–58.

In addition, in the period covered by the study (1899 to 1909) those new immigrants would be more likely to be predominantly males. In time, however, as with all of the earlier groups, wives and families would follow. If the commission had studied the same ethnic groups from southern Europe a decade later, the disproportionate sex ratio would have diminished.

ACQUISITION OF ISLAND TERRITORIES

Prior to 1867 the expansion of the American Empire involved the acquisition of contiguous territory. The effort to incorporate Canada in the War of 1812 ended in failure, but the desire remained. In 1867 the secretary of state, William Seward, purchased Alaska from the Russians. The annexation

> *was far from a white elephant. It was designed to sandwich British Columbia between American territory and thereby, Seward hoped, increase the pressure upon Canada to join the U.S.A. More important, however, it established what he called a "drawbridge" between America and Asia. Seward regarded Alaska as the Northern protected-flank in his aim to dominate the Pacific. The Southern flank would be ensured by an American controlled Panama Canal.*[100]

Hawaii and the Philippines would aid in the American control of the Pacific, but, as it turned out, their acquisition would have to wait until the end of the century. However, the Midway Islands were annexed in 1867, and they provided a safe coaling station for American ships.

A century before the war with Spain that enabled the Americans to acquire the Philippines, Puerto Rico, and Cuba and that indirectly affected the annexation of Hawaii, many Americans were interested in Cuba. Cuba was desired primarily because of the fear that it would fall into the hands of Britain or France. Later its economic potential became a motive. In 1848 President James K. Polk unsuccessfully attempted to purchase Cuba from Spain.[101] Nevertheless, later events on this island eventually provided the justification for the successful acquisition of Cuba as well as the Spanish islands in the Pacific—the Philippines.

Acquisition of the Philippines, Puerto Rico and Cuba

Revolutionary efforts on the part of the native peoples of the Philippines and of Cuba in the 1870s were the beginnings of the events that led to American dominance. Prior to 1872 there were some thirty-four revolts by the Filipino people against their Spanish overlords. Between 1872 and the American intervention in 1898, the Spanish government intensified efforts at control by the revival of Inquisition methods of torture and through wholesale execution. A Filipino ethnicity had developed under such circumstances, and, in the few months before the United States declared war on Spain, revolts were widespread.[102] An unsuccessful revolution against Spain in Cuba in 1878

destroyed many Spanish and Cuban planters by forcing them to sell their remaining holdings to pay debts. American capital entered the island in large quantities when the expansion of European beet sugar production drove down prices and bankrupted inefficient growers, who sold out cheaply. As the North American Review *boasted in 1888, this species of ownership gave Americans the financial fruits without political responsibilities.*[103]

Revolution in Cuba flared anew in 1897, but now American interests were threatened. A note from the American government to Spain stated this relationship:

Not only are our citizens largely concerned in the ownership of property and in the industrial and commercial ventures . . . but the chronic condition of trouble causes disturbance in the social and political conditions of our own peoples. . . . A continuous irritation within our borders injuriously affects the normal functions of business, and tends to delay the condition of prosperity to which this country is entitled.[104]

The Spanish efforts to crush the Cuban rebellion were described extensively in the Hearst newspapers; this "yellow journalism," coupled with the sinking of the U.S.S. *Maine* in the harbor of Havana, inflamed public opinion and created demands for intervention and war. Congress obliged and declared war on Spain at the end of April 1898.

Six weeks before the declaration, Admiral George Dewey had received orders that in the event of war the Spanish fleet was not to leave the Pacific. One week after the declaration, the American Pacific fleet sailed into Manila Bay in the Philippines and destroyed the Spanish fleet without the loss of a single American sailor. The leader of the Filipino insurgents, Emilio Aguinaldo, and Dewey agreed that the Filipinos would begin the seige of Manila on land while the American navy blockaded it by sea. An American army would then join the rebels and capture Manila. Aguinaldo naïvely believed that "the Americans, not from mercenary motives, but for the sake of humanity and the lamentations of so many persecuted people have considered it opportune to extend their protecting mantle to our beloved country. . . ."[105] Eventually the American army arrived, and Manila surrendered on August 13.

While the Filipinos and the American navy were occupied in the Pacific, eighteen thousand American soldiers landed in Cuba and Puerto Rico between June 20 and June 25 and were subsequently victorious in the battles of El Caney, San Juan, and Santiago. By the middle of July the conflict was over in the Caribbean.

The treaty that was eventually ratified between the American and Spanish governments in Paris ceded the Philippines, Puerto Rico, and Cuba to the United States. A preliminary agreement with Spain shortly after cessation of hostilities in the Caribbean had called only for the occupation of Manila. But the Republican administration and many of the economic elite wanted all of the Philippine territory because of its strategic value and its resources, particularly its sugar, tobacco, and Manila hemp. According to President McKinley, it was a difficult decision to make. He walked the floor of the White House at night, prayed to God, wrestled with his conscience, and finally arrived at truth: we can't give the islands back to Spain, which would be dishonorable; nor can we turn them over to France or Germany, which would be bad business. Since "they were unfit for government" we have no choice but to take all of the Philippine Islands and "educate the Filipinos, and uplift and civilize and Christianize them."[106] With the decision made, McKinley cabled the American representative at the treaty conference, stating that "the cession must be of the whole archipelago." Spain protested with no success, and took a token payment of $20 million for the loss of this remnant of its former empire.[107] In February 1899, notwithstanding bitter opposition from Democrats and some antiimperialist Republicans, Congress approved the treaty. America had its maritime empire.

The Philippine War, 1899–1901

While the treaty was being debated in Congress, American soldiers in the Philippines had been extending their own occupied area at the expense of the rebel Filipino army, which was forced into humiliating withdrawals. Two days before the treaty was signed, American sentries in a newly occupied sector fired on a number of Filipino soldiers, who returned their fire. The next day the American army attacked the Filipino forces, killing about three thousand. A two-and-a-half-year war for control of the Philippines had begun. Senator Patterson of Colorado believed that the attack had been instigated deliberately in order to increase the necessary votes for ratification.[108]

Between February 5, 1899, and July 4, 1902, over 126,000 American soldiers were engaged in crushing resistance to the incorporation of these islands and the subordination of the Filipino people. Over 4,000 Americans were killed and 3,000 wounded. The consequences for the Filipinos were far greater:

> By a "body-count," 16,000 Filipinos had been slain in combat—although 20,000 may be closer to the actual number. The suffering of the civilian population was intense and beyond measure. Possibly a quarter of a million noncombatants died as a result of the hostilities directly, and indirectly because pestilence and disease often raged uncontrolled.[109]

Indiscriminate shooting of any suspected "rebels" did occur and a "take no prisoners" policy was in effect, but without official authorization from

Washington. General Jake Smith was later admonished in a court martial hearing when it was revealed that he had said to his men: "I want no prisoners. I wish you to kill and burn; the more you kill and burn the better you will please me." The general's attorney stated that the order was to apply only to those over ten years of age.[110]

Theodore Roosevelt justified the incorporation of the Philippines in an address in 1901:

> *It is our duty toward the people living in barbarism to see they are freed from their chains, and we can free them only by destroying barbarism itself. The missionary, the merchant, and the soldier may each have a part to play in this destruction, and in the consequent uplifting of the people.*[111]

Annexation of Hawaii

In 1778, the British Captain James Cook initiated the contact between the Hawaiians and the Europeans by "discovering" Hawaii. The estimated population of the islands at this time was around three hundred thousand. Because of death from new diseases and a low birthrate, the ethnic Hawaiians had diminished to around thirty-nine thousand by 1896.[112] In the middle of the nineteenth century, whites (Europeans and Americans), or *haoles*, had begun to dominate the economy of Hawaii, although the government was still controlled by the native peoples. With the sharp decrease in available native labor, immigration of numerous groups was encouraged—Japanese, Filipinos, Chinese, Portuguese, Koreans, and Puerto Ricans, to name the largest of these immigrant groups.[113] Virtually four-fifths of the arable land was owned by a small population of haoles (primarily Americans, British, and French), with the major economic activity being the sugar industry.[114] Such was the class and ethnic nature of the islands when the American government began its involvement with this society.

In 1875 a reciprocity treaty was signed between Hawaii and the United States. According to this agreement, the principal products of each country were to be admitted duty free, and Hawaii agreed not to convey title of any of its territory to another power. By 1890 three-fourths of Hawaiian imports came from the United States, and 99 percent of its exports went to America. The treaty "virtually made Hawaii an economic colony of the U.S."[115]

In 1890 a new tariff put sugar on the free list—no tariffs would be placed on imported sugar into the United States, but sugar companies in the United States would receive a bounty of two cents a pound. Hence, Hawaiian sugar had to compete with other foreign sugar, and American companies enjoyed a competitive advantage. The tariff had drastic consequences for the Hawaiian planters, who had previously enjoyed a favored status with the United States. Prices fell and plantations depreciated.[116]

Prior to 1890, the planter class opposed annexation to the United States because American immigration restrictions on Oriental labor would prevent planters from using this cheap source. Now, however, the advantages of receiving the two-cents-a-pound bounty outweighed the disadvantages of losing Asian labor supplies. Other groups favored annexation also. Many believed the Hawaiian monarchy to be weak and incapable of controlling the problems between the natives and the foreigners. Some native leaders believed that annexation would increase their own power in government because population restrictions on legislative membership would be eliminated. Probably the majority of the Hawaiian population was undecided, while the Hawaiian monarchy under Queen Liliuokalani was adamantly opposed.[117]

American residents in Hawaii formed the Annexation Club, with the plan of convincing the queen to abdicate; if she refused, force would be used, and a provisional government controlled by the club would run the country until annexation was approved by the American Congress. In 1892 the club filed a report with the American State Department arguing the case for annexation on the basis of (1) the commercial and naval significance of the islands, (2) the corruption of the existing government, (3) the condition of the sugar industry, (4) the danger to white civilization by the increasing number of Orientals in the islands, (5) the potential danger of British control over the islands, and, as an added threat, (6) the diversion of Hawaiian sugar to Canada.[118]

The queen not only refused to abdicate but, in an unconstitutional act, proclaimed a new constitution by royal edict—a constitution that would increase the power of the monarchy at the expense of the planter class. This act, which took place on January 14, 1893, was just what the annexationists needed to justify the overthrow of the government. The Annexation Club declared the abrogation of the monarchy, drew up a provisional constitution, and asked for American aid. Two days later 164 sailors and marines from the U.S.S. *Boston* landed without permission from the queen "to protect American lives and property." The troops were stationed at the consulate and in a vacant building quite close to the Royal Palace and the legislature. The next day the Annexation Club declared that the provisional government was now in power, even though the military force of the queen still existed; the United States minister to Hawaii promptly recognized the new government.[119]

Later that same day Queen Liliuokalani stepped down, stating that she yielded

> *to the superior force of the United States of America whose minister . . . has caused United States troops to be landed at Honolulu, and declared that he would support the said Provisional Government. Now to avoid any collision of armed forces and perhaps loss of life, I do under this protest, and impelled by said forces, yield my authority until such time as the Government of the United States shall, upon the facts being presented to it, undo the actions of its representative and reinstate me in the authority which I claim as the constitutional sovereign of the Hawaiian Islands.*[120]

On February 1, 1893, the United States government declared Hawaii to be a protectorate, and on February 14 a treaty of annexation was signed by representatives of the provisional government and the United States State Department and sent to the Senate for approval.

So far the events had moved rapidly toward annexation. But the president of the United States, Benjamin Harrison, was a Republican and a lame-duck president. The treaty of annexation would have to wait until March, when the Democratic president, Grover Cleveland, took office. Cleveland was opposed to the whole idea of annexation and the underhanded methods that had transpired up to this point. He withdrew the protectorate, declared the illegitimacy of the provisional government, and advocated the restoration of the monarchy. Since the provisional government refused to accept Cleveland's policy and since restoration of the monarchy would have involved the use of American force, a stalemate ensued. Nothing was done until the next administration.[121]

In 1896, the antiexpansionism of the Democrats was repudiated at the polls, and the Republican candidate, William McKinley, took office. A new impetus for annexation came from the perception that Japan was seeking control of Hawaii, along with the older arguments about dominating the Pacific and the dangers to the white race. However, American sugar interests in the United States and antiimperialism votes in the Senate were still sufficient to prevent passage of the annexation treaty until the outbreak of war with Spain in 1898. In July 1898 the treaty passed both houses of Congress (209 to 91 in the House, 42 to 21 in the Senate). On August 12, 1898, Hawaii became part of the United States.

SUMMARY

All of the basic ways in which ethnic groups become subordinated occurred in American history: conquest, enslavement, immigration, and annexation. Conflict permeated all of these processes to a greater or lesser extent.

American civilians, the American army, and members of European ethnic groups invaded and occupied the territories of the approximately two hundred Indian ethnic groups that inhabited what is now the United States. This conquest had several general characteristics: unified whites against divided Indians; the signing of treaties with defeated groups and the placement of these groups on reservations; subsequent violation of these treaties by whites or by Indians who did not recognize the validity of the treaties; numerous guerrilla wars between Indians and whites on the expanding frontier, with a few major clashes between the army and an alliance of tribes; total war against the Indians on the frontier after the Civil War; and the complete subjugation of all Indians by the end of the nineteenth century.

Through a working arrangement between African leaders and European slavers, black slaves were taken to the New World in increasing numbers from 1501 to around 1850. In 1619 the first blacks arrived in the English colonies, and by the end of the first decade of the eighteenth century most of the colonies had passed laws making all blacks slaves for the rest of their lives, along with the children of female slaves. Earlier, inchoate forms of racism in the English colonies later crystallized as a legitimation of the developing slave system. Before 1830, such doctrines were based primarily on a belief in the environmental inferiority of Africans and black slaves. In response to the abolitionists' attacks on the institution of slavery in the nineteenth century, racists began to see the supposed inferiority of blacks as biological and hence permanent.

In the meantime, only a sparsely inhabited Spanish territory—in Florida and west of the Mississippi River—stood in the way of American expansion to the Caribbean and to the rich territory of California. Following the American Revolution, American immigrants entered these territories of Spain in increasing numbers, an immigration that preceded the exercise of American military power. Spain sold a huge section of this territory to France in 1800, and Bonaparte promptly turned around and sold it to the United States in 1803. A revolt of Americans with the support of the American government led to the acquisition of West Florida in 1812. After being invaded by the armies of Andrew Jackson, East Florida was sold to the United States by a Spanish government who could see the handwriting on the wall. Americans in Texas declared their independence and, after several losses, were successful in defeating the Mexican army at San Jacinto in 1836, thereby creating the Republic of Texas. The annexation of Texas by the United States (1845) and the sending of the American army across the traditional dividing line between Texas and Mexico brought about war between the United States and Mexico (1846–1848).

With few setbacks, the American Army entered the halls of Montezuma, and the Mexicans surrendered. One-half of what was then Mexico was added to the territory of the United States and approximately seventy-five thousand Mexicans became subordinate when the ink dried on the Treaty of Guadalupe Hidalgo.

Between 1820 and 1930 some 37 million immigrants from all over the world entered the United States to settle the new territories and to supply much needed labor. Economic opportunity was the pull factor; the push factors were unemployment, overpopulation, famine, poverty, and political persecution in the immigrants' native countries. The great majority of European immigration before 1880 came from northern Europe, and the majority of European immigration after 1880 came from southern and eastern Europe. To many native Americans these facts constituted the basis for believing that immigration was a severe threat to the American way of life, that the inundation of "inferior" southern and eastern Europeans would result in "mongrelization." This racist belief was an important factor in the establishment of immigration restrictions in the 1920s, in spite of the fact that more northern Europeans entered the United States after 1880 than before this date.

In 1867 the United States began to add noncontiguous territories to its empire. Alaska was purchased from Russia, and the Eskimo in this area became subordinate to Americans instead of to Russians. After a revolution of the Cubans against Spain threatened American economic interests on the island and after the Spanish sank the battleship Maine, the United States declared war on a hapless Spain in 1898. Within a few months the remnants of the empire of the conquistadores —Cuba, Puerto Rico, and the Philippines—became American possessions. The Filipinos, expecting independence from the Americans, were brutally suppressed by military force (1899–1901). Hawaii was annexed to the United States in 1898, after Americans in Hawaii were successful in overthrowing the Hawaiian monarchy. The delay between the coup by the American-Hawaiians (January 1893) and the annexation of Hawaii (July 1898) was due to the resistance of the Democratic party, the opposition of the sugar industry in the United States, and the belief held by many that annexation would only bring more inferior peoples into American society. With annexation, the dominant Hawaiians became a charter member subordinate minority within the American Empire.

211

8

MAINTENANCE OF DOMINANCE UP TO 1945: DISCRIMINATION AND RACISM

INTRODUCTION

As we have seen, ethnic minorities in the United States became subordinate to the dominant American group at different times and for different reasons. The treatment of these ethnic minorities also varied, depending upon the manner in which the groups became subordinate, the extent to which they differed phenotypically and culturally from the dominant group, and their population size and concentration in particular regions. Variation in dominant group treatment of these minorities was also affected by changes in the economy (expansion/contraction; prosperity/depression) and by America's foreign policy and relationships in certain cases. Without question the most severe and structured forms of discrimination and the most elaborate doctrines of racism were directed against Black-Americans. At the other extreme, the northern Europeans (excluding the Catholic Irish) experienced only minor and sporadic forms of discrimination and prejudice. In between these extremes, more or less in the following order according to severity of treatment, were the Mexicans, the Indians, the Asians, the Jews, the Irish, and the southern and eastern Europeans (other than the Jews from these regions, and the Italians in particular).

In this chapter and the next, the patterns of discrimination, racism, accommodation, and resistance that developed in regard to these groups will be broadly delineated. These patterns varied according to group, but they all maintained Anglo dominance—and in some instances even intensified this dominance.

BLACK-AMERICANS

Black-Americans were subordinate under two systems of relatively formalized and structured patterns of dominant-subordinate relationships—slavery and apartheid. Institutionalized by the middle of the seventeenth or early eighteenth century, the slave system lasted in the North until around 1800 and in the South until 1865. *Apartheid*, an Afrikaner term, can be defined as a policy of separate but unequal—coerced segregation in numerous areas of social life along with relatively consistent efforts to restrict blacks to the lowest strata of society. Apartheid was the pattern of relations between white and nonslave blacks in both the North and South before the Civil War and was greatly intensified in the South by the end of the nineteenth century. Apartheid was the dominant pattern of relationships between whites and blacks in the North on an informal basis between 1900 and 1945, while in the South in the same period it was institutionalized into the legal structure. Elements of this highly discriminatory and normative system have persisted until the present time.

Slavery

Between approximately 1640 and 1750 an increasing number of discriminatory norms developed that regulated the status of black slaves in both the North and the South. Emerging out of informal practices on the plantations and in the cities, many of these norms became part of the legal code as the result of judicial decisions and the acts of legislative bodies. The major norm which defined the blacks' status was that of chattel property—only Negroes could be bought and sold according to the wishes of their white masters. Numerous other constraints existed, which varied according to time and place as norms and in the extent to which they were enforced.

Generally, the following were the major restrictions on the slave population. Slaves were not allowed to own property, be educated, preach to other slaves without the presence of the master, vote, be witnesses in court against a white person, hire their own time or find their own employment, be legally married, or be abusive to any white person. Sexual relations between black males and white females were absolutely forbidden. Slaves were expected to step out of the way when a white person approached, and any gathering of more than five slaves, away from home and unattended by a white, was illegal. In some cities slaves were subjected to curfew laws (6:00 P.M.) and prohibited from working in a printing office, gambling, or assembling in any public place; in Charleston, no blacks, slave or free, could assemble at parades or other "joyful demonstrations."[1]

As Boorstin has stated regarding the enforcement of these norms:

> The severe laws on the books, even hostile observers noted, were not rigorously or regularly enforced. Many, passed in times of fear or hysteria, were kept through

inertia, only to be handy for a future emergency. Perhaps never before or since—except in modern totalitarian states—have legal rules been applied so whimsically, arbitrarily, and unpredictably. While defensive Southerners emphasized the amelioration of the slave's condition which made this possible, in fact the departures from the letter of the law often made the slave's condition worse than the law allowed.[2]

To enforce these norms, a number of positive and negative sanctions were utilized. These sanctions were designed to accustom the slave "to rigid discipline, demand from him unconditional submission, impress upon him his innate inferiority, develop in him a paralyzing fear of white men, train him to adopt the master's code of good behavior, and instill in him a sense of complete dependence."[3] Flogging was the most common negative sanction, carried out by the master, by an overseer (who might be a slave himself), or by a public flogger whose pay scale depended upon the number of lashes he inflicted. Other negative sanctions were the use of stocks, chaining a person to the ground to be exposed to the sun, branding or other forms of mutilation, extra work, and short rations. On the positive side, slaves might be given time off for good behavior, extra rations and clothing, cash payments, or a small plot of ground for their own use.[4]

On the whole it was better to be a slave in the North than the South, to work on small farms rather than on large plantations, and to be one of a few slaves belonging to a master rather than part of a large gang. But these better positions were only good in comparison to the alternative.

Although the great majority of whites accepted the legality of slavery (at least the legal if not the moral right of slave ownership), few whites were actual slave owners. According to the census of 1860, only 384,000 whites out of a white population of approximately 4 million were slave owners; of these, 10,781 owned 50 slaves or more, and only 1,733 possessed at least 100.[5] It was this small planter class that perpetuated the slave system and eventually convinced other Southerners that secession from the United States was necessary to maintain the southern way of life. "There is no better example in modern history of a handful of the ruling class so shaping public opinion as to bring on a war to preserve an institution which benefited themselves alone."[6] Assisting this class in preserving the "peculiar institution" were proslavery apologists—scholars, politicians, and scientists. Together they developed the most elaborate and systematic racist doctrines ever developed.

Prior to the 1830s there was little organized opposition to the system. As attacks from the abolitionist movement and other groups increased, however, slavery began to require an ideological defense, one that was superior to the earlier environmental-deterministic views of black inferiority. Two major ideas developed: black inferiority as biologically determined and permanently fixed, and slavery as a positive good.

Much of the literature of the period stressed the idea of the innate inferiority of blacks, whether as the result of natural causes or God's Will. According to one such example, ". . . the Negroes, whether physically or morally considered, are so inferior as to resemble the brute creation as nearly as they do the white species. . . ." Hence, ". . . no alteration of their present condition would be productive of the least benefit to them, in as much as no change of their nature can be expected to result there from" (1833).[7] Another states that it is "well established" that "the negro is now an inferior species, or at least a variety of the human race. . . . even when partly civilized under the control of the white man, he speedily returns to the same state if emancipated. . . ." (1863).[8]

A variety of arguments were advanced to show that slavery was a positive good. Blacks had been "saved from the pot" (from cannibalism) and had been given the advantages of Christianity and Western civilization. Slavery was also beneficial for whites since democracy and egalitarianism would not be possible among whites without it. According to a governor of Virginia, "break down slavery and you would with the same blow destroy the great democratic principle of equality among men."[9]

After the defeat of the South in the Civil War (or The War Between the States, or The War for Southern Independence), slavery was eliminated in December 1865 by the Thirteenth Amendment to the Constitution, which stated that "neither slavery nor involuntary servitude, except as punishment for crime whereof the party shall have been duly convicted, shall exist within the United States, or any place subject to their jurisdiction." Nevertheless, racism and discrimination continued.

Apartheid

The apartheid system began in white relationships with "free" Negroes (nonslaves) in the North and the South before the Civil War. During this period there was always a small percentage of blacks with a free status—7.9 percent in 1790, 13.7 percent in 1830, and only 11 percent in 1860.[10] Slaves gained freedom by running away and avoiding recapture, by military service in the colonial wars, by private manumission, by purchasing freedom through a friendly intermediary, and by the abolition of slavery in the northern states in the early nineteenth century.[11]

The free Negro was "a walking contradiction in terms, a social anomaly, a third party in a system built for two. Not only did the free Negroes provide an 'evil example' to slaves, but, much worse, their presence imposed a question mark on the rationale of slavery."[12] Because of this "threat," segregation in numerous areas of social life, disfranchisement, and restrictions on occupational and spatial mobility became part of the social reality of the free Negro and increased throughout the pre–Civil War period.

After the war all blacks were legally "free," and for a brief period from 1867 to around 1880 they enjoyed some improvement in their status.[13] For ten years immediately following the war (1867–1877) the South was treated as a conquered country and was occupied by Federal troops and military governors. Northern Republicans were quite concerned with their positions, and this meant the avoidance of a unified white South in the Democratic party. White liberals, North and South, wanted the end to black discrimination. The upper class in the South had no particular desire to stigmatize blacks by segregating them; labor exploitation was far more significant.[14] As a result of white dissensus and the organized efforts of blacks, for a period blacks voted in large numbers, dominated the skilled manual occupations, developed business enterprises, and elected members of their own group to the national Congress and to the state legislatures.

However, at least in the South (where 90 percent of all blacks resided before 1900), this period of improvement was temporary. After the troops were withdrawn in 1877, the white lower classes demanded racial separation and the relegation of blacks to menial occupations, which would guarantee white workers a "floor" (and would give the black workers a "ceiling"). Industrial capitalists in the North and their Republican spokesmen were now concerned with southern markets. And many liberals in both parts of the country became convinced that the "Negro problem" was the major factor in perpetuating a divided nation.[15] Thus, the South was to be allowed to handle its own affairs. The once fragmented white power structure had again become unified.

In the 1890s new techniques were developed to disfranchise the black electorate, and new ordinances were passed to segregate blacks from the mainstream and to prevent their moving into higher strata. And a code of "racial etiquette" rapidly became institutionalized. Lynchings became an effective tool in creating black conformity to this revived and more intense form of apartheid. Lynchings rose rapidly from 1882 to the early 1890s, and the downward trend from the middle of the 1890s thereafter was a barometer of the success of this intensified degradation. Banton notes that "the edifice of white supremacy was virtually completed by 1906."[16] Very little improvement in the position of blacks took place until after World War II.

Discrimination against Black-Americans.   The following are the major specific forms of discrimination imposed against nonslave blacks before the Civil War and against all blacks from the Civil War to 1945 by white Americans in a position to do so, with the support and approval of the great majority of the rest. In certain types of discriminatory norms there was a remarkable stability; the techniques changed but the discriminatory norms persisted.

1. *Discrimination in voting.*   After the American Revolution, state after state in both the North and the South overtly or covertly (through property requirements) disfranchised the free Negro. By 1860 only five states in New England legally permitted black voting, but even in those states informal tactics like threats or "losing" the black voter's registration form prevented large numbers from voting.[17]

In March of 1870 the Fifteenth Amendment to the Constitution was ratified, thus making at least all overt forms of voting discrimination illegal. From this point on there were only sporadic efforts in the North to restrict black voting. In the South, however, numerous practices were invented or revived to prevent the political participation of blacks. In the 1870s election returns were doctored, terrorizing tactics by such organizations as the Ku Klux Klan kept blacks from the polls, and Negro voters were falsely arrested the day before elections and then released shortly afterwards.[18]

In spite of such tactics, blacks managed to vote in sufficient numbers that whites competed for black votes. In the 1890s the southern legislatures moved to make disfranchisement legal. Mississippi, in 1890, came up with the poll tax and the literacy test. The poll tax was a voluntary annual payment of a small fee to the state for the privilege of voting. By 1910 this practice had spread to seven southern states, and a few of these states added modifications; for example, the levy was cumulative beginning when the voter reached twenty-one, or interest charges were added to each year in which the person did not vote. Both the white and black poor were affected, but the device still affected the black poor disproportionately.[19] The literacy test demanded that the potential voter show an ability to read, write, or speak English—usually to read the Constitution in English, or to answer questions about government. As a rule, whites would be given simple questions, and mispronunciations would be overlooked. Often a single error would disqualify blacks.

During this same period—the end of the nineteenth century—another widely used device was the grandfather clause, invented in Louisiana. According to this clause, a man might register permanently before September 1, 1898, if he had been entitled to vote in any state prior to and including January 1, 1867, or if he was the son or grandson of a man so entitled. Since few blacks could vote before this date, the act was clearly discriminatory. In Louisiana following World War I, Negroes attempting to register were required to give their age exactly in years, months, weeks, and days, and were disqualified if they were unable to do so.[20] Voters in a few states had to meet a character requirement—in practice this meant a black had to be approved by a white.[21] Other tactics included hiding the registration books and telling the Negro voter the book was somewhere else, or allowing a black to register on one day only, which always happened to be the wrong day when he appeared; the less subtle tactics of violence and intimidation were still prevalent.

In time, many of these "legal" stipulations for voting were declared unconstitutional by the courts under the Fourteenth or Fifteenth Amendments, but new devices would usually take their place. Whatever the technique, the norm of black disfranchisement was enforced, and enforced quite effectively. For example, a study of Mississippi counties in 1910 found only a handful of black registered voters—twenty-five in a county with a black population of eleven thousand.[22] In 1940 it was estimated that only 4 percent of all eligible black voters in eight southern states cast their ballots in this election year.[23] Because of voting discrimination, only a small percentage of those blacks legally qualified to vote did so until after the Voting Rights Act of 1965.

2. *Discrimination in housing.* Before the twentieth century, housing discrimination per se was sporadic and informal. Low income produced by job discrimination was a major factor in restricting blacks to the worst areas of the cities. As a consequence, segregation by race in northern or southern cities was rarely as pronounced as it would be in the twentieth century. In the South, well-to-do white neighborhoods had a sprinkling of poorer homes inhabited by blacks, who were often the servants in those white homes. In the large northern cities, such as Philadelphia, Boston, and Chicago, blacks were scattered throughout. Before 1915 blacks lived in almost all sections of Chicago, and one-third of the black population lived in sections that were less than 10 percent Negro.[24] Blacks, however, did pay higher rents than whites for equivalent residences.

In the twentieth century, discrimination against blacks in housing became normative—blacks were not to live in residential areas desired by whites. The black ghettos found in the major cities of the North today began with the large influx of rural southern blacks, particularly in the years 1915 to 1918 and 1940 to 1945. In 1910 only 10.4 percent of all blacks lived in the North. This proportion increased to 23.8 percent by 1940, a net migration of 1,750,000.[25] During the war and the postwar years from 1940 to 1950 another 1,244,700 entered the northern cities.[26] Between 1910 and 1950 72 percent of the total migration went to six states—California, Illinois, Michigan, New York, Ohio, and Pennsylvania.[27]

The major technique of housing discrimination in this period was the restrictive covenant. Areas of a city were covered by a single contract in which house owners in the particular area agreed not to sell or rent to blacks. A typical clause in a real estate contract stated that "... no part of said premises shall be sold, given, conveyed or leased to any Negro or Negroes, and no permission of license to use or occupy any part thereof shall be given to any Negro, except house servants or janitors or chauffeurs employed thereon as aforesaid."[28] The housing contract often specified what Negroes were—such as all persons with one-eighth or more Negro blood or anybody commonly known as colored. In a study of St. Louis and Chicago, the increase in racial covenants was directly correlated with the increase in the Negro population of these two cities. "As more and more Negroes came to these cities and the need for additional housing accommodation increased, at the same time, efforts to limit the available accommodations through the use of restrictive covenants were heightened."[29] It was the restrictive covenant, according to this study, that produced "the fact of residential racial segregation in the North in its present form."[30]

In addition, real estate agents would not handle transactions with Negroes who desired to move into white neighborhoods, and lending institutions would find that blacks were not qualified for mortgage loans if the property was in a white area.[31] Article 34 of the Realtor's Code of Ethics of the National Association of Realtors in the 1940s stated that "a realtor should never be instrumental in introducing into a neighborhood a character of property or occupancy, members of any race or nationality, or any individuals whose presence will clearly be detrimental to property values in that neighborhood."[32] Until 1950 the Federal Housing Authority (FHA) supported this norm in its own policy statements.

3. *Discrimination in public organizations—services, transportation, and accommodations.* Segregation in numerous areas of public interaction or in services offered to the public has a long history in the United States. Segregation practices between black and white that became widespread and institutionalized in the South in the early twentieth century were a common aspect of race relations in the North before the Civil War. According to Litwack, the "free" Negroes in the North

found themselves systematically separated from whites. They were either excluded from railway cars, omnibuses, stagecoaches, and steamboats or assigned to special "Jim Crow" sections; they sat, when permitted, in secluded and remote corners of theaters and lecture halls; they could not enter most hotels, restaurants, and resorts, except as servants; they prayed in "Negro pews" in white churches, and if partaking of the sacrament of the Lord's Supper, they waited until the whites had been served the bread and wine. Moreover, they were often educated in segregated schools, punished in segregated prisons, nursed in segregated hospitals, and buried in segregated cemeteries.[33]

In terms of public education in the North, "by the 1830s statute or custom placed Negro children in separate schools in nearly every northern community."[34] In some cases even a segregated education was not provided for Negroes—any form of education was proscribed. The black schools that did exist were often far from equal to the caliber and quality of the white schools. Black schools were ill equipped, were allocated limited funds, had a curriculum inferior to the courses offered white students, and paid low salaries to the teachers; white teachers faced social ostracism if they taught black children.[35]

The free Negro in the South before the Civil War faced similar conditions in some respects yet in other respects had closer contact with whites. As in the North, southern blacks, from the earliest period of this nation, sat in separate sections of the churches, and, like their northern brethren, they began to found separate churches around the beginning of the nineteenth century in reaction to this stigma. Education, what there was of it, was also segregated, while intermingling in restaurants occurred in some places. But *extreme* castelike separation formalized into laws was a post–Civil War development. In the 1850s a Presbyterian minister in the South described his view of this pattern:

They [the Negroes] belong to us. We also belong to them. They are divided among us and mingled up with us, eating from the same storehouses, drinking from the same fountains, dwelling in the same enclosures, forming parts of the same families . . . . See them all around you, in these streets, in all these dwellings; a race distinct from us, yet closely united to us . . . .[36]

This was neither integration nor equality, but contact was greater, and the almost pathological insistence on avoidance and separation that would be characteristic of the South around 1900 was not evident.

Almost immediately after the Civil War the climate in the South began to change. According to several scholars, blacks in the postbellum South became more competitive and organized. From the white point-of-view, they became "uppity niggers." In fact, for many whites thay had become dangerous.[37]

For a while blacks were successful in thwarting the attempts of city governments to create segregation in trains and streetcars. By the last decade of the nineteenth century white unification and favorable court decisions produced rapid changes. In 1891 Georgia passed a law segregating the races in streetcars. Between 1902 and 1910 virtually all the southern states and several border states followed suit.[38] Similarly, between 1881 (Tennessee) and 1907 (Oklahoma) all of the southern states had segregation laws for trains.[39] Earlier laws specified separation within cars by some form of partition, while later statutes created separate cars for black and white.

Segregation on public conveyances was given legal sanction in 1896 by the Supreme Court in *Plessy* v. *Ferguson*. The Court ruled that the Louisiana railway segregation law was constitutional as long as there were equal facilities. The majority opinion held that separation per se did not "stamp the colored race with a badge of inferiority." Justice J. M. Harlan, dissenting, wrote: "The arbitrary separation of citizens, on the basis of race, while they are on a public highway, is a badge of servitude wholly inconsistent with the civil freedom and the equality before the law established by the Constitution."[40]

Blacks were legally discriminated against and segregated in numerous other areas in the South. They used separate entrances and exits, separate drinking fountains, separate pay windows, separate red-light districts, separate hospital rooms and prison cells, separate public toilets, and separate play facilities in public recreation areas. No blacks were to be accommodated in any hotel that received white patronage. They could try on clothing in department stores along with whites, but only if they purchased the clothing.[41] The use of library facilities was generally prohibited. Only 99 out of 774 public libraries in thirteen southern states served Negroes, and more than half of these were concentrated in four states (Virginia, Kentucky, Texas, and North Carolina).[42]

Southern public and private schools continued to be segregated and were given legal sanction by the application of the *Plessy* v. *Ferguson* decision to education. However, although schools were separate, they were not equal. During 1935 and 1936 the average annual salary for teachers in Negro schools in seventeen southern states was $510, compared to $833 for teachers in white schools in the same states.[43] Public monies were predominantly allocated to white schools.[44] The curriculum for black high school students was primarily limited to craft and vocational training, and numerous counties did not even provide a four-year high school program for blacks.[45]

In the North, similar forms of segregation in public accommodations, public transportation, public services, and public education existed, although such discrimination was not part of the legal structure. By 1910 sixteen northern states had civil rights laws against these forms of discrimination, but they were rarely enforced.[46] Intimidation, harassment, and refusal of service were quite effective in maintaining black-white apartheid, northern style.

4. *Discrimination in the military.* Discrimination against blacks in the military and naval forces of the United States is another form of discrimination with a long history. For a brief period during the American Revolution, in spite of George Washington's directive not to enlist blacks, the Continental Congress authorized their recruitment. Supplying needed manpower, they served in integrated units in several northern colonies (with the exceptions of Massachusetts, Rhode Island, and Connecticut). In the South, however, blacks were not permitted to bear arms or to serve in the militia.[47]

Laws passed by states and the federal government in the late eighteenth century prevented blacks from enlisting in the militias, and these were not repealed until 1862.[48] Again under the pressure of manpower needs, blacks in the North were recruited for the Federal army during the Civil War; by the end of the war, over 9 percent of the Union army was Negro. Black soldiers in segregated units under the command of whites were actively involved in this war—they participated in over 499 military engagements, of which 39 were major battles.[49]

Between 1869 and the end of World War II, the core of black service in the army was restricted to four all-black units, two cavalry and two infantry. In the nineteenth century the blacks were stationed in the West, distinguishing themselves in the Indian wars.[50] Blacks were used in combat roles in the Spanish-American War, but only forty thousand out of four hundred thousand black soldiers in World War I saw combat; the remainder were in service units.[51] In 1922 the navy, which had always been highly discriminatory, adopted the policy of total exclusion of blacks except as messmen.[52]

Immediately preceding World War II, blacks made up only 5.9 percent of the army and served in segregated service units. There were only five black officers, three of whom were chaplains. There were no blacks in the U.S. Marine Corps, and only black messmen or stewards in the navy.[53] With the advent of war, black manpower was needed once again—not to fight but to free white service personnel for combat duties. Segregated units were formed in the army and the Marine Corps primarily in service-duty capacities, such as latrine services (digging trenches for toilets and then filling them after white troops had left).

Toward the end of the war, guidelines directed against discrimination were issued from the War Department, but these were poorly circulated and largely ignored. Integrated units and the reduction of discrimination did not take place until after 1948.

Two incidents during World War II symbolize the position of the black soldier in American history up to this point. In 1942, at an Army Day parade in Savannah, Georgia, black troops marched at the end of the parade behind the garbage trucks. In the winter of 1944, blacks on a troop train in Texas ate their food behind a curtain in the dining room car. Eating in the main section with the white American troops were German prisoners of war.[54]

5. *Occupational discrimination.* For the most part blacks have been restricted to menial jobs not valued by whites. Blacks have traditionally been cooks, coachmen, domestics, barbers, hod carriers, washerwomen, field hands, secondhand clothing dealers, garbage collectors, assembly line workers, and those who performed the hottest and dirtiest tasks in the factories. Thus, such occupations have become known as "Negro jobs."

There were exceptions to this. In the South many blacks were skilled artisans, a tradition stemming from the slave period. By the end of the Civil War five out of six skilled workers in the South were black.[55] With the increase in European immigration, however, many traditional unskilled and skilled occupations associated with blacks were taken over by whites. In addition, every depression or recession would redefine "Negro jobs" as occupations reserved for whites. Thus, by 1900 the proportion of black artisans to white dropped to one in twenty.[56] The other exception was the development of a small group of black businessmen and professionals; because of discrimination, however, their activities were generally limited to serving other blacks within black communities.

The earliest unions, such as the Knights of Labor and the National Labor Union, opposed racial discrimination, but these organizations declined in membership and ceased to exist by the 1890s. Antidiscrimination was also a policy of the American Federation of Labor in its earliest years, but by 1900, with the admission of anti-Negro craft unions into the federation, its policies changed to those which excluded Negroes or advocated separate Negro unions.[57]

The major techniques of discrimination utilized by unions in both the North and the South included voting formal restrictions into their constitutions, writing separate racial seniority and promotional provisions into union-business contracts; keeping blacks out of apprentice programs by reserving those openings to sons of existing members, denying access to union hiring halls, excluding blacks from craft occupations by controlling the policies of the licensing boards, sending a union applicant back and forth between offices until he was discouraged (the volley ball technique); filing the application under G (for garbage), and waving a pile of papers under the applicant's nose to indicate how many are ahead of him (the full house technique).[58]

Such techniques generally were quite effective in eliminating blacks from the skilled crafts, particularly in the building trades. Only the Congress of Industrial Organization (CIO), formed in the 1930s on the basis of workers in a given industry (such as automobiles or steel), engaged in nondiscriminatory policies toward blacks.

6. *Other forms of discrimination.* Blacks were excluded from jury duty from the beginning of this country's independence until after World War II. Generally, such discrimination has occurred in the absence of legal statutes prohibiting blacks from serving. And since 1880, when a Supreme Court decision declared unconstitutional a West Virginia statute by which only white males could serve, jury discrimination has been relatively consistent, even though proscribed by law. Major techniques have been to combine a number of procedures to ensure that blacks would not sit in the jury box—using property lists or lists of registered voters, avoiding addresses in black neighborhoods, requiring "good" character, using lists of members of organizations known to be reserved for whites only. If a black still managed to be in the courtroom as part of a jury pool, he or she would be challenged and dismissed by one or the other of the attorneys involved in the case.[59]

Numerous states, North and South, passed laws preventing intermarriage of whites and Negroes (or whites and "coloreds"). In a study of state laws on the subject in 1910, Stephenson found prevention-of-intermarriage statutes between whites and persons "of color" in twenty-six states and territories—all of the southern states plus Colorado, Idaho, Delaware, Indiana, Oregon, Nevada, Utah, and California. Some of the laws defined "of color" according to "blood" content, such as one-eighth, one-fourth, or one-half or more. Generally, the statutes declared an intermarriage to be null and void and imposed criminal liability on the act. Punishment called for imprisonment or a fine or both (Alabama law called for imprisonment of at least two years but no more than seven; Colorado stipulated a fine varying from fifty dollars to five hundred dollars or from three months' to two years' imprisonment or both).[60] Restrictions on racial intermarriage persisted in many states until declared unconstitutional by the Supreme Court in 1968.

In the South a code of "racial etiquette" or institutionalized social distance became part of southern life in the twentieth century. In this caste system interracial dining was prohibited. Negroes on service calls could enter white homes only through the back door. Black male pedestrians could not look at white women sitting on porches. White drivers were always given the right of way, and blacks were arrested for careless driving if they violated this norm. Negroes were not to make social calls on whites, offer their hand to a white man for handshaking, call a white man by his first name, or look a white person straight in the eyes while speaking. All blacks were called by their first names or by some patronizing term, such as boy, auntie, or grandad.[61] A black person who failed to adhere to these norms of interpersonal conduct or to other discriminatory norms was an "uppity nigger" and could suffer violent consequences.

Far more pervasive than the sporadic sanctioning of black "deviants" was what Dollard has termed the "atmosphere of intimidation":

> *Every Negro in the South knows that he is under a kind of sentence of death; he does not know when his turn will come, it may never come, but it may also be at any time. This fear tends to intimidate the Negro man. If he loves his family, this love itself is a barrier against any open attempt to change his status . . . . Southern white people do not like to believe they have created such an uncomfortable situation for the Negro and are likely to minimize the fact. They tend to rely on the openly ascertained statistics of lynching and violence and to point out that not many Negroes are killed; what the white caste does not take into account is the emotional climate that is established for the Negro by asocial violence and by the many aggressive pressures which are leveled against him whenever he tries to claim his full status as a man in the sense of the wider American conception of a human being. What matters is the fear of extra or extralegal violence, not knowing when or how the danger may appear, not being able to organize oneself with reference to it, uncertainty, and the mist of anxiety raised under such conditions.*[62]

In the North intimidation existed also, but the system was not as consistent or as structured. Inconsistencies were present in most of the states and areas of the North, creating an anxiety-producing set of circumstances for those blacks who did not restrict themselves to ghetto life. If one was unsure of acceptance, it was better to play safe and avoid the encounter or the situation. In 1896, W. E. B. Du Bois described such circumstances for those who interacted across the color line in Philadelphia:

> *In all walks of life the Negro is liable to meet some objection to his presence or some discourteous treatment; and the ties of friendship or memory seldom are strong enough to hold across the color line.*
>
> *If an invitation is issued to the public for any occasion, the Negro can never know whether he would be welcomed or not; if he goes he is liable to have his feelings hurt and get into unpleasant altercation; if he stays away, he is blamed for indifference.*[63]

These patterns of discrimination against blacks varied, of course, in different times and places during this rather extensive time period (1880–1945); nevertheless, when white discrimination against blacks is compared to the treatment of other groups in this country or to discrimination in other societies, past and present, one can see that such patterns have never been exceeded for consistency, duration, and severity, with the possible exception of discrimination against Jews in Christendom.

White Racism.   It is probably safe to say that between the end of the Civil War and 1945 the overwhelming majority of whites believed in the inferiority of Black-Americans. And within this large segment of the white population, regardless of ethnic affiliation, the majority believed this inferiority to be biologically determined. During this period there were the two general forms of racist thought and attitude—conflict racism and paternalistic racism. Many people, particularly intellectuals and writers between 1865 and 1900, held to both views simultaneously in their conception of "good and bad niggers."

As will be examined in more detail in Chapter 9, many blacks, North and South, took active roles in working for and supporting civil rights legislation. During the Reconstruction Period, with the support of the military governments, they actively participated in government at the state and federal levels. And in spite of efforts to disfranchise them in the South before 1900, blacks continued to play a part in the electoral process, even in the absence of federal protection. Clearly, to whites and particularly to southern whites, these were uppity Negroes. Given these circumstances, it was no wonder that the dominant racist theme was conflict racism, and more specifically, the Negro as beast.

The beast idea was not a unique invention of this period. In English literature *prior to the slave period*, such words as "brutish," "bestial," or "beastly" were applied to the blacks of Africa.[64] Such ideas, motivated by an almost pathological fear of miscegenation, were revived during and after the Civil War. In the minds of many whites, the black male was preoccupied with the desire to fornicate with white women. In addition, black people had disgusting features, had innate constitutional weaknesses as indicated by white perceptions of their disease and crime rates, and had been *degenerating* since emancipation. A professor of medicine in 1900 believed they were "reverting through hereditary forces to savagery."[65]

To many intellectuals and writers in the 1880s and 1890s, influenced by the works of Charles Darwin and the social Darwinists, the black race was doomed to extinction as a result of this degeneration.[66] However, this ultimate extinction would take time. The problem became "how to prevent the contamination of the white community while the doomed race reverted to savagery and declined morally, physically, and economically."[67] For others, the black race was already in such a state.

By the turn of the century numerous books had been written emphasizing the supposed biological traits of blacks, such as criminality, sexual excess, immorality, and animalistic body features. *The Negro as Beast* by Charles Carroll and *The Leopard's Spots* by Thomas Dixon are two of these books. Samuel Gompers, head of the American Federation of Labor wrote an article in 1904 describing Negroes who replaced striking white workers as "hordes of ignorant blacks," "possessing but few of those attributes we have learned to revere and love," "huge strapping fellows, ignorant and vicious, whose predominating trait was animalism."[68] Regarding the sexual aspect, one doctor claimed that the root of the problem was "the large size of the negro's penis" and the fact that he lacked "the sensitiveness of the terminal fibers which exists in the Caucasian." It followed, therefore, that "the

African's birthright" was "sexual madness and excess."[69] He could never gain sexual satisfaction.

Such a view justified numerous forms of discrimination and more violent conflict. Lynchings were legitimated as necessary to protect white women from rape and to curb other criminal tendencies.[70] Political disfranchisement was justified on the grounds that political equality would lead to social equality, and social equality would mean the worst of all possible evils—miscegenation. Segregation in all of its forms was believed to be necessary to avoid contamination, miscegenation, and the decline of the white race and American civilization.[71] Educational discrimination was also justified on the grounds of biological inferiority, and inferiority of the "beast" variety or of the more traditional view of the "retarded" but docile black. One scientist writing in the *American Journal of Anatomy* in 1906 argued that the black brain was smaller, had fewer nerve cells, and was shaped differently from the white brain. Because of this, blacks were more subjective and emotional and were meek and submissive except when passions were aroused. "The Caucasian and the Negro are fundamentally opposite extremes in evolution." Therefore, "it is useless to try to elevate the Negro by education or otherwise, except in the direction of his natural endowments."[72]

But arguments based upon the science of the times were not the only justifications for discrimination against blacks. A recurring idea with a high consensus throughout the period (and before) was religious in nature: "If God Almighty had intended these races to be equal, He would have so created them."[73] A variant on this was that if God had wanted integration he would not have created three separate races.

Whites more removed from the competition and conflict between the races in the lower strata were likely to subscribe to a paternalistic view of black "inferiority." In this more traditional view, blacks were generally considered childlike. They only became aggressive in reaction to hostile white treatment. According to the president of Roanoke College in Virginia in 1899, the Negro "is naturally docile and peaceable; and if we trust him with anything like fairness, justice, and consideration we claim for ourselves as men, we shall hear less of race antagonism in the future."[74] In this moderate perspective, all of the talk about blacks raping white women was severe distortion. The "good darky" was not gone and could be trained to do lower levels of work in capitalistic production. With the "proper" education, blacks could be elevated and taught to be productive. Such a view was popular among the educated and the liberals and in the philanthropic circles, as well as among many of the captains of industry.

A variant of paternalism was the "charming primitive" stereotype popular in some white circles in the 1920s. Robert Park, a famous sociologist, wrote in 1918 that while the Anglo-Saxon was basically a pioneer and frontiersman type, the Negro was essentially "an artist, loving life for its own sake. His *métier* is expression rather than action. He is, so to speak, the lady among the races."[75] The negrophiles of the twenties wrote novels and plays "emphasizing that the blacks were basically exotic primitives out of place in white society because of their natural spontaneity, emotionalism, and sensuality."[76] Of course such exotic and charming primitives were not capable of performing more advanced tasks in industry and the professions. Music and dance were their forte. Harlem became the equivalent of the protected native reserve where whites could take taxis and observe the dancing natives at the "Darktown Strutters' Ball."

For a while before 1900, some whites made a distinction between "good and bad niggers." Good Negroes were docile and respectful; bad Negroes were problems, with their insolence and disrespect and with their demands for equality. The good ones could be kept around; the bad had to be expelled from the society or severely segregated and controlled. However, according to Friedman in *The White Savage*:

> By the turn of the century, it was becoming increasingly difficult for a white Southerner to associate only with servile Negroes while he avoided the "uppity" ones. Attempts to exclude defiant Negroes were gradually producing an unwieldy system of public segregation. Extensive, complex, and impersonal, the system often unwittingly prevented the docile from crossing color lines.[77]

The large movement of blacks to the impersonal cities of the South, the problem of distinguishing between the good and the bad, and the growing belief that Negroes were bearers of contagious diseases all operated to reduce this good-bad distinction in the minds of many.[78]

These forms of white racism directed against Black-Americans had roots in England and in the later slave system. And many of these beliefs have continued in the thinking and verbal expressions of whites up to the present time. A final note: given the lower status position of most members of the European ethnic groups in this period, *discrimination* by whites should be translated as discrimination by Americans or Anglo-Americans since they had the power; however, white *racism* (or "prejudice") was prevalent among the European ethnics as well as the Anglos.

MEXICAN-AMERICANS

With the end of the Mexican War in 1848, Mexicans in the territory acquired by the United States became Mexican-Americans. Although they were subordinate, it took several decades of Anglo discrimination to deprive them of their lands, reduce them to menial labor, and make them politically impotent. This process of increased subordination or the placement of the great majority of Mexicans in the lower stratum occurred at different rates in different areas of the Southwest. In Texas, Arizona, and much of California the process was relatively rapid, involving blatant discrimination coupled with extensive violence. In New Mexico, on the other hand, "the process was indirect and subtle and took the form of gradual assertion of dominance through manipulation rather than by outright appropriation."[79]

With the gold rush in northern California and the subsequent extension of the railroad to this state, California was rapidly inundated by Americans and European immigrants. Within a relatively short period Mexican miners were driven from their camps and from their claims by the new arrivals. Camps were burned and numerous lynchings of Mexicans occurred throughout the period between 1849 and 1890 (the last reported lynching of a Mexican was in 1892). In the words of McWilliams, "the subordination of Mexicans in the social structure of California cannot be understood apart from the early-day pattern of violence and intimidation."[80]

The great majority of Mexican land passed into Anglo ownership not only in California but throughout the Southwest. A number of obvious discriminatory tactics were utilized in the process, but cultural differences, technological change, and natural disasters also were involved. Under the Spanish or Mexican system, land grants were not subject to taxes as land per se; only agricultural products and livestock were taxed. Land boundaries, in addition, were often quite vague and imprecise. "Under the jurisdiction of the Anglo legal system, property owned by Mexican-Americans became subject to property taxes, precise delineation of boundaries, and registration of land titles. Herein lies a major causal factor in the demise of Mexican-American land ownership."[81] Boundaries that could not stand up in court often meant the loss of the land to an Anglo with a more precise claim. Property taxes that were not paid on time accumulated interest (often compounded monthly), and eventually the land would be sold to pay the taxes. On the face of it, the acquisition of Mexican land by the Americans seems to be an excellent example of wholesome and normal competition; however, the rules of the game were Anglo, and the overwhelming majority of the judges and lawyers who played the game were also Anglo. Valdez explains one tactic used by Anglo lawyers: "One legal partner would file suit against an unregistered parcel of land while his associate would offer his services for the defense of the land title, *agreeing to accept land as retribution for his services*. Regardless of the outcome of the case, both lawyers would win; the Mexican-American landowner would be the sole loser."[82] Land tax assessments were often clearly discriminatory, as higher taxes were levied against Mexican landowners, and if Mexican land so taxed became Anglo due to tax delinquency, then the tax assessment would be lowered. Small Mexican farmers were also forced to sell their land in the face of highly organized and financed reclamation programs and large-scale farming and cattle industries owned by Anglos.

Political dominance by Anglos in California government was established in a short period. "By 1851, all native Mexicans had been excluded from the state Senate; by the 1860s, only a few Mexicans remained in the Assembly;

and by the 1880s, people with Spanish surnames could no longer be found in public offices."[83]

In Texas similar land-grabbing tactics were employed along with the utilization of barbed wire to acquire Mexican land. Barbed wire enclosed open cattle range and kept out the sheep and cattle ranchers who owned animals but little or no land.[84] Within a very short time after the Mexican War, most of the land was owned by a few wealthy Anglos. A census in 1860 found that 263 Texans owned over one hundred thousand dollars in real property, and all but two were Anglos.[85] In one county, Nueces, all but one of the Mexican land grants became Anglo.[86] With the introduction of the cotton plantations and the absence of sufficient slaves, most of the Mexican population was engaged either in the cattle industry as wage-earning cowboys or as workers in the cotton fields. Joan Moore has summarized the development of Mexican subordination in Texas:

> *By 1900 the Mexican laborer in both rural and urban Texas had become defined as an inferior person and as a member of a distinctive race entitled to neither political, educational, nor social equality. Remnants of Mexican equality survived only to a limited extent in some of the commercial towns of the Rio Grande valley where Mexicans remained in the majority.*[87]

Land theft was somewhat slower in New Mexico because of the preponderance of the Mexican population and its more cohesive social structure. However, the upper-class Hispanos (*rico* class), constituting around twenty families, allied themselves with Anglo merchants, bankers, and lawyers to dominate this local society; collectively, this alliance was termed "the Sante Fe Ring" by its opponents.[88] Since virtually all lawyers and judges in New Mexico were Anglos, and they had the cooperation of the *rico* class, Hispanos would continually lose in court cases over land grants and land titles. One device used by Anglos in alliance with the upper-class Hispanos was to file bogus claims on Spanish land grants. Such claims automatically kept the land from becoming public domain until the validity of the grant was established; but in the meantime the land could be grazed. Another device was to buy a small section of land from a Mexican resident, thus giving the buyer rights to the pasturage held in common by all landowners in the area under Spanish law. A surveyor appointed by President Grover Cleveland "contended that gross fraud had been committed through the machinations of Anglo-Americans in close alliance with a few large Spanish-American landowners."[89]

Until sufficient Anglos entered the territory, New Mexico was governed by federal American officials appointed to the government and to the courts. Thus, the much larger Mexican population was effectively denied political participation and the political control that democratic suffrage would have introduced. McWilliams has stated that ". . . the federal government ruled

New Mexico for sixty-three years as a dependent province."[90] New Mexico eventually became a state in 1912.

Arizona, the last major area acquired from Mexico, was extremely under-populated by both Mexicans and Americans throughout most of the nineteenth century. Until the end of the Apache wars in the 1880s, both Anglos and Mexicans were concentrated in a few areas, particularly around Tucson. Mining and railroads were introduced in the latter part of the nineteenth century, and Mexicans native to the area as well as Mexican nationals from Sonora supplied the labor.[91]

The large influx of several million legal and illegal immigrants from Mexico between 1900 and 1945 merely added members to the subordinate Mexican-American group in a system whose basic features had been struc-tured in the nineteenth century. Anglos made few distinctions between the old and the new Mexican populations.

In the twentieth century Anglo discrimination centered around exploit-ing the lower-class Mexican laborers (who made up the bulk of this group until after World War II), segregating them from Anglos in numerous areas of social life, and trying to prevent their political participation. Discrimina-tion against Mexican-Americans was never as formalized as discrimination against blacks and often varied widely by states in the Southwest and by counties within the states; however, in certain areas and at certain times, discrimination was equally severe and had drastic effects on Mexican equality and self-esteem.

Occupationally, Mexicans were restricted to the most menial tasks in the industries of the Southwest, particularly in agriculture, mining, and the railroads. They were generally paid less for the same labor done by poor Anglos or by European ethnic group members. They were prevented from entering most trade unions, and in times of general unemployment or when the introduction of machinery reduced the need for manual labor they were the first to be fired. That such exploitation was profitable can be seen by the tremendous growth of the vegetable and fruit industry that began in the Southwest around 1900 and that by 1930 was producing 40 percent of the country's total supply of these products.[92] Between 1900 and 1940 Mexicans constituted 65 to 85 percent of the work force in agriculture, 60 percent of the labor in the mining industry, and 60 to 90 percent of the laborers on eighteen western railroads.[93]

Various forms of segregation in different areas of social life were com-monplace in numerous counties, particularly in California and Texas. In 1942 the sheriff of Los Angeles County made a special report in relation to the problem of Mexican delinquency. Although the report stated racist rea-sons for Mexican juvenile delinquency—inborn character traits—it did present the following information about discrimination:

Discrimination and segregation, as evidenced by public signs and rules, such as appear in certain restaurants, public swimming plunges, public parks, theaters, and even in schools, cause resentment among the Mexican people. . . . There are certain parks in this state in which a Mexican may not appear, or else only on a certain day of the week. There are certain plunges where they are not allowed to swim, or else only on one day of the week, and it is made evident by signs reading to that effect, for instance, "Tuesdays reserved for Negroes and Mexicans. . . ." Certain theaters in certain towns either do not allow Mexicans to enter, or else segregate them in a certain section. Some restaurants absolutely refuse to serve them a meal and so state by public signs. . . . All this applies to both the foreign and American-born Mexicans.[94]

In Texas similar restrictions existed. McWilliams notes that Mexicans were denied burial in major cemeteries and denied attendance in white churches on Sundays, and that signs on the toilets in Texas courthouses stated: For Whites—Mexicans Keep Out.[95] Taylor, in his 1929 study of Nueces County, Texas, found that the class of the Mexican-American made a difference regarding service in restaurants, barber shops, and drug stores: "If a Mexican is high class, they admit him, and if of the lower class, they don't; they draw the line on the laboring class."[96] Taylor gave this statement by one white Texan that illustrates the mixture of class and ethnicity in regard to social distance: "We give social equality to educated Spaniards, but these (Mexicans) are a cross between Aztec Indian and Spanish, and are not white. They get no social equality."[97] Other forms of social distance in this country, presumably related to lower-class Mexicans, were given by a school executive: "If you give the Mexicans a meal, hand it out the back door like you would to a Negro. . . . You don't visit them. You holler and he comes out of his house and you have him come over to you. In the stores they tolerate the Mexicans' coming, but they must go to their own restaurants."[98]

In many of the older towns and cities of the Southwest with large Mexican populations, Mexican-Americans were restricted to certain areas, or *barrios*, which in many cases were sections of cities long inhabited by Mexicans (in some cases even before there were Anglos). Devices commonly used against blacks were also used to maintain residential segregation of Mexican-Americans—for example, restrictive covenants and refusal to sell to Mexicans any homes in the Anglo areas.[99]

Around some of the cities and towns in the Southwest, squatter camps made up of shacks grew up, inhabited by Mexican farm workers for the most part. These *colonias*, or "Mex towns," were generally separated from the Anglo community by physical space. One writer expressed the essence of the *colonia*: ". . . it was never intended that the *colonias* were to be part of the wider community; rather, it was meant that they were to be apart from it in every way; *colonia* residents were to live apart, work apart, play apart, worship apart, and unfortunately trade, in some cases, apart."[100]

Educational discrimination of various forms was widespread, particularly in those counties in rural or urban areas with large Mexican populations. In the larger cities, school segregation existed if for no other reason than because of residential segregation. Formal or de jure segregation efforts, which were applied to blacks, usually were not applied to Mexicans. For example, in Nueces County, Texas, Mexican children were legally white. "Nevertheless, the general practice in Nueces County in 1929 was to separate Mexican children from white American school children."[101] Other forms of discrimination in public education consisted of providing all-Mexican schools with inferior equipment and housing and inadequate funding, forcing Mexican students to speak English while in school or on the playgrounds, and the hazing of Mexican students by Anglos. One student reported to Taylor that "some Americans don't like to talk to me. I sat by one in high school auditorium and he moved away. Oh my God, it made me feel ashamed. I felt like walking out of school. In grammar school they used to call us 'dirty Mexicans,' *pelados*, and greasers."[102] Such an experience was not uncommon in schools of the Southwest that were supposedly integrated.

Poll taxes, threats, and voting count frauds were effective in some counties in preventing Mexican-Americans from voting. Mexicans on juries were rare. Complete disregard for civil rights was common in the arrests and trials of Mexicans. Kibbe, in her study of Texas in 1946, wrote:

> . . . there are some twenty-five or thirty far west, central west, central and southeast Texas counties in which, generally speaking, Latin Americans have no rights of any kind. Reports of mistreatment are seldom received from these counties for the simple reason that their Latin American residents, who were brought in originally as cheap labor, have been so consistently submerged by the Anglo Americans living there that they have more or less accepted their servile position.[103]

The racism that justified or legitimated discrimination against the Mexican-American, treatment that for many Anglos was highly advantageous, was overwhelmingly the "indolent hedonist" variety of conflict racism. The lazy, unclean, sexually prolific greaser stereotype has existed from the beginning of Anglo domination over the Mexican population to the present day. An author in Texas in the 1850s gave his opinion of the origin of the term "greaser"—a word applied originally to the Mexican rancheros and stemming from the Anglo perception of the conditions of any city in Mexico:

> The people look greasy, their clothes are greasy, their dogs are greasy, their houses are greasy—everywhere grease and filth hold divided dominion, and the singular appropriateness of the name bestowed by the western settlers, soon caused it to be universally adopted by the American army.[104]

Whatever the origin, this pejorative term, along with "spick," "Mex," and "chili eater," were commonly used by Anglos.

Taylor, in his study of Nueces County, recorded numerous racist statements by Anglos, of which the following are typical: "The Mexicans are like children. They have an average mentality of a nine-year-old child. If you tell them to do two things, they will do one of them wrong or forget to do it at all."[105] "Some Mexicans are very bright, but you can't compare their brightest with the *average* white children. They are an inferior race."[106] "The reason [for school segregation] is because of their filth. As a class they are dirty."[107] In general, according to Taylor, "belief in the inferiority of Mexicans was general, and was assumed by many to be axiomatic, although whether the inferiority was biological or social, whether it could be removed by education or not, occasioned more difference of opinion."[108]

Racism of this sort was not limited to the average Anglo. Scientists and scholars wrote learned tracts with the same theme. In 1929 the journal *Eugenics* included an article which stated that "eugenically as low-powered as the Negro, the peon is from a sanitation standpoint, a menace. He not only does not understand health rules: being a superstitious savage, he resists them."[109] A study done at the University of Southern California in 1938 concluded that "the Mexicans, as a group, lack ambition. The peon of Mexico has spent so many generations in a condition of servitude that a lazy acceptance of his lot has become a racial characteristic."[110] And a major textbook in 1940 (*Heredity and Social Problems*) contained this statement: "Mexicans present the second most serious race problem. They are apparently of distinctly low mental caliber, have not yet produced eminence and do contribute heavily to various dependent classes."[111]

INDIANS

The major forms of discrimination and racism directed against Indian-Americans prior to the end of World War II (and in some cases up to the 1970s) consisted of the denial of political participation in decisions affecting their destiny and efforts by governmental and private organizations to eliminate the cultures and forms of social organization of the Indian ethnic groups. Such efforts were often coercive. These general forms of discrimination were justified by the racist idea that Indians were an inferior and savage race but were capable of behavioral modification under the guidance of American administrators. Although this was the dominant racist theme, another view, held by many Westerners and by some intellectuals, was the belief that this savage race was doomed to extinction in the struggle for survival. Many nineteenth-century Westerners were eager to hasten this process.

The Reservation System

With the conquest and subordination of particular Indian tribes at different times, the continuing problem was what to do with them. One idea that never got off the ground was to create separate Indian states and admit them to the Union. The germ of this effort at solution goes back to a treaty with the Delaware Indians in 1778, which provided for the *possibility* of an Indian state. Later, in 1819, a governmental minister to the Indians in the then Northwest (Great Lakes region) recommended that "this territory be reserved exclusively for Indians, in which to make the proposed experiment of gathering into one body as many of the scattered and other Indians as choose to settle here to be educated, become citizens, and in due time to be admitted to all the privileges common to other territories and states in the Union."[112] Of course such a proposal was never accepted by Congress—the territory was too valuable to be given to "squalid savages" (a term of endearment used by Theodore Roosevelt). But even as late as 1871 President Grant recommended that a territory south of Kansas be created as an Indian state.[113]

Another effort at solving the problem, as has been previously described, was to move the Indians into unwanted territory. But by the 1850s it was apparent to the government that moving Indians around was no longer tenable—there was no more room, "no place in the West where Indians could be placed with a reasonable hope that they might escape molestation."[114]

Reservations, as political and administrative units, became the accepted solution, at least for a period, with the idea that the Indians would eventually be assimilated into American society. By the 1860s Indians were no longer treated as quasi nations but as "wards" of the government. According to Lurie, ". . . without ever really having legal sanction, the term 'ward' took on administrative connotations by which the Bureau exercised incredible control over the lives and property of individuals, much as a guardian would act for minor and even hopelessly retarded children."[115]

The implications of the reservation system for Indian-Americans has been stated by Washburn:

> *The reservation system in its final evolution represented a total reversal of roles for white and Indian. Political authority was withdrawn from the native leaders and assumed by the representatives of the United States. Dependence upon a subsistence system controlled by the Indian was replaced by dependence upon one controlled by the white man. Freedom to carry on intertribal warfare, tribal ceremonies, and traditional law was increasingly denied or restricted by the new authority.*[116]

In 1865 the government began to make contracts with missionary societies, primarily Protestant, to administer the reservations and to acculturate their wards—to give them Christianity and the English language and to teach them agriculture and the mechanical arts. Protestant and Catholic groups competed for reservation rights, while the army wanted the Indian Bureau back in the War Department.[117]* The army, and in particular General Sherman of Civil War fame, desired to thoroughly eliminate Indian

---

*In 1849 the Indian Bureau was moved from the War Department to the Department of the Interior.

resistance and only then to acculturate Indians, by force if necessary. Missionaries were at best do-gooders. This view was widely shared by Westerners in this post–Civil War period and was intensified by every act of hostile Indians on the frontier. For example, the *Cheyenne Daily Leader* in 1870 editorialized: "Let the snivelling quakers give place to bluff soldiers. Let the hell-hounds of the wilderness for once feel the power of the people whom they defy."[118]

Along with missionary groups and government-appointed Indian agents to supervise the activities of the Indians, the government in the early 1880s developed off-reservation boarding schools run by the Bureau of Indian Affairs. According to Farb:

> . . . *Indian children . . . were snatched from their families and shipped off to board-ing schools far from their homes. The children usually were kept at school for eight years, during which time they were not permitted to see their parents, relatives, or friends. Anything Indian—dress, langauge, religious practices, even outlook on life—was uncompromisingly prohibited. Ostensibly educated, articulate in the English language, wearing storebought clothes, and with their hair short and their emotionalism muted, the boarding-school graduates were sent out either to make their way in a white world that did not want them, or to return as strangers to their reservation.*[119]

Government agents in the nineteenth century were generally political appointees with low salaries and a need to make as much money as possible through graft. The agents, along with private contractors who supplied food and clothing to the Indians, falsified accounts, utilized dishonest weights, and substituted cheaper, even inedible, foods, pocketing the difference in the costs.[120] When they weren't crooked they were incompetent or self-righteous or both. The self-righteous type was exemplified by Nathan C. Meeker, agent to the Ute in Colorado. Meeker, in his crusade to civilize the Indians, tried to plow up their pasture lands, dig irrigation ditches, reduce their pony herds, and make them abandon their tribal culture. The Ute responded by killing him in an uprising in 1879.[121]

By the 1880s, many whites sincerely dedicated to Indian welfare were convinced that the reservation system, with all of its paternalism and corruption, would never accomplish its goal—the assimilation of the Indian people into mainstream America. The solution now became the abolishment of the reservation system and the transformation of the Indian into an individualistic Yankee farmer. This was the intended goal of the General Allotment Act of 1887, popularly known as the Dawes Act, after its sponsor, Senator Henry Dawes of Massachusetts.

The Dawes Act, supported by reformers and land grabbers alike and described by Theodore Roosevelt as "a mighty pulverizing engine to break up the tribal mass,"[122] set up procedures to break up reservation lands into individual plots. Each head of a family was given 160 acres, each single person over eighteen received 80 acres, and persons under eighteen received

40 acres. These grants were called trust patents, meaning that the individual could not sell the land for twenty-five years. When this period of time was over, the Indians would acquire "fee patent," or the right to hold or dispose of the property as they saw fit. The act stipulated that Indians acquiring allotted land as trust patents would become citizens of the United States and were under the jurisdiction of the state and local governments of which the land was a part. The Indians of Oklahoma Territory were exempted from the act until 1905 because of their special status.[123]

Subsequent laws in the next twenty years modified many of these provisions. Outs were provided whereby Indians with trust patent land could sell or lease sections to whites. Some reservation lands were declared "surplus" and sold to whites. And later citizenship was granted only after the land became a fee patent instead of when trust patents were acquired.

The act, like many government actions before and after, had unforeseen consequences. It did achieve its purpose of eliminating the reservations—of the approximately 130 million acres of reservation land in 1877, 60 percent was lost to the Indian people by 1934; 60 million acres were declared surplus and sold to whites, and 27 million acres of land allotted to Indian individuals and families were lost by sale to whites.[124] However, Indians with allotted lands, which were often unsuitable for agriculture in the first place, had numerous problems. For one thing, land was fractionalized within families. In two generations an 80-acre plot, for example, might be divided among thirty-nine living heirs. While 160 acres in some areas of the country might be sufficient for farming, in other, less arable lands it would be far from sufficient. And many Indians made no provisions for the state property taxes that were assessed. For whatever reasons, the majority of the allotted land was sold and the money given up for taxes or quickly spent.[125]

The second purpose of the Dawes Act—the assimilation of the Indian—did not occur. Instead, the thousands of Indians were deprived of whatever base they had on the reservations, even with all of its faults. Washburn summarized the consequences of this policy of the American government:

> *The policy, honestly believed by its supporters to be in the best interests of the Indian, can now be seen to have been in his worse interest. Ignorance of Indian culture, fatuous self-righteousness, and land hunger combined to push the Indian reeling into the twentieth century without any of the economic supports or cultural values that had previously given his life meaning.*[126]

In 1901 American citizenship was granted to the "Five Civilized Tribes" in Oklahoma, and in 1924 Congress passed a citizenship law that covered all other Indians not included in previous acts. However, until around 1940 seven states prevented Indians from exercising one privilege of citizenship—voting.[127]

Poverty conditions continued to exist on the remainder of the reservations, while nonreservation Indians struggled to survive in the lower-class "reservations" of the larger cities. Between 1929 and 1931 the Hoover administration did manage to nearly double the money appropriated for the BIA, money desperately needed by Indians as the nation went into depression. However, most of the money went to hire two thousand more bureaucrats (an increase of 300 percent) and to increase salaries 25 percent.[128]

In 1934, during the New Deal administration of Franklin D. Roosevelt, the government of the United States changed its policy toward the Indians. John Collier, the executive secretary of a private organization dedicated to assisting the Indian (the American Indian Defense Association) became the new commissioner of Indian Affairs, and Congress passed the Indian Reorganization Act. The act called for the return to tribal ownership of all surplus lands not yet leased, the formation of an Indian Civil Service, self-determination by tribal governments on the reservations, and the guarantee of the exercise of religious freedom and the use of Indian languages. In addition, the act stressed the use of cooperatives, such as salmon canneries, dairies, and cattlemen associations, as an organizational form more in keeping with Indian culture. Collier wanted to provide a sound political and economic base to allow the tribal groups to survive and to encourage sufficient development for the Indians to eventually move into the larger society; however, he stressed that such decisions were to be made by each group and were not to be the result of governmental actions.[129]

But this policy, which would have been the end to a hundred years of paternalistic discrimination, was never really implemented. By the time the program was explained to the various reservations for their approval or disapproval,* the nation was at war; the country had other, more important priorities.[130] A program of cultural, political, and economic pluralism for Indians would have to wait until the 1970s.

White Racism

As long as the Indians were fighting whites, either in resisting conquest or in revolting against their subordination, the "treacherous savage" form of racism predominated. Besides all of the published views of whites in the West that blatantly called for the extermination or at least the military suppression of the "red savage," a record of statements that would fill volumes, the scholars of the nineteenth century did their part. Typical of the "treacherous savage" viewpoint was that of the historian, Francis Parkman:

> *Nature has stamped the Indian with a hard and stern physiognomy. Ambition, revenge, envy, jealousy, are his ruling passions; and his cold temperament is little exposed to those effeminate vices which are the bane of milder races . . . . He loathes the thought of coercion; and few of his race have ever stooped to discharge a menial office. A wild love of liberty, an utter intolerance of control, lie at the basis of his character, and fire his whole existence . . . . With him the love of glory kindles into a burning passion; and to allay its cravings, he will dare cold and famine, fire, tempest, torture, and death itself.*

*And some Indian groups did reject the program, as will be examined in Chapter 9.

These generous traits are overcast by much that is dark, cold, and sinister, by sleepless distrust, and rankling jealousy. Treacherous himself, he is always suspicious of treachery in others. Brave as he is—and few of mankind are braver—he will vent his passion by a secret stab rather than an open blow.[131]

The experts disagreed as to whether Indian personality traits and their general inferiority were due to inherent biological conditions or to environment and whether or not the Indian was capable of being modified. One scientist, Dr. Daniel Brinton, in his book *The American Race* (1881), was convinced that little change would be possible. In a ridiculous argument he stated that the Indian had a special bone in the skull that retarded development. "The presence of the bone is due to a persistence of the transverse occipital suture, which is usually closed in fetal life. Hence it is a sign of arrested development, and indicative of an inferior race." He went on to argue that although the Indian was superior to some other races (Australian, Polynesian, and African) it was inferior to the white race. In spite of all that had happened to the American Indians and their current condition at the time of the writing, Brinton offered further "evidence" of Indian biological inferiority: " . . . individual instances of highly educated Indians are rare; and I do not recall any who have achieved distinction in art or science, or large wealth in the business world."[132]

By the twentieth century, with the Indian properly subdued and helpless, the major form of racism became one of liberal paternalism. The 1905 report of the Indian commissioners quite clearly stated this view, one that has continued with little modification until the present day in the "social work" mentality of many whites interested in the "Indian problem":

. . . we firmly believe that the way to preserve the best of what is distinctively characteristic in the North American Indians is to civilize and educate them, that they may be fit for the life of the twentieth century under our American system of self-government. . . . we wish to see children of Indian descent educated in the industrial and practical arts and trained to habits of personal cleanliness, social purity, and industrious family life. . . . We want to make the conditions for our less-favored brethren of the red race so favorable that the social forces which have developed themselves slowly and at great expense of time and life in our American race . . . shall be made to help in the uplifting of the Indians and to shorten that interval of time which of necessity must elapse between savagery and Christian civilization.[133]

Such gracious paternalism can be as debilitating to a people as the grossest forms of conflict racism. Perhaps the Indians should be asked their opinion in such matters.

IMMIGRANTS FROM ASIA

Japanese- and Chinese-Americans and Japanese and Chinese aliens have been subjected to discriminatory and racist treatment in the United States, and in California in particular, that far exceeded any possible threat they might have been to white Americans. Although small in actual population size, their numbers and their competitive strength were highly exaggerated by Americans in California in the nineteenth and early twentieth centuries. Perhaps this almost pathological fear of the Asians was due to the high degree to which they were racially and culturally differentiated from the American or Anglo group, their industriousness, and a racist climate that flourished after two centiries of relationships with blacks and Indians.

The Chinese in the Nineteenth Century

The Chinese, who were the first immigrant group to arrive in California, suffered more from the frontier climate of the times than the Japanese who arrived later in the nineteenth century. The initial arrival of a few Chinese in 1847 created little stir. But as early as 1849 a movement to expel Chinese laborers from the mining areas in California had begun. In the 1850s in California, and in the 1860s in Oregon, the Chinese were driven out of mining. Local ordinances were passed preventing Chinese from mining, and these acts were combined with discriminatory taxes and violence. An army captain who had traveled through Oregon in 1862 reported that the Chinese miners were "moving from one mining locality to the next, fleeing from the kicks of one to the cuffs of another, with no fixed abiding place."[134] In Alaska they were completely expelled by 1886.[135]

Besides a miners' tax, a discriminatory device used against Chinese in most western states, a tax to fish (four dollars a month) was applied only to the Chinese, and failure to pay was punished by seizure of the fishing boats. San Francisco made it illegal to carry baskets on a pole suspended across the shoulders and taxed horse-drawn vehicles only two to four dollars while assessing fifteen dollars for vehicles pulled by persons.[136] Numerous day-to-day acts of violence were perpetuated against the highly identifiable Chinese, acts that were rarely punished by the authorities. The Chinese were beaten and robbed, their queues (a braid of hair) were cut off, and their laundries were burned down; insults were common and murder not uncommon.

Article XIX of the California Constitution, in effect from 1879 to 1952, included the following restrictions on the Chinese: "No corporation . . . shall . . . employ, directly or indirectly, in any capacity, any Chinese or Mongolian"; "no Chinese shall be employed on any state, county, municipal, or other public work, except in punishment for crime"; "the legislature shall delegate all necessary power to the incorporated cities and towns of this state for the removal of Chinese without the limits of such cities and towns, or for their location within prescribed portions of those limits."[137]

From the early 1850s to 1882 there were continuous and increasing efforts to close off immigration from China. California exclusion laws were passed in 1852, 1855, 1858, and 1874, and each was declared unconstitutional by the United States Supreme Court. However, when the East, in the 1870s and 1880s, considered Chinese workers a source of cheap labor and strikebreakers, agitation to restrict Chinese immigration became more widespread. Eventually, federal laws passed in 1882, 1888, 1902, and 1904 virtually eliminated all further Chinese immigration into this country until World War II.

The racism that motivated or justified such discrimination was of the conflict variety, in which the "sinister foe" image predominated. The Chinese were considered unassimilable and unchangeable: ". . . they cannot be improved. Their virtues and their vices are bred in them by a civilization older than our ancient world. . . . If they become citizens, we have simply annexed a Chinese state."[138] They were defined as immoral and dangerous to American civilization. "I have frequent occasion to see the shocking results of the immorality of the Chinamen who come to this country, very few of them who bring their wives, and who prey upon white girls. . . . The Chinese are like the sponge; they absorb and give nothing but odors and worse morals. They are a standing menace to the women of this country. Their very presence is contaminating."[139] And because of their ability to live on little income they were dangerously competitive. "Living on the cheapest diet (mostly vegetable), wearing the poorest clothing, with no family to support, they enter the field of labor in competition with the American workman. . . . American citizens will not and can not afford to stand idly by and see this undesirable race carry away the fruits of the labor which justly belongs to them."[140] They were termed John Chinaman, John, Chinamen, or, more derogatorily, chinks. "In high places and low, in the United States Senate and in the streets of American slums, the Chinese were assaulted with this word and others like it."[141] Even the Secretary of State, John Hay, used the term "chink" and referred to the treaty between China and Russia as the Russo-Chink Treaty.[142] In the twentieth century, such images and prejudiced behavior toward Chinese-Americans would diminish, but even in the movies of the 1930s the sinister Oriental was often the heavy (for example, Fu Manchu).

The Chinese and Japanese in the Twentieth Century

The Japanese arrived in large numbers toward the end of the nineteenth century. As discrimination against the Chinese diminished significantly in the twentieth century, the Japanese took over the "yellow peril" role. As with the Chinese, the American fear of the Japanese "peril" and the discriminatory treatment the Japanese underwent until after World War II were far greater than one might expect, given their small population size; even by 1940 fewer than 135,000 Japanese in the whole United States were recorded by the census, with approximately 112,000 in California out of a population of 10 million.[143] Nevertheless, they were perceived as major threats, and World War II did not help the situation.

In the 1890s and 1900s the unions in California were successful in excluding Japanese. Whites attempting to compete with Japanese and Chinese laundries formed the Anti-Jap Laundry League, used anti-Japanese billboard advertising, boycotted Japanese laundries, and, on occasion, were successful in pressuring city governments to refuse permits to Japanese launderers.[144] But more significant than these forms of occupational discrimination were the land laws. In 1913 California passed the Alien Land Law. Under this act Japanese aliens (but not Japanese-American citizens) were not permitted to buy land, to bequeath land they already owned, or to lease land for more than three years.[145] When Japanese aliens got around the law by putting land in the name of their native-born children, who were American citizens, the government of California amended the law (1920). Under the new provisions aliens could not lease any land whatsoever and were denied a guardian role over the property of American-born minors, property they themselves could not legally acquire.[146] Virtually all other states with a sizable Japanese population, with the exception of Utah, followed California's lead in this form of discrimination.[147]

In one of the more absurd efforts at discrimination, in 1905 the San Francisco schools attempted to segregate all Asian children. The justification offered by the board was: ". . . our children should not be placed in any position where their youthful impressions may be affected by association with pupils of the Mongolian race."[148] A year later the resolution was implemented, and all Asian children were sent to the Oriental Public School. Out of a total school population of 28,736, only 93 Japanese children were in the San Francisco schools, and nearly half of these were already in two of the city's twenty-three schools.[149] What a threat from the "yellow hordes." The incident had international implication and threatened United States relations with Japan. President Theodore Roosevelt pressured the San Francisco School Board, and the segregation order was rescinded.

Racist attitudes about the Japanese before World War II were similar to the white views of the Chinese in the nineteenth century—that they were unassimilable, sneaky, dangerous, and immoral. According to one observer of the time, they were "wily and crafty"; "they have no morals. Why, I have seen one Jap woman sleepin' with half a dozen Jap men. . . . Nobody trusts a Jap. . . ."[150] Their unassimilable quality was stated in an article in *Harper's Weekly* in 1906: "For the Japanese in the United States will always be Japanese. They will not become Americans. They will neither wish to merge with our people nor shall we wish to have them."[151] And in an extreme view held by an anti-Japanese group called the Committee of One Thousand: "Wherever the Japanese have settled, their nests pollute the communities like the running sores of leprosy. They exist like the yellowed, smoldering discarded butts in an over-full ashtray vilifying the air with their loathsome smells, filling all who have misfortune to look upon them with a wholesome disgust and a desire to wash."[152]

Such racism led to the Immigration Act of 1924 and the total elimination of further Japanese immigration to this country. And by 1942 it led to the culmination of Anglo-American discrimination against the Japanese-American.

In February of 1942, after the attack on Pearl Harbor in December of 1941, President Roosevelt issued an executive order to "relocate" and "supervise" all people near military installations who might be a danger, in terms of espionage and sabotage. Under this general authority, the army on the West Coast rounded up about seventy thousand Japanese-Americans and forty thousand Japanese aliens and sent them to "relocation centers" in various states in the interior. No Italian or German aliens (much less American citizens) in the area were evacuated (fifty-eight thousand Italian and twenty-three thousand German aliens were on the West Coast); nor were over one hundred fifty-seven thousand Japanese in Hawaii subjected to this treatment, and Hawaii was in a more precarious situation than was the West Coast.[153] The commander in charge of putting the Japanese in concentration camps was General J. L. DeWitt, who in testimony to a House Committee in 1943 offered this justification: "A Jap's a Jap. They are a dangerous element, whether loyal or not. There is no way to determine their loyalty." He added that you did not have to worry about Germans or Italians except in individual cases, "but we must worry about the Japanese all the time until he is wiped off the map."[154] The Supreme Court concurred a few months later. "We cannot close our eyes to the fact, demonstrated by experience, that in time of war, residents having ethnic affiliation with an invading enemy may be a greater source of danger than those of a different ancestry."[155]

As for the Chinese between the turn of the century and World War II, they "retreated behind the invisible walls of Chinatown and were making the best of an extremely onerous situation."[156] But the Chinese benefited somewhat from the war, since China was an ally of the United States. They were exempted from land restrictions and granted citizenship, and with citizenship they could enter into professional and commercial activities that previously had been denied to them. In addition, a small number of special types of Chinese immigrants were allowed to enter the United States.[157]

EUROPEAN ETHNIC GROUPS

Compared to discrimination and racism against the racial-ethnic groups previously examined, discrimination and racism against the European ethnics was generally minor, temporary, and sporadic. Racism, in the form of verbal and written insults and derogatory stereotypes, was common in the nineteenth and early twentieth centuries, varying with different groups at different times, but it rarely became manifest in any continuing and systematic pattern of discrimination. In short, there was a large gap between racist expletives and literature and any effective efforts at discrimination. Such a situation was probably due to the fact that the immigrants were needed to settle the West and to satisfy the almost unquenchable demand for labor in an industrializing society, coupled with the fact that European ethnic groups became acculturated relatively rapidly—in a generation or two. One could add to this the political power of most of the groups in preventing the extensive and patterned forms of discrimination imposed upon the racial ethnic groups. To state these generalizations is not to ignore the exceptions, such as the treatment of the Irish Catholics before the Civil War, of the Italians around the turn of the century, and of the Jews, particularly in the 1920s. Nor do these generalizations de-emphasize the real and painful experiences that few of these Europeans could avoid or ignore the major act of discrimination against European ethnics—the immigration restriction laws of 1921 and 1924. What is emphasized here is simple enough: being a white ethnic subordinate group in America was never as disadvantageous as being nonwhite. And, within this racial category, Protestants generally received more favorable treatment than Catholics, Greek or Russian Orthodox, or Jews.

The Catholic Irish

The Catholic Irish (as opposed to the Scots-Irish Protestants from Ulster) experienced their worse difficulties at the hands of the native Americans in the period from 1830 to 1860. Even before the large influx of Irish during the potato famine in Ireland (1845–1850), the Irish in America encountered sporadic efforts to restrict their activities as well as mob violence. When several million more impoverished Irish arrived to escape the famine (one million entered New York City alone between 1847 and 1860), resistance to this threat to Protestant America and to the native-born manual laborers intensified.

Efforts to restrict the Irish centered around occupations and voting. Throughout this thirty-year period and, in some communities, continuing to the twentieth century, newspaper advertisments for job vacancies often stated: "No Irish need apply," or "No Blacks or Irish need apply." One advertisement in 1830 said this: "Wanted—A Cook or a Chambermaid. They must be American, Scotch, Swiss, or African—no Irish."[158] In certain companies and at different times Irish laborers on the railroads and the canals and in the mines received lower wages for their efforts than did native Americans. Employers soon recognized the abilities of the hard-working Irish, however, and much of this kind of discrimination soon dissipated. In most industries the Irish received low wages typical of the lower social class in this period, a condition made possible by the lack of union organization and by the large supply of labor from European immigration.

Efforts to restrict Irish political participation were equally sporadic and only somewhat successful. The Irish were particularly astute at politics and took to ward activities and political maneuverings with a joy unprecedented in America. According to one historian of the Irish in America:

243

What infuriated the nativists was the enthusiasm with which the Catholic Irish threw themselves into partisan politics, the noise they made in shouting up their favorite candidates, the assertiveness of their political opinions and their readiness to back up their views with physical force, and their belligerent rejection of the idea that in politics they should conduct themselves like well-behaved servants grateful for the privilege allowed them of voting, on the assumption that the native-born were endowed with a priority over the naturalized.[159]

Such a political threat, coupled with the intense anti-Catholicism of many Protestant Americans in the nineteenth century, led to the rise of at least two new political parties between the 1830s and the 1850s—the Know-Nothing party and the Native American party. Both of these parties had only a brief period of importance in American political life; and, split by regional differences, by the opposition by the major parties, and by lack of support from the American public as a whole, they soon disappeared. These parties basically aimed to prevent "aliens" from holding public office, to extend the period necessary for naturalization, and to keep the Bible in the public schools (to prevent priestly domination of student minds). In spite of a large amount of anti-Catholic rhetoric, these parties and other nativist organizations were successful in electing candidates in only a few cities in the East.[160]

The reduction of Irish influence in politics until the end of the nineteenth century was not obtained by efforts at political discrimination as much as by the even greater political skills of the Yankee politicians of the East. According to Potter, the native American politicians "surrounded and isolated the Catholic Irish vote—a maneuver to which the Irish contributed by their clannish huddles. . . ."[161] Boston illustrates the success of the American tacticians. In 1844 Boston was one-fourth Irish and in 1853 it was two-fifths Irish. Yet is wasn't until 1870 that the first Irish alderman was elected; the first Irish congressman from Boston took office in 1882, and the first Irish mayor of Boston had to wait until 1884.[162]

The Catholic Irish did experience mob violence on several occasions in this period, especially in Boston and Philadelphia. In Boston, in 1834, a mob of Whig supporters attempted to prevent the Irish from voting, leading to a large-scale riot when the Irish fought back. Two months later in Charlestown, across the river from Boston, a convent was burned to the ground by mob action. The police and fire department took no action at the time, though eventually several of the perpetrators were indicted but later acquitted. No restitution was ever made by the city. In 1844, in Philadelphia, a meeting of the Native American party was raided by Irish militants and dirt poured into the middle of the crowd that had gathered. The nativists reacted by destroying numerous Irish houses and churches. During five days of rioting (May 3–8) eighty-one houses were looted or destroyed; two churches, two convents, two rectories, one Catholic library, and one exclusively Irish firehouse were burned to the ground; forty were killed and sixty were wounded (not all Irish); and an estimated $150,000 of public property was damaged or destroyed. Two months later in the same city a second riot broke out when some Irishmen were seen carrying weapons into a church. A mob attacked the church, burned it down, and then fought against a military force sent to suppress the riot. Fourteen dead and fifty wounded were the results of this riot.[163] Numerous other incidents of violence involving fewer numbers occurred in this same thirty-year period.

The racism of the native Americans directed toward the Irish had two bases—an "indolent hedonist" view of the Irish and an extensive anti-Catholicism (most Catholics were Irish at this time). The following statement had a wide circulation in the 1830s and 1840s:

> *The children of bigoted Catholic Ireland, like the frogs which were sent out as a plague against Pharaoh, have come into our homes, bed-chambers, and oven and kneading troughs. Unlike the Swedes, the Germans, the Scots, and the English, the Irish when they arrive among us, too idle and vicious to clear and cultivate land, and earn a comfortable home, dump themselves down in our large villages and towns, crowding the meaner sort of tenements and filling them with wretchedness and disease. In a political point of view, what are they but mere marketable cattle.*[164]

According to George Potter, in his study of the Irish in America, "Americans saw the Catholic Irish through the eyes of English writings as the cabin companions of the pig, disturbers of the peace at fairs, lawless and rebellious, steeped in ignorance and superstition, whom the English . . . had tried unsuccessfully to civilize."[165] Other elements in this stereotype depicted the Irish as improvident and preferring play to work, as a happy-go-lucky type and a riotous, fighting drunk. While this image declined as the Irish improved their position in American society, anti-Catholicism persisted into the twentieth century. Given the mostly harmonious relations between Catholic and Protestant today, it is difficult to imagine the extreme hatred of Catholics that permeated numerous native American Protestant communities in the nineteenth and early twentieth centuries. The Irish Catholics and later European immigrants of the Catholic faith were depicted as more loyal to the Pope than the United States, as engaging in a vast papal conspiracy to overthrow the American government, and as superstitious idol worshipers led by lustful and immoral priests.[166] Anti-Catholicism came in waves of intensity in the nineteenth century and became quite prevalent again in the 1920s, corresponding to the revival and the new respectability of the Ku Klux Klan.

Other Northern Europeans

The Protestant immigrants from northern Europe experienced little discrimination compared to that directed against the Irish or to the southern and eastern Europeans. Swedes, Danes, Dutch, Germans, English, Welsh, and Norwegians were generally depicted as sober, industrious, and law abiding in most of their areas of settlement. Few restrictions were placed upon their activities, and these restrictions were always the result of individual actions instead of a concerted effort. Prejudice at best consisted of emphasizing the clannishness of these groups and their "dumbness." Jokes dealing with the "dumb Swede" or the "thick-headed Dutchman" were popular, as were similar jokes about the dumb Polacks, Russkis, and other groups from Europe. Anderson reports one popular joke of the time dealing with Swedes: Two Swedes ran to catch a departing ferryboat. The first made the jump from the dock to the boat, but the second missed, falling into the water. "Good man, Ole," said the first. "Ay dank you make it in two yumps."[167] In comparison with all of the other minority groups in the United States, the northern European Protestant groups were given a hospitable and friendly reception, a major factor in accounting for their relatively rapid successes and the disappearance of countless second- and third-generation members into the dominant American mainstream.

One notable exception to this otherwise favorable treatment occurred during World War I. German-Americans, prior to the war, were held in high esteem by native Americans for their patriotism, industry, and general capabilities. With the outbreak of the war, and assisted by British propaganda in the United States, German-Germans and German-Americans became dangerous threats, or "sinister foes." The *New York Times* editorialized that the German-Americans were "subservient to foreign influence and a foreign power." It was widely believed that Germans, operating under the direction of the German embassy, were plotting insurrection and acts of sabotage and that German-American Red Cross volunteers were putting ground glass in bandages and food sent to American soldiers. "Others were supposed to be selling court plaster containing tetanus bacilli, spreading influenza germs, or poisoning wells."[168] German operas were boycotted, some states banned the teaching of German, Congress repealed the charter of a major German organization (the German-American Alliance), mobs destroyed German property, and an occasional German-American was publicly flogged or tarred and feathered. The ultimate in this reaction to rumors and to deliberate propaganda was the movement to change the term "sauerkraut" to "liberty cabbage."[169] When the war was over, such anti-German attitudes rapidly disappeared and did not recur even in World War II.

Southern and Eastern Europeans

According to an educator in 1909:

> These southern and eastern Europeans are of a very different type from the north Europeans who preceded them. Illiterate, docile, lacking in self-reliance and initiative, and not possessing the Anglo-Teutonic conceptions of law, order, and government, their coming has served to dilute tremendously our national stock, and to corrupt our civic life.[170]

246

The habit of contrasting European ethnic groups by geographical origins was popular around the turn of the century, but words like "treacherous" or "dangerous" were often substituted for "docile." Other terms of endearment used to describe the groups from these areas of Europe were "anarchists," "dirty," or "disease ridden."

These images contributed to the growing demand for restrictions on the immigration of southern and eastern Europeans from the 1880s to the passing of the Immigration Act of 1924. This act was the major and most significant discriminatory action taken by the dominant Americans against these numerous minority groups—Russians, Greeks, Italians, Hungarians, Poles, Slovaks, Czechs, Romanians, and, the most important target of the act, the Jews. The Immigration Act of 1924 stated that "the annual quota of any nationality shall be two per centum of the number of foreign-born individuals of such nationality resident in continental United States as determined by the United States census of 1890, but the minimum quota shall be 100."[171] Since there were relatively few immigrants from southern and eastern Europe prior to 1890, the act was clearly discriminatory. For example, the quotas for 1924 would admit sixty-five thousand British and twenty-five thousand Germans, but only three thousand French and five thousand Italians.

There were a number of factors involved in this victory for the exclusionists in America over those opposed to immigration restrictions, and the victory did not come without considerable difficulty. At least four major social problems were directly related to the immigration and the presence of southern and eastern European ethnic groups: occupational conditions; the conditions of the large cities; the threat of anarchy, revolution, and "bolshevism"; and the threat of "mongrelization" and the loss of "Americanism."

1. *Occupational conditions.* In the 1870s and 1880s, the first wave from southern and eastern Europe, particularly the Italians and the Hungarians, met resistance from the American working class. In this period, class conflict between workers and owners was extensive. A solution for the owners was to bring in recent immigrants as strikebreakers. Higham describes their treatment in the coal fields of the East:

> *From the outset the Slavic and Italian immigrants ran a gamut of indignities and ostracisms. They were pelted on the streets, fined and imprisoned on the smallest pretext, cheated of their wages and crowded by the score into converted barns and tumble-down shanties that served as boarding houses. The first of them to arrive in western Pennsylvania, a group of Italian strikebreakers hired by the Armstrong Coal Works in 1874, were met by riots and armed attacks in which several of the newcomers were killed.*[172]

The unions, at this stage, were not in favor of restricting immigration, since many members believed that the immigrants were "captive workers"—not voluntary immigrants but ignorant serfs recruited en masse by the capitalist class in Europe and shipped in "as so many cattle" to break the unions.[173] In addition, many union members were themselves of immigrant background (northern European). However, the depression of the 1890s produced new insecurities. "The distinction between voluntary and induced immigration, which organized labor cultivated so assiduously through the eighties, was now wearing thin. As the new immigration continued to expand in the early nineties, the unions had to face the fact that this was no mere conspiracy on the part of the employers."[174] With the revival of prosperity in the 1900s and again during World War I, the immigrant threat to jobs did not seem to be a major issue. With the end of the war, however, the conditions in Europe were such that America could expect new waves of displaced ethnics inundating America in search of scarce jobs. Working-class agitation for restrictions intensified.

The working class was not alone in viewing the southern and eastern Europeans as economic threats. The Jews in particular, because of the rapid improvement of their position in American society, met the most structured forms of discrimination. Rising rapidly in the early twentieth century as real estate speculators, as clothing manufacturers, and as professionals, they were competitive threats to the native American middle class. Several state legislatures enacted laws prohibiting aliens (nonnaturalized inhabitants) from entering certain specialized occupations. Help-wanted ads in the newspapers after World War I and throughout the 1920s often specified Gentiles only. A Chicago employment office in 1922 reported that 67 percent of requests for employees specified no Jews, and a survey of teacher agencies in the midwest in 1925 reported that 95 percent to 98 percent specified Protestants only.[175] As Russian and Polish Jews began to attend college in relatively large numbers in the 1920s, numerous universities and colleges established quotas. Columbia University cut down the proportion of Jews from 40 percent to 20 percent between 1920 and 1922. The president of Harvard openly advocated a quota system, which was rejected by the board of trustees. According to Baltzell, "almost all other private Eastern colleges, as well as other types of institutions all over the nation, had some kind of covert or overt restrictions on the number of Jewish students admitted."[176] In some educational insitutions such discrimination continued until after World War II. In 1947 the Presidential Commission of Higher Education reported that during the period from 1935 to 1946 the proportion of Jewish students in professional schools had been greatly reduced, in some instances by as much as 50 percent.[177]

Members of all of the classes feared a Jewish banking conspiracy. In 1890 the American government decided to retain the gold standard. To many, it seemed that Jewish forces were behind this decision and would in time completely control the economy. This "sinister foe" image was stated quite clearly by the patrician Henry Adams: "The Russian Jews and the other Jews will completely control the finances and Government of this country in ten years, or they will be dead. . . . The hatred with which they are regarded . . . ought to be a warning to them. The people of this country . . . won't be starved and driven to the wall by Jews who are guilty of all the crimes, tricks and wiles that have hitherto been unknown and unthought of by civilized humanity."[178] Similarly, Henry Ford wrote in his newspaper, the *Dearborn Independent*: "I know who makes wars, the international Jewish bankers arrange them so that they can make money out of them." Jews exhibit "a decided aversion to industrial employment," and their true forte is banking—"the chain of international finance as it is traced around the world discloses at every link a Jewish capitalist, financial family, or a Jewish-controlled banking system."[179] These views were held by many Americans (and are held even to the present day) in spite of the fact that Jewish-Americans have had negligible representation in the banking industry in the United States.

2. *Conditions in the cities.* The large influx of impoverished immigrants from southern and eastern Europe was visually apparent in the major cities, particularly in the East. Distinctive and overlapping ethnic enclaves were formed, characterized by poverty, disease, slums, strange languages, peculiar customs, and a myriad of odors. In the minds of many native Americans, including the professional urban reformers, most of the major problems of the cities, such as crime, disease, poverty, slums, and vice, were the creations of the immigrant rabble.

The Italians, from the beginning, were depicted as the major source of crime and vice, with their associations with the Sicilian Mafia, their boisterous mannerisms, and their use of knives rather than their fists in street fights. One penologist wondered "how the country could build prisons which Italians would not prefer to their own slum quarters. On the typical Italian the prison expert commented: 'The knife with which he cuts his bread he also uses to lop off another "dago's" finger or ear. . . . He is quite as familiar with the sight of human blood as with the sight of the food he eats.' "[180] The police in several cities often indiscriminately arrested every Italian in sight whenever one was suspected of a crime. Mob action against this "criminal element" was not uncommon. In New Orleans, in 1891, a police chief was killed and the Mafia was believed to be responsible. A mob forced its way into the jail, shot ten Sicilian suspects, and hanged another in the street outside.[181] In other violent incidents in the nineteenth century, six Italians were killed by a mob in Walsenburg, Colorado, in 1895; two hundred were driven out of Altoona, Pennsylvania, in 1894; three were lynched in Hahnville, Louisiana, in 1896; and another five were similarly murdered by a mob in Tallalah, Mississippi, in 1899.[182]

The poor Jewish immigrants, with their beards, black coats, and peddler carts, were defined not so much as criminal as dirty and disease ridden—as pests to the native American. In 1882 the *New York Tribune* wrote:

Numerous complaints have been made in regard to the Hebrew immigrants who lounge about Battery Park, obstructing the walks and sitting on the chairs. Their filthy condition has caused many of the people who are accustomed to go to the park to seek a little recreation and fresh air to give up this practice.[183]

Other groups, including the Russians, the Poles, the Hungarians, the Greeks, the Bohemians, and others, were similarly defined as major contributors to the problems of the cities. The solution to these problems became obvious—prevent any further immigration of such types.

3. *Radicalism.* Many immigrant members of southern and eastern European groups participated in the numerous labor strikes of the late nineteenth and early twentieth centuries. The communist movement in Europe spread fears among native Americans, fears that were intensified by the communist revolution in Russia in 1917. The idea of the immigrant as anarchist or as revolutionist grew into the "red scare," following World War I. To most native Americans, the idea that native-born Americans could be radicals and anarchists was extremely untenable. Newspapers wrote such items about immigrants as: "These people are not Americans, but the very scum and offal of Europe." "There is no such thing as an American anarchist. . . ." "Our National existence, and, as well, our National and social institutions are at stake."[184] There *were* radical immigrants of course, and several were Bolsheviks; there were over fifty radical newspapers after World War I, operated primarily by southern and eastern Europeans. But their numbers always constituted but a small fraction of the total first-generation immigrant population, and even fewer of the American-born members of these ethnic groups.

Many businessmen and corporation leaders sincerely believed in the radical menace and in the stereotype of the bearded foreigner with a bomb under his cloak. Others utilized the fear as a tactic in the class conflict of the period. In Higham's words, ". . . employers inflamed the historic identification of class conflict with immigrant radicalism. In advertisements and interviews they confirmed impressions that the strikes represented alien outbreaks intended to inaugurate an actual revolution."[185]

4. *Fear of miscegenation and the elimination of the American Way of Life.* Probably more important than all of the preceding factors was the growing fear that America would be unable to assimilate foreigners and that miscegenation between the "swarthy" immigrants and the "true" Americans would create a mongrel race.

Prior to around 1880, most Americans firmly believed that all Europeans could be incorporated into American life. In the words of Oliver Wendell Holmes, "we are the Romans of the modern world, the great assimilating people."[186] Assimilation for many meant absorption. For others assimilation meant putting everyone into the "melting pot," in which the contributions of all of the groups would produce a new and distinctive blend of Americanism. But the flood of immigration around the turn of the century changed this optimism to pessimism. America was in danger. As Nathan Glazer has written: "When America's character as an Anglo-Saxon nation was most obvious, incoming immigrants formed no threat, for they were often in small enough numbers to be either invisible or exotic, and they did not reinforce a pre-existing mass of their compatriots."[187] But now the "mongrels" poured in, and ". . . they looked strange, swarmed everywhere, were too loud; they came from a Europe thick with revolutionary conspiracy to an America where the possessors were becoming insecure. Besides, there was always in the background the monstrous (and fascinating) sexual threat that the purity of America's blood would be polluted by miscegenation with swarthy foreigners."[188] Prior to immigration restriction, Kenneth Roberts, the novelist, wrote that "if a few million members of the Alpine, Mediterranean, and Semitic races are poured among us, the result must inevitably be a hybrid race of people as worthless and futile as the good-for-nothing mongrels of Central America and southeastern Europe."[189] The sociologist E. A. Ross, writing in 1914, was convinced that "the blood being injected into the veins of our people was sub-human" and that "race suicide" would be the end result.[190] Even the businessmen who wanted the cheap labor from Europe were caught up in the fear of mongrelization. A delegate to a large business convention summed up the dilemma with the confusing statement that "immigration from, and emigration to, countries peopled by races with which inter-marriage gives deteriorated (or 'halfbreed') and unsatisfactory results—races socially and politically unassimilable—should be permitted by all governments concerned only for commercial purposes."[191]

There were still optimists, however. Beginning around 1915 numerous organizations and civic groups became preoccupied with reducing ethnic differentiation in America through assimilation programs. Strong emphasis was placed upon naturalization ceremonies; the Fourth of July was designated Americanization Day; an earlier slogan of Many Peoples, But One Nation gave way to American First. Civic lessons appeared in the pay envelopes of immigrant workers, classes were taught in the factories, and programs to teach English in night schools to workers increased.[192]

Pessimism and fear continued, however. All of the factors that have been described came together, and the resistances and apathy of many segments of the American community were overcome. Immigration restriction became a reality in 1921 and 1924.* In the words of a major instigator of immigration restriction, "the passage of the Immigration Act of 1924 marks the close of an epoch in the history of the United States."[193] A discriminatory quota system on immigration into the United States would continue until 1965.

---

*The act of 1921 limited immigration in any given year to 3 percent of the population of each nationality according to the census of 1910. This act, superceded by the act of 1924, would have allowed around 44 percent of the total immigration to come from southern and eastern Europe, since by 1910 populations of these groups were quite large. However, by using the 1890 census and limiting the percentage to 2 percent, the 1924 act drastically reduced the southern and eastern European country totals. One final point: the 1924 act also eliminated Japanese immigration, a group not excluded by the immigration restrictions placed on the Chinese in the acts of 1882 and 1904.

THE ISLAND TERRITORIES

As a result of the Spanish-American War in 1898 and the annexation of Hawaii in the same year, American sovereignty was extended over new territories separated by water barriers and populated by diverse "charter member" minorities. Within two years Hawaii was granted American citizenship and the status of an incorporated territory, a prerequisite to statehood which had been fulfilled by all of the American states, with the exception of the original thirteen. However, quite different political statuses were created for Cuba, the Philippines, and Puerto Rico. In terms of economic and political reality, these territories were colonies, but colonialism was never officially recognized. No department for the colonies with a colonial secretary was ever created. Until World War II Puerto Rico and the Philippines were administered by the Bureau of Insular Affairs in the War Department, and smaller possessions, such as Guam, were controlled by the Navy Department. Cuba, until 1934, was an unofficial protectorate.

Cuba

Between 1898 and 1902, Cuba was occupied by the military forces of the United States under the authority of a military governor. During this brief period of occupation, yellow fever was drastically reduced by careful sanitation procedures; the criminal justice system was improved in numerous areas; interest rates were reduced; chaotic land titles were ordered to some extent; new schools were opened, increasing school attendance from around 21,000 children to 250,000; and lighthouses and numerous other public buildings were built, as well as new roads and telephone and telegraph lines. Cuba benefited tremendously from this brief period of American political occupation and from its military governor, Major General Leonard Wood.[194]

On May 20, 1902, Cuba became an "independent" republic under a constitution prepared by Cubans but including several provisions imposed upon their constitutional convention by the American government. Cuba was not to permit any foreign powers to obtain "lodgement or control" on the island, a number of American naval stations in Cuba were to be independent of Cuban control, and the United States had the authority to intervene in the internal affairs of Cuban society whenever there was a threat to order and the Cuban government was incapable of controlling such threats.[195] Unofficially, Cuba became an American protectorate.[196]

American dominance over the Cuban people was exerted by the landing of military forces in 1906 and 1917 to assist the Cuban government in the suppression of revolts and by economic colonialism. By the 1920s, the United States had over $1.5 billion invested in Cuban sugar and tobacco plantations, in public utilities and mines, and in other varied interests. Cuba had become "a land of great sugar and tobacco plantations, owned abroad and worked by a landless Cuban proletariat whose prosperity [was] almost entirely dependent upon the American market, which in turn [was] dependent upon the American tariff."[197] In 1934, as part of the New Deal's "Good Neighbor" policy, the protectorate status of Cuba was terminated. Economic domination continued, however, until the Castro revolution in the 1950s.

The Philippines

With the suppression of the Filipino "rebels" and the establishment of order, the Americans began the occupation and administration of the Philippine Islands, a period of domination that would not be terminated until 1946 (excluding Japanese domination of the islands between 1941 and 1944). The Philippines, an archipelago of 115,026 square miles of land occupied by approximately eighty-seven ethnic groups, were an economic and political liability from the outset. After centuries of Spanish domination the Philippines were in a deplorable condition, as judged by American administrators. Almost immediately, as in Cuba, the "colonial" administration set to work to americanize the islands.

Between 1901 and 1903 numerous changes were introduced: titles to land were organized, land was purchased from the friar orders and sold or leased to the Filipinos, the Bureau of Agriculture was created to introduce improved farming technology, church and state were separated, a public education system was established to reduce the widespread illiteracy, English became the language of instruction and government (only 5 percent spoke Spanish), health services were organized and numerous fatal diseases were sharply reduced, canals were cleaned, harbors were dredged, and over two thousand miles of roads were constructed, among numerous other construction projects.[198]

Between 1901 and 1913, Americans occupied the major positions of power, including those of governor-general and executive secretary and the important posts in the newly created organizations. As early as 1901, however, members of the Filipino elite (educated Spanish or Chinese mestizos) were entrenched in the local and municipal levels, and "it was this position within the local power structure that was never effectively challenged by the American colonial officials with all their efforts at supervision, intervention, and manipulation of institutional structures."[199] The Americans needed the elite to help in the maintenance of order, and these Filipinos benefited accordingly.

When the Democrats came into power under Woodrow Wilson in 1913, it was already apparent to many Americans that the Philippines offered few advantages and numerous problems. Businessmen did not find the opportunity for industrial and commercial profits they had expected. A new tariff in 1909 allowed Philippine products to enter the United States without an export tax. (For a brief period Philippine products were taxed when they left the islands on the way to the United States, a discriminatory requirement, since export taxes were unconstitutional in the United States). American sugar interests in the United States were seriously affected by competition with Philippine sugar and became the major advocates of Philippine independence.[200] Many naval experts were convinced that in case of war with Japan the islands would be indefensible. Many racists in America were opposed to any efforts to permanently incorporate such diverse and inferior peoples into the American Way of Life. And there had been opposition among many segments of the American public to the whole imperialistic venture from the very beginning.

The Democrats wanted to give the Philippines independence within no more than two to three years. However, Republican opposition produced the compromise act in 1916—American sovereignty was to be withdrawn "as soon as a stable government can be established therein."[201]

Within a short time Filipinos occupied virtually all of the major positions in government, with the exception of the top colonial offices. By the middle of the 1920s Filipinos filled 71 percent of the public service positions, 99 percent of all municipal offices, and over 90 percent of the provincial posts.[202] There were 2,623 Americans in Philippine administration in 1913, but by 1921 this number was reduced to 614.[203]

In 1920 President Wilson recommended to the Congress that the islands be granted independence. But upon taking office in 1921, the new Republican president, Warren G. Harding, sent a commission to study the situation. The commission recommended that American control be continued, and Harding accepted the report. The Great Depression, however, increased agitation for the elimination of control over this expensive and useless colony. The labor unions and the western states wanted immigration restriction on Filipinos entering the labor market in the United States. Labor also wanted to keep out "foreign" goods that competed with American products. Numerous industries and patriotic societies lobbied "for Philippine independence so that the Islands would lose their special status and become a foreign country susceptible to import quotas."[204] With the ascension of the Democrats again under Roosevelt, Congress in 1934 passed the Independence of the Philippines Act. The Philippines were to become an independent nation in ten years. The Japanese occupation of the Philippines during World War II upset the timetable, however, and in 1946 the United States terminated American dominance over these islands, thus ending America's most serious colonial effort.

Puerto Rico

Of all of the island acquisitions, Puerto Rico suffered the most under the control and exploitation of the United States. For a brief period, Puerto Rico, like Cuba, was under military occupation, but, unlike Cuba, it did not materially benefit. In 1900 the military rule was withdrawn, and Puerto

Rico became an "unincorporated territory" (a status that would not lead to statehood) technically termed "the People of Puerto Rico." Puerto Ricans were administered by a governor and an executive council appointed by the president of the United States and were allowed a representative to the United States Congress who could speak but not vote. Because of this status, the territory and its inhabitants were denied constitutional rights of trial by jury and indictment by a grand jury and the privilege of certain constitutional restrictions on the powers of taxation.[205] In 1917 Puerto Rico was granted American citizenship, an act opposed by the Puerto Rican Union party, which wanted independence, and that was meaningless in some respects, such as suffrage; however, constitutional rights previously denied to Puerto Ricans were granted.

Economic exploitation and the structural disadvantage of being part of the tariff system created the greatest problems for the Puerto Rican people. Large sugar and tobacco plantations owned by absentee Americans dominated the economy. Four sugar companies alone controlled 166,000 acres, and by 1930 virtually every aspect of social organization and daily life was geared to sugar. Even the local legislature was filled by Puerto Rican sugar lawyers.[206] In these absentee-owned companies, "no matter how well qualified by education or skill, Puerto Ricans were not permitted to hold top-level jobs in such enterprises. For the lesser jobs they did hold, they were paid less than any imported American or European would have been. As colonial subjects, and with rare exceptions, they were not admitted to the clubs and social life of the resident Americans."[207]

The interest rate paid by Puerto Ricans was twice as high as on the mainland, and, because of the tariffs, the most important foods in the diet of most people were often three or four times the price they would have been on the open market.[208] When Puerto Ricans attempted to open their own enterprises they were generally forced out of business by larger American companies, which lowered prices until the local industries could no longer compete.[209]

One scholar on the subject of Puerto Rico has summarized the economic condition of this island under the domination of the Americans: "Throughout the first four decades under the United States, Puerto Rico remained truly a stricken land, disease infested, hungry, beset by poverty so far as the bulk of its population was concerned, virtually without hope."[210]

This situation remained virtually unchanged until Puerto Rico was allowed to select one of its own people as governor in 1948 (Luis Muñoz Marín) and obtained a new political status on July 25, 1952—as the Commonwealth of Puerto Rico.

Hawaii

In direct contrast to Puerto Rico, and at the other extreme, was American dominance in the territory of Hawaii. As mentioned previously, Americans and other Europeans had established economic dominance in Hawaii prior to the incorporation of these islands as a territory in the United States. From 1898 to World War II, haoles, and particularly Anglo-Americans, overwhelmingly occupied the upper and upper-middle classes.

Because of a labor shortage, immigration from other parts of the world was encouraged. Even before annexation, Japanese, Chinese, and Portuguese immigrants arrived in such numbers that together they outnumbered the native population. After annexation, small numbers of Koreans, Puerto Ricans, and Spaniards arrived, in addition to more Japanese, Portuguese, and Chinese and a large influx of Filipinos. By 1920, the largest group in Hawaii was the Japanese, who constituted 42.7 percent of the total population; their numerical predominance has persisted to the present time.[211]

The upper-class haoles pitted immigrant group against immigrant group, encouraging new groups to enter the territory when others had become too entrenched. In this manner the working class or classes were ethnically divided, a circumstance favoring the corporate class and quite effective in preventing working-class solidarity from developing.

Americans dominated the territory of Hawaii by virtue of their class position; however, the forms of racism and overt efforts at ethnic or racial discrimination so prevalent on the mainland during this period were, by comparison, negligible in Hawaii. This is not to say that Hawaii was a paradise model of ethnic and race relations. Wage differences by race existed in certain industries and at particular times, and the upper class kept its distance from the other classes (a situation not unique to Hawaii, however). A pecking order of ethnic groups was evident, with haoles ranked the highest, followed by Chinese, Japanese, and Filipinos, and with native Hawaiians, Puerto Ricans, and Portuguese on the bottom.[212] However, the official policy and the stated position of most of the ethnic members of the islands has been, and is, one of racial and ethnic equality. Overt bigotry is frowned upon, segregation was (and is) voluntary rather than enforced, intermarriage rates then and now were relatively high, and discrimination was sporadic and covert. The sociologist Romanzo Adams has suggested that perhaps the relative absence of racism in Hawaii was due to the precedents established by the native Hawaiians when they were dominant—their lack of racial antipathy and the wide acceptance of intermarriage between haoles and Hawaiians.[213] Whatever the reason, given the patterns of ethnic and race relations in the continental United States before World War II and the multiethnic nature of the islands, the situation in Hawaii was truly remarkable.

SUMMARY

This chapter described the major patterns of discrimination, racism, and government policies directed against the subordinate ethnic groups and races in the United States prior to the end of World War II. Black-Americans, without question, have been subjected to the most extreme forms of discrimination and racism, as indicated by the normative quality of discrimination, the consistency of these norms and their sanctioning over the entire period of American history, the number *of areas in which blacks were denied rights available to white Americans, and the intellectual respectability and systematic elaboration of doctrines of black inferiority.*

The other racial-ethnic groups in America—Japanese, Chinese, Indian, and Mexican—experienced similar disadvantageous treatment at the hands of the government and the Anglo-American citizenry in many respects, although the duration of their experiences was somewhat shorter.

The white ethnic groups, particularly the Protestant groups, were subjected to only sporadic, inconsistent, and noninstitutionalized forms of discrimination and racism—the major exception being the institutionalization of the quota system of immigration directed against the southern and eastern Europeans.

Of the noncontiguous island territories, Cuba benefited considerably from American policy under its brief period of American military control and was granted independence after only a short period of incorporation within American society. Economic domination of Cuba continued until after World War II, but this form of economic imperialism over sovereign states is outside the scope of a text concerned with the internal ethnic and race relations of American society. In the Philippines, a semiautonomous section of the American state until 1946, the disadvantages of colonialism far outweighed any possible benefits. Because of the power of the Filipino elite, American dominance was held in check. According to one scholar of the subject, "through a combination of political tactics and republican principles, the American administrators, by granting to Filipino leaders as much influence as they did, renounced the necessary means to enforce their own conception of what the Philippines should become. The result was an odd mixture of theory and expediency, a perpetual compromise, a modern variant of indirect rule.''[214] *Puerto Rico alone was truly exploited and subordinated in the style of classic colonialism, and the Puerto Rican people suffered immensely from this governmental and corporate paternalism. Hawaii, possibly because of the liberal precedents in race relations established by the native Hawaiians and the fact that Americans within Hawaii were a dominant minority separated by several hundreds of miles from the mainland, became a unique case in the history of race and ethnic relations. What other society in human history has so effectively integrated a remote and noncontiguous territory populated with diverse peoples into its system of social organization?*

Discrimination, racism, and governmental policies are beliefs and actions directed against *the subordinate groups* by the dominant group *within a society. Chapter 9 will examine the manner in which subordinate groups have* reacted to *discrimination, racism, governmental policies, and their social class position.*

9

MAINTENANCE OF DOMINANCE
UP TO 1945: SUBORDINATE
GROUP ADAPTATION

INTRODUCTION

Subordinate groups in America faced numerous problems. Almost all of the groups were predominantly in the lowest stratum for at least one or two generations. Extreme poverty was a reality for many families and individuals who were slaves, struggling farmers or farm laborers, or unskilled residents of urban slums. With the exception of the blacks, subordinate groups were expected to integrate and eventually to assimilate into society, while at the same time they were subjected to various forms of discrimination. The culture of the dominant Americans posed innumerable problems of adjustment for many, if not all, of the groups. For the non-English-speaking there was the problem of language. Americans have been notoriously ethnocentric about their language, and every person of a foreign tongue was expected to learn English. Failure to do so meant a drastic isolation from the mainstream of American society and consignment to poverty. Catholic ethnics differed significantly from the primarily Protestant Americans and thus were subject to discrimination. Since the cultures of the Orientals and the American Indians were even more divergent from the American mainstream, they suffered even greater discrimination.

In adapting to these environmental problems or conditions, the subordinate groups behaved similarly in several respects. They all adopted numerous elements from the dominant culture while simultaneously developing cultural elements uniquely their own. They all chose to reside within segregated communities for at least a generation. And within these communities, which were often concentrated in particular regions of the country, they formed organizations to adjust to and change their conditions.

Within each ethnic group there were divisions that reflected both the general position of the group in the larger society and the relative successes and failures of individual adaptations. One source of division was dissensus over group goals: whether to maintain the culture and group unity in separation from others (pluralism), to become an integral part of the society except in primary relations (integration), or to disappear as a group altogether (assimilation). Second, whatever the goals were, there was dissensus over the means of achieving these goals: whether to conform or resist dominant group expectations, and, if resistance was the choice, whether to use the courts or to engage in illegal forms of coercion. Third, there were class divisions—divisions that often were indicative of successes and failures in adaptation to American society.

All of the subordinate groups in America became *unique* ethnic groups as a result of their adaptive efforts. Mexican-Americans (or Chicanos) are not the same as Mexican-Mexicans. Irish-Americans developed distinctive elements not found among the Irish in Ireland. And in the case of Black-Americans and Indian-Americans, totally new ethnic groups were formed out of racial categories.

As a result of their adaptive efforts, all of the subordinate groups improved their general stratification position, albeit the improvement was minor for some.

Another consequence of subordinate group adaptation was its contribution to the maintenance of American (Anglo) dominance. The groups that chose pluralism might have kept their culture and identity somewhat intact, but by so doing they remained identifiable and subordinate. The more extreme forms of resistance were rarely successful, and in some instances, subordinance was intensified as a result. The assimilation of numerous members from the northern European groups into the Anglo group increased its population and provided new talent.

All of the aspects of ethnic dominance were maintained. The upper class remained overwhelmingly Anglo (of British descent), and the majority of the wealth was still distributed within this dominant group. Cultural dominance persisted as well. Anglos adopted some minor elements of subordinate group cultures, such as foods and musical forms, but generally without acknowledging the origins of these traits. Anglo values and world views were not seriously challenged, but in fact were often emulated by many. It would take World War II and the changes that followed to create an upsurge in subordinate group resistance, not only to discrimination and racism, but also to Anglo lifestyles and national character.

The preceding are generalizations. Each group had its own specific problems to cope with and its own relatively unique methods of adaptation to these problems. The problems and the modes of adaptation were related to the manner in which each group differed from the dominant Americans, culturally and racially.

BLACK-AMERICANS

Adaptation to the Slave System

Among subordinate groups in the United States, the slave condition was unique to Black-Americans. In the earliest period of slavery, slaves were individuals wrenched from their peoples and forced to make individual adjustments without the benefit of ethnic support. Kramer explains this circumstance: "Each Negro encountered the condition of his enslavement alone, one by one facing the full force of white domination. Slaves could find little social support among themselves since few even spoke the same language, let alone shared the same values. Their culture was as remote as their country, and all continuity was disrupted. Only despair remained."[1] For the others, socialized into the rudiments of American culture and divided into slave and free, or house slave and field slave, nothing but skin color and the conditions of oppression could provide a sense of unity.

What choices were available to slaves? They could choose to die an isolated death that had no group significance, since there was no group. They could resist in cunning ways, but always with the threat of physical injury or death. They could escape, but this alternative was not a real choice until abolitionist whites and free Negroes in the North provided help. Or the slaves could accommodate. They could make do under the circumstances, and, at least overtly, conform to the expectations of the white master. As a last resort, with the help of other slaves, they might attempt a revolt, hoping that others would join the rebellion. But this alternative was a forlorn hope and a rarity in this system of virtually total dominance and subordinance. All of these choices were utilized by particular slaves, but accommodation was the norm, followed by acts of sabotage, individual aggression, running away, and only as a last resort, overt rebellion in groups. If one understands the nature of the slave system, then one can understand this hierarchy of adjustment. Any other race or ethnic group in the same circumstances would have behaved in this manner.

Conformity: Role Internalization or Role Playing? To what extent was the behavior of slaves characterized by "childlike" traits—irresponsibility, desire for immediate gratification, deference to "adults" (whites), a happy-go-lucky attitude, superstition—and was this overt behavior the result of internalization or merely role-playing? Given the nature of the system of social control involving total power over the life or death of a slave and white expectations about the proper behavior of slaves, *overt* "Sambo" behavior was probably more the rule than the exception. The real issue is whether such behavior was "sincere," as a result of the deep internalization of such conduct norms into the self; whether it was cynical role playing in the presence of whites; or whether both forms existed.

Professor Stanley Elkins has argued that the conditions of the large plan-tation systems were so oppressive and total in their control over slaves that the situation was analogous to German concentration camps during World War II. Under such total oppression, infantilism is bound to occur and becomes part of the self. Infantile behavior, such as giggling, stealing, and "snitching," by educated Jews at Dachau and Buchenwald has been noted by many survivors of those camps—behavior that manifested itself in an extremely short time period.[2]

Other social scientists, including Roy Simon Bryce-Laporte and Benja-min Quarles, believe that although such *overt* forms of behavior existed because of the coercive nature of the large plantation system, the slaves were only acting. In the words of Bryce-Laporte:

> *The overt aspects of culture among the slaves were subservient, submissive, and largely* primary adjustment *in response to the closed, routinized, regimented, coercive, and total nature of the slave plantation. The* underlife *of the slaves, however, consisted largely of* secondary adjustments *and these adjustments were in fact subtle, elusive roles and sociocultural relations which were prevalent and sustained among them. . . . [To believe that] the prevalent personality pattern among slaves was Sambo, Tom, or Thomasina . . . is to equivocate the* stereotype *with* reality *and* acting *with* being.[3]

Before we explore this controversy further, it will be helpful to examine the historical evidence of the resistance of slaves to the slavery system.

Resistance to Slavery. Although many slaves conformed to the system at least overtly, numerous forms of deviant behavior were widespread. The least spectacular but effective forms of resistance may be termed "day-to-day." Day-to-day resistance manifested itself in subtle ways: feigning stupidity, forgetting, forcing the master to make all requests at least twice, answering with a mocking smile, being overly deferential.[4] Such techniques are irritating to the dominant but are difficult to punish (as any teacher of young students can testify). Lying and other forms of subterfuge were also frequently used. A former slave gives this account of how a group of slaves increased their caloric intake as well as their self-esteem:

> *. . . Mammy told me about one master who almost starved his slaves. Mighty stingy, I reckon he was. Some of them slaves was so poorly thin they ribs would kinda rustle against each other like corn stalks a-drying in the hot winds. But they gets even one hog-killing time, and it was funny, too, Mammy said.*
>
> *They was seven hogs, fat and ready for fall hog-killing time. Just the day before Old Master told off they was to be killed, something happened to all them porkers. One of the field boys found them and come a-telling the master: "The hogs is all died, now they won't be any meats for the winter."*
>
> *When the master gets to where at the hogs is laying, they's a lot of Negroes stand-ing around looking sorrow-eyed at the wasted meat. The master asks: "What's the*

illness with 'em?" "Malitis," they tells him, and they acts like they don't want to touch the hogs. Master says to dress them anyway for they ain't no more meat on the place.

He says to keep all the meat for the slave families, but that's because he's afraid to eat it hisself account of the hogs' got malitis.

"Don't you all know what is malitis?" Mammy would ask the children when she was telling of the seven fat hogs and seventy lean slaves. . . .

"One of the strongest Negroes got up early in the morning," Mammy would explain, "long 'fore the rising horn called the slaves from their cabins. He skitted to the hog pen with a heavy mallet in his hand. When he tapped Mister Hog 'tween the eyes with that mallet, 'malitis' set in mighty quick. . . ."[5]

Stealing, or "toting," was also a widespread feature of day-to-day resistance. "If slaveholders are to be believed, petty theft was an almost universal 'vice'; slaves would take anything that was not under lock and key. Field-hands killed hogs and robbed the corn crib. House servants helped themselves to wine, whisky, jewelry, trinkets, and whatever else was lying about. Fugitives sometimes gained from their master unwilling help in financing the journey to freedom, the advertisements often indicating that they absconded with money, clothing, and a horse or mule."[6] Preventing theft by moral preachments seemed to be an integral part of the white preacher's sermons to the slaves. As a former slave put it, "the niggers didn't go to the church building; the preacher came and preached to them in their quarters. He'd just say, 'Serve your masters. Don't steal your master's turkey. Don't steal your master's chickens. Don't steal your master's hogs. Don't steal your master's meat. Do whatsoever your master tells you to do.' Same old thing all the time."[7]

Day-to-day resistance also occurred in more or less disguised forms of sabotage. Gates were left open, allowing animals to escape; arson was so commonplace that fire insurance companies were sometimes reluctant to write policies for slaveholders; the cinch on the master's saddle would not be correctly done; and expensive equipment and tools would be broken.[8] When slaves were detected, the common ploy was to act stupid—an act which was often successful because of racist whites' belief that Negroes *were* stupid.

A second form of resistance to dominance, and one considerably more dangerous, was flight. Slaves, for a variety of motives, fled to swamps or caves, to urban centers, to the North, or to Canada. Their flight was often unassisted, and unsuccessful as well, as dogs and hunting parties scoured the countryside to bring back this rebellious property. The fugitives forged passes or "free papers," stowed away on ships, or fled with a light-skinned Negro, attempting to pass as slave and master. One slave enclosed himself in a box containing food and water, and carefully marked This End Up, and shipped himself to Philadelphia.[9] Later the organized underground "railways" developed, allowing the slave, with abolitionist help, to move from hiding place to hiding place until he or she reached the North or Canada.

Running away became so frequent that Dr. Cartwright believed it to be caused by a disease, "drapetomania," which could be cured by "whipping the devil out of them."[10]

In spite of the extremely coercive nature of the slavery system, particularly on the large southern plantations, a number of revolts and rebellions occurred. White apologists for slavery during the slave period and up to the present time have de-emphasized the extent and causes of such rebellions, arguing that the revolts were few in number, that they were caused by northern agitators or a few criminally degenerate slaves, or that they were protests by a subservient *class* and not racial in motivation (similar arguments have been offered to explain the protests and rebellions of the 1960s). On the other hand, in the view of many modern militants, slave history was one long revolution against oppression. Social scientists disagree over the extent and severity of such uprisings. Herbert Aptheker, in his *American Slave Revolts*, argues that some 250 slave insurrections occurred, involving anywhere from ten to fifty thousand slaves.[11] Jordan and Elkins have de-emphasized such large-scale rebellion. In the words of Jordan, "on the American continent, it now seems clear that there were many more rumors than revolts and that the number of actual revolts was small; if it takes a score of persons to make a 'revolt' the number all-told before 1860 was probably not more than a dozen."[12]

The following is a brief description, in chronological order, of the major slave uprisings:

1. *Marcus Cato, 1739. Cato led a small uprising in North Carolina, in which the goal was to reach freedom in Spanish-controlled Florida. Twenty-five slaves were apprehended and executed.*[13]

2. *Gabriel Prosser, 1800. Gabriel, a plantation slave in Virginia, armed a thousand slaves with guns, knives, and clubs and planned to march on Richmond after killing slaveholders in the nearby areas. The plan never materialized, as heavy rains made the passage to Richmond impossible, and the plot was divulged by two slaves. Gabriel and thirty of his followers were hanged. Governor James Monroe put a standing army around the city to prevent further attempts.*[14]

3. *New Orleans, 1811. An uprising involving between 180 and 500 persons began at a plantation about thirty-six miles from New Orleans and then moved down the Mississippi to the beating of drums. The insurgents were defeated in a pitched battle with state troops. Many were executed and decapitated, and their heads were placed on poles along the river.*[15]

4. *Denmark Vessey, 1822. In Charleston, South Carolina, a free Negro, Denmark Vessey, planned to emulate the uprisings in the West Indies. Approximately sixty-nine Negroes collected numerous pike heads, bayonets, and daggers and then planned to raid the arsenal at Charleston. Charleston was to be burned, and the slaves would then sail to the West Indies and freedom. The plot was*

exposed by a slave, resulting in the execution of Vessey and thirty-four follow-
ers. The remainder were sold out of the state. [16]

5. *Nat Turner, 1831. In Southhampton County, Virginia, Turner organized an up-*
rising of not more than eight slaves, which eventually grew to include sixty or
seventy. After killing Turner's master and his family, the rebels seized and killed
fifty-five whites. Within forty-eight hours federal troops had broken the revolt,
resulting in the execution of Turner and nineteen other rebels. [17]

After the Turner uprising no other serious action occurred. But rumors were ever-present, and previous controls were improved and new forms of control developed. Nightly patrols, curfews, restrictions on assembly, more stringent slave codes, and an ever-ready militia all were evidence that Sambo could be dangerous. Two years after the Nat Turner scare, Governor Robert Hayne of South Carolina expressed the anxieties of the white South: "A state of military preparation must always be with us, a state of perfect domestic security. A period of profound peace and consequent apathy may expose us to the danger of domestic insurrection."[18]

Upon reexamination of the issue of infantilism, or Sambo, certain conclusions seem to be apparent. Certainly *some* slaves internalized Sambo norms of behavior and acted accordingly. Equally certain, a much larger segment of the slave population lived out their lives *acting* the part that the white dominants demanded in the presence of whites while simultaneously engaging in ego-building forms of subtle resistance to the degree that their courage permitted. At the other extreme, a minority attempted flight until they were successful in gaining freedom, were beaten into submission, or were killed; a few engaged in violent uprisings, which invariably resulted in death or in severe punishment. The rural slave system, ranging from small farms to large plantations, was never as total in its control over subordinate individuals as the concentration camps of the twentieth century. Although the system was extremely oppressive and dehumanizing as a whole, variations were of sufficient magnitude to make all-encompassing statements about slave character extremely tenuous. *All* slaves did not fit into the categories of child, two-faced role actor, or revolutionary. Role-playing conformity combined with subtle forms of resistance was probably the norm, true Sambos or radical aggressors the exceptions.

Cultural Adaptation and Cultural Change. Cultural differentiation between members of African ethnic groups and the dominant American culture was rapidly reduced by a number of slave practices. Fathers, mothers, and children were often separated and sold to different plantations and regions; children were socialized into the rudiments of Anglo culture so that they could perform their tasks; and missionaries and church groups were extremely successful in their proselytization. As a result of this severe "resocialization" or "deculturation" process, the dividing up of ethnic members, and the increasing difficulty of transmitting African cultural elements to children (which increased with each generation), most of the African heritage was lost. With the virtual end of the slave trade from Africa in the early nineteenth century, the process of cultural assimilation became virtually complete.

What elements of African culture, if any, were retained? This has been a controversial question for scholars and for modern Black-Americans interested in black culture and their identity. Le Roi Jones argues that certain elements of religion and music found in the culture of Afro-Americans go back to an African past, although they have been modified by the American experience. One African religious belief is that the stronger tribes' gods were to be revered, which may, in part, account for the blacks' rapid acceptance of Christianity. Particular magical elements found among rural blacks are believed by Jones to derive from African culture—elements such as charms, particular roots and herbs used in folk medicines, the significance of dreams, and voodoo elements. A number of superstitions or folk beliefs may have an African origin, such as the notions that one should "never go to bed on an empty stomach" (based on an African belief that evil spirits could steal your soul while you slept if your body was empty), or that "sweeping out the house after dark is disrespectful" (this refers to the African practice of praying each night for protection by an invisible guardian spirit, a spirit that could be swept away). In addition, such religious notions as "getting religion" or "feeling the spirit" in Afro-Christianity are related to "spirit possession" in African religions.[19] Jones argues that the musical intonation of blacks in America stem from an African past. "Rhythmic syncopation, polyphony, and shifted accents, as well as the altered timbral qualities and diverse vibrato effects of African music were all used by the Negro to transform most of the 'white hymns' into Negro spirituals. The pentatonic scale of the white hymn underwent the same 'aberrations' by which the early musicologists characterized African music. The same chords and notes in the scale would be flattened or diminished."[20]

In recent years, the linguist William Stewart and other members of the Center for Applied Linguistics in Washington have argued for other African survivals. According to their theories, the typical way in which many Negroes laugh is African and not an American adaptation—covering the mouth, lowering the head, and doing a little dance with the feet. American Negro eating habits, which consist of not eating on a schedule but when one is hungry and of taking food from a number of pots and dishes that steam continually on the stove, are believed to stem from the African custom of leaving food on a fire in the village for everybody to sample. Rolling one's eyes upward when daydreaming as opposed to staring vacantly into space, speaking loud and boisterously by white standards, and tongue clicking are all behavioral patterns believed to be rooted in African culture.[21]

In this matter of African cultural survival, certainty cannot be attained. In any case, culture is a dynamic process. Old elements are lost and new elements are added to the shared meanings of groups of people in social interaction. Black culture (Afro-American culture) is not limited to elements that survived from Africa. This culture also includes borrowed elements from white American culture, but, like all cultural borrowing, the process involves creative syncretization. And this culture includes the unique elements of the black experience in America—argot, forms of music, food preferences, religious forms, and others. In recent years, elements from Africa have also been consciously adopted and integrated into the total culture. The culture of each ethnic group is unique, and the culture of Afro-Americans should not be downgraded with the pejorative description of a "pathological mirror-image of Anglo-American culture." Nor is the denial of ethnic status to Black-Americans justifiable. Pierre van den Berghe has stated this extreme position:

> *Notwithstanding all the African mystique, Afro-Americans are in fact culturally Anglo-American. They are a caste group and lack all the characteristics of an ethnic group. If they had some kind of territorial base, they could perhaps in time become an ethnic group, but failing that, they will never achieve ethnic status.* [22]

Although in the slave period blacks were not an ethnic group but a racial estate or caste, they became an ethnic group in the nineteenth century. Their culture, then and now, is not sharply differentiated from the dominant culture, but enough elements exist along with their phenotype differences to provide for a sense of "peoplehood." A territorial base is an important factor in creating and in maintaining an ethnic group, but territory does not have to be a region; there are Black-American communities each with its own territory.

Adaptation to the Apartheid System

From the beginnings of the apartheid system before the Civil War to the present time, the more or less segregated black communities have been characterized by disagreement over the goals of integration and pluralism. For most blacks in the nineteenth century, integration was the value; to make race irrelevant, to eliminate discrimination and segregation, and to obtain equality was the goal. Tactically, blacks sought integration through favorable court decisions, by applying political pressure in those regions where they were entitled to vote, and by forming organizations to oppose efforts at discrimination and segregation. Thus, as early as the 1840s and 1850s, northern blacks, through petitions and court suits, attempted to abolish school segregation. Under their major leader, Frederick Douglass, they achieved some success in Massachusetts, where a few cities acquiesced to the pressure and accepted black children in the white schools. A notable victory occurred in Boston. [23]

Similar efforts to prevent segregation in public transportation took place in the South after the Civil War. In Savannah, Georgia, in 1869, Negroes were forced to ride in all-Negro streetcars (one Negro car for every three white cars on a given run). Blacks threatened a suit under the Civil Rights Act of 1866, and the company temporarily gave in. A local court case declared that separate but equal cars were within the law, and segregation was reasserted. But within months Negro boycotts forced an end to the practice. In 1899 the streetcar company tried segregation once again, but another boycott ended this attempt. Finally, in 1906, the company was successful. White hostility had become more drastic, and black resistance failed.[24]

According to Spear, in his study of Chicago around the turn of the century, the traditional elite in the black communities was strongly in favor of integration and opposed to any form of black separate development or pluralism. "To the integrationists, any type of separate Negro institution smacked of segregation and represented a compromise of principle. At times, a Negro institution might be necessary as a temporary expedient, but it could never be regarded as a substitute for the ultimate goal of integration."[25] But even if black organizations and institutions were conceived as temporary expedients, separate development was necessary. Whites demanded black-white segregation.

One of the oldest of the black institutions was the Negro church. The first black church as an organization was founded in Philadelphia in 1794 after a discriminatory incident. Prayers were interrupted in the St. George Methodist Episcopal Church to make several black leaders leave their seats and sit in the gallery. One of these men formed the all-black St. Thomas Protestant Episcopal Church. Two years later, in New York City, the African Methodist Episcopal Zion Church was organized, which then spread to other cities. The second major church, the Colored Methodist Episcopal Church, was founded after the Civil War, and numerous black Baptist churches also gained in popularity.[26] By 1900, there were 2.7 million church members in a black population of 8.3 million.[27] The black church not only provided a place of worship free from white dominance and hostility but also carried on education and provided a training ground for black leaders. The black church founded schools and colleges in the South, and was important in forming secular mutual aid organizations, such as insurance companies, burial societies, and lodges. In the words of the black sociologist E. Franklin Frazier, the church was the Negro's "refuge in a hostile white world."[28]

In the nineteenth century there were some blacks who opposed integration and did not conceive of parallel development as a temporary expedient, but they were in the minority. In the 1870s several black activists campaigned in a few cities with the slogan Colored Teachers for Colored Schools. The goal was not integration but the improvement of black schools and the creation of black control in the classroom and in the administration.[29] In the 1880s the separation idea was intensified with the founding of several all-black towns: South-Eatonville, Florida; Hobson City, Alabama;

Grambling, Louisiana; Boley, Oklahoma; Mound Bayou, Mississippi; and Columbia-Heights, Alabama. As envisioned by the founders, the all-black communities would foster racial pride and enable blacks to acquire wealth free from the restraints of whites. With few exceptions, however, these towns stagnated, unable to free themselves from dependence on nearby white financial resources and services.[30]

By the 1920s, renewed white discrimination and increased black migration from rural to urban areas had created the black ghetto in numerous cities, north and south. In Chicago, for example, there were few all-Negro blocks in the city in the nineteenth century, but by 1915 the South Side was virtually all black, with an offshoot on the West Side.[31] The pattern was similar in other major urban centers. Given these realities, the emphasis on integration as a viable option declined; accommodation within the black community was realistic. Within the separate communities, some degree of independence could develop, racial pride could be fostered, and a black subculture could be intensified.

One leading advocate of black accommodation was Booker T. Washington, the founder of the Tuskegee Institute in 1881. Washington, in his speeches and writings, advocated racial separation and the avoidance of conflict with whites. Within the isolated communities, blacks should work hard, master skilled manual trades, and avoid identifying with the white working class.[32] To many blacks of the time (and today), Washington was an Uncle Tom, a classic case of cooptation. In his speeches to white leaders, such a label seems appropriate. For example: "The wisest among my race understand that the agitation of questions of social equality is the extremest folly." Or, Negroes could be depended upon to "run your factories" and to labor "without strikes or labor troubles."[33] He did, however, work for equality of economic opportunity, the end to discrimination in the courts, and improved living conditions for blacks, and he emphasized racial consciousness and dignity.[34] Perhaps he was a realist.

An opponent of Washington was W. E. B. Du Bois. Although he agreed with Washington on several points, such as the need for racial pride and improved economic conditions and the unlikelihood of a union between white and black workers, Du Bois stressed the ballot and the courts as the means of obtaining equality and integration.[35] Du Bois and a number of white and black liberals formed the National Association for the Advancement of Colored People (NAACP) in 1909, an outgrowth of an earlier organization, the Niagara Movement (1905). The integrationist view, which can be traced back to Frederick Douglass, was not dead, in spite of the increased isolation of blacks, the apathy of much of the black masses, and the benefits segregation offered to some segments of the black middle class.

The NAACP and other local civil rights organizations in this period won a few victories in the struggle against apartheid. One such victory was against the federal government. Under the administration of Woodrow Wilson, several bureaus in 1913 instituted racial segregation—screens separating white and black employees and separate lavoratories and lunchrooms. The NAACP protested in petitions, in mass meetings, and in editorials. The government gave in. By March of 1914, the earlier, more integrated arrangement was reinstated.[36]

Civil rights organizations in Chicago in the 1920s and 1930s picketed white stores to employ blacks and were successful in getting two thousand blacks hired. They failed, however, to eliminate restrictive covenants, to reduce the rents of black tenants, or to get black milkmen hired by the dairies.[37]

In the 1930s and 1940s the NAACP initiated a number of civil suits against southern schools in order to obtain equal salaries for black teachers. In some of these cases the suits were denied by the courts or the teachers bringing the suits were fired. However, the NAACP won a favorable decision in a district court when unequal payments to black teachers were declared unconstitutional. Because of the threat of further suits, numerous other school districts in the South decided to provide equal salaries.[38] However, these were minor cracks in the wall of apartheid. The more drastic alteration of the segregation system would have to wait until after World War II.

A third leading figure of the time was Marcus Garvey. Garvey represented a pan-African movement totally out of keeping with either the integrationist or the pluralist strains within the black community, a movement opposed by most of the black leaders. The major organization of the movement was the Universal Negro Improvement Association (UNIA), founded in 1914, which had an estimated membership of one million by 1922.

The ideology of the UNIA stressed the total liberation of Africa from alien rule. There could be no hope for blacks anywhere until Africa had been freed from the domination of whites. Blacks from the New World were to be the vanguard and the leaders. Those with leadership ability and technological skills were to move to Africa and lead the African struggle for independence. Garvey stressed the common identity of "Africans" everywhere, and the need to develop "a distinct racial type civilization"[39] of their own. In the United States Black-Americans were to channel their resentment into constructive efforts to achieve these goals by preparing themselves for the struggle.

Negro leaders in the United States attacked the organization as a back-to-Africa movement (which it was not), and assaulted Garvey personally as an "alien" (he was Jamaican), and for his physical appearance— "protruding jaw," "heavy jowls," "bull-dog face." He was convicted on an unjust charge of mail fraud in 1923. In 1927, his sentence was commuted. Garvey was then deported as an undesirable alien, and he died in London in 1940.[40] As a pan-African, he was ahead of his time. In this first half of the twentieth century, the great majority of Black-Americans did not conceive of themselves as Africans in either a cultural or a spiritual sense.

An even more radical program was advocated and practiced by a small group of blacks in a religious sect known as the Nation of Islam, or, more commonly, the Black Muslims. The sect, founded in Detroit in the early 1930s by Elijah Muhammad, had its own peculiar form of adaptive strategies to the consequences of white racism and discrimination. According to the group's ideology, its major task (then and now) was to raise black pride, to improve their technological skills, and to deny the legitimacy of the whites' view of black people, a view too often accepted by the blacks themselves.

The first step in the process was the development of a theology containing a myth of the origin of the black and white races and the reason for white domination. The following summarizes the ideas of Malcolm X, a follower of Elijah Muhammad at this time:

In the beginning all people were black, being created 66 trillion years ago. About 6600 years ago, a scientist, Mr. Yacub, began preaching in Mecca and converted thousands to an unacceptable doctrine. In reaction, he was exiled along with 59,999 followers to the Island of Patmos. Embittered toward Allah he decided to create a devil race, the race of whites. Over hundreds of years his experimentation with genes managed to create brown people out of black, red people out of brown, and eventually the white race out of the red race—"blond, pale-skinned, cold-blue-eyed devils—savages, nude and shameless; hairy, like animals, they walked on all fours and they lived in trees." These savages were unleashed into Arabia where they stirred up discontent and fighting among blacks. Unable to control them the whites were rounded up and taken in chains to the caves of Europe. Allah, in time, instructed Moses to civilize them and bring them out of the caves; the first to be led out of savagery were the Jews. The white race overran the world creating capitalism and slavery. Moses had written, in a now-missing book, that the whites would rule the world for 6000 years, but after this time a black leader would restore the blacks to dominance as whites would destroy themselves. The leader of this restoration was W. D. Fard, who came from the Near East to America and gave this revelation to Elijah Muhammad.[41]

The Muslims have advocated "the separation of the so-called Negroes and the so-called white Americans." "We want our people in America whose parents or grandparents were descendents from slaves, to be allowed to establish a separate state or territory of their own—either on this continent or elsewhere." "As long as we are not allowed to establish a state or territory of our own, we demand not only equal justice under the laws of the United States, but equal employment opportunities—NOW!" Muslims demand the release of their members in prison, an end to police brutality, and an exemption from taxation as long as they are deprived of equal justice.[42] In their newspaper, *Muhammad Speaks*, great stress is placed upon the mastery of technological skills: "Get knowledge to benefit self!"; "Enter technology schools and do for self!"; "Learn agricultural engineering"; "Technicians-engineers of all types are wanted by the Nation of Islam." Although representing only a small proportion of Black-Americans (five thousand to fifteen thousand registered members and perhaps fifty thousand believers in 1960), the sect has had great success in rehabilitating numerous addicts, criminals, and alcoholics.[43] It is an alternative form of adaptation with particular appeal to many lower-class blacks, male and female, who no longer see any possibility of racial integration in America.

For the great mass of blacks in pre-World War II America, whether in rural towns in the South or in the urban ghettos of the North and the South, adaptation to subordination meant getting through the day—avoiding encounters with whites, particularly those in authority, making a living, and finding some sources of enjoyment and self-esteem. For those who had to leave the ghetto every morning in order to make a living, encounters with whites were unavoidable. Within the ghetto, however, blacks could carry out various lifestyles with only a minimal amount of contact with members of the dominant white community.

Although writing in the 1960s, St. Clair Drake has painted a picture of ghetto life that was probably typical throughout much of the twentieth century:

> The "ghettoization" of the Negro has resulted in the emergence of a ghetto subculture with a distinctive ethos, most pronounced, perhaps, in Harlem, but recognizable in all Negro neighborhoods. For the average Negro who walks the streets of any American Black Ghetto, the smell of barbecued ribs, fried shrimps, and chicken emanating from numerous restaurants gives olfactory reinforcement to a feeling of "at-homeness." The best of "gut music" spilling into the streets from ubiquitous tavern juke boxes and the sound of tambourines and rich harmony behind the crude folk art on the windows of store-front churches give auditory confirmation to the universal belief that "We Negroes have 'soul.'" The bedlam of an occasional brawl, the shouted obscenities of street corner "foul mouths," and the whine of police sirens break the monotony of waiting for the number that never "falls," the horses that neither win, place, nor show, and the "good job" that never materializes. . . .
>
> This is a world whose urban "folkways" the upwardly mobile Negro middle class deplores as a "drag" on "The Race," which the upper classes wince at as an embarrassment, and which race leaders point to as proof that Negroes have been victimized. But for the masses of the ghetto dwellers this is a warm and familiar milieu, preferable to the sanitary coldness of middle-class neighborhoods and a counterpart to the communities of the foreign-born, each of which has its own distinctive subcultural flavor. The arguments in the barbershop, the gossip in the beauty parlors, the "jiving" of bar girls and waitresses, the click of poolroom balls, the stomping of feet in the dance halls, the shouting in the churches are all theirs— and the white men who run the pawnshops, supermarts, drug stores, and grocery stores, the policemen on horseback, the teachers in blackboard jungles—all of these are aliens, conceptualized collectively as "The Man," intruders on the Black Man's "turf."[44]

The black ghettos, unlike the ethnic enclaves of the European ethnics, contained all of the classes. Successful European ethnics could flee from their segregated communities and purchase homes in affluent white areas. Because of housing discrimination, however, blacks were forced to coexist and intermingle within small and densely populated areas, regardless of class differences. Chicago in the 1940s, for example, had a heterogeneous population crowded together within an eight-square-mile enclave sur- rounded by whites. Within the ghetto, a small percentage of professionals, organizational executives, and businessmen made up a "respectable" elite competing for dominance and prestige with successful racketeers and gamblers (upper-class "shadies"). A middle level of white-collar workers and skilled manual workers attempted to maintain a respectable lifestyle in spite of the inability to avoid contact with the largest segment of the ghetto population, the lower stratum. And within this bottom layer, the church- going poor who attended numerous storefront churches attempted to keep their children out of trouble and away from the contamination of the lower-class "shadies."[45]

Although the ghetto was an "oasis" for black accommodation to white hostility and discrimination, the presence of "the Man" was a continuing source of friction and potential conflict, even violent rebellion. Houston, in 1917, witnessed a military revolt of sorts. Black soldiers attacked the white police when a Negro woman was believed to have been mistreated. In the action a Negro soldier was killed. The black soldiers mutinied against their white officers and stormed downtown Houston. When it was over, several whites and blacks had been killed and sixty-five Negro soldiers received prison sentences for their actions.[46]

In the summer of 1919 some twenty-five riots erupted in several American cities. In Chicago, the worst riot of the year led to the deaths of thirty-eight people, twenty-three of whom were black.[47]

In 1935 Harlem underwent a major rebellion. The spark was the alleged beating of a black boy caught stealing. Black speakers charged white mer- chants with discrimination and the police with brutality. As the crowds grew, police, many of them mounted, attempted to disperse the people and pull down the speakers' platforms. A full-scale riot followed, resulting in the looting of white stores and widespread property destruction—over two- hundred stores were looted and smashed, with an estimated property loss of $2 million. "White New York was almost panic-stricken as a nightmare of Negro revolt appeared to be a reality." Seven hundred white policemen and fifty radio cars suppressed the revolt.[48]

The last major riot in this period occurred during World War II in Detroit (1943). A number of Negro teenagers had been forcibly ejected from a park and had retaliated by attacking whites in indiscriminate rage. The violence spread to the ghetto when a rumor about the killing of a Negro woman and a child circulated within a night club, sending blacks into the streets. Looting and destruction of the property of white merchants were again widespread. Before order was restored by the police (the "thin blue line"), nine whites and twenty-five blacks had been killed.[49] These incidents of black-white urban conflict were the forerunners of the far more widespread uprisings of the 1960s.

In the twentieth century before World War II, the sporadic uprisings of urban blacks encountered a unified white power structure and were promptly suppressed. The nonviolent legal efforts of black integrationist groups also had little effect upon the stratification position of Black-Americans as a whole or on the extent of their segregation. Accommodation to apartheid was the norm for the great majority of blacks, whether in the ghettos of the cities or in the rural communities of the South. White dominance over black was maintained with little change.

INDIANS

From the very beginning of contact with whites, numerous Indian ethnic or tribal groups made cultural and organizational adaptations. The Iroquois responded to the fur trade by creating the Iroquois Federation. The Cherokee invented a new written language and founded schools and enterprises in addition to a bicameral form of governmental organization. The Navaho adopted the sheep and the horse of the Spanish and developed a new art of craftsmanship in silver jewelry and basket making.[50] "Other groups of Indians responded to the horse by rapidly elaborating a brilliant culture as horse-nomads, and today the popular stereotype of the Indian is precisely the mounted warrior chasing the buffalo and harassing the Anglo settlers."[51] The Fox in Iowa managed to keep their culture and identity somewhat intact, yet they accepted the American's techniques of land purchase and methods of agricultural production.[52] In keeping with the warrior tradition of exposing oneself to danger and of male bonding, the men of several Indian tribes in the twentieth century entered such occupational substitutes for war as mountain fire fighting in the West and skyscraper construction work in the East.

Indian religions have also adapted to the circumstances of subordination. As a result of the missionary pressures of the various Christian churches, most Indians eventually converted, at least nominally. For many the conversion was highly selective—they rejected some elements of Christian belief while accepting others, and they combined Christian and native religious elements in a unique syncretization.

One such religious adaptation has centered around the use of peyote, a nonaddictive drug used by a minority of Indians, mostly in the Southwest. The peyote cult became institutionalized as the Native American Church when the drug was legalized in Oklahoma in 1908. According to Washburn, the new church, rather than remaining an illegitimate cult, "found it easier to combat the attacks of organized Christian churches, who regarded the cult as a rival, and of the Indian Bureau, which looked upon it as an impediment to the Indian's adoption of the white man's way. With an organizational structure, the peyote worshippers could more easily claim the protection of the constitutional guarantees of religious freedom and more effectively defend themselves in court cases and administrative proceedings directed against them."[53] Psychologically, the peyote religion "created in the believer a new inner state which allowed necessary adaption to the dominant white culture while permitting pride and belief in Indianness, albeit not of the traditional variety."[54]

It should be added that the use of peyote has been opposed by many *Indians*. Antipeyote ordinances were passed by several tribal governments including those of the Navaho, the Tao, and the White Mountain Apache.[55]

The major form of social organization functioning in Indian adaptation has been the band. Every reservation is divided into informal social units of kith and kin. According to Murray Wax, " . . . it is the strength of the band organization—its vitality, tenacity, and flexibility—which has enabled Indian communities to survive at all. These patterns of sharing, voluntary cooperation, equality, and solidarity have sustained these communities under conditions which otherwise would have destroyed their membership."[56]

Indians have been torn between pluralism and integration. The Society of American Indians (SAI), a pan-Indian organization in existence between 1916 and 1923, favored the development of a common Indian ethnicity, temporary accommodation to the Bureau of Indian Affairs (BIA), but an eventual integration of all Indians into American society. The society's Seneca leader, Arthur C. Parker, was opposed in some respects by Carlos Montezuma, a Yavapai doctor who broke away from SAI and who advocated in his magazine, *The Wassaja*, the elimination of the BIA and the abolition of the reservation system. Integration, however, was the goal of both.[57]

A majority of all American Indians opposed John Collier's Indian Reorganization Act of 1934, an act designed to maintain and to improve the reservation system (pluralism). Many Indians were antitribal and in favor of assimilation. Those with private land holdings or allotments resulting from the Dawes Act of 1887 were opposed to a provision of the 1934 act through which family-owned land would be returned to the reservation. In addition, many Navaho voted against the act because of its intent to reduce the goat and sheep herds for ecological reasons. And some were opposed on principle—anything the government did "for them" was against their best interests.[58]

This latter objection to the Indian Reorganization Act was well taken. The act was designed to strengthen tribal governments in order to help develop a greater independence for the Indians. Yet its unintended effect was to increase federal control and Indian dependency:

Prior to the passage of the statute a tribe generally had the inherent power freely to make its own laws and to spend any funds not in the possession of the federal Treasury. Despite the fact that these rights and powers were in words confirmed by the Indian Reorganization Act, in actual practice every constitution adopted under the statute requires the secretary of the interior to review nearly all ordinances in various categories, notably those which define and punish offenses. Similarly, every Indian Reorganization corporate charter subjects to such approval almost the entire amount that a tribe can spend or make contracts for.[59]

A very large minority was in favor of the act in spite of such issues. The vote of the Navaho illustrates the pluralism-integration split: 8,197 opposed, 7,679 in favor.[60] The issue exists to this day.

Much of the organized resistance to American governmental policies was carried on *in behalf* of Indians by white liberals. The American Indian Defense Association, for example, was successful in 1923 in defeating government efforts to make executive-created reservations (as opposed to treaty reservations) open to leasing by private oil and gas interests. The Indian Rights Association and several church groups were instrumental in obtaining legislation authorizing the building of a dam in the Arizona territory of the Pima and Maricopa Indians. The water that was stored was used to benefit Indian farmers.[61]

However, not all resistance to governmental paternalism and exploitation came from the white liberals. A major success in a conflict situation was the accomplishment of the Pueblo Indian groups. In 1922, a bill was presented to Congress (the Bursum Lands Bill) that would have established a procedure through which white squatters who had taken over Pueblo lands at an earlier period could acquire title to the land. A key section of the bill put the burden of proof of ownership upon the Indians, a stipulation that violated established legal procedure. The Pueblos formed several organizations and defeated the bill. In 1924, the Pueblo Indian groups were successful in the passing of the Pueblo Lands Act, an act that guaranteed either the restoration of all Spanish land grants that had been lost to the Indians or reparation payments for the lost land.[62]

Such victories against the system, however, were rare. For the great majority of Indians on reservations, on independent farm plots, or in the segregated sections of urban slums, the major problem was survival (as it is today). Because of the inadequate economic base of the reservations, most Indians were reduced to accepting charity from the government, to doing odd jobs (often few and far between), to becoming prostitutes, or to escaping into alcoholic insensibility. Those who left the reservation and entered the asphalt jungles were totally unprepared for the competition, discrimination, and alien environment they found there. Many Indians, in an effort to cope with their problems, have "commuted," in a sense, from city to reservation and back again, without really adjusting to either environment.

The high rate of alcoholism among Indians, past and present, deserves some additional comment. In the earliest periods of contact with Indians, whites encouraged the use of alcohol as a tactic in land grabbing. Because they had no previous experience with such a powerful drug and because there were no social regulations that would constrain and ritualize the taking of alcohol, Indians were particularly prone to "binge" drinking—that is, rapid drinking with peers to get as drunk as possible for a prolonged period.[63] According to Washburn, the lack of negative sanctions among Indians for drunkenness was also a factor: "No stigma was attached by fellow Indians to Indian drinking or to acts committed while under the influence of liquor, however much such acts might be condemned when committed sober."[64] A genetic factor may also be involved. Studies of the Tarahumara Indians of Mexico (close relatives of the Pima tribe in Arizona) indicate that the introduction of refined sugar and distilled alcohol drastically upset a metabolism developed to utilize scarce glucose in their diet (from corn and beans); they now suffer from obesity, diabetes, and ischemic heart disease, as well as from alcoholism.[65] And, certainly, getting drunk has been an escape, at least temporarily, from the poverty and from the conditions of a people caught between two worlds.

MEXICAN-AMERICANS

The reduction of the majority of Mexicans to landless menial labor in the nineteenth century did not occur without Mexican resistance. Violent conflict erupted in New Mexico immediately after the Mexican War. Pablo Montoya, a Mexican peasant, Father Antonio José Martínez, a Mexican priest, and Tomasite Romero, a Pueblo Indian, fought back against the American occupation of their territory. Governor Charles Bent of New Mexico, along with five other important Americans, was killed in the initial uprising, and the revolt spread. The American army attacked some 1,500 Mexicans and Indians outside of Taos, and about 150 of the rebels were killed when artillery fire destroyed a church that had been fortified. Thirty-five more were immediately executed by firing squads upon surrendering, and, after a short trial, 15 rebels were sentenced to death. A large segment of the remainder were publicly flogged.[66]

Juan Cortina led another major effort of resistance to American dominance. Using Mexico as a base of operations, a small army under Cortina raided the lower Rio Grande area for fifteen years, killing American settlers, stealing cattle, and terrorizing Mexican-Americans suspected of being informers. Americans retaliated by burning the homes of any Mexican-American believed to be sympathetic to Cortina or to be giving him aid. To many Mexicans on both sides of the border, Cortina was a hero, but to others he was an outlaw. Under pressure from the American government and from Mexicans opposed to such tactics, Cortina was captured by the Mexican government, thus ending the "Cortina War" in 1873.[67]

A third attempt at resistance in the nineteenth century took place in San Miguel County, New Mexico, between 1889 and 1891. After the Civil War American squatters had settled on a Mexican land grant held in common—496,000 acres of land confirmed as Mexican-owned by the American Congress in 1860. The squatters purchased sections of land from individual Mexicans, an illegal practice since the property was communally owned. After the purchases, Americans fenced in their claims, thus denying Mexicans access to timber, water, and grazing land. A number of Mexicans retaliated, led by such organizations as *La Mano Negra* and *Las Gorras Blancas*. Fence wires were cut and property destroyed, particularly railroad tracks on land that had been appropriated as a right-of-way. Anglo power, combined with the loss of Mexican support, led to the demise of this movement by the turn of the century.[68]

Whether or not the large majority of the charter member Mexican-Americans supported these sporadic attempts at resistance is not known. However, whether or not they approved of resistance, most of them conformed to their new position, acquired jobs from Anglo employers, and carried on their traditional culture within their barrios.

Between 1900 and 1930 these segregated communities were inundated by legal and illegal Mexican nationals. In the words of Carey McWilliams:

> . . . the partial accommodation which had been achieved by 1900 was completely disrupted by the avalanche of immigration. As thousands of immigrants streamed across the border at a dozen points, the old conflict of cultures was renewed. The new immigrants were, of course, fitted into the mold of subordination which had previously crystallized in the border-lands. Once they had become conscious, however, of the way in which they were being subordinated in the social structure, the immigrants attempted to rebel. Dating from the late 'twenties, this rebellion was most decisively crushed.[69]

Much of this largely unsuccessful resistance to subordination was the work of Mexican labor unions. The following is a brief summary of the major incidents of ethnic and class conflict involving Mexican unions in the twentieth century prior to World War II:

1. *Arizona, 1903: A strike by Mexican copper miners was suppressed by the arrest and conviction of their leaders.*[70]
2. *Arizona, 1915–1917: Three Mexican copper mining unions involving 5,000 men went on strike over discriminatory pay (the "Mexican Rate") and the selling of jobs by foremen. The mouth of the mine was sealed with concrete by the owners, hundreds of miners were arrested, and eventually the National Guard ended a nineteen-week strike. Two years later a second strike was terminated by the use of Anglo vigilantes who rounded up 1,186 of the strikers, dumped them into boxcars, and shipped them to the deserts of New Mexico.*[71]
3. *Southern California, 1928–1930: A strike of agricultural workers in 1928 was broken by wholesale arrests and deportations to Mexico. Two years later the growers were surprised by a strike of 500 workers and met the workers' demands. "But a few months later, when the canteloupe harvest began, the union was*

> *viciously attacked before it could call a strike. Over 103 arrests were made and a local newspaper reported that 'the county has purchased more tear-gas guns, shells, and bombs than ever before.' "*[72]

4. *California, 1930–1932: Large-scale forced deportations of Mexican nationals and Mexican-Americans took place in the face of labor unrest. In 1932, over eleven hundred were sent to Mexico from Los Angeles alone.*[73]

5. *San Joaquin Valley, California, 1933: A strike by Mexican cotton workers brought in the National Guard. An arbitration board was established. The pickers received an increase from sixty cents a hundred pounds of cotton to seventy-five cents (workers had demanded a dollar a hundred pounds).*[74]

6. *Los Angeles County, California, 1933: Agricultural workers' demands for higher pay "provoked a whirlwind of violence." Union meetings were broken up by tear gas and with clubs, and several labor union lawyers and others were arrested.*[75]

7. *San Angelo, Texas, 1934: A strike by the predominantly Mexican Sheepshearers' Union was broken by vigilante activity and by the use of strikebreakers.*[76]

8. *Los Angeles County, California, 1936: Two thousand striking Mexican workers were met by police using tear gas. Some of the workers had barricaded themselves in a barn, which subsequently produced a miniature battle before resistance was eliminated by the police. Workers that had fled to their homes were followed and beaten.*[77]

9. *Orange County, California, 1936: Four hundred armed guards were recruited by the orange growers to crush a strike. Two hundred of the strikers were arrested and arraigned in an outdoor pen that served as the courtroom.*[78]

10. *Stockton, California, 1937: Striking cannery workers were forced back to work by the use of over twelve hundred Anglo farmers who had been deputized for the occasion.*[79]

Meier and Rivera have summarized the successes and failures of the Mexican unions in this period:

> *During the twenties and thirties the Southwest had small Mexican unions, whose energies and weak finances were quickly sapped by the oppressive tactics of growers, such as indiscriminate arrests, deportation, excessive bail, expensive litigation, vicious vigilante assaults, and other forms of intimidation. Although Mexican Americans gained much labor union experience from 1900 to 1940, their organizations achieved only limited success. Some gains were made in wages and working conditions; however, the hopes and aspirations of Mexican-American workers continued to be frustrated by repression and discrimination.*[80]

The Mexican-American communities developed other groups besides unions to aid in their adaptation to life in the American Southwest. Like the European immigrants and the blacks, they formed numerous mutual aid societies, which provided insurance, limited social welfare benefits, funeral funds, and forums for discussion of common problems. The *Alianza Hispano-Americana, Sociedad Mutua Hijos de Hidalgo, Sociedad Benito Juárez, and Sociedad Española de Beneficencia Mutua* are examples of these organizations.[81]

The League of United Latin American Citizens (LULAC), formed in Texas in 1929, was the major organization concerned with integration and the achievement of civil rights for Mexicans. The ideology of the organization was "to develop within the members of our race the best, purest and most perfect type of a true and loyal citizen of the United States of America (Article 1)"; "to use all the legal means at our command to the end that all citizens in our country may enjoy equal rights, the equal protection of the laws of the land and equal opportunities and privileges (Article 3)"; and "to assume complete responsibility for the education of our children as to their rights and duties and the language and customs of this country; the latter, insofar as they may be good customs (Article 6)." Further, "we solemnly declare once and for all to maintain sincere and respectful reverence for our racial origin of which we are proud (Article 7)" and "we shall oppose any radical and violent demonstration which may tend to create conflicts and disturb the peace and tranquility of our country (Article 18)."[82]

The cultural adaptation of the Mexican-Americans, like other subordinate groups, involved a changing mixture of diverse elements: rural Mexican peasant culture, American borrowings, and unique inventions, neither Mexican-Mexican nor American. Class and regional differences in culture existed as well. The language was Spanish, of course, but a Spanish different from Spain's, and major variations existed between the archaic forms spoken in the more isolated areas of northern New Mexico and southern Colorado—a dialect going back to the earliest periods of settlement—and the dialect of the more recent immigrants from Mexico.

As with all languages, the pronunciation and use of certain words and phrases varied by social class. The lower-class street gangs of the cities invented numerous terms that were neither Spanish nor English. This was known as the *pachuco* patois. The following examples show the differences between pachuco, Spanish, and English words: bolar (P), dólar (S), and dollar (E); canton (P), casa (S), house (E); huisa (P), muchacha (S), girl (E); jando (P), dinero (S), money (E); mostacho (P), bigote (S), mustache (E).[83]

A peasant folk culture characterized much of the Mexican population before World War II. This culture found greater adherence among the lower classes and the more recent arrivals, and was maintained to a greater extent in the more segregated barrios and *colonia* than in areas with greater residential integration.

At the risk of stereotyping, we can identify some elements of the peasant world view that seem to be the most important:

Life is a balance of opposites: pain and pleasure, life and death, illness and health. God maintains the balance, and there is no extreme without a counterbalance.

There is much suffering, but we should accept it for it comes from God. Life is sad but beautiful. The future is vague but the present is now and cannot be ignored.

The most important obligation is to one's family. The family must be self-sufficient and free from obligations to others. The old are to be respected, and the young must learn to obey. The husband and father are to be treated with deference by the women and by the young.

To be a man means to avoid weakness, to maintain one's honor and personal dignity, and to be sexually active. What a person "is" is more important than what he "does."

One must be prudent and conceal personal gains from one's friends and neighbors; to display success is to belittle and abase others.[84]

In addition to this world view—a view not too different from peasant cultures in other times and other parts of the world—traits of the peasant culture also included Catholicism, distinctive fiestas, music and dance forms, and the Spanish language.

The *colonia*, or "Mex towns," were generally homogeneous in social class—poor agricultural workers who gave their allegiance for the most part to the folk culture as much as this was possible. In many of the older and more stable communities, however, several classes existed along with class-linked cultural variations. Madsen's study of several communities in South Texas identified five strata. At the bottom were the immigrant laborers, often recent arrivals from rural Mexico, and "the stronghold of the folk value system of *La Raza*."[85] One step above were the agricultural laborers with some specializations and the semiskilled factory workers. In this upper-lower segment, the determinism of the folk culture on behavior had weakened as a result of the stress on economic advancement. The lower-middle stratum consisted of mechanics, clerks, small farmers, and cab drivers; the upper-middle stratum consisted of the owners of larger farms and the highly trained technicians. The middle stratum was more removed from the world view of the folk culture and far more anglicized, particularly the upper-middles, with their strong emphasis on the value of higher education. The small upper class was occupied by the self-made—the owners of large businesses, the important ranchers, and the professionals, such as lawyers and doctors—and by the old elite. The old elite were the descendants of Spanish land-grant families. Some lived in genteel poverty, while others had maintained or increased their family fortunes. The old elite looked down "on other Mexican-Americans as peasants, tradesmen, and upstarts." The were friendly with upper-class Anglos but tended to "regard them as boorish, ignorant, and lacking manners."[86]

With the exception of the old elite, the higher the class, the greater the similarity of the members' views to the dominant Anglo culture. This increasing acculturation by class was simultaneously a factor in vertical mobility and an effect of higher class attainment.

Acculturation continued in the postwar period (after 1945); however, the

Chicano movement of the 1960s and 1970s reasserted *La Raza* and partially stemmed the tide of anglicization.

CHINESE- AND JAPANESE-AMERICANS

The adaptive problems of the Chinese were unique, in part because of the circumstances of their immigration. The great majority of the immigrants were men responsible to families remaining in China. Because of the unreliable climate in China and the small size of family plots, Chinese men sought their fortune in various parts of the world, including America. The Chinese male's "only hope of improvement was to leave his village, earn money outside and purchase land. Whatever hard work lay before him, it had to be done to fulfill his obligations as a good son, husband, father, or brother."[87] His residency in a foreign country was to be temporary (a sojourn), and, after acquiring sufficient money to purchase land in China, he expected to return to his native village.* To come back with insufficient funds was to lose face with his entire family and village.

A second factor peculiar to Chinese immigration was their dependence on and subordinance to a few Chinese elite. This relationship began in China. The men sold what little property they had, borrowed at high interest rates (often using daughters as collateral), or signed promissory notes for passage stating that the debt would be paid back by wage deductions.[88] Once in the United States, debts had to be paid, and, because of language difficulties, these immigrants were dependent upon bilingual Chinese intermediaries for securing employment. According to Lyman, "the single most important feature of the occupations of the Chinese immigrants was their tendency to keep the Chinese in a state of dependency on bosses, contractors, merchants—ultimately on the merchant elites of Chinatown."[89]

The major Chinese organization engaged in hiring and negotiating with employers in the United States was known as the Chinese Six Companies, a federation of district associations based upon districts in the province of Canton. The organization, eventually termed the Chinese Consolidated Benevolent Association, not only functioned as a union hall or an employment bureau, but also as a pressure group to protect the rights of Chinese and as a welfare agency.[90]

Besides this federation of district associations, the Chinese developed clan organizations. Generally, these groups were made up of people with the same surnames. They offered eating and sleeping facilities and meeting rooms, handled savings and loans, provided a secretary to write or read letters for the illiterate members, and made employment arrangements.[91]

Around 350,000 Chinese came to the United States between 1840 and 1920, but only 61,639 were recorded in the census of 1920. This drop was due not only to the fact that many returned to China but also the lack of women and, hence, the lack of children. In 1890 there were twenty-seven males to every female (Charles F. Marden and Gladys Meyer, Minorities in American Society, 4th ed. [New York: Van Nostrand, 1973], pp. 362–63).

The Chinese word for any organization was *tong*. To most Americans and to the police, the term meant a criminal organization. Many were just that. To aid a large population of men without women struggling in an alien land, the tongs promoted prostitution, gambling, and opium. The kidnapping of a scarce resource, Chinese women, from other tongs led to numerous tong wars from the nineteenth century until the 1930s. Such "wars" were fought by hired assassins armed with hatchets or cleavers. It is estimated that in 1898 the number of such professional killers in the Chinese communities numbered between three and five hundred.[92] The stereotyped image of the Chinese communities held by many Americans was not completely without foundation.

In their initial employment, the Chinese worked in the mines in the hope of acquiring gold, and, when driven out of the gold fields, they turned to laboring on the railroads. Few became farmers.

When they also encountered white hostility in the railroad industry, particularly from the Irish, the Chinese then turned to occupations within the confines of segregated urban Chinatowns, occupations not in competition with the native whites. In 1870, there were 27,045 Chinese engaged in mining, but by 1920, there were only 151. The number of traders, dealers, and merchants increased from 779 in 1870 to 7,477 by 1920. Similarly, Chinese domestic service workers increased from 9,349 in 1870 to 26,440 by 1920.[93] Over 90 percent of the cigars and cigarettes sold on the Pacific Coast in 1862 were made by Chinese.[94] Many of the restaurants in California were Chinese, and several dishes, such as chop suey, were Chinese-American inventions to satisfy American tastes. Chinese laundries are proverbial; "no tickee, no washee" was not an isolated expression. San Francisco had over three hundred Chinese laundries in 1876, employing around five men each, with two firms often using the same establishment in night and day shifts. "What the first Chinese laundrymen, farmers by trade, knew about washing and ironing, heaven only knows! What they did know was that the regular price was $8 for doing a dozen shirts, and that there were very few women in California to do this kind of work, and that at $5 a dozen, they, the Chinese, could get the business."[95]

As long as the sojourner mentality prevailed, the Chinese clung to the culture of their villages and provinces and to a low level of ethnicity that even divided the Chinese communities into neighborhoods based on village origin. In time, however, many gave up the idea of returning and decided to become American citizens. Wives were sent for or arrangements were made to acquire them from China. The population began to increase, as did migration to eastern cities, and a Chinese-American sense of ethnicity developed. By World War II, however, the great majority of Chinese still remained within the safe confines of West Coast Chinatowns.

The circumstances of immigration, the problems of adaptation, and the modes of adaptation were somewhat different for the Japanese. Over 90 percent of the Japanese immigrants were peasant *families* and they came with the intention of staying. Rather than attempting to make quick money in whatever occupation paid the most, most Japanese entered the field they knew best—agriculture.

Initially, they labored as hired field hands, generally making more money under the piece-rate system than other ethnic workers. By saving their wages and by acquiring loans from a form of credit union (the *tanomoshi*), the Japanese aliens and Japanese-Americans began to acquire their own farms in spite of discriminatory efforts to restrict this development. In 1900, there were only thirty-nine Japanese farmers holding more than 5,000 acres; by 1909, over 210,000 acres were held by six thousand farmers.[96] In 1919, 1 percent of California's cultivated land was owned by members of this small minority, and this 1 percent accounted for 10 percent of the total volume of production, as measured in dollars.[97]

One success story was that of George Shima. He came to the United States in 1889, at the age of twenty-six. By 1926, he controlled 85 percent of the California potato crop, valued at $18 million, and employed over five hundred persons, many of them whites. At his death in 1926 his estate was estimated to be worth $15 million. Yet people had tried to make him move from an exclusive neighborhood.[98]

To increase their competitive ability, the Japanese farmers formed numerous agricultural associations, which marketed members' produce, protected the farmers' interests, regulated labor disputes and internal competition, controlled prices and wages, and worked to protect the social welfare of the members' families.[99] More informally, Japanese farmers would collectively buy up neighboring farms in economic trouble and then improve them, and they would shame any ethnic member who neglected his lands.[100]

Other Japanese worked in canneries, became section hands on the railroads, worked as domestics and gardeners, or entered business as merchants.

The Japanese as businessmen were as competitive as they were in farming, and they resisted Anglo efforts to reduce their competition. When threatened with boycotts, picketing, arson and mob violence, the Japanese trade guilds reacted by boycotting the boycotters, by bribing the thugs hired to terrorize them, and by using private police for protection. And, in the true business spirit, they undercut the prices of their white opposition.[101]

The Japanese culture contained several traits found in most preindustrial societies, particularly in the peasant class. "Familism" was a virtue; the acceptance of family responsibilities, the submission to and recognition of the authority and prestige of the parents, and the "maintenance of inviolate integrity of family status within the community" were esteemed.[102] The father (and the male in general) was superior in every respect; females and children must know their place. Marriages were arranged by the parents.

But there were important deviations from this traditional, preindustrial pattern. The Japanese believed that everything done for a person by another produced a debt that had to be repaid with devotion and loyalty. This emphasis on duty to others was coupled with a work ethic that even exceeded the belief of New England Yankee Calvinists. According to the first-generation Japanese (*issei*), the second-generation Japanese (*nisei*) were too Americanized. They were ambitionless, lazy, indolent, not serious minded, and took things too easy.[103] Work was not something necessary to satisfy immediate needs, as in many peasant cultures, but a virtue in itself.

In another respect, the Japanese were closer to Protestant Anglos than were the Catholic ethnics of Europe and Mexico. The Japanese emphasized planning and control in life. Excessive emotion was out of place. Cursing, weeping, or loud laughter would show that a person did not anticipate events and act as calmly as he or she should. Self-discipline was a virtue.[104]

Education was as important to the Japanese as it was for the Jews and the Anglo-Americans. By 1942, the second generation of Japanese-Americans exceeded the national average of years of schooling.

The culture of the Japanese changed, of course, as the result of adaptation to the American environment. The value of education, itself, was probably one such development, since schooling is not a necessity for peasants. Many became Christians, and the Buddhist churches took on many of the trappings of Protestantism: congregations, hymns, sermons, Sunday schools, and a God that could be supplicated.[105] Second-generation Japanese often objected to arranged marriages, preferring instead the idea of individual choice based upon love. And many females were no longer content to play the role of the retiring, shy, and home-oriented wife and mother.

In numerous small towns and cities in the West, however, at least through World War II, there existed a distinctive Japanese-American subculture, neither American nor Japanese, but a creative blend of both and with some elements not found in either.

OCCUPATIONAL DISTRIBUTION BY RACE, 1900 AND 1940

The type of occupations engaged in by members of particular ethnic groups and races is a function of cultural traditions, discrimination, and individual abilities. Before the adaptation of the European ethnic groups is examined, it might be useful to summarize the distribution of whites and the racial-ethnic groups—Black-Americans, Indians, Chinese, and Japanese*— within a number of broad occupational categories as a result of these factors.

Table 9.1 is compiled from census data and utilizes the Occupational Proportion Index (OPI). This index is derived by finding the percentage of a

*Data for Mexican-Americans are not available, since this group is included under "white" in the censuses of 1900 and 1940.

Table 9.1

Occupational Proportion Index in 1900 and 1940

Occupational Category	White		Black		Indian		Chinese		Japanese	
	1900	1940	1900	1940	1900	1940	1900	1940	1900	1940
1. Professionals	1.12	1.07	0.30	0.36	0.31	0.40	0.17	0.37	0.08	0.42
2. Farmers	1.01	0.96	0.98	1.31	1.75	3.20	0.19	0.12	0.12	1.33
3. Managers, Officials & Proprietors	1.15	1.10	0.08	0.13	0.12	0.13	1.30	2.50	0.21	1.42
4. Clerical & Sales	1.11	1.10	0.05	0.11	0.08	0.13	0.39	0.75	0.17	0.67
5. Craftsmen & Operatives	1.11	1.06	0.31	0.45	0.54	0.60	0.53	0.87	0.54	0.33
6. Service	0.67	0.80	2.04	2.76	1.79	0.67	4.11	3.00	0.96	1.25
7. Farm Laborers	0.80	0.82	2.20	2.57	1.25	2.87	1.17	0.37	3.91	3.75
8. Nonfarm Laborers	0.93	0.88	1.38	2.10	1.71	1.40	1.11	0.25	1.08	1.25

group's male and female workers in an occupational category and then dividing this percentage by the percentage of the group's membership in the total societal labor force. A score of 1.00 indicates the group is proportional—that it has as many members in this occupational area as would be expected, given the size of its labor force. For example, if a group constituted 4 percent of the labor force and 4 percent of farm laborers, then their OPI for farm laborers would be 1.00. If an OPI score is 0.50, then a group is underrepresented; it has only 50 percent, or half as many members in this occupational category as one would expect. A score of 2.00 means that a group has twice as many members in the category as there would be if the group was proportional. If race made no difference, then each group would have a score of 1.00 in each occupational area, but obviously race does make a difference. The table compares the OPIs of 1900 and 1940.

Table 9.1 (continued)

Occupational Category	White		Black		Indian		Chinese		Japanese	
	1900	1940	1900	1940	1900	1940	1900	1940	1900	1940
9. White Collar[a]	1.15	1.09	0.10	0.17	0.17	0.20	0.57	1.12	0.13	0.83
10. Blue Collar[b]	0.96	0.95	1.22	1.42	1.17	1.00	1.11	1.12	1.23	1.08
11. Percentage of Total Labor Force	85.48	89.75	13.65	9.93	0.26	0.15	0.36	0.08	0.24	0.12

SOURCES: *Occupation at the Twelfth Census, Special Reports* (Washington, D.C.: Department of Commerce and Labor, U.S. Bureau of the Census, Government Printing Office, 1904), Table 2, pp. 10–13; Table 3, pp. 14–15. *Sixteenth Census of the United States, 1940, Population, The Labor Force, Occupational Characteristics* (Washington, D.C.: U.S. Department of Commerce, Bureau of the Census, U.S. Government Printing Office), Table II, p. 5. *Sixteenth Census of the United States, 1940, Population, Characteristics of the Nonwhite Population by Race* (Washington, D.C.: U.S. Department of Commerce, Bureau of the Census, U.S. Government Printing Office), Table 8, p. 47. Census data for 1900 in terms of occupation is not categorized in the same manner as the data for 1940 and succeeding decades. In the 1900 tables the following itemized categories were utilized to correspond to the 1940 method of tabulation: Professional—12 (minus 18 and 24), 68; Farmers—5; Managers, Officials, and Proprietors—24, 32, 38, 39, 45, 46, 56, 57, 59, 140; Clerical and Sales—48, 49, 54, 62, 64; Craftsmen and Operatives—18, 47, 52, 60, 63, 65, 66, 67, 69, 70 (minus 140); Service—29, 30, 31, 33, 34, 36, 37, 40, 42, 43, 55, 61; Farm Laborers—3, 4, 11; Nonfarm Laborers or Other Laborers—6, 7, 8, 9, 10, 35, 51.

[a] Includes professionals; managers, officials, and proprietors; and clerical and sales. Excludes farmers.

[b] Includes craftsmen and operatives; service workers; farm and nonfarm laborers. Excludes farmers.

A few findings are worth emphasizing. Very little change took place in the occupational distribution of whites between 1900 and 1940. Blacks about doubled their membership in the unskilled nonfarm laboring category, which indicates their movement from rural areas to unskilled jobs in the cities. Blacks also increased their numbers in the service occupations (as domestics and waiters, for example) by about 75 percent. Other than in these categories, which make up the lower stratum, there was very little change for blacks.

Indians experienced a two-fold increase, in the farm laboring and the independent farmer categories, illustrating the effects of governmental policies to turn them into farmers.

The Chinese, who in 1900 already had more members in the manager, official, and proprietor category than would be expected, about doubled their representation by 1940. It should be noted that this increase came more in the proprietor field of small businesses than in management or as officials of organizations. The Chinese also dropped drastically in both the farm and nonfarm laboring areas.

Between 1900 and 1940 the Japanese raised their membership significantly in the professional and clerical occupations. The change from 0.12 to 1.33 in the farmer category is indicative of their acquisition of farm land in spite of Anglo efforts to prevent this development.

Since an individual's occupation is a major factor in affecting the acquisition of rewards—power, prestige, privilege, and wealth—the OPI is also an indirect measurement of social stratification by race or ethnicity.

EUROPEAN ETHNIC GROUPS

Urban Conditions

The great majority of European immigrants came from agricultural areas in their native lands. A large percentage of some of the groups decided to continue as farm laborers or as independent farmers; the Danes, Swedes, and Germans are examples. However, the largest number of immigrants within most of the groups opted for urban life, particularly the Irish, the Italians, the Austrians, the Hungarians, and the Jews.

In the large cities of the East and the Midwest, and in a few other urban centers, such as San Francisco and New Orleans, Europeans resided, for the most part, in the cheapest and least desirable sections of the cities. In the slum and tenement districts, Europeans clustered together as ethnic groups; sometimes entire city blocks contained families from particular regions or cities in Europe. Nevertheless, very few cities or sections of cities had large, ethnically homogeneous areas. A number of city blocks were inhabited by a majority from one group, but families from other groups could also be found, particularly on the boundaries of these areas.

The pattern of "invasion-succession" was quite prevalent. Later immigrant groups would settle into areas previously inhabited by the earlier group. Second- and third-generation family members that were successful often moved to the better residential areas or to the suburbs, leaving behind the less successful, the old, or the more traditionally inclined.

The Irish were the first major group to enter America from Europe in the nineteenth century. Crowded into sections of Boston, New York, Philadelphia, and a few other metropolises, many of the Irish lived in extreme poverty and under the most deplorable of slum conditions. Numerous "shanty" Irish lived in shacks built from rotten boards with a piece of stovepipe for a chimney, or in high-density tenement buildings.

The typical slum conditions experienced to a greater or lesser degree by most of the first-generation Europeans were particularly felt by the Irish, who were extremely impoverished to begin with. The death rates of the Irish in the nineteenth century were higher than they were in Ireland. The number of Irish in the charity wards or almhouses exceeded all other groups in the nineteenth century. And in this century, alcoholism and insanity have been major problems in the Irish communities. The stereotype of the drunken Irishman was based on reality, and the Irish temperance groups had little success in reducing alcohol intake.[106]

Studies of Italian communities around the turn of the century illustrate other urban conditions. In a Little Italy in Chicago, only 417 families out of 14,360 had tubs in their apartments. One-third of the families in Philadelphia lived in one-room apartments, only a few of which had tubs or toilets. In one area in New York City, 1,231 people were squeezed into 120 rooms.[107]

But probably the worst area at this time (1900) was the predominantly Jewish New York East Side. Three times as many Jews lived in this area as blacks do today. Thirty-seven of the city's fifty-one blocks housing more than three thousand people were on the Lower East Side. The population density of the East Side was extreme—seven hundred persons per acre. Crowded into the ghetto were 60 cigar shops, 172 garment shops, 65 factories, and 34 laundries. The tenements were firetraps; a few had fire escapes, but they were utilized as sleeping areas. Only 8 percent had baths, and most of these had cold water only. Families slept on the floors, on folding cots or beds, and lived within the most wretched sanitary conditions.[108]

Adaptation to these conditions did take the form of vices, crime, and juvenile gangs. But the great majority of the first- and second-generation immigrants stayed within the law, coping with their problems until it was possible to leave.* In spite of these circumstances, however, many preferred the sense of community found in their ethnic areas to the strange and impersonal world outside. And many of those who left would come back on occasion to renew ties with kith and kin and to renew their sense of ethnicity.

Organizational Adaptation

Virtually all of the European ethnics, whether in urban or farm communities, developed patriotic mutual aid organizations that provided health and death insurance, a place for meetings and ethnic social life, and, in some cases, entered the political arena to act as pressure groups. The major organization of the Irish was the Ancient Order of Hibernians, founded in 1836. The order provided charity, organized St. Patrick Day parades, supported the revival of the Gaelic language, and stimulated interest in Irish culture through its literary and debating groups. Politically, the

---

*Unlike black communities, with their close proximity of members from all the classes, European communities remained lower class, as the upper-strata Europeans moved out fairly soon.

organization sought the independence of Ireland from England by pressuring American foreign-policy makers and by making financial contributions to Ireland.[109]

The Italians had their Venetian Fraternal Order, the Italo-American National Union, and the Order of the Sons of Italy of America, with accommodation functions similar to those of the Irish Hibernian Order. And, like the Irish, the Italians were interested in their native land. With the successes of Mussolini, a renewed sense of "Italianness" was revived in the 1920s and 1930s. Italian-Americans formed the Fascist League of North America, which had eighty branches and a reported membership of 12,500. The Sons of Italy "became an important source of Fascist propaganda, with many of its chapters acting as unofficial organs of the Italian Ministry of Popular Culture."[110] However, this "fascism" was always more of a "nostalgic patriotism" than a political ideology, and World War II brought about a rapid repudiation of this identification of Italian ethnicity with fascism.[111]

The Jews had their Hebrew Immigrant Aid Society, the American Jewish Congress, the Antidefamation League of B'nai B'rith, the Jewish Labor Committee, and the Zionist Organization of America. Similar organizations of other groups were the Serb National Federation, the Slovene National Federation, the Sons of Norway and the Norwegian Bygdelag Society, the Caledonian clubs of the Scots, and the Polish National Alliance, to name but a few. Religious organizations also made up a major part of community life, functioning not only in their traditional spiritual sense, but also as agents of accommodation to subordination. Educational institutions, for example, were often outgrowths of the ethnic churches.

As the first large Catholic contingent, the Irish came to dominate the church. Along with their involvement in politics and the police departments, the Catholic church became a major source of social mobility for the Irish. As early as 1886, thirty-five of the sixty-nine bishops in the church were Irish. According to Wittke, "there is hardly a diocese or an archdiocese in the United States that has not been governed by prelates of Irish birth or descent."[112] The first private Catholic school system, founded in Boston in 1820, was an invention of the Irish. The Catholic schools functioned to keep Catholicism alive in the face of Protestant domination of the public school system, a domination exemplified by the reading of the Protestant Bible during school time.[113] About 50 percent of the Germans who eventually immigrated to the United States were Catholic, and they too staked their claim in the higher positions of the church.

When the Poles arrived in large numbers toward the end of the nineteenth century, they decided to build their own churches, parochial schools, and colleges, rather than attend organizations controlled by Germans or the Irish. By 1942, Polish communities in America (Polonia) had 831 churches, 553 elementary schools, 71 high schools, 6 colleges, 4 seminaries, and 34 hospitals.[114]

Although the Italians were overwhelmingly Catholic, they gave little support to the church, built very few churches of their own, and, when they did attend, participated in rituals carried on by Irish priests. In Italy the church was an oppressive landlord, and the reaction to this condition carried over into America. By 1940, an estimated two-thirds of Italians were outside the church or only nominal Catholics, using the church primarily for christening, marriage, and burial services.[115]

Various Protestant ethnic immigrants were dissatisfied with Anglo domination of their denominations and founded their own churches as well. The Scandinavian Lutherans in particular founded ethnic churches, private schools, and colleges.

The large number of Polish and Russian Jews that arrived in the late nineteenth and early twentieth centuries also found a situation of alien ethnic domination. Reform Judaism had begun in Europe and was brought to America by German Jews. Within a short period, there occurred a rapid acculturation in the direction of the dominant Anglo Protestants. Reform synagogues were characterized by hymns, Sunday schools, organs, choirs, sermons, the sitting together of men and women, and the abandonment of the canopy and the breaking of a glass in the traditional Jewish marriage rite. The services were primarily in English, and hats and prayer shawls were absent. According to Nathan Glazer, "the effect of these changes was to make the social atmosphere of the synagogue that of a Protestant church of the upper and upper-middle classes."[116] By 1880, most of the 250,000 Jews in the United States were Reform, and the remainder were Orthodox of a type different from that in Eastern Europe.

The over two million East European Jews did not like what they saw. Reform Judaism was not even Judaism to many, and the American Orthodox synagogues contained deviations from the traditions of their native areas in Russia and Poland. One reaction was to develop a new form of Judaism, the Conservative synagogue, which was neither Reform nor East European Orthodox but combined some elements of both—elements deemed appropriate for American society. Sixteen of the Conservative synagogues united together as the United Synagogue of America in opposition to the older federation of Reform synagogues, the Union of American Hebrew Congregations.[117]

The Orthodox variety of Judaism built new synagogues in competition with the other branches. And all of the divisions of Judaism organized their own educational institutions, such as the Hebrew Union College (Reform), the Jewish Theological Seminary (Conservative), and Yeshiva College (Orthodox), along with numerous "Saturday" schools for the younger Jews.

It should be mentioned that there were many atheist or secular Jews, just as there are now. "Jewishness" is ethnic, and being a Jew may or may not involve subscribing to the creed of one of the several divisions of Judaism.

Besides the mutual aid societies and the churches with their educational offshoots, another organization played an important function in the adaptation of the Europeans to American life—the newspaper. Very few ethnic communities were without a local or a national newspaper in their native language. The newspapers, primarily weeklies, carried local social news, coverage of events in the countries of origin, and reports on American governmental policies of importance to the European ethnics. Like all newspapers, they lived a precarious existence. Between 1884 and 1920, 3,444 foreign language papers were founded, and in the same period 3,186 folded.[118] While they existed, however, they functioned to maintain ethnic languages and cultures as well as to provide information on issues largely ignored in the dominant group press. The reduction of their numbers since World War II is one indicator of the integration and assimilation of the European ethnics into the American mainstream.

Occupational Adaptation and Change

A majority of the members of each of the immigrant ethnic groups in America engaged in relatively few types of occupations in the first generation. Over the generations, such occupational specialization was reduced, and ethnic Europeans began to approximate the Anglo occupational distribution more closely. Occupational choices were limited by the type of skills ethnic Europeans brought with them from the old countries, by their reading ability in their own language, by their ability to speak and to read English, and by whatever discrimination was being practiced.

The Irish largely came from rural areas, had high rates of illiteracy, but could speak the English language, more or less. The early immigrants who arrived before the potato famine in Ireland became urban laborers, small farmers, and artisans. The majority did, however, have sufficient resources to start their new lives. Those who came because of the famine in Ireland after 1845 had few resources, higher rates of illiteracy, and few skills of value in an urban setting. The vast majority went into domestic service or common unskilled labor. The Irish railroadman, bartender, servant girl, chambermaid, waiter, coachman, and factory worker were common correlations of ethnicity and occupation. Only about 10 percent went into farming.

In time, the Irish found several major organizational routes for advancement—the church, city government and the police and fire departments, and the labor unions. The Irish were particularly suited to the city politics of nineteenth- and early twentieth-century America. According to Wittke:

> The same genius for organization which made the Irish so successful as leaders in the Church and the field of labor helps account for their success in politics. To all three fields, warmhearted, sociable Irishmen brought a human touch that proved most important. In Ireland, politics had been a struggle, with not too much concern for the rules of the game, and Irishmen had few, if any, ethical scruples about the machine politics of American cities a century ago. Their wit, their flexibility in dealing with people, and their oratorical gifts made them natural leaders for a turbulent urban democracy which had neither accepted them nor mastered the techniques of orderly, honest, and efficient government.[119]

An Irishman who was not a Democrat was an anomaly. Irish affiliation with the Democratic party began with veneration of Andrew Jackson (himself the son of a poor Irish immigrant) and was intensified by a traditional hatred of aristocratic parties, such as the Whigs and Tories ("Tory" was originally an Irish word). Beginning with political meetings in saloons, the Irish eventually took over the major city machines, like Tammany Hall in New York. Excelling in the corrupt politics of the time, they paid immigrants to vote and sometimes to vote again. They became aldermen and mayors and a host of lesser officials.[120]

Their political positions in the urban centers of the East also enabled them to distribute jobs among the faithful, particularly within the police and fire departments. The Irish considered a police officer's job very important. And Anglos accepted the idea that only Irish cops could handle Irish drunks. Although a small minority, the Irish have been highly disproportionate in police work since the 1850s, and in some cities and during certain periods they made up the majority of the police force. In Chicago in 1850, six out of nine police officers were Irish. By 1870, the Irish constituted much of the rank and file of the police departments in cities with Irish populations. A study of the New York City police deparment in 1933 found that of the total of 20,000 men, 1,533 were foreign-born Irish and 5,671 were American-born Irish. The Irish were outnumbered only by the Anglos.[121] "The 'crime wave' which trembling Americans anticipated from the floodtide of Catholic Irish foreigners ended up with the Catholic Irish entrenched as the guardians of the law."[122]

Italians had a background similar to that of the Irish but without a knowledge of English. They did not limit themselves to urban areas but specialized in fruit growing, fishing, and tobacco growing in the South, truck gardening in New England, and wine making and fishing in California. Large numbers of miners in Colorado were Italians, as were factory workers in numerous urban areas. In other urban occupations, the Italians formed their own labor unions. In New York City, for example, there is the Italian Typographical Union, the Italian Medical Society, the Rapallo Association (for lawyers), and the Italian Actors Union.[123] The American Federation of Musicians has a large Italian membership. Typical business specializations were grocery stores, dry cleaning establishments, trucking and moving firms, and produce-handling concerns.[124]

One occupation that came to be dominated by Italians was (and is) organized crime. Finding politics and the police controlled by the Irish, and facing considerable business competition from the Jews, Italians turned to organized crime as an avenue of social mobility. Competing with Jewish and German racketeers after World War I, Italians, primarily of Sicilian background, increasingly came to dominate organized crime in the 1920s and 1930s. Obviously, only a small number of Italians are gangsters; however, the higher levels of organized crime are primarily occupied by Italians. In this land of opportunity, many criminals of whatever ethnicity have done quite well.[125]

German Jews, who arrived in large numbers in the 1840s and 1850s, rose rapidly within the occupational structure, meeting little Anglo resistance until the 1880s and 1890s. Extremely successful Jews made their fortunes in mining, banking, and merchandising. A United States government survey of German Jews in 1890 found that 50 percent were in business, 30 percent were in clerical work and sales, 5 percent were in the professions, 1 percent were peddlers, and only 0.5 percent were laborers. Forty percent had one servant, 20 percent had two, and 10 percent had three or more.[126]

The East European Jews, who arrived in the latter part of the nineteenth century, met opposition not only from the Anglo-Americans but also from the German Jews. Besides their strange Orthodox religion and their numbers, which seemed to many to be of tidal wave proportions, they were highly competitive. Approximately five-sixths of the Jews who immigrated between 1900 and 1925 were skilled workers,[127] and they took advantage of every opportunity open to them. "Nineteenth century immigrants from a peasant background seldom used the free libraries available, and resisted compulsory education laws. By contrast, Jewish immigrants crowded into every free educational institution available."[128] This value on education soon became apparent in educational attainment. In 1908, Jews made up only 2 percent of the population, yet 8.5 percent of the male student body in seventy-seven major universities and colleges were Jews.[129]

Without distinguishing between German and East European Jews, *Fortune* did a study of Jewish occupational distribution in 1936. The entire waste-processing industry (paper, scrap metal, rag) was controlled by Jews. Eighty to 90 percent of the underwear and dress-cutting trades were Jewish. Jews owned, controlled, or occupied 95 percent of the dress industry, 95 percent of the fur industry, 85 percent of men's clothing, 75 percent of the cigar-making industry, and 50 percent of the major liquor-distilling concerns. Three out of eight movie companies were Jewish owned, and fifty-three out of the eighty-five motion picture executives and producers were Jews. Although 16 percent of the members of the New York Stock Exchange were Jews, they were underrepresented in banking (with the exception of the few Jewish banking houses), either as directors or as employees of any kind. In heavy industries, such as rubber and automobile manufacturing and coal mining, there were few, if any, Jewish executives, a condition due more to discrimination than to choice.[130] It has been estimated that by 1940, 40 percent of all Jews were in commerce or trade (three times as many as would be expected, given their proportion in the labor market), 10 to 12 percent were in the professions, and 15 to 20 percent were in manufacturing, to name the major areas.[131]

German Protestants and Catholics came from diverse occupations in their native land. Many came as farmers and acquired their new farm lands in the Midwest and Texas. More than half of the German immigrants were skilled workers, professionals, and merchants and moved easily into similar vocations in the United States. Highly industrious, frugal, and occupationally diversified, the Germans spread themselves throughout the occupational categories. Those less skilled acquired education and technical knowledge and then moved up rapidly within the stratification system. "Mirroring the larger Protestant group, German Americans have been spread throughout the class structure. Few remained long near or at the bottom."[132] Within a short time, they became proportional with the business elite. One study in 1925 found 10 percent of all millionaires to be of German descent.[133]

The Scandinavian groups came as farmers, and, for the most part, they resumed this occupation in America. Settling primarily in the midwestern rural areas, they formed distinctive farm communities. While most Norwegians were farmers, there were many Norwegian as well as Swedish lumberjacks. And, as a result of their seagoing tradition, Norwegians were overrepresented in the Puget Sound trawling industry, in the nautical enterprises of San Francisco, and in the Great Lakes' schooner trade.[134] A smaller percentage of Scandinavians entered the cities, in particular, Minneapolis, St. Paul, Milwaukee, San Francisco, and Chicago, working in a wide variety of urban occupations with few hindrances upon their vocational choices except, perhaps, ignorance of English or lack of a particular skill. Second-generation Scandinavians moved from agriculture to urban occupations in great numbers. For example, while three-fourths of all Swedes were in agriculture in 1870, only one-third were so engaged by 1930.[135]

Like the Germans, the immigrants from the British Isles came from a wide variety of occupations and rapidly distributed themselves at all levels within the occupational structure of the United States. Being ethnically akin to the native Anglo-Americans, they formed few distinct ethnic communities and rapidly disappeared into the American group. The English in particular assimilated quickly. According to Anderson, the "English Americans were culturally assimilated with rather painless celerity; their hyphenated status was short-lived, if even recognized."[136]

Cultural Adaptation

If the English and other Protestant ethnic groups had little difficulty in making cultural adjustments in America, such was not the case with the Catholics. In *The Rise of the Unmeltable Ethnics*, Michael Novak presented his view of the contrasts between the WASPS and the PIGS (Poles, Italians, Greeks, and Slovaks), and what changes had to be undergone by those who aspired to the "new paradise." In his view, Catholics had to learn loneliness and to value independence from family, ethnic group, and community. They had to switch from the belief that life is sweet but that hardship, disaster, and heavy work is the fate of man to the WASP emphasis on optimism, competition, and the sky's the limit. Instead of trusting in a beneficent God who ran the world, one had to accept the idea of the individual against the world, a world that can be manipulated and conquered. Catholics had to learn "that it was *all right* just to think of themselves, to go after exactly what they wanted, to give free rein to avarice and ambition," that "the right way is to count only on yourself" in creating your own future.[137]

Control of their emotions was necessary if they were to become "true" Americans, according to Novak. "They had to learn order, discipline, neatness, cleanliness, reserve. They had to learn to modulate emotion, to control passion, to hold their hands still, to hold the muscles of their face placid, to find food and body odors offensive, to quieten their voices, to present themselves as coolly reasonable."[138] "How desperately many tried to prove they were proper, reliable, chaste, self-disciplined, controlled. How earnestly they worked against their instincts, impulses, gestures, feelings, drives, and perceptions. How urgently they worked to find sex 'dirty.' The melting pot was a cauldron of lead for the purging and the encasement of passion. If one could not be a WASP, one could make oneself into a good metallic soldier."[139]

While Novak's contrasts between the Anglo-Protestant American and the immigrant Catholic ethnics are too sharp, dichotomous, even stereotypic,* there were important differences, although more by degrees. If the Catholics were to move up in an organizational world controlled by upper and upper-middle class Anglos, they would have had to make the adaptations that Novak emphasized. Such circumstances force Novak to cry out: "In all God's world is there anything as cool as a Yale lawyer across the carpeted office of a philanthropic fund? How could any other race ever fashion its psyche to that style?"[140]

Many of the Catholics did acculturate in the direction of the dominant group, despite the problems of cultural differences, as did the Jews and the Protestant ethnics (the latter with less difficulty, of course). One factor that affects the extent of acculturation of any goup in any society is the degree of spatial segregation. The more ethnic groups were isolated in their own communities from other groups, the less the acculturation.

Two German communities are illustrations of this principle. The isolated town of Hermann, Missouri, was incorporated in 1839. For at least seventy-five years the community remained distinctively German. Visitors in 1907 found few changes from the descriptions that had been written in 1850. By 1929, German was still spoken by the older residents, although English church services had been introduced and coexisted with the German.[141] On the other hand, the town of Belleville, Illinois, was founded on a major route between St. Louis and Louisville. Although predominantly

---

For example, in The Rise of the Unmeltable Ethnics, *Novak describes the WASP as rational, suffering alone, clean with a disgust and fear of germs, reserved, controlled, independent, optimistic, inexpressive, considering pain as impersonal and mechanical, having belief in order and mastery. In the same book he describes Catholic ethnics as loyal, hard working, family oriented, having a fierce attachment to homes, less duty bound, more sensuous, less formal, more casual, having passions kindled by nature, people with roots, not atomic people. It is not hard to tell who are the good guys and the bad guys in Novak's view.*

German in the nineteenth century, by the late 1920s "nearly all relics of Germanism had disappeared. No German was spoken in the homes of the descendents of German immigrants any longer, nor was the growing generation even learning German."[142] By 1929, when Hermann was still a distinctively German community, the "German stock of Belleville was said to have no futher connections with German culture, and immigrants from Germany arriving in recent years had little or nothing in common with them. . . . Americanization, by contrast with Hermann, was all but complete."[143]

For those individuals and families who left the more segregated confines of the eastern cities and migrated West into more heterogeneous communities, acculturation was greater. In contrast to the slow acculturation of the Italians in the eastern cities, for example, was "their [the Italians'] virtual ethnic disappearance out West. Acculturation proceeded so rapidly that the story of Western immigrants can be constructed only with difficulty."[144] "One Italian wrote [about the West] that there he was indeed, 'born again,' and that he would have 'to take up as much as possible of the garb and language, of the habits of thought and of the nature and temperament of an alien race.'"[145]

The relationship of the East and the West *could* have been different. What would have happened if the Americans had stayed in the East and all the immigrants had gone West? Instead of absorbing American culture in the East, albeit slowly, ethnically differentiated states could have developed in the West—German states, Italian states, etc.[146] Acculturation would have been retarded by this reversal of regional concentration. This did not occur, however; for the Europeans, at least, the West was the melting pot.

Another factor that affected acculturation besides spatial concentration and distribution was the extent to which groups consciously attempted to maintain their cultures through social organizations designed for that purpose. Groups such as the Jews and the Poles perpetuated their cultures with special schools for the young, with "national" patriotic societies, and with foreign-language newspapers. At the other extreme were the Danes, who deliberately lacked such organizations. There was little intergenerational perpetuation of distinctively Danish subcommunities. "Danish customs and social ties were apparently short-lived, and nowhere did Danes long persist as a self-conscious and identifiable national origin group."[147]

Acculturation rates varied by generation, a circumstance that often created conflict between parents and children. According to Shibutani and Kwan:

Intergenerational conflicts have been commonplace in families of immigrants to the United States. Most of them came from peasant societies and settled in industrial centers, where their children attended American schools and acquired American middle-class values. The children quickly became aware of the low standing of their ethnic category, and many became contemptuous of the things that their schoolmates ridiculed.[148]

A study of Italian-Americans in Greenwich Village in 1935 gives evidence of the generation gap in acculturation and the sources of conflict between these generations. The study sampled the opinion of those over and those under age thirty-five as to agreement or disagreement with a number of traditional Italian norms. Table 9.2 gives the percentages of the "old" and the "young" who do *not* believe in seven norms related to the family.

Table 9.2

Do Not Believe That:	Over 35 Years	Under 35 Years
1. Marriages should be arranged.	70%	99%
2. Large families are a blessing.	48%	86%
3. Girls should not associate with men unless engaged.	45%	83%
4. Husband's authority should be supreme.	34%	64%
5. A child should sacrifice his or her personal ambitions to the welfare of the family group.	31%	54%
6. Divorce is never permissible	12%	61%
7. Children owe absolute obedience to parents.	2%	15%

SOURCE: Caroline F. Ware, *Greenwich Village* (New York: Harper & Row, 1935), p. 193.

As a general rule for most of the European ethnic groups (as well as for Japanese- and Chinese-Americans, and Mexican-Americans in certain regions), the first generation remained somewhat traditional; the second generation varied from trying to cope with two cultures to rejecting the culture of their parents; and the third generation, although highly acculturated, attempted in a greater or lesser degree to regain the sense of ethnicity of their grandparents. In many cases, this third-generation "nativism" was superficial and romanticized, restricted to learning the language or some phrases, eating the ethnic foods, taking a tour of the "ghetto," or going back to the old country on a visit. Today, for some of the third generation (and even later generations), a reassertment of ethnicity has become a political and a moral crusade.

ISLAND PEOPLES*

Puerto Rico

As has been described in Chapter 8, Puerto Rico was a poverty-stricken colony of the United States until after World War II. An excess of exports over imports and the drain of money to absentee owners amounted to

Since the subordination of Cuba was terminated after only a short period of occupation, this section will be concerned only with Puerto Rico, the Philippines, and Hawaii.

around a $10 million loss to the Puerto Ricans each year in the 1920s. The death rate from tuberculosis was 4½ times higher than that of the continental United States.[149] The Great Depression of the 1930s, severe as it was on the mainland, was a disaster in Puerto Rico. According to Hanson, "after 1930 Puerto Rico headed rapidly toward complete bankruptcy. Municipality after municipality could not pay its obligations in wages and salaries; the bonded indebtedness as well as private mortgages soared to unprecedented heights; personal suffering, amounting to near starvation, permeated the population."[150] Puerto Rican leaders, with hats in hand, attempted to present their problems to Washington but were largely ignored. Third-rate political appointees made up the bulk of the administrators sent from Washington to govern the island.[151]

The form of adaptation to such circumstances has been stated by Hanson: "Most of them bore their hunger, their illnesses, their abject poverty, their miserable housing, and their exploitation by a few large sugar companies with a hopeless fatalism."[152]

A small percentage moved to the mainland and dispersed themselves throughout the forty-eight states, primarily in the form of cheap labor. But this method of adaptation to the problems of subordination was limited to a few. Fatalism and apathy prevented most from migrating. And when darker-skinned Puerto Ricans who had migrated reported racist conditions not experienced at home, many were discouraged from migrating themselves. The large influx of Puerto Ricans to the mainland did not occur until after the war, when improving conditions at home raised the expectations of a better life for many.*

There was some resistance by the Puerto Ricans to their colonial status and condition. A small organization, the Nationalists, advocated independence and engaged in a few terrorist activities. Of greater political consequence was the growth of a new political party in the late 1930s—Partido Popular, or the Popular Democratic Party. Led by Luis Muñoz Marín, the party advocated a program of socioeconomic reform and avoided the issue of the political status of Puerto Rico. In 1940 the new party was successful in capturing 38 percent of the total vote and control of the island's legislative body.[153] This was the beginning of the transformation of Puerto Rico; extensive changes followed World War II.

The Philippines

The social and economic conditions of the Philippines under American rule were vastly superior to what they had been under Spanish dominance. In addition, American administrators made few demands upon the majority of the population and imposed few restrictions of a discriminatory nature.

There were 63,000 Puerto Ricans in New York City in 1940 and 970,000 by 1970, as a result of migration and natural increase. An estimated 600,000 native-born Puerto Ricans migrated to the continental United States between 1940 and 1960.

Numerous ethnic groups lived in their segregated communities in their traditional manner, with little need to make adaptations to the limited American control.

Nevertheless, there was discontent within many segments of this American colony. While numerous individuals and groups benefited from American dominance and were interested in maintaining the status quo, others wanted independence. The desire for political sovereignty (or nationalism) had developed under the Spanish and had continued with varying fervor throughout the period of American domination. Unarmed peasants made several unsuccessful efforts to overthrow the government in 1923–1924, 1927, 1931, and 1935. The culmination of violent efforts by the independence movement was led by the Sakdalista party in 1935. Believing they would receive military support from Japan, the Sakdalista party demanded immediate independence and began the rebellion. Says Mahajani: "The abortive revolt by about sixty thousand ill-equipped Sakdalistas was easily crushed. The American military units, alerted to stand by ready for action, were not employed. Hundreds of rebels died at the hands of government forces and thousands were taken prisoner. Neither the Japanese army nor aeroplanes so hopefully awaited by Filipino peasants appeared on the scene."[154]

A nonviolent organization that was part of the independence movement was the Partido Nacionalista. Founded in 1907, this party was successful in obtaining the creation of a Philippine assembly and worked within this structure to obtain its goal. The actions of the Partido Nacionalista, coupled with the increasingly popular American definition of the Philippines as a "colonial albatross," finally brought about political independence after World War II.

Hawaii

Having no persisting nationalistic sentiment, and benefiting from an atmosphere of racial toleration and economic opportunities, Hawaii experienced no revolts or rebellions of any significance. Haole dominance, however, was everywhere apparent—in their control of government, in the large plantations where they employed nonhaole labor, and in their occupation of the other major positions of power and wealth. (Anglo Americans made up the great majority of the haole or white category.) According to Burrows, when nonhaoles left school, ". . . they met with a rude shock. They found that the tolerance and friendliness among races, for which Hawaii has been justly celebrated, prevailed only within limits, and at a price. The price demanded by the dominant haoles—never in so many words, but nevertheless insistent—has been cheerful acceptance by other peoples of a subordinate place."[155]

The great majority conformed to these expectations, although not always cheerfully. Grumbling was the only significant form of aggression or resistance.[156] Other modes of adaptation, particularly by the native Hawaiians, consisted of "grasshopper" behavior (from the point of view of Anglo "ants")—dancing, ukulele playing, drinking, and fishing. Others, in particular, the Japanese and Chinese, moved rapidly up the stratification system from their agricultural beginnings, stopping short of the upper class. In a manner similar to their activities on the mainland, the Japanese and Chinese exceeded the islands' educational average and became overly disproportionate in the professional, the proprietary, and the managerial occupations.[157]

Culturally, as on the mainland, the subordinate groups moved in the direction of the Anglo-Americans. By 1930 (the last year the census ascertained this information), 75 percent of the islanders spoke English.[158] Public schools disseminated Anglo values, traditions, and conceptions of history. Japanese Buddhism became increasingly Christianized, as it did in California.[159] There were efforts to stem the tide of anglicization with revivals of traditional pageantries, Chinese art and drama, Hawaiian hula dancing, and Japanese dancing. But what remains today is largely ceremonial.

Acculturation was correlated with increasing spatial integration. At the beginning of the twentieth century, segregated sections of the cities and relatively homogeneous ethnic regions were prevalent. Growing urbanization, intermarriage, and improvements in stratification positions diminished these ethnic enclaves to a great extent. The Japanese, with their large population, remained somewhat together in spatial proximity, while a few remote islands were still native Hawaiian communities.

Acculturation and spatial desegregation were accompanied by an increase in racial intermarriages. In 1912–1913 only 13 percent of the marriages were interracial. Between 1931 and 1932, the rate increased to 32 percent, and between 1942 and 1944, 38.5 percent married a member of a different race or ethnic group.[160]

The general trend in the period under discussion (1898 until World War II) was adaptation by integration rather than by pluralism: try to become like the dominant group, and in the meantime, cooperate.

SUMMARY

Once an ethnic group became subordinate in the United States, the group was forced to adapt in some manner to the expectations of the dominant Anglos and to an unfavorable stratification position. In spite of pious statements to the contrary, the great majority of Americans have not tolerated cultural differences. Without exception, all of the subordinate groups were expected to acculturate in the direction of the dominant Anglo group, although pressure to do so varied with each group. Those groups without the stigma of "color" were expected not only to acculturate but to give up their previous ethnicity and to disappear into the dominant ethnic group. The nonwhites were to acculturate, but to keep their distance. Only official Indian policy was an exception to the norm against nonwhite assimilation. A "white melting pot" was the desired state of affairs, but this "pot" was not to be a mixture of elements that would create something new; rather, the foreign elements were to be absorbed into the dominant element. At the same time that the groups were expected to acculturate, even to assimilate, some degree of discriminatory barriers were imposed upon them. The discriminatory restrictions and requirements were greatest for the nonwhites and for the Catholics and Jews among the whites. In addition to these adaptation problems, a large percentage of most of the subordinate groups faced all of the conditions that are associated with the term "poverty."

Each group as a whole responded to its own peculiar problems differently. But no group enjoyed complete consensus as to just what the adaptive response would be. Within each subordinate group, some individuals and organizations strove to maintain their culture and their ethnic identity, while others tried to emulate the more successful members of the dominant group. Some members simply conformed to whatever was expected of them, feeling that nothing could be done about their condition. Others fought back in a variety of ways—through crime, violent revolts, legal actions, legislative lobbying, or with pressure on the in-group to "keep the faith." Avoidance of contact with dominant group members was an answer for a large percentage of any group. There was always the solution of escape into the comfort of drugs, alcohol, hedonism, or a religion that promised heavenly happiness for the true believers. Numerous individuals worked hard, legally and illegally, and moved up within the American system of inequality. And many members, when it was possible, solved their minority problems once and for all—they changed their names, moved away from friends and relatives, and disappeared into the American group.

Besides these tactics of conformity, resistance, avoidance, escape, status seeking, and assimilation, innovation occurred as a means of adaptation. New organizations were developed. New forms of religious worship, art, music, and foods came into existence—cultural elements unique to American society but not Anglo in origin.

The collective consequences of these different, and often contradictory, modes of adaption by the subordinate groups still reflect a few general patterns. With a few exceptions, such as the English immigrants, all of the subordinate groups had segregated communities for at least a few generations. These communities either existed prior to subordination and were continued (as in the case of some Mexican towns), or they were new developments for the particular ethnic groups. Although black segregation was primarily due to discrimination, most ethnic residential segregation reflected the desire to live among one's own people (inadequate income was also a factor, of course). While the regional concentration of Black-Americans was reduced in the twentieth century, urban segregation within ghettos increased. All of the other ethnic communities on the mainland and in Hawaii experienced a reduction of regional and urban area concentrations.

A second consequence that developed despite whatever efforts there were to the contrary was the Americanization, to a greater or lesser degree, of the subordinate groups. The acculturation rate was greatest among the middle and upper strata within each group. This relationship between social class and acculturation is not without significance. One explanation is that people who were in the upper strata prior to subordination, such as the Mexican or "Spanish" upper social classes, acculturated due to a greater association with the elites and professionals within the dominant Anglo group. In some cases, this was true; however, a more frequent relationship was acculturation prior to the movement from the lower strata to the upper. Becoming Americanized was necessary if improvement was to occur.

The third consequence of subordinate group adaptation was the maintenance of Anglo dominance. Accommodation and cooperation by subordinate groups that maintained their ethnic integrity produced no challenges to the system. Resistance was largely ineffective. Violent challenges were suppressed, and most of the efforts to reduce or eliminate racial and ethnic discrimination met with little success. The assimilation of thousands of individuals, primarily from the northern European groups, enhanced the dominant group. The great majority of *the important positions in state and federal government, in the corporations, in the universities, and in other significant organizations remained in the hands of Protestants of British descent. The basic institutions formed in the early period of American history by British-Americans were little affected. Although the English language was enriched by words and phrases borrowed from some of the subordinate groups, it remained unchallenged as the medium of public and organizational discourse. American history was Anglo history and was required learning for every child in the public school system. History from the view of the minorities, with very few exceptions, was not part of the curricula of the public schools or the universities. If such a historical interpretation was taught at all, it was taught in the private schools of the minorities. And, of course, given their numerical size and their control of the upper classes, the great majority of the society's wealth still went to the dominant Anglo-Americans.*

In this period many members of subordinate groups naïvely believed they were "Americans," only to be assigned a hyphen or to be referred to in more pejorative terms. Even the successful ones were made aware of this reality. Joseph Patrick Kennedy, Boston millionaire, Ambassador to the Court of St. James, and father of the first Catholic president, once exclaimed, "How long does our family have to be here before we are called Americans rather than Irish-Americans?" [161]

The few years before and after 1900 were significant. If a period of time were to be selected in which the greatest cultural differences existed between all of the groups in the United States, in which ethnic segregation was at its peak, and in which the greatest stratification differences existed between the dominant Anglos and any other ethnic group, it would be around 1900. The Indians had been conquered and confined to reservations or to plots of impoverished farm land; the blacks had been pushed back down into the institutionalized apartheid system; the Mexicans had been reduced to landless laborers; the greatest volume of immigrants from Europe, many of whom could not speak English, was arriving and settling into segregated urban poverty; and imperialistic ventures had just added Hawaii, Cuba, the Philippines, and Puerto Rico to American territory.

An overall examination of the social pattern of race and ethnic relations shows that between 1900 and World War II there was a slight reduction in discrimination, segregation, cultural differentiation, and stratification, but the major changes would be a postwar development.

10

CHANGING DOMINANCE:
SOCIAL MOVEMENTS
SINCE WORLD WAR II

INTRODUCTION

In the period preceding World War II, the pattern of dominance between Anglo-Americans and the European ethnic groups was already undergoing transformation by integration: there was an increase in acculturation, a decrease in geographical segregation, a reduction in lower-strata concentration, and the absorption of many individual members into the American group. The pattern between the Anglos and the *racial-ethnics*, however, remained relatively stable: few, if any, nonwhites were in higher organizational positions; the government practiced discrimination and condoned such efforts in the private sector; geographical segregation continued within regions and within sections of cities; a majority of whites held to racist conceptions; there was a lower rate of subordinate group acculturation among racial-ethnics (with the exception of blacks); the concentration of the majority of blacks, Indians, and Mexicans in the lowest stratum continued; and a pattern of subordinate group accommodation rather than one of organized resistance was, for the most part, affirmed.

Following World War II, a number of subordinate group social movements developed. The first of these was the civil rights movement, divided into a legalistic phase and a nonviolent confrontation stage. This movement was largely superseded in the late 1960s and 1970s by a power movement—Black Power, Chicano Power, and Red Power. Coexisting with this racial-ethnic power movement has been a white ethnic social movement. Although integrated to a far greater extent than the racial-ethnics, many white ethnics (largely Catholic ethnics in the working class) have felt they have been left out and ignored by the government. The demands by the racial-ethnics for equality and pluralism and the government's actions to meet these demands stimulated a white ethnic reaction. This chapter focuses on the first of the major postwar changes—the change from subordinate group accommodation to organized resistance in the form of social movements.

EFFECTS OF WORLD WAR II

The involvement of the United States in World War II (1941–1945) had a number of effects that stimulated the development of subordinate group social movements. The first of these effects was the creation of employment opportunities and skills. Regarding blacks, Broom and Glenn have written:

> *With the entry of the United States into World War II, Negro workers for the first time took a giant step toward equality with whites. The drafting of hundreds of thousands of civilian workers into the Armed Services created an acute labor shortage, and the dearth of qualified white males led to the recruitment of white women and Negroes of both sexes into types of work that previously had been largely closed to them. . . . With the return of veterans to the civilian labor force at the end of the war, with the end of the Fair Employment Practices Committee in 1946, and with the decline of industries that mainly served the war effort, Negroes suffered losses in occupational status. However, not all wartime gains were lost, and conditions remained more favorable for Negro advancement than they had been before the war. Negro servicemen and workers in war industries gained valuable training and experience that enabled them to compete more effectively, and their employment in large numbers in unionized industries during the war left them in a stronger position in the labor movement.[1]*

Mexican-Americans underwent a similar experience. In the defense industries, they acquired salaries and standards of living far exceeding their prewar conditions. Their membership in unions increased. Numerous Mexican-Americans took advantage of federal programs to learn job skills that American society needed. In New Mexico, for example, thirty-five hundred men learned welding and mechanics, among other skills, and were quickly employed in the factories and shipyards.[2]

Japanese-Americans acquired new occupational skills, but in an entirely different context. Although the Japanese in Hawaii were employed in industries related to the war effort, the mainland Japanese suffered internment in the interior of California and in other western states. Internment, however, had an unanticipated consequence. According to Kitano:

> *In the evacuation centers, a whole range of occupations was open to them that had never been available before. For the first time, with their race no longer a factor in competition, Nisei were able to fill every job a community requires (except the administrative, reserved for Caucasians). Japanese competed against other Japanese, so that education, training, and ability determined success. . . . For many, the experience and training in camp jobs served to help them relocate later in Eastern communities.*

Perhaps the most important thing gained from camp job experience was confidence. Nisei found they could do good work in varied and important roles. The satisfaction of being allowed to do what they were capable of doing and trained to do ultimately made them dissatisfied with anything less.[3]

For minority veterans, new job opportunities also developed during the war. Although blacks and Japanese-Americans served in segregated military units while Indians, Chinese, and Chicanos were integrated, all of the members of the armed forces were exposed to a much wider range of experiences through vocational training, leadership skills, and contact with other peoples. In addition, all military personnel, white and nonwhite alike, were bombarded with propaganda that this was a war of a freedom-loving people against the racist ideologies and practices of the Axis powers. When the war was over, the G.I. Bill gave all veterans the opportunity to further their education or to go into business for themselves.

In the years immediately following the war, the veterans returned to their communities and sought employment. However, the transition from the high rate of wartime production to a peacetime economy resulted in economic dislocations, firings, and temporary layoffs. Needless to say, a greater percentage of racial minorities were affected in the adjustments that followed. White veterans, in an economy with a labor supply now exceeding demand, were far more likely to be hired than the ex-soldiers of darker complexion.

Nevertheless, conditions had improved for many members of the racial minorities during the war, and as a result expectations had also risen. The economic conditions and discriminatory practices of white Americans, once accepted as circumstances that one could do little about, now became intolerable. To paraphrase an old saying, they had got their inch and now they legitimately wanted a mile. Anger and frustration began to swell among peoples who had contributed greatly to an undertaking ideologically justified as a war against racism and oppression. Paradoxically, the Japanese-Americans that left their camps or returned from the service met the least resistance to their new aspirations.

A less direct effect of World War II was the psychological consequences of the end of European colonialism upon nonwhite Americans. Britain, France, and the Netherlands, drastically affected by the war and faced with independence movements, gave up their colonies in Asia and Africa. Supposedly inferior "coloreds" had been successful against their white masters. Many Black-Americans were particularly affected by these developments. Says de Riencourt, "the rise of free and independent African states had a profound impact on the American Negro by restoring his pride in his *negritude* and confirming the possibility open to him of separate development; henceforth, he would be different from the white man, but not inferior. Before World War II, Africa made a powerful contribution to Negro self-contempt; now, suddenly, it contributed as much to his self-pride."[4] The writings of African leaders increased in popularity among black intellectuals and their audiences, and rhetoric comparing the ghettos of America to the European colonies in Africa emerged.

The first social movement that developed after World War II was the civil rights movement. By the middle of the 1960s, however, a second movement—the power movement (Black, Red, and Brown)—gained the headlines as the first declined in impact.

CIVIL RIGHTS MOVEMENT

Although each racial-ethnic group had one or more organizations—each utilizing different tactics—representing their specific ethnic interests, the civil rights movement did have a common ideology. The movement was basically reformist in nature, and its major goals were (1) the elimination of discrimination in government and in the private sector; (2) the establishment of the principle of legal equality as public policy and the principle that the federal government must protect the constitutional rights of citizens;[5] and (3) the eventual integration of racial minorities into the American system through the elimination of segregation, the placement of racial-ethnic members into more prestigious occupations and in the higher positions within organizations, and the maximization of minority participation in the political process.

The first step for the civil rights movement was to eliminate the legal basis of discrimination, or the denial of civil rights through court decisions and enacted laws. The second step was to gain the support of governments—local, state, and federal—to actively pursue a policy of eliminating discrimination within government and within the private sector, and to assist the governments in the implementation of these actions. Many civil rights supporters (white and nonwhite) believed that integration would occur when the previous steps had been accomplished.

As a reform social movement the civil rights organizations were not demanding radical changes in society in the form of new values and new structures; they demanded only the guarantee of the basic civil rights of all Americans, rights that originated in the beginnings of American society. Tactically, this reform movement stressed nonviolence. To achieve their goals, different organizations used different techniques, including legal proceedings through the courts, lobbying and political pressure, speeches at outdoor rallies, and, on occasion, boycotts, sit-ins, strikes, and obstruction tactics, such as lying down on streets at construction sites.

The beginning of the civil rights movement can be traced to an incident during World War II. In 1941, the president of the Brotherhood of Sleeping Car Porters (a black union), A. Philip Randolph, threatened a mass march on Washington unless discrimination was eliminated in all industries with a federal government contract. President Roosevelt reacted by issuing an executive order establishing a Fair Employment Practices Commission. The march was called off.[6] Although the commission had no powers of enforcement and was disbanded right after the war (1946), precedents had been set. Job discrimination was a violation of civil rights, and the government could be coerced into doing something about discrimination.

First Phase: Legalism

The period between 1945 and 1955 was one largely dominated by legalistic tactics—taking, or threatening to take, cases involving discrimination into the courts. By such procedures, the National Association for the Advancement of Colored People (NAACP) was successful in eliminating the legality of the white primary in the Supreme Court decisions of 1944 (*Smith* v. *Allwright*) and in 1952 (*Terry* v. *Adams*). In 1948, in a case initiated by the NAACP, the Supreme Court ruled that restrictive covenants could no longer be enforced by the courts (*Shelly* v. *Kraemer*). And, in 1954, the Supreme Court declared de jure racial school segregation to be unconstitutional (*Brown* v. *The Board of Education of Topeka, Kansas*). In a similar vein, Mexican-American unity leagues that were founded right after the war, along with the once accommodationist League of United Latin American Citizens (LULAC), were instrumental in making the courts declare the illegality of the separation of Anglo and Mexican students in the schools of California (1946 and 1947) and in Texas (1948).

Legal inroads, then, were made by these organizations and others, such as the American G.I. Forum, founded by Mexican-American veterans in 1948, and the Congress of Racial Equality (CORE), founded in 1942. However, "impressive as it was to cite the advances—especially legal advances—made in the postwar years, in spite of state laws and supreme court decisions something was clearly wrong. Negroes were still disfranchised in most of the Deep South; Supreme Court decisions in regard to transportation facilities were still largely ignored there; discrimination in employment and housing was the rule, even in states with model civil rights laws; and after 1954, the Negro unemployment rate grew constantly due to recession and automation."[7] Similarly, the other racial-ethnic groups saw little improvement from prewar conditions. Because the executive and legislative branches of government were relatively inactive on these issues, legalistic tactics, alone, would not be sufficient to correct the problems.

Second Phase: Confrontation

The second phase of the civil rights movement began around the mid-fifties. In this phase a more active and direct approach to eliminating discrimination developed, using the nonviolent tactics of boycotts, sit-ins, and voter registrations.

In December 1955, in Montgomery, Alabama, Rosa Parks, a black seamstress, refused to move to the back of the city bus. From this violation of a discriminatory norm came a boycott of the bus system, a new organization for black improvement, and a new leader, Dr. Martin Luther King, Jr. With the arrest of Ms. Parks, the blacks in Montgomery organized a boycott led by Reverend King and the Montgomery Improvement Association. The initial demands of the black leaders were hardly revolutionary: that Negroes be given courteous treatment; that bus riders be seated on a first-come-first-served basis, with blacks entering from the back and moving to the front; and that Negro bus drivers would be used in predominantly Negro neighborhoods. The white community reacted by arresting of ninety-five blacks and refusing to negotiate.[8] The Montgomery Improvement Association changed its demands to full integration and, with the support of the NAACP, boycotted bus services for 381 days, inflicting large financial losses on the bus company. The company did not give in, however, until the issue was decided in the courts. In November 1956, the Supreme Court of the United States upheld a lower court decision that discriminatory segregation in the Alabama transportation system was unconstitutional. In this case legal action was still useful, but it was black activism that made the integration possible.

As a result of this incident, Dr. King became a national celebrity, and, after leaving Montgomery to return to Atlanta, he and a number of other black clergymen formed the Southern Christian Leadership Conference (SCLC). The new organization expressed the belief that the black church had to be involved in the struggle for civil rights.[9] The ideology of the organization stressed nonviolent civil disobedience, a tactic that originated in India with Gandhi but that was also practiced in the United States during the Depression by a pacifist organization named the Fellowship of Reconciliation. For King's group, the first problem was to define what constituted the need for civil disobedience: "How does one determine whether a law is just or unjust? A just law is a man-made code that squares with the moral law or the law of God. An unjust law is a code that is out of harmony with the moral law." More specifically, "an unjust law is a code that a numerical or power majority group compels a minority group to obey but does not make binding on itself. . . . A law is unjust if it is inflicted on a minority that, as a result of being denied the right to vote, had no part in enacting or devising the law."[10] The tactics of civil disobedience would involve resisting the desire to fight violence with violence, by accepting blows from police, and making no aggressive effort to resist arrest.

Between April 3, 1963, and May 11, 1963, the SCLC led a demonstration in Birmingham, Alabama. In order to test compliance with a recent Supreme Court decision on the illegality of discrimination in public facilities, the organization and hundreds of young whites and blacks engaged in restaurant sit-ins and boycotts of businesses that continued to discriminate. After disobeying a court order to cease and desist, King was arrested. After eight days he was released, and the protest seemed at an end. However, students tried a new tactic—getting arrested to fill up the jails. When this succeeded and over 2,500 demonstrators were in custody, the local authorities turned to using fire hoses and dogs to break up the protests. The event received national television coverage, thus dramatizing the cause of blacks, and a group of businessmen capitulated. Pledges were made to desegregate public facilities and to hire blacks in nontraditional positions. Birmingham had set the pattern. In the ten weeks that followed, there were 758 demonstrations in seventy-five Southern cities, resulting in 13,786 arrests.[11] Later in the same year, the organization directed more than 250,000 whites and blacks in a march on Washington, demonstrating for an end to discrimination.

After a civil rights act was finally passed in 1964, with major provisions to end discrimination in public accommodation and transportation, the SCLC turned to voting discrimination. In 1965, Dr. King led a march of several hundred blacks from Selma, Alabama, to the capitol at Montgomery. Local police attacked the group as it approached the capitol. The publicity of the confrontation brought numerous church leaders from numerous faiths and other civil rights leaders to Montgomery and won a federal injunction against any further efforts to stop the march. A new voting rights act stemmed from this protest, where a racially mixed group sang, "Black and white together," "We shall Overcome."[12]

Earlier, in 1960, four black college students in Greensboro, North Carolina, took seats at a Woolworth lunch counter and refused to leave until they were served. The example spread and thousands of black students formed a new base of power. Under the initial direction of the SCLC, the students were mobilized as the Student Nonviolent Coordinating Committee (SNCC). For a year, students applied sit-in tactics in the public facilities of 140 southern cities. When this initial impetus died down, SNCC members joined CORE in the Freedom Rides in the summer of 1961, testing a Supreme Court decision that outlawed segregation in transportation terminals. When white mobs attacked the group in Birmingham, the federal government gave the group members protection to ride to Jackson, Mississippi, where they were jailed by the local police for violating segregation ordinances.[13] In the early sixties, SNCC was active in voting registration drives in the Deep South, particularly in Mississippi.

The older organizations, such as the NAACP and CORE, became more militant as the result of the new competition within the civil rights movement. Branches of the NAACP disagreed on whether or not the new tactics should be adopted, but, while continuing their legalistic tradition, many branches did engage in protest and confrontation methods. In 1961, President John F. Kennedy established the Committee on Equal Employment Opportunity. The NAACP filed complaints under this new policy and broke the historic pattern of discrimination in the southern industries of tobacco, textile, steel, and pulp. After a four-year campaign in the Lockheed plant at Marietta, Georgia, the association forced the hiring of two hundred blacks in skilled jobs. In 1964, after demonstrations organized by the NAACP in forty-one cities, General Motors gave in and employed blacks in clerical and administrative positions for the first time.[14]

CORE focused much of its attention on job discrimination by boycotting or demonstrating against particular businesses concerned with their public image. Working with SNCC in Philadelphia, CORE was successful in opening up nine-thousand jobs for blacks in the consumer-goods industries between 1960 and 1963 through the use of selective buying and boycotting. A boycott of the A & P grocery stores in New York in 1964 resulted in an agreement promising that 90 percent of all new employees hired in the next year would be nonwhite. Boycotts and highly visible public demonstrations against the Bank of America in California in 1964 made possible the hiring of eight thousand black workers in the next twelve-month period.[15]

Mexican-American organizations, such as the G.I. Forum and the LULAC, continued their legal efforts to end discrimination, but they were also active in forming political organizations to get out the vote. The first organizations specifically designed to gain political power through democratic means came in 1958 when the Mexican-American Political Association (MAPA) was founded in California, the Political Association of Spanish-Speaking Organizations (PASO) in Texas, and the American Coordinating Council on Political Education (ACCPE) in Arizona.[16] Political activity through institutionalized procedures was largely unsuccessful except in Crystal City, Texas. In 1962 Mexican-Americans elected their own ethnic candidates to public office, in spite of the obstruction efforts by the Texas Rangers. This was a first in Texas, and "this symbolic victory would spark an increased activism in the decade-and-a-half to follow."[17]

The nonviolent confrontation stage of the civil rights movement did have some successes in opening up public accommodations and public facilities, in securing the passage of several civil rights acts, and in enforcing antidiscrimination procedures in voting. Before World War II, these organizations probably would not have been successful in achieving their goals, and they might even have been ruthlessly suppressed. Eschen, Kirk, and Pinard suggest the following reasons for the movement's success:

> . . . *the movement did not depend on large numbers for success. It could not, for* active *participation required the participant to be highly deprived, but such persons were held out of the movement by feelings of low political efficacy. Instead the movement relied on the creation of disorder—disorder which could mobilize friends and sanction opponents, and which could be created by small numbers. That this method did not lead to suppression was due to several factors: that there existed in the society a dilemma, a dilemma to which the most powerful were the most sensitive; that the movement chose the least illegitimate of all non-routine means while its opponents responded without restraint; and that, because of its small numbers, the movement was forced to concentrate its efforts geographically, permitting most people to refer the issue to their abstract values rather than their self-interest.*[18]

The local authorities in the southern communities overreacted: they kicked women, had their dogs attack the protesters, and beat nonresisting people—all on national television. Powerful white liberals could not condone such actions nor ally themselves with such men as Sheriffs Bull Connors and Jim Clark. People outside the areas under attack could be self-righteous and criticize the actions of the whites in these communities on the basis of abstract values of equality and without feeling personally threatened. Communities that gave in felt virtuous, and, because they were worried that if other communities did not desegregate their customers would go elsewhere, businessmen tended to support the movement.[19] In spite of these successes, however, the nonviolent confrontation phase disintegrated in the latter part of the 1960s. New movements began that eventually eclipsed the older civil rights tactics of legalism and nonviolent activism: first Black Power, then Chicano Power and Indian Power.

POWER MOVEMENT

Black Power

Eschen, Kirk, and Pinard have identified some factors that contributed to the rise of the power movement and the demise of the nonviolent confrontation phase. Numerous conditions of inequality and discrimination remained—poverty, unemployment, poor housing conditions and housing segregation, and the concentration of black workers in the less desirable occupations. Greater numbers of blacks demanded to be involved in the movement, and, with the new goals, lower-class blacks became participants. The increase in size of the movement made it difficult to socialize members into the discipline required for nonviolence (for example, allowing someone to spit on you without striking back). Many of the new participants mistook the disorder that had been created by the confrontation tactics for violence and concluded that violence worked. Slogans of Black Power and Black Culture became popular. The elites in the civil rights organizations had to become sensitive to these mass demands and popular outcries or be replaced. With these changes in the movement came an increase in white resistance and the development of new forms of resistance. White officials learned how to respond to confrontations without the use of extreme measures and the creation of disorder. When the movement shifted to less legitimate goals, in the opinion of white liberals, the liberals had second thoughts. It was one thing to grant the freedom to use public facilities and accommodations and to allow blacks to vote; it was quite another to desegrate housing or to accept a program of compensatory hiring (affirmative action). "Black Power" as a term was perceived as a threat, and "Black Culture" to many whites was nothing more than poverty culture.

When spontaneous riots broke out and the rioters began chanting "Black Power," it was difficult for whites to distinguish between the civil rights movement and criminal rioters. White resistance in turn made a power movement even more necessary in order to overcome the low political efficacy of the black masses.[20]

The highly charged term "Black Power" has meant several things to whites and to blacks, including "colored self-help," political and cultural pluralism, black unity, black revolution, black nationalism (secessionism), and black domination of whites. To Stokely Carmichael and Charles Hamilton in 1967, Black Power was "a call for black people in this country to unite, to recognize their heritage, to build a sense of community. It is a call for black people to define their own goals, to lead their own organizations, and to support those organizations. It is a call to reject the racist institutions and values of this society."[21] A year earlier Carmichael wrote: "There must be reallocation of land, of money. . . . The economic foundations of this country must be shaken if black people are to control their lives. The colonies of the United States—and this includes the black ghettos within its borders, North and South—must be liberated. . . . For racism to die, a totally different America must be born . . . integration is a subterfuge for the maintenance of white supremacy. . . . The society we seek to build among black people . . . is not a capitalistic one. It is a society in which the spirit of community and humanistic love prevail."[22] Roy Wilkins of the NAACP reacted negatively to the term, believing that it meant "anti-white power. . . . It has to mean going it alone. It has to mean separatism."[23] Martin Luther King stated that it was absolutely necessary for the Negro to gain power, but the term 'black power' is unfortunate because it tends to give the impression of black nationalism. . . . We must never seek power exclusively for the Negro, but the sharing of power with the white people."[24] In a study of the opinions of black and white respondents in Detroit in 1967, the term "Black Power" meant numerous things: black rule over whites (38.6 percent of the whites and 8.5 percent of the blacks believed this), black unity or a fair share for black people (42.2 percent of blacks and 10.7 percent of whites), or "trouble," or rioting (11.9 percent of whites and 4.1 percent of blacks).[25]

Except for a few small fringe groups with little support in the black community (the Black Liberation Army, the Black Crusaders, the Republic of New Africa), Black Power was and is a pluralist movement. It is anti-integration, places a strong emphasis on black culture and black pride, and aims for local control of its own communities, an end to discrimination, and economic parity with whites.

It is difficult to ascertain just when the Black Power movement began, but quite possibly the year was 1966. Early in that year, Stokely Carmichael was elected president of SNCC and announced a new "black power" policy—the removal of whites from major roles in the civil rights organizations and a shift from a prointegration program to an "integration is irrelevant" stance.* In the same year, the Black Panther party was formed in Oakland, California. With three to four thousand members and forty store-front headquarters around the country, and with their black berets, leather jackets, guns, and Black Power rhetoric, they became, in the words of *Newsweek*, the "bad niggers of white America's nightmares."[26] The Pan-thers, led by Huey Newton, Eldridge Cleaver, and Bobby Seale, advocated a ten-point program to accomplish: (1) black determination of the destiny of black communities, (2) full employment, (3) an end to robbery by whites, (4) decent housing, (5) an education that would teach the true history of racism and the role of blacks in America, (6) the exemption of blacks from military service, (7) an end to police brutality and murder, (8) freedom for all black prisoners, (9) trials of blacks by blacks, and (10) a United Nations–supervised plebiscite to be held throughout the black "colony" "for which only black colonial subjects will be allowed to participate, for the purpose of determining the will of black peoples as to their national destiny."[27] The group rejected pan-Africanism, using the argument that blacks are united with all oppressed peoples and that American society must be totally re-structured.

Other militant organizations were formed in subsequent years. In Au-gust of 1968, the Black Crusaders were organized with around two hundred members. The group advocated self-defense against the police and viewed itself as a liberation army. Lacking black support, it folded by February of 1969. The Republic of New Africa was founded in Detroit in 1968, with the goal of establishing a black nation-state out of five states in the Deep South. Little has been heard from this group since.

One of the more absurdly unrealistic organizations was the Black Economic Development Conference, founded in Detroit in 1969. Their man-ifesto contained the following flights of black power rhetoric: "We are the Vanguard Force. We shall liberate all the people in the U.S. and we will be instrumental in the liberation of colored people the world around." The revolution "will be an armed confrontation" and will involve "long years of sustained guerilla warfare." "We are dedicated to building a socialist soci-ety inside the United States where the total means of production are in the hands of the State and that must be led by black people. . . ." Their mani-festo demanded a reparation of $500 million from white churches and synagogues as restitution for the past, and "to win our demands we will have to declare war on the white Christian churches and synagogues and this means we may have to fight the total government structure of this country."[28] Nothing ever happened.

For this group and other extremists on the fringe of the Black Power Movement, Robert F. Williams wrote a manual on how to make a revolution. Williams, self-appointed premier of the African-American government in exile (Williams fled the country to avoid a federal warrant in 1961), lists "the

*In 1969, SNCC changed the N in its name from Nonviolent to National.

weapons of defense" to be "employed by Afro-American freedom fighters": Molotov cocktails, light bulbs injected with lye or acid, homemade flame throwers, and all sorts of conventional military weapons that could be bought from servicemen. Sabotage would be the basic tactic: choking gas tanks with sand or sugar, dropping boards with nails in them on the freeways, derailing trains, putting booby traps on police call boxes, shooting oil storage tanks from a distance, and dropping kitchen matches into air conditioning systems in large buildings.[29]

More in the pluralistic mainstream of the power movement, CORE in 1970 joined SNCC in rejecting integration as a method of obtaining equal opportunity. The organization espouses black capitalism.

James Foreman, one of the leaders of the Black Economic Development Conference, has strongly criticized the idea of black capitalism, arguing that any black who advocated this approach to equality was "seeking not only his ultimate destruction and death, but is contributing to the continuous exploitation of black people all around the world."[30]

Black Riots in Urban Centers, 1964–1968

Between 1964 and 1968, hundreds of major and minor disorders involving blacks and white political authorities occurred throughout the United States. During these years black-white conflict escalated according to the number of incidents, major incidents, deaths, and arrests, the extent of property damage or loss, the number of police and National Guardsmen involved, and the number of times troops were called in to restore order. In 1964 there were 8 major riots, all in the North, resulting in 8 deaths, 1,056 reported injuries, and 2,643 arrests. In 1965 the number of major riots dropped to 5 but in Watts, a black section of Los Angeles, riots resulted in 34 deaths, 1,032 reported injuries, 3,952 arrests (three-fourths of which were for burglary or theft), and an estimated $40 million in property loss and damage. In 1966 the number of major riots increased to 20, with a total of 43 disorders and riots, leaving 13 dead, 366 injured, and 1,647 arrested. Chicago experienced the greatest racial conflict of 1966, with 3 deaths, the use of 4,200 National Guardsmen, and 433 arrests. Racial conflict rose dramatically in 1967, with 76 major riots and a total of 164 disorders, major and minor (56 alone in the month of July). The riots in this year spread to 28 states and 128 cities and resulted in 16,000 arrests, the use of 27,700 National Guardsmen and 4,800 federal troops, the deaths of 89 people, and an estimated property loss of $67 million. The two most serious incidents of racial unrest were in Newark, New Jersey (23 deaths, 1,400 arrests, and $10 million in property loss) and Detroit, Michigan (43 deaths, 7,200 arrests, and $40–45 million in property loss). During the following year, 1968, racial conflict reached its peak. In April alone, there were almost as many civil disorders as there were in the entire year of 1967, with more injuries, more arrests, more troops called in more times, and nearly as much property damage as in 1967. Altogether, 313 riots and racial disorders occurred in 138 cities in 36 states, resulting in 78 deaths and $78 million in property loss.[31] According to Skolnick, ". . . 1968 represented a new level in the massiveness of the official response to racial disorder. . . . *Never* before in this country has such a massive military response been mounted against racial disorder."[32] In April of 1968, for example, 34,900 National Guardsmen and 23,700 federal troopers were called in to suppress disorder.[33]

In an effort to explain these disorders, the National Advisory Commission on Civil Disorders (more popularly known as the Kerner Commission)* undertook a study of twenty-four disorders that had occurred in twenty-three cities in 1967. Some of the commission's major findings were:

1. *The disorders involved Negroes "acting against local symbols of white America —property and authority—rather than against white individuals.*

2. *Blacks seemed to be demanding "fuller participation in the social order and the material benefits enjoyed by the vast majority of American citizens" rather than trying to subvert the social order.*

3. *These disorders were the result not of one single cause or triggering event but of an accumulation of tension-heightening incidents linked to underlying grievances.*

4. *The major grievances of the populations in the riot-stricken cities were unemployment and underemployment, verbal and physical abuse by police, occupational discrimination, inadequate housing, inadequate and segregated education, discrimination in the courts, inadequate recreational facilities, and white racism.*

5. *The riot areas were characterized by severely disadvantaged conditions in contrast to the conditions of white areas of the same cities, by an unresponsive local government, by a large increase in the black population (the black population increased at a median rate of 75 percent between 1950 and 1960), and by the beginnings of federal programs to improve conditions, programs that had not yet reached most of the black citizens.*

6. *Fifty percent of the incidents immediately prior to the outbreak of disorder involved routine arrests by the police; 40 percent of the incidents prior to the final events involved alleged police discrimination.*

7. *The initial disturbance took place within crowded street areas, primarily between 6:00 P.M. and 6:00 A.M. during the summer months when temperatures were high.*

8. *The typical rioter was not a criminal, a recent migrant, a member of the uneducated underclass, or a person lacking broad social and political concerns. The typical rioter was a teenager or a young adult, a lifelong resident of the city, a high school dropout, somewhat better educated than most residents, underemployed or unemployed, proud of race, hostile to whites and middle-class blacks, and politically informed but distrustful of the system.*[34]

President Lyndon Johnson established this Commission in 1967, in Executive Order 11365, to investigate these racial disorders. The commission was chaired by Otto Kerner, governor of Illinois, and the vice-chairman was John V. Lindsay, mayor of New York City.

The general conclusion of the commission was: "Our nation is moving toward two societies, one black, one white—separate but unequal."[35] However, the condition could be reversed or arrested. The overriding and general cause of the disorders was white attitudes and actions (racism and discrimination): "What white Americans have never fully understood—but what the Negro can never forget—is that white society is deeply implicated in the ghetto. White institutions created it, white institutions maintain it, and white society condones it."[36]

A study of the Detroit riot in 1967 by Geschwender and Singer suggests at least one modification of the commission report. Black interviewers questioned 10 percent of those arrested (499 black males out of 6,500) and interviewed 499 black males who had not been arrested but who lived in the riot area. They found that the commission study had not examined age differences. The arrestees were generally younger and less educated than those not arrested; they also had lower occupational status, lower weekly income, and had experienced greater unemployment. "Thus, it appears that it is the more deprived segment of a deprived black community who participates in ghetto disorders."[37]

A study of Detroit and Newark by Caplan and Paige supported several of the commission report's findings. The research team examined the differences between those who identified themselves as rioters (11 percent of the 437 respondents in Detroit and 45 percent of the 236 respondents in Newark) and those who did not. Rioters were more likely than nonrioters to be long-term residents, to be angry with society, and to have strong race pride, even a sense of racial superiority; they were also likely to have more education than the nonrioters. The researchers found little difference between rioters and nonrioters in terms of income, alienation, and judgment of ghetto conditions. The researchers concluded that the "continued exclusion of Negroes from American economic and social life is the fundamental cause of riots." Since black exclusion is nothing new, why did the riots occur at this particular time? Caplan and Paige answer: "Our data suggest that Negroes who riot do so because of their conception of their lives and their potential has changed without commensurate improvement in their chances for a better life."[38]

While the Detroit-Newark study found that a sense of alienation did not distinguish rioters from nonrioters, research by Ransford in Los Angeles found this factor to be quite important. The greater the isolation from whites (lack of communication), the greater the feelings of powerlessness; and the greater the racial dissatisfaction, the greater the probability that the black person would engage in violence.[39] In another study of the Watts area, Ransford found that the darker the skin color of male respondents, the more willing they were to use violence to improve their positions and to reject integration. Because of discrimination, the darker the skin, the greater the probability of menial occupation or unemployment.[40]

It is probably not too useful to ascertain factors that distinguish those ghetto blacks who pick up the bricks, light the fires, and loot the stores from those who do not. Distinctions between active looters, active arsonists, nonactivists but sympathizers, and counterrioters (those who tried to cool things down) are also unbeneficial. Virtually all blacks in the ghettos of American cities are alienated and deprived to a greater or lesser extent. The important findings from the riot studies seem to be that the riots were not the work of criminals, riffraff, or militant "communist" agitators but were the result of long-standing white discrimination and economic deprivation. The timing of the revolt—and a revolt it was, although unplanned and unorganized—was related to the successes of the civil rights movement. This movement represented the interests of its middle-class black partici-pants—integrating restaurants and hotels, eliminating college discrimina-tion, securing voting rights, and putting an end to discrimination in the purchasing of homes. Securing these rights, however, meant little to the black lower class, which comprised a large majority of the black population. Much closer to home were the problems of slums, low income, unemploy-ment, job discrimination, and contact with the police, the courts, the slum lords, and the white merchants. Yet changes affecting black people in gen-eral had occurred as the federal government had become more responsive, and further improvement seemed to be forthcoming. The conclusion of Cap-lan and Paige about the timing of the riots (1964–1968) bears repeating: " . . . their conception of their lives and their potential . . . changed without commensurate improvement in their chances for a better life." And in 1968 the authors added, "Negroes are still excluded from economic opportunity and occupational advancement, but they no longer have the psychological defenses or social supports that once encouraged passive adaption to this situation. The result has been the most serious domestic violence in this century."[41]

Why did these major uprisings of ghetto blacks cease after 1968? Jerome Skolnick, director of a task force on the study of violence and protest, suggests an answer: "The specific explanation is far from clear. It lies somewhere in the interaction between more massive and immediate 'riot control' efforts by authorities and the apparent perception by many blacks that the 'spontaneous riot,' as a form of political protest, is too costly in terms of black lives."[42]

The Chicano Movement— Brown Power

While the Mexican-Americans benefited from the successes of the black organizations and from their own civil rights groups, they nevertheless began to raise shouts of "Brown Power," "Chicano Power," "La Raza," and "Aztlán." Mexican-Americans, particularly the more militant individuals, began to refer to themselves as Chicanos instead of Spanish-Americans or

Mexican-Americans. Essentially, the Chicano Movement, like most expressions of Black Power, is a pluralist social movement, emphasizing the cultural distinctiveness of Mexican-Americans, the desire for local control of their institutions, the demand for the end of Anglo discrimination, and an educational and artistic reassertion of the Mexican heritage. Some of the members slip into a nationalist (secessionist) rhetoric focusing on the idea of Aztlán, the legendary homeland (in what is now the American Southwest) of the Aztec and Toltec peoples. For some, Aztlán is a symbol of the spiritual unity of the Mexican people. For others, it is a geographical area to be reclaimed as an independent state-society through secession from the United States by force of arms.

The following seems to be representative of the ideology of the Chicano Movement and is taken from the *Chicano Manifesto* by Armando B. Rendon:

1. On Aztlán: *Aztlán represents the unifying force of our nonmaterial heritage . . . the dynamic principle upon which to build a deep unity and brotherhood among Chicanos. . . . The quest for Aztlán will never be fulfilled, for Aztlán is not just a thing or a place to the Chicanos. Land and power will come into the Chicanos' hands, but Aztlan will remain an inspirational ideal and a goal ever drawing us forward. [However] the concept of Aztlán is undergirded by a desire for restitution of the land of Aztlán. The Chicano does not wish to have merely an empty dream. [Rendon goes on to say that an effort to acquire this land would result in violent suppression by the Anglos.]*[43]

2. On Chicano Identity and the Name "Chicano": *[Mexico is our cultural homeland] . . . but the true Chicano, while he always feels an affinity to Mexico, also must face the reality of the time and place in which he lives, and establish an internal reality of himself that can be independent of the need for the physical surroundings of the Mexican culture, traditions, and language. . . . Chicano is a beautiful word. . . . Chicano is a unique confluence of histories, cultures, languages, and traditions . . . [Chicano] portrays the fact that we have come to psychological terms with circumstances that might otherwise cause emotional and social breakdowns among our people if we only straddle cultures and do not absorb them. Chicano is a very special word. Chicano is a unique people. Chicano is a prophecy of a new day and a new world.*[44]

3. View of Social Problems: *We proclaim that we are not a conquered people but that the gringo has treated us as if we were subject to him and denied us opportunities that he has lavished on his own. This must stop. . . . Culture, history, language —the roots of the Chicano—have been suppressed and forgotten by the Anglo society's chief instrument of character assassination, the educational system . . . too many Mexican-Americans have remained passive . . . better futures for our families will not come by passively waiting for them.*[45]

4. Goals: *. . . Chicanos in essence desire three things: To fulfill our peoplehood, Chicano; To reclaim our land, Aztlán; To secure the future for ourselves and our countrymen. To achieve these goals Chicanos must have political, social, and economic freedom.*[46]

5. Tactics: *How do we accomplish this? Outright revolution—that is, armed insurrection appears to be only a device of the rhetoricians. Our revolt may cause violence, but we will be the chief victims of it if it occurs. . . . The Chicano revolt will become more physical, more activist, and more direct than school walkouts, product boycotts, marches, and rallies. . . . The final answer lies in the Chicano revolution of unionization, barrio organization, and political control.*[47]

The Chicano Movement, which began around 1965 or 1966, is made up of several organizations that reflect differences in goals, tactics, and interests. One of the earliest organizations was the United Farm Workers (UFW). After World War II, Anglo growers in the Southwest utilized large numbers of Mexican nationals for menial labor. These workers (*braceros*) were legally permitted to enter the United States for a stated period of time, and their presence drastically lowered the wages of all Mexican workers, whether Mexican nationals or Mexican-Americans. In 1964 Congress ended the bracero program, thus reducing the supply of potential strikebreakers and making the organization of field workers possible. In 1965 a number of Philippine workers walked away from the vineyards in Delano, California, in protest over low wages. With the support of the Mexican and Philippine workers, César Chavez became the leader of the strike and formed the first truly effective union for farm workers. After five years of conflict involving a nation-wide boycott of grapes, the UFW was victorious in 1970 in forcing the growers to recognize it as the bargaining agent for workers. The representation of other farm workers in California, however, was lost by the UFW to the Teamsters Union. And in the same year (1973), the UFW began its boycott efforts to force the Gallo wine organization to the bargaining table.

In 1965, the Crusade for Justice was formed in Denver, Colorado, under the leadership of Rudolfo (Corky) Gonzalez. The organization has been active in Chicano education programs, in boycotting and striking against Coors Brewery in Golden, Colorado, over job discrimination, and in combating alleged police abuses. Gonzalez is an avowed separatist and strongly opposed to integration. At the national Chicano Youth Liberation Conference held in Denver in 1969, Gonzalez made the statement that La Raza was a separate and independent nation.[48] But such rhetoric does not make reality.

In New Mexico in 1963, the first openly militant Chicano organization was formed—the Alianza de Las Mercedes—under the charismatic leadership of Reies Lopez Tijerina. Tijerina and his organization wanted the return of 1.7 million acres of community land (public) and 2 million acres of private holdings to the Hispanos of New Mexico. Needless to say, the federal government did not turn over the national parks, nor did Anglo individuals give up their holdings. The organization engaged in several other activities with no results: in 1966, they marched from Albuquerque to Sante Fe to present their case to the governor of New Mexico; later in the year they drove one hundred cars into Carson National Forest; shortly after this incident, they "arrested" national park rangers and in a "trial" convicted the rangers of trespassing; the group also took over a section of the national park for the weekend, building fires and killing game. In 1967 arson and fence-cutting incidents increased in the land-grant forests. The final act of this ill-fated organization occurred in June of 1967. The plan was to make a citizen's arrest of a district attorney, Alfonso Sanchez. Because of his efforts to eliminate their organization, the group wanted to charge him with unlawful conduct in exceeding the authority of his office. Twenty men from the organization arrived at the courtroom in Rio Arriba. Sanchez was not there, but during the search shots were fired that wounded a state policeman and a jailer. Grabbing two hostages (who managed to escape shortly thereafter), the group headed for the mountains. Over five hundred men, including members of the state police, the FBI, the National Guard, the New Mexico Mounted Patrol, and the Apache Police, set out after Tijerina and his men. Within a few days all of the courthouse raiders were arrested.[49] After appeals were exhausted, Tijerina served two years in a federal prison and was released in the summer of 1971. Since this time, he has ceased to be a militant and seeks reform by working within the two-party system.

Numerous organizations were formed in the universities of California, Texas, New Mexico, and Colorado dedicated to the promotion of Chicano students, to increasing Chicano faculty, and to eliminating perceived discrimination against Chicanos in the education field. Among these organizations are the United Mexican American Students (UMAS), Movimiento Estudiantial Chicano de Aztlán (MECHA), the Mexican American Student Association (MASA), and the Mexican American Youth Organization (MAYO). A group active in the lower-class barrios of major cities in the Southwest has been the Brown Berets. Primarily composed of young people who were formerly engaged in gang warfare, the organization is concerned with the education of high school students and with the conduct of the police.

Conflicts between the police and Mexican-American high school students opposed to school authorities broke out in Los Angeles in 1968 and 1970 and in Denver in 1969. However, there has been no large-scale rioting comparable to the black urban riots. The major incident occurred in Los Angeles in 1970. Over seven thousand Chicanos and numerous leaders of the movement had gathered to protest the involvement of Mexican-Americans in the Vietnam War. Violent conflict broke out between the demonstrators and the police, involving the throwing of bottles and bricks by the rioters and the use of tear gas by the police. Over four hundred demonstrators were arrested, and in the melee one of the most respected Chicano leaders, Reuben Salazar, was killed.[50]

The Brown Power movement, like the Black Power variety, has diminished sharply since 1970, at least in terms of open confrontation with authority. According to Stoddard, there has been a shift in strategy from

"short-run gains of the activist period to a long-range strategy of consolidat-
ing these gains for future, viable planning."[51] There is now a pragmatic
focus on improving the positions of Chicanos in organizations and on emphasizing and creating Chicano art, music, and literature.[52]

Red Power

The power movement among American Indians also has been essentially a
pluralist social movement, demanding greater political and economic autonomy on reservations, an improvement of the economic base of reservation life, and the revival or intensification of Indian culture. The major
activists in the Red Power movement have been city Indians and college-
educated young people.

One of the earliest Red Power organizations was the National Indian
Youth Council (NIYC), founded in 1961. Primarily composed of college-
educated Indians, the organization seeks to replace the Bureau of Indian
Affairs with governmental agencies that would provide specific counsel and
advice. The NIYC and other organizations, such as the Coalition of American Indian Citizens and the United Native Americans, want federal funds to
go directly to the Indian communities and not through bureaucratic agencies that have control over the distribution of funds. Local Indian communities would decide on their own programs and use federal funds accordingly. Organizations in the Red Power movement, like those among blacks
and Chicanos, generally perceive their respective ethnic groups to be colonial subjects seeking self-determination.[53] In 1964 the NIYC came to the aid
of various tribes in the Northwest engaged in a struggle over fishing rights.
The state of Washington opposed the unrestricted fishing of Indians off their
reservations, and, with NIYC help, Indians staged a "fish-in" in areas closed
to them. Members of the Washington tribes are still attempting to maintain
their fishing rights in the major rivers of this state.[54]

While active confrontation of blacks and Chicanos with established authority has diminished in the seventies, militant Indian groups have been
capturing the headlines, if nothing else. The major militant organization
today is the American Indian Movement (AIM), a group of city Indians led
by Russell Means and Dennis Banks. AIM first became nationally prominent when the group took over the abandoned prison Alcatraz in November
of 1969. Claiming squatter's rights, a few Indians managed to survive on the
desolate place until June of 1970 when federal officers surprised the few remaining Indians and reestablished governmental authority. In November
1972, members of AIM took over the Bureau of Indian Affairs (BIA) in
Washington, D.C., damaged $1 million worth of property, and sent numer-
ous BIA files to Jack Anderson, the newspaper columnist. The project was
quite successful. After seven days of occupation, negotiation with the White
House began. The government agreed to increase the BIA budget from $50
million to $593 million and to change the leadership of the Bureau of Indian

Affairs. The Indians were sent home without being charged with any offense and were given $60,000 in travel money. A retired Sun Oil Company executive from the Pawnee tribe said, "For 148 years, the tribal leaders have been going to the BIA and trying to get things done. They could never get in contact with the White House. By taking over that building, AIM ended up negotiating with the White House in seven days."[55]

Soon after this victory, on February 27, 1973, over 150 Indians in war paint took over the historic village of Wounded Knee on the Sioux reservation in South Dakota. Russell Means of AIM at first demanded the return of the Dakotas, Montana, and Nebraska to the Indians. Later, he reduced his demands to the creation of a full-scale probe of historical treaty violations, to making most of South Dakota an Indian reservation, and to the ouster of the Sioux Tribal Council president, Dick Wilson (an Indian). The federal government reacted by sending in 300 FBI agents and marshalls, two U.S. Air Force Phantoms, and armored personnel carriers. For seventy days, the Indians shouted at the government officials, looted the trading post, and destroyed a museum. Although a few shots were exchanged, the government attempted to avoid a second massacre at Wounded Knee. Eventually, after making the most out of the publicity, the Indians surrendered. The incident cost the government $5 million, and the case against the AIM defendants was dismissed in September of that year because of prosecution ineptness and mishandling of the case.[56]

Members of AIM and other Indian organizations have also occupied an electronics plant at Shiprock, New Mexico, to protest discrimination; blocked construction projects; set up roadblocks in the state of Washington, closing off fifty miles of seashore in protest over the litter on their beaches; taken Indian artifacts and Indian bones and mummies out of museums; and formed "Indian Patrols" to monitor police activity.

As a result of the activities of power movement organizations, people have been killed, property has been destroyed, and officials have been embarrassed; but has change occurred? The effects of the civil rights movement were often quite direct—a court case was won, a company changed its policy in order to end a boycott, a president promised a new law that was subsequently enacted. A few instances of conflict actions in the power movement did have similar direct effects. But the major consequences have been indirect and more diffuse. The ethnic consciousness of these minority groups has undoubtedly been intensified. For whites, these racial-ethnic groups are no longer invisible. Another consequence of the militant activity and the militant rhetoric has been a redefinition of what is radical and what is moderate. When the civil rights movement started, conservatives viewed its organizations as dangerous, radical threats to the social order. When the power movement came along, the same conservatives began to view these civil rights organizations as moderate, reasonable, even acceptable alternatives to the other groups. Through the efforts of the power movements, the government, too, has become an active agent in promoting change in race and ethnic relations. Without the violence, the threats, and the confrontations, the government could have continued to say ad infinitum: "Here are your rights; it's up to you to make sure they are implemented and adhered to. We've removed the barriers; it's up to you to improve your position and economic circumstances." The civil rights movement eliminated the legitimacy of racial and ethnic discrimination as well as the most overt varieties of discrimination. The power movement challenged the government to engage in affirmative action programs and to take an active part in changing economic conditions. The alternatives seemed to be civil war or the garrison state.

"WHITE ETHNIC" MOVEMENT

Beginning in the late 1960s and continuing to the present time, another ethnic-based social movement has developed, largely in response to the black movements. The core of the movement is composed of members of white Catholic ethnic groups, primarily Italian-Americans and Polish-Americans but members of other Catholic groupings as well, and with an essentially working-class base. Major Catholic spokespersons, leaders, and organizations of this incipient movement are Monsignor Geno Baroni, head of the National Center for Urban Ethnic Affairs; Andrew W. Greeley, director of the Center for the Study of American Pluralism and author of *Why Can't They Be Like Us? America's White Ethnic Groups;* Michael Novak, author of *The Rise of the Unmeltable Ethnics;* Steve Adubato, head of the North Ward Cultural and Educational Center in Newark, New Jersey; and the Italian-American Civil Rights League in New York, formerly headed by Joseph Colombo. Other important spokespersons are Ralph Nader, Mayor Frank Rizzo of Philadelphia, Reverend James E. Groppi, Casimir Lenard, Barbara Milkulski, Carl Holman, and numerous politicians of white ethnic extraction at the federal level.[57]

At the periphery of the movement are two Jewish organizations—the militant Jewish Defense League, headed by Rabbi Meir Kahane, and the American Jewish Committee, with its subdivision, the National Project on Ethnic America, directed by Irving Levine.[58]

According to Weed, " . . . white ethnics have become a new minority. Though an important part of American life for the past 100 years, they have been largely ignored. But black self-assertion, followed by the backlash in the urban North, the Kerner Report, and the 1968 Wallace vote, all served to promote self-awareness among white ethnics."[59] In the words of Monsignor Baroni, "today there is a budding national movement of white workers wonderfully parallel to where the Blacks were a few years ago. My hunch is this one is going to move even faster."[60]

The social problems that have given rise to the movement are numerous and come from a mixture of conditions relevant to being a non-Anglo white ethnic in America and to being working class. Many or all of the following conditions are perceived to be social problems: degrading treatment by the mass media, inflation, higher taxes, preferential treatment of blacks, continuing Anglo discrimination, being ignored by the liberal WASP establishment, student radicals, defamation (such as Polish jokes or the belief of many native Americans that "Italian" and "gangster" are synonymous), and the widely prevalent idea that white ethnics are racist. According to a study done by the National Project on Ethnic America, white ethnics "saw their values, way of life and ethnic characteristics being consistently ridiculed by the media and the liberal intellectual establishment. Often when they were mentioned at all they were characterized as the 'silent majority,' hardhats, racist pigs, honkies and bigots. Thus relegated to this verbal junk heap, they were no longer allowed any sense of importance in American society."[61] The study found that the groups believed that they were politically impotent, that political leaders had deserted the working class for the welfare poor, and that the leadership of their unions no longer represented their interests. In particular, " . . . these people saw their traditional areas of employment—which they struggled as individuals to obtain—being invaded by groups worse off than they, i.e., blacks and Puerto Ricans . . . that it was more likely for a black child to be awarded a scholarship or receive a summer job than for their own children. Many felt they were unfairly ridiculed in Polish, Irish, and other ethnic jokes while black power and African culture were celebrated by the media. While they deprived themselves and their families of many benefits and comforts to pay their taxes, those same tax dollars were benefiting blacks in the form of housing, job training, and education, which they need almost as badly."[62]

Although studies indicate that white ethnics are no more racist in their attitudes than Anglos (or non-hyphenated Americans),[63] there is a strain of resentment against blacks due to the perception of competition with blacks in the core cities, the belief that blacks are being given preferential treatment by the government, and the association of blacks with crime in the minds of many white ethnics. In the words of Stephen Adubato, a leading Italian-American politician in Newark, New Jersey, "blacks have got all these special programs to help them get to college, or to rehabilitate their houses, or to help them find jobs. We white ethnics don't get any of these things. All we want is equity." "A lot of people confuse us with white Americans, which we're not." "We are the working-class people who haven't made it in America, like the blacks, and we are still in the inner city competing with them."[64] Frank Rizzo of Philadelphia was elected mayor on a strong law-and-order campaign in 1971, and, as police commissioner and mayor, he has been strongly opposed to all black militant groups. In addition, numerous gun clubs and vigilante groups have been formed by white ethnic members in several major cities in which there are large black populations.[65]

Contrary to this antiblack strain in the movement is the belief in a minority coalition. Several of the white ethnic leaders, such as Greeley, Novak, and Baroni, have stressed the need for an alliance between all working-class and poor people or all minorities dissatisfied with conditions in American—white ethnics, blacks, the Spanish-speaking, Jews, and even the poor WASPs of Appalachia.[66]

The movement up to now has been strongly pluralist and nonviolent and concerned with rectifying the stratification position of its members. Novak has written that " . . . America will assimilate *individuals*. It will not assimilate groups. The new ethnic politics is a direct challenge to the WASP conception of America. It asserts that *groups* can structure the rules and goals and procedures of American life. It asserts that individuals, if they do not wish to, do not have to 'melt.' "[67] At a national conference of the National Center for Urban Ethnic Affairs held in Washington, D.C., in 1971, the following was part of a policy statement: "What can be done about the fundamental inequities of our society? How can our social policies benefit all sections of the population rather than increase the power of a few? These are the fundamental challenges of the seventies. Thus, the central issue becomes that of redistribution of rewards, goods, and services . . . the change in distribution must be toward the needs of a multi-racial pluralistic society."[68]

The American Jewish Committee (AJC) supports this value of pluralism, saying that " . . . a society which protects pluralism and combats polarization is in the best interest of Jews and other minority groups."[69] But the AJC seeks to prevent working-class ethnic Catholics "from congealing into a negative monolithic force," according to Weed.[70] "Pluralism" means different things to different groups.

Besides the forming of citizen patrols to curb the crime rate in several central cities, there have been a few other incidents of social action within this fledgling movement. In the school years 1968-1969, in the Ocean Hill-Brownsville section of New York City, the predominantly Jewish United Federation of Teachers clashed with blacks on the issues of teacher seniority rights versus decentralization and black control of local schools. On June 29, 1970, an estimated crowd of forty thousand (or two hundred thousand, depending on whose estimates are used) Italian-Americans in New York City held a protest. Waving Italian flags, the crowd heard numerous speeches protesting the FBI's use of such terms as "Mafia" and "Cosa Nostra." The gathering was the culmination of a year of picketing the FBI headquarters in Washington and New York. Shortly after the rally, the FBI agreed to substitute "organized crime" and "the syndicate" for the inflammatory terms. And the Jewish Defense League, a highly militant organization formed to actively combat anti-Semitism, has, in recent years, carried out protests against Soviet embassies for the USSR's treatment of its Jewish minority.[71]

How much appeal does the movement have to white ethnic members, and what are the possibilities of the movement's becoming more militant? Andrew Greeley has answered the first question this way: "At the present time I do not think the ethnic movement has a very wide base of popular support. Indeed, it can scarcely be said to exist at all."[72] This is perhaps an overstatement, but certainly there are many white ethnics who reject that label and who regard themselves only as Americans. What could increase participation in the movement and perhaps make it more militant? Greeley speculated on two possible developments. "First, the efforts to impose quotas on every dimension of American life. . . . If these efforts are successful, the ethnics may demand *their* quotas, and if they don't get them they may become inflamed. Second, it is also possible that a serious attempt to redistribute income in American society might lead to a violent outburst of the ethnics. . . . Rightly or wrongly, those ethnics who are either just above or just below the line separating blue- from white-collar worker seem to be convinced that any major attempt to redistribute income will be done especially at their expense."[73]

SUMMARY

World War II had several consequences that gave rise to subordinate group demands for change. Taking form after the war, the civil rights movement focused on a number of specific areas for change — public accommodations and transportation, school segregation, voting, employment, and housing. By the middle of the 1960s, the movement had made several notable gains and was instrumental in eliminating the legitimacy of racial discrimination in America. But the more entrenched problems of economic conditions remained, only slightly affected by civil rights agitation and governmental policies. Riots, protests, and revolts broke out in numerous American cities, and a power movement was born. Many militant blacks, Chicanos, and Indians demanded equality and pluralism, while others threatened revolution or secession.

As will be examined in the Chapter 11, the federal government moved to meet many of these demands, grudgingly at first, and then with more active efforts at change. Racial anarchy was the alternative.

Governmental programs to aid the groups that were the most vociferous ("the squeaky wheel gets the grease"), coupled with long-standing grievances and stagnating economic conditions, gave rise to the beginnings of another social movement—the White Ethnic movement. Government programs for certain groups, however ineffective they may be, have opened up a Pandora's box.

11

CHANGING DOMINANCE:
GOVERNMENT POLICIES
SINCE WORLD WAR II

INTRODUCTION

The United States emerged from World War II as the most powerful country in the world. Its only rival was the Soviet Union. An American-Soviet conflict relationship was established in the last few months of the war, and this relationship has lasted until the present time in the form of a tenuous accommodation.

One of the main causes of this conflict was competition for influence in other parts of the world, particularly in Africa and Asia. Nonwhite populations became the center of a tug-of-war between the capitalists and the socialists, as each group sought spheres of influence. For the United States, the effort to win the "hearts and minds" of "colored" populations posed a serious problem. A society with a tradition of racism and racial discrimination would be at a competitive disadvantage with the USSR, a society that at least presented a nonracist image. Moreover, the United States government had taken an active part in the formation of the United Nations, an organization with a charter containing a bill of rights strongly in opposition to all forms of racism and racial discrimination; the government would have to do something about the implementation of these rights.

If the racial minorities in the United States had remained quiet in a pattern of conforming accommodation, it might have been possible for the American government to present some form of a fraudulent equalitarian and democratic image to the "third world." But as we have seen, such was not the case. The government after World War II was faced with increasing internal discord and an unfavorable image in its foreign relations. President Eisenhower, forced to call out the troops in the school integration conflict in Little Rock, Arkansas (1957), made the following statement:

At a time when we face grave situations abroad because of the hatred that Communism bears toward a system of government based on human rights, it would be difficult to exaggerate the harm that is being done to the prestige and influence and indeed to the safety of our nation and the world. Our enemies are gloating over this incident and using it everywhere to misrepresent our whole nation. We are portrayed as violator of those standards of conduct which the peoples of the world united to proclaim in the Charter of the United Nations.[1]

The government's reaction to these problems occurred in a developmental fashion. The stages in the development, which varied according to the particular problem, such as housing or employment, seem to be the following: (1) the issuance of proclamations by governors, administrators, or presidents stating in effect that discrimination is bad or un-American; (2) the passage of antidiscrimination laws, the issuing of antidiscrimination executive orders, and the striking down of particular discriminatory practices as unconstitutional (although such actions undermined the legitimacy of discrimination, they rarely provided effective mechanisms for enforcement); (3) legislative, executive, and judicial actions improving the sanctioning ability of older laws or the establishment of additional laws with greater enforcement powers; and (4) the initiation of programs of affirmative action—active involvement by government agencies in seeking out discrimination and in enforcing antidiscrimination laws along with programs to reduce or eliminate the effects of *past* discrimination.

Before the war, government (local, state, and national) actively participated in racial and ethnic discrimination and condoned this form of conflict in the private sector. After the war the government gradually moved to policies of antidiscrimination, first by undermining the legitimacy of discriminatory actions, and then by designing programs to eliminate existing discrimination and the effects of past discrimination.

The effectiveness of these efforts, however, is another story. Government policy in the abstract sense has a number of aspects. Of concern in this section are two of these aspects: policy *statements* and policy *outputs.** Policy statements are the formal or written result of policy decisions, and they take the form of court decrees, laws, and government agency rules, regulations, and guidelines. There are two basic components of policy statements: directives and implementation. The policy directive is the norm or goal of the policy—what should or should not be (for example, the norm that school

*In Public Policy-Making (New York: Praeger, 1975, pp. 2–6), James E. Anderson distinguishes between five aspects of public policy. Two of these are policy statements and policy outputs. In addition, there are policy demands, or the pressures put upon government officials for action or inaction on some perceived social problem; policy decisions, or those processes involved in formulating policy statements; and policy outcomes, the objective and actual intended or unintended consequences of the policies upon society. Policy outcomes will be examined in Chapter 12.

segregation is illegal). The effectiveness of a policy directive depends on how clear it is. If a policy directive is ambiguous, it probably will not be effective. Policy statements generally, but not always, contain procedures for implementing the directives—the agencies to be established, an authorized budget, the authority to sanction, the modes of sanctioning or enforcing, the size of the agency staff. A policy statement containing a directive but no implementation procedures is clearly inadequate. If implementation procedures are included in the policy statement, they must be adequate to accomplish what is intended. Programs must have sufficient financial resources, sufficient numbers of trained personnel, and sufficient powers to produce compliance to the directives.

The second aspect of policy of concern here is policy outputs, or those acts performed in pursuance of policy decisions and statements; outputs are what the government *does* as distinguished from what it says it will do.[2] The effectiveness of policy outputs can be determined by answering the following questions. If more than one agency is involved, is there coordination, or is there duplication of efforts or bureaucratic infighting? Are the agencies keeping up with their work load? If the agencies have power to produce compliance, do they use sanctions when necessary? Is data being collected —data that will enable implementation of a policy and evaluation of the results?

In this chapter, government policies in a number of areas—employment, education, housing, voting, public accommodations and transportation, the armed forces, and immigration—will be summarized and evaluated to determine their effectiveness. In addition, policies directly related to Mexican-Americans, to Indian-Americans, and to Puerto Rico will be examined.

INSTITUTIONS

Employment

Government policies directed against discrimination and structural disadvantage in employment began in 1941 with a federal fair employment practices law and a commission to supervise employment in all companies having a federal contract. In 1946, however, Congress did not act to grant the commission funds, and this effort expired. In 1945 New York State established the first Fair Employment Practices Commission (FEPC) at the state level, and this was followed by the creation of FEPCs in a majority of the states and in many major cities. But with the exception of the Philadelphia FEPC and the New York State FEPC, these state and local commissions were and still are limited to acting upon individual complaints and to using only persuasion and conciliation in efforts to produce compliance.

Powers to investigate, hold hearings, and turn complaints over to the courts for prosecution are notably lacking.[3]

In 1948 and in 1955, Presidents Truman and Eisenhower, respectively, issued executive orders stating the goal of fair employment, but both orders lacked implementation procedures and Congress did not act to set up any administrative machinery for implementation.

Federal Agencies and Their Jurisdiction. Not until the 1960s did the federal government take any significant action to eliminate discrimination in employment. During that decade, by legislative action and by executive orders, four federal bureaucracies were authorized to carry out policies designed to create fair employment: the Civil Service Commission (CSC), the Department of Justice, the Equal Employment Opportunity Commission (EEOC), and the Office of Federal Contract Compliance (OFCC). The CSC and the Department of Justice were given new functions, while the other two agencies were especially created for the purpose of achieving fair employment.

For all practical purposes, federal policy to eliminate discrimination in employment began with the passage of the Civil Rights Act of 1964. This act contains two sections relevant to employment discrimination—Title VI and Title VII. Title VI prohibits discrimination within any organization or by any program that receives federal financial assistance, such as colleges, universities, urban renewal programs, hospitals, and small businesses that have received government loans. The Civil Rights Division within the Department of Justice coordinates and supervises all federal agencies that provide federal monies to private organizations or state and local governments. Cancellation of this financial assistance upon recommendation by the Justice Department is the ultimate sanction against those who persist in discriminatory employment practices.

While Title VI covers all forms of discrimination, including employment, Title VII is specifically concerned with equal employment opportunity. Title VII extends federal antidiscrimination controls to all private companies with twenty-five or more employees, to all labor unions with twenty-five or more members, and to all private employment agencies. A 1972 statute (the Equal Employment Opportunity Act) amends Title VII, reducing the minimum number of employees and union members to fifteen and extending coverage to state and local governments.

The 1964 act (Title VII) authorized the establishment of an independent agency, the Equal Employment Opportunity Commission (EEOC), to implement and enforce the policy directive. Until the 1972 amendment, the EEOC had little power; it was restricted to arranging a conference with a company or union accused of discriminating in order to resolve employment problems through conciliation and persuasion. If no satisfactory resolution took place, the EEOC could only tell the complainant that he or she should take the dispute to the Justice Department for further action. Since 1972, the EEOC can itself initiate court action by referring a complaint to the Department of Justice. In March of 1974, the EEOC was further strengthened when Congress granted it the exclusive power to initiate court action in cases of "patterned" discrimination (widespread and systematic discrimination) in an industry or organization.

In 1965 President Johnson, in Executive Order 11246, authorized the Civil Service Commission (CSC) to "supervise and provide leadership and guidance in the conduct of equal employment opportunity programs . . . with the executive departments and agencies. . . ."[4] Hiring and promotion within the federal government was to be supervised by special divisions within the CSC with the power to handle discrimination complaints and to hear agency appeals on any decision the CSC might render. The CSC was directed to issue regulations with which all federal agencies were directed to comply. The 1972 Equal Employment Opportunity Act authorizes the CSC to require from each federal agency a semiannual report consisting of provisions for a training and education program designed to increase the opportunity for advancement and a description of the resources each agency is devoting to its opportunity program.[5]

Under the same executive order (11246), the Office of Federal Contract Compliance (OFCC) within the Department of Labor was created. The function of the OFCC is to oversee all of those federal agencies,* such as the Treasury Department and the Department of Defense, that issue contracts of more than ten thousand dollars to private companies. The OFCC is expected to monitor all federal agencies issuing contracts and all companies granted contracts. The OFCC has the power to revoke any government contract if compliance is not forthcoming.† In addition, the OFCC can revoke a federal agency's jurisdiction over a particular contractor or remove the agency's entire compliance responsibility.

Thus, to summarize the particular responsibility of each agency in securing equal employment: the CSC under authorization of Executive Order 11246 (1965) supervises employment in the federal government; the OFCC, also under the authority of Executive Order 11246 (1965), regulates employment in all private companies that have been granted a federal contract in excess of ten thousand dollars; the EEOC, under Title VII of the Civil Rights Act of 1964, as amended by the Equal Employment Opportunity Act of 1972, controls employment in all private businesses and labor unions with fifteen or more members as well as in all employment agencies and state and local governments (since some business might have federal

---

*Twenty-six agencies in 1964, reduced to fifteen in 1969, and increased to nineteen in 1973. The largest of the contracting agencies is the Department of Defense, which has responsibility for approximately 75 percent of all government contracts.

†A contract with a company can be cancelled if the company subcontracts certain work and the subcontractor violates the fair employment regulations. Union-company contracts must have an equal employment clause, and if a union discriminates, the company's contract can be voided.

contracts, there is a jurisdictional overlap with the OFCC); and the Department of Justice, Civil Rights Division, under Title VI of the Civil Rights Act of 1964, regulates all organizations that receive federal financial assistance.

Affirmative Action Policies. In the late 1960s, these federal bureaucracies began a policy of "affirmative action." A CSC policy statement in 1969 provides one general definition of affirmative action: "An affirmative action program must go beyond mere nondiscrimination. It must be devised to overcome obstacles that impede equality of opportunity for minority group persons. . . . "[6] But this is quite general. The specific policy statements and programs classified together as affirmative action are varied, and some are more controversial than others. There have been at least eight major forms of affirmative action programs or policy statements:

1. The investigation of discrimination (intended discrimination) without waiting for complaints from minority individuals (or from women) and the prosecution of these cases. Such investigations have included public hearings, where information about discrimination in a given industry may be acquired. Data from employers have also been required in order to ascertain patterns of discrimination. Investigations of entire industries have ensued, as well as court actions directed against all of the divisions of a company or against several companies and unions in the same industry.[7]

2. The extension of the search for qualified job applicants beyond the traditional techniques. For example, the CSC has posted job vacancies in post offices and sent announcements to minority organizations and to unions and employment agencies. Spanish language notices have also been used. Private organizations have been required to submit affirmative action hiring plans that spell out in detail the procedures for enlarging the application pool (as opposed to reliance upon the old-boy network).

3. The establishment of quotas and timetables. Efforts have been made to hire a certain percentage of minorities or to place a certain percentage in particular occupational rankings. Generally, this percentage quota for employment or union membership is equal to the population percentage of the group in the community. Incremental increases of minority employment within a given time period (annually, for example) have been specified. A major example of this form of affirmative action is the Philadelphia Plan, in which the OFCC has dictated that an annually increasing proportion of the city's minorities be hired in the skilled trades. In principle, the minority applicants must be qualified and not admitted solely to make a quota.

4. The reevaluation and modification of appointment and promotion requirements to reduce structural disadvantage (or "institutional

racism"). The OFCC prohibits seniority systems that exclude minorities from employment or act to deprive minorities of promotion rights. Government agencies can no longer use a written test as the sole basis for hiring or promotion. The requirement of certain types of knowledge (such as algebra) that are not germane to the job have been dropped by government agencies and many companies. More emphasis is being placed on personal presentation in an interview and on job experience than on test scores.[8] In the *United States v. Sheet Metal Workers, Local 36* (1969), the court ruled that the seniority principle means illegal discrimination if a union "counts white seniority prior to when blacks were permitted to join," or if blacks cannot count seniority acquired in one job with a company when moving into a new job in the same company, a job previously denied blacks.[9] In *Griggs* v. *Duke Power Co.* (1971), all admission and promotion prerequisites (such as tests and educational requirements) that disproportionately exclude blacks are illegal unless it can be demonstrated that these requirements are necessary in the business. The burden of proof is on the company.[10]

5. The initiation of special training programs, either prior to admission or as on-the-job training. Job training, often a joint enterprise between government and business, has consisted of programs designed to impart specific skills or to provide some form of general work experience to people not accustomed to the routine of working. Underlying this form of affirmative action is the idea that even if discrimination is eliminated or vacancies are publicized many people will not be able to take advantage of the opportunity. A number of such programs have been established, including the training of experienced workers displaced by changes in technology and of the "disadvantaged" workers in classrooms or on the job (Manpower Development and Training Act), the subsidizing of businesses that hire and train welfare recipients (Work Incentive Program), the providing of public service jobs for poor youths between sixteen and twenty-one who are out of school as well as part-time employment for those still in school (Neighborhood Youth Corps), and the reimbursing of businesses that train the disadvantaged worker (Job Opportunities in the Business Sector).[11]

6. The providing of monetary compensation to workers who have previously suffered discrimination. In 1974, the EEOC negotiated with nine companies and the steelworker's union in order to have $31 million in back wages paid to fifty thousand workers. After EEOC action, American Telephone and Telegraph paid $15 million in back pay to minority workers and female employees, as well as granting raises totaling $23 million.[12]

7. The promotion of equal employment through the use of propaganda and publicity. The EEOC has printed and distributed numerous

pamphlets, has held conferences with minority groups and community organizations, and has even had films produced to proselytize for equal employment.[13]

8. The granting of temporary preferential treatment to minorities in hiring and in promotion. In a Circuit Court of Appeals case (*Associated General Contractors of Mass., Inc.* v. *Altshuler*, 1973), it was stated that

> *It is by now well understood . . . that our society cannot be completely color-blind in the short term. After centuries of viewing through colored lenses, eyes do not quickly adjust when the lenses are removed. . . . Preferential treatment is one partial prescription to remedy our society's most intransigent and deeply rooted inequalities.*[14]

There have been several other court decisions about preferential treatment.[15] Around 40 percent of all state and local governments use a pass-fail certification procedure, which means that those hired are selected from all candidates that pass the employment examination rather than from the top scorers.[16] With a quota system in effect and with the principle of preferential treatment (or "reverse discrimination," as some would say), less qualified members of subordinate groups can be selected over more qualified dominant group members. It should be added, however, that the Supreme Court, in *Griggs* v. *Duke Power Co.* (1971), stipulated that Title VII of the 1964 Civil Rights Act does not require the hiring of a person solely because he or she has been the subject of discrimination.[17]

As can be seen, the definition of "affirmative action" is quite varied. It has become a catchall term to mean anything from eliminating restrictions to promoting proportional representation.

Adequacy of Federal Agency Output.   Have the policy outputs of the federal agencies been adequate? Do the agencies have sufficient resources to implement policy directives? How much coordination, if any, exists between the numerous agencies? And do the bureaucracies themselves practice what they preach (that is, not discriminate)? The United States Commission on Civil Rights, created in 1957 and given powers of investigation by Title V of the 1964 act, has served as a watchdog on government efficiency. If one could draw a general conclusion from the commission's numerous reports on employment, the answer might be: government action or policy output is inadequate, inefficient, and uncoordinated and is hindered by limited budgets, by refusal to act when cause exists, and by a limited and untrained personnel staff.

The EEOC has come under particular attack. Its budget has been limited and its personnel too few, but this is a fault of Congress, not the EEOC. The backlog of cases awaiting action increases each year: 23,642 in September 1971; 53,410 in June 1972; 98,000 in June 1974.[18] In its first seven years the EEOC investigated 41,000 cases but successfully resolved only 6 percent of these (and according to a chairman of EEOC, around 80 percent of the complaints were probably valid).[19] The investigations that are done and that are referred to the Justice Department for court action have often been inadequate for litigation.[20] When conciliation agreements are obtained, compliance with them has not been systematically monitored; until 1974, monitoring was all but completely absent.[21] In 1975 the Civil Service Commission issued a report on its fellow bureaucracy and stated that in the EEOC "internal equal employment opportunity program direction and leadership is virtually nonexistent."[22] But inefficiency is one thing, hypocrisy another. Prior to 1972, 220 charges of discrimination *within the agency* were filed by its employees. The CSC report in 1975 also charged the EEOC with having three dozen internal discrimination cases open for six months, and with filling top positions in the agency through the method of "colleague referral" (the standard old-boy procedure).[23]

The CSC criticism of the EEOC is a case of the pot calling the kettle black. The official view of discrimination in the CSC is that it is the result of individual bigotry rather than systematic practice.[24] Accordingly, the Civil Service Commission is concerned only with individual complaints. The burden of proof is upon the complainant, who must specify the individual source of the discrimination. Complaints on behalf of a particular class or category of employees of which the alleged victim is a member are not reviewed.[25] In fiscal year 1974 the average time to process a complaint was 201 days, and discriminatory violations were found in only 12.8 percent of all complaints.[26] The CSC still uses hiring and promotion tests that are not validated according to EEOC guidelines and several court decisions (for example, no statistical evidence has been presented that link test items to job performance).[27]

The Office of Federal Contract Compliance (created in 1965) has not been a model of bureaucratic efficiency either. Not until two and one-half years after it was founded did the OFCC issue any regulations to companies, and it remained deliberately vague on affirmative action until 1968. Between 1965 and 1968, no contractor was debarred (made ineligible for future contracts and deprived of the present contract). Finally, in May 1968, debarment notices were sent to five companies. By September of 1971, one contractor had been debarred.[28] By 1975, only nine contracts had been cancelled.[29] Only a small percentage of the total organizations with government contracts are monitored by the contracting agencies under the supervision of OFCC. And "despite strong indications that compliance agencies ... routinely commit violations," the OFCC has never sanctioned a single agency.[30] The OFCC is expected to use conciliation procedures, but nobody in the agency has received any training in this method, nor has the office even issued a manual to assist its agents.[31] Besides the general inadequacy of the OFCC policy output, there is another reason for the poor effort of the OFCC and its contracting agencies to ensure equal employment. According to Howard Glickstein, a member of the U.S. Commission on Civil Rights in 1969, "federal agencies are loath to upset their relations with contractors.

Effective enforcement might result in the disqualification of low bidders or other preferred contractors, or cause delays in the letting or performance of contracts."[32]

Since the Department of Justice, the EEOC, and the OFCC are all concerned with employment in the private sector, one would think there would be some coordination between the agencies and an attempt to avoid duplicating efforts. According to the U.S. Commission on Civil Rights, however, "only ad hoc coordination measures have been initiated. The agencies have adopted their own program goals, priorities, and mechanisms on an independent basis. . . . The failure to join forces has resulted in a critical misuse of limited staff resources and the dissipation of enforcement potential."[33] For example, the Treasury Department, a contracting agency under OFCC, only accidentally learned that a bank with which it was negotiating was also under investigation by the EEOC. In another case, the Crown Zellerbach Company accepted an EEOC seniority plan, which was subsequently attacked by the OFCC. Further, in a court suit, the Justice Department "urged the court to reject the seniority plan that OFCC has requested and adopt an entirely new test." "In commenting on this lack of Federal coordination, the U.S. Court of Appeals said: 'We cannot help sharing Crown Zellerbach's bewilderment at the twists and turns indulged in by Government agencies in this case.' "[34]

A pathetic effort at coordination was authorized by the 1972 Equal Employment Opportunity Act. An Equal Employment Opportunity Coordinating Council (EEOCC) has been established in which the secretary of labor, the attorney general, and the heads of EEOC, CSC, and the U.S. Commission on Civil Rights are members. The committee meets infrequently, has no permanent staff, and has no authority to make its decisions binding on the agencies in its membership.[35]

Legitimacy of Government Policies in Employment. Are government efforts to create equal opportunity in employment legitimate? According to one study that sampled white opinion in fifteen cities (1968), most whites accept the legitimacy of laws to prevent discrimination against blacks in job hiring and promotion: 67 percent were in favor, 19 percent were opposed, 10 percent of the opinions could not be ascertained, and 4 percent believed that whites should have job preferences over blacks.[36] Questions about the legitimacy of *federal* laws and programs in the area of employment opportunity, however, elicit a different response. In national surveys conducted in 1964 and 1968, only 33 percent (in both years) of whites believed that the federal government "should see to it that Negroes get fair treatment in jobs." Blacks, on the other hand, strongly believed in the legitimacy of federal government intervention in employment opportunities: 87 percent in 1964, and 84 percent in 1968.[37] A study in six cities in 1967 indicated that only a minority of whites believed in the legitimacy of affirmative action programs, and this percentage diminished when it came to certain forms of affirmative action. In terms of the general principle of fair employment, 66.2 percent of whites approved of equal employment opportunity. However, when it came to various forms of affirmative action, 38.1 percent of whites approved of on-the-job training by industry so blacks not fully qualified could be hired permanently, 27.2 percent of whites approved of special government training programs for blacks, 7.2 percent of whites approved of giving blacks with the necessary skills a chance ahead of whites in promotions, and only 3.5 percent approved of giving blacks a chance ahead of whites in hiring for jobs that blacks had not held in the past. There was a similar decline in the legitimacy of affirmative action when evaluated by blacks. Surprisingly, only 70.8 percent of nonwhites (primarily blacks) approved of equal opportunity in employment. The majority of nonwhites did not approve of affirmative action beyond business-sponsored on-the-job training (61.1 percent). Black response to other programs were as follows: government training programs, 42.5 percent in favor; preference for blacks in equal ability promotions, 19.3 percent in favor; and giving blacks a chance ahead of whites in hiring for jobs that blacks had not held in the past, 13.2 percent in favor.[38]

Education

Phase One.   Although not completely unprecedented,[39] the U.S. Supreme Court decision in *Brown* v. *The Board of Education* (of Topeka, Kansas), 1954, marked the first national decision on the subject of educational discrimination. The decision declared that "separate educational facilities are inherently unequal." The *Plessy* v. *Ferguson* (1896) decision was reversed.* Procedures for implementation of the *Brown* decision were delayed until 1955, when the court ruled that desegregation must begin "with all deliberate speed." Lower courts were to ensure compliance, but to be guided by "equitable principles," and a "practical flexibility."

The delay in the implementation decision and the vagueness of the implementation procedures gave the South new hope. According to Vander Zanden, "from across the South came slightly suppressed expressions of elation from officials at the nature of the decree. Of particular joy was the failure of the Supreme Court to set a deadline for compliance. Some even called it 'a victory for the South' and felt that the decree was the 'mildest' possible without the high court's actually reversing itself."[40] Responsibility for enforcement was left in the hands of lower court judges, who were native Southerners and who "knew only too well that they would be ostracized in their own communities if they enforced the law; and some of the judges disagreed with the decision. Generally, therefore, the Supreme Court was abandoned by the lower courts."[41]

*Since Plessy v. Ferguson *related to public transportation and not specifically to education, the* Brown *decision has been interpreted to mean that all forms of racial segregation (discriminatory segregation) are unconstitutional.*

For the next ten years, desegregation efforts in the South were minimal. Congress made no effort to implement the *Brown* decision. In 1963, the House of Representatives summarily defeated antidiscrimination amendments on two education bills after five minutes of debate on one and ten minutes on the other.[42] President Eisenhower only reluctantly intervened in the Little Rock, Arkansas, crisis in 1957. Enforcement, in fact, was left to the NAACP, which used the tactics of selecting court cases and presenting desegregation petitions signed by local Negroes to southern school boards. Southern resistance then became intense in response to the actions of the "communist" NAACP. White citizens councils sprang up everywhere, but particularly in areas that were heavily black. In reaction to NAACP activity, sanctions were imposed on petitioners as their names were published in newspapers or they were fired from their jobs.[43] By November of 1962, 379 new laws were passed by the legislatures of sixteen states to avoid or to impede school desegregation.[44] At the end of the ten years, only 2 percent of black students in the South could be said to be "integrated."

Phase Two. A second phase of government policy in the area of education began in 1964 and 1965, with the passing of the Civil Rights Act of 1964 and the Elementary and Secondary Education Act of 1965. The national publicity given to the Birmingham incident (1963), the assassination of President Kennedy, President Johnson's desire to erect a memorial to Kennedy (because of Kennedy's concern with civil rights), and public pressure led to the passing of the Civil Rights Act. The law authorized the attorney general to file civil suits to compel desegregation if a complainant was unable to bring the action (Title IV), but, more important, Title VI specified that federal aid to education could be cut off if a school district engaged in discrimination. This latter provision had little significance at the time, as there was no federal aid to education to be terminated. In the following year, however, Congress passed the Elementary and Secondary Education Act, providing federal monies to local schools. Administrative sanctioning power now existed. But nobody knew what constituted cause for termination.

The Office of Education in the Department of Health, Education and Welfare was responsible for ascertaining violations, but it was unclear when money should be withheld from a school district for failure to desegregate. Disagreement and inactivity in the agency allowed a recently hired consultant, Professor G. W. Foster, Jr., of the Wisconsin Law School, to initiate action on the problem. Professor Foster wrote up his own guidelines and, without official sanction, had them published in the *Saturday Review of Literature* (March 20, 1965). Once this article had received wide circulation and had broken the ice, the Office of Education made Foster's guidelines official policy the following month.[45] Isn't it marvelous how bureaucracies operate?

The guidelines, which were based on the idea of freedom of choice, initiated phase two of government policy (phase one being lower court action based on individual complaints). In phase two black and white students could "choose" to attend certain selected schools in each district. The school boards had to make public the schools that could be selected and could not require complicated forms and embarrassing personal interviews of blacks to discourage transfer.[46]

Needless to say, "freedom of choice" plans were only moderately effective in reducing segregation. In 1969, the U.S. Commission on Civil Rights stated:

> *There are a number of reasons why freedom-of-choice is ineffective as a means of desegregating schools. Since white families almost always choose to have their children attend the predominately white school, the burden of desegregating the schools in a district falls entirely upon the black families living there. Accordingly, most Negro families choose to have their children attend the all-black school, and those few black families who choose to send their children to the predominately white school can be—and are—singled out and subjected to pressure and abuse.*[47]

In 1968, in *Green* v. *New Kent County School Board,* the U.S. Supreme Court ruled that if freedom of choice "fails to undo segregation, other means must be used to achieve this end."[48]

Phase Three.   On July 3, 1969, the attorney general and the secretary of HEW jointly announced a new policy. The new emphasis would be upon litigation brought by the Department of Justice. Administrative action by HEW, backed by the threat of termination of federal funds, would be de-emphasized. "Freedom of choice" plans would continue to be accepted, but only if such plans "genuinely promised" to achieve desegregation at an early date. In addition, the government would begin a "substantial program of desegregation in areas of the North, the Midwest, and the West, where de facto racial segregation in schools results from discriminatory housing patterns."[49]

There were several problems with the new policy. First, in 1968 a greater percentage of black students attended desegregated schools in seven states of the Deep South under the administration of HEW (an average of 21 percent) than under individual-initiated court orders (9.4 percent).[50] Yet the government was to emphasize the court approach, hoping that this tactic would be more effective if government attorneys took the initiative. Second, if any school district was placed under a court order to desegregate, HEW could not enforce compliance by withdrawing federal funds unless HEW found that the district was not implementing the court order. Third, a program to eliminate de facto segregation in the North and West had no legal support in the form of court decisions.

Phase Four.   The emphasis on actions (or inactions) taken by the executive branch of the federal government has continued into the present. But since 1971 there has been a *coexisting* fourth phase involving the judicial branch.

As the result of court decisions, the following new policy developments have taken place: the meaning of de jure segregation has been expanded and reinterpreted, district courts can impose desegregation plans of their own upon school districts, several school districts within a metropolitan area can be forced to integrate across their boundaries if evidence of de jure segregation exists in each district, and northern and western school systems have come under attack.

The U.S. Supreme Court decision in *Swann* v. *Charlotte-Mecklenburg Board of Education et al.* (1971) had numerous implications for desegregation policy. As a result of this decision, (1) school boards are obligated to achieve *immediate* desegregation; (2) district courts can impose their own plans on school districts that default; (3) in these plans, courts have the authority to alter attendance zones, to require busing, to close certain schools, to specify ratios for the assignment of students, faculty, and staff, and to pair or group schools together; and (4) the mere existence of segregated attendance patterns is not sufficient to constitute a violation of the law, for discrimination must be demonstrated; however, the burden of proof is upon the school board to show that segregation is not the result of discrimination.[51]

The meaning of de jure school segregation has been broadened by several court decisions. De jure segregation exists not only if state and local governments have practiced overt discrimination, but also if such school segregation can be shown to be the result of indirect discrimination, such as real estate discrimination.[52] In 1973, in *Keyes et al.* v. *School District No. 1, Denver, Colorado*, the Supreme Court expanded the meaning of "de jure" even further. If a community no longer practices intentional segregation but it can be established that the community practiced intentional segregation in the past, de jure segregation still exists. In other words, the past history indicates that the effects of discrimination are still present, and the remoteness in time of the discriminatory acts is not important. The court in *Keyes* stated that the burden of proof is upon the school board to show that its past policies did not contribute to present segregation.[53] Regarding this latter ruling, Rodgers has written: "For Northern boards to prove that their policies have not contributed to, or caused, segregation should be extremely difficult since the specified school board activities that the Supreme Court has identified as evidence of discrimination are activities that are practiced widely both North and South."[54]

A major problem in attempting to desegregate schools is that if a city has a large percentage of black students there will not be enough white students to achieve integration. And if a city core is desegregated, many white families may move to the suburbs. The answer, of course, is to impose integration on the entire metropolitan area. However, the U.S. Supreme Court has ruled that desegregation across school district boundaries can only be imposed if the de jure principle operates in *all* of the school units in question. In *Bradley* v. *School Board* (Richmond, Virginia, 1972), a district court ruled that the Richmond schools must be combined with two neighboring predominantly white counties. The Richmond decision was reversed by a court of appeals, and the reversal was upheld by the Supreme Court; no constitutional violations on the part of the white counties were established. In 1971, in a case involving Detroit, Michigan, and fifty-three suburbs (*Bradley* v.*Milliken*), a district court and an appeals court ruled that the metropolitan area had to be integrated and that the court had the authority to impose a desegregation plan. In 1974 the case was appealed to the Supreme Court (*Milliken* v.*Bradley*), which overruled the previous decisions by a vote of 5 to 4. According to the ruling, a school district cannot rectify its own segregation situation by imposing busing on others that have not been shown to have practiced segregation. An interdistrict remedy cannot be applied unless there is an interdistrict violation.[55]

In 1976 and 1977, the Supreme Court, in decisions related to housing, employment, and education, has come out strongly for the principle that only de jure, or intentional, discrimination is unconstitutional. Regarding education, in December 1976 the Court struck down an order of the Fifth Circuit Court of Appeals designed to desegregate Austin, Texas, schools by busing up to twenty-five thousand students. Justice Lewis F. Powell, Jr, speaking on behalf of the majority, stated that "the remedy ordered appears to exceed that necessary to eliminate the effect of any official acts or omissions. . . . large-scale busing is permissible only where the evidence supports a finding that the extent of integration sought to be achieved by busing would have existed had the school authorities fulfilled their constitutional obligations in the past." In the majority view there must be evidence of discrimination, and the existence of segregated schools per se "doesn't in itself amount to racial discrimination." Schools cannot be held responsible for racial imbalances caused by a city's residential patterns.[56] This decision seems to indicate a more conservative position and a retreat from the broadening of the meaning of de jure.

While the courts were taking educational desegregation into their own hands, what was the executive branch of the federal government doing? The answer is, not much. In the late 1960s, the U.S. Commission on Civil Rights referred 101 complaints to HEW or to the Department of Justice for action. Of the total, the government acted on only 7 cases. In many of these cases, HEW or the Justice Department did not even acknowledge the fact that the complaint had been received.[57] In 1973 a U.S. District Court ruled in *Adams* v.*Richardson* that HEW and its subdivision, the Office of Civil Rights, had been extremely negligent in the enforcement of Title VI of the 1964 Civil Rights Act. The suit exposed these facts: federal funds were still given to numerous school districts two years after those districts were judged noncompliant, and 640 school districts under court-ordered desegregation were judged by HEW as in compliance, even though no investigation of these districts ever took place.[58] The court ordered HEW to begin immediate action to secure compliance to Title VI through its power to withdraw federal funding. HEW appealed this ruling three times without success, and, as of 1975, the agency was still involved in paper work with only a slight improvement in performance.[59]

Legitimacy of School Desegregation. What does the American public think about the legitimacy of school desegregation policies? What do Americans feel about busing as one technique to achieve racial desegregation? In 1964, 1968, and 1970, the Center for Political Studies of the Institute for Social Research conducted a national survey of black and white opinion. One item in the survey stated: "Some people say that the government in Washington should see to it that white and Negro children are allowed to go to the same schools. Others claim this is not the government's business. Do you think the government in Washington should:"[60]

	White			Black		
	1964	1968	1970	1964	1968	1970
See to it that white and Negro children go to the same schools	38%	33%	41%	68%	84%	84%
It depends	7	7	10	4	3	3
Stay out of this area as it is none of its business	42	48	36	12	6	7
Don't know	3	1	1	7	3	1
Not interested	10	11	12	9	4	5

Leaving out the role of the government, national polls are somewhat inconsistent on the public's view of the legitimacy of school integration in general, but the majority of both black and white in recent years find this social arrangement to be legitimate. *Newsweek*-Gallup surveys of blacks found that the following percentages accepted integration in the schools: 70 percent in 1963, 70 percent in 1966, and 78 percent in 1969.[61] National polls on white opinion found that in 1971, 75 percent of whites approved of school integration, and that in 1972 only 65 percent approved.[62] The legitimacy of busing to achieve racial desegregation, however, receives a positive response from only a minority of white Americans. In 1971, 81 percent of whites opposed busing to achieve school desegregation; only 14 percent approved.[63] In 1972 a national poll indicated a slight decline in white opposition to busing; 73 percent were not in favor of busing.[64] In 1971 a Harris poll reported that 47 percent of whites would not oppose the busing of their children if required by a court; this percentage declined to 25 percent by 1972.[65] Black parents are also not overwhelmingly happy about busing. Busing was acceptable to 50 percent of black respondents in 1963, 49 percent in 1966, and 45 percent in 1969.[66]

But whether or not white and black parents perceive busing as legitimate, most communities have accepted the court-ordered plans without violent opposition, although there has been much bombastic rhetoric and several demonstrations. Two notable exceptions to nonviolence occurred in Boston, Massachusetts, and Louisville, Kentucky. Riots broke out in the largely Irish-Catholic areas of South Boston at the beginning of the school year in 1974 and in 1975. In the September 1975 riot, over five hundred police in riot gear were called out to supervise the entrance of black students into previously all-white schools.[67] In Louisville in the same month, the opposition and violence were even more intense. An estimated ten thousand whites blocked highways with cars, lighted fires on the highways, burned or otherwise damaged school buses, and stoned the police. As the riot became more uncontrollable, it spread to the suburbs, where stores were looted and gas station pumps ripped out. Over eight hundred armed National Guardsmen were called in to suppress the busing disturbance.[68]

Housing

State and Local Government Policies.   Fair housing policies by government began in New York City in 1939 and then spread to other cities and states. By 1970, twenty-six states had fair housing laws. These state and local laws primarily cover discrimination in multiple housing accommodations that are privately owned and in public and publicly assisted housing. The laws are typically administered by a board or commission made up of appointed citizens and a small professional staff. Their methods of enforcing compliance vary—some can only investigate on the basis of a complaint and then use persuasion and conciliation, while others can instigate their own investigations and issue cease-and-desist orders that are enforced by the courts.[69] With the establishment of fair housing policies at the federal level, complaints made to the federal government are often referred to these fair housing commissions when appropriate.

Federal Policy Statements and Jurisdiction of Federal Agencies.   The major federal agencies concerned with eliminating discrimination in the sale and rental of housing are the Federal Housing Administration (FHA), the Department of Housing and Urban Development (HUD), the Veterans Administration (VA), and the Department of Justice.

In 1948, in *Shelley* v. *Kraemer,* the Supreme Court ruled that restrictive covenants in real estate contracts were nonenforceable in the courts. Prior to this decision, the FHA* supported a policy of residential segregation by race. With *Shelley,* the FHA reversed itself and ruled that it would not insure mortgages on property with such covenants filed after February 15, 1950. In 1960 the FHA ruled that it could stop business with real estate brokers who discriminated in the selling and renting of property listed with them.[70]

Founded in 1934 by the National Housing Act and given responsibility for mortgage insurance (individuals borrow money from banks to finance the purchase or the building of homes, and these mortgages are insured by the federal government and are subject to FHA regulations).

In 1962 President Kennedy issued Executive Order 11063, directing "all departments and agencies in the executive branch of the Federal Government, insofar as their functions relate to the provision, rehabilitation, or operation of housing and related facilities, to take all action necessary and appropriate to prevent discrimination because of race, color, creed, or national origin." The order covered housing owned by the government, housing purchased through loans insured by FHA and VA, and housing provided by federally funded urban renewal programs. The order authorized conciliation and persuasion to produce compliance, but, if this failed, the agencies involved could cancel or terminate agreements and contracts.[71] Not included in the order were all conventional mortgages (non-FHA or non-VA) financed by banks and savings and loan companies insured by the federal government. Coverage was limited to around 25 percent of the new housing market and only 1 percent of the country's entire housing inventory.[72]

Title VI of the 1964 Civil Rights Act increased the scope of federal controls to all federally assisted housing in addition to FHA- or VA-insured housing. Failure of organizations to comply would result in cancellation of financial assistance. HUD was given responsibility for supervising enforcement and was authorized to turn over to the Justice Department cases of noncompliance.

In 1968 a new law and a Supreme Court decision extended antidiscrimination provisions to virtually all of the rest of housing in America. Title VIII of the Civil Rights Act of 1968 covered all federally assisted housing and most private housing. Excluded from controls were rental housing with fewer than five units (one of which was owner occupied) and single-family homes owned by an individual and sold without using a real estate broker. HUD has the major responsibility for enforcement of Title VIII, but its powers are limited since it is empowered only with informal methods of conference, conciliation, and persuasion. Court action can be brought, however, by individuals or by the Department of Justice. The 1968 act further prohibited discrimination in the financing of housing and in the advertising of houses for sale or rent, and it prohibited "blockbusting."* Title VIII extended federal coverage to about 80 percent of all housing.[73]

Two months later, in *Jones* v. *Mayer and Co.*, the Supreme Court completed the extension of government regulations on discrimination in housing. The court declared that a civil rights law passed during Reconstruction (1866) "bars all racial discrimination, private as well as public, in the sale or rental of property." Enforcement of the decision, however, is left to privately instigated litigation.[74]

---

*The law defines blockbusting this way: "For profit, to induce or attempt to induce any person to sell or rent any dwellings by representations regarding the entry to prospective entry into the neighborhood of a person or persons of a particular race, color, religion, or national origin." This refers to the attempt by real estate agents to get whites to sell their houses because Negroes are moving into the area—"sell now or take a big loss later."

Another major policy statement in the area of housing was a U.S. district court decision in Detroit—*Vincent Luch et al.* v. *John H. Hussey et al.*(1973). The court ruled that heavy real estate solicitation in a neighborhood is a violation of the 1968 Civil Rights Act because of the panic and fear that such solicitation generates.[75]

In January 1977 the Supreme Court followed the Austin, Texas, school desegregation case by applying to housing the same principle of intended discrimination. Arlington Heights, Illinois, a suburb of Chicago, has a zoning law prohibiting apartment houses or multifamily dwellings in most of the areas of the city. A proposed housing development was blocked by this ordinance, a housing development that would have benefited low-income people, many of whom would be black. According to Justice Lewis F. Powell, Jr, speaking for the majority, "official action will not be held unconstitutional solely because it results in a racially disproportionate impact. . . . Proof of racially discriminatory intent or purpose is required to show a violation of the equal protection clause."[76]

Adequacy of Federal Agency Output. In its responsibility for Title VI of the 1964 act, HUD's output has been highly inadequate; yet it is under this title that the agency has the greatest sanctioning powers. HUD has concentrated primarily on local governmental housing authorities while neglecting builders and housing developers. Between July 1972 and March 1973, HUD managed to conduct eighty-nine compliance reviews of organizations receiving federal assistance. Of the eighty-nine cases, twenty-nine were found to be in violation, and in thirteen of these cases voluntary compliance was achieved by persuasion and conciliation. The other sixteen reviews were still involved in drawn-out negotiations into 1974.[77] But more significantly, "Hud has never debarred a recipient for noncompliance with Title VI."[78] In 1972, HUD required all builders and developers receiving federal monies to submit affirmative action plans and, on a monthly basis, to submit information on the racial and ethnic occupancy of their projects. HUD, in its preoccupation with Title VIII (1968) responsibilities, has inadequately monitored this program to see if compliance is occurring.[79]

Under Title VIII of the 1968 act, HUD waits for individual complaints before it takes action, although it did engage in a major publicity campaign that resulted in a 25 percent increase in complaints from 1972 to 1973. Between July 1972 and March 1973, HUD handled 1,601 Title VIII complaints. Twenty percent of these cases (262) went to conciliation, while the rest were closed (because of lack of proof of discrimination, withdrawal of the complaint, or insufficient information). Fifty-four percent of the 262 complaints were conciliated successfully.[80] Once agreements are reached, however, HUD frequently does not ascertain if the conciliation is being implemented.

Compared to other federal agencies responsible for fair housing, HUD is a marvel of efficiency. The policy of the Veterans Administration, which is authorized by Title VIII (1968) to assure fair housing for minority veterans, seems to be limited to receiving written promises of nondiscrimination from builders, brokers, and lenders. In addition, brokers who have not signed such agreements are still permitted to sell VA properties. The only equal employment opportunity staff exists in the central agency; field stations have no such personnel. And neither the central bureau nor the field stations ever monitor their charges.[81]

Title VIII declares discrimination by banks and savings and loan companies to be illegal. Four federal agencies* are given the task of enforcement. Only one has issued any regulations of any sort, and none have required affirmative action or required builders and developers who get loans from these private financers to put into writing that they will not discriminate. The four bureaucracies have included little assessment of nondiscrimination compliance in their periodic reviews of banks and loan companies. And, as might be expected, no violations have ever been found.[82]

Government Policies in Other Institutional Areas

Voting. Voting discrimination was declared illegal by the Fifteenth Amendment to the U.S. Constitution (1870) and, as we have seen, prior to 1945, particular voting discrimination techniques were declared unconstitutional by the courts. Nevertheless, voting discrimination in the Deep South and in Texas persisted after the war.

Prior to 1965, three weak voting laws were passed. A 1957 law states that the federal government has the authority to enforce voting rights with court orders. A 1960 act declares that states and voting registrars can be sued for discriminating, that voting records must be preserved, and that the attorney general has the right to inspect those records. Title I of the Civil Rights Act of 1964 proclaims that: denial of voting cannot be permitted on the basis of minor mistakes or omissions; that only written literacy tests may be used; that, in voting discrimination suits, anybody with a sixth-grade education is literate unless a state can prove otherwise; and that a special three-judge federal court can be convened to hear a voting suit in which a claim is made that there is a pattern or practice of voting discrimination.

The Voting Rights Act of 1965 was especially designed to provide the federal government with powers to eliminate voting discrimination in eight states where discriminatory devices were still prevalent: Alabama, Alaska, Georgia, Louisiana, Mississippi, South Carolina, Virginia, and twenty-six counties in North Carolina. Any examinations or devices that tested literacy, education, moral character, or ability to speak English or asked for

---

The Federal Reserve System, the Federal Deposit Insurance Corporation, the Comptroller of the Currency, and the Federal Home Loan Bank Board.

proof of being qualified (such as being vouched for by a registered voter) were declared illegal. "Voting" was broadly defined as including registering, balloting, and counting the vote. The use of federal examiners appointed by the attorney general is authorized by the law to guarantee enforcement, if necessary. Violation of voting rights is a federal crime.

A seven-year extension of the Voting Rights Act was passed in August 1975. Federal enforcement of voting was authorized for the states of Alabama, Georgia, Louisiana, Mississippi, thirty-nine counties in North Carolina, South Carolina, three counties in New York, and nine counties in Arizona. Each of the stigmatized jurisdictions has to report any political change, such as moving a ballot box or enacting a new voting law, and these changes must be approved by the attorney general. Literacy tests anywhere in the United States were declared illegal (a 1970 act suspended literacy tests in the United States until a 1975 act declared them illegal). The 1975 act included Mexican-Americans in its coverage within the specified areas, but this did not include Texas, where voting discrimination against Chicanos persists.*

Public Accommodations and Transportation. Court decisions and state laws began the process of eliminating discrimination in public accommodations, such as hotels and restaurants, and in public transportation, such as buses, trains, and streetcars. In 1946, segregation on interstate buses was declared unconstitutional by the Supreme Court. In March of 1955, a circuit court of appeals in Virginia, basing its decision on *Brown* (1954), ruled that segregation in public parks and playgrounds was unconstitutional. In November of 1956, the Supreme Court upheld a lower court ruling on the illegality of segregated public transportation in Alabama. By 1970, thirty-eight states had passed laws declaring that discrimination in public accommodations and transportation was illegal. The state laws either make violation a criminal misdemeanor or permit the alleged victim to initiate civil action.[83]

Titles II and III of the 1964 Civil Rights Act make discrimination illegal in certain types of public accommodations and facilities: hotels, motels, restaurants, places of amusement if their operations affect interstate commerce or if discrimination is supported by actions of state governments, parks, libraries, hospitals, and other state or municipally owned or operated public facilities. If no local or state discriminatory laws exist, then barbershops, hotels, retail stores that do not serve food, and private clubs are excluded from Title II of the Civil Rights Act. Enforcement of Titles II

*In 1975 the Mexican-American Legal Defense and Education Fund testified in Congress to have the Voting Rights Act extended to cover Texas, but without success. The NAACP was opposed to extension; in the words of Clarence Mitchell, an NAACP executive, it was feared that extending coverage would improve the present law "out of existence." (Denver Post, March 24, 1975). Seemingly, the NAACP was afraid that adding new states would strain the already inadequate enforcement efforts.

and III takes the form of court litigation initiated either by individuals or by the attorney general of the United States.

The Military. The beginning of the end of black discrimination and segregation in the military came in a committee report from the War Department in 1946 (the Gillem Board Report). Segregation would be continued, black units were not to exceed regimental size, and a quota on the number of blacks who could join the armed forces would be maintained. However, whites and blacks were to be employed together in "appropriate special and overhead units," and qualified black officers could replace white officers in the Negro units.[84]

A Navy Department directive in 1946 stated: "Effective immediately, all restrictions governing the type of assignment for which Negro naval personnel are eligible are hereby lifted. Henceforth, they shall be eligible for all types of assignments in all ratings in all activities." The directive was generally ignored or only slowly implemented for several years.[85]

In 1948, President Truman issued Executive Order 9981, which stated that " . . . there shall be equality of treatment and opportunity for all persons in the armed services without regard to race, color, religion, or national origin." A presidential committee was established to investigate conditions in the armed forces and to recommend changes. Each branch of service submitted its plans for ending segregation, and, with the exception of the army's plan, they were approved by the committee. After three plans were turned down, the army issued a directive in 1950 that was acceptable: racial quotas for units and restrictions on assignments were eliminated.[86]

In spite of policy directives, little was done by the respective services to implement them. The Korean War, however, eventually broke down segregation in the armed forces when a shortage of white troops and an excess of black personnel made integration necessary. For the Southern congressmen, the change was legitimized on the grounds that battlefield casualties would be equalized—let the blacks get killed, too. A major study of the integration process found that black-white conflict was minimal and that the fear of inept and cowardly performances by black soldiers was unfounded.[87]

Off-base discrimination against blacks remained a problem, and in 1970 the Defense Department issued a directive giving base commanders authority to declare off-limits all accommodations such as apartment houses, stores, and bars that discriminated against blacks. The department also ordered the removal or reassignment of military officers and civilian officials who failed to achieve satisfactory results in acting against discrimination on or off the bases.[88]

Immigration. The quota system regulating immigration to the United States that was established in the Immigration Acts of 1921 and 1924 was reaffirmed in the Immigration and Naturalization Act of 1952. But in 1965 national quotas were eliminated and replaced with hemisphere limits. For Western Hemisphere countries, a maximum of 120,000 immigrants per year would be accepted into the United States, with no limitations placed on particular countries; 170,000 persons a year from the Eastern Hemisphere would be accepted by the United States, with a maximum of 20,000 immigrants from any given country.

MEXICAN-AMERICANS

Although Chicanos have benefited somewhat from the policies and programs previously described, their specific needs and problems have been largely ignored by the federal government. The resources and activities of governmental agencies have been concentrated for the most part upon problems of black inequality and white discrimination against blacks. The second largest subordinate ethnic group in America has been labeled "the forgotten minority," and, in the case of Federal concern, the label is appropriate.

The only program of any significance has been the Inter-Agency Committee on Mexican-American Affairs, established in 1967. The heads of seven major executive departments in the federal government made up the committee, and its chairman was a Mexican-American. The mandate of the committee was "to insure that Mexican-Americans were receiving the Federal assistance they needed; to promote new programs to deal with the unique problems of the Mexican-American community; to establish channels of communication with Mexican-American groups; and to suggest how the Federal government could best work with State and local governments, with private industry, and with Mexican-Americans, themselves, in solving the problems facing Mexican-Americans throughout the country.[89]

In 1967 the committee held the Mexican-American Conference in El Paso, Texas. The committee heard numerous complaints from the fifteen hundred delegates at the conference, but the most common complaints were the lack of bilingual and bicultural executives and staff in the federal government; the failure to incorporate bilingualism into all phases of public activity, especially education; and the failure of the government to make a commitment in good faith that would produce action.[90]

The committee was successful in persuading the Census Bureau to include a question in the 1970 census that would permit persons of Spanish heritage to identify themselves. In addition, the committee convinced the Department of Agriculture to buy grazing land in the Southwest and to encourage Chicanos to work on it. It failed to influence the Labor Department to ban "green-card holders" (Mexican nationals who worked in the United States by day and went back to Mexico at night).[91]

In December, 1969, the committee was enlarged to include other Latin Americans, such as Puerto Ricans and Cubans, and its name was changed to the Cabinet Committee on Opportunity for the Spanish-Speaking. Four more agencies were added, a full-time chairman and staff were established, and the committee was granted a budget independent of the member agencies. Today the new committee is working to increase "Spanish" employment in government and to create manpower training programs. However, in the words of one expert on Mexican-American problems, the committee has a "low priority on the roster of government programs."[92]

Although the Chicano or Mexican-American is a "forgotten minority" in terms of government policy, Mexican nationals have not been. Since World War II the government has had a changing policy toward immigrants from Mexico, with consequences for the Mexican-American. During the war the government initiated the *bracero*, or contract labor program, whereby Mexican nationals were granted temporary visas to work in the United States. The program of importation of labor dropped significantly in the years immediately following the war but was resumed during the Korean War as a result of the pressure of growers in the Southwest for cheap labor. Coupled with the *bracero* program was "Operation Wetback," conducted by the U.S. Immigration and Naturalization Service, which rounded up illegal immigrants from Mexico and sent them packing. In a five-year program beginning in 1951, around 3.8 million illegal migrants were returned to Mexico, only 63,515 of which were deported under formal proceedings. In 1964 the *bracero* program was terminated (with a few minor exceptions).

Mexican-Americans were adversely affected by the immigration of Mexican nationals in two ways. First, Mexican-Americans were often accosted by Immigration Department officials and required to show proof of American citizenship. And second, the supply of cheap labor from south of the border forced down the wages of Chicanos engaged in unskilled labor in the Southwest.[93]

INDIAN RESERVATIONS

Between 1934 and 1953 the federal government was committed, at least in principle, to improving the Indian reservations and to maintaining the pluralist status of these enclaves.

In 1946 Congress passed the Indian Claims Commission Act, which enabled whole tribes to sue the federal government as a method of redressing historical grievances and of recovering financial losses.* According to Brophy and Aberle, "as of January 1, 1964, Indian tribes had filed 588 claims; 108 were dismissed and 50 awards totaling $94,915,000 have been made."[94] But the pressing of claims had repercussions upon the pluralist status of Indian reservations. If Indians could be assimilated, then such claims would end.

Indians could sue the government prior to this act, but only by obtaining special acts from Congress to present specific cases.

On August 1, 1953, the House of Representatives issued a "termination resolution" (number 108), resolving that Congress should move:

> ... *as rapidly as possible to make the Indians within the territorial limits of the United States subject to the same laws and entitled to the same privileges and responsibilities as are applicable to other citizens of the United States, to end their status as wards of the United States, and to grant them all the rights and prerogatives pertaining to American citizenship.* [95]

A few days later, on August 15, Congress enacted Public Law 280, transferring civil and criminal jurisdiction over reservations in Oregon, Nebraska, California, Minnesota, and Wisconsin to the governments of these states. Reservations in Alaska lost their autonomy with a later amendment. The act further specified that the elimination of the pluralist status of reservations by the states could be done without the consent of the Indian tribes; however, the states would then have to assume financial and other responsibilities as well. [96]

Although the congressmen had various motives for taking such actions, one scholar believes that Indian claims against the government were an important factor. Many congressmen were convinced that the special relationship of the Indians to the federal government could not continue indefinitely:

> *It was clear that so long as many tribes had apparently legitimate unsettled claims, this relationship could not be easily terminated. Thus, the bill [No. 108] attracted support from Congressmen who considered it a means to withdraw programs designed solely for Indian benefit. Many of them believed that the claims awards could help to make tribes self-sustaining, thereby reducing the justification for such programs.* [97]

Reservations were to be eliminated as federal units having a particular status and were to become counties within state government. In addition to termination, Indians were encouraged to "relocate" in the cities. However, Congress and the executive branch were not in agreement, as usual, and considerable confusion existed over what the government's policy toward Indians would be. In 1958 the secretary of interior stated that no tribe would be involuntarily terminated, in spite of Public Law 280. And in 1961 the new secretary of interior under Kennedy and the president's Task Force stated a policy of developing Indian resources. [98] By the middle 1960s, termination as a policy was dead, and the opposition of the Indian tribes to that concept brought about an amendment in 1968 to Public Law 280: termination could not occur without the consent of the Indians within reservations.

Before termination as a policy ceased, several tribes were drastically affected, particularly the Klamaths of Oregon, the Menominees of Wisconsin, and the Paiutes of Utah. The Klamath reservation was terminated in 1954. The government gave the Indians a choice of taking individual shares of the total assets or keeping the property in trust for the group. The great majority (1,660) voted to take checks amounting to $44,000 apiece, while 84 voted to keep their share in a group trust. In 1969, because of the high property taxes they now had to pay, the trust group voted to sell. Checks averaging around $120,000 were eventually paid by the government in 1973. Most of the money has been spent and Klamaths are now on the state's relief rolls. Most of the reservation land became a national park; the remainder was sold to individuals in small plots (some Indians bought their own private land).[99] Prior to termination in 1954, the Menominees were quite wealthy and independent by Indian standards; they even paid for most of the federal services. After termination, the tribe kept most of its assets in a private organization, Menominee Enterprises, Inc., and the reservation was incorporated into the state as a county. In a short time, it was the poorest county. Much of the land held in common has been sold to pay taxes and expenses. Similarly, Paiute land was put in trust in a Salt Lake City bank, 160 miles away. Ill equipped to understand the complexities of their new status or to make payments which they did not expect, the Paiutes have become helpless dependents within the state of Utah.[100]

The policy directive of the sixties and seventies can be illustrated by a speech of President Nixon to Congress in 1970:

This, then, must be the goal of any new national policy toward Indian people: to strengthen the Indian's sense of autonomy without threatening his sense of community. We must assure the Indian that he can assume control of his own life without being separated involuntarily from the tribal group. And we must make it clear that Indians can become independent of federal control without being cut off from federal concern and federal support.[101]

A number of federal agencies, such as HEW, the Department of Labor, and HUD, as well as the Bureau of Indian Affairs (BIA), have been involved in programs to revitalize the reservations. Economic programs have consisted of loans to businesses that locate near or in reservations, technical assistance, public work projects, conservation programs and job training.[102] The federal government provides financial aid to states and school districts that have large Indian student populations, and Indian day schools receive a per capita funding that is higher than the national average. The BIA also has a college scholarship fund ($3.8 million for forty-three hundred students in 1969–1970). A few showcase schools have been founded with high funding and high community involvement, including the Navaho Community College, the Rough Rock Demonstration School, and the Institute for American Indian Arts. All of these are bilingual and bicultural.[103] Health care has improved (although it is still far from adequate) and is better on reservations in numerous isolated areas elsewhere in the United States. Medical appropriation monies for reservations were four times higher in 1970 than 1955; between 1955 and 1968 there was an 84 percent increase in hospital and clinic admissions. In 1971 Levitan and Hetrick stated that " . . . the Federal government annually spends more than half a billion dollars on Indian programs, or some $5,500 per Indian reservation family. This amount is much greater than the federal government spends per family for the rest of the population, even if all defense expenditures are included."[104]

On the negative side, paternalism and bureaucratic inefficiency still predominate, along with the loss of Indian resources to outsiders. Since 1951 a policy for increasing community involvement in schools has existed; yet by 1970 only four schools with a total of 950 students had been turned over to tribal control. The BIA has done little in this regard, preferring to provide *for* the Indians; however, tribal leaders have contributed to the problem because of their fear of termination if the reservation becomes too independent.[105] Another problem is that there is no one agency coordinating the overall development process. Federal agencies have curtailed or limited water supplies on the grounds that "Indians do not need the water because they do not have any immediate uses—but they do not have any immediate uses because irrigation expenditures have been limited."[106] Scarce water in the Southwest has been diverted by whites, and the government has failed to protect the water rights of Indians.[107] Oil and gas leases on reservations bring only limited benefits to Indians. The oil industry workers are generally non-Indian; there are no programs or strategies to develop firms owned by Indians, and systematic exploration by Indians to find new oil and gas sources is lacking.[108]

In 1976 and 1977 the government faced new problems produced by a renewal of Indian land-claim cases. Indian tribes and Indian organizations, particularly the Native American Rights Fund, asked for the return of thousands of acres of land. In 1977, more than half of the 266 federally recognized tribes were pressing their claims in the courts. Indians in Maine wanted the return of 8 million acres, and around 350,000 acres are in the process of being claimed by the Wampanoags in Massachusetts, the Pequots and Schaghticokes in Connecticut, the Narragansetts in Rhode Island, and the Oneidas in New York. Hundreds of smaller land claims were made, primarily in the East, but including forty of the fifty states. In most of these cases the Indians contended that the land was taken from them without congressional approval authorized by the Nonintercourse Act of 1790.[109]

Quite probably these cases will be settled through mediation, which will result in the granting of limited sections of land, and by financial compensation of the Indian claims. The issue is serious and one that threatens many white communities and property holders, but it is unlikely that large-scale land transfers will occur. As *Time* concludes, "whatever settlements are reached in the U.S. must, of course, be weighed by Congress. Congress should be able to be fair without suffering the delusion that the country can really be given back to the Indians. The time for that passed forever with the vanishing of the pioneers who took it from them."[110]

As will be seen in Chapter 12, Indian-Americans have made some progress in reducing their inequality and in improving their economic, health, and educational position. But they remain the most impoverished of all ethnic groups in America.

As a final point, in principle, reservations have a pluralist status. Tribal governments are technically autonomous in governing reservations except for a few explicit areas spelled out by statute. But this pluralism remains a facade. "In reality, the federal government reserves the right to veto all tribal laws, codes, ordinances, and financial arrangements. While Congress uses the rhetoric of giving Indians freedom of action, it also empowers the Secretary of the Interior to regulate in utmost detail the administration of federal programs for the Indians, a mandate which the federal officials exercise with great diligence."[111]

THE ISLAND TERRITORIES

Postwar American government policy toward the three major island territories took quite different forms: independence for the Philippines, integration for Hawaii, and pluralism for Puerto Rico. The United States government terminated dominance over the Philippines in 1946. At the other extreme, the territory of Hawaii became a state in 1959. The admission of Hawaii into the Union had been delayed long past its meeting the requirements for statehood, primarily because of racist resistance on the mainland to the incorporation of such diverse peoples.

In 1946 Washington appointed the first Puerto Rican governor and in 1948 the U.S. government granted the Puerto Rican people the right to democratically elect their own governor. In March 1949 a special pluralist status was authorized by Congress as Public Law 600. This status was that of a "commonwealth," or, in Spanish, *Estado Libre Asociado* (Free Associated State). The Puerto Rican people approved Public Law 600 by a four-to-one margin in a referendum held in June 1951. Under this unique status, Puerto Rico receives social security benefits and federal aid for economic and social improvements, but the people on the island pay no federal income taxes, no tariffs are imposed upon goods shipped to the mainland, and excise taxes collected in Puerto Rican ports go to the Puerto Rican treasury rather than to the Treasury Department in Washington, D.C. On the negative side, however, on the grounds of no representation without taxation, a resident commissioner from Puerto Rico sits in the American Congress but cannot vote. The political arrangement at the present time seems to be satisfactory to a majority of the Puerto Ricans; a large minority favors statehood and a small minority advocates complete independence.[112]

SUMMARY

World War II initiated numerous changes in the pattern of race and ethnic relations in the United States. Beginning with a civil rights movement supported by white liberals but actively involving members of the racial-ethnic minorities, and followed by a power movement, the racial conflicts in postwar America signaled an end to accommodation and acquiescence to extreme subordination. The federal government, under cold war pressures and internal discord, began a halting and inconsistent effort to reverse its previous explicit and implicit supports of discrimination. Government antidiscrimination policies, limited and vague at first, gradually became stronger as appropriate agencies gained the resources and sanctioning authority sufficient to produce at least the beginnings of change. If nothing else occurred, at least government support of a system of inequality justified by racism was eliminated. Programs were begun to redress the consequences of past discrimination and to reduce existing restrictions. At the very least, there were three significant changes from the prewar pattern: the organization of subordinate groups in an active effort to promote change, the enactment of government programs to reduce discrimination and inequality, and the perception that racial oppression was illegitimate.

But the efforts of the civil rights movement were limited by inadequate resources; the power movement was largely marked by rhetoric, although words are not without effect; the white ethnic movement has just begun; and government programs have been inadequate compared to what they might have accomplished. In reference to government programs, in January 1973 the U.S. Commission on Civil Rights issued a reassessment of federal civil rights enforcement efforts. The following is a portion of this evaluation quoted here at length:

> Our findings are dismayingly similar to those in our earlier reports. The basic finding of our initial report, issued in October, 1970, was that executive branch enforcement of civil rights mandates was so inadequate as to render the laws practically meaningless. Many deficiencies ran throughout the overall effort. We found, for example, that the size of the staff with full-time equal opportunity responsibilities was insufficient. At the same time, because of their low position in their organizational hierarchy, civil rights officials lacked authority to bring about change in the substantive programs conducted by their agencies.

Moreover, it became abundantly clear that agency civil rights enforcement efforts typically were disjointed and marked by a lack of comprehensive planning and goals. . . .

The enforcement failure was the result, to a large extent, of placing responsibility for ensuring racial and ethnic justice upon a massive Federal bureaucracy which for years had been an integral part of a discriminatory system. Not only did the bureaucrats resist civil rights goals; they often viewed any meaningful effort to pursue them to be against their particular program's self-interest. . . .

In this, our most recent assessment, we have found that the inertia of agencies in the area of civil rights has persisted. . . . This latest Commission study has reinforced the finding of the three preceding reports that the Government's civil rights program is not adequate or even close to it. . . .

In the past the Government's vast resources frequently have been effectively marshaled to cope with natural disasters, economic instability, and outbreaks of crime. Can we afford to do less when dealing with the country's greatest malignancy—racial and ethnic injustice?

The answer is clearly "no." But days pass into weeks, then into months, and finally into years, and Federal civil rights enforcement proceeds at a snail's pace. . . . Time is running out on the dream of our forebearers.[113]

In spite of the inadequacy of government efforts to produce change, has there been any significant reduction in ethnic and racial stratification? Has the activity of the social movements made any impression? Have changes occurred other than what has been intended by government policies and by minority organizations? What is the direction of these changes, if any—toward integration or toward pluralism? Chapter 12 will try to answer some of these questions.

12

CONTEMPORARY DOMINANCE: STRUCTURAL CHANGES AND CONTINUITIES

INTRODUCTION

Two major changes in race and ethnic relations since World War II have been described in the two preceding chapters. First, the accommodation of minority groups to subordinance has been replaced by resistance, activism, and the crystallization of ethnic and racial minorities as interest groups. Second, the government has become more or less committed to a policy of antidiscrimination and black-white integration. Other changes have also developed; yet several elements of the prewar pattern of relationships persist. In some cases, the patterns of change and of continuities with the past are relatively easy to discern because there is "hard data" to make interpretations. In other cases, there is conflicting evidence, a dearth of evidence, or different interpretations of the same evidence.

This chapter will present evidence for change or lack of change in racial and ethnic stratification in occupational placement, educational attainment, and family income distribution; in racial and ethnic discrimination; in the geographical distribution of selected ethnic groups and races within regions and urban areas; and in social and personal distance between blacks and whites. The extent of black-white school desegregation since the Supreme Court decision of 1954 will also be reviewed.

OCCUPATION, EDUCATION, AND INCOME

Occupational Placement

Occupation in an industrial society probably has the most significant effect on the distribution of rewards; it affects income, prestige, power, and privilege. As explained in Part 1, the distribution of an ethnic group or race among occupations and occupational categories is rarely, if ever, proportional to the group's population size or to its percentage of the total employed labor force. Discrimination, the effects of past discrimination, and "competitive ability" (a group's organization, technology, cohesiveness, leadership, and values are important factors) combine to influence occupational placement. Tables 12.1 and 12.2 give the percentage of each selected race or ethnic group in the occupational categories devised by the U.S. Census Bureau in four census years: 1940, 1950, 1960, and 1970. The tables also provide a white-collar and a blue-collar category.

As can be seen, with only a few exceptions, the proportions of members of the white race have barely changed; the exceptions include the doubling of whites in professional and semiprofessional occupations and the significant reduction of white farmers from 1940 to 1970. The percentage of blacks and Indians in the professions, however, quadrupled between 1940 and 1970; the percentage of Mexican-Americans quadrupled in a shorter period, between 1950 and 1970. What is outstanding is the twelvefold increase of Chinese-Americans and the sixfold increase of Japanese-Americans in the professions. Puerto Ricans in the continental United States experienced little change in the professional category, but in the Commonwealth of Puerto Rico the percentage quadrupled. All groups seem to be turning away from farming. All groups have larger representation in the white-collar occupations at the expense of blue-collar jobs and farming, especially the blacks (five times as many as in 1940) and the Indians (four times as many as in 1940).

Tables 12.3 and 12.4 provide the occupational proportional index (OPI)* for the same seven groups in the same time periods. While the OPI of the white race has been consistent over the thirty-year period, the OPIs of other groups have changed quite a bit.

Several interesting comparisons can be noted: (1) the remarkable improvement of the Chinese and Japanese in the professional category; (2) the decline in the number of Chinese and Japanese managers and proprietors (largely in small retail stores or restaurants); (3) the persistence of black employment as domestics at a rate five to six times higher than it should be; (4) the rather general similarity of the white- and blue-collar scores for blacks, Indians, Puerto Ricans, and Mexicans in all time periods, in contrast to whites, Japanese, and Chinese; (5) the fact that by 1970 Indians exceeded

---

*Again, a score of 1.00 means that a group is proportionally represented in this particular occupation—that is, the group's percentage in the total labor force is equal to the percentage of its members in the occupation. A score of 2.00 indicates that a group has twice as many workers as would be expected, given its percentage of the total U.S. labor force; 0.50 means one half as many as would be expected. The OPI is derived by taking the percentage of a group's membership in a particular category and dividing it by the group's percentage of the total labor force. For this reason, whites, with their high percentage of the total labor force, will never have a OPI score much above 1.00. For example, the highest white score in 1970 could only be 1.12, even if only whites were to be found in the occupation (100 percent of an occupation divided by 89.2 equals 1.12).

Table 12.1

Percentage of Selected Races and Ethnic Groups' Membership in Occupational Categories: 1940, 1950, 1960, 1970

Occupational Category	White				Black				Indian			
	1940	1950	1960	1970	1940	1950	1960	1970	1940	1950	1960	1970
1. Professional & semiprofessional	8.0	9.4	12.4	15.6	2.7	3.4	5.1	8.3	2.8	3.2	6.2	9.8
2. Farmers	11.1	7.6	4.2	2.0	15.0	9.4	3.0	0.6	37.0	20.5	7.4	1.6
3. Managers, officials & proprietors	9.2	9.8	9.6	9.0	1.1	1.9	˙.6	2.2	1.4	1.9	2.6	4.1
4. Clerical & sales	18.6	21.1	24.2	26.0	1.8	4.7	7.9	16.0	2.7	4.5	8.7	16.6
5. Craftsmen & operatives	31.7	35.2	34.2	31.3	13.4	24.3	28.1	32.7	18.7	25.2	31.0	36.1
a. Craftsmen	12.3	15.0	15.0	14.4	3.0	5.3	6.7	9.1	4.8	9.1	11.2	14.1
b. Operatives	19.3	20.2	19.2	16.9	10.4	19.0	21.4	23.6	13.9	16.1	19.9	22.0
6. Service & domestics	10.0	8.1	9.3	11.0	34.3	30.9	34.7	28.3	8.2	10.3	17.1	19.0

a. Domestics	2.7	1.2	1.4	0.8	22.5	15.4	16.4	8.3	3.9	3.3	5.2	2.6
b. Service	7.2	6.9	7.9	10.2	11.7	15.4	18.4	20.0	4.2	7.0	11.9	16.4
7. Farm laborers	5.6	3.7	2.0	1.1	17.5	9.4	5.8	2.4	19.7	20.1	12.2	4.2
8. Other laborers	6.0	5.1	4.2	3.9	14.3	15.9	13.7	9.3	9.5	14.4	14.7	8.6
9. White collar[a]	35.7	40.4	46.2	50.6	5.5	10.0	14.6	26.6	7.0	9.6	17.5	30.5
10. Blue collar[b]	53.2	52.0	50.0	47.4	79.5	80.4	82.3	72.8	56.1	70.0	75.1	68.0

SOURCES: *Sixteenth Census of the United States, 1940, Population, The Labor Force, Occupational Characteristics* (Washington, D.C.: U.S. Department of Commerce/Bureau of the Census, Government Printing Office, 1943), Table II, p. 5. *Sixteenth Census of the United States, 1940, Population Characteristics of the Nonwhite Population by Race* (Washington, D.C.: U.S. Department of Commerce/Bureau of the Census, Government Printing Office, 1943), Table 8, p. 47. *Special Reports, Nativity and Parentage, 1950* (Washington, D.C.: U.S. Department of Commerce/Bureau of the Census, Government Printing Office, 1954), Table 10, pp. 3A–58. *1950 United States Census of Population, Special Reports, Nonwhite Population by Race* (Washington, D.C.: U.S. Department of Commerce/Bureau of the Census, Government Printing Office, 1953), Tables 9 and 10, pp.: 3B–27 and 3B–32. *United States Census of Population, 1960, United States Summary, General Social and Economic Characteristics* (Washington, D.C.: U.S. Department of Commerce/Bureau of the Census, Government Printing Office, 1963), Table 88, pp. 1–217. *United States Census of Population, 1960, Nonwhite Population by Race* (Washington, D.C.: U.S. Department of Commerce/Bureau of the Census, Government Printing Office, 1963), Tables 32 and 33, pp. 101, 104. *1970 Census of the Population, Subject Reports, Occupational Characteristics* (Washington, D.C.: U.S. Department of Commerce/Bureau of the Census, Government Printing Office, 1973), Table 39, pp. 593–608.

[a]The sum of categories 1, 3, and 4.

[b]The sum of categories 5, 6, 7, and 8. The sum of categories 2, 9, and 10 is approximately 100 percent.

Table 12.2

Percentage of Selected Races and Ethnic Groups' Membership in Occupational Categories: 1940, 1950, 1960, 1970

Occupational Category	Chinese				Japanese				Mexican[a]		P. Rican (Cont. U.S.)			P. Rican (Island)		
	1940	1950	1960	1970	1940	1950	1960	1970	1950	1970	1950	1960	1970	1940	1950	1970
1. Professional & semiprofessional	2.8	7.2	19.2	26.5	3.2	6.8	14.2	19.0	2.7	7.7	4.6	3.2	5.5	3.1	4.8	13.4
2. Farmers	1.3	1.2	0.6	0.3	14.9	11.1	7.9	2.0	4.0	0.5	0.2	0.1	0.1	9.4	6.5	1.1
3. Managers, officials & proprietors	20.4	20.1	13.6	8.9	11.5	7.1	7.7	8.4	4.3	4.2	3.8	2.7	3.4	4.8	5.9	6.2
4. Clerical & sales	11.3	16.2	21.9	21.2	11.0	15.4	22.8	26.4	10.3	19.4	10.2	12.6	20.9	8.1	10.1	21.7
5. Craftsmen & operatives	23.7	20.3	21.6	20.2	9.8	18.7	26.4	23.0	31.9	40.4	55.6	57.7	47.1	23.5	24.0	33.4
a. Craftsmen	1.2	2.9	5.5	5.4	2.2	5.5	12.9	11.6	10.8	14.0	7.6	8.3	11.5	5.5	7.5	12.2
b. Operatives	22.4	17.4	16.1	14.8	7.6	13.2	13.5	11.4	21.1	26.4	48.0	49.4	35.6	18.0	16.5	21.2
6. Service & domestics	36.2	31.9	21.2	20.4	15.6	15.2	11.7	13.1	17.1	15.7	19.0	15.2	16.2	10.7	11.1	14.2
a. Domestics	6.1	2.6	1.1	0.8	7.8	6.5	3.6	1.7	3.0	1.7	0.9	0.4	0.3	7.7	5.8	2.4

b. Service	30.1	29.2	20.1	19.6	7.8	8.7	8.1	11.4	8.1	14.0	18.1	14.8	15.9	3.0	5.3	11.8
7. Farm laborers	2.6	1.4	0.5	0.3	25.4	16.2	5.3	1.9	20.7	4.1	1.8	2.2	1.1	35.0	30.9	4.7
8. Other laborers	1.6	1.7	1.4	2.3	8.5	9.5	4.0	6.3	15.0	7.2	4.9	6.2	5.8	5.2	5.6	5.3
9. White collar[b]	34.6	43.5	54.6	56.5	25.7	29.3	44.7	53.7	17.3	31.3	18.6	18.6	29.8	16.0	20.8	41.3
10. Blue collar[c]	64.2	55.3	44.7	43.2	59.4	59.6	47.4	44.3	78.7	67.4	81.3	81.3	70.2	74.4	71.6	57.6

SOURCES: Sixteenth Census of the United States, 1940, Population, Characteristics of the Nonwhite Population by Race (Washington, D.C.: U.S. Department of Commerce/Bureau of the Census, Government Printing Office, 1943), Table 8, p. 47. 1950 United States Census of Population, Special Reports, Nonwhite Population by Race (Washington, D.C.: U.S. Department of Commerce/Bureau of the Census, Government Printing Office, 1953), Tables 11 and 12, pp. 3B–37, 3B–42. 1950 United States Census of Population, Special Reports, Persons of Spanish Surname (Washington, D.C.: U.S. Department of Commerce/Bureau of the Census, Government Printing Office, 1953), Table 6, pp. 3C–23, 3C–27, 3C–31, 3C–35, 3C–39. United States Census of Population, 1960, Nonwhite Population by Race (Washington, D.C.: U.S. Department of Commerce/Bureau of the Census, Government Printing Office, 1963), Tables 34 and 35, pp. 108, 111. 1970 Census of the Population, Subject Reports, Occupational Characteristics (Washington, D.C.: U.S. Department of Commerce/Bureau of the Census, Government Printing Office, June 1973), Table 39, pp. 593–608. 1950 Census of Population, Volume II, Characteristics of the Population, Parts 51–54, Territories and Possessions (Washington, D.C.: U.S. Department of Commerce/Bureau of the Census, Government Printing Office, 1953), Table 26, pp. 53–39. 1950 Census of Population, Puerto Ricans in Continental United States (1950 Population Census Report P-E, No. 3D, Washington, D.C.: U.S. Department of Commerce/Bureau of the Census, Government Printing Office, 1953), Table 4, pp. 3D–13. Volume I, Characteristics of the Population, Part 53, Puerto Rico, 1970 Census of Population (Washington, D.C.: U.S. Department of Commerce/Bureau of the Census, Government Printing Office, June 1973), Table 48, pp. 53–201, 53–202. 1970 Census of Population, Puerto Ricans in the United States (Washington, D.C.: U.S. Department of Commerce/Bureau of the Census, Government Printing Office, 1973), Table 7, p. 69. United States Census of Population, 1960, Puerto Ricans in the United States (Washington, D.C.: U.S. Department of Commerce/Bureau of the Census, Government Printing Office, 1963), Table 5, p. 26.

a Mexican, 1950, refers to those with "Spanish surname in 5 Southwestern states"; Mexican, 1970, refers to those of Spanish origin, U.S. The comparison is tenuous since there are some Spanish surnamed in the Southwest that are not Mexican or of Mexican descent.

b The sum of categories 1, 3, and 4.

c The sum of categories 5, 6, 7, and 8. The sum of categories 2, 9, and 10 is approximately 100 percent.

Table 12.3

Occupational Proportional Index (OPI) by Race and Racial-Ethnic Group: 1940, 1950, 1960, 1970

Occupational Category	White				Black				Indian			
	1940	1950	1960	1970	1940	1950	1960	1970	1940	1950	1960	1970
1. Professional & semiprofessional	1.07	1.07	1.06	1.04	0.36	0.38	0.44	0.56	0.40	0.36	0.53	0.64
2. Farmer	0.96	0.97	1.02	1.08	1.30	1.22	0.74	0.30	3.20	2.54	1.87	0.84
3. Managers, officials, & proprietors	1.10	1.09	1.08	1.08	0.13	0.20	0 18	0.27	0.13	0.21	0.27	0.48
4. Clerical & sales	1.10	1.08	1.07	1.04	0.11	0.24	0.35	0.64	0.13	0.21	0.40	0.64
5. Craftsmen & operatives	1.06	1.03	1.02	1.00	0.45	0.71	0.84	1.04	0.60	0.64	0.93	1.16

a. Craftsmen	1.08	1.07	1.06	1.04	0.26	0.38	0.47	0.66	0.40	0.57	0.80	1.00
b. Operatives	1.05	1.01	0.99	0.96	0.57	0.94	1.11	1.35	0.73	0.71	1.07	1.24
6. Service & domestics	0.80	0.78	0.80	0.86	2.76	3.00	2.98	2.21	0.67	0.93	1.47	1.48
a. Domestics	0.58	0.46	0.51	0.52	4.78	6.04	5.82	5.45	0.80	1.21	1.87	1.68
b. Service	0.94	0.89	0.89	0.91	1.52	2.00	2.08	1.78	0.67	0.79	1.40	1.44
7. Farm laborers	0.82	0.87	0.84	0.88	2.57	2.17	2.50	1.96	2.87	4.54	5.33	3.32
8. Other laborers	0.88	0.83	0.82	0.88	2.08	2.59	2.72	2.08	1.40	2.14	3.00	1.92
9. White collar	1.09	1.08	1.07	1.05	0.17	0.26	0.34	0.55	0.20	0.21	0.40	0.64
10. Blue collar	0.95	0.95	0.94	0.95	1.42	1.47	1.56	1.46	1.00	1.14	1.47	1.36
11. % of total labor force	89.7	90.0	90.2	89.2	9.9	9.6	9.1	9.6	0.15	0.13	0.15	0.25

Sources: Same as for Table 12.1.

Table 12.4

Occupational Proportional Index (OPI) by Race and Racial-Ethnic Group: 1940, 1950, 1960, 1970

Occupational Category	Chinese				Japanese				Mexican		P. Rican (Cont. U.S.)			P. Rican (Island)		
	1940	1950	1960	1970	1940	1950	1960	1970	1950	1970	1950	1960	1970	1940	1950	1970
1. Professional & semiprofessional	0.37	0.78	1.68	1.75	0.42	0.82	1.20	1.26	0.30	0.51	0.53	0.27	0.36	0.42	0.55	0.90
2. Farmer	0.12	0.11	0.13	0.12	1.33	1.45	1.93	1.06	0.52	0.29	0.01	0.02	0.02	0.82	0.84	0.60
3. Managers, officials, & proprietors	2.50	2.11	1.53	1.04	1.42	0.82	0.87	1.00	0.47	0.51	0.42	0.30	0.40	0.58	0.66	0.75
4. Clerical & sales	0.75	0.78	0.93	0.83	0.67	0.82	1.00	1.03	0.53	0.78	0.53	0.55	0.84	0.48	0.52	0.87
5. Craftsmen & operatives	0.87	0.56	0.67	0.62	0.33	0.55	0.80	0.71	0.93	1.29	1.58	1.70	1.50	0.79	0.71	1.06

a. Craftsmen	0.12	0.22	0.40	0.37	0.17	0.36	0.90	0.83	0.76	1.01	0.21	0.59	0.84	0.42	0.54	0.88
b. Operatives	1.25	0.78	0.80	0.83	0.42	0.64	0.70	0.66	1.04	1.54	2.32	2.52	2.02	0.98	0.83	1.21
6. Service & domestics	3.00	3.00	1.80	1.58	1.25	1.55	1.00	1.00	1.07	1.23	1.79	1.30	1.28	0.87	1.10	1.11
a. Domestics	1.37	1.00	0.40	0.50	1.67	2.64	1.27	1.11	1.17	1.10	0.37	0.16	0.24	1.65	2.30	1.58
b. Service	5.00	3.67	2.27	1.71	1.25	1.18	0.93	1.00	1.04	1.25	2.26	1.61	1.40	0.39	0.70	1.05
7. Farm laborers	0.37	0.33	0.20	0.21	3.75	3.91	2.27	1.49	4.80	3.24	0.42	0.93	0.84	5.18	7.27	3.74
8. Other laborers	0.25	0.22	0.27	0.50	1.25	1.64	0.80	1.40	2.44	1.61	0.79	1.23	1.30	0.75	0.92	1.19
9. White collar	1.12	1.11	1.27	1.17	0.83	0.82	1.03	1.11	0.46	0.65	0.47	0.43	0.62	0.49	0.56	0.86
10. Blue collar	1.12	1.00	0.87	0.83	1.08	1.09	0.90	0.89	1.43	1.35	1.42	1.52	1.40	1.34	1.32	1.16
11. % of total labor force	0.08	0.09	0.15	0.24	0.12	0.11	0.30	0.35	1.12	3.77	0.19	0.44	0.50	1.13	1.00	1.10

SOURCE: Same as for Table 12.2.

blacks in the professional, the managerial-proprietor-official, the craftsmen, and the white-collar categories.

While Japanese- and Chinese-Americans have improved their occupational positions dramatically, the rate of change for blacks, Mexicans, and Indians has been much smaller. Using the rate of change in certain occupations between 1960 and 1970, one can predict when blacks will be proportional to other groups. In 1974, occupational data for blacks and whites also became available. In Table 12.5 the OPIs for the white and black races in 1940, 1950, 1960, and 1970 are repeated from Table 12.3 and the 1974 OPIs are added. Changes between 1970 and 1974 can, therefore, be used along with the 1960–1970 change rate to make predictions.

The rate of change between 1960 and 1970 in the professional and semiprofessional category for blacks (an increase of 0.12) indicates that blacks will not be proportional in the professions until about 2006. The increase of 0.5 between 1970 and 1974 gives the same data for a score of 1.00. According to the rate of change between 1960 and 1970 (0.9), blacks will not be proportional in the managerial and official occupations until 2050. According to the 1970–1974 rate of change, however (an estimated 0.15 increase between 1970 and 1980), proportional attainment will be thirty years sooner, in 2020. In the clerical and sales category, blacks showed an increase of 0.29 points between 1960 and 1970, and at this rate will be proportional in 1982; however, the number of blacks entering this occupational area as a percentage of the black labor force declined somewhat between 1970 and 1974. At this rate of change (about 0.15 a decade), it will be 1994 before blacks are proportionally represented in this area.

Since the Mexican, Indian, and Puerto Rican (mainland) OPIs are similar to blacks in these areas, the predicted dates when occupational proportion will be attained are also similar.

One way to indicate quantitatively an increase or a decrease in the *overall* occupational differentiation by ethnicity or race in a society is simply to add each group's deviation from 1.00 in each year, regardless of the direction of the deviation (higher or lower), and then compare the years. For such a procedure to be meaningful, *all* of the ethnic groups in the society would have to be included. However, by using a few groups for which data is available, some idea of the direction in occupational differentiation can be ascertained. Table 12.6 gives the deviation from 1.00 (OPI) of whites, blacks, Indians, Chinese, and Japanese, along with the total deviation of these groups and the average deviation in the years 1940, 1950, 1960, and 1970.

For some reason, occupational differentiation by race or ethnic group, in terms of total and average deviations, increased between 1940 and 1950 and then declined between 1950 and 1970. Although there never will be perfect equality in occupational proportions (a total or average deviation score of 0.0), at least in terms of the groups listed in Table 12.6, occupational differentiation by race and ethnicity is diminishing (from an average deviation of 5.64 in 1940 to 2.99 in 1970).

Table 12.5

Occupational Proportional Index (OPI) by White and Black Race, 1940, 1950, 1960, 1970, 1974

Occupational Category	White					Black				
	1940	1950	1960	1970	1974	1940	1950	1960	1970	1974
1. Professional & semiprofessional	1.07	1.07	1.06	1.04	1.03	0.36	0.38	0.44	0.56	0.61
2. Farmers	0.96	0.97	1.02	1.08	1.08	1.30	1.22	0.74	0.30	0.33
3. Managers, officials, & proprietors	1.10	1.09	1.08	1.08	1.07	0.13	0.20	0.18	0.27	0.33
4. Clerical & sales	1.10	1.08	1.07	1.04	1.03	0.11	0.24	0.35	0.64	0.70
5. Craftsmen & operatives	1.06	1.03	1.02	1.00	0.99	0.45	0.71	0.84	1.04	1.11
a. Craftsmen	1.08	1.07	1.06	1.04	1.04	0.26	0.38	0.47	0.66	0.71
b. Operatives	1.05	1.01	0.99	0.96	0.96	0.57	0.94	1.11	1.35	1.44
6. Service & domestics	0.80	0.78	0.80	0.86	0.89	2.76	3.00	2.98	2.21	1.99
a. Domestics	0.58	0.46	0.51	0.52	0.69	4.78	6.04	5.82	5.45	3.97
b. Service	0.94	0.89	0.89	0.91	0.91	1.52	2.00	2.08	1.78	1.76
7. Farm laborers	0.82	0.87	0.84	0.88	0.97	2.57	2.17	2.50	1.96	1.32

(continued on p. 372)

Table 12.5 (continued)

Occupational Proportional Index (OPI) by White and Black Race, 1940, 1950, 1960, 1970, 1974

Occupational Category	White					Black				
	1940	1950	1960	1970	1974	1940	1950	1960	1970	1974
8. Other laborers	0.88	0.83	0.82	0.88	0.91	2.08	2.59	2.72	2.08	1.85
9. White collar	1.09	1.08	1.07	1.05	1.04	0.17	0.26	0.34	0.55	0.59
10. Blue collar	0.95	0.95	0.94	0.95	0.98	1.42	1.47	1.56	1.46	1.22
11. % of total labor force	89.7	90.0	90.2	89.2	89.2	9.9	9.6	9.1	9.6	9.4

Sources: Sixteenth Census of the United States, 1940, Population, The Labor Force, Occupational Characteristics (Washington, D.C.: U.S. Department of Commerce/Bureau of the Census, Government Printing Office, 1943). Table II, p. 5. Sixteenth Census of the United States, 1940, Population, Characteristics of the Nonwhite Population by Race (Washington, D.C.: U.S. Department of Commerce/Bureau of the Census, Government Printing Office, 1943), Table 8, p. 47. Special Reports, Nativity and Parentage, 1950 (Washington, D.C.: U.S. Department of Commerce/Bureau of the Census, Government Printing Office, 1954), Table 10, pp. 3A–58. 1950 Census of Population, Special Reports, Nonwhite Population by Race (Washington, D.C.: U.S. Department of Commerce/ Bureau of the Census, Government Printing Office, 1953), Table 9, pp. 3B–27. United States Census of Population, 1960, United States Summary, General Social and Economic Characteristics (Washington, D.C.: U.S. Department of Commerce/Bureau of the Census, Government Printing Office, 1962), Table 88, pp. 1–217. United States Census of Population, 1960, Nonwhite Population by Race (Washington, D.C.: U.S. Department of Commerce/ Bureau of the Census, Government Printing Office, 1962), Table 32, p. 101. 1970 Census of the Population, Subject Reports, Occupational Characteristics (Washington, D.C.: U.S. Department of Commerce/Bureau of the Census, Government Printing Office, 1973), Table 39, pp. 593–608. Current Population Reports, The Social and Economic Status of the Black Population in the United States, 1974, Special Studies, Series P-23, No. 54, U.S. Department of Commerce/Bureau of the Census, July 1975), Table 50, p. 75.

Table 12.6

Deviations from Occupational Proportional Index (OPI)
of 1.00 in 1940, 1950, 1960, 1970

Group	1940	1950	1960	1970
White	0.85	0.72	0.79	0.62
Black	7.66	7.45	7.63	5.52
Indian	7.54	8.87	9.54	4.28
Chinese	6.77	6.33	4.81	2.99
Japanese	5.38	5.44	2.93	1.53
Total	28.20	28.81	25.70	14.94
Average	5.64	5.76	5.14	2.99

Sources: Same as for Tables 12.1 and 12.2.

Stratification information for European-derived ethnic groups within the white race is difficult to obtain and to compare for several reasons. In some cases, U.S. Census Bureau data is limited to first and second generations (foreign born and native born with a parent or parents who were foreign born). The Census Bureau and the National Opinion Research Center (NORC) also sample the heads of households by asking, "What is your nationality background, or what is your origin or descent, or what country or countries did most of your ancestors come from?" This second procedure elicits information about several generations, but there are other problems: a person's ancestors may come from a certain country, but he or she may have no particular affinity with that country; multiple origins are not uncommon; a person may feel pressured to choose one of several origins, even though "American" may be the only ethnic affiliation of importance to that person.

Tables 12.7 and 12.8 should be examined with these limitations in mind. Table 12.7 gives occupational percentages of several selected white ethnic groups in 1950 and 1970; Table 12.8 provides OPIs for the same groups in 1950 and 1970, with the addition of OPIs for the year 1900 to indicate how far these groups have come. Both Tables 12.7 and 12.8 utilize census data for first and second generation only. The country "Russia" appears as a category, since this is how the census information was categorized; however, the data refers predominantly to Russian Jews.

Between 1963 and 1972, the National Opinion Research Center sampled the heads of households in the United States to determine "ethnic identification" and the relationship of ethnicity and religion to other social data.

Table 12.7

Percentage of the Total Labor Force in Each Occupational Category by Selected White Ethnic Groups, 1950 and 1970

Occupational Category	Irish		Italian		Polish		Swedish		German		British[a]		Russia[b]	
	1950	1970	1950	1970	1950	1970	1950	1970	1950	1970	1950	1970	1950	1970
1. Professional & semiprofessional	11.3	17.7	5.0	10.6	6.2	13.4	10.6	17.0	8.4	15.1	12.7	19.7	12.6	21.7
2. Farmers	1.8	0.5	1.1	0.4	2.0	0.6	9.4	4.2	10.4	4.2	3.8	0.9	3.5	1.5
3. Managers, officials, & proprietors	9.2	10.3	9.4	9.7	9.1	9.0	10.6	12.1	11.2	9.9	12.4	11.5	23.4	16.5
4. Clerical & sales	27.3	31.4	18.6	24.9	17.8	24.8	19.6	26.9	18.2	25.8	23.7	30.4	27.7	34.2
5. Craftsmen & operatives	29.5	22.0	48.6	38.1	49.5	38.3	34.8	26.1	35.4	28.9	33.6	24.2	24.6	18.0
a. Craftsmen	13.7	11.8	16.7	17.0	16.9	15.9	21.0	15.4	18.5	15.4	17.2	13.3	10.1	8.8
b. Operatives	15.7	10.2	31.9	21.1	32.6	22.4	13.8	10.7	16.9	13.5	16.5	10.9	14.5	9.2

6. Service & domestics	15.4	14.9	8.4	11.8	8.1	10.4	8.8	10.4	9.8	12.6	9.4	10.6	4.5	6.3
a. Domestics	2.7	1.3	0.3	0.3	0.8	0.5	2.4	1.3	2.0	1.4	1.7	1.0	0.4	0.4
b. Service	12.7	13.6	8.2	11.5	7.3	9.9	6.4	9.1	7.8	11.2	7.7	9.6	4.1	5.9
7. Farm laborers	0.7	0.2	0.6	0.2	1.2	0.2	2.4	0.8	2.7	0.8	1.1	0.3	1.5	0.3
8. Other laborers	4.7	2.9	8.2	4.3	6.1	3.2	4.3	2.5	3.6	2.6	3.3	2.3	2.2	1.5
9. White collar	47.8	59.4	33.0	45.2	33.1	47.2	40.8	56.0	37.8	50.8	48.8	61.6	63.7	72.4
10. Blue collar	50.3	40.0	65.8	54.4	64.9	52.1	50.3	39.8	51.5	44.9	47.4	37.4	32.8	26.1

SOURCES: *1950 United States Census of Population, Nativity and Parentage* (Washington, D.C.: U.S. Department of Commerce/Bureau of the Census, Government Printing Office, 1954), Table 20, pp. 3A–136 to 3A–139, 3A–142 to 3A–147, 3A–152 to 3A–155. *1970 Census of Population, Subject Reports, National Origin and Language* (Washington, D.C.: U.S. Department of Commerce/Bureau of the Census, Government Printing Office, June 1973), Table 13, pp. 125, 126, 128, 132, 133, 138, 141.

Note: Data available only for first and second generation (foreign born and native born of one or both foreign-born parents).

[a]England and Wales in 1950; United Kingdom in 1970.

[b]By country; includes Jews; excludes Ukrainians in 1970.

Table 12.8

Occupational Proportional Index (OPI):
Selected White Ethnic Groups in 1900, 1950, 1970

Occupational Category	Irish			Italian			Polish		
	1900	1950	1970	1900	1950	1970	1900	1950	1970
1. Professional & semi-professional	0.88	1.28	1.18	0.38	0.56	0.71	0.25	0.70	0.90
2. Farmers	0.37	0.23	0.24	0.08	0.14	0.21	0.26	0.26	0.32
3. Managers, officials & proprietors	1.01	1.02	1.24	1.26	1.04	1.17	0.87	1.00	1.08
4. Clerical & sales	1.32	1.40	1.25	0.70	0.95	1.00	0.70	0.91	0.99
5. Craftsmen & operatives	1.46	0.86	0.70	1.51	1.42	1.21	1.76	1.45	1.22
a. Craftsmen	NA	0.98	0.85	NA	1.19	1.23	NA	1.21	1.15
b. Operatives	NA	0.78	0.58	NA	1.59	1.20	NA	1.62	1.27
6. Service & domestics	1.56	1.49	1.17	0.92	0.82	0.92	0.59	0.78	0.81
a. Domestics	NA	1.06	0.85	NA	0.11	0.16	NA	0.31	0.32
b. Service	NA	1.63	1.20	NA	1.05	1.02	NA	0.94	0.87
7. Farm laborers	0.27	0.16	0.16	0.25	0.14	0.14	0.35	0.28	0.17
8. Other laborers	1.28	0.78	0.64	2.66	1.34	0.97	2.09	0.99	0.71
9. White collar	1.12	1.28	1.23	0.84	0.88	0.94	0.67	0.88	0.98
10. Blue collar	1.18	0.92	0.81	1.37	1.20	1.09	1.70	1.18	1.04
11. % of total labor force	8.3	1.9	0.8	1.1	4.1	2.9	0.8	2.6	1.7

Table 12.8 (continued)

Occupational Proportional Index (OPI):
Selected White Ethnic Groups in 1900, 1950, 1970

Swedish			German			Britishª			Russiaᵇ		
1900	1950	1970	1900	1950	1970	1900	1950	1970	1900	1950	1970
0.45	1.20	1.15	0.75	0.95	1.02	1.32	1.44	1.32	0.53	1.42	1.47
0.83	1.21	2.26	0.80	1.34	2.29	0.68	0.48	0.50	0.28	0.47	0.80
0.60	1.17	1.46	1.14	1.24	1.19	1.42	1.38	1.38	2.43	2.59	1.99
0.64	1.00	1.07	1.21	0.94	1.03	1.35	1.22	1.21	2.07	1.42	1.37
1.34	1.02	0.83	1.35	1.04	0.92	1.56	0.99	0.77	1.80	0.72	0.57
NA	1.50	1.11	NA	1.32	1.12	NA	1.23	0.96	NA	0.72	0.64
NA	0.68	0.61	NA	0.84	0.77	NA	0.82	0.62	NA	0.73	0.53
1.54	0.86	0.83	1.02	0.96	0.98	0.73	0.92	0.84	0.49	0.44	0.49
NA	0.93	0.89	NA	0.79	0.95	NA	0.64	0.67	NA	0.17	0.25
NA	0.83	0.80	NA	1.01	0.99	NA	1.01	0.86	NA	0.53	0.53
0.66	0.55	0.61	0.52	0.64	0.68	0.34	0.25	0.27	0.27	0.34	0.24
1.09	0.70	0.57	0.87	0.59	0.59	0.73	0.55	0.53	0.61	0.37	0.35
0.59	1.08	1.15	1.09	1.01	1.06	1.40	1.31	1.27	1.87	1.71	1.51
1.18	0.92	0.80	1.03	0.94	0.93	1.01	0.87	0.76	1.04	0.60	0.53
1.5	1.1	0.5	11.3	3.8	1.8	3.6	1.6	1.4	0.8	2.1	1.4

SOURCES: Same as for Table 12.7 and *Occupation at the Twelfth Census, Special Reports* (Washington, D.C.: Department of Commerce and Labor/Bureau of the Census, Government Printing Office, 1904), Table 22, pp. 64–67.

NOTE: Data available only for first and second generation (foreign born and native born of one or both foreign-born parents).

NA = not available.

ªEngland and Wales in 1900 and 1950; United Kingdom in 1970.

ᵇExcludes Ukrainians in 1970.

Whites were asked to identify their main nationality background or the country from which most of their ancestors came (different questions were asked in different years). Summaries of these samples (presumably obtained by averaging) and the composite are presented in Table 12.9. The term "religio-ethnic" group is used because of the importance of religious differences within certain ethnic groups.

Although Table 12.9 is not directly comparable to Table 12.7 for the year 1970, certain similarities to the U.S. census data can be seen as well as the difference religion makes. Generally, this NORC table indicates smaller percentages in most white-collar areas and the white-collar total than the 1970 census data does. There are several reasons for this. NORC used heads of households, who are predominantly male, while the Census Bureau used *everybody* twenty-five years or older. The census information is limited to first and second generations; the NORC material is a composite stretching back to 1963. In a few cases, however, the NORC table has higher percentages than the 1970 Census Bureau table. This appears with Protestant and Catholic farmers and craftsmen; British managers and owners, farmers, and craftsmen; Italian professionals and craftsmen; and both Protestant and Irish Catholic managers and owners, farmers, craftsmen, and operatives.

The NORC samples highlight the difference religion makes in employment. Jews and Catholics make up four of the five highest white-collar percentages. When Germans are divided by religion, the order is Jewish, Catholic, and Protestant. Similarly, there is a greater percentage of Irish Catholics in the white-collar occupations than Irish Protestants (largely Scots-Irish, with a large percentage in the South).

Before one concludes that WASP dominance is over, it must be understood that the occupational categories presented in these tables are broad. The highest organizational positions in the general category of managers, officials, and proprietors are statistically overwhelmed by junior governmental officials, small businessmen, and middle- and lower-level corporation officials.

A few studies of elites have been conducted, although they are somewhat dated. A 1953 study by Suzanne Keller found that 85 percent of those who claimed a religion and who held top executive positions in the 200 largest corporations were Protestant.[1] In a 1955 study, 93 percent of the top executives in manufacturing, mining, and finance were WASPs.[2] A study of "influentials" in 1963 revealed that Protestants are "overwhelmingly predominant in education, the military, and business, overrepresented in government, but slightly underrepresented in labor and religion."[3] According to research by *Look* magazine in 1968, WASPs made up 88 percent of the 790 directors of the 50 largest corporations and 83 percent of the 241 directors of the 10 largest commercial banks, and nearly all of the presidents of the 775 colleges and universities were WASPs, as well as 80 percent of the trustees of the 10 largest universities.[4] Protestants have been overrepresented in

Congress; there has only been 1 Catholic President; and between 1789 and 1957, of the 91 justices of the U.S. Supreme Court, 6 were Catholic, 3 were Jewish, and the rest were Protestant.[5]

Nevertheless, Catholic improvement in occupational statuses, particularly for the Irish and German Catholics, is highly significant. The occupational findings (and, as we shall see, income and educational findings) challenge the stereotype of the "white ethnic."

Further Evidence

A 1965 study of Cook County, Illinois, showed that blacks constituted 20 percent of the county's population and 28 percent of the residents of Chicago. If blacks really had power (Black Power is more normative than cognitive), they would have had similar percentages of the major policy-making positions. As it turned out, blacks occupied only 2.6 percent of the 10,997 policy-making positions in Cook County organizations. In the public sector, 5 percent of local-government-appointed officials, 8 percent of elected officials, slightly more than 1 percent of locally or federally appointed officials, and 2 percent of the top federal civil service officials were blacks. In the private sector, blacks made up only 2 percent of the major positions: 0.6 percent in the corporations, 0.3 percent in banking, and 1 percent of the major university officials in the area.[6] According to Barron, "the power structure of Chicago is hardly less white than that of Mississippi."[7]

A similar situation existed in Milwaukee in 1972, a city with a population that was 12 percent black at the time. There was only *one* black in the 1,867 key positions in the business sector; there were *no* blacks in 26 positions in organized labor. Although 26.5 percent of 472 policy-making positions in voluntary organizations concerned with poverty and minority problems were black, the majority of these organizations had only limited community influence. Many of the blacks appointed to policy-making positions were the same individuals holding several posts.[8]

Nationwide, with the increasing ability of blacks to use their voting power, the number of black elected officials is slowly increasing. In 1964 there were only 103 elected black officials in the entire country. Increasing each year, the number of elected black officials reached 3,503 in May 1975. Yet this total still only represented 1 percent of all elected officials in the United States.[9] In 1975 there were 135 black mayors, 104 of whom governed communities with fewer than twenty-five thousand residents; however, there were black mayors in eleven of the metropolitan areas with one hundred thousand or more inhabitants. In this same year the number of major black elected officials included 1 U.S. senator, 17 U.S. congressmen, and 281 state legislators and executives.[10]

The armed forces were "integrated" after World War II, and in the middle 1960s there was considerable stress on affirmative action by the government. How have blacks actually fared in the military and the federal government? Table 12.10 compares the number of blacks in each of the ranks

Table 12.9

Occupation of Head of Household and Ethnic Identification, Percentage

Religio-Ethnic Group	Professional & Technical	Managers & Owners	Farmers	Clerical	Sales	Craftsmen	Operatives	Service	Farm Workers	Other Labor
Protestants										
British	19.2	17.3	6.2	8.6	7.4	19.2	12.3	5.7	0.7	3.6
German	13.9	13.1	11.7	6.4	6.2	22.2	15.9	5.9	0.7	4.0
Scandinavian	14.6	12.2	14.6	9.0	5.8	17.8	18.1	5.2	0.6	2.0
Irish	10.0	14.4	7.9	6.9	6.7	23.4	18.3	6.7	1.4	4.3
Catholics										
Irish	19.4	16.8	3.0	5.9	6.6	25.3	15.5	5.3	0.3	2.0

German	16.1	15.8	9.6	7.1	5.6	22.6	14.2	4.6	0.0	4.3
Italian	14.7	11.6	0.6	8.2	4.4	24.5	19.7	13.5	0.0	2.8
Polish	9.5	7.1	0.8	11.9	5.6	28.6	27.0	7.1	0.0	2.4
Slavic	13.5	6.3	3.1	7.6	3.6	29.6	20.2	8.5	0.0	7.6
French	10.3	13.7	2.7	5.5	5.5	24.0	26.0	7.5	1.4	3.4
Spanish-speaking	6.0	6.0	0.9	8.5	3.4	17.9	29.1	12.8	6.0	9.4
Jews										
German	0.0	20.0	0.0	13.3	13.3	6.7	10.0	3.3	0.0	3.3
Eastern European	29.0	21.4	0.0	15.2	13.1	10.3	6.9	3.4	0.0	0.7
National Average	13.7	12.5	6.5	7.7	5.4	20.2	18.5	8.7	1.0	5.8

SOURCE: Andrew M. Greeley, *Ethnicity in the United States: A Preliminary Reconnaissance* (New York: John Wiley & Sons, Wiley-Interscience, 1974), Table 12, pp. 54–55, with modification by approval of the publisher.

Table 12.10

Percentage of Black Servicemen by Rank and Branch of Service, 1964 and 1970

Rank	Army 1964	Army 1970	Navy 1964	Navy 1970	Air Force 1964	Air Force 1970	Marines 1964	Marines 1970
Officers	3.4	3.4	0.3	0.7	1.5	1.7	0.4	1.3
Generals/Admirals	0.0	0.2	0.0	0.0	0.2	0.2	0.0	0.0
Colonels/Captains	0.2	1.2	0.0	0.1	0.2	0.4	0.0	0.0
Lt. Colonels/Commanders	1.1	4.7	0.6	0.3	0.5	1.2	0.0	0.2
Majors/Lt. Commanders	3.6	5.2	0.3	0.5	0.8	1.7	0.3	0.3
Captains/Lieutenants	5.4	3.7	0.5	0.6	2.0	2.2	0.4	1.4
1st Lieutenants/Lieutenants J.G.	3.8	2.5	0.2	0.6	1.8	1.4	0.4	1.5
2nd Lieutenants/Ensigns	2.7	1.7	0.7	1.2	2.5	1.2	0.3	1.9
Enlisted Men	13.4	13.5	5.8	5.4	10.0	11.7	8.7	11.2
E-9, Sgt. Major	3.5	6.0	1.5	1.5	1.2	3.0	0.8	2.3
E-8, Master Sgt.	6.1	11.8	1.9	3.1	2.2	4.4	1.2	5.3
E-7, Sgt. 1st Class	8.5	17.8	2.9	5.3	3.2	6.2	2.3	10.5
E-6, Staff Sgt.	13.9	22.0	4.7	6.8	5.3	10.1	5.0	13.4
E-5, Sergeant	17.4	11.3	6.6	4.4	10.8	14.7	11.2	10.6
E-4, Corporal	14.2	10.9	5.9	2.8	12.7	10.7	10.4	8.1
E-3, Pvt. 1st Class	13.6	13.4	6.6	5.0	9.7	11.8	7.8	10.4
E-2, Private	13.1	15.0	5.7	10.2	11.7	14.8	9.5	13.6
E-1, Recruit	6.8	13.3	7.1	13.0	14.4	18.3	9.1	14.2

SOURCE: 1964–Department of Defense statistics, cited in Charles C. Moskos, "Racial Integration in the Armed Forces," *American Journal of Sociology* 72 (September 1966): 136–37; 1970—National Urban League from data in U.S. Department of Defense (Equal Opportunity), *The Negro in the Armed Forces: A Statistical Fact Book, 1971*.

Table 12.11

Black Federal Employment (General Schedule):
OPI and Percent of Pay Categories, 1965, 1970, 1974

Salary Categories	OPI			% of Categories		
	1965	1970	1974	1965	1970	1974
GS— 1–4	2.11	2.00	1.72	19	22	21.9
GS— 5–8	1.11	1.27	1.31	10	14	16.6
GS— 9–11	0.33	0.45	0.57	3	5	7.2
GS—12–18	0.11	0.27	0.50	1	3	6.4
% Employed	9.0	11.0	12.7	9	11	12.7

SOURCES: *Current Population Reports, Special Studies, The Social and Economic Status of Negroes in the United States, 1970*, Series P-23, No. 38, BLS Report No. 394 (Washington, D.C.: U.S. Department of Commerce/Bureau of the Census, Government Printing Office, July, 1971), Table 55, p. 67. *Current Population Reports, Special Studies, The Social and Economic Status of the Black Population in the United States, 1974*, Series P-23, No. 54 (Washington, D.C.: U.S. Department of Commerce/Bureau of the Census, Government Printing Office, July 1975), Table 52, p. 77.
Note: General Pay Schedule 1–4 is the lowest: GS—12–18 is the highest.

for the various services in 1964 and in 1970. Table 12.11 shows the percentage of blacks in each of the four pay ranks in the federal civil service in 1965, 1970, and 1974 and the OPIs for the same years and pay categories.

In the military organizations at the officer level, there have been very few significant improvements between 1964 and 1970; in the army the percentage of blacks in the ranks of captain down to second lieutenant declined. At the enlisted level, there was notable improvement in the ranks of E-6 to E-9 in all of the services, with the exception of E-9 in the navy. The top two levels of the service hierarchies remained very white, with the exception of a fourfold increase in black lieutenant colonels.

In the federal civil service, blacks remained extremely underrepresented in the highest pay categories, although some improvement occurred between 1965 and 1974. At the rate of progress made between these years, however, blacks will be proportional in the GS-9–11 pay categories in the year 1991 and in the highest seven ranks (GS-12–18) by 1986.

As anyone who watches television can see, blacks have considerably increased their percentage in professional athletics. Five percent of the players in the National Basketball Association in 1954 were black. By 1970 this percentage increased to 56 percent (with an OPI of around 5.0). In 1957 14 percent of the players in the National Football League were black; the percentage was 34 percent by 1971. There was one black baseball player,

Jackie Robinson, in the major leagues in 1947; by 1970 36 percent of major league baseball players were black.

But even this remarkable success poses problems for black people. According to one writer on the subject of the black athlete:

> *Given the functions of sport for the fan, the successful black athlete stimulates black people's individual hopes for eventually competing successfully as* equals *in society. A major consequence, however, is that young blacks are encouraged toward attempts at "making it" through athletic participation, rather than through pursuit of other occupations that hold greater potential for meeting the real political and material needs of both themselves and their people. Athletics, then, stifles the pursuit of rational alternatives by black people.* [11]

The high-salaried and successful athletes, regardless of race, are few in number, and there is little room for the less successful. A few make it, but most are failures in athletics. The same can be said for the field of popular music, another area of appeal and accomplishment for blacks.

Educational Attainment

Educational attainment, as measured by the number of years of schooling (even if nothing rubs off) and the acquisition of those accreditation prizes, the high school diploma and the college degree, may be conceived of as a reward that is unequally distributed. To most people, however, schooling is an unpleasant task rather than a reward, although a college degree does have some prestige value (declining, however, with accreditation inflation). More important, years of schooling is positively, if not perfectly, related to income and to occupational placement.

Tables 12.12 and 12.13 give the percentage of a given race or racial-ethnic group in each educational category (male and female together, twenty-five years of age or older) and the median years of education completed in 1940, 1950, and 1970. Table 12.14 gives the same for certain white ethnic groups (first and second generation only), except that data for 1940 is not available.

All of the groups listed in these tables have increased the percentages of their members graduating from high school and college and reduced the percentage of their members in the category of eight years of schooling or less. The most remarkable change is the increase of college degrees among Chinese-Americans. In the thirty years between 1940 and 1970, the percentage of Chinese with college degrees increased eight and one-half times (853 percent); by 1970 one in four Chinese had a college degree (more than twice that of whites). In the same thirty years, whites increased the percentage of their members with college degrees by two and one-half times (241 percent), blacks by more than three and one-half times (367 percent), Indians by four and three-fourths times (475 percent), and Japanese-Americans by more than three times (320 percent).

When blacks and Indians are compared to whites in 1940 and 1970 at the level of the college degree (four years of college or more), one can see marked

Table 12.12

Years of Education Completed: Percentage of Selected Races and Ethnic Groups
in Each Educational Category, 1940, 1950, 1970

Years of Schooling, 25 Years or Older		White			Black			Indian		
		1940	1950	1970[b]	1940	1950	1970	1940	1950	1970
No school completed		3.0	2.1	0.9	10.0	6.3	3.3	25.2	18.0	7.7
Elementary	1–4	7.7	6.6	2.7	31.3	25.4	11.3	18.3	15.7	7.7
	5–8	46.5	35.9	20.1	41.2	37.2	29.2	37.2	36.3	38.0
High School	1–3	15.6	17.4	19.3	8.4	13.1	24.8	9.4	13.1	23.3
	4	15.0	21.4	33.5	4.1	7.7	21.2	4.9	8.6	22.0
College	1–3	5.8	7.6	11.8	1.8	2.8	5.9	1.9	2.3	7.5
	4 +	4.9	6.4	11.8	1.2	2.0	4.4	0.8	1.3	3.8
Eight years or less		57.2	44.6	22.9	82.5	68.9	43.8	80.7	70.0	43.4
% high school graduates[c]		25.7	35.4	57.1	7.1	12.5	31.4	7.6	12.2	33.3
Median years completed		7.5[a]	9.7	12.2	5.7	6.5[a]	9.8	5.7	6.6[a]	9.8

SOURCES: *Sixteenth Census of the United States, 1940, Population, Characteristics of the Nonwhite Population by Race* (Washington, D.C.: U.S. Department of Commerce/Bureau of the Census, Government Printing Office, 1943), Table 6, p. 34. *Sixteenth Census of the United States, 1940, Population, Nativity and Parentage of the White Population, General Characteristics* (Washington, D.C.: U.S. Department of Commerce/Bureau of the Census, Government Printing Office), Table IX, p. 5. *1950 United States Census of Population, Special Reports, Nonwhite Population by Race* (Washington, D.C.: U.S. Department of Commerce/Bureau of the Census, Government Printing Office, 1953), Tables 9 and 10, pp. 3B–27 and 3B–32. *Subject Reports, Negro Population, 1970 Census of Population* (Washington, D.C.: U.S. Department of Commerce/Bureau of the Census, Government Printing Office), Table 3, p. 20. *Subject Reports, American Indians, 1970 Census of Population* (Washington, D.C.: U.S. Department of Commerce/Bureau of the Census, Government Printing Office, 1973), Table 3, p. 18. *United States Census of Population, Subject Reports, National Origin and Language* (Washington, D.C.: U.S. Department of Commerce/Bureau of the Census, Government Printing Office, 1973), Table 4, p. 21. *1950 United States Census of Population, Nativity and Parentage* (Washington, D.C.: U.S. Department of Commerce/Bureau of the Census, Government Printing Office, 1954), Table 9, p. 3A–57.

[a] Estimated.

[b] 1970 white is native parentage only; statistics for combined foreign and native parentage are not available.

[c] Includes persons younger than 25 years as well as older.

Table 12.13

Years of Education Completed: Percentage of Selected Races and Ethnic Groups in Each Educational Category, 1940, 1950, 1970

Years of Schooling, 25 Years or Older		Chinese			Japanese			Mexican[b]			P. Rican (Cont. U.S.)			P. Rican (Island)		
		1940	1950	1970	1940	1950	1970	1940	1950	1970	1940	1950	1970	1940	1950	1970
No school completed		23.3	18.3	11.1	6.9	3.1	1.8	NA	18.0	9.9	NA	8.0	5.8	NA	33.3	14.4
Elementary	1–4	21.4	14.3	5.1	8.0	5.0	2.4	NA	27.2	15.0	NA	20.6	14.8	NA	31.5	23.4
	5–8	32.4	23.0	16.3	38.8	21.8	14.8	NA	30.3	29.0	NA	45.4	34.3	NA	23.2	24.2
High School	1–3	7.7	8.9	9.7	11.7	10.7	12.2	NA	10.0	17.3	NA	12.2	22.1	NA	4.7	10.9
	4	6.7	13.2	21.2	23.1	39.1	39.3	NA	7.8	19.3	NA	8.6	17.1	NA	3.6	15.0
College	1–3	2.0	5.8	11.0	4.5	9.2	13.6	NA	2.0	6.0	NA	2.7	3.6	NA	1.6	6.0
	4+	3.0	9.0	25.6	5.0	7.3	16.0	NA	1.3	3.4	NA	2.4	2.3	NA	1.8	6.1

Eight years or less	77.1	55.6	32.5	53.7	29.9	19.0	NA	75.5	53.9	NA	74.0	54.9	NA	88.0	62.0
% high school graduates[c]	11.7	28.0	57.8	32.6	55.6	68.8	NA	11.1	28.7	NA	13.7	23.0	NA	7.0	27.1
Median years completed	5.5	7.5[a]	12.4	8.7	11.5[a]	12.5	NA	5.4	8.6	NA	NA	8.6	NA	3.7	6.9

SOURCES: Sixteenth Census of the United States, 1940, Population, Characteristics of the Nonwhite Population by Race (Washington, D.C.: U.S. Department of Commerce/Bureau of the Census, Government Printing Office, 1943), Table 6, p. 34. 1950 United States Census of Population, Special Reports, Nonwhite Population by Race (Washington, D.C.: U.S. Department of Commerce/Bureau of the Census, Government Printing Office, 1953), Tables 11 and 12, pp. 3B–37 and 3B–42. 1950 United States Census of Population, Special Reports, Persons of Spanish Surname (Washington, D.C.: U.S. Department of Commerce/Bureau of the Census, Government Printing Office, 1953), Table 3, p. 3C–16. 1950 Census of Population, Volume II, Characteristics of the Population, Parts 51–54, Territories and Possessions (Washington, D.C.: U.S. Department of Commerce/Bureau of the Census, Government Printing Office, 1953), Table 16, p. 53–32. 1950 Census of Population, Puerto Ricans in Continental United States, P-E, No. 3D (Washington, D.C.: U.S. Department of Commerce/Bureau of the Census, Government Printing Office, 1953), Table 4, p. 3D–13. Subject Reports, Japanese, Chinese, and Filipinos in the United States, 1970 Census (Washington, D.C.: U.S. Department of Commerce/Bureau of the Census, Government Printing Office, 1973), Tables 3 and 18, pp. 9 and 68. Subject Reports, Persons of Spanish Surname, 1970 Census of Population (Washington, D.C.: U.S. Department of Commerce/Bureau of the Census, Government Printing Office, 1973), Table 4, p. 32, "Persons of Mexican Origin." Volume I, Characteristics of the Population, Part 53, Puerto Rico, 1970 Census of Population (Washington, D.C.: U.S. Department of Commerce/Bureau of the Census, Government Printing Office, June 1973), Table 38, p. 53–188. 1970 Census of Population, Puerto Ricans in the United States (Washington, D.C.: U.S. Department of Commerce/Bureau of the Census, Government Printing Office, 1973), Table 4, p. 34.

NA = not available.

[a] Estimated.

[b] Figures for Mexicans in 1950 limited to five southwestern states. Figures for Mexicans in 1970 from total U.S.

[c] Includes persons younger than 25 years as well as older.

Table 12.14

Years of Education Completed: Percentage of Selected White Ethnic Groups in Each Educational Category, 1950 and 1970

Years of Schooling, 25 Years or Older	Irish 1950	Irish 1970	Italian 1950	Italian 1970	Polish 1950	Polish 1970	Swedish 1950	Swedish 1970	German 1950	German 1970	British 1950	British 1970	Russian[a] 1950	Russian[a] 1970
No school completed	0.7	0.5	7.8	3.9	7.2	3.8	0.5	0.4	0.7	0.7	0.6	0.5	7.9	4.1
Elementary 1–4	4.7	1.7	14.0	6.3	11.9	4.5	3.5	1.3	6.6	2.8	4.3	1.3	7.7	2.9
5–8	42.3	25.2	38.5	28.9	40.0	30.7	44.7	29.2	53.6	37.7	37.0	20.4	27.9	19.1
High School 1–3	17.1	17.9	17.6	20.8	16.8	19.6	15.5	16.7	13.7	16.5	17.7	17.8	13.5	13.9
4	22.7	33.8	16.4	28.3	16.4	25.8	22.0	30.5	15.7	25.6	24.4	35.1	25.5	30.4
College 1–3	6.4	10.2	2.8	5.8	3.8	7.1	7.9	12.0	5.0	8.9	8.4	12.9	7.8	12.2
4+	6.1	10.6	2.7	5.8	3.8	8.4	5.9	9.8	4.5	7.8	7.6	11.9	10.2	17.3
Eight years or less	47.7	27.4	60.3	39.1	59.1	39.0	48.7	30.9	60.9	41.2	41.9	22.2	43.5	26.1
% high school graduates[b]	35.2	54.6	21.9	39.9	24.0	41.3	35.8	52.3	25.2	42.3	40.4	59.9	43.5	60.0

SOURCES: 1950 United States Census of Population, Nativity and Parentage (Washington, D.C.: U.S. Department of Commerce/Bureau of the Census, Government Printing Office, 1954), Table 20, pp. 3A–136 to 3A–139, 3A–142 to 3A–147, 3A–152 to 3A–155. 1970 Census of Population, Subject Reports, National Origin and Language (Washington, D.C.: U.S. Department of Commerce/Bureau of the Census, Government Printing Office, June 1973), Table 12, pp. 99, 100, 102, 106, 107, 112, 155.

[a] Predominantly Russian Jews.

[b] Includes persons younger than 25 years as well as older.

improvement. In 1940 whites had 4.08 times as many college graduates as blacks, but only 2.68 times as many in 1970. In 1940 there were 6.12 times more whites with a college degree than Indians, but this declined to only 3.11 times as many in 1970.

A major problem in making comparisons is the years that are selected. Comparing 1940 with 1970 will give a different rate of change than comparing 1960 with 1970, since many groups improved their circumstances between 1940 and 1960. Moreover, projections into the future will differ depending on the years compared. Nevertheless, using the rate of change between 1950 and 1970, since data on several groups are available in these years, when will certain ethnic groups approach equality with whites in terms of college degrees? The answer seems to be never, unless the percentage of whites obtaining a degree drops dramatically and a far greater percentage of minority groups obtain college degrees. Between 1950 and 1970, the white race increased the percentage of its members with a college degree by 5.4 percent (from 6.4 percent of all whites in 1950 to 11.8 percent in 1970). In the same twenty-year period, blacks increased their percentage of degree holders by 2.4 percent (from 2.0 to 4.4), Indians by 2.5 percent (from 1.3 to 3.8), Mexicans by 2.1 percent (from 1.3 to 3.4), and mainland Puerto Ricans lost ground (− 0.1 percent). At this rate of change, blacks in the year 2030 will have the same percentage of members with a college degree as whites did in 1970. At the same future date Indians will have 11.3 percent with a degree, Mexicans, 9.7 percent and mainland Puerto Ricans will be about the same as they were in 1970. Whites, however, will have increased the percentage of members with a college education to 28.0 percent by the year 2030. Moreover, the ratio of whites to each of these groups, with the exception of Puerto Ricans, will have declined only slightly. In 1970 whites had 2.68 times as many college degrees as blacks; in 2030 whites will have 2.37 times as many college degrees as blacks. Similarly, the white-Indian ratio in 1970 was 3.11/1 and in 2030 it will be 2.48/1; the white-Mexican ratio in 1970 was 3.11/1 and will be 2.89/1 in 2030. For the hypothetically stagnant Puerto Ricans in the continental United States, the ratio will increase from 4.95/1 to 12.17/1.

Of course this projection is hypothetical. Changes for each of the groups relative to whites can increase quite rapidly in the very near future. But this is the point of the projection. Mexicans, blacks, Indians, and Puerto Ricans will have to increase the percentage of members in the college education category dramatically if they are to achieve equality with whites even at the beginning of the twenty-first century.

At the lowest level of educational attainment—eight years of schooling or less—the situation for blacks, Mexicans, Puerto Ricans and Indians compared to whites is just as depressing. In 1940 only 1.44 times as many blacks as whites had eight years of schooling or less. By 1970 twice as many blacks were in this category (1.91). Figures for Indians were 1.41 in 1940 and 1.90 in 1970. In 1950 Mexican-Americans had 1.69 times more members in this educational category than whites did; by 1970 there were 2.35 times as many Mexican-Americans in this category. Similarly, in 1950 there were 1.66 times as many Puerto Ricans as whites with eight years or less of education; this figure increased to 2.4 times as many in 1970. With the exception of the Puerto Ricans, the disadvantaged groups are slightly improving their education position at the higher levels in relation to whites, but all four of the groups are falling behind at the lowest level of education.

If one compares the educational attainment of whites in general in 1970 (Table 12.12) with years of schooling of specific white ethnic groups in the same year (Table 12.14), a peculiarity is found. With the exception of those ethnic groups from Britain and from Russia, the percentage of the white ethnics with a high school degree is below that of whites as a whole. Similarly, with the exception of Swedes and white ethnic groups from Russia and Britain, the white ethnics have a lower percentage of college degree holders than whites in general. One reason for this paradox is the fact that in 1970 the data for whites, collectively, were limited to *native* whites of *native* parentage (Table 12.12) while data for the specific groups excluded this category, including only foreign born of foreign parentage and native born of foreign parentage (Table 12.14). Taking Table 12.14 by itself, however, one finds that the data does indicate the relatively superior educational attainment of Russian Jews, British, and Swedes in contrast to the other white ethnic groups.*

Family Income Distribution

Census data about income are available for families classified by the ethnic or racial status of the head of the household. However, in its infinite wisdom, the Census Bureau makes it difficult to make comparisons between groups in a given year or between years. In some years and in some groups, family income data are missing or individual income is given only for males. In some cases, the income categories used (for example, $1,000 to $1,999) are different from those used in other years or for other groups. For the races and the racial-ethnic groups, income data for families are available for 1959 and 1969 (censuses of 1960 and 1970). Table 12.15 gives the percentage of all of the families in particular races and racial-ethnic groups in each income category in 1959 and 1969. Data for families with a head of

*Instead of using the categories of foreign born of foreign parentage, native born of foreign parentage, or native born of native parentage, in 1972 the Census Bureau simply asked heads of households, "What is your ethnic origin?" It did not matter how long a person or family had been in this country. Educational data were then ascertained. Even though the technique for ascertaining ethnic group membership differed, the information indicated a similar rank order of educational attainment: Russian Jews, British, German, and then Irish and Italian at about the same level. ("Characteristics of the Population by Ethnic Origin: March, 1972 and 1971," Current Population Reports, Population Characteristics, Series P-20, No. 249 [Washington, D.C.: U.S. Department of Commerce/Bureau of the Census], pp. 1, 23.)

Mexican origin are not available for 1959, nor for median family income in 1959 for all groups except the white race. In 1974 family income data for the year 1973 were collected for whites, blacks, and Mexican-Americans. Percentages in each income category for 1959 and 1969 are reproduced along with the 1973 information in Table 12.16.

Again, the significant improvement of the stratification position of the Japanese- and Chinese-Americans must be noted. By 1959 the percentage of Japanese and Chinese families making $15,000 or more was greater than that of whites, and this relationship continued to exist in 1969. At the poverty level in 1959, both the Chinese- and the Japanese-Americans had a lower percentage of families with an income of $3,000 or less than the white race did. In 1969 the Chinese-Americans slipped somewhat; that year they had a slightly higher percentage of poor families (10.3 percent) than the whites did (9.0 percent). Japanese-Americans, however, continued to have a smaller percentage in that category than the whites. (6.4 percent compared to 9.0 percent).

From 1959 to 1969, blacks, Indians, and Puerto Ricans not only failed to reduce their percentage of families in poverty relative to whites, but they lost ground. In 1959 2.7 times more black families were in poverty than whites, but by 1969 3.3 times more black families than whites were below the poverty line. Similarly, 2.9 times as many Indian families as white families were in poverty in 1959; this increased to 2.7 times as many by 1969. And while mainland Puerto Ricans had only 1.7 times as many families in poverty as whites in 1959, by 1969 they had 3.3 times more poor families. For these groups, the initial "battles" in the "war on poverty" were won by the "enemy." Blacks, for example, had a higher percentage in poverty relative to whites in 1973 than they did in 1959.

Although no data are available for heads of families of Mexican origin in 1959, in 1969 there were 2.7 times as many Mexican-American families as white families in poverty, a ratio that is better than that for the other disadvantaged groups. By 1973 this ratio had been slightly reduced (2.3 times as many Mexican-American families as whites if the poverty base is $4,000 a year or less and 2.1 times if a base of $5,000 a year or less is used).

At the highest level of family income—$15,000 a year or more—blacks, Indians, Mexican-Americans, and Puerto Ricans have made considerable progress in reducing the gap between themselves and whites as a whole. In 1959 10.0 times as many white families as black families received an income of $15,000 or more, 7.1 times as many white families as Indian families, and 7.1 times as many white families as Puerto Rican families. By 1969 only 2.6 times as many white families as blacks received this income, 2.9 times as many white families as Indian families, and 3.3 times as many white families as Puerto Rican families. Since Mexican-Americans have been similar to the other three groups according to other indicators of stratification, in the absence of 1959 data it can be assumed that the ratio of Mexican families to white families at this income level was also reduced by 1969. By

Table 12.15

Family Income: Percentage of Families in Each Income Category by Selected Races and Ethnic Groups, 1959 and 1969

Income Category	White		Black		Indian		Chinese		Japanese		Mexican		P. Rican (Cont. U.S.)		P. Rican (Island)	
	1959	1969	1959	1969	1959	1969	1959	1969	1959	1969	1959	1969	1959	1969	1959	1969
Less than $1,000	4.5	2.1	15.8	6.5	22.5	7.9	3.3	2.5	3.1	2.1	NA	4.2	6.7	7.0	42.4	21.4
$1,000 to 2,999	14.1	6.8	33.6	17.1	31.8	17.4	12.7	5.8	8.1	4.5	NA	12.0	25.3	11.9	36.4	27.9
$3,000 to 4,999	20.0	9.2	25.2	17.6	21.4	17.6	21.5	9.2	17.5	5.9	NA	16.9	35.2	19.6	11.4	19.7
$5,000 to 6,999	23.9	11.9	14.0	16.1	13.0	16.2	20.8	11.5	23.1	7.3	NA	17.2	19.2	19.8	7.2	20.7
$7,000 to 9,999	21.2	21.7	8.0	18.8	7.7	18.4	20.1	17.4	25.9	15.4	NA	22.7	9.9	20.2		
$10,000 to 14,999	11.2	28.0	2.9	16.1	2.9	15.4	14.4	25.1	16.0	29.2	NA	19.0	3.1	15.3	1.4	6.3
$15,000 or more	5.0	20.3	0.5	7.8	0.7	7.0	7.2	28.5	6.3	35.6	NA	7.9	0.7	6.1	0.7	4.0

a. 15,000 to 24,999	3.6	15.9	NA	6.9	NA	6.0	NA	21.5	NA	28.3	NA	6.9	NA	5.3	NA	3.1
b. 25,000 or more	1.4	4.4	NA	0.9	NA	1.0	NA	7.0	NA	7.3	NA	1.0	NA	0.8	NA	0.9
% below poverty line	18.6	9.0	49.4	29.9	54.3	33.3	16.0	10.3	11.2	6.4	24.5	32.0	27.1	78.8	60.3
Median	5893	9977	NA	6063	NA	5832	NA	10,610	NA	12,515	NA	6962	NA	6115	NA	3063

SOURCES: *United States Census of Population, 1960, Nonwhite Population by Race,* (Washington, D.C.: U.S. Department of Commerce/Bureau of the Census, Government Printing Office, 1963) Table 14, p. 25; Table 15, p. 26; Table 16, p. 27; Table 17, p. 28. *United States Census of Population, 1960, General Social and Economic Characteristics* (Washington, D.C.: U.S. Department of Commerce/Bureau of the Census, Government Printing Office, 1963) Table 95, p. 225. *Volume I, Characteristics of the Population, Part 53, Puerto Rico, 1970 Census of Population* (Washington, D.C.: U.S. Department of Commerce/Bureau of the Census, Government Printing Office, 1973) Table 40, p. 53–190. *1970 Census of the Population, Puerto Ricans in the United States* (Washington, D.C.: U.S. Department of Commerce/Bureau of the Census, Government Printing Office, 1973) Table 5, p. 26. *Subject Reports, Source and Structure of Family Income, 1970 Census of Population* (Washington, D.C.: U.S. Department of Commerce/Bureau of the Census, Government Printing Office, January 1973), Table 1, p. 4. *Subject Reports, Negro Population, 1970 Census of Population* (Washington, D.C.: U.S. Department of Commerce/ Bureau of the Census, Government Printing Office, 1973), Table 9, p. 143. *Subject Reports, American Indians, 1970 Census of Population* (Washington, D.C.: U.S. Department of Commerce/Bureau of the Census, Government Printing Office, 1973), Table 9, p. 120. *Subject Reports, Japanese, Chinese, and Filipinos in the United States, 1970 Census of Population* (Washington, D.C.: U.S. Department of Commerce/Bureau of the Census, Government Printing Office, 1973), Tables 9 and 24, pp. 42 and 101. *Subject Reports, Persons of Spanish Origin, 1970 Census of Population* (Washington, D.C.: U.S. Department of Commerce/Bureau of the Census, 1973), Table 10, p. 121, "Head of Mexican Origin." *United States Census of Population, 1960, Puerto Ricans in the United States* (Washington, D.C.: U.S. Department of Commerce/Bureau of the Census, Government Printing Office, 1963), Table 4, p. 25.

NA = not available.

Note: 1959 poverty line is $3,000; 1969 poverty line is $3,388.

393

Table 12.16

Family Income, 1959, 1969, 1974: Percentage of Families in Each Income Category—
White, Black, and Mexican-American

Income Category	White			Black			Mexican-American		
	1959	1969	1974	1959	1969	1974	1959	1969	1974
Less than $3,000	18.6	8.9	4.0	49.4	23.6	14.0	NA	16.2	10.5
$3,000 to 4,999	20.0	9.2	7.0	25.2	17.6	17.0	NA	16.9	12.8
$5,000 to 6,999	23.9	11.9	88.0	14.0	16.1	14.0	NA	17.2	15.5
$7,000 to 9,999	21.2	21.7	14.0	8.0	18.8	17.0	NA	22.7	21.9
$10,000 to 14,999	11.2	28.0	26.0	2.9	16.1	19.0	NA	19.0	23.4
$15,000 or more	5.0	20.3	42.0	0.5	7.8	19.0	NA	7.9	25.8
a. 15,000 to 24,999	3.6	15.9	NA	NA	6.9	NA	NA	6.9	13.9
b. 25,000 or more	1.4	4.4	NA	NA	0.9	NA	NA	1.0	1.9
% below poverty line	18.6	9.0	7.0	49.4	29.9	23.0	NA	24.4	16.4

SOURCES: *United States Census of Population, 1960, Nonwhite Population by Race* (Washington, D.C.: U.S. Department of Commerce/Bureau of the Census, Government Printing Office, 1963), Table 14, p. 25. *United States Census of Population, 1960, General Social and Economic Characteristics* (Washington, D.C.: U.S. Department of Commerce/Bureau of the Census, Government Printing Office, 1963), Table 95, p. 225. *Subject Reports, Persons of Spanish Origin, 1970 Census of Population* (Washington, D.C.: U.S. Department of Commerce/Bureau of the Census, Government Printing Office, 1973), Table 10, p. 121. *Subject Reports, Negro Population, 1970 Census of Population* (Washington, D.C.: U.S. Department of Commerce/Bureau of the Census, Government Printing Office, 1973), Table 9, p. 143. *Subject Reports, Sources and Structure of Family Income, 1970 Census of Population* (Washington, D.C.: U.S. Department of Commerce/Bureau of the Census, Government Printing Office, 1973), Table 1, p. 4. *Current Population Reports, Population Characteristics, Persons of Spanish Origin in the United States,* Series P-20, No. 280 (Washington, D.C.: U.S. Department of Commerce/Bureau of the Census, Government Printing Office, April 1975), Table 14, p. 33, "Mexican Origin." *Current Population Reports, The Social and Economic Status of the Black Population in the United States,* Special Studies, Series P-23, No. 54 (Washington, D.C.: U.S. Department of Commerce/Bureau of the Census, Government Printing Office, July 1975), Table 11, p. 27.

NOTE: 1959 poverty line is $3,000; 1969 poverty line is $3,388. 1974 poverty line is $4,000.

NA = not available.

the end of 1973, affluent white families exceeded affluent Mexican families by only 1.6 times, a drop from 1969, when the ratio was 2.6 to 1.

Another aspect of black-white inequality in terms of family income is the relatively stable relationship of black median family income as a percentage of white median family income between 1947 and 1974. Table 12.17 gives the median income of nonwhite families as a percentage of white

Table 12.17

Median Income of Nonwhite and Black Families as a Percentage
of White Median Income, 1947–1974

Year	% of White	Year	% of White
1947	51	1960	55
1948	53	1961	53
1949	51	1962	53
1950	54	1963	53
1951	53	1964	56 (54)
1952	57	1965	55 (54)
1953	56	1966	60 (58)
1954	56	1967	62 (59)
1955	55	1968	63 (60)
1956	53	1969	63 (61)
1957	54	1970	64 (61)
1958	51	1974	.. (58)
1959	52		

SOURCES: *Special Studies, The Social and Economic Status of Negroes in the United States, 1970, Current Population Reports,* Series P-23, No. 38 (Washington, D.C.: U.S. Department of Commerce/Bureau of the Census, Government Printing Office), Table 16, p. 25. U.S. Department of Labor, *The Negroes in the United States: Their Economic and Social Situation,* Bulletin No. 1511 (Washington, D.C.: U.S. Department of Labor, Government Printing Office, 1966), Table III, A-1, p. 138. *Current Population Reports, The Social and Economic Status of the Black Population in the United States, 1974,* Series P-23, No. 54 (Washington, D.C.: U.S. Department of Commerce/ Bureau of the Census, Government Printing Office, July 1975), Table 11, p. 27.

NOTE: Nonwhite percent of white available only between 1947 and 1963. From 1964 to 1970, black percentage of white is given in parentheses. Only black percentage of white is available for 1974.

median family income annually from 1947 to 1963. From 1964 to 1970 both nonwhite and black percentages are given. The black percentage of white median income between 1947 and 1963 can be estimated by subtracting two to three percentage points from the nonwhite figures for these years. Very little progress has been made between the end of World War II and the present in reducing the black-white inequality in terms of this indicator, despite all of the activity of the government and the social movements. At the rate of change in the twenty-year period from 1949 (a low point) to 1969 (a high point), equality between white and black in the form of median family income will not exist until around 2032. But the trend in the first half of the 1970s suggests that perhaps no such improvement will take place.

Data on family income of white ethnic groups of European descent are not available for 1959; however, 1969 information is provided in Table 12.18 for certain selected groups limited to first-generation (foreign born) and second-generation (native born with one or both parents being foreign born) heads of families. The total median family income and the total percentage

Table 12.18

Percentage of Families in Each Income Category by Selected White Ethnic Groups, 1969

Income Category	Irish	Italian	Polish	Swedish	German	British	Russian[a]
Less than $1,000	1.4	1.7	1.3	1.5	2.1	1.6	1.5
$1,000 to 2,999	5.7	5.4	4.8	8.9	10.0	6.5	5.4
$3,000 to 4,999	8.2	6.9	6.4	11.8	12.3	9.6	6.7
$5,000 to 6,999	9.2	9.2	8.4	10.5	11.2	9.5	7.5
$7,000 to 9,999	16.8	20.0	18.3	17.1	17.2	16.7	13.8
$10,000 to 14,999	28.6	30.7	30.4	24.9	24.5	27.2	23.9
$15,000 or more	30.0	26.2	30.4	25.3	22.6	28.9	41.2
a. 15,000 to 24,999	23.4	20.9	23.1	19.5	17.1	21.9	25.0
b. 25,000 or more	6.6	5.3	7.3	5.8	5.5	7.0	16.2
Median income — native born	11,776	11,857	12,275	10,568	9,353	11,374	14,281
Median income — foreign born	10,112	8,397	9,631	6,931	10,064	10,347	8,571
% in poverty —native born	5.1	4.5	3.8	6.2	8.4	5.4	3.8
% in poverty —foreign born	7.0	10.9	8.5	10.4	8.6	7.4	9.9

Source: *1970 Census of Population, Subject Reports, National Origin and Language* (Washington, D.C.: U.S. Department of Commerce/Bureau of the Census, Government Printing Office, June 1973), Table 14, pp. 151, 152, 154, 158, 159, 164, 167.

[a] Predominantly Russian Jews.

in poverty were not provided by the Census Bureau; this information was subdivided by generations. Table 12.19 gives 1971 family income for the same groups (with the exception of the Swedes, for whom data were not available), but in this year ethnic identification was derived by asking the heads of households, "What is your origin or descent?" Table 12.18, therefore, is not limited to first and second generations. Because of inflation, the years 1969 and 1971 are not exactly comparable, but the findings are quite similar.

In 1969, with the exception of German families, families headed by native-born persons in all of the selected white ethnic groups had a higher median family income than whites ($9,977). All of these white ethnic groups (with either foreign- or native-born heads of families) also exceeded the white percentage of families making $15,000 to $24,999 (white: 15.9 percent), and $25,000 or more (white: 4.4 percent). Russian Jews (first and second generation) are easily the most successful group in America in terms of family income. This is an extreme change from the impoverished status of the

Table 12.19

Percentage of Families in Each Income Category by Selected White Ethnic Groups, 1971: All Generations

Income Category	Irish	Italian	Polish	German	British	Russian[a]
Less than $1,000	1.1	1.0	0.9	1.0	1.0	0.9
$1,000 to 2,999	6.0	3.8	3.8	4.8	4.8	3.7
$3,000 to 4,999	8.9	7.4	7.6	9.0	9.3	5.8
$5,000 to 6,999	11.4	9.1	7.8	10.7	10.1	6.7
$7,000 to 9,999	16.5	18.6	16.8	18.9	17.5	14.4
$10,000 to 14,999	29.4	31.1	30.3	28.5	27.9	23.9
$15,000 or more	26.8	29.0	32.7	27.1	29.5	44.5
a. 15,000 to 24,999	20.9	23.7	27.1	21.5	22.3	29.2
b. 25,000 or more	5.9	5.3	5.6	5.6	7.2	15.3
Median Family $	11,060	11,646	12,182	10,977	11,345	13,929

SOURCE: *Current Population Reports, Characteristics of the Population by Ethnic Origin: March 1972 and 1971*, Series P-20, No. 249 (Washington, D.C.: U.S. Department of Commerce/Bureau of the Census, Government Printing Office, April 1973), Table 9, p. 26.

NOTE: Ethnic origin was ascertained by the answer to the question "What is your origin or descent?"

[a] Predominantly Jews.

Eastern European Jews around the turn of the century. The high percentage of Polish families with a native-born head making $15,000 to $24,999 or $25,000 or more counters the "dumb Polack" jokes so popular in recent years. Polish-Americans are exceeded only by second-generation Jewish families and Japanese-Americans at these high levels of family income.

Other data show the greater income success of Jews and Catholic ethnic groups as opposed to Protestant. In 1975 the National Opinion Research Center sampled eighteen thousand Americans of several generations. A comparison of the annual average (mean) income of individuals of different ethnic and religious groups indicates the decline of the WASP (as a whole): Jews—$13,340; Irish Catholics—$12,426; Italian Catholics—$11,748; German Catholics—$11,632; Polish Catholics—$11,298; and Episcopalians—$11,032. The poorest religious groups are the white Baptists ($8,693) and the Irish Protestants ($9,147). The study determined that Jews and Irish Catholics are now the wealthiest and most educated; they are "more successful than the American Protestants which constitute the host culture." The study added that "they [Catholics] have the best education and best income of any gentile group in the country. Still, in cities in the North, British Protestants have a higher rate of occupational mobility than do Irish Catholics—they get higher prestige jobs than do Irish Catholics with the same education."[12] For Italian Catholics, the disparity is even greater. The study concluded with the inference that discrimination at the upper echelons of the occupational strata still exists.

Ethnic and Racial Stratification: A Rank Order

Ethnic groups and races in the United States may be ranked according to a number of stratification indexes and on the average. Table 12.20 ranks fourteen ethnic groups and races in 1950 according to percentage of members in white-collar occupations; percentage of members in professional, managerial, and proprietor occupations (part of white collar but excludes clerical and sales personnel); percentage of members with a high school degree, and percentage of members with a college degree. From these rankings an average overall rank is determined for each group. In 1970 these same indicators are used, along with the percentage of families with incomes of $25,000 or more (income data not available for 1950), and the average rank of each group is again determined.

Some may object to the ranking of groups. One objection might be that we are all Americans and that ranking is invidious and divisive as well as embarrassing for certain groups. Ignoring group differences, however, will not make them go away. Although every group contains successful members, average members, and unsuccessful members, the groups do not contain equal proportions of these members. Groups vary according to differences in competitive ability (organization, values, technology, leadership) and according to the extent of discrimination imposed upon them. Another

Table 12.20

Rank Order of Ethnic Groups and Races: Selected Indexes

1950 Group	White Collar	Prof. & Man.	High School	College	Average or Overall Rank	1970 Group	White Collar	Prof. & Man.	High School	College	$25,000 Plus	Average or Overall Rank
1. Russian[a]	1	1	2	1	1.25	1. Russian[a]	1	1	2	2	1	1.40
2. British	2	3	3	3	2.75	2. Chinese	4	2	4	1	4	2.80
3. Chinese	4	2	7	2	3.75	3. British	2	3	3	4	5	3.40
4. Swedish	5	4	4	7	5.00	4. Japanese	6	6	1	3	2	3.60
5. Irish	3	5	6	6	5.00	5. Irish	3	5	6	6	6	5.20
6. White[b]	6	7	5	5	5.75	6. Swedish	5	4	7	7	7	6.33
7. Japanese	10	10	1	4	6.25	7. White[b]	8	8	5	5	10	7.20
8. German	7	6	8	8	7.25	8. Polish	9	9	9	8	3	7.60
9. Polish	8	8	9	9	8.50	9. German	7	7	8	9	8	7.80
10. Italian	9	9	10	10	9.50	10. Italian	10	10	10	10	9	9.80
11. P. Rican[c]	11	11	11	11	11.00	11. Indian	12	11	11	12	12	11.60
12. Black	13	13	12	12	12.50	12. Mexican	11	12	13	13	11	12.00
13. Mexican	12	12	14	13	12.75	13. Black	14	13	12	11	13	12.60
14. Indian	14	14	13	13	13.50	14. P. Rican[c]	13	14	14	14	14	13.80

SOURCE: Compiled from the following previous tables: 12.1, 12.2, 12.7, 12.9, 12.12, 12.13, 12.14, 12.15, 12.18, and 12.19.

[a] Predominantly Russian Jews.

[b] "White" is a race with ethnic subdivisions and is included here along with some of the subdivisions since many people use this term.

[c] Mainland.

objection could be the indicators themselves. Certainly, making $25,000 or more a year is more important than having a high school diploma, but the indicators are not weighted according to significance. However, the use of "weighting" or of other indicators will produce only a few changes in relative positions.*

Probably the most interesting aspect of the table is the relatively minor change between 1950 and 1970. Most of the groups moved up or down one position or remained in the same position, with the exceptions of the Japanese, who moved from seventh to fourth place; the Indians, who moved from last to eleventh place; and the Puerto Ricans (mainland United States), who dropped from eleventh to last place.

A Further Note on Indian Stratification

As can be seen in the various tables, there is considerable diversity within the white race category. Although the differences are not as great, there are also variations within the Indian race. Tables 12.21 and 12.22 give the median family income and the percentage of families in poverty for selected Indian groups and selected Indian reservations. According to these indicators, the eastern Indian groups—Mohawk, Oneida, and Seneca—are the most successful. Their median family income is highest and the percentage of their families below the poverty line is lowest. Even the most successful of the Indian ethnics, however, were below the white median family income in 1969 ($9,977) and had a greater percentage of families in poverty than the whites did (9.0 percent). The Navajo, who have the most impoverished reservations, are poorest among Indians.

In 1973 the U.S. Commission on Civil Rights issued the Southwestern Indian Report, which was primarily about the Navajo but also covered other groups in the Southwest (such as the Zuni, Hopi, and Apache). The unemployment rate for Indians was 40 percent in New Mexico and between 50 and 60 percent in Arizona. The median income of persons was $3,000 below the general population of New Mexico and $4,500 below the median income of the general population in Arizona. The infant mortality rate in the area served by the Albuquerque Indian Health Service was 37.1 per 1,000, compared to 22.4 per 1,000 for the nation as a whole. The tuberculosis rate was 8 times higher than the average for the United States; death from overuse of alcohol was 6.5 times higher than the national average; and the suicide rate was twice as high.[13]

In September 1975 the U.S. Commission on Civil Rights reported that the Navajo are suffering "not only [from] a shocking and disgraceful condition of neglect, but [from] an alarming acceptance of the status quo emanating from key federal programs that should be providing the means for Navajo

---

*If the income indicator in 1970 is left out to make the categories between the time periods constant the Germans and the Poles in 1970 change places, and blacks move from thirteenth place to tie with the Mexicans for twelfth.

Table 12.21

Median Family Income and Percentage of Families Below the Poverty Line
of Selected Indian Ethnic Groups, 1970: Rank Order by Median Family Income

Selected Indian Ethnic Groups	Median Family Income	Percentage of Families Below Poverty Level
1. Mohawk	$9,064	17.8
2. Oneida	8,183	19.2
3. Seneca	7,580	18.7
4. Zuni	6,401	35.6
5. Cherokee	6,329	26.5
6. Creek, Alabama, Coushatta	6,248	27.6
7. Menominee	6,124	27.9
8. Yakima	6,123	32.4
9. Comanche	6,102	28.7
10. Seminole	5,956	29.7
11. Chickasaw	5,928	20.3
12. Chippewa	5,928	33.0
13. Choctow and Houma	5,925	30.2
14. Hopi	5,644	41.6
15. Blackfeet	5,588	33.9
16. Cheyenne	5,567	38.0
17. Kiowa	5,285	38.0
18. Lumbee	5,157	37.3
19. Apache	5,106	41.4
20. Ute	4,761	32.4
21. Sioux, Dakota	4,734	44.2
22. Navajo	3,434	58.2

SOURCE: See Table 12.22.

self-development."[14] Navajo per capita income was only one-fourth the
national average, infant mortality was twice as high as in the nation as a
whole, education was one-half the national median in terms of years of
schooling completed, and unemployment was 10 times higher than the
national rate.[15]

Most of the Indian groups, particularly the largest—the Navajo—
continue to have the highest percentage of families in poverty. Although the
national average for Indian families in poverty in 1969 was 33 percent, it
can be seen from Tables 12.21 and 12.22 that several major tribes and many
reservations in 1970 exceeded this percentage.

DISCRIMINATION

Until 1960, discrimination was relatively easy to ascertain. As described in
previous chapters, discriminatory laws were found at the local, state, and
federal levels. Organizations often had discriminatory rules or procedures

Table 12.22

Median Family Income and Percentage of Families Below the Poverty Line
of Selected Reservations, 1970: Rank Order by Median Family Income

Reservations	Median Family Income	Percentage of Families Below Poverty Level
1. Menominee, Wisconsin	$5,729	38.0
2. Zuni, New Mexico	5,291	56.7
3. Northern Cheyenne, Montana	5,278	39.8
4. Yakima, Washington	5,167	45.5
5. Flathead, Montana	5,045	32.4
6. Ft. Apache, Arizona	4,343	53.3
7. Blackfeet, Montana	4,258	47.8
8. Cherokee, No. Carolina	4,125	52.2
9. Pine Ridge, So. Dakota	3,912	54.3
10. Cheyenne River, So. Dakota	3,802	54.8
11. Standing Rock, No. & So. Dakota	3,652	58.3
12. Hopi, Arizona	3,454	61.8
13. Rosebud, So. Dakota	3,423	62.9
14. Papago, Arizona	2,500	78.1
15. Joint Use Area (Navajo & Hopi), Arizona	2,052	79.3

SOURCE: *Subject Reports, American Indians, 1970 Census of Population* (Washington, D.C.: U.S. Department of Commerce, Bureau of the Census, 1973), Table 14, pp. 171–77.

in their policy manuals and constitutions. Much of the discrimination, particularly against racial-ethnic groups, was normative, and it did not take too much effort to get members of the dominant group to admit to such norms. And when minority individuals challenged or violated the norms, they met readily observable enforcement of the norms.

Since the 1960s, and particularly in the 1970s, ascertaining discrimination has been extremely difficult in most cases. The problem is intensified by the difficulty of defining discrimination. To many social scientists and government officials, the mere existence of inequality by race or ethnicity, the presence of residential segregation, or the existence of only a few minority members in some organization or occupation is enough to show the existence of discrimination. Discrimination is automatically inferred as the cause of such phenomena, even though there may be other causes. From this perspective, any policy, program, or practice that has a disproportionately negative impact on ethnic groups or races is discriminatory. In June 1976 in Colorado, for example, a state advisory committee to the U.S. Commission on Civil Rights argued that the Colorado bar examination, a test administered to prospective lawyers by the Colorado Supreme Court, was discriminatory. The committee argued that since a smaller percentage of minorities than Anglos passed the test the examination "has a disparate and therefore discriminatory effect on minority applicants."[16] According to this logic, if the test has a disparate effect, then it must be discriminatory.

It is doubtful that the committee meant that the test discriminated against all minorities. A "disparate effect" means discrimination not against all minorities but only against certain "designated" minorities— generally, the four most disadvantaged groups in America as indicated by the stratification indexes: blacks, Indians, Mexicans, and Puerto Ricans. The "disparate treatment" of other groups, including Americans of British descent or Jewish Americans, as a result of affirmative action programs does not indicate that discrimination has occurred. Jews, British, Germans, Irish, and many others are no longer minorities in the eyes of the bureaucrats. An interesting footnote to the Colorado bar exam incident is that in the same month and year a male Italian-American attempted to enter the University of Colorado law school with the preferential treatment afforded to a "designated" minority. A district court ruled that the law school did not have to admit him as a minority group member because he was Italian-American.

When discrimination is so broadly defined, even when restricted to certain minorities, discrimination will, of course, be widespread. According to this broad definition, all forms of structural disadvantages become discrimination.

In June 1976 the United States Supreme Court developed a far narrower view of discrimination, a view that this book shares. The Court ruled that it is not enough merely to show that a government action has a disparate impact upon groups. According to Justice White, "disproportionate impact isn't irrelevant, but it isn't the sole touchstone of an invidious racial discrimination forbidden by the Constitution."[17] In this particular case, which concerned a District of Columbia examination, even though blacks failed the test four times as often as whites, "discriminatory racial purpose" in the tests was unproven. In other words, intent was not proven.

When this definition of discrimination is used, the extent of ethnic or racial discrimination will be less than under the broader meaning of the term. Because this definition includes the *intentional* effort to limit the alternatives of one status, it is often difficult to ascertain discrimination, even with this narrower meaning.

Today, few people in positions of authority will admit to the existence of racial or ethnic discrimination in their organizations. Written discriminatory provisions have been almost entirely eliminated. How, then, can the existence and extent of discrimination be ascertained? One approach, which is not necessarily reliable, is to talk to minority members. Minorities may, on the one hand, find discrimination everywhere as a rationalization for their own failures and inadequacies. Dick Gregory, the comedian, tells the story of the black man with a bad stutter who complained of racial discrimination when he was not hired as a radio announcer. On the other hand, subordinate group members may not be aware of existing discrimination because they have not been in the situation to experience it. For example, if they have not applied for a home loan, they will not know whether or not discrimination exists in that situation.

Minority as well as majority opinions about the existence or nonexistence of discrimination should be used only with the qualifying understanding that they are, finally, opinions. For the most part, discrimination has to be discovered by inference, and this procedure is also difficult and subject to error. The fact that a union has no members or only a few members from minority groups (for example, no Eskimos) does not automatically mean that discrimination is occurring. If, however, there are qualified minority group members working in a craft within a community and they have unsuccessfully sought admission to a union, the presence of discrimination is a valid inference. Merely citing percentages of ethnic group members who have been turned down for a bank loan does not prove discrimination. If, however, the qualifications of any of the minority applicants who have been turned down are equal to or exceed those of dominant group members whose applications have been approved, discrimination is a valid inference.

Because of these problems and the lack of systematic "hard data," any presentation of the existence of and the extent of discrimination in the last ten to fifteen years will have to be tentative and speculative. At best, the presentation must rely upon a few studies, the investigation of the Civil Rights Commission, the opinions of "experts," the opinions of individuals sampled in polls, and the effort to make valid inferences from data on membership, income, occupational placement, etc. The following presentation describes what *seems to be the case.*

One development that seems to be certain is the diminishing of discrimination since World War II. Formal and overt discrimination is virtually nonexistent. Few, if any, large-scale organizations engage in open discriminatory practices because of the continuing threat of sanctions imposed upon them by the government or by civil rights organizations. "Institutional racism," in the *precise* meaning of this term, is very rare.*

In spite of individual paranoia, most members of the white Catholic ethnic groups encounter little discrimination from Anglos in their daily activities, such as renting an apartment, buying a home, getting a job, being promoted, voting, or joining an organization of their choice (the KKK might be an exception). Their success as a group in getting good jobs, achieving high levels of education, and earning high incomes seems to indicate few barriers except at the very top of the stratification order. It seems logical to infer that Anglo discrimination at the elite level exists, given the evidence of the competitive abilities shown by Poles, Irish, and Italians (who are predominantly Catholic).

Organizations practicing formalized, intentional discrimination justified on institutionalized doctrines of the superiority and inferiority of ethnic groups and races. An exception might be the Bureau of Indian Affairs.

The major area in which discrimination against Japanese-Americans still exists is in housing, and this is primarily in California. Writing in 1956, Harry Kitano emphasized the great change since the war but noted the new problem of housing discrimination:

[In California] there is still prejudice and discrimination, but the reduction in both from before the war is striking. The area that is perhaps of more concern to Japanese than any other area is housing. . . . This is not to say there is no discrimination in jobs and elsewhere, but in the experience and thinking of Japanese-Americans, housing looms as the single most important area of discrimination. [18]

Housing discrimination began when the improvement in the class position of the Japanese-Americans led them to seek new housing outside of their traditional ethnic enclaves. In 1956 Kitano found that 39 percent of the Japanese respondents had experienced housing discrimination and that two out of five persons knew of other individuals who had been refused housing because of race.[19] Ten years later, however, in a repeat study, Kitano found very little discrimination against Japanese in housing.[20]

Endo, writing in the 1970s, was more pessimistic:

Though difficult to measure and often more subtle than in earlier years, discrimination persists, for instance, in the unavailability of housing in certain neighborhoods, the exclusion policies of private social clubs, the reluctance of some employers to hire or promote Japanese Americans, some evidence of quota systems in education for students and teaching-administrative staffs, the omission of the Japanese-American experience from textbooks and curriculum materials except in cursory or inaccurate treatments, the stereotyping of Asians in films and television programs and commercials, and the less frequent but existing discourtesies, insults, and stereotyping that occur in everyday face-to-face interaction. [21]

California is not yet a paradise for the Japanese-American, yet little evidence exists for any major patterns of discrimination. The improvement of the stratification position of the Japanese-American since the war would indicate few occupational and educational barriers.

The biggest problem for Mexican-Americans seems to be in the area of justice (the courts and the police), a condition which persists from the past. U.S. Civil Rights Commission studies in 1968 and 1970 found that "there is evidence of widespread patterns of police misconduct against Mexican-Americans in the Southwest."[22] Reported were incidents of police brutality, discourtesy, discriminatory enforcement of motor vehicle ordinances, excessive use of arrests for "investigation," and repeated use of stop-and-frisk practices.

Chicanos were inadequately represented on juries: ". . . neither lack of English ability nor low income of Mexican-Americans could explain the wide disparities between Mexican-American percentage of the population and their representation on juries."[23] This seems to be a valid inference regarding the existence of discrimination.

Bail abuses were also reported to the commission:

> . . . *the system of bail in the Southwest frequently is used more severely against Mexican Americans than against Anglos as a form of discrimination. In certain cases, Mexican American defendants are faced with excessively high bail. Defendants in other cases are held without any opportunity to put up bail or are purposely confused by local officials about the bail hearing so that they unknowingly forfeit their bail. In one area the local farmers put up bail or pay fines for migrant workers and make them work off the amount in a situation resembling peonage or involuntary servitude.*[24]

The major form of discrimination against Indians is a century old—the paternalistic dominance of the Bureau of Indian Affairs over the behavior and activities of the reservation Indians. Although Indians do have some control over the decisions that affect them (a change from the past), white administrators still make the major decisions or approve tribal decisions, often with extensive delays. A 1961 U.S. Civil Rights Commission report made such a charge, and the committee repeated the accusation in reports made in 1973 and 1975.[25]

In the 1960s, at least, evidence exists for discrimination against Indians in welfare programs administered by state and local governments, in the arrest practices of local police, and in occupational discrimination by white members in communities near reservations.[26]

Antisemitism is still prevalent in America, particularly in communities inhabited by the less educated and more fundamentalist Gentiles. However, prejudice (categorical antipathy) is not discrimination. Jews, like the Catholic white ethnics, still face discriminatory barriers to the elite positions in many corporations. This seems to be the major area of discrimination, an area that affects only a small percentage of the Jewish population. Although little evidence is available, housing discrimination in higher income areas of some cities and suburbs is quite probably a reality.

The greatest discrimination against ethnic and racial groupings in the United States still is against Black-Americans. In the all-important area of occupation, discrimination is still apparent at both high and low employment levels. Blacks receive lower wages or salaries than whites who have equal education and are employed in the same specific or general occupational areas. Blacks, as described previously, have improved their educational attainments, but this does not guarantee other rewards. In 1970 *all* males twenty-five or older with a high school degree had a median income of $8,554 and a mean income of $9,042. Black males with the high school diploma, however, had a median income of $6,368 and a mean income of $6,295. In 1970 all males with a college degree had a median income of $12,277 and a mean income of $14,229. Black college-educated males, on the other hand, had a median income of $8,022 and a mean income of $8,218.[27] A college-educated black male on the average made less per year than the national average for males with only a high school degree. Such a circumstance can hardly be due to chance. Either black college-educated males did not find jobs commensurate with their education, as white college-educated males did, or blacks got similar jobs as whites but were paid less. In either case, discrimination seems to be the explanation for the variance.

College-educated females twenty-five years or older in 1970 received less income for their educational efforts than males, but, interestingly enough, black females did better than the national averages for all females (of which the great majority are whites). In 1970 all females with four years of college had a median income of $5,269 and a mean income of $5,635. Black females similarly accredited had a median income of $6,267 and a mean of $6,137. Is discrimination in reverse the answer here? Why would black females receive preferential treatment and not black males?

At the high school level of accreditation, all females in 1970 had a median income of $3,369 and a mean income of $3,759. Black females with a high school degree had a median income of $3,400 and a mean of $3,554.[28] Perhaps the slightly larger average income for black females than the national average for all females (with the exception of the high school mean income figure) is not due to preferential treatment; black women, perhaps, are more likely than white women to be full-time employees rather than part-time.

Table 12.23—which gives the median earnings in 1973 of different categories of workers by white and black race and by gender—offers further evidence of occupational discrimination based upon inference rather than direct observation.

On the average, white males make more money than black males, regardless of the occupational category. One reason for this might be that black males are in the lower positions in each of these categories (for example, they might be public school teachers rather than professors, or dental assistants rather than dentists). Another reason may be that black males receive less income than whites for the same jobs. Both black and white females have lower income than either black or white males (sex discrimination is clearly the reason for this discrepancy). There is, however, little difference between the incomes of black and white females, at least according to occupational category. As we have seen, a comparison according to education does indicate a difference.

Blacks are still underrepresented in skilled craft unions. Since there are many skilled craftsmen in the black population, and since the desire to become a skilled blue-collar worker is in the cultural traditions of Black-Americans, discrimination would account for this underrepresentation. In 1967 Ray Marshall, an expert in the field of labor relations, wrote:

Table 12.23

Median Earnings in 1973 of Full-time Workers 14 Years or Older
by Occupation, Race, and Sex

Occupational Category	Men		Women		Ratio: Black to White	
	Black	White	Black	White	Men	Women
Professional and technical	$10,682	$14,455	$9,015	$9,076	0.74	0.99
Managers and administrators	11,498	14,662	(B)	7,602	0.78	(B)
Farmers and farm managers	(B)	6,824	(B)	(B)	(B)	(B)
Clerical and kindred	9,241	10,811	6,522	6,462	0.85	1.01
Sales workers	(B)	12,415	(B)	4,632	(B)	(B)
Craft and kindred	8,857	11,387	(B)	6,224	0.78	(B)
Operatives	7,830	9,782	4,824	5,449	0.80	0.89
Private household workers	(B)	(B)	2,232	1,827	(B)	1.22
Service workers (except private household)	6,397	8,618	4,495	4,577	0.74	1.00
Farm laborers	(B)	5,104	(B)	(B)	(B)	(B)
Laborers, except farm	6,554	8,423	(B)	4,722	0.78	(B)

SOURCE: *Current Population Reports, The Social and Economic Status of the Black Population in the United States, 1974,* Special Studies, Series P-23, No. 54 (Washington, D.C.: U.S. Department of Commerce/Bureau of the Census, Government Printing Office, July 1975), Table 55, p. 80, "Year-Round Full-Time Workers."

B = base too small for figure to be shown.

The decline in formal exclusion by international unions does not mean that discrimination has declined, because local affiliates of these unions, as well as others which never had formal race bars, exclude Negroes by a number of informal means. These include agreements not to sponsor Negroes for membership; refusal to admit Negroes into apprentice programs or to accept their applications, or simply to ignore their applications; general "understandings" to vote against Negroes if they are proposed (for example, as few as three members of some locals can bar applicants for membership); refusal of journeymen status to Negroes by means of examinations which are rigged so that Negroes cannot pass them; exertion of political pressure on governmental licensing agencies to ensure that Negroes fail the tests; and restrictions of membership to sons, nephews, or other relatives of members.[29]

Government pressure in the form of yearly quotas of blacks to be admitted into craft unions has had some effect, but continued underrepresentation of blacks in several unions and the existence of all-white locals in certain areas indicate that techniques described by Marshall in the 1960s are still used.

In 1965 the Voting Rights Act was passed, an act designed to eliminate racial discrimination in registration and voting in those geographical areas historically identified with the most flagrant and severe forms of discrimination. In accordance with the act, federal authorities monitored the registration and voting procedures. To what extent has the law been successful? The U.S. Civil Rights Commission estimated that the year before the act was passed, in seven southern states 73.4 percent of voting-age whites and 29.3 percent of voting-age blacks registered to vote, leaving a gap of 44.1 percent. In 1971 and 1972, an estimated 67.8 percent of voting-age whites were registered in these same states and 56.6 percent of voting-age blacks, reducing the gap to 11.2 percent.[30] Of the 2,621 elected black officials holding office in 1973, 45 percent were in the South (22 percent in the North, 26 percent in the Midwest, and 7 percent in the West).[31] Obviously, the act has had an effect.

Political participation by blacks in the South has been remarkable; yet in spite of the Voting Rights Act, discrimination still exists in varying forms from county to county and region to region. In 1968 the U.S. Civil Rights Commission reported the following forms of political discrimination against blacks in the South:

1. *Abolishing offices sought by Negroes.*
2. *Omitting names of registered Negro voters from the voting list.*
3. *Switching to at-large elections if black voting strength is concentrated within certain political subunits (for example, elimination of district voting for specific councilmen making the city as a whole the voting unit.)*
4. *Redrawing of boundary lines of political units to divide concentrations of black voting strength (gerrymandering).*
5. *Use of full-slate voting procedures (for example, twenty candidates are running to fill ten offices and three of the candidates are black; the voter must vote for ten candidates; failing to do so voids the ballot; blacks vote for the three black candidates but must also vote for seven whites; the ten candidates with the highest vote totals are elected).*
6. *Extending the term of office of white incumbents if there is a possibility of a black's being elected.*
7. *Establishing polling places in white areas and white establishments.*
8. *Withholding information from blacks about party precinct meetings.*
9. *Refusing to provide or to permit assistance to illiterate Negro voters.*
10. *Disqualifying ballots of blacks on technical grounds.*
11. *Failure to afford Negro voters the same opportunity as whites to cast absentee ballots.*
12. *Excluding or harassing black poll watchers (individuals who watch and report any voting irregularities).*
13. *Intimidating Negro voters, particularly with the threat of economic sanctions.*
14. *Marking the ballots of Negro illiterates contrary to their wishes.*[32]

In 1975 the Civil Rights Commission published another report on the election process in the South entitled *The Voting Rights Act: Ten Years After.* The commission found that some progress had been made but that it was uneven; in some counties with substantial black populations, the situation was typical of prewar South. Gerrymandering, abolition of elected offices if blacks might win, lack of poll watchers, economic intimidation and vocal harassment of voters, inability to find the names of black voters on the registration lists, uncooperative and hostile behavior on the part of election officials, the use of at-large elections, and turning elected offices into appointed positions were discriminatory techniques still being utilized at one place or another. Another tactic, not reported in 1968, was found in South Carolina. Innocent blacks were charged with serious crimes and threatened with imprisonment if a not-guilty plea was made in court. By pleading guilty, the individual would receive a fine or suspended sentence; pleading guilty would also void the individual's voting rights.[33]

Although housing discrimination against blacks in the 1960s continued, it was somewhat reduced and more covert. In the words of John Denton, writing in 1967:

> *The history of concerted action to force minority people to live in ghettos breaks sharply with the* Shelley v. Kraemer *decision in 1948. Prior to that decision, the force exerted against minorities was open and undisguised; since then it has become covert and hypocritical. Some forms of organized racial discrimination have disappeared, but the* most effective *ones prevail, and new subtle forms beyond the reach of existing law have been developed.*[34]

Denton argued that "the dominant force in creating and maintaining ghettos is the activity of professionals in the real estate industry."[35] Real estate professionals include agents, brokers, property managers, appraisers, mortgage loan officers, home builders and escrow and title company officers.

The persistence of black-white housing segregation in the 1960s, ascertained by the sociologists Karl and Alma Taeuber, prompted the question "What causes segregated housing?" They concluded that "neither free choice nor poverty is a sufficient explanation for the universally high degree of segregation in American cities. Discrimination is the principal cause of Negro residential segregation, and there is no basis for anticipating major changes in the segregated character of American cities until patterns of housing discrimination can be altered."[36]

Several discriminatory techniques have been used to maintain white-black housing segregation in the 1960s, and quite possibly in the 1970s as well. Although real estate professionals will deny it, "steering" and "redlining" seem to be practiced in many communities. Blacks are "steered" away from white areas, or a red line is drawn around areas on city maps that are designated to be the next addition to the black ghetto. Mortgage loans are given to blacks for housing in the red-lined areas, but loan officials make it difficult for whites to buy in the same area. Other techniques include the requirement that perspective buyers belong to membership clubs in order to purchase real estate in an area; the use of buy-back agreements that require owners who are selling property to give an association or neighbors first chance at purchasing a home when the owner decides to sell; the strict enforcement of zoning ordinances when blacks try to buy; harassment by building inspectors; raising the cost of city services to open-occupancy areas.[37]

It is difficult to determine the extent of housing discrimination against blacks in the 1970s, but there is little doubt that some forms of housing discrimination still exist, although they vary widely by region and community. In 1974 the U.S. Commission on Civil Rights remained convinced that housing discrimination was prevalent and was sharply critical of the inadequacy of the federal agencies in implementing fair housing. Moreover, the commission cited several court suits and agency investigations in which alleged violations of fair housing laws had occurred. In addition, a total of 2,053 Title VIII complaints were made to HUD in the first nine months of fiscal 1973. Although an increasing number of complaints does not indicate the extent of discrimination (any more than the number of crimes known to the police indicates the total crime rate), it does indicate that white discrimination against blacks in housing remains a persistent phenomenon in many American communities.

It is interesting to find out what people *think* about the existence or nonexistence of discrimination against blacks, even though such opinions may have little congruence with objective reality. In 1969 and again in late 1972 the Harris Survey polled a sample of white and black households across the country. The spokesperson for the family was asked if he or she believed that discrimination against blacks existed in specific areas. Table 12.24 gives the results in each of the two years and the percentage point change between the years.

With all of the publicity engendered by the black social movements and by government actions, it is apparent that more whites became sensitized to the existence of discrimination against blacks. During the same period, greater numbers of blacks felt that discrimination was being reduced.

A much larger percentage of blacks than whites in each of the years believed in the existence of discrimination against blacks. From the subjective view of discrimination as a social problem it is significant that, with one exception (housing, 1972), a majority of whites in all areas and in both years did not believe that discrimination against blacks was part of American life. On the other hand, in 1969 the majority of blacks believed that discrimination was a reality in all areas, and, with the exception of four areas, a majority of blacks continued to believe this in 1972.

Table 12.24

The Perception of Discrimination by Whites and Blacks, 1969 and 1972:
Harris Surveys—Percent Agreeing
"Let me ask you about some specific areas of life in America. For each tell me if you think blacks are discriminated against in that area or not."

Discriminated against in:	1969	1972	Point Change
1. Getting decent housing			
Whites	46	51	+5
Blacks	83	66	−17
2. Getting full equality			
Whites	43	40	−3
Blacks	84	72	−12
3. Getting white-collar jobs			
Whites	38	40	ı2
Blacks	82	68	−14
4. Getting skilled-labor jobs			
Whites	35	40	+5
Blacks	83	66	−17
5. Way treated as human beings			
Whites	35	38	+3
Blacks	77	64	−13
6. Getting into hotels, motels			
Whites	35	31	−4
Blacks	68	44	−24
7. Getting quality education			
Whites	23	29	+6
Blacks	72	53	−19
8. Getting into labor unions			
Whites	22	28	+6
Blacks	64	47	−17
9. Way treated by police			
Whites	19	25	+6
Blacks	76	66	−10
10. Wages paid			
Whites	22	22	0
Blacks	73	61	−12
11. Getting manual-labor jobs			
Whites	18	20	+2
Blacks	58	47	−11
12. Prices paid in grocery stores			
Whites	12	16	+4
Blacks	51	35	−16
13. Way treated by federal government			
Whites	x	10	xx
Blacks	x	41	xx

SOURCE: Harris Surveys, 1969 and 1972.

GEOGRAPHICAL DISTRIBUTION

Prior to World War II, the majority of members of most ethnic groups were concentrated in a particular region or within a few states. Although there has been a reduction in such concentration as ethnic groups disperse, the majority of each of the groups remain somewhat concentrated geographically.

Table 12.25 shows the regional distribution—Northeast, North Central, South, and West—for several racial-ethnic groups between 1940 and 1970.

The majority of blacks remain in the South, although the percentage of blacks residing in the South declined from 77 percent in 1940 to 53 percent by 1970. In 1940 the majority of blacks lived in seven southern states in the following order: Georgia, North Carolina, Mississippi, Alabama, Texas, Louisiana, and South Carolina. By 1970 50 percent or more of all blacks were found within eleven states, including three states with the largest numbers of blacks not in the South: New York, Illinois, California, Texas, Georgia, North Carolina, Louisiana, Florida, Pennsylvania, Michigan, and Alabama.

The Chinese have undergone very little internal migration since 1940; in both 1940 and 1970 the majority lived in the West and a quarter of the Chinese population lived in the Northeast. In 1940 51 percent of all Chinese (excluding those in Hawaii) lived in California and 18 percent in New York. In 1970 the percentage of Chinese in California dropped to 39 percent, while 12 percent resided in Hawaii and 18 percent still made their home in New York.

Between 1940 and 1970 the Japanese remained overwhelmingly concentrated in the West, predominantly in California and Hawaii: in 1970, 217,000 of the 591,000 Japanese lived in Hawaii (37 percent) and 213,000 (36 percent) lived in California.

Approximately 50 percent of Indian-Americans reside in the West in all four census years (1940, 1950, 1960, and 1970) but close to another 50 percent was divided between the north central and the southern states. In 1940 50 percent or more of the 334,000 Indians were found in four western states in the following order: Oklahoma, Arizona, New Mexico, and South Dakota. By 1970 at least a majority of Indians resided in five states: Oklahoma, Arizona, California, New Mexico, and North Carolina.

Mexican-Americans have continued to live primarily within two states, California and Texas (77 percent in 1970). The other major Spanish-speaking group, the Puerto Ricans, are still concentrated in New York, particularly New York City, followed by New Jersey (and in Puerto Rico, of course).

A measure of a group's relationship to the total distribution of American society by region can be derived by determining the percentage point deviation of each ethnic group from the total regional percentages and then dividing by four (four regions). For example, blacks in 1940 deviated from

Table 12.25

Regional Distribution of Selected Ethnic Groups, 1940, 1950, 1960, 1970

Ethnic Group	1940				1950				1960				1970			
	% No. East	% No. Cent.	% South	% West	% No. East	% No. Cent.	% South	% West	% No. East	% No. Cent.	% South	% West	% No. East	% No. Cent.	% South	% West
Blacks	10.6	11.0	77.0	1.3	13.4	14.8	68.0	3.8	16.0	13.3	60.0	5.7	19.2	20.2	53.0	7.5
Chinese	25.3	7.9	6.4	60.4	24.5	9.0	8.9	57.6	22.4	7.6	7.2	62.9	26.7	8.8	7.5	57.1
Indians	3.5	21.4	28.2	46.9	4.6	22.4	20.1	53.0	6.4	19.2	24.3	50.1	6.0	18.9	25.5	49.7
Japanese	2.7	1.2	0.8	95.3	5.2	13.2	2.2	79.5	4.0	6.1	3.7	86.2	6.7	7.2	4.8	81.2
Mexicans	...	...	...	...	...	...	...	...	...	...	...	...	1.0	8.3	37.5	53.3
Puerto Ricans[a]	93.0	1.3	2.6	3.1	88.7	3.8	4.3	3.2	...	...	...	...	80.9	9.8	5.0	4.3
Total U.S.	27.2	30.4	31.5	10.9	26.1	29.4	31.2	13.3	24.9	28.8	30.7	15.6	24.1	27.8	30.9	17.1

SOURCES: *Sixteenth Census of the United States, 1940, Population, Characteristics of the Nonwhite Population by Race* (Washington, D.C.: U.S. Department of Commerce/Bureau of the Census, Government Printing Office, 1943), Tables 1 and 3, pp. 5 and 7–8. *1950 United States Census of Population, Nonwhite Population by Race* (Washington, D.C.: U.S. Department of Commerce/Bureau of the Census, Government Printing Office, 1953), Tables 2–5 and 16–18, pp. 3B-16 to 3B-19 and 3B-60 to 3B-64. *1950 United States Census of Population, Puerto Ricans in Continental United States* (Washington, D.C.: U.S. Department of Commerce/Bureau of the Census, Government Printing Office, 1953), Table 1, p. 3D-11. *United States Census of Population, 1960, Nonwhite Population by Race* (Washington, D.C.: U.S. Department of Commerce/Bureau of the Census, Government Printing Office, 1963), Table 1-4, pp. 1–4. *United States Census of Population, 1960, Puerto Ricans in the United States* (Washington, D.C.: U.S. Department of Commerce/Bureau of the Census, Government Printing Office, 1963), Table 1, p. 2. *Subject Reports, Puerto Ricans in the United States, 1970* (Washington, D.C.: U.S. Department of Commerce/Bureau of the Census, Government Printing Office, 1973), Tables 1 and 2, pp. 1 and 4. *Subject Reports, Negro Population, 1970 Census of Population* (Washington, D.C.: U.S. Department of Commerce/Bureau of the Census, Government Printing Office, 1973), Table 1, p. 1. *Subject Reports, Japanese, Chinese, and Filipinos in the United States, 1970 Census of Population* (Washington, D.C.: U.S. Department of Commerce/Bureau of the Census, Government Printing Office, 1973) Table 1, p. 1. *Subject Reports, American Indians, 1970 Census of Population* (Washington, D.C.: U.S. Department of Commerce/Bureau of the Census, Government Printing Office, 1973) Table 1, p. 1, 2, 16 and 17, pp. 1, 2, 60 and 61. *Current Population Reports, Persons of Spanish Origin in the United States* (Washington, D.C.: U.S. Department of Commerce/Bureau of the Census, Government Printing Office, 1973), Table 1, p. 2, "Persons of Mexican Origins."

a Puerto Ricans born in Puerto Rico and living in the continental U.S. in 1940 and 1950 columns; Puerto Ricans born in Puerto Rico or in the continental U.S. in 1960 and 1970 columns.

the national northeastern percentage by 16.6 points, from the north central by 19.4 points, from the southern total by 45.5 points, and from the western total by 9.6 points; the sum of these deviations (91.1) divided by the four regions equals 22.8. The average deviation of each of the groups can in turn give an overall indication of at least these groups' relationships to the national population distribution by region. The average deviation from the national distribution for several groups is given in Table 12.26.

Each of the groups and the groups collectively are gradually moving in the direction of the overall national population distribution. The Japanese remained the most concentrated and the farthest away from the total population distribution in all four census periods, and, with the exception of 1940, blacks have had the greatest approximation to the national regional distributions. Ethnicity not only continues to make a difference in terms of stratification, it also persists in differentiating the residences of a population. When all of the groups or when a particular group has a score of 0.0, perfect congruence to the total societal distribution by region will have occurred. At the rate of change between 1940 and 1970, the relationship of ethnicity to residence by regions will remain significant until well into the twenty-first century for most of the groups.

The American population as a whole is increasingly urbanized, and, with the exception of the Indians, the racial-ethnic groups are exceeding the national increase. Table 12.27 gives the percentage of the racial-ethnic groups and the white race that were residents of urban centers in 1950, 1960, and 1970.

Table 12.26

Regional Distribution of Selected Ethnic Groups:
Average Deviation from National Distribution

Ethnic Group	1940	1950	1960	1970
Black	22.8	18.4	14.6	11.1
Indian	18.0	19.8	17.3	16.3
Mexican	NA	NA	NA	21.4
Chinese	24.7	22.1	23.6	21.2
Puerto Rican	32.9	31.3	NA	28.4
Japanese	42.2	33.1	35.3	32.1
Average	28.1	24.9	22.7	21.8

SOURCES: Same as for Table 12.25.

NA = not available.

416

Table 12.27

Percentage of Selected Ethnic Groups and Races
in Urban Residences, 1950, 1960, 1970

Ethnic Group	1950	1960	1970
Black	62.4	73.2	81.3
Indian	16.3	16.3	44.6
Mexican	NA	NA	85.5
Chinese	93.1	95.5	96.6
Japanese	71.0	81.5	89.1
Puerto Rican	NA[a]	96.3	97.7
White	64.3	69.5	NA[b]
National	64.0	69.9	73.5

SOURCES: Same as for Table 12.25.

NA = not available

[a] 82.9 percent of all Puerto Ricans in continental U.S. were in New York City.

[b] Would be slightly less than national.

Chinese and Japanese-Americans have long been highly urbanized and remained so in the decades following World War II. The large influxes of Puerto Ricans from the Commonwealth of Puerto Rico to the continental United States has overwhelmingly been into the large cities, particularly New York City. Indians, long associated with reservations, almost tripled their urban residence percentage between 1960 and 1970, and, although 55 percent remain rural, 39 percent of the 45 percent classified as urban reside in large metropolitan centers.

The movement of blacks to the urban areas has largely been into the core of the metropolitan areas: 82.5 percent of the increase of four million in metropolitan black populations between 1960 and 1970 took place in central cities. By 1974 58 percent of blacks lived in central cities, compared to 26 percent of whites; 41 percent of whites resided in the metropolitan "rings" surrounding the core cities, compared to 17 percent of blacks.[38] The populations within the metropolitan rings have remained virtually white: 95 percent white between 1956 and 1960, 96 percent white in 1966, 94 percent white in 1970, and 93 percent white in 1974. By 1970 blacks made up a majority of the population in four central cities: Washington, D.C.; Newark, New Jersey; Gary, Indiana; and Atlanta, Georgia; and were close to becoming a majority in five or six other major cities. Table 12.28 gives the rank

Table 12.28

Rank Order of Negro Population by Percentage of City and by Size
of Negro Population: 15 Cities

Rank Order, 1970 by Percentage of Blacks	1970 %	1960 %	1950 %	Rank Order, 1970 by No. of Blacks
1. Washington, D.C.	71	54	35	1. New York, N.Y.
2. Newark, N.J.	54	34	17	2. Chicago, Ill.
3. Gary, Ind.	53	39	39	3. Detroit, Mich.
4. Atlanta, Ga.	51	38	37	4. Philadelphia, Pa.
5. Baltimore, Md.	46	35	24	5. Washington, D.C.
6. New Orleans, La.	45	37	32	6. Los Angeles, Calif.
7. Detroit, Mich.	44	29	16	7. Baltimore, Md.
8. Richmond, Va.	42	42	32	8. Houston, Tex.
9. Birmingham, Ala.	42	40	10	9. Cleveland, Ohio
10. St. Louis, Mo.	41	29	18	10. New Orleans, La.
11. Memphis, Tenn.	39	37	37	11. Atlanta, Ga.
12. Cleveland, Ohio	38	29	16	12. St. Louis, Mo.
13. Oakland, Calif.	35	23	12	13. Memphis, Tenn.
14. Philadelphia, Pa.	34	26	18	14. Dallas, Tex.
15. Chicago, Ill.	33	23	14	15. Newark, N.J.

SOURCES: *Special Studies, The Social and Economic Status of Negroes in the United States, 1970,*
Series P-23, No. 38 (Washington, D.C.: U.S. Department of Commerce/Bureau of the Census,
Government Printing Office), Table 11, p. 17. Modified by author.

order of the black population within fifteen cities in 1970 by percentage of
the population of each city and by the numerical size of the black population. The percentages of blacks in these cities in 1950 and 1960 are also
provided.

According to a demographer, "a review of recent special census data for
ten large cities offers little assurance that patterns of residential segregation are giving way to a racially integrated urban society. On the contrary, it
is evident from these observations that established Negro areas are becoming more, rather than less, racially distinct, and that the general trend is
toward polarization rather than dispersion of the nonwhite population."[39]
Perhaps a significant factor in this trend has been government efforts to
create integrated schools.

SCHOOL DESEGREGATION

Efforts by the federal government to promote black-white desegregation in
the public schools generally have been inadequate, given the number of
years that have transpired since the Supreme Court decision in 1954 and the
amount of resources, time, and energy that has gone into this government

policy. For the first ten years after *Brown* v. *The Board of Education of Topeka*, little change took place in the South. In the late 1960s desegregation accelerated, but the change rate in the 1970s has become minimal, particularly in the Northeast, the border states, and the West. By 1974 the South was the least segregated and the Northeast the most segregated.

Between 1954 and 1964, only Texas and Tennessee had more than 2 percent of their black students in "integrated" schools, with only 1 percent in the South as a whole.[40] In the North during approximately this same period (1950–1965), a U.S. Civil Rights Commission study of fifteen large northern cities found an increase in segregation, as increases in black enrollment in northern city schools were largely absorbed by already predominantly black schools; 84 percent of the increase was absorbed by schools already more than 90 percent black.[41]

In the South, between 1968 and 1972, a considerable amount of desegregation took place, compared to the previous inaction. Between 1968 and 1972 the percentage of black students attending predominantly white schools increased from 18.4 percent to 44.4 percent, and while 68 percent of the black students in the South in 1968 went to schools with 100 percent black enrollment, by 1973 only 10 percent of black students were in schools that were totally black.[42]

However, in the border states (Kentucky, Maryland, Delaware, Missouri, Oklahoma, and West Virginia) and in the North, progress toward desegregation was considerably slower. In 1968 28.9 percent of black students in the border states attended predominantly white schools, increasing to only 33.8 percent by 1972. In the northern states the percentage increase between 1968 and 1972 was even less—from 27.6 percent to 29.1 percent.[43] A U.S. Commission on Civil Rights report in 1972 stated that integration had virtually halted in the previous four years in the North and in the border states, and that the number of black students in totally segregated schools in the border states was increasing.[44]

Government desegregation efforts were quite possibly related to changes in the black-white population composition of several American cities. For example, white enrollment in the public schools in Houston declined by 20 percent between 1970 and 1972 as whites moved to suburban schools.[45] In New York City in 1958, 58 percent of the students attending academic public high schools were white; by 1971 whites had become a minority population of 48 percent.[46] In Memphis, since a court-ordered desegregation ruling in 1973, the percentage of whites enrolled in school declined from 50 percent to 30 percent by 1975.[47] Three years after busing to achieve racial balance was introduced in Atlanta, the black student population increased from 56 percent to 87 percent.[48] And in Inglewood, California, the student population was 62 percent white when schools were ordered to integrate in 1970; by 1975 the school district was 80 percent nonwhite.[49]

Busing students out of their neighborhoods in order to achieve racial balance (black-white racial balance) is certainly a reason why many white parents decide to move to suburban areas. The reality of racial busing, however, has been greatly distorted. In 1972 about 43 percent of the total public school population in the United States was bused; however, only around 3 percent of the student population was bused to achieve racial desegregation.[50] And between 1920 and 1962 the number of children transported to schools by buses increased from one out of fifty to one out of three, with no public outcry.[51] Experts at the present time estimate that only 2 to 4 percent of all students are bused for the purpose of racial integration.

Merely decreasing the ratio of black and white pupils within schools is not integration, of course, as black and white students may keep to themselves within desegregated schools. Further, it is important to know how desegregation of the public schools affects black and white achievement. Do black students improve? Do white students at least maintain previous levels of academic achievement?

In a review of 120 studies on these issues since the Brown decision, one social scientist, Nancy H. St. John, found the evidence to be inconclusive and often contradictory. On the whole, desegregation did not seem to have either negative or positive effects on the relationship between blacks and whites or on scholastic achievement.[52]

Studies by Bertram Koslin and Richard Pargament had more negative results. Black male elementary students in classes from 5 percent to 15 percent black felt more distant from whites than blacks who comprised half of the students in a class. With these low percentages, the students were more likely to use race as a criterion for selecting their friends. Varying the proportion of blacks in a school from 15 percent to 50 percent also had no systematic effect on black or white students' racial attitudes or on their academic achievement scores (regardless of IQ and socioeconomic status).[53]

A study of the effects of busing in Riverside, California, between 1965 and 1975 was similarly negative. Using a sample of virtually all of the school district's nine hundred minority students (blacks and Chicanos) and their parents, plus a matched sample of nine hundred white children and their parents, the researchers found that anxiety among black students had increased substantially; there was little change in minority motivation to achieve; in terms of test scores, the minority children, overall, did not gain, either absolutely or relative to national norms; teacher bias was not reduced; and minority student grades went down after desegregation. White students, however, were not adversely affected.[54] One of the researchers' conclusions dealt with a major assumption of such programs:

We cannot expect busing programs to lead straight to better minority education. It was quixotic, if not arrogant, to have thought at the outset that sitting next to white classmates would cause Mexican-American and black students to take on good, white middle-class values, and enter the mainstream of American society. It just did not happen. We found, instead, that the children in each ethnic group became more and more cliquish over the years and less accepting of those outside their own group.[55]

SOCIAL AND PERSONAL DISTANCE

A number of polls sampling white and black attitudes in the 1960s and 1970s indicate that social and personal distance between the races is declining. Findings from these polls are itemized below:

1. *Segregation and Desegregation in General.* In 1964, when whites were asked to number the whites in their area who favored strict segregation of the races (social distance), 12 percent said they believed that all of them did and 23 percent said they believed that most of them did; by 1970 the percentage of whites making these estimations declined to 9 percent and 18 percent, respectively. When asked how they personally felt about desegregation (personal distance), the percentage of whites believing in desegregation increased from 27 percent to 35 percent between 1964 and 1970, while those advocating strict segregation declined from 24 percent to 17 percent in the same period. The percentage of whites who wanted something in-between, however, changed very little—from 46 percent in 1964 to 44 percent in 1970.[56]

In 1964, when blacks were asked, "In general, how many of the Negroes in this area would you say are in favor of desegregation?" 26 percent of black respondents estimated that all of them were and 32 percent estimated that most of them were. By 1970 26 percent still believed that all of the blacks in their area were in favor of desegregation, while the percentage that believed that most of them were in favor rose to 42 percent. In 1964 72 percent of blacks personally valued desegregation, increasing to 78 percent by 1970. Only a very small percentage of blacks were in favor of strict segregation of the races—6 percent in 1964 and 3 percent in 1970.[57] Although the majority of blacks were generally in favor of desegregation in these years, in 1964 only 23 percent of whites believed that all or most blacks wanted this condition; this figure declined to 20 percent by 1970.[58]

In a 1968 study of fifteen major cities, at least a slim majority of whites of whatever demographic characteristic (religion, size of community of origin, region of birth, occupation, age, income, sex, country of national origin) favored increased interracial contact, with only a few exceptions. (Exceptions were women aged fifty to fifty-nine (47 percent favored interracial contact); and persons of Polish background (45 percent favored interracial contact).[59]

2. *Neighborhoods.* In 1964 29 percent of whites believed that white people have the right to keep Negroes out of their neighborhoods if they want to; this percentage declined to 21 percent in 1970.[60] In another poll

that goes back somewhat further, whites were asked, "Would it make any difference to you if a Negro with the same education and income as you moved into the block?" In 1942 62 percent responded that it would make a difference; this percentage declined to 21 percent in 1968.[61] In another comparison, in 1958 77 percent of whites said they would move out of the neighborhood if large numbers of blacks moved in; in 1967 71 percent said they would move out under such a circumstance.[62]

3. *Friends.* A sample of white respondents in 1964 showed that 81 percent of those interviewed had *only* white friends; this percentage declined to 66 percent by 1970 and to 50 percent by 1974.[63] Of black respondents, 40 percent had *only* black friends in 1964, declining to 23 percent in 1968, increasing somewhat to 28 percent in 1970, and then declining again to 23 percent in 1974.[64]

4. *Work.* In 1964 54 percent of whites estimated that their place of employment was all white, while another 39 percent said it was mostly white. By 1970 47 percent of whites worked in all-white concerns and 41 percent in mostly white. Twenty-three percent of blacks in 1964 worked in concerns where all or most of the employees were black; in 1970 this figure declined only slightly to 21 percent.[65] Another set of surveys of black workers in 1963 and 1969 found that the great majority of blacks would rather work in a mixed racial group than with mostly other blacks—76 percent in 1963, increasing to 82 percent in 1969.[66]

5. *Schools.* In 1963 61 percent of southern white parents objected to sending their children to schools where even a few students were black. By 1975, however, only 15 percent objected to such token integration. In the North, opposition to this condition was minimal—10 percent were opposed in 1963 and 3 percent in 1975. Far more white parents object to sending their children to schools where more than half of the students are black, but even this percentage has declined. In 1963 86 percent of southern white parents and 53 percent of northern white parents objected to sending their children to a school with a predominantly black student body. In 1975 a majority of southern parents still objected (61 percent), but this was a greater percentage decline than in the North, where 47 percent of white parents in 1975 did not favor such a racial mix for their children (a slim majority would not object).[67]

Newsweek magazine surveys in 1963 and 1969 asked a sample of black parents, "Would you like to see the children in your family go to school with white children or not?" In 1963 70 percent said they would prefer to see their children go to school with whites, 10 percent would not, and 20 percent were not sure. By 1969 those favoring school integration increased to 78 percent, those opposed declined slightly to 9 percent, and the not-sure category declined to 14 percent.[68]

One can conclude that at least the attitudes of blacks and whites are moving in the direction of integration, even if the structural conditions that would make such integration possible show less change.

SUMMARY

Since World War II, quite possibly as a result of the combination of subordinate group social movement activity and government actions, a number of significant changes from the prewar pattern have occurred. Yet, particularly in the case of Black-Americans, there are continuities with the racist system of the past.

Occupationally, all of the racial-ethnic groups have increased their percentages in the more remunerative white-collar occupations at a greater rate than have whites. At the same time, the more disadvantaged racial-ethnic groups (Blacks, Puerto Ricans, Chicanos, and Indians) will not be equal to whites until well into the twenty-first century if the change rate is not increased dramatically. Although Anglos (primarily those Americans of British descent, but perhaps German and Scandinavian as well) continue to control the elite positions, the group has been seriously challenged and even surpassed at the slightly lower occupational levels. The proportion of Jews, Japanese, Irish Catholics, and Chinese-Americans in the higher occupational levels below the elite is now equal to or greater than that of the dominant group.

All of the ethnic groups and subordinate races have increased the percentages of their members having college degrees, increased the median years of schooling of their members, and have reduced the percentage of members in the lowest educational category (eight years of schooling or less). But again, the rate of improvement has varied by groups. With the exception of the Puerto Ricans on the mainland, all of the racial-ethnics have exceeded the growth rate of whites in acquiring diplomas—both high school and college. Jews, Chinese, Japanese, and Irish Catholics all exceed whites as a whole in the obtainment of these degrees, and quite probably they exceed Americans of British descent as well. Educationally, as with occupational placement, the four most disadvantaged minorities have improved significantly in most cases; yet, given their low educational attainments before and right after the war, their rate of improvement will have to be greatly increased to obtain an educational level on a par with whites or the society as a whole.

Family income distribution by race and ethnicity has followed a similar line. All of the groups have improved, but some have improved more than others. At the higher income levels all of the disadvantaged

423

racial-ethnic groups have reduced the gap between themselves and whites, but the change rate will have to improve significantly if the gap is to be closed before the twenty-first century. At higher income levels, again, several ethnic groups exceed whites in general (regardless of what level is used—$15,000 and over, $15,000 to $24,999, or $25,000 and over). These groups include the Irish, Italians, Poles, Swedes, Germans, British, Russian Jews, Chinese, and Japanese. In a number of groups the percentage of families obtaining high income is equal to or exceeds that of Americans of British descent. These groups include the Japanese, the Chinese, Jews, Poles, and the Irish (particularly the Catholic Irish). At the poverty level, the percentage of families in the four disadvantaged groups has been reduced in the last twenty years, yet, relative to whites *(and the country as a whole), there has been no improvement.*

Whatever stratification data are utilized to rank the major ethnic groups in this country, a sharp line can be drawn between those ethnic groups of European and Asian descent and the bottom four: Puerto Rican-Americans, Mexican-Americans, Indian-Americans, and Black-Americans.

Discrimination against the white Catholic and Jewish ethnics seems to still exist at the elite level. Discrimination against Chicanos seems prevalent in the area of the criminal justice system, a continuity from the past, and somewhat less in the area of employment. Blacks are still discriminated against in several areas, although discrimination is more inconsistent than in the past. Evidence exists for continuing discrimination against blacks in housing, in some unions, in voting procedures in the South, and in employment. Less pronounced, but still apparent in some communities, is discriminatory treatment in hotels, restaurants, the criminal justice system, and the schools. Nevertheless, compared to discrimination in pre–World War II America, white discrimination against blacks has been sharply curtailed.

Regional dispersement of the racial-ethnic minorities has taken place to some degree, moving in the direction of the total societal distribution. However, the majority of each of the racial-ethnic groups remains concentrated in a few traditional regions and states within the country. By 1970 blacks most closely approximated the national population distribution, followed by Indians, Mexican-Americans, Chinese, and Puerto Ricans. Japanese-Americans remained, as they were in 1940, the group most deviant from national population distributions.

The movement of blacks from rural areas to central cities has intensified, while at the same time the metropolitan suburban rings that surround the major cities have remained overwhelmingly white.

Black-white school desegregation made little progress for ten years after the 1954 Supreme Court decision to integrate the schools, then increased somewhat in the late 1960s, and now has tapered off. The South, by 1974, was far more integrated than the Northeast, the Midwest, the border states, or the West.

Studies of the effects of school integration on academic achievement and relationships between the races seem to be inconclusive, but several indicate negative effects. Preparing students from highly disadvantaged groups for adult roles may not be possible within the context of so-called desegregated schools. At the very least, it is too soon to expect significant improvements in children after only a brief period of desegregation. The handicaps with which these students enter school and the present structure of the public school system are obstacles not easily overcome.

A final change that must be noted is the reduction of social and personal distance between whites and blacks in the last ten to fifteen years. The change in social distance may be both an effect and a cause of the reduction in black inequality.

13

THE DIRECTION OF CHANGE:
PLURALISM OR INTEGRATION?

INTRODUCTION

Although value judgments have periodically slipped into this analysis, Part 2 of this book has primarily been concerned with describing and evaluating the history of race and ethnic relations in the United States from the beginnings of this nation to the present time. We have seen how a new ethnic group, the Americans, emerged out of confrontation with the British Empire and established dominance by secession. With the acceptance of the Constitution in 1787, blacks and Indian groups became subordinate to the ethnic Americans in the new society. In time, numerous other groups became subordinate through military conquest, annexation, and voluntary immigration. All of the subordinate groups struggled successfully or unsuccessfully to adapt to American dominance and to improve their relative statuses in the face of varying degrees of discrimination, racism, exploitation, and dominant group arrogance. Within each subordinate group there was always some disagreement about whether the goal of adaptation was integration, assimilation, pluralism, or secession. American dominance, under which the definition of American was limited to descendents of Protestant British ancestors and northern Europeans who were willing to give up all other ethnic loyalties, faced few serious challenges until after World War II. Since that war new social movements have developed, the federal government has officially adopted policies designed to rectify conditions faced by the more seriously disadvantaged groups, and numerous important changes in the relative inequality of the groups have occurred.

What *is* the direction of these postwar changes, and what should be the direction of relationships between the races and ethnic groups that constitute American society? In the 1970s traditional Anglo-American dominance, revolution, and secession are unrealistic forms of race and ethnic relations. The choice is thus limited to pluralism or integration. This final chapter will present, in the manner of a debate, the case for pluralism and the case for integration and then will offer a few conclusions about the direction of race and ethnic relations in the United States.

THE CASE FOR PLURALISM

Ethnicity and race in America have always significantly affected the behavior, motives, values, beliefs, and patterns of interaction within American society. Ethnic and racial competition and conflict have probably been more significant in this country than class conflict and competition, Marxist rhetoric to the contrary. There never has been a melting pot. Individuals have managed to disappear into the majority if they had the "correct" phenotype, but, with very few exceptions, virtually all of the ethnic groups that ever existed in this country remain today. The idea of "one nation, one people" has been a hypocritical ploy used by the majority either to eliminate competition and intolerable diversity or to raise the hopes of a group while simultaneously denying that group any genuine participation in American life.

Although many American minority individuals accepted the value of integration in the past, there is a resurgence of ethnicity in the present. And this resurgence is found not only among racially identifiable groups but also among the ethnic sub-divisions of the white population. Weed points out aspects of this resurgence among "white ethnics":

> The social activist uses ethnic origins to personalize causes and polarize ethnics on certain issues. The ethnic business or professional man, the ethnic priest, politician, or community leader often builds his career within the confines of his group and thus for him ethnicity serves as a means of social mobility and economic betterment. . . . With the expanding ethnic middle class, and in reaction to the recent emphasis on black studies, scholarly and artistic interest in the customs of white ethnic groups has greatly increased. Educators are establishing ethnic studies programs. Scholars are investigating the immigrant experience and the persistence of ethnicity. . . . Ethnic book clubs and educational and cultural journals are beginning to appear. Visits to the country of one's ancestors have become popular. Ethnic first names are becoming increasingly popular, and few ethnics are now modifying or discarding their surnames. This preservation of cultural links is deliberate. It is highly self-conscious and is limited neither to the lower middle class nor to the inhabitant of the ethnic enclave.[1]

Weed also points to such events as the passage in the Senate of an ethnic studies bill in 1971, the requests to the post office for stamps commemorating ethnic heroes, the development of ethnic fairs and cultural exhibitions, and the recognition by New York City of Puerto Rico Discovery Day with appropriate activities. Black studies and a return to African costumes, languages, and first and last names have become popular in recent years.

Third-generation Japanese and Chinese in particular are reasserting what they believe to be important elements of their traditional culture. Chicanos are stressing their unique ethnic identity and, at the same time, the common identity of all members of *La Raza*. Culturally and personally, the elements in the melting pot are reasserting their distinctive qualities.

Ethnic diversity has always existed in American history. Except during the first half of the nineteenth century, there never has been a majority ethnic group in America; there certainly is no ethnic majority today. Table 13.1 gives the estimated percentages of the major ethnic groups in the United States for the year 1970–1971.

Table 13.1

Ethnic Percentages of the Total United States Population, 1970–1971: Estimated

1. British[a]	14.5
2. German	13.8
3. Black	11.2
4. Irish	8.3
5. Italian	4.1
6. Scandinavian[b]	3.7
7. Jews	2.5
8. Slavic	2.5
9. Mexican	2.4
10. Polish	2.0
11. French	1.6
12. Canadian	1.5
13. Puerto Rican[c]	0.7
14. Indian	0.4
15. Japanese	0.3
16. Cuban	0.3
17. Chinese	0.2
18. Filipino	0.2
19. Other[d]	30.0

SOURCES: *Current Population Reports, Population of the United States, Trends and Prospects: 1950–1990*, Series P-23, No. 49 (Washington, D.C.: U.S. Department of Commerce/Bureau of the Census, Government Printing Office, 1974), Table 3.18, p. 93. Andrew M. Greeley, *Ethnicity in the United States: A Preliminary Reconnaissance* (New York: John Wiley & Sons, 1974), Table 4, pp. 42–43. *Characteristics of the Population by Ethnic Origin, March 1972 and 1971, Current Population Reports*, Series P-20, No. 249 (Washington, D.C.: U.S. Department of Commerce/Bureau of the Census, Government Printing Office, April 1973), p. 1.

[a] Scots, English, and Welsh.   [b] Norwegians, Swedes, Danes.

[c] Continental U.S. only.

[d] Includes all individuals identifying with some other group that is not listed above, individuals giving multiple group identifications, individuals reporting only American, and individuals reporting no ethnic identity.

428

If Anglo or Anglo-Saxon refers to persons of British, German, Scandinavian, or English-Canadian descent, then the group forms only about 33 to 34 percent of the population. If Anglo-Saxons are to be considered to be Protestant only, then the exclusion of German Catholics leaves a figure of 30 percent. Even if half of the "other" category is added to the Anglo-Saxon category, we are still speaking of a minority group of 45 to 49 percent of the total population.

The term "American" was appropriated by British Protestant groups and their descendents. It was a term that, even in the past, did not effectively conceal the differences between the Scot, Welsh, and English subgroups. As a nationality we are all Americans but with ethnic subdivisions, even though some of us claim no ethnic identity. Anglo is an appropriate name for those descendents of the British colonials and for others with an extremely mixed ancestry and no specific ethnic identity. Anglos are no more American than any other group in this country, and the first Americans, or the native Americans, were not British, but Indian.

This Anglo, WASP, or "English" dominance and arrogance is now exposed for what it is—one ethnic identification among many. Even though this group has been relatively successful in the past in identifying its view of the world as *the* American view, such an identification is now challenged. In the words of Michael Novak:

> English conceptions of order, decorum, social planning, the free marketplace (of goods and ideas), friction-free consensus, etc., dominate American life so thoroughly that most WASPs seem unaware of them as ethnic preferences. For them, such matters are so much a part of their sense of reality, so integral to their own life story, so symbolically familiar, so inherently self-validating, that charges of partiality and bias must seem to them faintly insane. Their conception of sanity is, in fact, in question. They are obliged to see themselves as ethnically one-sided for perhaps the first time. What used to be regarded as dignified reserve is now mocked as uptightness; what used to be regarded as good character is analyzed now for its "hangups"; the individualism of the Marlboro man, once a cherished aspiration, is regarded as alienation; the smooth-talking managerial style of liberal WASP authoritarianism is hissed as manipulative and venal; competitiveness is laughed at by those to whom it is closed. American cultural pluralism, fed by Jews, Blacks, Indians, and other ethnic groups, has thrown WASP ideals into a new and unflattering light.[2]

But the resurgence of the multiple ethnicity of Ameria (and the exposure of Anglo ethnicity and arrogance that masquerade under the term "American") is just one form of the pluralistic direction America is now taking. Indian groups will not be denied political and economic control over their own reservations. The Bureau of Indian Affairs is an anachronism of paternalistic Anglo dominance over the Indian people. With the dissolution of this agency—and this will most surely come about—Indians will obtain pluralistic status to accompany the reemphasis of their ethnicity. Government services will still be provided to Indians, but Indians will make the major decisions about available services and will manage the administration of those services within their own political units. Government assistance only violates the idea of ethnic autonomy when the peoples affected have no say in the form and extent of such assistance. Political pluralism for the Indian peoples will accomplish what a century and a half of paternalism has not—the improvement of the economic status and the self-esteem of Indian peoples.

For Black-Americans, concentrated in the core of metropolitan centers because of persisting white discrimination, political and economic pluralism will produce significant improvements in their stratification position. Piecemeal court actions, ineffective government programs, and social movement rhetoric have not improved the position of the ghetto black in any significant manner. At the present snail's pace of change, blacks will not see anything like equality until well into the twenty-first century. The argument that statistically blacks are better off today than in the past is irrelevant. They also are better off as a whole than the great majority of the people in India. But blacks do not live in India, and it is no consolation that their ancestors were in a far worse condition. Blacks live in the present, and inequality and white discrimination persist. When blacks obtain local political control over cities in which they make up most of the population, they will have a number of power bases from which to influence national policies. The establishment of black economic enterprises in ghettos will enable the development of those skills necessary for economic activities and for economic influence in the large society.

Because blacks have been the most severely repressed group in America, their subordinance has had far-reaching effects. As a result, blacks are sure to make mistakes, but the mistakes will be their own and they will benefit by such mistakes. Jesse L. Jackson, a major black leader, has stressed the problems and what he feels must be done:

> There are now 130 black mayors in the United States. We blacks have populated the cities; we must now learn to run them. The need is urgent: the ethical collapse, the heroin epidemic, the large numbers of our people who are out of work and on welfare, and the disruptive violence in our schools all indicate that the cities may be destroying us.
>
> . . . black Americans must begin to accept a larger share of responsibility for their lives. For too many years we have been crying that racism and oppression have kept us down. That is true, and racism and oppression have to be fought on every front. . . .
>
> It is time, I think, for us to stand up, to admit to our failures and weaknesses and begin to strengthen ourselves. Here are some of the things I am thinking about:
>
> We have become politically apathetic. Only 7 million out of 14 million black voters are registered to vote. Yet politics is one key to self-development. In terms of

votes, we have more potential strength than labor or any other single bloc. We have a responsibility to use it to the full.

We too often condemn blacks who succeed and excel, calling them Toms and the like, when the ideal ought to be for all of us to succeed and excel.

We are allowing a miniscule minority of criminals in our midst to create disorder, ruin our schools and sap the energy we need to rebuild our neighborhoods and our cities.

Many leaders who are black, and many white liberals, will object to my discussing these things in public. But the decadence in black communities—killings, destruction of our businesses, violence in the schools—is already in the headlines; the only question is what we should do about it.

Others will object that to demand that we must meet the challenge of self-government is to put too much pressure on the victims of ancient wrongs. Yet in spite of these objections, in spite of yesterday's agony, liberation struggles are built on sweat and pain rather than tears and complaints.[3]

Jackson also stresses that massive federal assistance is not the complete answer to black problems, as past urban programs have shown. He emphasizes commitment, hard work, a moral authority, and education— elements he feels have been lacking in the black community. He points out that "in the last 10 to 12 years, many of us missed the chance to grow intellectually and chased Superfly instead. Many of us spent more time on lottery and luck than looking for a job. . . . I know young black workers who talk with pride about going to work any hour they feel like it and taking a day off when they feel like it. They're rebelling against the system, they say. . . . What they're really exhibiting is ignorance of a tradition of work in the black community that is one of our proudest legacies."[4] Political and economic pluralism, whether for reservations or ghettos, is not a magic solution to one's problems but a condition to be won, to be diligently pursued, and to be constantly maintained.

Chicanos also have a "spatial" basis for a realistic development of political and economic pluralism. In many large cities in the Southwest, Chicano *barrios* still exist. Poverty, discrimination in housing, and a genuine desire to maintain a sense of ethnic community have contributed to this condition. In some of the smaller towns, Chicanos are a majority of the population.

There is no technological or instrumental reason why sections of cities, whether termed ghetto, *barrios*, or enclaves, cannot have some degree of autonomy on an ethnic basis. Schools, police departments, borough legislative bodies, and other organizations can be quasi-autonomous within the larger metropolitan unit. Such subdivisions already exist within many metropolitan areas, and cities completely surrounding smaller cities are not uncommon. Based on ethnic boundary lines, each unit could have responsibility for its own areas and maintain its interests against the encroachment of other units. The political structure of urban life would be fragmented to some extent, but no more than it is presently. Urban political pluralism would officially recognize urban ethnic reality and would pre-vent ruthless urban renewal programs from taking place as well as inte-grationist efforts to undermine the ethnic sense of community.

Not all ethnic groups, particularly some white ethnic groups, would feel that political and economic pluralism is desirable or advantageous. And in some communities, members of one ethnic group might opt for pluralism while members of other groups would not. But the choice would belong to the ethnic group. Structured pluralism (as opposed to the mere existence of more than one ethnic group or the fact of cultural differences) does not mean that every group in every community must have this arrangement.

Admittedly, for structured pluralism to exist, members of ethnic groups must be concentrated within communities or regions. In spite of the in-creased dispersion of the members of many ethnic groups throughout the country, there still remain numerous communities in America with large concentrations of specific ethnic group members. Structured pluralism can therefore exist even in the absence of regional concentrations. The integra-tionist, of course, claims that ethnic pluralism would be divisive, that it would destroy social unity and create great potentials for conflict. This argument rings hollow, however, in view of the fact that American society has always been diverse and that ethnic and racial conflict has not been an exceptional occurrence. Integration proposals mask Anglo dominance, whether intentionally or not. Pluralism recognizes the reality of a multi-ethnic society and would structure society accordingly. It is possible to develop institutionalized methods of preserving ethnic interests and resolv-ing ethnic conflicts, methods that in the final analysis would prevent the more violent forms of conflict from developing. Pluralism legitimizes and would probably minimize the ethnic conflicts that do in fact occur in our society. If conflict is not reduced, better pluralism than oppressive order produced by ethnic dominance.

THE CASE FOR INTEGRATION

Few people who have some knowledge of the history of race and ethnic relations in America deny the existence of majority group discrimination and severe exploitation of at least some of the minorities in the past and in the present. Racial and ethnic inequality and conflict have existed through-out American history. Since World War II, however, and particularly since the 1960s, significant changes have taken place. Racial and ethnic inequal-ity has been reduced. Yet, for the more severely treated groups, particularly the blacks, the Indians, the Chicanos, and the Puerto Ricans, much must still be accomplished to achieve equality. Racial discrimination, wide-spread before the war, is now officially illegal, and most of the overt forms of discrimination no longer exist. Subtle and covert discrimination, particu-larly against Black-Americans, can still be found in many areas and communities, but the trend is towards the elimination of the most damaging varieties.

Minorities, once highly concentrated in particular regions and communities, have become more dispersed throughout particular cities and towns and throughout the regions of America. As with discrimination, the major exception to this decline in community segregation has been the blacks. Although black-white differences have persisted in spite of programs and organizational activities to reduce them, more and more whites have become sensitized to the conditions of Black-Americans. Some evidence exists that social distance between the two groups is being reduced; greater percentages within these races advocate greater integration.

No one, even the most doctrinaire pluralist, can truly claim that American society is more culturally differentiated today than in the past. Around the turn of the twentieth century truly significant cultural differences did exist, but today there are few cultural elements distinctive to particular groups. Black music has become American music. Ethnic foods are widely shared. Ideological and behavioral differences between Protestants, Catholics, and Jews are far fewer than they were in the past. Many define Jews not in ethnic terms but in religious terms—as Americans of Jewish persuasion and part of the Judaic-Christian tradition. Mass communication, mass transportation, and the development of the "chains"—hotels, motels, restaurants, department stores—have created a major standardization of American life. Today the ethnic groups of European descent, in the words of Nathan Glazer,

> ... do not find justification in separate language, religion, and culture, all of which have succumbed to the eroding process of American life. The descendents of European nations in America are now completely divorced from their origins: they speak English, participate in American culture, and observe Americanized forms of the ancestral religions. Their justification for existence might be called on one level nostalgia, on another ideology. And this ideology has no organic relation to their real individual pasts but is rather in large measure a reaction to the conditions of life in the twentieth-century United States and the twentieth-century world.[5]

The present revival of ethnicity is at best a temporary reaction to the massive acculturation of ethnics in American society and the development of a mass culture. Some members, *and only some*, are preoccupied with preserving ethnic cultures when there is very little left to preserve. The so-called resurgence of ethnicity is a form of nativism, a part of the general nostalgia for an idealized past in the face of contemporary problems and conditions. Columbus Day, St. Patrick parades, and children wearing native costumes once a year on Ethnic Day are but vestiges of a once viable and diverse cultural tradition. Ethnicity exists but ethnic groups are disintegrating.

Pluralists confuse all of the rhetoric about ethnic cultures with the existence of cultural differences, and then this confusion is termed "pluralism."

Paradoxically, in 1900, when ethnic cultural diversity was greatest in this country, the intellectuals and ethnic spokespersons advocated integration. Today, when little diversity remains, "pluralism" is all the rage.

Much of what some people refer to as ethnic culture is more likely to be behavioral and attitudinal responses of people in the lowest strata to their stratification position. According to one expert on Indian-white relations, "American Indian composite households and family household cycles are not retentions of aboriginal customs, but are products of their meager and unstable incomes, lack of skills, and lack of control over resources."[6] Few cultural differences exist between ethnic groups within the middle and upper strata. The conditions of poverty seemingly produce "ethnic" culture, but all the stress on ethnicity simply compounds a problem that today is largely one of social class. The lower-class conditions that disproportionately affect some ethnic groups can be changed, without worrying about the preservation of "ethnic" heritages.

Like the pluralist, the integrationist believes that we are all Americans. If we are not yet, we will be soon. Admittedly, the meaning of "American" was quite limited in the past. But today the core of Protestant British has been expanded to include numerous other groupings of Catholic and Jewish faith. What is a "typical" American family name is no longer limited to the British Smith and Martin but includes surnames of many other groups as well.* What continues to limit the expansion of the meaning of "American" is race. Phenotypic differences will be with us for many generations; however, race (phenotypic categories) is increasingly irrelevant to more and more Americans. Even this boundary is being weakened.

As has been emphasized, pluralism is much more than the preservation of ethnic cultural differences. Pluralism is the relative autonomy of two or more ethnic groups within a society in the conduct of their institutional activities. To what extent is this condition possible today? Will it be much less possible in the future? Classic pluralism exists in societies where regional concentrations of ethnic groups provide a territorial base for social, political, and economic (in some cases) autonomy. In the United States extreme regional concentration is a thing of the past, although a few groups are still concentrated in a few states or in single regions. Even in those regions, however, viable ethnic communities—communities perpetuating

---

Many celebrities, however, still find it necessary to change their names (in order to become more mainstream as well as to fit on the marquees). Some interesting name changes of entertainment celebrities have been: Lazlo Lowenstein (Peter Lorre), Antonio Benedetto (Tony Bennett), Vito Farinola (Vic Damone), Dino Crocetti (Dean Martin), Joseph Levitch (Jerry Lewis), Allen Konigsberg (Woody Allen), Emanuel Goldenberg (Edward G. Robinson), Raquel Tejada (Raquel Welch), Ricky Orrico (John Saxon), Mladen Sekulovich (Karl Malden), Krekor Ohanion (Mike Connors), Bernie Schwartz (Tony Curtis), Tadewurz Wladzui Knopka (Ted Knight), Charles Buchinsky (Charles Bronson), Ramon Estevez (Martin Sheen), Izzie Itskowitz (Eddie Cantor), Florencia Bisenta de Casillas Martinze Cardona (Vikki Carr), Doris Kapplehoff (Doris Day), Margarita Carmen Cansino (Rita Hayworth), Frederick Austerlitz (Fred Astaire), and Issur Danielovitch (Kirk Douglas).

the culture of their ancestors and engaging in limited interaction with members of other communities—are not likely to exist. There are white ethnic neighborhoods in many urban centers, particularly in the Northeast, New Orleans, and Chicago. But they are just that—neighborhoods; they are places to associate with friends, relatives, and mates, but they are usually not places of work. Neighborhoods hardly provide the territorial basis necessary for political, much less economic, autonomy.

Some small towns have a high concentration of particular minority groups. But these communities, in many cases, are already autonomous in a very negative sense—impoverished and isolated from the mainstream economic and social life of American society. Pluralism does not thrive on poverty and isolation.

Mexican *barrios* and black ghettos still exist, of course, and, from an integrationist perspective, they indicate what must still be done. Pluralists may glorify these places as the repositories of ethnic heritages, but, to many members forced to live in these poorer sections of the cities, they are places to leave if humanly possible. They are lower-class communities plagued with all the traditional problems indigenous to such areas. Very few successful Chicanos or Black-Americans stay in these areas or move back to preserve their heritage. The pluralists live in suburbia along with the integrationists and discuss their ideological differences at backyard barbecues or at lawn parties. In the meantime, their lower-class ethnic members in the central cities are as isolated from the mainstream as rural Appalachians. The solution is not to preserve such poverty traps, but to eliminate them.

What about "black capitalism" or "Chicano capitalism" (or socialism, for that matter)? What do such terms mean? Are such pluralistic endeavors possible? In a society dominated by giant corporations, increasing in economic activities and capital every year, can there be any form of ethnic capitalism? If the idea of ethnic capitalism means a number of production-based corporations owned predominantly by particular ethnic groups, then this is possible, but generally improbable. If ethnic capitalism means an increase in the number and quality of ethnic-owned service-oriented enterprises, then this is possible and even probable in the case of the more disadvantaged groups. From an integrationist viewpoint, such developments are desirable, since they mean a more proportional-distribution of all groups in the various economic sectors. But if black capitalism (or any other ethnic capitalism) means some relatively autonomous sector of the economy controlled and operated by blacks, it becomes absurd, given the structure of an industrialized state.

The only true pluralism that exists in the United States is in the Commonwealth of Puerto Rico. Puerto Rico is truly pluralist; one Puerto Rican writer has described it as an "'independent' country within the framework of the United States, sharing the broader independence of the latter."[7]

The only other territory in which a pluralist status would be a possibility is the Indian reservation, but only as a temporary arrangement. The development of Indian skills, particularly in government, in managerial activities, and in various forms of industrial technology, would best be accomplished by the Indians themselves, without the suffocating paternalism of the Bureau of Indian Affairs. Such an improvement in the Indian position becomes a necessary condition for their subsequent integration into the social mainstream.

Integration *is* the direction and *should be* the direction of race and ethnic relations in the United States, and the majority of the members of ethnic groups think so too. The true "minorities" in America are those that advocate pluralism as a goal or who interpret contemporary society as being "pluralistic."

AND A FEW JUDGMENTS MORE:
OPINIONS OF THE AUTHOR

The reader may have additional arguments to make for a particular position or may object to certain ideas that have been stated as representative of the integrationist or the pluralist positions. Nevertheless, the direction of race and ethnic relations in America from World War II to the present time and the direction these relations will take and should take in the future are open to discussion.

The opinion of this author is that the direction of change in America is towards integration. Race and ethnicity are increasingly irrelevant, particularly at the secondary level of social relationships. The *process* of integration is taking place; the *condition* of integration will not be realized for several generations.

At the present time, there is a reassertion of ethnicity; this cannot be denied. But this ethnic resurgence is not pluralism per se, although it could lead to pluralistic statuses for at least a few groups as a necessary precondition of eventual integration. The renewed sense of ethnicity seems to be a response by ethnics to an increasingly impersonal society that does not provide sufficient roots for many people, despite political oratory. A second factor seems to be a reaction by many nonblacks to the seemingly preferential treatment accorded to Black-Americans by the federal government.

Russell Endo has described two apparently contradictory trends among Japanese-Americans. On the one hand, there is a "reawakening of interest in things Japanese American," along with a developing political consciousness based upon ethnicity. At the same time, "there has been a gradual but continuing trend toward less participation in the ethnic community and more within the institutions of American society."[8] Something similar could be said about virtually all of the subordinate groups in America. Perhaps the paradox can be explained by the idea of a stage in the integration process. For many decades, even centuries in some cases, subordinate groups in America have been culturally oppressed. The prestige and worth of the dominant culture have been so taken for granted, even among most members of the minorities, that psychic damage has resulted. These groups are now challenging the assumption of Anglo-American cultural dominance and reevaluating their own worth. Integration does not take place between superiors and inferiors, but between equals. In this sense, the increase in ethnic identification that is so much a part of the modern scene is a necessary stage in the process of integration. Ethnicity in the American context has to become more relevant before it can become irrelevant. And, at the same time, subordinate group challenges to mainstream culture have been cathartic. Assumptions about the world, long taken for granted, are being reevaluated, particularly by the younger generation of the dominant group. In time, perhaps, a new synthesis can take place.

To say that integration is occurring is not to argue that assimilation is taking place. Many scholars confuse the two concepts or make them synonymous. The United States will remain a multiethnic society for generations to come, with some degree of ethnic identification (lower-level ethnicity as opposed to higher-level American ethnicity) within many American communities. The United States is not a closed society. Immigration still occurs (5 percent of the total population in 1960 and in 1970 were foreign born), helping to keep alive ethnic subdivisions. And although ethnicity has and will become increasingly insignificant in affecting secondary relationships, it will remain a factor in the choice of marriage partners and even friends.

From a normative perspective, not only is integration the best label to identify what *is* taking place in American society, but integration *should be* the goal of our country. A qualification, however, is in order. Integration should develop as a "natural" process, without government efforts to accomplish this end state. The effort to eliminate discrimination (intentional actions and policies) is legitimate. Policies and programs that broaden the meaning of discrimination to include virtually all conditions in which more members of some groups are more likely to receive disadvantageous treatment than other groups are not legitimate. Nor are "benign quotas," "affirmative action," "preferential treatment," and "reverse discrimination" legitimate methods of changing the system. Such policies are often ineffective, but, more important, they create more problems than they intend to solve, retarding integration rather than enhancing it. Sowell has criticized "affirmative action" this way: "While doing little or nothing to advance the position of minorities and females, it [affirmative action] creates the impression that the hard-won *achievements* of these groups are *conferred* benefits."[9] Gilbert and Eaton have suggested four possible latent or unintended consequences of policies of preferential treatment or discrimination in reverse, policies that emphasize ascribed status at the expense of technical qualifications: (1) performance breakdown—minorities who are employed because of their status and not on merit might ultimately fail in their tasks, thereby validating stereotypes of inferior minorities; (2) occupational stigmatization—discrimination in reverse can be practiced with less risk in occupations that do not require highly technical skills, and, hence, the admission of unqualified people into these occupations would eventually lower the status of the occupations; a treadmill effect would be produced in which minorities step up to a higher occupation only to find that this position has depreciated; (3) backlash—from majority group members or white ethnic members not designated as minorities; and (4) erosion of credentialism—if minority individuals can attain a position without fulfilling all requirements for the credentials necessary for the position, then others will question the value of such credentials.[10]

The backlash factor needs further elaboration. The selection by the government of some minorities to be given preferential treatment (the "designated minorities" or the *only* minorities) opens up a serious divisive element that constitutes discrimination. There is no reason why every group in this country should not ask for occupational quotas, for different tests of admission, or for other ethnic-based privileges. Weed has written:

The more public recognition given to America's ethnic diversity and to specific ethnic groups, the more likely it becomes that each group will assert itself and demand greater recognition. Each time an important politician singles out one group for mention in his public utterances, others feel slighted for seemingly intentional omission of their group. It is the politicians and ethnic leaders who foster divisions in American group life.[11]

And what about backlash from the dominant group, the nonhyphenated Americans, or the Anglo-Americans? If the government continues to offer preferential treatment to some groups and not others, and if representatives of ethnic minorities continue to challenge what these people conceive of as traditional values, there is going to be a reaction. American or Anglo ethnicity will be intensified. Instead of a continuing broadening of the meaning of ethnic American, there will be a contraction. There is a very large minority, possibly even a majority of the citizens of the United States, who have no other name for themselves but American and feel no sense of identification with peoples in other countries, and a good percentage of these feel that the whole idea of ethnicity is a lot of nonsense. This category, with all the "pluralistic" clamoring that is going on, will become more ethnic than they were in the past. If they can't have the name "American" as their exclusive possession, the insipid and relatively meaningless term "Anglo" may be glorified and celebrated. People who, for the most part, have competed as individuals will increasingly compete as a group. Given the advantages already acquired from two centuries of dominance, the subordinate groups will face serious disadvantages.

The answer, of course, is to continue to expand the meaning of ethnic American rather than to limit it, and to seek to end most of the formalized aspects that emphasize the ethnic subdivisions within American society. Some emphasis on the importance of the contributions of the ethnic minorities to American life should be part of the educational process for many years. Such programs will enhance the probabilities of integration rather than impede it.

With this expanded meaning of American, Americans will remain nominally dominant by the sheer factor of numbers; however, the meanings implied by the concepts of dominance and subordinance, which have been the theme of this book, will have lost their significance. Dominance will be transformed by becoming irrelevant.

NOTES

Chapter 1

1. Tamotsu Shibutani and Kian M. Kwan, *Ethnic Stratification: A Comparative Approach* (New York: Macmillan Co., 1965), p. 47.

2. R. A. Schermerhorn, *Comparative Ethnic Relations: A Framework for Theory and Research* (New York: Random House, 1970), p. 12.

3. Shibutani and Kwan, *Ethnic Stratification*, p. 42.

4. Edward Shils, "Deference," in *Social Stratification*, ed. J. A. Jackson (London: Cambridge University Press, 1968), p. 112.

5. Pierre van den Berghe, *Race and Ethnicity* (New York: Basic Books, 1970), pp. 144–45.

6. E. Digby Baltzell, *The Protestant Establishment: Aristocracy and Caste in America* (New York: Random House, 1964), pp. 58–60.

7. Simon Davis, *Race Relations in Ancient Egypt*, (New York: Philosophical Library, 1952), p. 1.

8. William W. Howells, "The Meaning of Race," in *The Biological and Social Meaning of Race*, ed. Richard H. Osborne (San Francisco: W. H. Freeman and Co., 1971), pp. 3–6; John Buettner-Janusch, *Origins of Man: Physical Anthropology* (New York: John Wiley and Sons, 1966), pp. 9–12, 367–74, 395–425.

9. W. Farnsworth Loomis, "Skin Pigment Regulation of Vitamin D Biosynthesis in Man," *Science* 157 (August 1967): 501–506.

10. Paul T. Baker, "Human Biological Diversity as an Adaptive Response to the Environment," in Richard H. Osborne, *Meaning of Race*, pp. 29–30; Buettner-Janusch, *Origins of Man*, pp. 366–74, 409.

11. Theodosius Dobzhansky, "Race Equality," in Osborne, *Meaning of Race*, p. 17.

12. John Geipel, *The Europeans* (New York: Pegasus, 1970), p. 266.

13. Buettner-Janusch, *Origins of Man*, p. 612.

14. The term "society" has numerous meanings in sociology. One meaning makes the term synonymous with social organization. The other major usage conceives of society as a social unit—a unit of social organization with boundaries. The problem is to ascertain the boundaries and to distinguish between a society and other social units, such as communities, ethnic groups, and organizations. A common method of specifying the boundaries is to identify different culture regions; hence, a society becomes a pattern of social organization with a common culture. The problem with this meaning is the tremendous overlap of cultures among groups. Another problem, when there are numerous ethnic groups, is determining "whose" culture. Theorists have also stressed "autonomy" of activities as the method of ascertaining the boundary. If economic autonomy is the criterion, then there are few, if any, societies in the world today. Some consider territory and a division of labor to be delineating factors; however, organizations such as universities also have these characteristics. Because of these difficulties, the idea of sovereign norms has been taken to be the boundary. In the modern period, society refers to a country or a "nation-state." Past political divisions, such as a city-state, a tribe (not part of some empire), a kingdom, and an empire, would all be societies as defined here.

15. Brewton Berry, "America's Mestizos," in *The Blending of Races,* ed. Noel P. Gist, and Anthony Gary Dworkin (New York: Wiley-Interscience, 1972), pp. 191–210.

16. Noel P. Gist, "The Anglo-Indians of India," in Gist and Dworkin,*The Blending of Races,* p. 43.

17. Ibid., p. 48.

18. Richard Slobodin, "The Métis of Northern Canada," in Gist and Dworkin,*The Blending of Races,* pp. 144–64.

Chapter 2

1. Power, as defined here, is always manifest. Either decisions are implemented (power) or they are not (lack of power, or powerlessness). However, one can speak of potential power, in that resources can be ascertained that *may* be utilized, or a prediction of potential power can be made on the basis of past performances. The term "balance of power" raises some problems, if power is manifest. In this meaning of power, "balance of power" means stalemate or balance of resources. Power per se does not exist because each of the groups in the relationship cannot secure compliance to or suppress resistance to particular decisions or expectations related to the others.

2. As will be examined in Chapter 4, efforts to acquire privileges or to maintain privileges is discrimination. Discrimination, in turn, is one form of conflict.

3. Other meanings for this concept have been: (1) a class is a segment of a single-reward distribution—a division of wealth, such as the rich and the poor; a division of prestige; or a division of power, such as the power elite and the masses; (2) a class is an "open" stratum, as opposed to those types of strata that restrict social mobility, such as estates and castes; (3) classes are divisions of authority within organizations—those with authority and those without authority; there are as many classes in a society as there are organizations times two.

Besides these definitions, theorists may or may not emphasize any of the following as essential to the meaning of class: the existence of a subculture; some degree of continuity of members over at least a few generations; an awareness of one's class and the classes of others; engagement in conflict with another class.

4. Sammy Smooha, "Black Panthers; The Ethnic Dilemma," *Society* 9 (May 1972): 34–35.

5. Wlodzimierz Backzkowski, "Russian Colonialism in its Soviet Manifestation, 1958," in *The Imperialism Reader,* ed. Louis L. Snyder (Princeton: D. Van Nostrand Co., 1962), pp. 572–73.

6. Quoted by Cynthia H. Enloe,*Ethnic Conflict and Political Development* (Boston: Little, Brown and Co., 1973), p. 105, from T. H. Rigby,*Communist Party Membership in the USSR, 1917–67* (Princeton: Princeton University Press, 1968), pp. 398–99.

7. Backzkowski, "Russian Colonialism," p. 571.

8. Sidney Harcave, *Russia: A History* (New York: J. B. Lippincott Co., 1953), p. 506.

9. D. Stanley Eitzen, "Two Minorities: The Jews of Poland and the Chinese of the Philippines," in *Ethnic Conflicts and Power: A Cross-National Perspective,* ed. Donald E. Gelfand and Russell D. Lee (New York: John Wiley and Sons, 1973), p. 142. Previously published in the *Jewish Journal of Sociology* X (December 1968).

10. Carl Solberg, *Immigration and Nationalism: Argentina and Chile, 1890–1914,* (Austin: University of Texas Press, 1970), pp. 51–52.

11. *Denver Rocky Mountain News*, February 6, 1972, p. 4.

12. Enloe, *Ethnic Conflict and Political Development*, pp. 213–14.

13. Will Durant, *Caesar and Christ* (New York: Simon and Schuster, 1944), p. 462.

14. Herbert J. Muller, *Freedom in the Ancient World* (New York: Harper and Brothers, 1961), p. 99.

15. Quoted by Charles H. Anderson, *Toward a New Sociology: A Critical View* (Homewood, Ill.: Dorsey Press, 1971), p. 91, from Ferdinand Lundberg, *The Rich and the Super Rich* (New York: Bantam Books, 1969), p. 11. Regarding preindustrial societies and income distribution, see Gerhard Lenski and Jean Lenski, *Human Societies* (New York: McGraw-Hill Book Co., 1974), p. 230.

16. Pierre van den Berghe, *Race and Racism* (New York: John Wiley and Sons, 1967), pp. 61, 62.

17. Roy Lewis and Yvonne Foy, *Painting Africa White: The Human Side of British Colonialism* (New York: Universe Books, 1971), p. 209.

18. Howard J. Ehrlich, *The Social Psychology of Prejudice* (New York: John Wiley and Sons, 1973), p. 62.

19. Ibid.

20. Tamotsu Shibutani and Kian M. Kwan, *Ethnic Stratification: A Comparative Approach* (New York: Macmillan Co., 1965), p. 142.

21. Virginia Gayda, *Modern Austria: Her Racial and Social Problems* (London: T. Fisher Unwin, 1915), pp. 66–82.

22. Harry H. L. Kitano, *Japanese Americans* (New York: Prentice-Hall, 1969), p. 76.

23. Solberg, *Immigration and Nationalism*, pp. 48–49.

24. Ibid., p. 47.

25. Ibid., p. 49.

26. Ibid., p. 50.

27. Philip Mason, *Patterns of Dominance* (London: Oxford University Press, 1970), pp. 232–33.

28. Richard J. Coughlin, *Double Identity: The Chinese in Modern Thailand* (London: Oxford University Press, 1960), p. 137.

29. Lewis Coser, *The Functions of Social Conflict* (New York: Free Press, 1956), p. 37.

30. Bruce H. Mayhew and Robert L. Levinger, "On the Emergence of Oligarchy in Human Interaction," *American Journal of Sociology* 81 (March 1976): 1043–44.

31. James Morris, "Jubilee Day," in *The Horizon History of the British Empire*, ed. Stephen W. Sears (New York: American Heritage Publishing Co., 1973), pp. 11–12.

32. C. Wagley and H. Harris, *Minorities in the New World* (New York: Columbia University Press, 1958), p. 243.

33. This classification of three types of societies based upon patterns of race and ethnic relations was influenced by the work of M. G. Smith, Pierre van den Berghe, and Leo Kuper in *Pluralism in Africa*, edited by Leo Kuper and M. G. Smith (Berkeley and Los Angeles: University of California Press, 1969). However, there are several changes in approach and terminology for which these authors are not to blame. The "empire society" approximates Smith's model of a plural society, with its emphasis on a dominant minority, cultural diversity, and origins through conquest. If a plural society is one characterized by "(1) segmentation into corporate groups that frequently, though not necessarily, have different cultures or subcultures; and (2) a social structure compartmentalized into analogous, parallel, noncomplementary but distinguishable sets of institutions," (van den Berghe, p. 67), then an empire society is a plural society; however, so is a "pluralistic" society, as described in the text. Switzerland is plural but does not have a dominant ethnic group. This author feels that the "empire" type and the "pluralistic" should not be included together. "National" societies approximate what these authors have termed integrated societies, homogeneous societies, and nonplural societies.

Chapter 3

1. T. W. Moody and F. X. Martin, *The Course of Irish History* (Cork, Ireland: Mercier Press, 1967), p. 188.

2. Colonel G. Hamilton-Browne, "A Lost Legionary in South Africa (1879)," in *The Horizon History of Africa*, ed. Alvin M. Josephy, Jr. (New York: American Heritage Publishing Co., 1971), pp. 427–28.

3. Will Durant, *Our Oriental Heritage: The Story of Civilization, Part I* (New York: Simon and Schuster, 1954), p. 266.

4. Quoted by Klaus E. Knorr, *British Colonial Theories, 1570–1850* (Toronto: University of Toronto Press, 1944), p. 31.

5. Quoted by Harold Underwood Faulkner, *American Economic History*, 5th ed. (New York: Harper and Brothers, 1943), p. 36.

6. D. K. Fieldhouse, *The Colonial Empires* (New York: Delacorte Press, 1965), p. 393.

7. Ibid., pp. 380–94.

8. Stanlake Samkange, "Wars of Resistance," in Josephy, *The Horizon History of Africa*, p. 404.

9. Quoted by Louis L. Snyder, ed., *The Imperialism Reader* (Princeton, N.J.: D. Van Nostrand Co., 1962), p. 89, from A. Wirth, *The Race and World Power in History* (Berlin, 1904).

10. Moody and Martin, *Course of Irish History*, p. 174.

11. High Seton-Watson, *The Decline of Imperial Russia, 1855–1914* (New York: Frederick A. Praeger, 1964), p. 86.

12. Ibid.

13. Amaury de Riencourt, *The American Empire* (New York: Dial Press, 1968), p. 115.

14. Michael Edwardes, *British India, 1772–1947* (New York: Taplinger Publishing Co. 1967), pp. 18–19.

15. Quoted in Snyder, *The Imperalism Reader*, p. 453.

16. Ibid.

17. Ibid., p. 395.

18. The effects of the initial conquest of large numbers of white settlers on small numbers of indigenous natives have been studied by Grenfell A. Price in *White Settlers and Native Peoples: An Historical Study of Racial Contacts Between Whites and Aboriginal Peoples in the United States, Australia and New Zealand* (Melbourne: Georgian House, 1950). Contrasts between the two patterns of conquest have also been noted by Pierre van den Berghe in *Race and Racism* (New York: John Wiley and Sons, 1967), pp. 125–26.

19. Jim Hicks and Michael Edwardes, "Warfare on India's Borders," in Josephy, *The Horizon History of Africa*, pp. 155–58.

20. A. M. Carr-Saunders, *World Population* (Oxford: Clarendon, 1936), pp. 49, 56.

21. Arnold M. Rose, *Migrants in Europe* (Minneapolis: University of Minnesota Press, 1969), pp. 20–21.

22. Ibid., p. 22.

23. Sidney Harcave, *Russia: A History* (New York: J. B. Lippincott Co., 1953), p. 106.

24. Eugene M. Kulischer, *Europe on the Move: War and Population Changes, 1917–47* (New York: Columbia University Press, 1948), p. 139.

25. C. P. Kindleberger, "Mass Migration Then and Now," in *World Migration in Modern Times*, ed. Franklin D. Scott (Englewood Cliffs, N.J.: Prentice-Hall, 1968), p. 148.

26. Tamotsu Shibutani and Kian M. Kwan, *Ethnic Stratification: A Comparative Approach* (New York: Macmillan Co., 1965), p. 182.

27. Edward Wakin, *The Lebanese and Syrians in America* (Chicago: Claretian Publications, 1974), pp. 11–13.

28. Louise Holborn, "Refugee Migration in the Twentieth Century," in Scott, *World Migration in Modern Times*, p. 154.

29. Ibid., pp. 154–55.

30. Quoted by Andrew F. Rolle, *The Immigrant Upraised* (Norman: University of Oklahoma Press, 1968), pp. 38–39.

31. Lewis M. Alexander, *World Political Patterns* (Chicago: Rand McNally and Co., 1963), pp. 237–38.

32. Philip Mason, *Patterns of Dominance* (London: Oxford University Press, 1971), p. 116.

33. David Brion Davis, *The Problem of Slavery in Western Culture* (Ithaca, N.Y.: Cornell University Press, 1966), p. 32.

34. M. J. Finley, *Slavery in Classical Antiquity* (Cambridge: W. Heffer and Sons, 1960), p. 145.

35. Davis, *Slavery in Western Culture*, p. 47.

36. Ibid., p. 51.

37. Ibid., p. 52.

Chapter 4

1. The word "discrimination" comes from the Latin, *discriminatio*, meaning to perceive distinctions among phenomena or to be selective in one's judgment. In this broad meaning, a person is discriminating in his or her choice of food, art, friends. As used in the field of race and ethnic relations (and sexual relations), the meaning has been narrowed. According to Vander Zanden, for example, discrimination "entails overt action in which members of a group are accorded unfavorable treatment on the basis of their religious, ethnic, or racial membership" (James W. Vander Zanden, *American Minority Relations* [New York: Ronald Press, 1972], p. 26). This unequal or disadvantageous treatment is selective, as in the broad meaning, but unequal treatment is given to the category of human beings so selected as opposed to another category (for example, women as opposed to men). Unequal treatment, however, can range from verbal insults to genocide. In addition, this definition of Vander Zanden's (which is similar to many others) doesn't make clear whether or not the treatment is intentional. For these reasons, the definition offered in the text is even more narrow in scope than these two general meanings.

2. Tamotsu Shibutani and Kian M. Kwan, *Ethnic Stratification: A Comparative Approach* (New York: Macmillan Co., 1965), p. 329.

3. *Christian Science Monitor*, December 14, 1972, p. 11.

4. Frank F. Lee, *Negro and White in Connecticut Town* (New Haven, Conn.: College and University Press, 1961), p. 94.

5. William K. Tabb, "Race Relations Models and Social Change," *Social Problems* 18 (Spring 1971): 438.

6. Lester C. Thurow, *Poverty and Discrimination* (Washington, D.C.: Brookings Institution, 1969), pp. 130–34.

7. Gwendolen M. Carter, *The Politics of Inequality* (New York: Frederick A. Praeger, 1968), p. 25.

8. Norval D. Glenn, "White Gains from Negro Subordination," in *Blacks in the United States*, ed. Norval D. Glenn and Charles M. Bonjean (San Francisco: Chandler Publishing Co., 1969), p. 289. Originally published in *Social Problems*, Fall 1966, no. 14, pp. 159–78.

9. Richard J. Coughlin, *Double Identity: The Chinese in Modern Thailand* (London: Oxford University Press, 1960), pp. 129–31, 133.

10. Norval D. Glenn, "The Role of White Resistance and Facilitation in the Negro Struggle for Equality," in *Power and the Black Community*, ed. Sethard Fisher (New York: Random House, 1970), p. 416.

11. Prosser Gifford and Timothy C. Weiskel, "African Education in a Colonial Context: French and British Styles," in *France and Britain in Africa*, ed. Prosser Gifford and William Roger Louis (New Haven, Conn: Yale University Press, 1971), pp. 673–74.

12. Norval D. Glenn, "White Resistance and Facilitation," p. 417.

13. Ibid.

14. *Time*, May 15, 1972, pp. 39–40.

15. Robert Conquest, *The Nation Killers: The Soviet Deportation of Nationalities* (London: Macmillan and Co., 1970), p. 62.

16. Will Durant, *The Reformation: The Story of Civilization, Part VI* (New York: Simon and Schuster, 1957), pp. 217–18.

17. R. A. Schermerhorn, *Comparative Ethnic Relations: A Framework for Theory and Research* (New York: Random House, 1970), p. 198.

18. Vincent Cable, "The Asians of Kenya," *African Affairs* 68 (July 1969): 218–31.

19. Samuel Lear, "The Concept of Institutionalization," *Sociology and Social Research* 36 (January-February 1952): 178.

20. Durant, *The Reformation*, p. 734; and Will and Ariel Durant, *Rousseau and Revolution: The Story of Civilization, Part X* (New York: Simon and Schuster, 1967), p. 631.

21. T. A. Jackson, *Ireland Her Own* (New York: International Publishers Co., 1947), pp. 65–66.

22. United Nations, *Apartheid in Practice* (New York: United Nations, 1969), pp. 7, 9.

23. Shibutani and Kwan, *Ethnic Stratification*, p. 323.

24. C. H. Haring, *The Spanish Empire in America* (New York: Oxford University Press, 1947), p. 218.

25. Lillian Estelle Fisher, *The Last Inca Revolt, 1780–1783* (Norman: University of Oklahoma Press, 1966), pp. 7–8.

26. Ibid., pp. 11–12.

27. Ibid., p. 15.

28. Haring, *The Spanish Empire in America*, p. 216.

29. Gilbert Thomas Stephenson, *Race Distinctions in American Law* (New York: D. Appleton and Co., 1910), p. 255.

30. Ibid., p. 254.

31. United Nations, *Apartheid in Practice*, p. 25.

32. Donald R. Matthews and James W. Prothro, "Political Factors and Negro Voter Registration in the South," *American Political Science Review* 57 (June 1963): 366.

33. Melvin L. Kohn and Robin M. Williams, "Situational Patterning in Intergroup Relations," in *Race, Class, and Power*, ed. Raymond Mack (New York: American Book Co., 1968), p. 153. Originally published in *American Sociological Review* 21 (April 1956): 164–74.

34. Ibid., pp. 154–58. The words in parentheses are a condensation by this author.

35. Chester L. Hunt and Lewis Walker, *Ethnic Dynamics: Patterns of Intergroup Relations in Various Societies* (Homewood, Ill.: Dorsey Press, 1974), pp. 107–108.

36. Richard Wright, "The Ethics of Living Jim Crow," in *Justice Denied: The Black Man in White America*, ed. William M. Chace and Peter Collier (New York: Harcourt, Brace and World, 1970), p. 280; an excerpt from *Uncle Tom's Children* (New York: Harper and Row, 1937 and 1965).

37. Pierre van den Berghe defines racism as "any set of beliefs that organic genetically transmitted differences (whether real or imagined) between human groups are intrinsically associated with the presence or absence of certain socially relevant abilities or characteristics, hence that such differences are a legitimate basis of invidious distinctions between groups socially defined as races." Pierre van den Berghe, *Race and Racism: A Comparative Perspective* [New York: John Wiley and Sons, 1967], p. 11). Professor van den Berghe limits racism to races and to beliefs based upon biological determinism; the definition, however, does emphasize that racism is a doctrine that justifies actions.

In Michael Banton's meaning of the term, racism is "the doctrine that a man's behaviour is determined by stable inherited characters deriving from separate racial stocks having distinctive attributes and usually considered to stand to one another in relations of superiority and inferiority. It is to be distinguished from *racialism*, which does not refer so much to the doctrine as to the practice of it . . ." (Michael Banton, *Race Relations* [New York: Basic Books, 1967], p. 8). Banton's meaning is similar to van den Berghe's, although ideas of inferiority and superiority are definitely stated, and racism as a belief system is clearly distinguished from actions (actions which he terms racialism).

For William J. Wilson, racism includes beliefs based upon one form of environmental determinism—cultural: racism is "an ideology of racial domination or exploitation that (1) incorporates beliefs in a particular race's cultural and/or inherent biological inferiority and (2) uses such beliefs to justify and prescribe inferior unequal treatment for that group" (William J. Wilson, *Power, Racism, and Privilege* [New York: Macmillan Co., 1973], p. 32). Again, in this meaning racism is a doctrine that justifies actions, but it does not include such actions in the meaning of term.

Donald Baker fuses beliefs about inferiority and superiority with actions taken in his definition of the concept: racism is "where a group of one color, or common social heritage, viewing itself as superior, utilizes its power to suppress and/or exploit those of another color or community group . . ." (Donald G. Baker, "Australian and Anglo Racism: Preliminary Explorations," in *Racism: The Australian Experience,* vol. 3, Colonialism, ed. F. S. Stevens [New York: Taplinger Publishing Co., 1972], p. 19). Baker's view does include ethnic groups, however.

Vander Zanden's usage is all-encompassing: "an inclusive concept that embraces the notion of prejudice, discrimination, and structural racism" (James W. Vander Zanden, *American Minority Relations,* 3d ed. [New York: Ronald Press, 1972], p. 29).

38. Simon Davis, *Race Relations in Ancient Egypt* (New York: Philosophical Library, 1952), p. 2.

39. James Bardin, "Science and the 'Negro Problem,'" in *The Development of Segregationist Thought,* ed. I. A. Newby (Homewood, Ill.: Dorsey Press, 1968), p. 34.

40. George Frederickson, *The Black Image in the White Mind* (New York: Harper and Row, 1971), p. 314.

41. William Robertson, "History of America," in *Historians at Work,* vol. 2, ed. Peter Gay and Victor G. Wexler (New York: Harper and Row, 1972), p. 264.

42. Leo J. Hannett, "Niugini Black Power," in F. S. Stevens, *Racism,* p. 48.

43. Titus Livius, *The History of Rome,* vol. IV, book 38, trans. William A. M'Devitte (London: George Bell and Sons, 1888), p. 1740.

44. Winthrop D. Jordan, *White over Black* (Chapel Hill: University of North Carolina Press, 1968), pp. 508–509.

45. Robert Bennett Bean, "The Nose of the Jew and the Quadratus Labii Superioris Muscle," *American Anthropologist,* January 1913, pp. 106–108. Reproduced in *In Their Place: White America Defines Her Minorities, 1850–1950,* ed. Lewis H. Carlson and George A. Colburn (New York: John Wiley and Sons, 1972), p. 269.

46. Howard J. Ehrlich, *The Social Psychology of Prejudice* (New York: John Wiley and Sons, 1973), pp. 25–27.

47. Shibutani and Kwan, *Ethnic Stratification,* pp. 83–84.

48. Livius, *The History of Rome,* vol. III, book 34, p. 1514.

49. Ibid., vol. II, book 23, p. 840.

50. John West, *The History of Tasmania* (Sydney: Angus and Robertson, 1971) p. 333.

51. Adolph Hitler, *Mein Kampf* (New York: Reynal and Hitchcock, 1940), pp. 417–50.

52. Quoted in Raphael Patai, *Israel Between East and West* (Philadelphia: The Jewish Publication Society of America, 1953), pp. 294–95.

53. Quoted in Sammy Smooha, "Pluralism: A Study of Intergroup Relations in Israel" (Ph.D. diss., University of California, Los Angeles, 1973) pp. 102–103.

54. W. B. Lighton, "The Greaser," in Carlson and Colburn, *In Their Place,* pp. 137, 138. Originally published in *Atlantic Monthly,* June 1899, pp. 750–60.

55. Howard Odum, "The Education of Negroes," in *The Development of Segregationist Thought,* ed. I. A. Newby (Homewood, Ill.: Dorsey Press, 1968), pp. 64, 67. Reprinted from Howard Odum, *Social and Mental Traits of the Negro* (New York: Columbia University Press, 1910).

56. Ibid., p. 68.

57. A. J. Alfaro Cardoso, "A Portuguese Defense of Paternalism in the African Colonies, 1950," in *The Imperialism Reader,* ed. Louis L. Snyder (Princeton, N.J.: D. Van Nostrand Co., 1962), p. 498.

58. van den Berghe, *Race and Racism*, p. 72.

59. David C. Gordon, "Algeria, 1962–1967: An Essay on Dependence in Independence," in *France and Britain in Africa*, ed. Prosser Gifford and William Roger Louis (New Haven, Conn.: Yale University Press, 1971), p. 769.

60. Stephen S. Baratz and Joan C. Baratz, "Early Childhood Intervention: The Social Science Base of Institutional Racism," in *Majority and Minority*, ed. Norman R. Yetman and C. Hoy Steele (Boston: Allyn and Bacon, 1971), p. 473. Previously published in *Harvard Educational Review* 40 (Winter 1970): 29–50.

61. Kenneth B. Clark, *Dark Ghetto: Dilemmas of Power* (New York: Harper and Row, 1965), p. 131.

62. Several of these examples are cited in Louis L. Knowles and Kenneth Prewitt, *Institutional Racism in America* (Englewood Cliffs, N.J.: Prentice-Hall, 1969), pp. 5, 21, 37–39, 88–89.

63. The concept of institutional racism is probably the most ambiguous idea of recent invention. All of the following ideas have been found in the meaning of this concept, with particular theorists selecting some or all of these aspects: intentional discrimination motivated by racist attitudes; unintended policies and practices *not* based upon racism (as a doctrine) but with similar effects; all practices of organizations ("institutions") and their consequences, whereby one race is disadvantaged regardless of the motives of the members; racial inequality or stratification generally; the indirect *or* the direct effects of intentional *or* unintentional practices and policies (for example, low income on the average, high infant mortality rates, slums). See: Stokely Carmichael and Charles Hamilton, *Black Power: The Politics of Liberation in America* (New York: Random House, 1967); Louis Knowles and Kenneth Prewitt, eds., *Institutional Racism in America* (Englewood Cliffs, N.J.: Prentice-Hall, 1969); Robert Blauner, *Racial Oppression in America* (New York: Harper and Row, 1972); Jerome H. Skolnick, *The Politics of Protest* (New York: Ballantine Books, 1969); Robert Friedman, "Institutional Racism: How to Discriminate without Really Trying," in *Racial Discrimination in the United States*, ed. Thomas F. Pettigrew (New York: Harper and Row, 1975).

64. Shibutani and Kwan, *Ethnic Stratification*, p. 331.

65. Michael Edwardes, *British India, 1772–1947* (New York: Taplinger Publishing Co., 1967), p. 182.

66. Ibid.

67. Haring, *The Spanish Empire in America*, p. 215.

68. Judith R. Kramer, *The American Minority Community* (New York: Thomas Y. Crowell Co., 1970), p. 260.

69. Ibid., p. 264.

70. Will Durant, *The Age of Faith: The Story of Civilization*, Part IV (New York: Simon and Schuster, 1950), p. 393.

71. Schermerhorn, *Comparative Ethnic Relations*, pp. 24–25.

72. Will Durant, *Caesar and Christ: The Story of Civilization, Part III* (New York: Simon and Schuster, 1944), pp. 542–45.

73. Lillian Estelle Fisher, *The Last Inca Revolt, 1780–1783*.

74. Sidney Harcave, *Russia: A History* (New York: J. B. Lippincott Co., 1953), p. 264.

75. Michael Edwardes, "The Great Mutiny," *The Horizon History of the British Empire*, ed. Stephen W. Sears (New York: American Heritage Publishing Co., 1973), pp. 168–74.

76. Stuart Legg, "From Suez to Khartoum," in Sears, *History of the British Empire*, p. 237.

77. John L. Phelan, *The Hispanization of the Philippines* (Madison: University of Wisconsin Press, 1959), p. 145.

78. Hugh Seton-Watson, *The Decline of Imperial Russia, 1855–1941* (New York: Frederick A. Praeger, 1964), pp. 162–64.

79. Stanlake Samkange, "Wars of Resistance," in *The Horizon History of Africa*, ed. Alvin M. Josephy, Jr. (New York: American Heritage Publishing Co., 1971), p. 422.

80. George Shepperson, "Under Colonial Rule," in Josephy, *The Horizon History of Africa*, p. 449.

81. Victor-L. Tapié, *The Rise and Fall of the Habsburg Monarchy* (New York: Praeger Publishers, 1971), p. 286.

Chapter 5

1. This definition of a social movement is a composite of the following: (1) "a group venture extending beyond a local community or a single event and involving a systematic effort to inaugurate changes in thought, behavior, and social relationships" (C. Wendell King, *Social Movements in the United States* [New York: Random House, 1956], p. 27); (2) "a social movement is a conscious, collective, organized attempt to bring about or resist large-scale change in the social order by noninstitutionalized means" (John Wilson, *Introduction to Social Movements* [New York: Basic Books, 1973], p. 8). King's emphasis on transcending a local community or a single event is important in distinguishing a social movement from a localized issue or event; however, Wilson's usage of "organized collective venture" is more accurate than the "group venture" used by King—social movements generally involve a number of groups. Wilson's stress on "noninstitutionalized means" is too restrictive—reform movements and sometimes radical movements rely on institutionalized means on occasion. Wilson's idea of *resisting* change is important; however, groups that attempt to resist change nevertheless want change—restoration of the status quo.

2. Social scientists place different emphasis on particular factors involved in the origins of social movements. For views emphasizing external structural changes and threats to established positions, see: Talcott Parsons, "Social Strains in America," in *The Radical Right*, ed. Daniel Bell, Garden City (New York: Doubleday (Anchor), 1964); Neil J. Smelser, *Theory of Collective Behavior* (New York: Free Press, 1962); Tamotsu Shibutani and Kian M. Kwan, *Ethnic Stratification: A Comparative Approach* (New York: Macmillan Co., 1965), pp. 343–51. Regarding rising expectations and relative deprivation, see: James C. Davies, "Toward a Theory of Revolution," *American Sociological Review* 27 (February): 5–19; John Wilson, *Introduction to Social Movements* (New York: Basic Books, 1973), pp. 68–69; Ted Robert Gurr, *Why Men Rebel* (Princeton, N.J.: Princeton University Press, 1970). For views on the perception of power differentials and success, see: William J. Wilson, *Power, Racism, and Privilege* (New York: Macmillan Co., 1973), pp. 48–61; Charles Tilly, "Collective Violence in European Perspective," in *The History of Violence in America*, ed. Hugh Davis Graham and Ted Robert Gurr (New York: Bantam Books, 1969).

3. Social problem theorists have stressed these three elements but have added others, elements or aspects that may more usefully be conceived of as dimensions or variations in social problems. For example: (1) A number of significant or competent observers define the problems (as opposed to insignificant and incompetent people).

This dimension can be labeled—attributes of the definers. (2) A significant number of people must be aware of the condition and make the same judgment (as opposed to an insignificant number)—a dimension of the number of people aware of the problem. (3) Social problems are within a society (as opposed to being international); this dimension can be termed the range of the problem. And (4), social problems are serious in nature (as opposed to being trivial)—the dimension of magnitude or degree of seriousness.

4. Integration, as defined in this text, is the opposite of segmentation, or one meaning of pluralism. There are, of course, other meanings. Ethnic integration for Hunt and Walker is more of an end state, and something corresponding to assimilation in this book: "a situation in which all citizens of the nation, or possibly even all members of the society regardless of citizenship, participate freely in all forms of social interaction without concern for ethnic affiliation. . . . The integrated society is not directly concerned with ethnic group equality, inequality, survival, or disappearance. Its legal and social structure is not concerned with ethnicity" (Chester L. Hunt and Lewis Walker, *Ethnic Dynamics: Patterns of Intergroup Relations in Various Societies* [Homewood, Ill.: Dorsey Press, 1974], p. 8). I would use this meaning as a form of extreme integration, and as a condition rather than a process.

Another use of the term involves the idea of cohesiveness, or "bondedness," as the opposite of *disintegration*. In one variant of this idea of cohesiveness, Max Gluckman emphasizes cohesiveness and consensus: "Cohesion arises from high articulation of the parts of a system or subsystem. If cohesion exists in a system where there is also a high degree of consensus, we may speak perhaps of a society with a high degree of integration. Integration is lacking where there is cohesion but relatively little consensus, or the consensus exists only within restricted groups" (Max Gluckman, "The Tribal Area in South and Central Africa," in *Pluralism in Africa*, ed. Leo Kuper and M. G. Smith [Berkeley and Los Angeles: University of California Press, 1969], p. 389). A second variant involving the idea of cohesiveness but emphasizing behavioral compliance and dominance as well is the definition of R. A. Schermerhorn: integration is "a process whereby units or elements of a society are brought into an active and coordinated compliance with the ongoing activities and objectives of the dominant group" (R. A. Schermerhorn, *Comparative Ethnic Relations: A Framework for Theory and Research* [New York: Random House, 1970], p. 66).

5. Charles H. Anderson, *White Protestant Americans* (Englewood Cliffs, N.J.: Prentice-Hall, 1970), pp. 58, 68, 70.

6. A. L. Kroeber, *Anthropology* (New York: Harcourt, Brace and Co., 1948), p. 425.

7. Ibid., p. 433.

8. Howard J. Ehrlich, *The Social Psychology of Prejudice* (New York: John Wiley and Sons, 1973), p. 62.

9. Ibid.

10. Kroeber, *Anthropology*, p. 432.

11. Tamotsu Shibutani and Kian M. Kwan, *Ethnic Stratification: A Comparative Approach* (New York: Macmillan Co., 1965), p. 130.

12. Ibid.

13. Pierre van den Berghe, *Race and Racism: A Comparative Perspective* (New York: John Wiley and Sons, 1967), pp. 45–58.

14. Michael Edwardes, *British India, 1772–1947* (New York: Taplinger Publishing Co., 1967), p. 288.

15. See: Sammy Smooha, "Black Panthers: The Ethnic Dilemma," *Society* 9 (May

1972): 31–36; and Mark Iris and Avraham Shama, "Black Panthers: The Movement," ibid., pp. 37–44.

16. Smooha, "Black Panthers: The Ethnic Dilemma," p. 32.

17. Iris and Shama, "Black Panthers: The Movement," p. 44.

18. Stated in *Racism: The Australian Experience*, vol. I, Prejudice and Xenophobia, ed. F. S. Stevens (New York: Taplinger Publishing Co., 1972), p. 37.

19. Walter Kolarz, *Russia and Her Colonies* (New York: Frederick A. Praeger, 1952), p. 208; as quoted in Schermerhorn, *Comparative Ethnic Relations*, p. 139. Similarly, in 1961 Khruschev stated, "Communists will not conserve and perpetuate national distinctions. . . . Even the slightest vestiges of nationalism should be eradicated with uncompromising Bolshevik determination." Quoted in Hunt and Walker, *Ethnic Dynamics*, pp. 64–65.

20. The concept of modernization has two meanings in the literature. The first is quite narrow—the introduction of industrial technology (mechanization, factories, credit). The broader meaning includes this plus all of the changes that are assumed to go with new technology. According to Wilbert E. Moore, "what is involved in modernization is a 'total' transformation of a traditional or pre-modern society into the type of technology and associated social organization that characterize the 'advanced,' economically prosperous, and relatively politically stable nations of the Western World" Wilbert E. Moore, *Social Change* (Englewood Cliffs, N.J.: Prentice-Hall, 1963), p. 89.

21. Cynthia H. Enloe, *Ethnic Conflict and Political Development* (Boston: Little, Brown and Co., 1973), p. 137.

22. *Newsweek*, September 3, 1973, p. 32.

23. Hugh Seton-Watson, *From Lenin to Malenkov* (New York: Frederick A. Praeger, 1955), p. 164.

24. Ibid., p. 242.

25. Carl Solberg, *Immigration and Nationalism: Argentina and Chile, 1890–1914* (Austin: University of Texas Press, 1970), p. 154.

26. Ibid.

27. Ibid., pp. 170–71.

28. Lewis M. Alexander, *World Political Patterns* (Chicago: Rand McNally and Co., 1963), pp. 248–49.

29. Doral McCartney, "From Parnell to Pearse (1891–1921)," in *The Course of Irish History*, ed. T. W. Moody and F. X. Martin (Cork, Ireland: Mercier Press, 1967), pp. 295–96.

30. *Denver Post*, October 3, 1973, p. 3.

31. H. J. Hanham, *Scottish Nationalism* (Cambridge: Harvard University Press, 1969), p. 75.

32 .Virginio Gayda, *Modern Austria: Her Racial and Social Problems* (London: T. Fisher Unwin, 1915), p. 91.

33. Victor-L. Tapié, *The Rise and Fall of the Habsburg Monarchy* (New York: Praeger Publishers, 1971), p. 78.

34. Enloe, *Ethnic Conflict and Political Development*, pp. 141–42.

35. Michael Edwardes, "The Threatened Raj," in *The Horizon History of the British Empire*, ed. Stephen W. Sears (New York: The American Heritage Publishing Co., 1973), p. 440.

36. Edwardes, *British India, op. cit.*, pp. 295–296.

37. Ibid., pp. 161, 198.

38. Joan Gillespie, *Algeria: Rebellion and Revolution* (New York: Frederick A. Praeger, 1960).

39. David Horowitz, *The Free World Colossus* (New York: Hill and Wang, 1965), p. 146.

40. Ibid., pp. 141–62.

41. *Time*, May 6, 1974, pp. 18–24; *International Herald Tribune*, September 4, 1973, byline by Peter Younghusband.

42. Ved P. Nanda in *Denver Rocky Mountain News*, December 7, 1971, pp. 18–19.

43. *Denver Rocky Mountain News*, November 27, 1973, p. 54.

44. Stanley Lieberson, "Stratifications and Ethnic Groups," *Sociological Inquiry* 40 (Spring 1970): 173.

45. Joseph Ward Swain, *The Ancient World*, vol. 1 (New York: Harper and Brothers, 1950), pp. 191–92.

46. Will Durant, *Age of Faith: The Story of Civilization, Part IV* (New York: Simon and Schuster, 1950), p. 196.

47. John A. Wilson, *The Culture of Ancient Egypt* (Chicago: University of Chicago Press, Phoenix Books, 1951), pp. 168, 292–93.

48. Roy Lewis and Yvonne Foy, *Painting Africa White: The Human Side of British Colonialism* (New York: Universe Books, 1971), p. 203.

49. Ibid., p. 205.

50. Ibid., p. 207.

51. William J. Wilson, *Power, Racism, and Privilege* (New York: Macmillan Co., 1973), p. 176.

52. Ibid., pp. 176–77.

53. Enloe, *Ethnic Conflict and Political Development*, pp. 226–27.

54. Ibid., p. 227.

55. Schermerhorn, *Comparative Ethnic Relations*, p. 270.

56. Ibid.

57. Shibutani and Kwan, *Ethnic Stratification*, pp. 123–24.

58. Lucien Bodard, "The Massacre of the Amazonian Indians," *Interplay*, March, 1970. See also, Lucien Bodard, *Green Hell: Massacre of the Brazilian Indians* (New York: Outerbridge and Dienstfrey, distributed by E. P. Dutton, 1972).

Chapter 6

1. Leonard Dinnerstein and Frederic Cople Jaher, "The Colonial Era," in *The Aliens: A History of Ethnic Minorities in America*, ed. Leonard Dinnerstein and Frederic Cople Jaher (New York: Appleton-Century-Crofts, Meredith Corporation, 1971), p. 17.

2. Harold Underwood Faulkner, *American Economic History*, 5th ed. (New York: Harper and Brothers, 1943), p. 105.

3. Nathan Glazer, *American Judaism* (Chicago: University of Chicago Press, 1957), pp. 14–19.

4. Charles H. Anderson, *White Protestant Americans* (Englewood Cliffs, N.J.: Prentice-Hall, 1970), p. 44.

5. Donald Reed Taft, *Human Migration* (New York: Ronald Press Co., 1936), p. 71.

6. Anderson, *White Protestant Americans*, p. 2.

7. Maldwyn Allen Jones, *American Immigration* (Chicago: University of Chicago Press, 1960), p. 44.

8. Ibid.

9. Glenn Weaver, "Benjamin Franklin and the Pennsylvania Germans," in Dinnerstein and Jaher, *The Aliens*, p. 50.

10. Maldwyn Allen Jones, *American Immigration*, p. 45.

11. Quoted in Louis M. Hacker, "The First American Revolution," in *The Causes of the American Revolution*, ed. John C. Wahlke (Boston: D.C. Heath and Co., 1950), p. 4. Reprinted from *Columbia University Quarterly*, vol. XXVII, no. 3, September 1935).

12. Faulkner, *American Economic History*, p. 116.

13. Ibid.

14. Hacker, "The First American Revolution," p. 10.

15. Faulkner, *American Economic History*, p. 118.

16. Hans Kohn, "The Meaning of Imperialism, Colonialism, and Their Variations, 1958," in *The Imperialism Reader*, ed. Louis L. Snyder, (Princeton, N.J.: D. Van Nostrand Co., 1962), p. 47.

17. Samuel Eliot Morison, *The Oxford History of the American People* (New York: Oxford University Press, 1965), pp. 181–82.

18. Ibid., p. 169.

19. Lawrence Henry Gipson, "The American Revolution as an Aftermath of the Great War for the Empire, 1754–1763," in Wahlke, *The Causes of the American Revolution*, p. 93. Reprinted from *Political Science Quarterly* LXV (March 1950).

20. Gareth Stedman Jones, "The Specificity of U.S. Imperialism," in *The Poverty of Progress*, ed. Milton Mankoff (New York: Holt, Rinehart and Winston, 1972), p. 135.

21. Faulkner, *American Economic History*, p. 121.

22. Hacker, "The First American Revolution," p. 9.

23. Morison, *History of the American People*, p. 235.

24. Daniel J. Boorstin, *The Americans: The Colonial Experience* (New York: Vintage Books, Random House, 1958), p. 368.

25. Ibid., p. 370.

26. Maldwyn Allen Jones, *American Immigration*, p. 51.

27. Russel Blaine Nye, *The Cultural Life of the New Nation* (New York: Harper and Brothers, 1960), p. 40.

28. Ibid., p. 39.

29. Howard Mumford Jones, *O Strange New World, American Culture: The Formative Years* (New York: Viking Press, 1964), p. 288.

30. Ibid.

31. Ibid., p. 319.

32. Ibid., p. 317.

33. Nye, *Cultural Life*, pp. 40–41.

34. Maldwyn Allen Jones, *American Immigration*, p. 39.

35. Ibid., pp. 75–76.

36. Max Lerner, *America as a Civilization* (New York: Simon and Schuster, 1957), p. 20.

37. Boorstin, *The Americans*, p. 275.

38. Ibid. p. 276.

39. Ibid., p. 275.

40. Howard Mumford Jones, *American Culture*, pp. 228–33, 264–65, 270.

41. John D. Hicks, *The Federal Union* (Boston: Houghton Mifflin, 1957), p. 327.

42. Ibid., pp. 326–28.

43. Lerner, *America as a Civilization*, p. 63.

44. Ralph Barton Perry, *Characteristically American* (New York: Alfred A. Knopf, 1949), pp. 8–33.

45. Ibid., p. 11.

46. Ibid.

47. Ibid., pp. 28–29.

48. Ibid., p. 15.

49. Ibid., pp. 15–16.

50. Robin M. Williams, Jr., *American Society* (New York: Alfred A. Knopf, 1952), p. 389.

51. Ibid., pp. 390–440.

52. Amaury de Riencourt, *The Coming Caesars* (New York: Coward-McCann, 1957), p. 196.

53. Quoted in C. Wright Mills, *The Power Elite* (New York: Oxford University Press, 1956), p. 177, footnote.

54. Amaury de Riencourt, *The American Empire* (New York: Dial Press, 1968), pp. 10–11.

Chapter 7

1. Alvin M. Josephy, Jr., *The Indian Heritage of America* (New York: Alfred A. Knopf, 1969), p. 12.

2. Ibid., pp. 24–28.

3. Ibid., pp. 283–84.

4. Ibid., pp. 279–80.

5. Robert M. Utley, *Frontier Regulars: The United States Army and the Indians, 1848–1865* (New York: Macmillian Co., 1967), p. 5.

6. Josephy, *The Indian Heritage of America*, p. 282.

7. Peter Farb, *Man's Rise to Civilization as Shown by the Indians of North America from Primeval Times to the Coming of the Industrial State*, (New York: E. P. Dutton and Co., 1968), p. 255.

8. Robert M. Utley, *Frontiersmen in Blue: The United States Army and the Indians, 1866–1890* (New York: Macmillan Co., 1973), p. 8.

9. Ibid., pp. 8–9.

10. Ibid., pp. 53–57.

11. Utley, *Frontiersmen in Blue*, p. 110.

12. Ibid., p. 111.

13. John Upton Terrell, *Apache Chronicle* (New York: World Publishing Co., 1972), p. 261.

14. Utley, *Frontiersmen in Blue*, p. 296.

15. Terrell, *Apache Chronicle*, p. 319.

16. Utley, *Frontiersmen in Blue*, pp. 346–47.

17. Samuel Eliot Morison, *The Oxford History of the American People* (New York: Oxford University Press, 1965), pp. 342–43.

18. Ibid., p. 381.

19. Ibid., pp. 381–82.

20. Josephy, *The Indian Heritage of America*, pp. 323–24; Morison, *History of the American People*, pp. 447–50.

21. Ray Allen Billington, *Westward Expansion* (New York: Macmillan Co., 1950), pp. 298–301.

22. Josephy, *The Indian Heritage of America*, pp. 145–46.

23. Ibid., pp. 328–29.

24. Morison, *History of the American People*, p. 750.

25. Utley, *Frontiersmen in Blue*, p. 295.

26. Dee Brown, *Bury My Heart at Wounded Knee* (New York: Holt, Rinehart and Winston, 1970), pp. 14–36.

27. Ibid., pp. 273–313.

28. Terrell, *Apache Chronicle*, p. 243.

29. Ibid., pp. 243–385.

30. Brown, *Bury My Heart at Wounded Knee*, pp. 431–45.

31. Basil Davidson, *The African Slave Trade* (Boston: Little, Brown and Co., 1961), p. 20. Published in the hardcover edition under the title of *Black Mother*.

32. Ibid., pp. 35–36.

33. Ibid., pp. 45–48.

34. Ibid., p. 51. See also: A. Adu Boahen, "The Coming of the European," in *The Horizon History of Africa*, ed. Alvin M. Josephy, Jr. (New York: American Heritage Publishing Co., 1971), p. 315.

35. Boahen, p. 315.

36. Davidson, *The African Slave Trade*, p. 50; Boahen, *History of Africa* pp. 312–13.

37. Boahen, *History of Africa* pp. 317–18.

38. Roy Lewis and Yvonne Foy, *Painting Africa White: The Human Side of British Colonialism* (New York: Universe Books, 1971), pp. 8–10.

39. Davidson, *The African Slave Trade*, p. 85.

40. Boahen, *History of Africa*, p. 318.

41. Robert Walsh, Jr., *An Appeal from the Judgments of Great Britain Respecting the United States of America*, 2d ed. (New York: Negro Universities Press, 1819, 1969), p. 336.

42. Charles E. Silberman, *Crisis in Black and White* (New York: Random House, 1964), p. 90.

43. Daniel Mannix and Malcolm Cowley "The Middle Passage," in *Justice Denied: The Black Man in White America*, ed. William M. Chace and Peter Collier (New York: Harcourt, Brace and World, 1970), p. 20.

44. Ibid., pp. 30–31.

45. Boahen, *History of Africa*, pp. 315–16.

46. Winthrop D. Jordan, *White over Black* (Chapel Hill: University of North Carolina Press, 1968), p. 73.

47. Ibid., p. 74.

48. Ibid., p. 75.

49. Ibid., p. 74.

50. Ibid., pp. 74–75.

51. Benjamin Quarles, *The Negro in the Making of America* (New York: Collier Books, Macmillan, 1964), p. 36.

52. Jordan, *White over Black*, p. 81.

53. Arthur Zilversmit, *The First Emancipation: The Abolition of Slavery in the North* (Chicago: University of Chicago Press, 1967), pp. 226–29.

54. Harold Underwood Faulkner, *American Economic History*, 5th ed. (New York: Harper and Brothers, 1943), p. 323.

55. Ibid., p. 325.

56. Jordan, *White over Black*, p. 28.

57. Ibid., p. 80.

58. Ibid., p. 34.

59. Ibid.

60. Ibid.

61. George M. Fredrickson, *The Black Image in the White Mind* (New York: Harper and Row, 1971), p. 2.

62. Joan W. Moore, *Mexican-Americans* (Englewood Cliffs, N.J.: Prentice-Hall, 1970), p. 12.

63. Jack D. Forbes, "Mexican-Americans," in *Mexican-Americans in the United States*, ed. John H. Burma (Cambridge: Schenkman Publishing Co., 1970), p. 9.

64. Rodolfo Acuna, *Occupied America: The Chicano's Struggle toward Liberation* (San Francisco: Canfield Press, 1972), p. 56.

65. Julius W. Pratt, *Expansionists of 1898: The Acquisition of Hawaii and the Spanish Islands* (Baltimore: John Hopkins Press, 1936).

66. Carey McWilliams, *North from Mexico: The Spanish-Speaking People of the United States* (Philadelphia: J. B. Lippincott Co., 1949), p. 90.

67. Pratt, *Expansionists of 1898*, p. 63.

68. Ibid., pp. 75–76.

69. Ibid., pp. 110–15.

70. Ibid., pp. 222, 249, 253.

71. Morison, *History of the American People*, p. 551.

72. J. F. C. Fuller, *Decisive Battles of the U.S.A. (New York: Beechhurst Press, 1953)*, p. 139; Acuna, *Occupied America*, p. 7.

73. Acuna, *Occupied America*, pp. 17–18.

74. Fuller, *Decisive Battles of the U.S.A.*, pp. 142–45.

75. Acuna, *Occupied America*, p. 18.

76. McWilliams, *North from Mexico*, pp. 120–21.

77. Morison, *History of the American People*, p. 559.

78. Ibid., p. 561.

79. Fuller, *Decisive Battles of the U.S.A.*, pp. 148–67.

80. McWilliams, *North from Mexico*, p. 103.

81. *1974 Annual Report: Immigration and Naturalization Service* (Washington, D.C.: Government Printing Office), Table 13, pp. 56–58.

82. John Higham, *Strangers in the Land: Patterns of American Nativism, 1860–1925* (New York: Atheneum, 1965), p. 16.

83. Ibid.

84. Ibid., p. 18.

85. Maldwyn Allen Jones, *American Immigration* (Chicago: University of Chicago Press, 1960), p. 95.

86. McWilliams, *North from Mexico*, pp. 185–86.

87. Ibid.

88. Ibid., pp. 179, 185.

89. Arnold Schrier, *Ireland and the American Emigration, 1850–1900* (Minneapolis: University of Minnesota Press, 1958), pp. 11–12.

90. Mack Walker, excerpted in *World Migration in Modern Times*, ed. Franklin D. Scott (Englewood Cliffs, N.J.: 1968), p. 22.

91. Leonard Dinnerstein and Frederic Cople Jaher, "The Young Republic," in *The Aliens: A History of Ethnic Minorities in America*, ed. Leonard Dinnerstein and Frederic Cople Jaher (New York: Meredith Corporation, Appleton-Century-Crofts, 1970), pp. 78–79.

92. Daniel J. Boorstin, *The Americans: The National Experience* (New York: Vintage Books, Random House, 1965), p. 179.

93. Ibid.

94. Ibid.

95. Andrew F. Rolle, *The Immigrant Upraised* (Norman: University of Oklahoma Press, 1968), p. 57.

96. Higham, *Strangers in the Land*, p. 113.

97. Ibid., p. 114.

98. *Annual Report of the Commissioner General of Immigration* (Washington, D.C.: Government Printing Office, 1929), Table 82, p. 184.

99. Maldwyn Allen Jones, *American Immigration*, pp. 180–81.

100. Gareth Stedman Jones, "The Specificity of U.S. Imperialism," in *The Poverty of Progress*, ed. Milton Mankoff (New York: Holt, Rinehart and Winston, 1972), p. 141.

101. Morison, *History of the American People*, p. 578.

102. Moorfield Storey and Marcial P. Lichauco, *The Conquest of the Philippines by the United States* (New York: G. P. Putnam's Sons, 1926), pp. 20–23, 10–31.

103. Gareth Stedman Jones, "The Specificity of U.S. Imperialism," p. 141.

104. Ibid., p. 144.

105. Storey and Lichauco, *Conquest of the Philippines*, p. 45.

106. Ray Allen Billington, Bert James Loewenberg, and Samuel Hugh Brockunier, eds., *The Making of American Democracy*, vol. II (New York: Rinehart and Co., 1950), pp. 277–78.

107. Storey and Lichauco, *Conquest of the Philippines*, pp. 67–70.

108. Ibid., p. 96.

109. Henry F. Graff, *American Imperialism and the Philippine Insurrection* (Boston: Little, Brown and Co., 1969), p. xiv.

110. Storey and Lichauco, *Conquest of the Philippines*, p. 142.

111. Frederickson, *The Black Image in the White Mind*, p. 308.

112. Andrew W. Lind, *Hawaii's People* (Honolulu: University of Hawaii Press, 1955), pp. 15–17.

113. Ibid., pp. 4, 27–30.

114. Pratt, *Expansionists of 1898*, p. 35.

115. Ibid., pp. 34–35.

116. Ibid., pp. 36–37, 43–45.

117. Ibid., pp. 58–59.

118. Ibid., p. 68.

119. Ibid., pp. 79, 83, 89.

120. Ibid., p. 93.

121. Morison, *History of the American People*, pp. 797, 807.

Chapter 8

1. Kenneth M. Stampp, *The Peculiar Institution: Slavery in the Ante-Bellum South* (New York: Vintage Books, Random House, 1956), pp. 149–50, 197–98, 207–209, 222–27.

2. Daniel J. Boorstin, *The Americans: The National Experience* (New York: Vintage Books, Random House, 1965), p. 205.

3. Stampp, *The Peculiar Institution*, p. 148.

4. Ibid., pp. 151, 154, 164–69, 172–73, 210–14.

5. Harold Underwood Faulkner, *American Economic History*, 5th ed. (New York: Harper and Brothers, 1943), p. 327.

6. Ibid.

7. George M. Frederickson, *The Black Image in the White Mind* (New York: Harper and Row, 1971), p. 50.

8. Ibid.

9. Ibid., p. 62.

10. E. Franklin Frazier, *The Negro in the United States* (New York: Macmillan Co., 1949), p. 62.

11. Benjamin Quarles, *The Negro in the Making of America* (New York: Collier Books, Macmillan Co., 1964), pp. 83–85.

12. Winthrop Jordan, *White over Black* (Chapel Hill: University of North Carolina Press, 1968), p. 134.

13. Charles S. Johnson, *Patterns of Negro Segregation* (New York: Harper and Brothers, 1943), p. 83; C. Vann Woodward, *The Strange Career of Jim Crow* (New York: Oxford University Press, 1966), pp. 25–29.

14. Frederickson, *The Black Image in the White Mind*, p. 203.

15. Woodward, *The Strange Career of Jim Crow*, pp. 70–82.

16. Michael Banton, *Race Relations* (New York: Basic Books, 1967), p. 141.

17. Leon F. Litwack, *North of Slavery* (Chicago: University of Chicago Press, 1961), pp. 91–92.

18. Quarles, *The Negro in the Making of America*, pp. 139–40.

19. Maurice R. Davie, *Negroes in American Society* (New York: McGraw-Hill Book Co., 1949), p. 267.

20. Ibid., p. 265.

21. Gunnar Myrdal, *An American Dilemma* (New York: Harper and Brothers, 1944), pp. 483–84.

22. Gilbert Thomas Stephenson, *Race Distinctions in American Law* (New York: D. Appleton and Co., 1910), p. 320.

23. Chuck Stone, *Black Political Power in America* (New York: Bobbs-Merrill Co., 1968), pp. 228–29.

24. Charles Abrams, "The Housing Problem and the Negro," in *Racial Discrimination in the United States*, ed. Thomas F. Pettigrew (New York: Harper and Row, 1975), p. 45. First printed in *Daedalus, The Negro American* 95 (Winter 1966).

25. Arnold Rose, *The Negro in America: The Condensed Version of Gunnar Myrdal's an American Dilemma* (New York: Harper Torchbooks, Harper and Row, 1964), p. 63.

26. Philip M. Hauser, "Demographic Factors in the Integration of the Negro," *Daedalus, The Negro American* (Richmond, Va.: American Academy of Arts and Sciences, Fall 1965), p. 351.

27. Ibid.

28. Herman H. Long and Charles S. Johnson, *People* vs. *Property*, in *Race Restrictive Covenants in Housing* (Nashville, Tenn.: Fisk University Press, 1947), p. 21.

29. Ibid., p. 15.

30. Ibid.

31. Ibid., p. 57.

32. Ibid., p. 58.

33. Litwack, *North of Slavery*, p. 97.

34. Ibid., p. 115.

35. Ibid., pp. 132–34.

36. Quoted in Lawrence J. Friedman, *The White Savage: Racial Fantasies in the Postbellum South* (Englewood Cliffs, N.J.: Prentice-Hall, 1970), p. 25.

37. See Friedman, *The White Savage*, pp. 32, 126–32; Frederickson, *The Black Image in the White Mind*, pp. 256–82.

38. Stephenson, *Race Distinctions in American Law*, p. 228.

39. Ibid., p. 216.

40. Quoted in Joel B. Grossman and Mary H. Grossman, *Law and Change in Modern America* (Pacific Palisades, Ca.: Goodyear Publishing Co., 1971), p. 221.

41. See Myrdal, *An American Dilemma*, pp. 346–47, 634–35; Johnson, *Patterns of*

Negro Segregation, pp. 27–29, 44–52, 56–57, 65–66, 72; John Dollard, *Caste and Class in a Southern Town* (Garden City, N.Y.: Doubleday, Anchor Books, 1957), pp. 352–53.

42. Myrdal, *An American Dilemma*, p. 347.

43. Johnson, *Patterns of Negro Segregation*, p. 15.

44. Ibid., pp. 13–14.

45. Ibid., pp. 18–19.

46. Stephenson, *Race Distinctions in American Law*, p. 122; Allan H. Spear, *Black Chicago: The Making of a Negro Ghetto, 1890–1920* (Chicago: University of Chicago Press, 1967), pp. 41–42.

47. Quarles, *The Negro in the Making of America*, pp. 46–51.

48. Ibid., pp. 111–112.

49. Ibid., p. 118.

50. Lee Nichols, *Breakthrough on the Color Front* (New York: Random House, 1954), pp. 30, 138; Arlen Fowler, *The Black Infantry in the West, 1869–1891* (Westport, Conn.: Greenwood Publishing Corporation, 1971), pp. 12–13, 38–40, 86–87.

51. Quarles, *The Negro in the Making of America*, pp. 182–85; Emmett J. Scott, *The American Negro in the World War* (Chicago: Homewood Press, 1919), pp. 22–23.

52. Dennis Nelson, *The Integration of the Negro into the United States Navy, 1776–1947*, (NAVEXOS-P-526, 1948), p. 30.

53. Charles C. Moskos, Jr., *The American Enlisted Man: The Rank and File in Today's Military* (New York: Russell Sage Foundation, 1970), pp. 109–110; also in Charles C. Moskos, Jr., "Racial Integration in the Armed Forces," *American Journal of Sociology* 72 (1966): 132–48.

54. These incidents and others are noted in: Lucille Milner, "Jim Crow in the Army," *The New Republic* 110 (March 13, 1944): 341; John Swomley, Jr., *The Military Establishment* (Boston: Beacon Press, 1964), p. 71; Samuel Stouffer et al., *The American Soldier: Adjustment during Army Life*, vol. I (Princeton: Princeton University Press, 1949), p. 561. Another general source for discrimination against blacks in the military is Jay Crane and Elaine Crane, eds., *The Black Soldier: From the American Revolution to Vietnam* (New York: William Morrow and Co., 1971).

55. Quarles, *The Negro in the Making of America*, p. 151.

56. Ibid.

57. Ibid., pp. 153–54.

58. Herbert Hill, "The Racial Practice of Organized Labor," in *The Negro and the American Labor Movement*, ed. Julius Jacobson (Garden City, N.Y.: Doubleday, 1968), pp. 297–98.

59. Charles Morgan, Jr., "Segregated Justice," in *Race, Crime, and Justice*, ed. Charles E. Reasons and Jack L. Kuykendall (Pacific Palisades, Ca.: Goodyear Publishing Co., 1972), pp. 279–80.

60. Stephenson, *Race Distinctions in American Law*, pp. 81–85.

61. Myrdal, *An American Dilemma*, pp. 607, 613; Johnson, *Patterns of Negro Segregation*, pp. 59, 76, 125, 128, 136, 143, 147–48; Dollard, *Caste and Class in a Southern Town*, pp. 184–85, 351–352.

62. Dollard, *Caste and Class*, p. 117.

63. W. E. Burghardt DuBois, *The Philadelphia Negro* (New York: Benjamin Blom, 1967, 1899), p. 325.

64. Jordan, *White Over Black*, p. 28.

65. Frederickson, *The Black Image in the White Mind*, p. 253.

66. Ibid., pp. 246–55.

67. Ibid., p. 258.

68. Quoted in Bernard Mandel, "Samuel Gompers and the Negro Workers, 1886–1914," in *The Making of Black America*, vol. II, *The Black Community in Modern America*, ed. August Meier and Elliott Rudwick (New York: Atheneum, 1971), p. 84. Originally published in *Journal of Negro History* XL (January 1955): 34–60.

69. Frederickson, *The Black Image in the White Mind*, p. 279.

70. Ibid., pp. 274–75.

71. Ibid., pp. 132–36, 266–70.

72. Robert Bennett Bean, "The Negro Brain," in *The Development of Segregationist Thought*, ed. I. A. Newby (Homewood, Ill.: Dorsey Press, 1968), p. 53. Originally published as "Some Racial Peculiarities of the Negro Brain," *American Journal of Anatomy* V (September 1906): 353–432.

73. Frank Clark, "A Politician's Defense of Segregation," in Newby, *The Development of Segregationist Thought*, p. 95.

74. Frederickson, *The Black Image in the White Mind*, p. 286.

75. Ibid., p. 327.

76. Ibid.

77. Friedman, *The White Savage*, p. 121.

78. Ibid., pp. 121–25.

79. Carey McWilliams, *North from Mexico: The Spanish-Speaking People of the United States* (Philadelphia: J. B. Lippincott Co., 1949), pp. 116–17.

80. Ibid., p. 131.

81. Armando Valdez, "Brown Power," in *Cracks in the Melting Pot*, 2d ed., ed. Melvin Steinfield (Beverly Hills, Ca.: Glencoe Press, 1973), p. 335. Originally published as "Insurrection in New Mexico—the Land of Enchantment," *El Grito* (Fall 1967).

82. Ibid., pp. 335–36.

83. Rodolfo Acuna, *Occupied America: The Chicano's Struggle toward Liberation* (San Francisco: Canfield Press, 1972), p. 106.

84. Joan W. Moore, *Mexican Americans* (Englewood Cliffs, N.J.: Prentice-Hall, 1970), p. 13.

85. Acuna, *Occupied America*, p. 44.

86. Moore, *Mexican Americans*, p. 13.

87. Ibid., p. 14.

88. McWilliams, *North from Mexico*, pp. 122–23.

89. Ibid., pp. 76–77.

90. Ibid., p. 121.

91. Moore, *Mexican Americans*, pp. 16–17.

92. McWilliams, *North from Mexico*, p. 185.

93. Ibid., pp. 185–86.

94. Ibid., pp. 233–34.

95. Ibid., p. 272.

96. Paul Schuster Taylor, *An American-Mexican Frontier: Nueces County, Texas* (Chapel Hill: University of North Carolina Press, 1934), p. 251.

97. Ibid., pp. 254–55.

98. Ibid., pp. 253–54.

99. Ibid., pp. 226–27; Pauline R. Kibbe, *Latin Americans in Texas* (Albuquerque: University of New Mexico Press, 1946), p. 229; McWilliams, *North from Mexico*, p. 219.

100. McWilliams, *North from Mexico*, p. 219.

101. Taylor, *An American-Mexican Frontier*, p. 215.

102. Ibid., p. 210.

103. Kibbe, *Latin Americans in Texas*, p. 220.

104. Cecil Robinson, *With the Ears of Strangers: The Mexican in American Literature* (Tucson: University of Arizona Press, 1963), p. 37.

105. Taylor, *An American-Mexican Frontier*, p. 127.

106. Ibid., p. 203.

107. Ibid., p. 217.

108. Ibid., p. 255.

109. C. M. Goethe, "The Influx of Mexican Amerinds," in *In Their Place: White America Defines Her Minorities, 1850–1950*, ed. Lewis H. Carlson and George A. Colburn (New York: John Wiley and Sons, 1972) p. 152. Originally published in *Eugenics*, January 1929.

110. Moore, *Mexican Americans*, p. 77.

111. Carlson and Colburn, *In Their Place*, p. 156. Originally published in L. L. Burlingame, *Heredity and Social Problems* (New York: McGraw-Hill Book Co., 1940), p. 257.

112. Daniel J. Boorstin, *The Americans: The National Experience* (New York: Vintage Books, Random House, 1965), p. 261.

113. Ibid., p. 262.

114. Henry E. Fritz, *The Movement for Indian Assimilation, 1860–1890* (Philadelphia: University of Pennsylvania Press, 1963), p. 18.

115. Nancy Oestreich Lurie, "The American Indian: Historical Background," in *Majority and Minority*, ed. Norman R. Yetman and C. Hoy Steele (Boston: Allyn and Bacon, 1971), p. 221.

116. Wilcomb E. Washburn, *The Indian in America* (New York: Harper and Row, 1975), p. 214.

117. Fritz, *The Movement for Indian Assimilation*, pp. 56–58, 71, 76–79.

118. Ibid., p. 115.

119. Peter Farb, *Man's Rise to Civilization as Shown by the Indians of North America from Primeval Times to the Coming of the Industrial State* (New York: E. P. Dutton and Co., 1968), p. 257.

120. Fritz, *The Movement for Indian Assimilation*, pp. 20–34.

121. Washburn, *The Indian in America*, p. 217.

122. Ibid., p. 242.

123. James E. Officer, "The American Indian and Federal Policy," in *The Ameri-*

can Indian in Urban Society, ed. Jack O. Waddell and O. Michael Watson (Boston: Little, Brown and Co., 1971), p. 34; Washburn, *The Indian in America*, pp. 244–49.

124. Washburn, *The Indian in America*, p. 243.

125. Fritz, *The Movement for Indian Assimilation*, pp. 212–214; Samuel Eliot Morison, *The Oxford History of the American People* (New York: Oxford University Press, 1965), p. 754.

126. Washburn, *The Indian in America*, p. 249.

127. Charles F. Marden and Gladys Meyer, *Minorities in American Society*, 4th ed. (New York: D. Van Nostrand Co., 1973), pp. 292–93.

128. Kenneth Philip, "Herbert Hoover's New Era: A False Dawn for the American Indian, 1929–1932," *Rocky Mountain Social Science Journal* 9 (April 1972): 54.

129. Washburn, *The Indian in America*, pp. 254–55; Lurie, "The American Indian" p. 227.

130. Lurie, "The American Indian," pp. 227–28.

131. Francis Parkman, *The Conspiracy of Pontiac and the Indian War after the Conquest of Canada*, rev. ed. (Boston: Little, Brown and Co., 1888), pp. 39–44. Excerpt from Carlson and Colburn, *In Their Place*, pp. 38–40.

132. Daniel G. Brinton, *The American Race* (New York: N.D.C. Hodges, 1891), pp. 38–43. Excerpt from Carlson and Colburn, *In Their Place*, pp. 33–34.

133. Carlson and Colburn, *In Their Place*, pp. 13–14.

134. Stanford M. Lyman, *Chinese Americans* (New York: Random House, 1974), pp. 59–61.

135. Ibid., p. 62.

136. Maurice R. Davie, *World Immigration* (New York: Macmillan Co., 1947), pp. 311–12.

137. Steinfield, *Cracks in the Melting Pot*, pp. 36–37.

138. Carlson and Colburn, *In Their Place*, p. 177.

139. Ibid., pp. 187–88.

140. Ibid., p. 186.

141. Robert McClellan, *The Heathen Chinee: A Study of American Attitudes towards China, 1890–1905* (Columbus: Ohio State University Press, 1971), p. 45.

142. Ibid.

143. Carlson and Colburn, *In Their Place*, p. 211.

144. Ivan H. Light, "Kenjin and Kinsmen," in *The Social Reality of Ethnic America*, ed. Rudolph Gomez et al. (Lexington, Mass.: D.C. Heath and Co., 1974), p. 289. Excerpt from *Ethnic Enterprise in America* (Berkeley and Los Angeles: University of California Press, 1972).

145. Harry H. L. Kitano, *Japanese Americans* (Englewood Cliffs, N.J.: Prentice-Hall, 1969), p. 17.

146. Ibid., pp. 17–18; William Petersen, *Japanese Americans* (New York: Random House, 1971), p. 52.

147. Petersen, *Japanese Americans*, p. 52.

148. Stephenson, *Race Distinctions in American Law*, p. 160.

149. Ibid.

150. Quoted in Kitano, *Japanese Americans*, p. 26.

151. Carlson and Colburn, *In Their Place*, p. 50.

152. Dennis Ogawa, *From Japs to Japanese: The Evolution of Japanese-American Stereotypes* (Berkeley, Ca.: McCutchan Publishing Corporation, 1971), p. 13.

153. Carlson and Colburn, *In Their Place*, p. 239; Petersen, *Japanese Americans*, pp. 67–69.

154. Ogawa, *From Japs to Japanese*, p. 11; Carlson and Colburn, *In Their Place*, p. 245.

155. Kitano, *Japanese Americans*, p. 39.

156. Lyman, *Chinese Americans*, p. 86.

157. Ibid., p. 126.

158. George Potter, *To the Golden Door: The Story of the Irish in Ireland and America* (Boston: Little, Brown and Co., 1960), p. 168.

159. Ibid., p. 259.

160. Carl Wittke, *The Irish in America* (Baton Rouge: Louisiana State University Press, 1956), pp. 117–22; Maldwyn Allen Jones, *American Immigration* (Chicago: University of Chicago Press, 1960), pp. 158–60.

161. Potter, *To the Golden Door*, p. 281.

162. Ibid.

163. Ibid., pp. 421–426.

164. Ibid., p. 167.

165. Ibid.

166. Wittke, *The Irish in America*, p. 117.

167. Charles H. Anderson, *White Protestant Americans* (Englewood Cliffs, N.J.: Prentice-Hall, 1970), p. 49.

168. John Higham, *Strangers in the Land: Patterns of American Nativism, 1860–1925* (New York: Atheneum, 1965), pp. 196–209.

169. Ibid.

170. Quoted in Milton Gordon, "Assimilation in America: Theory and Reality," in Yetman and Steele, *Majority and Minority*, pp. 267–68. Originally published in *Daedalus, Journal of the American Academy of Arts and Sciences* 90 (Spring 1961): 263–85.

171. Ray Allen Billington, Bert James Loewenberg, and Samuel Hugh Brockunier, eds., *The Making of American Democracy: Readings and Documents*, vol. 2 (New York: Rinehart and Co., 1950), p. 431.

172. Higham, *Strangers in the Land*, pp. 47–48.

173. Ibid., p. 48.

174. Ibid., pp. 70–71.

175. Carlson and Colburn, *In Their Place*, p. 281; C. Wagley and H. Harris, *Minorities in the New World* (New York: Columbia University Press, 1958), p. 222.

176. E. Digby Baltzell, *The Protestant Establishment* (New York: Random House, 1964), p. 211.

177. Carlson and Colburn, *In Their Place*, p. 286.

178. Higham, *Strangers in the Land*, p. 93; see also Carlson and Colburn, *In Their Place*, pp. 253–78, and Baltzell, *The Protestant Establishment*, pp. 90–93.

179. Carlson and Colburn, *In Their Place*, p. 260; see also Baltzell, *The Protestant Establishment*, pp. 205–206.

180. Higham, *Strangers in the Land*, p. 66.

181. Luciano J. Iorizzo and Salvatore Mondello, *The Italian-Americans* (New York: Twayne Publishers, 1971), pp. 67–69.

182. Ibid.

183. Higham, *Strangers in the Land*, p. 67.

184. Ibid., p. 55.

185. Ibid., p. 226.

186. Ibid., p. 21.

187. Nathan Glazer, "Ethnic Groups in America: From National Culture to Ideology," in *Minority Responses*, ed. Minako Kurokawa (New York: Random House, 1970), p. 84. Originally published in *Freedom and Control in Modern Society*, ed. Morroe Berger et al. (New York: Octagon Books, 1954), pp. 158–73.

188. Max Lerner, *America as a Civilization* (New York: Simon and Schuster, 1957), p. 91.

189. Ibid.

190. Quoted in Baltzell, *The Protestant Establishment*, p. 106; taken from Edward Alsworth Ross, *The Old World in the New* (New York: Century Co., 1914).

191. Higham, *Strangers in the Land*, p. 317.

192. Ibid., pp. 242–45.

193. Ibid., p. 324.

194. Russell H. Fitzgibbon, *Cuba and the United States, 1900–1935* (Menasha, Wis.: Collegiate Press, George Banta Publishing Co., 1935), pp. 32–66.

195. Morison, *History of the American People*, p. 808; Fitzgibbon, *Cuba and the United States*, pp. 78–79.

196. Fitzgibbon, *Cuba and the United States*, pp. 90–91.

197. Faulkner, *American Economic History*, pp. 569, 571.

198. D. R. Williams, *The United States and the Philippines* (Garden City, N.Y.: Doubleday, Page and Co., 1924), pp. 122–28; Moorfield Storey and Marcial P. Lichauco, *Conquest of the Philippines by the United States, 1898–1925* (New York: G. P. Putnam's Sons, 1926), pp. 233–34.

199. Michael Cullinane, "Implementing the 'New Order': The Structure and Supervision of Local Government during the Taft Era," in *Compadre Colonialism: Studies on the Philippines under American Rule*, ed. Norman G. Owen (Ann Arbor: University of Michigan Center for South and Southeast Asian Studies, 1971), p. 25.

200. Joseph F. Hutchinson, Jr., "Quezon's Role in Philippine Independence," in Owen, *Compadre Colonialism*, p. 162; Faulkner, *American Economic History*, p. 578; Amaury de Riencourt, *The American Empire* (New York: Dial Press, 1968), p. 27.

201. Storey and Lichauco, *Conquest of the Philippines*, p. 232.

202. Cullinane, "Implementing the 'New Order,'" pp. 16–17.

203. Williams, *The United States and the Philippines*, p. 154.

204. Hutchinson, "Quezon's Role in Philippine Independence," p. 162.

205. Clifford A. Hauberg, *Puerto Rico and the Puerto Ricans* (New York: Twayne Publishers, 1974), p. 39.

206. Earl Parker Hanson, *Transformation: The Story of Modern Puerto Rico* (New York: Simon and Schuster, 1955), pp. 30–31.

207. Ibid., p. 42.

208. Hauberg, *Puerto Rico and the Puerto Ricans*, p. 47.

209. Hanson, *Transformation*, pp. 74–75.

210. Ibid., p. 36.

211. Andrew W. Lind, *Hawaii's People* (Honolulu: University of Hawaii Press, 1955), pp. 4, 27–30.

212. Jitsuichi Matsuoka, "Race Preference in Hawaii," *American Journal of Sociology* 41 (1935–1936): 635–41.

213. Romanzo Adams, *Interracial Marriage in Hawaii* (New York: Macmillan Co., 1937), pp. 47–48, 53.

214. Norman G. Owen, "Introduction: Philippine Society and American Colonialism," in Owen, *Compadre Colonialism* p. 6.

Chapter 9

1. Judith R. Kramer, *The American Minority Community* (New York: Thomas Y Crowell Co., 1970), p. 203.

2. Stanley M. Elkins, *Slavery: A Problem in American Institutional and Intellectual Life* (Chicago: University of Chicago Press, 1968, pp. 104–139.

3. Roy Simon Bryce-Laporte, "The American Slave Plantation and Our Heritage of Communal Deprivation," in *Majority and Minority*, ed. Norman R. Yetman and C. Hoy Steele (Boston: Allyn and Bacon, 1971), p. 175. Originally published in *American Behavioral Scientist* XII (March–April 1969).

4. Kenneth M. Stampp, *The Peculiar Institution: Slavery in the Ante-Bellum South* (New York: Vintage Books, Random House, 1956), pp. 97–100.

5. B. A. Botkin, ed., *Lay My Burden Down: A Folk History of Slavery* (Chicago: University of Chicago Press, 1945), pp. 4–5.

6. Stampp, *The Peculiar Institution*, pp. 125–26.

7. Botkin, *Lay My Burden Down*, p. 25.

8. Benjamin Quarles, *The Negro in the Making of America* (New York: Collier Books, Macmillan Co., 1964), p. 75.

9. Ibid., p. 78.

10. Stampp, *The Peculiar Institution*, p. 109.

11. Herbert Aptheker, "American Negro Slave Revolts," in *Racial Violence in the United States*, ed. Allen D. Grimshaw (Chicago: Aldine Publishing Co., 1969), p. 30.

12. Winthrop D. Jordan, *White over Black* (Chapel Hill: University of North Carolina Press, 1968), p. 113.

13. Samuel Eliot Morison, *The Oxford History of the American People* (New York: Oxford University Press, 1965), p. 149.

14. Stampp, *The Peculiar Institution*, p. 135; Harvey Wish, "American Slave Insurrections before 1861," in *Justice Denied: The Black Man in White America*, ed. William M. Chace and Peter Collier (New York: Harcourt, Brace and World, 1970), pp. 85–86. (Originally published in *Journal of Negro History* XXII (July 1937), pp. 299–320.

15. Wish, "American Slave Insurrections before 1861," p. 92.

16. Stampp, *The Peculiar Institution*, p. 135; Quarles, *The Negro in the Making of America*, p. 81; Wish, "American Slave Insurrections before 1861," p. 90.

17. Stampp, *The Peculiar Institution*, pp. 132–34; Quarles, *The Negro in the Making of America*, p. 82; Aptheker, *American Negro Slave Revolts*, pp. 30–36.

18. Wish, *The Negro in the Making of America*, p. 82.

19. LeRoi Jones, "Afro-Christian Music and Religion," in Chace and Collier, *Justice Denied*, pp. 99, 100. Excerpt from LeRoi Jones, *Blues People: Negro Music in White America* (New York: William Morrow and Co., 1963).

20. Ibid., p. 105.

21. *Time*, May 9, 1969, pp. 75–76.

22. Pierre L. van den Berghe, "The Benign Quota: Panacea or Pandora's Box," in *Report on the International Research Conference on Race Relations* (paper presented at this conference held in Aspen, Colorado, June 7–9, 1970), p. 181.

23. Leon F. Litwack, *North of Slavery* (Chicago: Phoenix Books, University of Chicago Press, 1961), pp. 142–49.

24. August Meier and Elliott Rudwick, "A Strange Chapter in the Career of 'Jim Crow'," in *The Making of Black America*, vol. II, *The Black Community in Modern America*, ed. Meier and Rudwick (New York: Atheneum, 1971), pp. 15–18.

25. Allan H. Spear, *Black Chicago: The Making of a Negro Ghetto, 1890–1920* (Chicago: University of Chicago Press, 1967), p. 51.

26. George C. Bedell, Leo Sandon, Jr., and Charles T. Wellborn, *Religion in America* (New York: Macmillan Co., 1975), pp. 378–79.

27. Ibid., p. 393.

28. Ibid., p. 395.

29. Lawrence J. Friedman, *The White Savage: Racial Fantasies in the Postbellum South* (Englewood Cliffs, N.J.: Prentice-Hall, 1970), p. 134.

30. Ibid., pp. 135–36.

31. Spear, *Black Chicago*, p. 11.

32. Ralph J. Bunche, "The Programs of Organizations Devoted to the Improvement of the Status of the American Negro," in Meier and Rudwick, "Career of 'Jim Crow,'" p. 247. Originally published in *Journal of Negro Education* VIII (July 1939); 539–50.

33. Quoted in Martin Carnoy, *Education as Cultural Imperialism* (New York: David McKay Co., 1974), p. 294.

34. Bunche, "Programs of Organizations," p. 247.

35. Ibid.

36. Kathleen Wolgemuth, "New Freedom and Old Hypocrisy," in *Cracks in the Melting Pot*, 2d ed. (New York: Glencoe Press, 1973), pp. 270–85. Originally published as "Woodrow Wilson and Federal Segregation," *Journal of Negro History* (April 1959).

37. St. Clair Drake and Horace R. Cayton, *Black Metropolis: A Study of Negro Life in a Northern City*, vol. II (New York: Harper Torchbooks, Academy Library, Harper and Row, 1962), pp. 743–44.

38. Doxey A. Wilkerson, "The Negro School Movement in Virginia: From 'Equalization' to 'Integration,'" in Meier and Rudwick, "Career of 'Jim Crow,'" pp. 261–67. Originally published in *Journal of Negro Education* XXIX (Winter 1960): 17–29.

39. E. U. Essien-Udom, "Garvey and Garveyism," in Chace and Collier, *Justice Denied*, p. 242. Excerpt from *The Philosophy and Opinions of Marcus Garvey*, 2d ed., with introduction by E. U. Essien-Udom (New York: Humanities Press, 1967).

40. Ibid., pp. 239–45.

41. Malcolm X, *The Autobiography of Malcolm X* (New York: Grove Press, 1964), pp. 157–68.

42. *Muhammad Speaks* 9 (February 27, 1970): 32.

43. Ibid., pp. S-2 to S-14; C. Eric Lincoln, *The Black Muslims in America* (Boston: Beacon Press, 1961).

44. St. Clair Drake, "The Social and Economic Status of the Negro in the United States," in *Daedalus, The Negro American* (Richmond, Virginia: American Academy of Arts and Sciences, Volume 94, No. 4), pp. 777–78.

45. Drake and Cayton, *Black Metropolis*, pp. 526–715.

46. Allen D. Grimshaw, "Lawlessness and Violence in America and Their Special Manifestations in Changing Negro-White Relationships," in *Racial Violence in the United States*, ed. Allen D. Grimshaw (Chicago: Aldine Publishing Co., 1969), pp. 24–25.

47. Alphonso Pinkney, *Black Americans* (Englewood Cliffs, N.J.: Prentice-Hall, 1969), p. 32.

48. Roi Ottley and William Weatherby, "The Depression," in Chace and Collier, *Justice Denied*, pp. 265–66. Excerpt from *The Negro in New York: An Informal Social History* (New York: New York Public Library and Oceana Publications, 1967).

49. Thurgood Marshall, "The Gestapo in Detroit," in Grimshaw, *Racial Violence in the United States*, pp. 140–44.

50. Murray and Rosalie Wax, "Federal Programs and Indian Target Populations," in Yetman and Steele, *Majority and Minority*, pp. 500–501.

51. Ibid., p. 501.

52. Tamotsu Shibutani and Kian M. Kwan, *Ethnic Stratification: A Comparative Approach* (New York: Macmillan Co., 1965), p. 240.

53. Wilcomb E. Washburn, *The Indian in America* (New York: Harper and Row, 1975), p. 223.

54. Ibid., p. 226.

55. Ibid., p. 225.

56. Murray L. Wax, *Indian Americans* (Englewood Cliffs, N.J.: Prentice-Hall, 1971), p. 76.

57. Washburn, *The Indian in America*, pp. 251–52.

58. Ibid., pp. 256–57.

59. William A. Brophy and Sophie D. Aberle et al., *The Indian: America's Unfinished Business* (Norman: University of Oklahoma Press, 1966), pp. 34–35.

60. Washburn, *The Indian in America*, p. 257.

61. James E. Officer, "The American Indian and Federal Policy," in *The American Indian in Urban Society*, ed. Jack O. Waddell and O. Michael Watson (Boston: Little, Brown and Co., 1971), p. 41.

62. Ibid., pp. 40–41.

63. Wax, *Indian Americans*, pp. 151–53.

64. Washburn, *The Indian in America*, p. 109.

65. Ibid.

66. Rodolfo Acuna, *Occupied America: The Chicano's Struggle toward Liberation* (San Francisco: Canfield Press, 1972), pp. 58–59; Carey McWilliams, *North from Mexico: The Spanish-Speaking People of the United States* (Philadelphia: J. B. Lippincott Co., 1949), p. 118.

67. Acuna, *Occupied America*, pp. 47–50.

68. Ibid., pp. 73–77.

69. McWilliams, *North from Mexico*, p. 189.

70. Matt S. Meier and Feliciano Rivera, *The Chicanos: A History of Mexican Americans* (New York: Hill and Wang, 1972), p. 170.

71. Ibid., p. 173; McWilliams, *North from Mexico*, p. 197.

72. McWilliams, *North from Mexico*, p. 191.

73. Ibid., p. 193.

74. Meier and Rivera, *The Chicanos*, pp. 178–79.

75. McWilliams, *North from Mexico*, p. 191.

76. Meier and Rivera, *The Chicanos*, pp. 182–83.

77. McWilliams, *North from Mexico*, p. 192.

78. Ibid.

79. Meier and Rivera, *The Chicanos*, pp. 181–82.

80. Ibid., p. 184.

81. Ibid., p. 239.

82. Paul Schuster Taylor, *An American-Mexican Frontier: Nueces County, Texas* (Chapel Hill: University of North Carolina Press, 1934), pp. 243–44.

83. McWilliams, *North from Mexico*, pp. 292–93.

84. This is the author's synthesis of several studies and interpretations of Mexican folk culture. The following were utilized: William Madsen, *The Mexican Americans of South Texas*, 2d ed. (New York: Holt, Rinehart and Winston, 1973), pp. 18–26; Lyle Saunders, *Cultural Differences and Medical Care: The Case of the Spanish-Speaking People of the Southwest* (New York: Russell Sage Foundation, 1954), pp. 118–21, 129, 132; Florence Rockwood Kluckhohn and Fred L. Strodtbeck, *Variations in Value Orientations* (Evanston, Illinois: Row, Peterson and Co., 1961), pp. 13–18, 192–97.

85. Madsen, *Mexican Americans of South Texas*, p. 33.

86. Ibid., pp. 33–44.

87. Calvin Lee, *Chinatown, U.S.A.* (Garden City, N.Y.: Doubleday and Co., 1965), p. 13.

88. Ibid., pp. 10–11.

89. Stanford M. Lyman, "Contrasts in the Community Organization of Chinese and Japanese in North America," in *Majority and Minority*, 2d ed., ed. Norman R. Yetman and C. Hoy Steele (Boston: Allyn and Bacon, 1975), p. 293. Originally published in *The Canadian Review of Sociology and Anthropology* 5 (1968): 2.

90. Lee, *Chinatown, U.S.A.*, pp. 11–12; Stanford M. Lyman, *Chinese Americans* (New York: Random House, 1974), pp. 32–33.

91. Lee, *Chinatown, U.S.A.*, p. 31; Lyman, *Chinese Americans*, pp. 30–31.

92. Lyman, *Chinese Americans*, pp. 40–42; Lee, *Chinatown, U.S.A.*, pp. 35–36.

93. D. Y. Yuan, "Voluntary Segregation: A Study of New York Chinatown," in *Minority Responses*, ed. Minako Kurokawa (New York: Random House, 1970), p. 137.

94. Lee, *Chinatown, U.S.A.*, p. 14.

95. Ibid., p. 15.

96. William Petersen, *Japanese Americans* (New York: Random House, 1971), p. 29.

97. Roger Daniels, "The Japanese-American Experience: 1890–1940," in *The Social Reality of Ethnic America*, ed. Rudolph Gomez et al. (Lexington, Mass.: D. C. Heath and Co., 1974), pp. 218–19. Excerpt from *Concentration Camps U.S.A.: Japanese-Americans and World War II* (New York: Holt, Rinehart and Winston, 1971).

98. Ibid., p. 219.

99. Ibid., p. 292.

100. Ibid., p. 293.

101. Ibid., pp. 288–89.

102. Forrest E. La Violette, *Americans of Japanese Ancestry: A Study of Assimilation in the American Community* (Toronto: Canadian Institute of International Affairs, 1945), p. 175.

103. Ibid., p. 142.

104. R. A. Schermerhorn, *These Our People* (Boston: D. C. Heath and Co., 1949), pp. 203–204. See also La Violette, *Americans of Japanese Ancestry*, p. 18, and Harry H. L. Kitano, *Japanese Americans* (Englewood Cliffs, N.J.: Prentice-Hall, 1969), p. 107.

105. Shibutani and Kwan, *Ethnic Stratification*, p. 527.

106. Carl Wittke, *The Irish in America* (Baton Rouge: Louisiana State University Press, 1956), pp. 42–45.

107. Leonard Dinnerstein and Frederick Cople Jaher, *The Aliens: A History of Ethnic Minorities in America* (New York: Appleton-Century-Crofts, Meredith Corporation, 1970), p. 216.

108. Moses Rischin, "The Lower East Side," in *Racial and Ethnic Relations*, 2d ed., ed. Bernard E. Segal (New York: Thomas Y. Crowell Co., 1972), pp. 203–204. Excerpt from *The Promised City: New York's Jews, 1870–1914*. (Cambridge: Harvard University Press, 1962).

109. Wittke, *The Irish in America*, pp. 196–97.

110. John P. Diggins, *Mussolini and Fascism, The View From America* (Princeton: Princeton University Press, 1972), p. 93.

111. Ibid., p. 108.

112. Wittke, *The Irish in America*, pp. 92, 95.

113. Ibid., p. 99.

114. Schermerhorn, *These Our People*, p. 287.

115. Ibid., pp. 251, 255.

116. Nathan Glazer, *American Judaism* (Chicago: University of Chicago Press, 1957), p. 46.

117. Ibid., pp. 56–59, 77.

118. Donald Taft, *Human Migration* (New York: Ronald Press, 1936), p. 281.

119. Wittke, *The Irish in America*, p. 103.

120. Ibid.

121. Ibid., pp. 59–60; George Potter, *To The Golden Door: The Story of the Irish in Ireland and America* (Boston: Little, Brown and Co., 1960), p. 531.

122. Potter, *To the Golden Door*, p. 531.

123. Schermerhorn, *These Our People*, pp. 253–54.

124. Joseph Lopreato, *Italian Americans* (New York: Random House, 1970) p. 145.

125. See Daniel Bell, "Crime as an American Way of Life," *The Anitoch Review* 13 (June 1953): 131–54.

126. Glazer, *American Judaism*, p. 44.

127. Schermerhorn, *These Our People*, p. 410.

128. Thomas Sowell, *Race and Economics* (New York: David McKay Co., 1975), p. 145.

129. Glazer, *American Judaism*, p. 181.

130. Editors of *Fortune Magazine*, "Jews in America," in Dinnerstein and Jaher, *The Aliens*, pp. 238–43. Originally publsihed in *Fortune Magazine*, February 1936.

131. Schermerhorn, *These Our People*, p. 411.

132. Charles H. Anderson, *White Protestant Americans* (Englewood Cliffs, N.J.: Prentice-Hall, 1970), p. 82.

133. Ibid. The study was by Pitirim Sorokin, "American Millionaires and Multi-Millionaires," *Social Forces* III (May 1925): 627–40.

134. Ibid., pp. 61–62.

135. Ibid., p. 47.

136. Ibid., p. 21.

137. Michael Novak, *The Rise of the Unmeltable Ethnics* (New York: Macmillan Co., 1971), pp. 91–96.

138. Ibid., p. 106.

139. Ibid., p. 110.

140. Ibid., pp. 106–107.

141. John A. Hawgood, "The Attempt to Found a New Germany in Missouri," in Dinnerstein and Jaher, *The Aliens*, pp. 132–34. Excerpt from *The Tragedy of German-America* (New York: G.P. Putnam's Sons, 1940).

142. Ibid., p. 136.

143. Ibid.

144. Andrew F. Rolle, *The Immigrant Upraised* (Norman: University of Oklahoma Press, 1968), pp. 12–13.

145. Ibid., pp. 33–34.

146. Amaury de Riencourt, *The Coming Caesars* (New York: Coward-McCann, 1957), p. 128.

147. Anderson, *White Protestant Americans*, p. 70.

148. Shibutani and Kwan, *Ethnic Stratification*, p. 485.

149. Earl Parker Hanson, *Transformation: The Story of Modern Puerto Rico* (New York: Simon and Schuster, 1955), p. 63.

150. Ibid., p. 35.

151. Ibid., pp. 10–11.

152. Ibid., p. 3.

153. Ibid., p. 186.

154. Usha Mahajani, *Philippine Nationalism* (St. Lucia, Queensland, Australia: University of Queensland Press, 1971), pp. 324–26.

155. Edwin G. Burrows, *Hawaiian Americans* (New Haven: Yale University Press, 1947), p. 85.

156. Charles F. Marden and Gladys Meyer, *Minorities in American Society*, 4th ed. (New York: D. Van Nostrand Co., 1973), p. 417.

157. Ibid., pp. 417, 418, 421; Andrew W. Lind, *Hawaii's People* (Honolulu: University of Hawaii Press, 1955), p. 78.

158. Charles F. Marden and Gladys Meyer, *Minorities in American Society*, 2d. ed. (New York: American Book Co., 1962), p. 365.

159. Walter Kolarz, "The Melting Pot in the Pacific," *Social Process in Hawaii* 19 (1955): 23–26. Quoted in Marden and Meyer, *Minorities in American Society*, 2d ed., p. 366.

160. Lind, Hawaii's People, p. 103.

161. E. Digby Baltzell, *The Protestant Establishment* (New York: Random House, 1964), p. xiii.

Chapter 10

1. Leonard Broom and Norval D. Glenn, "The Occupations and Income of Black Americans," in *Blacks in the United States*, ed. Norval D. Glenn and Charles M Bonjean (San Francisco: Chandler Publishing Co., 1969), pp. 23–24. Originally published in Leonard Broom and Norval D. Glenn, *Transformation of the Negro American* (New York: Harper and Row, 1967), pp. 105–134.

2. Matt S. Meier and Feliciano Rivera, *The Chicanos: A History of Mexican Americans* (New York: Hill and Wang, 1972), pp. 197–98.

3. Harry H. L. Kitano, *Japanese Americans: The Evolution of a Subculture* (Englewood Cliffs, N.J.: Prentice-Hall, 1969), p. 49.

4. Amaury de Riencourt, *The American Empire* (New York: Dial Press, 1968), p. 237.

5. Alphonso Pinkney, *Black Americans* (Englewood Cliffs, N.J.: Prentice-Hall, 1969), p. 202.

6. August Meier, "Civil Rights Strategies for Negro Employment," in *Employment, Race, and Poverty*, ed. Arthur M. Ross and Herbert Hill (New York: Harcourt, Brace and World, 1967), pp. 184–85.

7. August Meier, "Negro Protest Movements and Organizations," in *Conflict and Competition: Studies in the Recent Black Protest Movement*, eds. John H. Bracey, Jr., August Meier, and Elliott Rudwick (Belmont, Calif.: Wadsworth Publishing Co., 1970), p. 23. Originally published in *Journal of Negro Education* XXXII (Fall 1963; 437–50.

8. Ralph H. Hines and James E. Pierce, "Negro Leadership after the Social Crisis: An Analysis of Leadership Changes in Montgomery, Alabama," in Bracey, *Conflict and Competition*, p. 46. Originally published in *Phylon* XXVI (2d Quarter 1965): 162–72.

9. Benjamin Quarles, *The Negro in the Making of America* (New York: Collier Books, Macmillan Co., 1964), p. 251.

10. George C. Bedell, Leo Sandon, Jr., and Charles T. Wellborn, *Religion in America* (New York: Macmillan Co., 1975), p. 341.

11. Ibid., p. 334; Louis H. Masotti et al., *A Time to Burn?* (Chicago: Rand McNally and Co., 1969), pp. 26–30.

12. Bedell, Sandon, and Wellborn, *Religion in America*, pp. 334–35.

13. Allen J. Matusow, "From Civil Rights to Black Power: The Case of SNCC, 1960–1966," Bracey, *Conflict and Competition*, pp. 135–38.

14. August Meier, "Negro Protest Movements and Organization," in Bracey, *Conflict and Competition*, pp. 22–25; August Meier, "Civil Rights Strategies for Negro Employment," in Ross and Hill, *Employment, Race, and Poverty*, pp. 191–94.

15. Meier, "Civil Rights Strategies for Negro Employment," in Ross and Hill, *Employment, Race, and Poverty*, pp. 196–98.

16. Meier and Rivera, *The Chicanos*, pp. 242–48; Ellwyn R. Stoddard, *Mexican Americans* (New York: Random House, 1973), pp. 188–90.

17. Stoddard, *Mexican Americans*, p. 191.

18. Donald von Eschen, Jerome Kirk, and Maurice Pinard, "The Disintegration of the Negro Non-violent Movement," in Bracey, *Conflict and Competition*, p. 127. Originally published in *Journal of Peace Research*, issue no. 3 (1969): 216–34.

19. Ibid., pp. 122–27.

20. Ibid., pp. 127–32.

21. Stokely Carmichael and Charles Hamilton, *Black Power* (New York: Random House, 1967), p. 44.

22. Stokely Carmichael, "What We Want," in *Racial Conflict*, ed. Gary T. Marx (Boston: Little, Brown and Co., 1971), pp. 186–93.

23. Joel D. Aberbach and Jack L. Walker, "The Meaning of Black Power: A Comparison of White and Black Interpretations of a Political Slogan," in Bracey, *Conflict and Competition*, p. 158. Originally published in *American Political Science Review* LXIV (June 1970): 367–88.

24. Ibid.

25. Ibid., p.161.

26. *Newsweek*, September 16, 1968, vol. 72, no. 12, p. 30.

27. Huey P. Newton, "The Black Panther Party," in Marx, *Racial Conflict*, pp. 203–204.

28. "Manifesto," in *Africa Today* (August/September 1969): 21–24.

29. Robert F. Williams, "For Effective Self Defense," in *Negro Protest Thought in the Twentieth Century*, ed. Francis L. Broderick and August Meier (New York: Bobbs-Merrill, 1965), p. 331.

30. Quoted in William K. Tabb, "Race Relations Models and Social Change," *Social Problems* 18 (Spring 1971): 432.

31. Masotti et al., *A Time to Burn?* pp. 35, 124, 171; *Report of the National Advisory Commission on Civil Disorders* (New York: Bantam Books, 1968), pp. 107, 113, 115; Jerome H. Skolnick, *The Politics of Protest* (New York: Ballantine Books, 1969), pp. 172–74.

32. Skolnick, *The Politics of Protest*, p. 173.

33. Ibid.

34. *Report of the National Advisory Commission on Civil Disorders* (New York: Bantam Books, 1968), pp. 109–150.

35. Ibid., p. 1.

36. Ibid., p. 2.

37. James A. Geschwender and Benjamin D. Singer, "Deprivation and the Detroit Riot," *Social Problems* 17 (Spring 1970): 457–63.

38. Nathan S. Caplan and Jeffery M. Paige, "A Study of Ghetto Rioters," *Scientific American* 219 (August 1968): 15–21.

39. H. Edward Ransford, "Skin Color, Life Chances, and Anti-White Attitudes," *Social Problems* 18 (Fall 1970): 164–78.

40. Caplan and Paige, "A Study of Ghetto Rioters," p. 21.

41. Ibid.

42. Skolnick, *The Politics of Protest*, p. 173.

43. Armando B. Rendon, *Chicano Manifesto* (New York: Collier Books, Macmillan Co., 1972), pp. 10, 304, 309.

44. Ibid., pp. 21, 325.

45. Ibid., pp. 113, 142, 192.

46. Ibid., p. 278.

47. Ibid., pp. 114, 156, 278, 279.

48. Stoddard, *Mexican Americans*, pp. 203–204.

49. Ibid., pp. 197–201.

50. Ibid., pp. 216–18.

51. Ibid., p. 225.

52. Ibid., pp. 220–21.

53. Murray L. Wax, *Indian Americans* (Englewood Cliffs, N.J.: Prentice-Hall, 1971), pp. 146–47.

54. Robert C. Day, "The Emergence of Activism as a Social Movement," in *Native Americans Today: Sociological Perspectives*, ed. Howard M. Bahr, Bruce A. Chadwick, and Robert C. Day (New York: Harper and Row, 1972), pp. 507–509, 527.

55. *Time*, March 19, 1973, p. 18.

56. Ibid., pp. 16–18, Armand L. Mauss; *Social Problems as Social Movements* (Philadelphia: J. B. Lippincott Co., 1975), p. 542.

57. Perry L. Weed, *The White Ethnic Movement and Ethnic Politics* (New York: Praeger Publishers, 1973), pp. 14–21.

58. Ibid., pp. 20–24, 63–64.

59. Ibid., p. 17.

60. Ibid., pp. 33–34.

61. Stanley Felstein and Lawrence Costello, *The Ordeal of Assimilation* (Garden City, N.Y.: Anchor Books, Anchor Press/Doubleday, 1974), p. 417.

62. Ibid.

63. Andrew M. Greeley, *Ethnicity in the United States: A Preliminary Reconnaissance* (New York: Wiley-Interscience, 1974), pp. 284–85.

64. Weed, *The White Ethnic Movement*, pp. 74–75.

65. Ibid., pp. 68–69, 77–78.

66. Ibid., pp. 16, 30

67. Michael Novak, *The Rise of the Unmeltable Ethnics* (New York: Macmillan Co., 1971), p. 270.

68. Weed, *The White Ethnic Movement*, p. 29.

69. Ibid., p. 24.

70. Ibid., p. 21.

71. Ibid., pp. 51–54, 63–64.

72. Greeley, *Ethnicity in the United States*, p. 288.

73. Ibid., p. 287.

Chapter 11

1. Quoted in Harold R. Isaacs, *The New World of Negro Americans* (New York: Viking Press, 1963), p. 13.

2. James E. Anderson, *Public Policy-Making* (New York: Praeger Publishers, 1975), p. 5.

3. See Michael Sovern, *Legal Restraints on Racial Discrimination in Employment* (New York: Twentieth Century Fund, 1966); Paul H. Norgren, "Fair Employment Practice Laws—Experience, Effects, Prospects," in *Employment, Race, and Poverty*, ed. Arthur M. Ross and Herbert Hill (New York: Harcourt, Brace and World, 1967); Jack Greenberg, *Race Relations and American Law* (New York: Columbia University Press, 1959).

4. U.S. Commission on Civil Rights, *Federal Civil Rights Enforcement Effort* (Washington, D.C.: Government Printing Office, 1971), pp. 20–21.

5. Ibid., p. 21; U.S. Commission on Civil Rights, *Federal Civil Rights Enforcement Effort–A Reassessment* (Washington, D.C.' Government Printing Office, 1973), pp. 14, 25.

6. U.S. Commission on Civil Rights, *Civil Rights Enforcement Effort* (1971), p. 35.

7. Ibid., pp. 2-9.

8. Ibid., p. 31.

9. Cited in Charles S. Bullock, III, "Expanding Black Economic Rights," in *Racism and Inequality: The Policy Alternatives*, ed. Harrell R. Rodgers, Jr. (San Francisco: W. H. Freeman and Co., 1975), pp. 87–88.

10. Ibid., p. 87.

11. Ibid., pp. 99–107.

12. Ibid., p. 86.

13. U.S. Commission on Civil Rights, *Civil Rights Enforcement Effort* (1971), p. 115.

14. U.S. Commission on Civil Rights, *The Federal Civil Rights Enforcement Effort—1974*, vol. V, *To Eliminate Employment Discrimination* (Washington, D.C.: Government Printing Office, 1975), p. 60.

15. Ibid. For example: *NAACP* v. *Allen*, 5th Circuit, 1974; *Morrow* v. *Crisler*, 5th Circuit, 1974. No preferential treatment cases have been decided upon by the U.S. Supreme Court, however.

16. U.S. Commission on Civil Rights, 1974, *Civil Rights Enforcement Effort*, vol. V (1974), p. 57.

17. Ibid., p. 39.

18. Ibid., p. 645; U.S. Commission on Civil Rights, *Civil Rights Enforcement Effort* (1973), p. 27.

19. U.S. Commission on Civil Rights, *One Year Later* (Washington, D.C.: Government Printing Office, 1971) p. 29.

20. U.S. Commission on Civil Rights, *Civil Rights Enforcement Effort* (1971), p. 109.

21. U.S. Commission on Civil Rights, *Civil Rights Enforcement Effort*, vol. V (1974), pp. 527–28.

22. Jack Olsen, Jr., byline, *Denver Rocky Mountain News*, January 30, 1976, p. 8.

23. Ibid.

24. U.S. Commission on Civil Rights, *Civil Rights Enforcement Effort*, vol. V (1974), p. 61.

25. Ibid., pp. 61, 67–68.

26. Ibid., pp. 79 (supra 272), 80.

27. U.S. Commission on Civil Rights, *Civil Rights Enforcement Effort* (1973), p. 17.

28. U.S. Commission on Civil Rights, *Civil Rights Enforcement Effort* (1971), p. 52.

29. U.S. Commission on Civil Rights, *Civil Rights Enforcement Effort*, vol. V (1974), p. 637.

30. Ibid., p. 636.

31. U.S. Commission on Civil Rights, *Civil Rights Enforcement Effort* (1973), p. 23.

32. U.S. Civil Rights Commission, "Statement of Howard A. Glickstein, Staff Director-Designate, U.S. Commission on Civil Rights, Before the Senate Subcommittee on Labor of the Committee on Labor and Public Welfare," (unpublished pamphlet, September 10, 1969), p. 30.

33. U.S. Commission on Civil Rights, *Civil Rights Enforcement Effort* (1971), p. 124.

34. Ibid., p. 124.

35. U.S. Commission on Civil Rights, *Civil Rights Enforcement Effort*, vol. V (1974), p. 647.

36. Angus Campbell, *White Attitudes toward Black People* (Ann Arbor: Institute for Social Research, University of Michigan, 1971), p. 23.

37. Ibid., p. 129.

38. Cited in Neil Gilbert and Joseph W. Eaton, "Favoritism as a Strategy in Race Relations," *Social Problems* 17 (Summer 1970): 40.

39. One such precedent was *Westminster School District* v. *Mendez et al.* in 1945. A district judge ruled that the segregation of Mexicans violated the equal protection clause of the 14th Amendment and that there was no legal basis for such segregation. An important case relating to blacks but to higher education only was *Gaines* v. *the University of Missouri* before the Supreme Court in 1938. The University of Missouri would not accept Gaines in the law school but would pay the tuition of the Missouri resident at any university for blacks in adjacent states. The Court overturned the state supreme court and ruled the practice to be unconstitutional.

40. James W. Vander Zanden, *Race Relations in Transition* (New York: Random House, 1965), p. 88.

41. Harrell R. Rodgers, Jr., "On Integrating the Public Schools: An Empirical and Legal Assessment," in Rodgers, *Racism and Inequality*, pp. 128–29.

42. Gary Orfield, *The Reconstruction of Southern Education* (New York: Wiley-Interscience, 1969), p. 32.

43. Vander Zanden, *Race Relations in Transition*, pp. 88–90.

44. George Eaton Simpson and J. Milton Yinger, *Racial and Cultural Minorities*, 4th Ed. (New York: Harper and Row, 1972), p. 550.

45. Orfield, *The Reconstruction of Southern Education*, pp. 85–94.

46. Rodgers, *Racism and Inequality*, pp. 129–30; U.S. Commission on Civil Rights, "Federal Enforcement of School Desegregation" (unpublished pamphlet, September 11, 1969), p. 14.

47. U.S. Commission on Civil Rights, *Federal Enforcement of School Desegregation*, p. 20.

48. *Green v. New Kent County School Board*, 391 U.S. 438.

49. U.S. Commission on Civil Rights, *Federal Enforcement of School Desegregation*, p. 7.

50. Ibid., p. 35.

51. Rodgers, *Racism and Inequality*, pp. 132–34, 139.

52. Ibid., p. 137.

53. Ibid., pp. 139–40.

54. Ibid., p. 140.

55. Ibid., pp. 141–44.

56. *Denver Post*, December 7, 1976, p. 10.

57. U.S. Commission on Civil Rights, "Federal Enforcement of School Desegregation," September 11, 1969, Appendix B.

58. Rodgers, *Racism and Inequality*, pp. 135–36.

59. Ibid., p. 136; see also U.S. Commission on Civil Rights, *The Federal Civil Rights Enforcement Effort–1974*, vol. III, *To Ensure Equal Educational Opportunity* (Washington, D.C.: Government Printing Office, 1975), p. 362.

60. Campbell, *White Attitudes toward Black People*, p. 130.

61. Peter Goldman, *Report from Black America* (New York: Clarion Books, Simon and Schuster, 1971), p. 267.

62. Charles S. Bullock, III, and Harrell R. Rodgers, Jr., *Racial Equality in America* (Pacific Palisades, Ca.: Goodyear Publishing Co., 1975), pp. 159, 160.

63. Ibid., p. 159.

64. Ibid., p. 160.

65. Ibid., pp. 159–60.

66. Goldman, *Report from Black America*, p. 268.

67. *Time*, September 15, 1975, p. 36; *Time*, September 22, 1975, p. 7.

68. *Time*, September 15, 1975, pp. 35–36.

69. Lynn W. Eley and Thomas W. Casstevens, *The Politics of Fair-Housing Legislation: State and Local Case Studies* (San Francisco: Chandler Publishing Co., 1968), pp. 4–6; U.S. Commission on Civil Rights, *Civil Rights Enforcement Effort* (1971), p. 147.

70. U.S. Commission on Civil Rights, *Civil Rights Enforcement Effort* (1971), p. 156.

71. Ibid., p. 139.

72. Ibid.

73. Ibid., pp. 141–42.

74. Ibid., p. 142.

75. Robert E. Forman, "Housing and Racial Segregation," in Rodgers, *Racism and Inequality*, p. 69.

76. *Time*, January 24, 1977, p. 52.

77. U.S. Commission on Civil Rights, *The Federal Civil Rights Enforcement Effort–1974, vol. II, To Provide for Fair Housing* (Washington. D.C.: Government Printing Office, 1974), p. 62.

78. Ibid., p. 67.

79. Ibid., p. 89.

80. Ibid., pp. 39–40.

81. Ibid., pp. 339–40.

82. Ibid., pp. 334–35.

83. Simpson and Yinger, *Racial and Cultural Minorities*, pp. 418–19.

84. Report of the Gillem Board, "Utilization of Negro Manpower," War Department Circular 124, April 27, 1946.

85. The President's Committee on Equality of Treatment and Opportunity in the Armed Services, *Freedom to Serve* (Washington, D.C.: Government Printing Office, 1950), p. 20.

86. Executive Order 9981, "Establishing the President's Committee on Equality of Treatment and Opportunity in the Armed Services," July 26, 1948.

87. Leo Bogart, *Social Research and the Desegregation of the Army* (Chicago: Markham Publishing Co., 1969), p. 182.

88. *Denver Post*, December 17, 1970, p. 1.

89. U.S. Commission on Civil Rights, *Civil Rights Enforcement Effort* (1971), p. 316.

90. Ibid.

91. Ibid., p. 318.

92. Ibid., pp. 319–20; Ellwyn R. Stoddard, *Mexican Americans* (New York: Random House, 1973), p. 236.

93. Joan Moore, *Mexican Americans* (Englewood Cliffs, N.J.: Prentice-Hall, 1970), pp. 43–44.

94. William A. Brophy and Sophie D. Aberle, *The Indian: America's Unfinished Business* (Norman: University of Oklahoma Press, 1966), p. 29.

95. Quoted in James E. Officer, "The American Indian and Federal Policy," in *The American Indian in Urban Society*, ed. Jack O. Waddell and O. Michael Watson (Boston: Little, Brown, and Co., 1971), p. 48.

96. Ibid.; Brophy and Aberle, *The Indian*, pp. 184–85.

97. Officer, "The American Indian and Federal Policy," p. 45.

98. Brophy and Aberle, *The Indian*, pp. 182–83.

99. Ibid., pp. 196–99.

100. Ibid., pp. 199–207.

101. *Denver Post*, July 8, 1970, p. 31.

102. Sar A. Levitan and Barbara Hetrick, *Big Brother's Indian Programs–With Reservations* (New York: McGraw-Hill Book Co., 1971), pp. 160–61.

103. Ibid., pp. 54–60.

104. Ibid., p. 193.

105. Ibid., pp. 53–55.

106. Ibid., p. 137.

107. Ibid.

108. Ibid., pp. 146–149.

109. *Time*, April 11, 1977, pp. 51–2.

110. Ibid., p. 52.

111. Levitan and Hetrick, *Big Brother's Indian Programs*, p. 10.

112. Earl Parker Hanson, *Transformation: The Story of Modern Puerto Rico* (New York: Simon and Schuster, 1955), pp. 388–92.

113. U.S. Commission on Civil Rights, *Civil Rights Enforcement Effort* (1973), pp. 2–11.

Chapter 12

1. Suzanne I. Keller, "The Social Origins and Career Lines of Three Generations of American Business Leaders" (Ph.D. dissertation, Columbia University, 1954); cited in Charles H. Anderson, *White Protestant Americans* (Englewood Cliffs, N.J.: Prentice-Hall, 1970), p. 143.

2. Ibid.

3. Mary R. Koch, "The Family Background of Influentials" (Ph.D. dissertation, St. Louis University, 1963); cited in Anderson, *White Protestant Americans*, pp. 144–45.

4. Fletchen Knebel, "The WASP: 1968," *Look*, July 23, 1968, pp. 69–72; cited in Anderson, *White Protestant Americans*, pp. 144–45.

5. Donald W. Matthews, *The Social Background of Political Decision Makers* (New York: Random House, 1954), pp. 26–27; Edwin S. Gaustad, "America's Institutions of Faith," in Donald Cutler, ed., *The Religious Situation: 1968* (Boston: Beacon Press, 1968), pp. 851–54; John R. Schmidhauser, "The Justices of the Supreme Court: A Collective Portrait," *Midwest Journal of Political Science* III (February 1959): 1–57; cited in Anderson, *White Protestant Americans*, p. 146.

6. H. M. Baron, "Black Powerlessness in Chicago," *Transaction* (November 1968): 27–33.

7. Ibid., p. 33.

8. K. H. Flaming, J. J. Palen, G. Ringlien, and C. Taylor, "Black Powerlessness in Policy-Making Positions," *The Sociological Quarterly* (1972): 126–33.

9. *Current Population Reports*, "The Social and Economic Status of the Black Population in the United States, 1974," Special Studies, series P-23, no. 54 (Washington, D.C.: U.S. Department of Commerce/Bureau of the Census, July 1975) p. 151.

10. Ibid.

11. Harry Edwards, "20th Century Gladiators for White America," *Psychology Today*, November 1973, p. 44.

12. *Denver Rocky Mountain News*, October 19, 1975, p. 43.

13. U.S. Commission on Civil Rights, *The Southwest Indian Report* (Washington, D.C.: Government Printing Office, May 1973), pp. 3–6.

14. Jack Olsen, Jr., byline, *Denver Rocky Mountain News*, September 17, 1975, p. 9.

15. Ibid.

16. Jack Olsen, Jr., byline, *Denver Rocky Mountain News*, June 3, 1976, pp. 5, 28.

17. *Denver Post*, June 8, 1976, p. 6.

18. Harry H. L. Kitano, "Housing of the Japanese-Americans in the San Francisco Bay Area," in Nathan Glazer and Davis McEntire, *Studies in Housing and Minority Groups* (Berkeley and Los Angeles: University of California Press, 1960), p. 178.

19. Ibid., p. 193.

20. Harry H. L. Kitano, *Japanese Americans* (Englewood Cliffs, N.J.: Prentice-Hall, 1969), p. 138.

21. Russell Endo, "Japanese Americans: The 'Model Minority' in Perspective," in *The Social Reality of Ethnic America*, ed. Rudolph Gomes et al. (Lexington, Mass.: D.C. Heath and Co., 1974), pp. 203–204.

22. U.S. Commission on Civil Rights, "Mexican-Americans and the Administration of Justice in the Southwest," March 1970, in *Cracks in the Melting Pot*, 2d ed., ed. Melvin Steinfield (New York: Glencoe Press, 1973), p. 97.

23. Ibid., p. 99.

24. Ibid., pp. 99–101.

25. U.S. Commission on Civil Rights, *Report of the U.S. Commission on Civil Rights, 1961*, in *Cracks in the Melting Pot*, 1st ed., ed. Melvin Steinfield (Beverly Hills, Ca.: Glencoe Press, 1970), pp. 64, 66; U.S. Commission on Civil Rights, *The Southwest Indian Report* (Washington, D.C.: Government Printing Office, May, 1973).

26. Steinfield, *Cracks in the Melting Pot*, 1st ed., pp. 66–70.

27. *Educational Attainment, Subject Reports, 1970 Census of the Population*, (Washington, D.C.: Department of Commerce/Bureau of the Census, March 1973) pp. 149, 151, 182, 184.

28. Ibid.

29. Ray Marshall, *The Negro Worker* (New York: Random House, 1967), p. 63.

30. U.S. Commission on Civil Rights, *The Voting Rights Act: Ten Years After* (Washington, D.C.: Government Printing Office, January 1975), p. 43.

31. *The National Roster of Black Elected Officials*, vol. 3 (Washington, D.C.: Joint Center for Political Studies, May 1973), p. viii.

32. United States Commission on Civil Rights, *Political Participation* (Washington, D.C.: Government Printing Office, 1968), pp. 171–74.

33. United States Commission on Civil Rights, *The Voting Rights Act: Ten Years After*, pp. 82–89, 92, 100–106, 341–43.

34. John H. Denton, *Apartheid American Style* (Berkeley, Ca.: Diablo Press, 1967), p. 43.

35. Ibid., p. 48.

36. Ibid., p. 43.

37. Ibid., pp. 37, 48, 50–51; Davis McEntire, *Residence and Race* (Berkeley: University of California Press, 1960), pp. 287–90; Rose Helper, *Racial Policies and Practices of Real Estate Brokers* (Minneapolis: University of Minnesota Press, 1969), pp. 42, 46.

38. George A. Davis and O. Fred Donaldson, *Blacks in the United States: A Geographic Perspective* (Boston: Houghton Mifflin, 1975), p. 46; (Washington, D.C.: *The Social and Economic Status of Negroes in the United States, 1970, Current Population Reports*, series P-23, no. 38, BLS Report No. 394 (Washington, D.C.: U.S. Department of Commerce/Bureau of the Census, 1971), p. 21.

39. Theodore G. Clemence, "Residential Segregation in the Mid-Sixties," in *Racial Discrimination in the United States*, ed. Thomas F. Pettigrew (New York: Harper and Row, 1975), p. 59. Originally published in *Demography* 4 (1967): 562–68.

40. Gary Orfield, *The Reconstruction of Southern Education* (New York: Wiley-Interscience, 1969), p. 20.

41. U.S. Commission on Civil Rights, *Racial Isolation in the Public Schools* (Washington, D.C.: Government Printing Office, 1967), p. 8.

42. *Christian Science Monitor*, June 1, 1973, p. 1; see also *Fall, 1972 Racial and Ethnic Enrollment in Public Elementary and Secondary Schools* (Washington, D.C.: Office for Civil Rights, 1973), pp. 12–15; Harrell R. Rodgers, Jr., "On Integrating the Public Schools: An Empirical and Legal Assessment," in *Racism and Inequality: The Policy Alternatives*, ed. Harrell R. Rodgers, Jr. (San Francisco: W. H. Freeman and Co., 1975), pp. 126–28.

43. *Christian Science Monitor*, June 1, 1973, p. 1.

44. *Denver Post*, January 13, 1972, p. 13.

45. *Denver Post* (from the *New York Times*), December 3, 1972, p. 36.

46. Ibid.

47. *Time*, September 22, 1975, p. 14.

48. *Time*, September 15, 1975, p. 41.

49. *Time*, September 22, 1975, p. 14.

50. Thomas F. Pettigrew, "The Racial Integration of the Schools," in Pettigrew, *Racial Discrimination in the United States*, pp. 230–31.

51. Davis and Donaldson, *Blacks in the United States*, p. 179.

52. Nancy H. St. John, *School Desegregation: Outcomes for Children* (New York: John Wiley and Sons, 1975).

53. S. Koslin, B. Koslin, R. Pargament, and H. Waxman, "Classroom Racial Balance and Students' Interracial Attitudes" (Riverside Research Institute, New York City, 1970).

54. Norman Miller and Harold B. Gerard, "How Busing Failed in Riverside," *Psychology Today*, June 1976, pp. 66–70, 100.

55. Ibid., p. 100.

56. Angus Campbell, *White Attitudes toward Black People* (Ann Arbor: Institute for Social Research, The University of Michigan, 1971), pp. 135, 136.

57. Ibid., pp. 134, 136.

58. Ibid., p. 134.

59. Ibid., pp. 45–55.

60. Ibid., p. 133.

61. Thomas F. Pettigrew, "Black and White Attitudes toward Race and Housing," in Pettigrew, *Racial Discrimination in the United States*, p. 93.

62. Ibid., p. 94.

63. Campbell, *White Attitudes toward Black People*, p. 147.

64. Ibid.

65. Ibid., p. 145.

66. Peter Goldman, *Report from Black America* (New York: Clarion Books, Simon and Schuster, 1971), p. 266.

67. Gallup Poll, 1973, reported in *Denver Post*, September 9, 1973, p. 8.

68. Goldman, *Report from Black America*, p. 267.

Chapter 13

1. Perry L. Weed, *The White Ethnic Movement and Ethnic Politics* (New York: Praeger Publishers, 1973), p. 42.

2. Michael Novak, *The Rise of the Unmeltable Ethnics* (New York: Macmillan Co., 1971), p. 114.

3. Jesse L. Jackson, "New Ideas, New Values to Improve the Plight of Blacks," *Denver Post*, May 9, 1976, p. 16.

4. Ibid., p. 17.

5. Nathan Glazer, "Ethnic Groups in America: From National Culture to Ideology," in *Minority Response*, ed. Minako Kurokawa (New York: Random House, 1970), p. 85. Previously published in *Freedom and Control in Modern Society*, ed. Morre Berger et al. (New York: Octagon Books, 1954), pp. 158–73.

6. Joseph G. Jorgensen, "Indians and the Metropolis," in *The American Indian in Urban Society*, ed. Jack O. Waddell and O. Michael Watson (Boston: Little, Brown and Co., 1971), p. 79.

7. Earl Parker Hanson, *Transformation: The Story of Modern Puerto Rico* (New York: Simon and Schuster, 1955), p. 5.

8. Russell Endo, "Japanese Americans: The 'Model Minority' in Perspective," in *The Social Reality of Ethnic America*, ed. Rudolph Gomez et al. (Lexington, Mass.: D.C. Heath and Co., 1974), p. 207.

9. Thomas Sowell, "'Affirmative Action' Reconsidered," *The Public Interest* Number 42, (Winter 1976); 63.

10. Neil Gilbert and Joseph W. Eaton, "Favoritism as a Strategy in Race Relations," *Social Problems* (Summer 1970); pp. 45–58.

11. Weed, *The White Ethnic Movement*, p. 201.

BIBLIOGRAPHY

Aberbach, Joel D., and Walker, Jack L. "The Meanings of Black Power: A Comparison of White and Black Interpretations of a Political Slogan." *American Political Science Review* LXIV (June 1970); 367–88.

Abrams, Charles. "The Housing Problem and the Negro." In *Racial Discrimination in the United States*, edited by Thomas F. Pettigrew. New York: Harper and Row, 1975.

Acuna, Rodolfo. *Occupied America: The Chicano's Struggle toward Liberation.* San Francisco: Canfield Press, 1972.

Adams, Romanzo. *Interracial Marriage in Hawaii.* New York: Macmillan Co., 1937.

Alexander, Lewis M. *World Political Patterns.* Chicago: Rand McNally and Co., 1963.

Anderson, Charles H. *Toward A New Sociology: A Critical View.* Homewood, Ill.: Dorsey Press, 1971.

———. *White Protestant Americans.* Englewood Cliffs, N.J.: Prentice-Hall, 1970.

Anderson, James E. *Public Policy-Making.* New York: Praeger Publishers, 1975.

Annual Report of the Commissioner General of Immigration. Washington, D.C.: Government Printing Office, 1929.

Aptheker, Herbert. "American Negro Slave Revolts." In *Racial Violence in the United States*, edited by Allen D. Grimshaw. Chicago: Aldine Publishing Co., 1969.

Backzkowski, Wlodzimierz. "Russian Colonialism in its Soviet Manifestation, 1958." In *The Imperialism Reader*, edited by Louis L. Snyder. Princeton, N.J.: D. Van Nostrand Co., 1962.

Baker, Donald G. "Australian and Anglo Racism: Preliminary Explorations." In *Racism: The Australian Experience*, edited by F. S. Stevens. Colonialism, vol. 3 New York: Taplinger Publishing Co., 1972.

Baker, Paul T. "Human Biological Diversity as an Adaptive Response to the Environment." In *The Biological and Social Meaning of Race*, edited by Richard H. Osbourne. San Francisco: W. H. Freeman and Co., 1971.

Baltzell, E. Digby. *The Protestant Establishment: Aristocracy and Caste in America.* New York: Random House, 1964.

Banton, Michael. *Race Relations.* New York: Basic Books, 1967.

Baratz, Stephen S., and Baratz, Joan C. "Early Childhood Intervention: The Social Science Base of Institutional Racism." *Harvard Educational Review* 40 (Winter 1970): 29–50.

Bardin, James. "Science and the 'Negro Problem.'" In *The Development of Segregationist Thought*, edited by I. A. Newby. Homewood, Ill.: Dorsey Press, 1968.

Baron, H. M. "Black Powerlessness in Chicago." *Transaction* 5 (November 1968); 27–33.

Bean, Robert Bennett. "The Negro Brain." In *The Development of Segregationist Thought*, edited by I. A. Newby. Homewood, Ill.: Dorsey Press, 1968.

———. "The Nose of the Jew and the Quadratus Labii Superioris Muscle." In *In Their Place: White America Defines Her Minorities, 1850–1950*, edited by Lewis H. Carlson and George A. Colburn. New York: John Wiley and Sons, 1972.

Bedell, George C.: Sandon, Leo Jr.; and Wellborn, Charles T. *Religion in America.* New York: Macmillan Co., 1975.

Bell, Daniel. "Crime as an American Way of Life." *The Antioch Review* 13 (1953): 131–54.

Berry, Brewton. "America's Mestizos." In *The Blending of Races,* edited by Noel P. Gist and Anthony Gary Dworkin. New York: Wiley-Interscience, 1972.

Bierstedt, Robert. *The Social Order.* New York: McGraw-Hill Book Co., 1970.

Billington, Ray Allen. *Westward Expansion.* New York: The Macmillan Co., 1950.

Billington, Ray Allen; Loewenberg, Bert James; and Brockunier, Samuel Hugh, eds. *The Making of American Democracy,* Volume II. New York: Rinehart and Company, 1950.

Blauner, Robert. *Racial Oppression in America.* New York: Harper and Row, 1972.

Boahen, A. Adu. "The Coming of the Europeans." In *The Horizon History of Africa,* edited by Alvin M. Josephy, Jr. New York: American Heritage Publishing Co., 1971.

Bodard, Lucien. *Green Hell: Massacre of the Brazilian Indians.* New York: Outerbridge and Dienstfrey, 1972.

———. "The Massacre of the Amazonian Indians." *Interplay,* March 1970: 18–23.

Boorstin, Daniel J. *The Americans: The Colonial Experience.* New York: Vintage Books, Random House, 1958.

———. *The Americans: The National Experience.* New York: Vintage Books, Random House, 1965.

Botkin, B. A., ed. *Lay My Burden Down: A Folk History of Slavery.* Chicago: University of Chicago Press, 1945.

Bracey, John H., Jr.; Meier, August; and Rudwick, Elliott, eds. *Conflict and Competition: Studies in the Recent Black Protest Movement.* Belmont, California: Wadsworth Publishing Company, Inc., 1970.

Brinton, Daniel G. *The American Race.* New York: N.D.C. Hodges, 1891.

Broom, Leonard, and Glenn, Norval D. "The Occupations and Income of Black Americans." In *Blacks in the United States,* edited by Norval D. Glenn and Charles M. Bonjean. San Francisco: Chandler Publishing Co., 1969.

Brophy, William A., and Aberle, Sophie D. *The Indian: America's Unfinished Business.* Norman: University of Oklahoma Press, 1966.

Brown, Dee. *Bury My Heart at Wounded Knee.* New York: Holt, Rinehart and Winston, 1970.

Bryce-Laporte, Roy Simon. "The American Slave Plantation and Our Heritage of Communal Deprivation." *American Behavioral Scientists* XII (March-April 1969): pp. 2–8.

Buettner-Janusch, John. *Origins of Man: Physical Anthropology.* New York: John Wiley and Sons, 1966.

Bullock, Charles S., III. "Expanding Black Economic Rights." In *Racism and Inequality: The Policy Alternatives,* edited by Harrell R. Rodgers, Jr. San Francisco: W. H. Freeman and Co., 1975.

Bullock, Charles S., III, and Rodgers, Harrell R., Jr. *Racial Equality in America.* Pacific Palisades, Ca.: Goodyear Publishing Co., 1975.

Bunche, Ralph J. "The Programs of Organizations Devoted to the Improvement of the Status of the American Negro." *Journal of Negro Education* VIII (July 1939): 539–50.

Burrows, Edwin G. *Hawaiian Americans.* New Haven: Yale University Press, 1947.

Cable, Vincent. "The Asians of Keyna." *African Affairs* 68 (July 1969): 218–31.

Campbell, Angus. *White Attitudes toward Black People.* Ann Arbor: Institute for Social Research, University of Michigan, 1971.

Caplan, Nathan S., and Paige, Jeffrey M. "A Study of Ghetto Rioters." *Scientific American* 219 (August 1968): 15–21.

Carlson, Lewis H., and Colburn, George A., eds. *In Their Place: White America Defines Her Minorities, 1850–1950.* New York: John Wiley and Sons, 1972.

Carmichael, Stokely, "What We Want." In *Racial Conflict,* edited by Gary T. Marx. Boston: Little, Brown and Co., 1971.

Carmichael, Stokely, and Hamilton, Charles. *Black Power: The Politics of Liberation in America.* New York: Random House, 1967.

Carnoy, Martin. *Education as Cultural Imperialism.* New York: David McKay Co., 1974.

Carr-Saunders, A. M. *World Population.* Oxford: Clarendon, 1936.

Carter, Gwendolen M. *The Politics of Inequality.* New York: Frederick A. Praeger, 1968.

Clark, Frank. "A Politician's Defense of Segregation." In *The Development of Segregationist Thought,* edited by I. A. Newby. Homewood, Ill.: Dorsey Press, 1968.

Clark, Kenneth B. *Dark Ghetto: Dilemmas of Power.* New York: Harper and Row, 1965.

Clemence, Theodore G. "Residential Segregation in the Mid-Sixties." In *Racial Discrimination in the United States,* edited by Thomas F. Pettigrew. New York: Harper and Row, 1975.

Conquest, Robert. *The Nation Killers: The Soviet Deportation of Nationalities.* London: Macmillan and Co., 1970.

Coser, Lewis. *The Functions of Social Conflict.* New York: Free Press, 1956.

Coughlin, Richard J. *Double Identity: The Chinese in Modern Thailand.* London: Oxford University Press, 1960.

Crane, Jay, and Crane, Elaine, eds. *The Black Soldier: From the American Revolution to Vietnam.* New York: William Morrow and Co., 1971.

Cullinane, Michael. "Implementing the 'New Order': The Structure and Supervision of Local Government During the Taft Era." In *Compadre Colonialism; Studies on the Philippines under American Rule,* edited by Norman G. Owen. Ann Arbor: University of Michigan Center for South and Southeast Asian Studies, 1971.

Daniels, Roger. *Concentration Camps U.S.A.: Japanese-Americans and World War II.* New York: Holt, Rinehart and Winston, 1971.

Davidson, Basil. *The African Slave Trade.* Boston: Little, Brown and Co., 1961.

Davie, Maurice R. *Negroes in American Society.* New York: McGraw-Hill Book Co., 1949.

———. *World Immigration.* New York: Macmillan Co., 1947.

Davies, James C. "Toward A Theory of Revolution," *American Sociological Review* 27: 5–19.

Davis, David Brion. *The Problem of Slavery in Western Culture.* Ithaca: Cornell University Press, 1966.

Davis, George A., and Donaldson, O. Fred. *Blacks in the United States: A Geographic Perspective.* Boston: Houghton Mifflin, 1975.

Davis, John P., ed. *The American Negro Reference Book.* Englewood Cliffs, N.J.: Prentice-Hall, 1966.

Davis, Simon. *Race Relations in Ancient Egypt.* New York: Philosophical Library, 1952.

Day, Robert C. "The Emergence of Activism as a Social Movement," in *Native Americans Today: Sociological Perspectives,* edited by Howard M. Bahr, Bruce A. Chadwick, and Robert C. Day. New York: Harper and Row, 1972.

Denton, John H. *Apartheid American Style.* Berkeley, Ca.: Diablo Press, 1967.

de Riencourt, Amaury. *The American Empire.* New York: Dial Press, 1968.

———. *The Coming Caesars.* New York: Coward-McCann, 1957.

Diggins, John P. *Mussolini and Fascism, The View From America.* Princeton: Princeton University Press, 1972.

Dinnerstein, Leonard, and Jaher, Frederick Cople, eds. *The Aliens: A History of Ethnic Minorities in America.* New York: Appleton-Century-Crofts, Meredith Corporation, 1970.

Dobzhansky, Theodosius. "Race Equality." In *The Biological and Social Meaning of Race,* edited by Richard H. Osborne. San Francisco: W. H. Freeman and Co., 1971.

Dollard, John. *Caste and Class in a Southern Town.* Garden City, N.Y.: Doubleday Anchor Books, 1975.

Drake, St. Clair, and Cayton, Horace R. *Black Metropolis: A Study of Negro Life in a Northern City.* Vol. II. New York: Harper Torchbooks, Academy Library, Harper and Row, 1962.

———. "The Social and Economic Status of the Negro in the United States." *Daedalus, Journal of American Academy of Arts and Sciences, The Negro American* 94: 717–814.

DuBois, W. E. Burghardt. *The Philadelphia Negro.* New York: Benjamin Blom, 1967, 1899.

Durant, Will. *Age of Faith: The Story of Civilization, Part IV.* New York: Simon and Schuster, 1950.

———. *Caesar and Christ: The Story of Civilization, Part III.* New York: Simon and Schuster, 1944.

———. *Our Oriental Heritage: The Story of Civilization, Part I.* New York: Simon and Schuster, 1954.

———. *The Reformation: The Story of Civilization, Part VI.* New York: Simon and Schuster, 1957.

Durant, Will, and Durant, Ariel. *Rousseau and Revolution: The Story of Civilization, Part X.* New York: Simon and Schuster, 1967.

Edwardes, Michael. *British India, 1772–1947.* New York: Taplinger Publishing Co., 1967.

———. "The Great Mutiny." *The Horizon History of the British Empire,* edited by Stephen W. Sears. New York: American Heritage Publishing Co., 1973.

———. "The Threatened Raj." In *The Horizon History of the British Empire,* edited by Stephen W. Sears. New York: The American Heritage Publishing Co., 1973.

Edwards, Harry. "20th Century Gladiators for White America." *Psychology Today,* November 1973: pp. 43–52.

Ehrlich, Howard J. *The Social Psychology of Prejudice.* New York: John Wiley and Sons, 1973.

Eitzen, D. Stanley. "Two Minorities: The Jews of Poland and the Chinese of the

Philippines." In *Ethnic Conflicts and Power:A Cross-National Perspective*, edited by Donald E. Gelfand and Russell D. Lee. New York: John Wiley and Sons, 1973.

Eley, Lynn W., and Casstevens, Thomas W. *The Politics of Fair-Housing Legislation: State and Local Case Studies*. San Francisco: Chandler Publishing Co., 1968.

Elkins, Stanley M. *Slavery: A Problem in American Institutional and Intellectual Life*. Chicago: University of Chicago Press, 1959.

Endo, Russell. "Japanese Americans: The 'Model Minority' in Perspective." In *The Social Reality of Ethnic America*, edited by Rudolph Gomez et al. Lexington, Mass.: D.C. Heath and Co., 1974.

Enloe, Cynthia H. *Ethnic Conflict and Political Development*. Boston: Little, Brown and Co., 1973.

Essien-Udom, E.U. *The Philosophy and Opinions of Marcus Garvey*. 2d ed. New York: Humanities Press, 1967.

Executive Order 9981, "Establishing the President's Committee on Equality of Treatment and Opportunity in the Armed Services," July 26, 1948.

Farb, Peter. *Man's Rise to Civilization as Shown by the Indians of North America from Primeval Times to the Coming of the Industrial State*. New York: E. P. Dutton and Co., 1968.

Faulkner, Harold Underwood. *American Economic History*. 5th ed. New York: Harper and Brothers, 1943.

Felstein, Stanley, and Costello, Lawrence. *The Ordeal of Assimilation*. Garden City, N.Y.: Anchor Books, Anchor Press/Doubleday, 1974.

Fieldhouse, D. K. *The Colonial Empires*. New York: Delacorte Press, 1965.

Finley, M. J. *Slavery in Classical Antiquity*. Cambridge: W. Heffer and Sons, 1960.

Fisher, Lillian Estelle. *The Last Inca Revolt, 1780–1783*. Norman: University of Oklahoma Press, 1966.

Fitzgibbon, Russell H. *Cuba and the United States, 1900–1935*. Menasha, Wis.: Collegiate Press, George Banta Publishing Co., 1935.

Flaming, K. H., Palen, J. J.; Ringlien, G; and Taylor, C. "Black Powerlessness in Policy-Making Positions," *The Sociological Quarterly* 13 (1972): 126–33.

Forbes, Jack D. "Mexican-Americans." In *Mexican-Americans in the United States*, edited by John H. Burma. Cambridge: Schenkman Publishing Co., 1970.

Forman, Robert E. "Housing and Racial Segregation." In *Racism and Inequality: The Policy Alternatives*, edited by Harrell R. Rodgers, Jr. San Francisco: W. H. Freeman and Co., 1975.

Fowler, Arlen. *The Black Infantry in the West, 1869–1891*. Westport, Conn.: Greenwood Publishing Corporation, 1971.

Frazier, E. Franklin. *The Negro in the United States*. New York: Macmillan Co., 1949.

Frederickson, George M. *The Black Image in the White Mind*. New York: Harper and Row, 1971.

Friedman, Lawrence J. *The White Savage: Racial Fantasies in the Postbellum South*. Englewood Cliffs, N.J.: Prentice-Hall, 1970.

Friedman, Robert. "Institutional Racism: How to Discriminate without Really Trying." In *Racial Discrimination in the United States*, edited by Thomas F. Pettigrew. New York: Harper and Row, 1975.

Fritz, Henry E. *The Movement for Indian Assimilation, 1860–1890*. Philadelphia: University of Pennsylvania Press, 1963.

Fuller, J. F. C. *Decisive Battles of the U.S.A.* New York: Beechhurst Press, 1953.

Gaustad, Edwin S. "America's Institutions of Faith." In *The Religious Situation, 1968*, edited by Donald Cutler. Boston: Beacon Press, 1968.

Gayda, Virginio. *Modern Austria: Her Racial and Social Problems.* London: T. Fisher Unwin, 1915.

Geipel, John. *The Europeans.* New York: Pegasus, 1970.

Geschwender, James A., and Singer, Benjamin D. "Deprivation and The Detroit Riot." *Social Problems* 17 (Spring 1970): 457–63.

Gifford, Prosser, and Weiskel, Timothy C. "African Education in a Colonial Context: French and British Styles." In *France and Britain in Africa*, edited by Prosser Gifford and William Roger Louis. New Haven: Yale University Press, 1971.

Gilbert, Neil, and Eaton, Joseph W. "Favoritism as a Strategy in Race Relations." *Social Problems* 17 (Summer 1970).

Gillespie, Joan. *Algeria: Rebellion and Revolution.* New York: Frederick A. Praeger, 1960.

Gipson, Lawrence Henry. "The American Revolution as an Aftermath of the Great War for the Empire, 1754–1763." In *The Causes of the American Revolution*, edited by John C. Wahlke. Boston: D.C. Heath and Co., 1950).

Gist, Noel P. "The Anglo-Indians of India." In *The Blending of Races*, edited by Noel P. Gist and Anthony Gary Dworkin. New York: Wiley-Interscience, 1972.

Glazer, Nathan. *American Judaism.* Chicago: University of Chicago Press, 1957.

———. "Ethnic Groups in America: From National Culture to Ideology." In *Minority Responses*, edited by Minako Kurokawa. New York: Random House, 1970.

Glenn, Norval D. "The Role of White Resistance and Facilitation in the Negro Struggle for Quality." In *Power and the Black Community*, edited by Sethard Fisher. New York: Random House, 1970.

———. "White Gains from Negro Subordination." In *Blacks in the United States*, edited by Norval D. Glenn and Charles M. Bonjean. San Francisco: Chandler Publishing Co., 1969.

Gluckman, Max. "The Tribal Area in South and Central Africa." In *Pluralism in Africa*, edited by Leo Kuper and M. G. Smith. Berkeley and Los Angeles: University of California Press, 1969.

Goethe, C. M. "The Influx of Mexican Amerinds." In *In Their Place: White America Defines Her Minorities, 1850–1950*, edited by Lewis H. Carlson and George A. Colburn. New York: John Wiley and Sons, 1972.

Goldman, Peter. *Report from Black America.* New York: Clarion Book, Simon and Schuster, 1971.

Gordon, David C. "Algeria, 1962–1967: An Essay on Dependence in Independence." In *France and Britain in Africa*, edited by Prosser Gifford and William Roger Louis. New Haven, Conn.: Yale University Press, 1971.

Gordon, Milton J. *Assimilation in American Life.* New York: Oxford University Press, 1964.

———. "Assimilation in America: Theory and Reality." *Daedalus, Journal of the American Academy of Arts and Sciences* 90 (Spring 1961): 263–85.

Graff, Henry F. *American Imperialism and the Philippine Insurrection.* Boston: Little, Brown and Co., 1969.

Greeley, Andrew M. *Ethnicity in the United States: A Preliminary Reconnaissance.* New York: Wiley-Interscience, 1974.

Greenberg, Jack. *Race Relations and American Law.* New York: Columbia University Press, 1959.

Grimshaw, Allen D., ed. "Lawlessness and Violence in America and Their Special Manifestations in Changing Negro-White Relationships." In *Racial Violence in the United States.* Chicago: Aldine Publishing Co., 1969.

Grossman, Joel B., and Grossman, Mary H. *Law and Change in Modern America.* Pacific Palisades, Ca.: Goodyear Publishing Co., 1971.

Hacker, Louis M. "The First American Revolution." In *The Causes of the American Revolution,* edited by John C. Wahlke. Boston: D.C. Heath and Co., 1950.

Hamilton-Browne, Colonel G. "A Lost Legionary in South Africa (1879)." In *The Horizon History of Africa,* edited by Alvin M. Josephy, Jr. New York: American Heritage Publishing Co., 1971.

Hanham, H. J. *Scottish Nationalism.* Cambridge: Harvard University Press, 1969.

Hannett, Leo J. "Niugini Black Power." In *Racism: The Australian Experience,* edited by F. S. Stevens. Colonialism, vol. 3. New York: Taplinger Publishing Co., 1972.

Hanson, Earl Parker. *Transformation: The Story of Modern Puerto Rico.* New York: Simon and Schuster, 1955.

Harcave, Sidney. *Russia: A History.* New York: J. B. Lippincott Co., 1953.

Haring, C. H. *The Spanish Empire in America.* New York: Oxford University Press, 1947.

Hauberg, Clifford A. *Puerto Rico and the Puerto Ricans.* New York: Twayne Publishers, 1974.

Hauser, Philip M. "Demographic Factors in the Integration of the Negro." *Daedalus, The Negro American* 94 (Fall 1965): 847–77.

Hawgood, John A. *The Tragedy of German-America.* New York: G. P. Putnam's Sons, 1940.

Helper, Rose. *Racial Policies and Practices of Real Estate Brokers.* Minneapolis: University of Minnesota Press, 1969.

Hicks, Jim, and Edwardes, Michael. "Warfare on India's Borders." In *The Horizon History of Africa,* edited by Alvin M. Josephy, Jr. New York: American Heritage Publishing Co., 1971.

Hicks, John D. *The Federal Union.* Boston: Houghton Mifflin, 1957.

Higham, John. *Strangers in the Land: Patterns of American Nativism, 1860–1925.* New York: Atheneum, 1965.

Hill, Herbert. "The Racial Practice of Organized Labor." In *The Negro and the American Labor Movement,* edited by Julius Jacobson. Garden City, N.Y.: Doubleday, 1968.

Hines, Ralph H., and Pierce, James E. "Negro Leadership after the Social Crisis: An Analysis of Leadership Changes in Montgomery, Alabama." *Phylon* XXVI (2d Quarter 1965): 162–72.

Hitler, Adolph. *Mein Kampf.* New York: Reynmal and Hitchcock, 1940.

Holborn, Louise. "Refugee Migration in the Twentieth Century." In *World Migration in Modern Times,* edited by Franklin D. Scott. Englewood Cliffs, N.J.: Prentice-Hall, 1968.

Horowitz, David. *The Free World Colossus.* New York: Hill and Wang, 1965.

Howells, William W. "The Meaning of Race." In *The Biological and Social Meaning of Race,* edited by Richard H. Osborne. San Francisco: W. H. Freeman and Co., 1971.

Hunt, Chester L., and Walker, Lewis. *Ethnic Dynamics: Patterns of Intergroup Relations in Various Societies.* Homewood, Ill.: Dorsey Press, 1974.

Hutchinson, Joseph F., Jr. "Quezon's Role in Philippine Independence." In *Compadre Colonialism: Studies on the Philippines under American Rule,* edited by Norman G. Owen. Ann Arbor: University of Michigan Center for South and Southeastern Asian Studies, 1971.

Iorizzo, Luciano J., and Mondello, Salvatore. *The Italian-Americans.* New York: Twayne Publishers, 1971.

Iris, Mark, and Shama, Avraham. "Black Panthers: The Movement." *Society* 9 (May 1972): 37–44.

Isaacs, Harold R. *The New World of Negro Americans.* New York: Viking Press, 1963.

Jackson, T. A. *Ireland Her Own.* New York: International Publishers Co., 1947.

Johnson, Charles S. *Patterns of Negro Segregation.* New York: Harper and Brothers, 1943.

Jones, Gareth Stedman. "The Specificity of U.S. Imperialism." In *The Poverty of Progress,* edited by Milton Mankoff. New York: Holt, Rinehart and Winston, 1972.

Jones, Howard Mumford. *O Strange New World, American Culture: The Formative Years.* New York: Viking Press, 1964.

Jones, LeRoi. *Blues People: Negro Music in White America.* New York: William Morrow and Co., 1963.

Jones, Maldwyn Allen. *American Immigration.* Chicago: University of Chicago Press, 1960.

Jordan, Winthrop. *White over Black.* Chapel Hill: University of North Carolina Press, 1968.

Josephy, Alvin M., Jr. *The Indian Heritage of America.* New York: Alfred A. Knopf, 1969.

Kibbe, Pauline R. *Latin Americans in Texas.* Albuquerque: University of New Mexico Press, 1946.

Kindleberger, C. P. "Mass Migration Then and Now." In *World Migration in Modern Times,* edited by Franklin D. Scott. Englewood Cliffs, N.J.: Prentice-Hall, 1968.

King, C. Wendell. *Social Movements in the United States.* New York: Random House, 1956.

Kitano, Harry H. L. "Housing of the Japanese-Americans in the San Francisco Bay Area." In *Studies in Housing and Minority Groups,* edited by Nathan Glazer and Davis McEntire. Berkeley and Los Angeles: University of California Press, 1960.

————. *Japanese Americans.* Englewood Cliffs, N.J.: Prentice-Hall, 1969.

Kluckhohn, Rockwood, and Strodtbeck, Fred L. *Variations in Value Orientations.* Evanston, Ill.: Row, Peterson and Co., 1961.

Knebel, Fletchen. "The WASPs: 1968," *Look,* July 23, 1968, pp. 69–72.

Knorr, Klaus E. *British Colonial Theories, 1570–1850.* Toronto: University of Toronto Press, 1944.

Knowles, Louis, and Prewitt, Kenneth. *Institutional Racism in America.* Englewood Cliffs, N.J.: Prentice-Hall, 1969.

Kohn, Melvin L., and Williams, Robin M. "Situational Patterning in Intergroup Relations." *American Sociological Review* 21 (April 1956): 164–74.

Kolarz, Walter. "The Melting Pot in the Pacific." *Social Process in Hawaii* 19 (1955): 23–26.

Kolarz, Walter. *Russia and Her Colonies.* New York: F. A. Praeger, 1952.

Kramer, Judith R. *The American Minority Community.* New York: Thomas Y. Crowell Co., 1970.

Kroeber, A. L. *Anthropology.* New York: Harcourt, Brace and Co., 1948.

Kulischer, Eugene M. *Europe on the Move: War and Population Changes, 1917–47.* New York: Columbia University Press, 1948.

La Violette, Forrest E. *Americans of Japanese Ancestry: A Study of Assimilation in the American Community.* Toronto: Canadian Institute of International Affairs, 1945.

Lee, Calvin. *Chinatown, U.S.A.* Garden City, N.Y.: Doubleday and Co., 1965.

Lee, Frank F. *Negro and White in Connecticut Town.* New Haven, Conn.: College and University Press, 1961.

Legg, Stuart. "From Suez to Khartoum." In *The Horizon History of the British Empire,* edited by Stephen W. Sears. New York: The American Heritage Publishing Company, Inc., 1973.

Lenski, Gerhard, and Lenski, Jean. *Human Societies.* New York: McGraw-Hill Book Co., 1974.

Lerner, Max. *America as a Civilization.* New York: Simon and Schuster, 1957.

Levitan, Sar A., and Hetrick, Barbara. *Big Brother's Indian Programs—With Reservations.* New York: McGraw-Hill Book Co., 1971.

Lewis, Roy, and Foy, Yvonne. *Painting Africa White: The Human Side of British Colonialism.* New York: Universe Books, 1971.

Lieberson, Stanley. "Stratification and Ethnic Groups." *Sociological Inquiry* 40 (Spring 1970): 172–81.

Light, Ivan H. *Ethnic Enterprise in America.* Berkeley and Los Angeles: University of California Press, 1972.

Lincoln, C. Eric. *The Black Muslims in America.* Boston: Beacon Press, 1961.

Lind, Andrew W. *Hawaii's People.* Honolulu: University of Hawaii Press, 1955.

Litwack, Leon F. *North of Slavery.* Chicago: University of Chicago Press, 1961.

Livius, Titus. *The History of Rome.* Vol. III. Translated by William A. M'Devitte. London: George Bell and Sons, 1888.

———. *The History of Rome.* Volume IV. Translated by William A. M'Devitte. London: George Bell and Sons, 1888.

Long, Herman H., and Johnson, Charles S. *People vs. Property; Race Restrictive Covenants in Housing.* Nashville, Tenn.: Fisk University Press, 1947.

Loomis, W. Farnsworth. "Skin Pigment Regulation of Vitamin D Biosynthesis in Man." *Science* 157 (August 1967): 501–506.

Lopreato, Joseph. *Italian Americans.* New York: Random House, 1970.

Lurie, Nancy Oestreich. "The American Indian: Historical Background." In *Majority and Minority,* edited by Norman R. Yetman and C. Hoy Steele. Boston: Allyn and Bacon, 1971.

Lyman, Stanford M. "Contrasts in the Community Organization of Chinese and Japanese in North America." *Canadian Review of Sociology and Anthropology* 5 (1968): 2.

Lyman, Stanford M. *Chinese Americans.* New York: Random House, 1974.

Madsen, William. *The Mexican Americans of South Texas.* 2d rev. ed. New York: Holt, Rinehart and Winston, 1973.

Mahajani, Usha. *Philippine Nationalism.* St. Lucia, Queensland, Australia: University of Queensland Press, 1971.

Mandel, Bernard. "Samuel Gompers and the Negro Workers, 1886–1914." *Journal of Negro History* XL (January 1955): 34–60.

"Manifesto." *Africa Today* 15, (August/September 1969): 21–24.

Mannix, Daniel, and Cowley, Malcolm. "The Middle Passage." In *Justice Denied: The Black Man in White America,* edited by William M. Chace and Peter Collier. New York: Harcourt, Brace and World, 1970.

Marden, Charles F., and Meyer, Gladys. *Minorities in American Society.* 2d ed. New York: American Book Co., 1962.

———. *Minorities in American Society.* 4th ed. New York: D. Van Nostrand Co., 1973.

Marshall, Ray. *The Negro Worker.* New York: Random House, 1967.

Marshall, Thurgood. "The Gestapo in Detroit." In *Racial Violence in the United States,* edited by Allen D. Grimshaw. Chicago: Aldine Publishing Co., 1969.

Masotti, Louis H.; Hadden, Jeffrey K.; Seminatore, Kenneth F.; and Corsi, Jerome R. *A Time to Burn?* Chicago: Rand McNally and Co., 1969.

Matthews, Donald R., and Prothro, James W. "Political Factors and Negro Voter Registration in the South." *American Political Science Review* 57 (June 1963): 28–44.

———. *The Social Background of Political Decision Makers.* New York: Random House, 1954.

Matusow, Allen J. "From Civil Rights to Black Power: The Case of SNCC, 1960–1966." In *Conflict and Competition: Studies in the Recent Black Protest Movement,* edited by John H. Bracey, Jr., August Meier, and Elliott Rudwick. Belmont, Ca.: Wadsworth Publishing Co., 1970.

Mason, Philip. *Patterns of Dominance.* London: Oxford University Press, 1970.

Mauss, Armand L. *Social Problems as Social Movements.* Philadelphia: J. B. Lippincott Co., 1975.

Mayhew, Bruce H., and Levinger, Robert L. "On the Emergence of Oligarchy in Human Interaction," *American Journal of Sociology* 81 (March 1976): pp. 1017–49.

McCartney, Doral. "From Parnell to Pearse (1891–1921)." In *The Course of Irish History,* edited by T. W. Moody and F. X. Martin. Cork, Ireland: Mercier Press, 1967.

McClellan, Robert. *The Heathen Chinee: A Study of American Attitudes Towards China, 1890–1905.* Columbus: Ohio State University Press, 1971.

McEntire, Davis. *Residence and Race.* Berkeley: University of California Press, 1960.

McWilliams, Carey. *North from Mexico: The Spanish-Speaking People of the United States.* Philadelphia: J. B. Lippincott Co., 1949.

Meier, August. "Civil Rights Strategies for Negro Employment." In *Employment, Race and Poverty,* edited by Arthur M. Ross and Herbert Hill. New York: Harcourt, Brace and World, 1967.

———. "Negro Protest Movements and Organizations." In *Journal of Negro Education* XXXII (Fall 1963): 437–50.

Meier, August, and Rudwick, Elliott, eds. "A Strange Chapter in the Career of 'Jim Crow.'" In *The Making of Black America. The Black Community in Modern America,* vol. II. New York: Atheneum, 1971.

Meier, Matt S., and Rivera, Feliciano. *The Chicanos: A History of Mexican Americans.* New York: Hill and Wang, 1972.

Miller, Norman, and Gerard, Harold B. "How Busing Failed in Riverside." *Psychology Today,* June 1976, p. 66.

Mills, C. Wright. *The Power Elite.* New York: Oxford University Press, 1956.

Moody, T. W., and Martin, F. X. *The Course of Irish History.* Cork, Ireland: Mercier Press, 1967.

Moore, Joan W. *Mexican Americans.* Englewood Cliffs, N.J.: Prentice-Hall, 1970.

Moore, Wilbert E. *Social Change.* Englewood Cliffs, N.J.: Prentice-Hall, 1963.

Morgan, Charles Jr. "Segregated Justice." In *Race, Crime and Justice,* edited by Charles E. Reasons and Jack L. Kuykendall. Pacific Palisades, Ca.: Goodyear Publishing Co., 1972.

Morison, Samuel Eliot. *The Oxford History of the American People.* New York: Oxford University Press, 1965.

Morris, James. "Jubilee Day." In *The Horizon History of the British Empire,* edited by Stephen W. Sears. New York: American Heritage Publishing Co., 1973.

Moskos, Charles C., Jr. "Racial Integration in the Armed Forces." *American Journal of Sociology* (1966) Vol. 72, 132–148.

————. *The American Enlisted Man: The Rank and File in Today's Military.* New York: Russell Sage Foundation, 1970.

Muller, Herbert J. *Freedom in the Ancient World.* New York: Harper and Brothers, 1961.

Myrdal, Gunnar. *An American Dilemma.* New York: Harper and Brothers, 1944.

The National Roster of Black Elected Officials. Vol. 3. Washington, D.C.: Joint Center for Political Studies, May 1973.

Nelson, Dennis. *The Integration of the Negro into the United States Navy, 1776–1947.* NAVEXOS-P-526, 1948.

Newton, Huey P. "The Black Panther Party." In *Racial Conflict,* edited by Gary T. Marx. Boston: Little, Brown and Co., 1971.

Nichols, Lee. *Breakthrough on the Color Front.* New York: Random House, 1954.

Norgren, Paul H. "Fair Employment Practice Laws—Experience, Effects, Prospects." In *Employment, Race, and Poverty,* edited by Arthur M. Ross and Herbert Hill. New York: Harcourt, Brace and World, 1967.

Novak, Michael. *The Rise of the Unmeltable Ethnics.* New York: Macmillian Co., 1971.

Nye, Russel Blaine. *The Cultural Life of the New Nation.* New York: Harper and Brothers, 1960.

Odum, Howard. "The Education of Negroes." In *The Development of Segregationist Thought,* edited by I. A. Newby. Homewood, Ill.: Dorsey Press, 1968.

Officer, James E. "The American Indian and Federal Policy." In *The American Indian in Urban Society,* edited by Jack O. Waddell and O. Michael Watson. Boston: Little, Brown and Co., 1971.

Ogawa, Dennis. *From Japs to Japanese: The Evolution of Japanese-American Stereotypes.* Berkeley, Ca.: McCutchan Publishing Corporation, 1971.

Orfield, Gary. *The Reconstruction of Southern Education.* New York: Wiley-Interscience, 1969.

Ottley, Roi, and Weatherby, William. *The Negro in New York: An Informal Social History.* New York: New York Public Library and Oceana Publications, 1967.

Owen, Norman G., ed. "Introduction: Philippine Society and American Colonialism." In *Compadre Colonialism: Studies on the Philippines under American Rule*. Ann Arbor: University of Michigan Center for South and Southeast Asian Studies, 1971.

Parkman, Francis. *The Conspiracy of Pontiac and the Indian War after the Conquest of Canada*. Rev. ed. Boston: Little, Brown and Co., 1888.

Parsons, Talcott. "Social Strains in America." In *The Radical Right*, edited by Daniel Bell. Garden City, N.Y.: Doubleday, Anchor, 1964.

Patai, Raphael. *Israel between East and West*. Philadelphia: Jewish Publication Society of America, 1953.

Perry, Ralph Barton. *Characteristically American*. New York: Alfred A. Knopf, 1949.

Petersen, William. *Japanese Americans*. New York: Random House, 1971.

Pettigrew, Thomas F. "Black and White Attitudes toward Race and Housing." In *Racial Discrimination in the United States*, edited by Thomas F. Pettigrew. New York: Harper and Row, Publishers, 1975.

―――― ed. "The Racial Integration of the Schools." In *Racial Discrimination in the United States*. New York: Harper and Row, Publishers, 1976.

Phelan, John L. *The Hispanization of the Philippines*. Madison, Wis.: University of Wisconsin Press, 1959.

Philip, Kenneth. "Herbert Hoover's New Era: A False Dawn for the American Indian, 1929–1932." *Rocky Mountain Social Science Journal* 9 (April 1972): 53–60.

Pinkney, Alphonso. *Black Americans*. Englewood Cliffs, N.J.: Prentice-Hall, 1969.

Potter, George. *To the Golden Door: The Story of the Irish in Ireland and America*. Boston: Little, Brown and Co., 1960.

Pratt, Julius W. *Expansionists of 1898: The Acquisition of Hawaii and the Spanish Islands*. Baltimore: John Hopkins Press, 1936.

The President's Committee on Equality of Treatment and Opportunity in the Armed Services. *Freedom to Serve*. Washington, D.C.: Government Printing Office, 1950.

Price, Grenfell A. *White Settlers and Native Peoples: An Historical Study of Racial Contacts between Whites and Aboriginal Peoples in the United States, Australia and New Zealand*. Melbourne: Georgian House, 1950.

Quarles, Benjamin. *The Negro in the Making of America*. New York: Collier Books, Macmillan Co., 1964.

Ransford, H. Edward. "Skin Color, Life Chances, and Anti-White Attitudes." *Social Problems* 18 (Fall 1970): 164–78.

Rendon, Armando, B. *Chicano Manifesto*. New York: Collier Books, Macmillan Co., 1972.

Report of the National Advisory Commission on Civil Disorders. New York: Bantam Books, 1968.

Rischin, Moses. *The Promised City: New York's Jews, 1870–1914*. Cambridge: Harvard University Press, 1962

Robertson, William. "History of America." In *Historians at Work*, edited by Peter Gay and Victor G. Wexler, vol. 2. New York: Harper and Row, 1972.

Robinson, Cecil. *With the Ears of Strangers: The Mexican in American Literature*. Tucson: University of Arizona Press, 1963.

Rodgers, Harrell R., Jr., "On Integrating the Public Schools: An Empirical and Legal Assessment." In *Racism and Inequality: The Policy Alternatives*, edited by Harrell R. Rodgers, Jr. San Francisco: W. H. Freeman and Co., 1975.

Rolle, Andrew F. *The Immigrant Upraised*. Norman: University of Oklahoma Press, 1968.

Rose, Arnold M. *Migrants in Europe*. Minneapolis: University of Minnesota Press, 1969.

———. *The Negro in America: The Condensed Version of Gunnar Myrdal's An American Dilemma*. New York: Harper and Row, Harper Torchbooks, 1964.

Samkange, Stanlake. "Wars of Resistance." *The Horizon History of Africa*, edited by Alvin M. Josephy, Jr. New York: American Heritage Publishing Co., 1971.

Saunders, Lyle. *Cultural Differences and Medical Care: The Case of the Spanish-Speaking People of the Southwest*. New York: Russell Sage Foundation, 1954.

Schermerhorn, R. A. *Comparative Ethnic Relations: A Framework for Theory and Research*. New York: Random House, 1970.

———. *These Our People*. Boston: D.C. Heath and Co., 1949.

Schmidhauser, John R. "The Justices of the Supreme Court: A Collective Portrait." *Midwest Journal of Political Science* III (February 1959): 1–57.

Schrier, Arnold. *Ireland and the American Emigration, 1850–1900*. Minneapolis: University of Minnesota Press, 1958.

Scott, Emmett, Jr. *The American Negro in the World War*. Chicago: Homewood Press, 1919.

Scott, Franklin D. *World Migration in Modern Times*. Englewood Cliffs, N.J.: Prentice-Hall, Inc. 1968.

Seton-Watson, Hugh. *From Lenin to Malenkov*. New York: Frederick A. Praeger, 1955.

———. *The Decline of Imperial Russia, 1855–1914*. New York: Frederick A. Praeger, 1964.

Shepperson, George. "Under Colonial Rule." In *The Horizon History of Africa*, edited by Alvin M. Josephy, Jr. New York: American Heritage Publishing Co., 1971.

Shibutani, Tamotsu, and Kwan, Kian M. *Ethnic Stratification: A Comparative Approach*. New York: Macmillan Co., 1965.

Shills, Edward. "Deference." In *Social Stratification*, edited by J. A. Jackson. London: Cambridge University Press, 1968.

Silberman, Charles E. *Crisis in Black and White*. New York: Random House, 1964.

Simpson, George Eaton, and Yinger, J. Milton. *Racial and Cultural Minorities*. 4th ed. New York: Harper and Row, 1972.

Slobodin, Richard. "The Métis of Northern Canada." In *The Blending of Races*, edited by Noel P. Gist and Anthony Gary Dworkin. New York: Wiley-Interscience, 1972.

Smelser, Neil J. *Theory of Collective Behavior*. New York: Free Press, 1962.

Smith, M. G., and Kuper, Leo, eds. *Pluralism in Africa*. Berkeley and Los Angeles: University of California Press, 1969.

Smooha, Sammy. "Black Panthers: The Ethnic Dilemma." *Society* 9 (May 1972): 31–36.

———. *Pluralism: A Study of Intergroup Relations in Israel*. Ph.D. dissertation, University of California, Los Angeles, 1973.

Snyder, Louis L., ed. *The Imperialism Reader*. Princeton, N.J.: D. Van Nostrand Co., 1962.

Solberg, Carl. *Immigration and Nationalism: Argentina and Chile, 1890–1914*. Austin: University of Texas Press, 1970.

Sorokin, Pitirim. "American Millionaires and Multi-Millionaires." *Social Forces* III (May 1925): 627–40.

Sovern, Michael. *Legal Restraints on Racial Discrimination in Employment.* New York: Twentieth Century Fund, 1966.

Sowell, Thomas. "'Affirmative Action' Reconsidered." In *The Public Interest* Number 42, (Winter 1976): 47–65.

———. *Race and Economics.* New York: David McKay Co., 1975.

Spear, Allan H. *Black Chicago: The Making of a Negro Ghetto, 1890–1920.* Chicago: University of Chicago Press, 1967.

Stampp, Kenneth M. *The Peculiar Institution: Slavery in the Ante-Bellum South.* New York: Vintage Books, Random House, 1956.

Stephenson, Gilbert Thomas. *Race Distinctions in American Law.* New York: D. Appleton and Co., 1910.

Stevens, F. S., ed. *Racism: The Australian Experience. Prejudice and Xenophobia,* vol. 1. New York: Taplinger Publishing Co., 1972.

St. John, Nancy H. *School Desegregation: Outcomes for Children.* New York: John Wiley and Sons, 1975.

Stoddard, Ellwyn R. *Mexican Americans.* New York: Random House, 1973.

Stone, Chuck. *Black Political Power in America.* New York: Bobbs-Merrill, 1968.

Storey, Moorfield, and Lichauco, Marcial P. *Conquest of the Philippines by the United States, 1898–1925.* New York: G. P. Putnam's Sons, 1926.

Stouffer, Samuel A. *The American Soldier: Adjustment during Army Life.* Vol. 1. Princeton, N.J.: Princeton University Press, 1949.

Swain, Joseph Ward. *The Ancient World.* Vol. I. New York: Harper and Brothers, 1950.

———. *The Ancient World.* Vol. II. New York: Harper and Brothers, 1950.

Swomley, John, Jr. *The Military Establishment.* Boston: Beacon Press, 1964.

Tabb, William K. "Race Relations Models and Social Change." In *Social Problems* 18 (Spring 1971): 431–44.

Taft, Donald Reed. *Human Migration.* New York: Ronald Press Co., 1936.

Tapié, Victor-L. *The Rise and Fall of the Habsburg Monarchy.* New York: Praeger Publishers, 1971.

Taylor, Paul Schuster. *An American-Mexican Frontier: Nueces County, Texas.* Chapel Hill: University of North Carolina Press, 1934.

Terrell, John Upton. *Apache Chronicle.* New York: World Publishing Co., 1972.

Thurow, Lester C. *Poverty and Discrimination.* Brookings Institution, 1969.

Tilly, Charles. "Collective Violence in European Perspective." In *The History of Violence in America,* edited by Hugh Davis Graham and Ted Robert Gurr. New York: Bantam Books, 1969.

United Nations, *Apartheid in Practice.* New York: United Nations, 1971.

U.S. Commission on Civil Rights. *Federal Civil Rights Enforcement Effort.* Washington, D.C.: Government Printing Office, 1971.

U.S. Commission on Civil Rights. *Federal Civil Rights Enforcement Effort–A Reassessment.* Washington, D.C.: Government Printing Office, 1973.

U.S. Commission on Civil Rights. "Federal Enforcement of School Desegregation." Unpublished pamphlet, September 11, 1969.

U.S. Commission on Civil Rights. *To Provide for Fair Housing.* The Federal Civil Rights Enforcement Effort—1974, vol. II. Washington, D.C.: Government Printing Office, 1974.

U.S. Commission on Civil Rights. *To Ensure Equal Educational Opportunity.* The Federal Civil Rights Enforcement Effort—1974, vol. III. Washington, D.C.: Government Printing Office, 1975.

U.S. Commission on Civil Rights. *To Eliminate Employment Discrimination.* The Federal Civil Rights Enforcement Effort—1974, vol. V. Washington, D.C.: Government Printing Office, 1975.

U.S. Commission on Civil Rights. *Mexican Americans and the Administration of Justice in the Southwest.* Washington, D.C.: Government Printing Office, March 1970.

U.S. Commission on Civil Rights. *One Year Later.* Washington, D.C.: Government Printing Office, 1971.

U.S. Commission on Civil Rights. *Political Participation.* Washington, D.C.: Government Printing Office, 1968.

U.S. Commission on Civil Rights. *Racial Isolation in the Public Schools.* Washington, D.C.: Government Printing Office, 1967.

U.S. Commission on Civil Rights. *The Southwest Indian Report.* Washington, D.C.: Government Printing Office, May, 1973.

U.S. Civil Rights Commission. "Statement of Howard A. Glickstein, Staff Director-Designate, U.S. Commission on Civil Rights, Before the Senate Subcommittee on Labor of the Committee on Labor and Public Welfare." Unpublished pamphlet, September 10, 1969.

U.S. Commission on Civil Rights. *The Voting Rights Act: Ten Years After.* Washington, D.C.: Government Printing Office, January, 1975.

United States Department of Commerce/Bureau of the Census. *Characteristics of the Population by Ethnic Origin: March, 1972 and 1971, Current Population Reports.* Series P-20, no. 249. Washington, D.C.: Government Printing Office, April 1973.

United States Department of Commerce/Bureau of the Census. *Educational Attainment, Subject Reports, 1970 Census of the Population.* Washington, D.C.: Government Printing Office, March 1973.

United States Department of Commerce/Bureau of the Census. *The Social and Economic Status of the Black Population in the United States, Current Population Reports.* Special studies, series P-23, no. 54. Washington, D.C.: Government Printing Office, July 1975.

United States Department of Commerce/Bureau of the Census. *The Social and Economic Status of Negroes in the United States, 1970, Current Population Reports.* Series P-23, no. 38, BLS report no. 394. Washington, D.C.: Government Printing Office, 1972.

Utley, Robert M. *Frontier Regulars: The United States Army and the Indians, 1848–1865.* New York: Macmillan Co., 1967.

———. *Frontiersman in Blue: The United States Army and the Indians, 1866–1890.* New York: Macmillan Co., 1973.

Valdez, Armando. "Brown Power." In *Cracks in the Melting Pot.* 2d ed., edited by Melvin Steinfield. Beverly Hills, Ca.: Glencoe Press, 1973.

van den Berghe, Pierre L. "The Benign Quota: Panacea or Pandora's Box." *Report on the International Research Conference on Race Relations,* Aspen, Colorado, 1970.

————, ed. *Race and Ethnicity*. New York: Basic Books, 1970.

————. *Race and Racism: A Comparative Perspective*. New York: John Wiley and Sons, 1967.

Vander Zanden, James W. *American Minority Relations*. 3d ed. New York: Ronald Press, 1972.

————. *Race Relations in Transition*. New York: Random House, 1965.

von Eschen, Donald; Kirk, Jerome; and Pinard, Maurice. "The Disintegration of the Negro Nonviolent Movement." *Journal of Peace Research* 6 (1969): 216–34.

Wagley, C. and Harris, H. *Minorities in the New World*. New York: Columbia University Press, 1958.

Wakin, Edward. *The Lebanese and Syrians in America*. Chicago: Claretian Publications, 1974.

Walsh, Robert, Jr. *An Appeal from the Judgments of Great Britain Respecting the United States of America*. 2d ed. New York: Negro Universities Press, 1819, 1969.

Ware, Caroline F. *Greenwich Village*. New York: Harper and Row, 1935.

Washburn, Wilcomb E. *The Indian in America*. New York: Harper and Row, 1975.

Wax, Murray, and Wax, Rosalie. "Federal Programs and Indian Target Populations." In *Majority and Minority*, edited by Norman R. Yetman and C. Hoy Steele. Boston: Allyn and Bacon, 1971.

Wax, Murray L. *Indian Americans*. Englewood Cliffs, N.J.: Prentice-Hall, 1971.

Weaver, Glenn. "Benjamin Franklin and the Pennsylvania Germans." In *The Aliens: A History of Ethnic Minorities in America*, edited by Leonard Dinnerstein and Frederic Cople Jaher. New York: Appleton-Century-Crofts, Meredith Corporation, 1971.

Weed, Perry L. *The White Ethnic Movement and Ethnic Politics*. New York: Praeger Publishers, 1973.

West, John. *The History of Tasmania*. Sydney: Angus and Robertson Publishers, 1971 (1st ed. in 1852).

Wilkerson, Doxey A. "The Negro School Movement in Virginia: From 'Equalization' to 'Integration'." *Journal of Negro Education* XXIX (Winter 1960): 17–29.

Wilkes, Laura. "Missing Pages in American History: Revealing the Services of Negroes in the Early Wars in the United States of America, 1641–1815." In *The Negro Soldier: A Select Compilation*. New York: Negro Universities Press, 1970.

Williams, D. R. *The United States and the Philippines*. Garden City, N.Y.: Doubleday, Page and Co., 1924.

Williams, Robert F. "For Effective Self Defense." In *Negro Protest Thought in the Twentieth Century*, edited by Francis L. Broderick and August Meier. New York: Bobbs-Merrill, 1965.

Williams, Robin M., Jr. *American Society*. New York: Alfred A. Knopf, 1952.

Wilson, John A. *The Culture of Ancient Egypt*. Chicago: The University of Chicago Press, Phoenix Books, 1951.

Wilson, John. *Introduction to Social Movements*. New York: Basic Books, 1973.

Wilson, William J. *Power, Racism, and Privilege*. New York: Macmillan Co., 1973.

Wish, Harvey. "American Slave Insurrections before 1861." In *Justice Denied: The Black Man in White America*, edited by William M. Chace and Peter Collier. New York: Harcourt, Brace and World, 1970.

Wittke, Carl. *The Irish in America*. Baton Rouge: Louisiana State University Press, 1956.

Wolgemuth, Kathleen. "New Freedom and Old Hypocrisy." In *Cracks in the Melting Pot*. 2d rev. ed., edited by Melvin Steinfield. New York: Glencoe Press, 1973.

Woodward, C. Vann. *The Strange Career of Jim Crow*. New York: Oxford University Press, 1966.

Wright, Richard. *Uncle Tom's Children*. New York: Harper and Row, 1937 and 1965.

X, Malcolm. *The Autobiography of Malcolm X*. New York: Grove Press, 1964.

Yuan, D. Y. "Voluntary Segregation: A Study of New York Chinatown." In *Minority Responses*, edited by Minako Kurokawa. New York: Random House, 1970.

Zilversmit, Arthur. *The First Emancipation: The Abolition of Slavery in the North*. Chicago: University of Chicago Press, 1967.

AUTHOR INDEX

SUBJECT INDEX

accommodation, 42, 103–104, 269
acculturation
　defined, 119
　forms of, 120
　in United States, 265–66, 274, 281,
　　297–98, 301
adaptation, of subordinate groups in United
　　States
　Black-Americans, 50, 261–74
　Chinese-Americans, 282–83
　general characteristics, 259–60
　German-Americans, 294–95
　Indian-Americans, 274–77
　Irish-Americans, 50, 288–93
　Italian-Americans, 9, 289–90, 293, 298
　Japanese-Americans, 45, 283–85,
　　306–307
　Jewish-Americans, 49–50, 289, 291, 294
　Mexican-Americans, 277–82
　Puerto Rican-Americans, 299–300
　Swedish-Americans, 295
affirmitive action, 335–37, 437–38
Africa
　ethnic groups in, 23
　European colonies in, 110–11, 307
　kingdoms in, 183
　Nigeria, 23
　Republic of South Africa, 37, 38, 63, 76,
　　80, 82, 84, 89, 139–40
　slavery in, 183
　slave trade with New World, 75, 184–90
　Uganda, 36, 85
Alaska, 204
American Empire
　Alaska, 204
　annexation of Hawaii, 207–209
　conquest of Indians, 173–82
　conquest of Mexico, 192–95
　Cuba, 252–53
　New Spain, 190–92
　overview of, 151–52, 166–69
　Philippines, 206–207, 253–54
　Puerto Rico, 254–55
　Spanish-American War, 204–206
American, as ethnic group
　character, culture, and language, 161–66
　maintenance of dominance, 260
　meaning of, 151, 429, 434
　origins of dominance, 148
　origins of ethnicity, 148, 152–53, 159–61
　subordinate group assimilation into,
　　250–51
American, as nationality, 22, 148
American Revolution
　causes of, 154–57
　events and battles, 158–59

Anglo-American, see American, ethnic
Anglo-Indians of India, 20–21
annexation
　factor in dominance, 72–73
　forms of, 73
　meaning of, 72–73
Argentina, 35–36, 45–46, 129
assimilation
　defined, 121, 122
　emphasis on in U.S., 251
　meaning of ethnic, 121–23
　meaning of racial, 123–25
　relationship to integration, 121, 437
Australia and Tasmania, 96, 127, 142
Austrian-Hungarian Empire, 43–44, 134,
　　141

Black-Americans
　adaptation of, 50, 261–67, 267–74
　apartheid system, 213, 215–27, 267–74
　class and, 273
　cultural elements of, 265–67, 272
　discrimination against, 80, 84, 88, 89, 90,
　　213–14, 216–24, 267–70, 406–12
　education of, 213, 219, 267–68, 385, 389,
　　418–21
　ethnic group, 21 (footnote), 267
　family, 47–48
　housing, 218–19, 270, 410–11
　income of, 391–96, 406–408
　integration and, 267–68, 269–70, 435
　occupations of, 270, 286–88, 306–307,
　　311–12, 362–63, 366–67, 370, 371–72,
　　379, 382–84, 407, 408
　organizations of, 269, 270, 271–72, 309,
　　311–15, 316
　　Black Crusaders, 314, 315
　　Black Panthers, 315
　　Congress of Racial Equality (CORE),
　　　309, 311, 312, 316
　　Nation of Islam (Black Muslims),
　　　271–72
　　National Association for the
　　　Advancement of Colored People
　　　(NAACP), 269–70, 309, 310
　　Southern Christian Leadership
　　　Conference (SCLC), 310–11
　　Student Non-Violent Coordinating
　　　Committee, 311, 312, 314, 316
　　Universal Negro Improvement
　　　Association, 270
　pluralism, and, 268–69, 270–72, 430–31
　public transportation and
　　accommodation, 267–68, 310–11
　racism against, 93, 94, 99, 189–90,
　　214–15, 224–27